MW01026939

MODELING PEACE

TANG CENTER SERIES IN EARLY CHINA

TANG CENTER SERIES IN EARLY CHINA

Editors
___

Anthony Barbieri-Low

Li Feng

The dramatic increase of information about China's early past made possible by recent archaeological discoveries has reenergized the study of Early China. The Tang Center Series in Early China, sponsored by the Tang Center for Early China at Columbia University and published by Columbia University Press, presents new studies that make major contributions to our understanding of early Chinese civilization and break new theoretical or methodological grounds in Early China studies, especially works that analyze newly discovered paleographic and manuscript materials and archaeological data. The disciplinary focus of the series includes history, archaeology, art history, anthropology, literature, philosophy, and the history of sciences and technology. The time period covered spans from the Neolithic to the end of the Han Dynasty (220 CE) or to the end of the Tang Dynasty (907 CE) for titles in archaeology.

Forthcoming from the series:

Kingly Crafts: The Archaeology of Craft Production in Late Shang China, Yung-Ti Li

Modeling Peace

ROYAL TOMBS AND POLITICAL IDEOLOGY
IN EARLY CHINA

Jie Shi

Columbia University Press
New York

Columbia University Press wishes to express its appreciation to the Tang Center for Early China for funding and editorial support in the publication of this book.

Columbia University Press
Publishers Since 1893
New York   Chichester, West Sussex
cup.columbia.edu
Copyright © 2020 Columbia University Press
All rights reserved

Library of Congress Cataloging-in-Publication Data
Names: Shi, Jie, 1979– author.
Title: Modeling Peace : Royal Tombs and Political Ideology in Early China / Jie Shi.
Other titles: Royal Tombs and Political Ideology in Early China
Description: First Edition. | New York : Columbia University Press, 2019. |
Series: Tang center series in early China | Includes bibliographical references and index.
Identifiers: LCCN 2018060751 (print) | LCCN 2019004768 (ebook) |
ISBN 9780231549202 (ebook) | ISBN 9780231191029 (Cloth : alk. paper)
Subjects: LCSH: Mancheng Qu (Baoding Shi, China)—Antiquities. |
Baoding Shi (China)—Antiquities. | China—Kings and rulers—Tombs. |
China—Politics and government—221 B.C.-220 A.D. |
Social archaeology—China—Baoding Shi. | Ethnoarchaeology—China—Baoding Shi. |
Archaeology and history—China—Baoding Shi.
Classification: LCC DS797.39.M363 (ebook) | LCC DS797.39.M363 S55 2019 (print) |
DDC 931—dc23
LC record available at https://lccn.loc.gov/2018060751

Columbia University Press books are printed on permanent and durable acid-free paper.
Printed in the United States of America

Cover design: Noah Arlow
Cover image: © Hebei Museum

CONTENTS

CONTENTS

LIST OF MAPS, FIGURES, AND TABLE

THE DISTINCTION OF ROYAL TOMBS IN EARLY CHINA

Royal tombs, here defined as burials prepared for the rulers of territorial states and their spouses, are among the most important material remains of early Chinese civilization.[1] More than a hundred of them have been discovered, and their monumental scale, sophisticated design, and marvelous contents crystalize the highest artistic and technological ingenuity of ancient China. These royal spectacles were so precious that constructing just one of them might take years or even decades and might consume as much as one-third of the state's annual income. They set the highest standard for the lower classes, including officials or commoners, who yearned to emulate but could not surpass them.

The importance of these royal tombs cannot be properly understood without appreciating the fact that they are physically and conceptually distinguished from all other lesser tombs in early China. Our study must take this fact as the point of departure.

The physical distinction of royal tombs has been sufficiently revealed by modern archaeologists, who have conventionally treated royal (and imperial) tombs as an independent typological category—the top tier of the highest-ranking burials. Among the many excavated early Chinese royal tombs, whose dates range from the Shang 商 (seventeenth to mid-eleventh century BCE) to the Western Han 西漢 (206 BCE–8 CE), the earliest examples include a

FIGURE 0.1 Excavation photo of Houjiazhuang tomb no. 1001, Anyang, Henan, ca. thirteenth to twelfth centuries BCE. Courtesy of Academia Sinica, Taiwan.

group of twelve large, vertical, pit graves dating back to the twelfth century BCE at the famous site called the "Ruins of the Yin" (Yinxu 殷墟) in present-day Anyang, Henan Province.[2] The average labor cost of these royal tombs was far superior to that of ordinary ones. For example, the largest of the Shang royal tombs, Houjiazhuang tomb no. 1001, measures nineteen by fourteen meters in area and penetrates more than ten meters into the ground, which is about two hundred times larger than ordinary burials for commoners (fig. 0.1).[3] Not surprisingly, in their studies of the Shang burial practice, archaeologists often single out these largest tombs of the Shang kings at Anyang as an independent group different from all other lesser graves of the same period.[4]

Although burials of the Western Zhou 西周 (mid-eleventh century to 771 BCE) kings are yet to be identified, archaeologists have unearthed at least sixty-six tombs of Western Zhou vassals or their principal wives, including such local polities as Wei 衛, Jin 晉, Guo 虢, Rui 芮, and Yan 燕.[5] The best-studied examples of this type are located in the cemetery of the marquises of Jin located in present-day Tianma-Qucun in Shanxi Province, which has yielded nineteen magnificent tombs attributed to the marquises or their principal wives.[6] Even though these local vassals' tombs technically were not "royal," in that the occupants did not assume the title of king, they neverthe-less might have been scaled-down reflections of the Zhou royal tombs and supported the Zhou ideology. Although their average scale cannot rival that of the Shang royal tombs, their richness in grave goods offers a glimpse of the royal grandeur of the Western Zhou kingly tombs. For example, in tomb no. 2009 at the Guo state cemetery, so far the most richly furnished tomb ever excavated from the Western Zhou period, the excavators uncovered more than three thousand six hundred objects—including more than one hundred and twenty bronze ritual vessels—from an area less than thirty square meters.[7]

The discoveries of the royal cemeteries dated to the Eastern Zhou 東周 period (771–221 BCE), particularly the later Warring States period, have been ample. Up to the present day, about a dozen cemeteries from these regional royal houses have been identified and partially excavated, presenting a com-plex picture of the social realities of pre-imperial China.[8] In terms of the scale of the tombs, the Eastern Zhou lords continued to push the limits. The greatest known kingly grave during this period was attributed to Duke Jing 景公 of the Qin 秦 state (d. 537 BCE). It penetrates twenty-four meters below ground and occupies a total area of 5,334 square meters, dwarfing the largest Shang precursor.[9] Moreover, unlike the earlier Shang and Western Zhou precedents, royal tombs in this period often feature a spectacular pyr-amid-shaped tumulus above the tomb pit, hence doubling the labor cost. Eastern Zhou royal burials, as Alain Thote has noted, share many formal and iconographical features in architecture and material content that distinguish them from burials of lower-ranking individuals.[10]

After the fall of the Eastern Zhou, China marched into the age of empire. The First Emperor, Qin Shihuangdi 秦始皇帝 (r. 247–210 BCE), who unified China by force in 221 BCE, abolished all the regional kingdoms to ensure his unchallengeable authority. The enthusiasm for constructing ever-greater tombs also reached its zenith. The massive mausoleum of the First Emperor at Mt. Li in present-day Lintong, Shaanxi—the largest tomb ever built in China, which features the world-famous terra-cotta army pits—is estimated to cover an area as vast as 56.25 square kilometers. After forty-five years of continuous excavation, only a small portion of this site has been exposed. The central tomb pit, beneath a fifty-five-meter-tall earth mound, measures 355 by 345 meters in area.[11]

During the Western Han dynasty, which replaced the Qin, China witnessed a second wave of constructing lavish royal tombs in the eastern principali-ties as well as imperial mausoleums near the capital of Chang'an (map 1).[12]

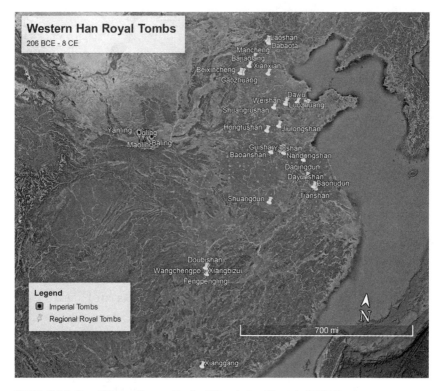

MAP 1 Distribution of Western Han royal tombs, 202 BCE to 8 CE. Map data ©2018 Google

Although the Western Han imperial or royal tombs could hardly compete with the First Emperor's in terms of total scale, they were similarly labor-intensive. The largest of the fully excavated monuments, located in Yongcheng, Henan Province, cuts into a limestone mountain and has an interior space of 6,500 cubic meters.[13] Within these vast mausoleums and burial chambers, the royal establishment deposited numerous grave goods, including many splendid works of art. Only intact tombs give us a sense of how densely furnished the royal burial chambers once were. For example, in the tomb of Zhao Mo 趙眜 (fl. late second century BCE), the self-proclaimed Emperor Wen of Southern Yue (Nanyue 南越), in present-day Guangzhou, the excavators discovered nearly seven thousand artifacts in a burial chamber nearly seventy square meters in area, about a hundred pieces per square meter.[14] Even the relatively simpler tombs of the King of Jibei 濟北 in present-day Changqing and that of the King of Shanyang 山陽 in Juye contained more than two thousand and one thousand objects, respectively (map 2).[15] The Western Han imperial and royal tombs have been the focus

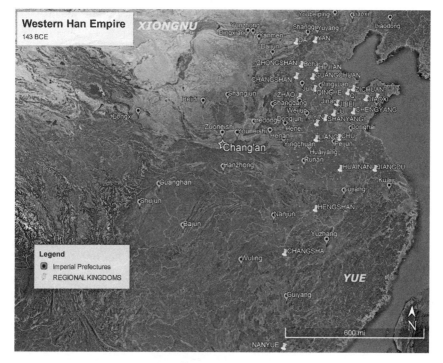

MAP 2 Western Han prefectures and kingdoms, 143 BCE. Map data ©2018 Google

of several monographs and dissertations, as well as a number of special-
ized scholarly articles, which have nearly established a subfield in the study
of Han funerary art.[16] To this day, Chinese archaeologists have uncovered
about eighty regional royal tombs distributed in almost every kingdom of
the empire from present-day Beijing to Guangzhou.[17] Whereas the Western
Han imperial mausoleums, such as the Shang, Zhou, and Qin precedents,
either were plundered or have not yet been (fully) excavated, those regional
royal tombs are generally far better preserved and published, constituting
an ideal data group that has already attracted scholarly attention worldwide.

Lothar von Falkenhausen has observed that from the Western Zhou to
the Eastern Zhou period, the differentiation between the tombs of the rulers
and the ruled changed from "one of degree to one of kind."[18] In other words,
this period witnessed a process of polarization as the multilevel hierarchical
system was reduced to just two opposite categories: the royal and the nonroyal. This fundamental "incipient gap" in mortuary ritual corresponded to
the basic distinction in the social responsibilities of the ruler and the ruled.
Early Western Han tombs continued to maintain the "incipient gap" between

the great ruler and his lesser subjects. The tombs of kings and queens were overwhelmingly larger than those of commoners or lower-ranking nobles. For example, in the Zhongshan royal cemetery at Mancheng, Hebei, the size of the king's burial equals that of his twenty-five satellite graves combined.[19]

Separating royal tombs from other lesser tombs as an independent category was not only a modern practice in archaeology but also an ancient idea with a metaphorical implication. By definition, royal tombs were not just large or richly furnished tombs but tombs built for a special social group, namely kings and their principal wives. Although the people who lived in what is now China learned to build great tombs as early as the Neolithic period (5000 to 3000 BCE), it was not until these skills were combined with an ideology of kingship that royal tombs came into being.

During the Shang and Western Zhou periods, the kings (*wang* 王) distinguished themselves from all other members of society not only by actually reigning over an independent state, running a government, and commanding an army but also by ideologically conceptualizing themselves as the supreme, ultimate ruler of the world, second to none.[20] This absolute sovereignty was expressed in a poem collected in the *Book of Poetry* (*Shijing* 詩經) that

> Under the vast heaven,
> There is nothing that is not the land of the king.
> Of all the subjects (tributaries) on the earth,
> There are none who are not the servants of the king.[21]

During the Eastern Zhou period, with the decline of the authority of the Zhou royal house, many local lords (vassals) also declared themselves "kings." The change took place first in the peripheral regions of the Zhou cultural sphere. Xiong Tong 熊通, the Lord of the Chu 楚, a polity in the middle Yangzi River valley in south China, first declared himself as King of Chu in 704 BCE. Rulers of the Wu 吳 and Yue 越 states in the lower Yangzi River valley in southeast China followed suit about the late sixth century BCE. But the political situation spiraled out of control during the fourth century BCE, when major vassals in the heartland of the Zhou cultural sphere, including the rulers of Qi 齊, Wei 魏, Qin 秦, Yan 燕, Zhao 趙, Han 韓, and Zhongshan 中山, began to adopt kingship one by one.[22] These self-made and mutually recognized kings rivaled their previous Zhou master, the "Son of Heaven" (*tianzi* 天子), through political and bureaucratic institutions, as well as through ostentatious symbolic royal spectacles, including their tombs.

Classifying royal mausoleums as an independent concept coincided with the growing ideology of kingship. Beginning in the mid–Warring States period, royal tombs acquired a specific name, *ling* 陵 (literally, "hill," so, by extension, "mausoleum"), which distinguished them from all other lower-ranking burials.[23] The first ruler we know of whose tomb was called *ling* was Marquis Su of the Zhao state 趙肅侯 (d. 326 BCE), whose successor, the famous King Wuling 武靈王 (r. 325–299 BCE), changed his title from marquis to king. In 325 BCE, Ying Si 嬴駟 (r. 338–331 BCE) proclaimed himself to be the first king (King Huiwen 惠文王) of the Qin state and began to call his tomb the mausoleum of the state (*gongling* 公陵). Afterward, this practice of calling a king's tomb "mausoleum" (*ling*) was established.[24] For example, King Daowu 悼武王 of Qin (r. 310–307 BCE) was buried in the mausoleum titled Yong (*yongling* 永陵), meaning "eternity," and King Xiaowen 孝文王 of Qin (r. 250 BCE) was buried in the mausoleum titled Shou (*shouling* 壽陵) or "longevity."[25] There was a clear parallel relationship between the two terms: *wang* ("king") and *ling* ("mausoleum") during the mid–Warring States period. To historian Yang Kuan, the burgeoning power of the regional king was embodied by the augmented scale of the king's tomb—towering like a mountain.[26]

In 221 BCE, after the unification of China, the First Emperor of Qin, renamed himself as *huangdi* 皇帝 (emperor) to enhance his religio-political authority and rendered the old title *wang* obsolete. The emperor also upgraded the title of his unique mausoleum from *ling* (hill) to *shan* 山 (mountain) to emphasize its unprecedented grandeur.

Emperor Gao 漢高祖 (r. 202–195 BCE), the founder of the Western Han, followed the example of the Qin and adopted the new imperial title of *huangdi* for himself. He also departed from the Qin in carving out several regional kingdoms in his eastern provinces to reward those who fought with him, though he later replaced these individuals with his sons, brother, and nephew on whose kingdoms he believed he could safely rely as a defensive zone to shield the empire from possible rebels or invaders (map 2). The rulers of the regional kingdoms were called *wang*, reminiscent of their Eastern Zhou predecessors. These regional kingdoms, which enjoyed a relatively independent status, were subject to the new political agenda of building and sustaining the empire.

The concepts of *ling* and *shan* were widely used in Warring States and Western Han literature as metaphors for the mountain-like stature of rulers, and the collapse of mountains and hills (*shanling beng* 山陵崩) became a popular idiom to describe the death of emperors and kings.[27] Meanwhile, as the term *shanling* 山陵 was widely accepted as a synonym for royal or imperial mausoleums, it also turned into a trope for the kings or emperors themselves.[28]

But why did people during the late Warring States period conceptually distinguish royal tombs from all other tombs and conceive of them as a unique category? In the study of ancient Chinese art and culture, such questions are yet to be investigated.

The previous scholarship on royal tombs was built upon two major, essentially anthropological, frameworks. The first one tended to emphasize that tombs, royal or ordinary, were defined in terms of cultural distinction.[29] This perspective led scholars to divide tombs by geographical location into Qin, Chu, Zhongshan, Dian 滇, and other categories and to study each of the groups as representing a different local tradition. From this point of view, for example, the tomb of a Qin king was regarded as categorically closer to a Qin commoner's burial than it was to the tomb of a Zhao king built during the same period.

The second major framework was religious. Scholars working from this perspective contended that a royal burial, and indeed any burial, was ultimately about one man's (the tomb occupant's) personal welfare, whose guarantee in the posthumous universe was symbolized by mortuary architecture and goods. Royal burials either simulated a new "afterlife universe" beyond the reach of and parallel to this world[30] or served the purpose of a happy selfish afterlife, wherever that afterlife was.[31] Despite their apparent differences, both theories point ultimately to the deceased's personal well-being in an immortal afterlife, either up in the sky, midway in the mountains, or down below in the Yellow Springs (*huangquan* 黃泉).

Despite their value and validity, these two frameworks fail to address a number of important questions. For example, what distinguished the tomb of the First Emperor of Qin from other Qin-period tombs, beyond the fact that it was larger and richer? In other words, is the difference between a royal tomb and a commoner's tomb merely a matter of size or is it a matter of basic nature? Let us imagine for a moment that, somehow, against all government regulations, a very rich merchant built himself a tomb as large and rich as a royal one. Would it be possible for the tombs to be considered the same?

Of course, it was the royal attribution that separated royal tombs fundamentally from tombs of the other members of society. Therefore, the

previous question can be converted to another simpler question: how was
royalty different from other social actors, or what did it mean to be king
as opposed to non-king? The most obvious difference, as anthropologists
have pointed out, was the king's actual political power over his people.[32]
However, the ways in which royal power was represented must also be
understood in the context of the political philosophy of the time, a subject
on which intellectual historians have achieved remarkable results. From
their scholarship, we have learned that philosophers from the Warring
States period to the Western Han period frequently discussed kingship,
which was grounded in the tomb occupants' royal status. Both Mozi 墨子
(fifth century BCE) (and later Mohists) and Xunzi 荀子 (third century BCE)
(and other Confucians) were concerned only with noble tombs, which
involved higher social and moral obligations than personal benefits. These
broader interests were derived from the tomb occupant's higher social status and responsibilities; as a ruler, a king had more in his world to worry
about than a commoner did. The kingly tombs were built for the "great
people" (daren 大人), the rulers, in accord with their lofty business of ruling the world rather than such trivial affairs as personal welfare, which
might have meant everything to the "small people" (xiaoren 小人), namely,
the commoners.[33]

Thus, in royal tombs, culture and religion served only as the means to a
higher goal: political ideology. Despite its importance, the cultural distinction represented in the royal tombs was not an objective reflection of the
social reality in which the deceased lived as much as a subjective demon-
stration of the "correct" social order that the patron aimed to achieve and
maintain. Furthermore, being physically sealed and hidden from this world
did not necessarily remove the worldly implications of the burials. Rather,
the cultural and religious characteristics of royal tombs were ideological
statements by their royal patrons in response to the pressing challenges
that they faced.

So what possibly might be those more advanced concerns that were
expressed in a ruler's burial? Although personal welfare was the most long-
lasting "substrate" of early Chinese religion and applied to all people at all
social levels,[34] this personal concern lay at the very bottom of a multilevel
social consciousness. For the elite (noblemen or bureaucrats), the situation
was much more complex.[35] If Martin Powers is correct in his study of decorated tombs and shrines of the Eastern Han 東漢 (25–220 CE) period—that

bureaucrats expressed a strong position between Ru 儒 (Confucianism) and Fa 法 (Legalism)[36]—then what ideology did the rulers, who were neither commoners nor officials, hold? If, as the excavation of Yinwan tomb no. 6 (dated to 10 BCE) has demonstrated, even a local official ought to consult registration books of governmental personnel and carry out his routine administrative duty while in his burial site, then what responsibility would the rulers assume while occupying their tombs?[37]

For rulers such as kings and emperors (*zhu* 主 or *jun* 君), a burial was more than an investment in personal welfare. It was relevant not only to the ruler himself but ultimately also to his family, his country, or further even, to all under heaven (*tianxia* 天下). Von Falkenhausen suggests that Chinese funerary customs toward the end of the Eastern Zhou period represented a ritual transformation from expressing the hierarchical aristocratic rank order of the early Zhou into expressing "a system of a philosophical ethics based on propositions of universal validity."[38] Jessica Rawson, in her study of the mausoleum of the First Emperor of Qin, hinted at such a "universal ethic": "The emperor . . . had set himself in the line of sage kings who, according to legend, had first paced out and ordered the world."[39] In stone inscriptions, the emperor directly identified himself as the "great sage" (*dasheng* 大聖) in the contemporary period who not only "brought peace to the world" (*zhi taiping* 致太平) but also personified all ancient political wisdom.[40]

Considering the conceptual link between kingship (*wang*) and royal tombs (*ling*) established during this period, we have good reason to ask: Did a ruler's inherent sagely identification and political responsibility, which eventually distinguished him from all his subjects, have an impact on the design of his tomb, which also marked his royal identity?

This previously unexamined question is the focus of this book. Although tombs were associated with the afterlife, it is more important to realize that the purpose of a tomb varied with the tomb occupant's social status. Beginning during the late Eastern Zhou period, royal tombs included facilities that simulated government agencies. This trend of governmentalizing mausoleums reached an extreme in the First Emperor's mausoleum, which contained various symbolic civil and military bureaus orbiting the imperial grave at the center.[41] Needless to say, these symbolic state organs—which were appropriate, perhaps even necessary, in a ruler's tomb—made little sense for the tombs of ordinary people, no matter how rich they were. Likewise, if a ruler's tomb blatantly ignored all the royal obligations (duties) and cared just about personal well-being like a selfish commoner, then it would be equally unthinkable, would it not?

A question like this leads us into the underground crypt—the secret heart of the mausoleum—to examine if each royal tomb during the Western Han period was made for each ruler to fulfill his political role as a "great man." To determine whether or not this was the case, extensive analysis of different royal tombs across different historical and geographical contexts should be supplemented by intensive analysis of individual sites. In other words, we must also delve into one site to analyze a complete organic system. Such a case study, which Robert K. Yin defined as "an empirical inquiry that investigates a contemporary phenomenon within its real-life context,"[42] has never been attempted for early Chinese royal burials. The reason for this absence is probably twofold: (1) the dearth of undisturbed or well-preserved archaeological sites and (2) the shortage of historical records regarding the tomb occupants and their social context. Without these two bodies of information, a systematic case study of a royal tomb would be impossible.

Whereas none of the discovered Warring States royal tombs has escaped plundering and disruption, a handful of Western Han royal tombs were miraculously preserved upon discovery. Among them, the most complex, richly furnished, and innovative example is the Mancheng site, the final resting place of Liu Sheng 劉勝 (r. 154–113 BCE), King Jing of Zhongshan 中山靖王, and his queen.

THE TWIN TOMBS AT MANCHENG: A ROYAL EXEMPLAR FROM THE WESTERN HAN

On May 23, 1968, near Baoding City, Hebei, a company of Chinese soldiers was digging into a rocky mountain called Mt. Ling (Lingshan 陵山) to construct an air-raid shelter when they accidentally broke into what appeared to be an ancient burial chamber (map 3, fig. 0.2). Local archaeologists were immediately called in to assess the situation. The result was astonishing: They had discovered a secret tomb of monumental scale that had remained intact for more than two thousand years. An excavation team was promptly assembled and was dispatched into the tomb six days later. After over two months of intense work, it was clear that this was no ordinary tomb, but the tomb of Liu Sheng, King Jing of the Zhongshan state, a half-brother of the famous Emperor Wu 武帝 (r. 141–87 BCE) of the Western Han.[43] According to the historian Ban Gu 班固 (32–92 CE), Liu's father (the emperor), in 154 BCE,

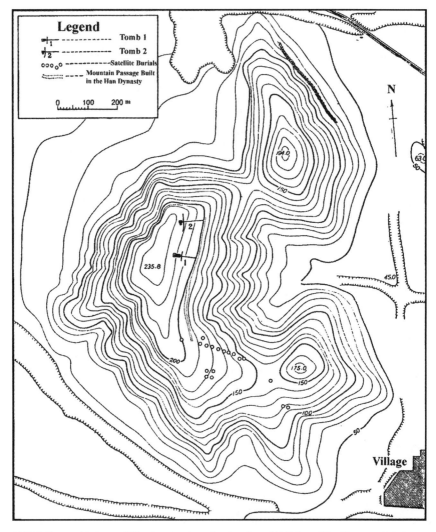

MAP 3 Topographical map of Mancheng tombs no. 1 and no. 2, ca. 118–104 BCE. After Zhongguo shehui kexueyuan kaogu yanjiusuo 中國社會科學院考古研究所, *Mancheng Han mu fajue baogao* 滿城漢墓發掘報告, 2 vols. (Beijing: Wenwu chubanshe, 1980), 1: 8, fig. 3. Courtesy of Wenwu Press.

sent him to revive a "barbaric" kingdom called Zhongshan in present-day Hebei Province, in order to gain effective control over the northern provinces of the young empire and to rule the local people, a hybrid population with ethnic-Han and non-ethnic-Han cultural origins.

Liu Sheng's nearly half-century reign witnessed a critical moment in Chinese history when the young Western Han dynasty, after winning a tumultuous civil war (209–202 BCE), struggled to strengthen its grip on

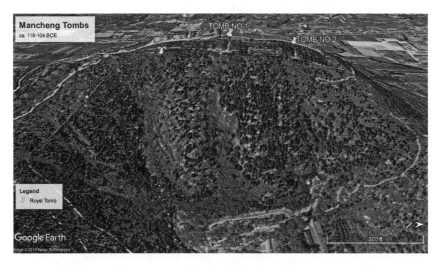

FIGURE 0.2 Distant view (looking westward) of Mancheng tombs no. 1 and no. 2 in Mt. Ling, Mancheng, Hebei, ca. 118–104 BCE. Map data ©2018 Google.

the vast territory. The Han rulers adopted the new idea of an empire run by a bureaucratic system from the Qin, whose rapid disintegration proved it to be an unsuccessful model, but they modified and developed that system to make it workable. One of the greatest challenges was to govern the frontiers and newly conquered lands without provoking such disastrous rebellions as the 209 BCE uprising that triggered the demise of the mighty Qin. Liu Sheng's Zhongshan kingdom sat right in this troublesome zone. He also experienced the well-known ideological battle at the imperial court in which Confucianism eventually emerged victorious. All these events helped shape the future course of Chinese history in the two thousand years that followed.

During the excavation, the excavation team uncovered a second tomb, the burial site of Liu Sheng's wife, Queen Dou Wan 竇綰, located only 120 meters away in the same mountain (map 3, fig. 0.2). Though her name was not recorded in any extant historical sources, she was very likely related to Liu Sheng's grandmother, the powerful Empress Dowager Dou Yifang 竇猗房 (d. 135 BCE).[44] The author of the 1980 excavation report suggests that Dou Wan might have been buried between 118 and 104 BCE.[45]

The main body of the burial site consists of both open and hidden structures. On the main mountain peak of Mt. Ling, at an altitude of 236 meters above sea level, the excavators found architectural remains of a ritual structure with ruins of broken roof tiles dating from the Western Han period

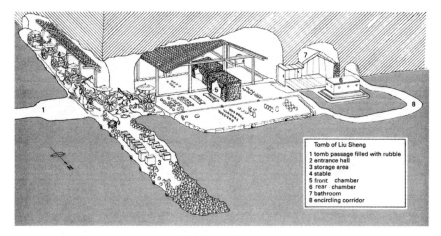

FIGURE 0.3 Tentative reconstruction of Mancheng tomb no. 1, Mancheng, Hebei, ca. 113 BCE. After Wen Fong, ed., *The Great Bronze Age of China* (New York: Metropolitan Museum of Art, 1980), p. 326, fig. 112. Courtesy of the Metropolitan Museum of Art, New York City.

approximately thirty meters above where Liu Sheng's tomb was concealed in the mountain. Scholars have identified this structure as the royal couple's funerary shrine.[46] An ascending passage was constructed to assist people below in accessing the lofty ritual structure.[47]

Thirty meters below the shrine, the two parallel tombs lie deep inside the limestone mountain. To cast a quick glance at the interior architectural structure, let us use the better-known tomb no. 1 (Liu Sheng's) as an example (fig. 0.3).

Oriented toward the east, the tomb consists of a group of interconnected passages and chambers sealed behind a cast-iron wall. In the front, an open passage penetrates into the mountain slope and leads toward the door of the concealed tomb. Past the door, a short tunnel flanked by two elongated side chambers leads to a spacious, crudely vaulted front cave[48] in which a timber house-shaped structure once stood. Behind the front cave, another roughly vaulted cave (the rear chamber) tightly holds a stone house-shaped construction in which the coffined body rested. At the threshold of the rear chamber, artisans dug both sides of the door to form a poorly polished narrow corridor or gallery embracing the rear chamber on three sides.[49]

Inside this hidden complex, the unprecedented richness of the grave goods dazzled the excavators, who found 5,509 different objects in tomb no. 1 and 5,124 in tomb no. 2 (Dou Wan's). This discovery brought to light the first archaeologically excavated jade suits and the hitherto unique lamp of the imperial "Palace of Lasting Trust," which were officially declared national treasures of China and widely regarded as icons of the Han dynasty and its culture.

Among hundreds of scientifically excavated burials in China, the Mancheng tombs truly excel as one of the landmark sites, and their discovery has become legendary in the history of Chinese archaeology. Fifty years after their discovery, despite numerous new findings, the twin tombs at Mancheng still stand out as the highest-ranking, most complex, and best-preserved funerary site fully available for scholarly investigation. As of the end of 2018, tens of thousands of tombs dated to the Han dynasty had been excavated in China. A large number of them, belonging to the highest ranks, stand out in size, content, and form. Among them, the top tier of this prestigious group includes more than seventy royal tombs associated with Western Han kings,[50] heads of a number of regional kingdoms that extended imperial authority to the newly conquered lands and defended against foreign enemies such as the Xiongnu 匈奴 or the Yue 越 (maps 1 and 2).[51] As the cream of the crop, the Mancheng tombs are part of only a handful of royal tombs that remained miraculously undisturbed until the moment they were opened; many others had been plundered or destroyed to varying degrees.[52] The discovery's archaeological significance, far beyond anyone's expectation, was immediately recognized.[53] Yu Weichao, an influential Chinese archaeologist, hailed the two novel tombs as the beginnings of a new era of Han culture, which was paradigmatically different from the previous Zhou culture.[54]

The significance of case study research has been established by many social scientists.[55] Nevertheless, it is legitimate for people to wonder to what extent these two tombs could represent all royal tombs during the Western Han, or even all of early China. If the selected data are extraordinary or unique, rather than average, one might worry that the case study could yield little of theoretical value. This suspicion comes from one of the greatest misunderstandings about case study research. Among nine case study types classified by John Gerring, only three fall into the average category: "typical," "representative," and "most-similar." The other six all describe nonaverage cases, including "deviant," "influential," "crucial," "pathway," "extreme," and "most-different."[56] In fact, it is often the nonaverage cases that yield the most insightful results, shedding light on how average samples may vary under unusual conditions. When compared to all other royal tombs in early China, the Mancheng tombs are neither "most similar" nor "most different," but they open a door to broader historical knowledge far more significant than the tombs themselves.

As I will demonstrate in the following chapters, the Mancheng tombs stand between a generic and an individual example of Western Han royal tombs. On the one hand, the unknown tomb designer always consulted earlier or contemporary royal examples by copying, modifying, and synthesizing. On the other hand, the plan of the tombs also honored the unique history of the name and locality of Zhongshan, as well as Liu Sheng's own faith and ideology.

THE ROYAL TOMB AS AN ARENA FOR ARTIFACTS AND VISUAL SPECTACLE

The Chinese tomb, even without any images, is a rich book—one that we are only beginning to learn how to read properly. Compared with the aboveground cemetery plan, the belowground part of a mausoleum has never been systematically studied. First, it must be noted that concealing something from the public view does not necessarily make what is concealed private—just like locking up top secret files in a government agency does not turn these files into personal property. What really matters is the political nature of the concealment and how it is connected to the public interest.

The best way to understand what ideas a Western Han ruler or his representatives integrated in his mausoleum, and what particular public good the state sought in sponsoring the tombs, is to observe the things themselves—that is, to closely examine the hidden structure and content of the tombs and to identify the cognitive patterns behind them.

To do so, we need to devise an analytical method that synthesizes insights from various fields, including material culture studies and art history.

It is a widely accepted idea that visual forms can encode thoughts. Mathematicians draw diagrams to demonstrate abstract proofs without resorting to words; yet grasping the unspoken argument requires an intelligent eye.[57] Artists or artisans can do the same with artifacts, and humanities scholars are increasingly aware of hidden unwritten expressions. One of the most active areas of such inquiry is the interdisciplinary field called "material culture studies." Under the sway of hermeneutics, a group of anthropologists, archaeologists, and historians have taken an ontological approach to manmade things and have assumed that all such works are agents of "frozen" meanings that can be experienced as concepts and statements.[58] This theory applies not only to modern consumer society but also to past cultures and ethnological contexts.[59] From this perspective, early Chinese royal tombs were unquestionably physical artifacts, so their material properties can be treated in a manner similar to the treatment of anthropological things, which embody "habits of thinking and acting" associated with the culture and people who made them.[60]

Despite its recent popularity in early Chinese studies, the material culture studies approach has its limits.[61] A lavishly furnished and decorated royal tomb, unlike "stuff" in a shopping cart as Daniel Miller describes, was also a visual spectacle, even though that spectacle was eventually concealed. The lavish ritual banquets set up in both the front and rear chambers of the tombs at the Mancheng site, a topic I will examine closely in the following chapters, were a dazzling display of numerous jades and bronzes. In terms of decoding visual messages, art history has much research experience to contribute.

Form can communicate meaning. Egyptian pyramids hail monumentality just as much as modern political cartoons parody it. In the eighteenth century, the founding masters of the modern discipline of art history already understood the language of images and had begun to ponder how a concrete Greek statue might be visually eloquent about contemporaneous aesthetic or sociopolitical ideas such as democracy.[62] Such a mysterious semantic association between the form of art and an idea has a psychological basis because, as Rudolph Arnheim has shown, "the visible pattern represents a symbolic statement about the human condition,"[63] which is both personal and social. To push this idea further, theorists such as Norman Bryson have argued that any work of art consists of both "discursive" and "figural" dimensions.[64] While the latter ("figural") addresses the pure form that charms a viewer, the former ("discursive") registers meanings that are intelligible to a reader. An early Chinese ideograph perhaps represents the purest and simplest discursive aspect of images as both an image and a word.[65]

There have been two major approaches to uncovering the meaningful "discursive" aspect of visual art. One is diachronic. The formalists, represented by Heinrich Wölflin and Alois Riegl, extracted hidden historical information from the changing artistic style of artwork through the ages (in the West).[66] In the 1990s, Riegl's sensitive reading of even the most "insignificant" forms, rather than the represented content of art, inspired a new generation of scholars to pursue what has been called "neo-formalism."[67] Martin Powers executed the formalist idea within the sociopolitical context of early China in his book, *Pattern and Person: Ornament, Society, and Self in Classical China.* Through an analysis of the changing decorations of early Chinese bronzes and lacquerware, he showed how the seemingly meaningless "ornamental" art embodied the various philosophies from the late Eastern Zhou to the early Western Han.[68]

The other approach to uncover the discursive aspect of visual art is synchronic. Erwin Panofsky developed a new methodology out of traditional biblical iconography that decoded the meaning of pictures by comparing the pictorial content with contemporary textual descriptions on the neo-Kantian basis that both pictures and texts, as more sophisticated, "higher" cultural forms, shared the same "symbolic form," which lies at a deeper, autonomous level of spiritual life.[69] Panofsky's influence on the interpretation of early Chinese pictorial art is obvious. Recently, Lilian Lan-ying Tseng applied Panofsky's idea of iconology self-consciously in her study, *Picturing Heaven in Early China,* to explore the correlation between the textual and pictorial representations of heaven during the period from the Eastern Zhou to the Han.[70]

These two approaches, diachronic and synchronic, are apparently contradictory because they express two different types of historical consciousness. By analyzing visual materials, the diachronic focuses on the logical connections between changing formal and cognitive paradigms that occurred subsequently over time, whereas the synchronic penetrates deeply into one of the paradigms from the past and reveals its inner structural mechanism. However, the contradiction may be overcome if the researcher is able to, on the one hand, delve into one paradigm and, on the other hand, constantly remain alert as to the chosen paradigm's historical particularity: where it comes from and how it is similar to and different from its precedent(s). In the case of early Chinese royal tombs, whose mechanism is both structurally complex and time-specific, it seems mandatory to combine the two approaches to gain a full understanding of the subject.

However, the traditional methods developed in the fields of material culture studies and art history are not enough to deal with Chinese royal tombs because none of the sophisticated analytical tools they have introduced is fully capable of analyzing the spectacle of displaying large numbers of objects in an architectural space as a meaningful installation. My book adds another approach into the research—analysis of the "arena for artifacts."

Royal mausoleums such as the Mancheng tombs were neither hordes of mingled artifacts nor sets of programmed murals but rather webs of meaningful relations of spatially interconnected things, including various kinds of ritual and everyday artifacts, arranged in an architectural setting. Taken as a whole, an archaeological site as complex as the Mancheng tombs should be regarded as a monumental, multilevel work of art. At the object level, it consists of various types of tangible things including architecture, burial objects, and corpses, which are physically independent of one another. The traditional way of studying tombs focuses on this typological level.[71]

In typology, "a system used for putting things into groups according to how they are similar,"[72] each type is defined by external morphological or material characteristics shared among its specimens. In Chinese archaeology, a tomb is conventionally classified either by material into stone, brick, or timber, or by form, into vertical pit grave or horizontal chamber grave. Each of these general types (*xing* 型) can further divide into smaller subtypes (*shi* 式). Each type or subtype is associated with a particular cultural disposition, convention, or social community. An important task for typologists is to map the genealogical relationship among these types and subtypes, tracing how closely or distantly they are related to one another and how they have evolved stylistically across time and space.[73] The same method applies to everything contained in the tomb, such as the ceramics, bronzes, ironware, jades, lacquerware, fabrics, and so forth. In the basic sense, this mode of thinking may be related to biological taxonomy, which identifies species and positions them properly in the evolutionary tree.[74]

However, royal tombs are more than a collection of various things to be cataloged. On the relational level, the entombed objects are bound together by intangible, internal structures of meaning, which are essentially topological.

Although it may sound somewhat alien to humanistic scholars, in mathematics, topology is a well-established branch of knowledge specifically concerned with connectivity and continuity of a set of points or surfaces. It describes a type of geometry in which quality is more important than quantity, and connection is more relevant than distance.[75] In the natural sciences, such as chemistry and physics, topology usually denotes a study of relationships among family members or a group of elements rather than the individual elements themselves. Briefly summarized, topology is all about boundary, linkage, passage, connectivity, mediation, and itinerary. Traditional ways of looking at a Chinese tomb generally have fallen into rigid typological fashions of classification—the object's "hard," external, physical characteristics and have ignored the topological side of things—the "soft," internal, symbolic structures of meaning between or among objects. For example, in the case of ceramic pots, what matters in typology is the object's physical shape: whether the side is straight or curved might account for a distinct tradition of craftsmanship. But typologists usually do not consider, for example, how the curving shape fits with the decorative pattern on the surface or how this correspondence reflects any cultural identification or ideas. In light of this, typology is especially effective when dealing with large quantities of specimens with relatively simple features, such as plain ceramics, and becomes less and less accurate as objects grow artistically more sophisticated. One of the best research models to uncover these intangible relationships is Gaston Bachelard's *topoanalysis*, or "analysis of space," which was used to analyze homes.[76] Whereas for Bachelard *topoanalysis* describes "the systematic psychological study of the sites of our intimate lives," in the study of Chinese tombs this topological method can be appropriated to unravel the intentional relationships embedded among actual things and images placed across the burial chambers. With such internal artfulness, many materials traditionally regarded as "purely archaeological" can be alternatively approached as works of art.

What makes the Mancheng tombs a perfect target for such a topological investigation is the site's unique state of preservation: two almost perfectly intact parallel tombs, one for the king and one for the queen. The pristine state of the site allows us to see beyond its *hard* physical contents into its *soft* relational aspects, that is, we do not see the site only as individual objects (including architectural elements) or as a category/group of objects but also as spatial relations among the objects, such as placement and assemblage. For example, ritual vessels positioned as an orderly set are different from ritual vessels scattered at several different locations. The former expresses the display (visual spectacle), while the latter indicates the substance. As I will show in chapters one through three, the relational aspect of things, despite being extremely vulnerable to disruption, registers a comprehensive and perhaps fundamental pattern of thought that permeated the minds of early Chinese rulers, including Liu Sheng, during the formative period of the Chinese Empire.

THEME AND OUTLINE OF THE BOOK

Using a primarily topological analysis, employed in conjunction with a typological reading of the royal tombs at Mancheng in comparison with other related archaeological sites dating from the late Eastern Zhou to the Western Han period, this book demonstrates that the Mancheng tombs embody three major relational motifs. These patterns represent three religious, social, and political tasks for a king in second century BCE China: harmonizing the body and soul, the husband and wife, and the Chinese (*Han* 漢) and the "barbarians" (*Hu* 胡). By comparing archaeological analysis with textual evidence, this book further argues that Liu Sheng's political ideology, as embodied in his royal burial, culminates in the concept of tripartite "pacification" (*jing* 靖) of the self, the family, and the state, just as Liu Sheng's official posthumous honorific title "king of peace" (*jingwang* 靖王) suggests.

This book concludes that the construction of the Mancheng tombs as a public rather than a private project was a necessary "decoration" (*shi* 飾) of the "way of the sages" (*shengwang zhidao* 聖王之道), whose ultimate goal was to "pacify all under heaven" (*pingtianxia* 平天下), where the concept of *tianxia* (the public) was held in opposition to the *jun* 君, or the ruler himself. In this complex project, sustaining the ruler's individual life (or afterlife) was only the basis for, and hence subject to, the higher purpose of harmonizing the world.

This book consists of six chapters, organized into two parts. Part I, including chapters one through three, is an in-depth look at the two tombs themselves. The first chapter demonstrates that each of the Mancheng tombs was designed as an artistic model of everlasting longevity. Each tomb was shaped into a multilayered "Chinese box" of inner coffins and outer chambers to arrest the volatile remains of the dead (*shen* 神) and make them recurrently embrace and "attend" (*shou* 守) the solid remains (*xing* 形). This model of "cultivating the self" (*xiushen* 修身) modifies and elaborates the relatively simple Eastern Zhou prototypes and echoes the latest theories of longevity (*shou* 壽) and immortality (*xian* 僊) in early Chinese religion and science during the second century BCE. As claimed in many early Chinese politico-philosophical texts, this sustained selfhood serves as the primary basis for successful rulership.

Chapter two proves that the two parallel Mancheng tombs were a physical articulation of the union of husband and wife as each other's mirror image. Unlike the earlier Eastern Zhou models, the Mancheng model represents not only husband and wife as parallel but also their sharing "one united body" (*yiti* 一體) and "matching each other as the two halves of one body" (*panhe* 判合). The new model allows the wife's space (inner sphere) and her presence to merge and extend into the husband's space (outer sphere), which echoes the powerful intrusion of the emperors' in-laws into the imperial court. The stable power structure in the family further paved the way toward the harmonious functioning of the world.

Chapter three argues that both tombs at the Mancheng site synthesized the ethnic-Han and non-ethnic-Han visual elements from architecture to small objects across the royal couple's personal and social spaces to mediate between the two different cultures. The syncretic design of the tombs demonstrates that the suppressed cultural traditions of the Rong-Di 戎狄 survived or were revived in the Zhongshan kingdom during the second century BCE as an important force to maintain the cultural diversity of the region, which, in contemporary political thought, ensured peace.

The second part of the book, consisting of chapters four through six, shifts the primary attention from object to subject (i.e., from the tombs to the social agents that made or viewed them). Chapter four focuses on the public nature of royal tombs during the Western Han dynasty by analyzing the inscribed labels or seals on entombed artifacts as well as historical texts concerning Han governmental institutions. This chapter argues that, during the Western Han, because the duty of funding, building, and maintaining royal tombs belonged to the public treasury rather than the private purse of the ruler, the royal mausoleum became a property of the government and held a public function. It no longer served just the purpose of the ruler himself or of his family but rather contributed to the welfare of the state and "all under heaven." This result corroborates the previous chapters, showing that the royal tomb represented more than a happy home for the ruler himself.

Chapter five analyzes the historical and philosophical texts related to Liu Sheng to investigate his political ideology of pacification and harmonization, which was articulated in his tomb design. This chapter argues that Liu, posthumously titled "king of peace," might have been a follower of the Huang-Lao 黄老 philosophy, which advocated for "ruling through taking no deliberate action" (*wuwei erzhi* 無為而治) in governing the state, and also a proponent of Confucianism, which lauded the material elaboration of royal burials. The results from this textual analysis echo those from the visual and material investigation of the tombs, seeing them as an embodiment of political ideology.

Chapter six examines the problem of the audience of the Mancheng tombs, which were eventually hidden from public view and buried underground. By putting the tomb back into its ritual and intellectual context, this section argues that the Western Han royal tombs were still subject to the gaze of both the living authority of the government and the ancestors, believed to exist "underground" (*dixia* 地下). This gaze justified the arrangement of burial objects in the tomb space as an expression of the ideal social order, which has not yet been witnessed in any earlier Chinese tomb.

PART I

Chapter One

THE EMBRACE OF BODY AND SOUL

In archaeology, one basic issue is "the concept and operation of classification."[1] The ten thousand objects housed in the Mancheng tombs fall, in both functional and morphological terms, into two major groups that I categorize as "outfits" and "instruments."[2] An outfit clothed, equipped, or decorated the body. These consist of small, portable, and personal objects, such as hairpins, belt hooks, seals, and swords, and usually feature no legs (or bases) on which they could stand on their own but sometimes have holes so they can be suspended from the body. Either worn or carried, they traveled with the human subject. In contrast, instruments, including kitchenware, couches, tables, and food vessels, are usually large, heavy, or cumbersome, and often had feet or bases that allowed them to remain firm on a level surface. Rarely related to a specific body part such as the head, neck, chest, waist, or hands, these objects were not made to move with the body but were usually sacrificial objects for the ancestors to eat, see, scent, and so forth.

This binary classification finds historical justification in early Chinese texts, which also juxtaposed "outfits" (*fu* 服) and "instruments" (*qi* 器) as *the* two basic categories of ritual objects. In the *Discourses of the States* (*Guoyu* 國語, compiled third century BCE) text, the author recalled that in the good ancient times when rituals were not corrupted, people held orderly sacrifices to the gods and "made sacrificial instruments and outfits in accord with the proper season."[3] According to the *Book of Rites* (*Liji* 禮記, dated fourth to second centuries BCE), a proper gentleman should never place too much emphasis on his outfits and instruments.[4] Ancient Chinese people recognized that what divided these two categories were their differing relationships to the human subject: outfits were to be "worn" (*fu* 服) while instruments were to be "used" (*yong* 用).[5]

In the thick forest of objects furnishing the Mancheng tombs, it may seem that everything, be it *fu* or *qi*, could be placed anywhere in the chambers, but in fact the distribution of objects is highly regular. Some basic patterns are easy to recognize. For example, the front chamber was filled with various utensils (i.e., "instruments") but almost no small personal paraphernalia such as garment hooks, seals, hairpins, and mirrors (i.e., "outfits").[6] But in the two nested coffins in the rear chamber, we see exactly the opposite: No utensils were deposited at all, and all objects could be put on the human body. In the rear chamber, a space situated between the coffins and the front chamber, archaeologists found a modest number of both utensils and personal items. The same pattern is repeated in Mancheng tomb no. 2 as well as in some other royal tombs from the same period.[7] Does this variation in object placement, which has always been taken for granted, yield any significance?

In this chapter, through a close analysis of the type and placement of material remains, I will argue that the various interred outfits symbolize the changing postmortem appearance of the deceased. First, I will examine the "jade suit" as the imperishable jade body and man; second, by studying the placement of the objects in their original positions, I will discuss a hitherto ignored ritual outfit in the outer coffin, which was arranged as if it were worn by an invisible body of the deceased. Third, I will show that the outfit in the casket is reduced and scattered without holding to an anthropomorphic form. Next, by situating the three outfits (the "jade suit," the invisible outfit, and the scattered outfit) in the larger context of the tomb, I will demonstrate that their presence is not a coincidence but rather part of a program of showing the deceased's varying appearance, which might echo the metaphorical notions of "the form breaking down" (*xingjie* 形解) and "people flowing into form" (*liuxing* 流形) found in early Chinese texts. Finally, I will demonstrate that the spatial arrangement of different objects at Mancheng embodied a religious and philosophical understanding of longevity during the Western Han. The body and soul of the king were harmonized in order to attain an inseparable unity of life (or afterlife), which served as the basis for King Liu Sheng's political mission of restoring social order and stability among the local people of Zhongshan.

I will begin with the overall structure of the tomb and then proceed to examine the tomb, layer by layer, from the innermost zone (the inner coffin) to the outermost zone (the front chamber). This chapter will conclude with a discussion of the religious and political meaning of the embrace of body and soul.

ENCASING: THE HORIZONTAL "CHINESE BOX"

The first step in understanding the patterns within the tomb furnishings is to study the architectural setting. This space not only framed all objects within it but also defined their relationships with one another.

As mentioned in the introduction, Mancheng tomb no. 1 is an artificial cave complex cut horizontally into the east slope of Mt. Ling (map 3, figs. 0.2, 0.3). Visitors could only approach the Mancheng tombs through a lateral door, albeit permanently sealed, which defined the burial space horizontally into *inner* and *outer*. Inside the door, the concealed area was further divided into a front and a rear section. Offerings lay on sacrificial tables in the front, while the coffin rested in the rear. For a human subject standing before the doors, the deceased's body was located at the "back" of the tomb complex rather than in the center, as in earlier tombs.

Although Liu Sheng's tomb does represent a new principle of organizing burial space—horizontality—the Mancheng tombs also retained the traditional structure of nested coffins and caskets, which turned the tomb into a kind of multilayer box characteristic of large pit graves during the Shang and Zhou periods.[8] This fact is most obvious in the rear chamber. Holding the two nested coffins, the rear chamber was designed essentially like a box within a box. The outer case, namely the stone casket, was a compound assembled with stone slabs to imitate a two-room apartment under a hip-gabled roof (fig. 1.1). The main room in the north (fig. 1.1, no. 8) housed a set of two nested coffins, while the side room in the south was used as a bathroom (fig. 1.1, no. 9). Whereas the stone casket was constructed on site, the wooden coffins, with bronze wheels fitted beneath them, must have been pushed or pulled into the casket before they finally settled on the rectangular stone platform located on the north side of the main chamber.

Although the front chamber (fig. 1.1, no. 7) appears to be forward of the rear chamber, it was ingeniously modified to also serve as the outermost "box" that encases the rear chamber. The structure that fulfills this role is the gallery surrounding the rear chamber (fig. 1.1, no. 10). Although this

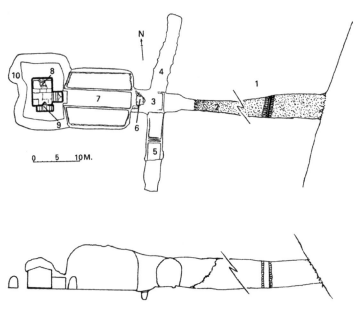

FIGURE 1.1 Plan and section of Mancheng tomb no. 1, Mancheng, Hebei, ca. 113 BCE. After Wen Fong, *The Great Bronze Age of China*, p. 325, fig. 111. Courtesy of Metropolitan Museum of Art, New York City.
1 Sealed doorway; 2 Tomb passage filled with rubble; 3 Entrance hall; 4 Storage area; 5 Stable; 6 Well; 7 Front chamber; 8 Rear chamber (house-shaped stone *guo* casket); 9 Bathroom; 10 Encircling corridor

gallery might relate to some slightly earlier prototypes found in other Western Han royal tombs (discussed in chapter 3), the architects revised the plan to make the gallery look like a physical extension of the front chamber. Instead of following the traditional practice of opening entries in the walls of a passage between the front chamber and the rear chamber, the gallery opens directly in the front chamber's rear wall with its two entries (exits) flanking the door to the rear chamber. In doing so, the tomb designer virtually encased the rear chamber within the front chamber and its connected gallery. Thus the king's tomb (no. 1) was designed essentially as a four-layer "Chinese box," while the neighboring tomb no. 2, which lacks the gallery, appears to be less archaizing.

This intention of editing the tomb plan to make it cohere with the traditional pit grave design finds further evidence in the special modification of the rear chamber. Liu Sheng's stone "house" almost completely occupies the entire rock-cut shell of his rear chamber, leaving only a narrow gap of less than ninety centimeters that was filled in with gravel (fig. 0.3).[9] In the adjacent Mancheng tomb no. 2, earth was used to fill this gap.[10] This filling transformed the stone house into an architectural interior; no free space was left for a viewer to circumambulate the house and inspect its exterior. At first glance, this extra effort might appear pointless because the stone house could stand on its own without any external structural support. In fact, the practice of filling the exterior space shows the designer's intention of imitating a traditional vertical pit grave, in which the assembled stone casket situated on the floor of a larger earthen shaft was completely enveloped by a wall of earth, sand, or gravel fill. The use of pebbles and ash (or charcoal) as fill was also derived from the local burial practice during the Eastern Zhou period that is referred to in the *Annals of Lü Buwei* (*Lüshi chunqiu* 呂氏 春秋, compiled in the third century BCE) as "filling with stones and charcoal" (*jishi jitan* 積石積炭).[11] These walls, which are a hallmark of vertical pit graves, are also called "the second-level ledge" (*ercengtai* 二層臺) in Chinese archaeological literature.[12] Considering the very limited room for maneuvering between the rock-cut shell and the stone house in the Mancheng tombs, the job of filling this gap with solid materials up to the height of the walls might have been much harder than filling the same interstice in a vertical pit grave, which only required workers to pour down the materials from above and pound them hard. This further increased the labor to install the casket but yielded no real function. However, the determination to include these details reveals the designer's mindset: to preserve, at least partially, the tradition of vertical pit graves, even though the plan of the tomb had fundamentally changed.

The purpose of painstakingly constructing the nested caskets and coffins, even if they were superfluous in function, was to preserve the basic structure of embracing and being embraced. The determination of modifying the otherwise horizontal tomb into a traditional pit grave shaped the architectural context in which the burial objects were organized into meaningful patterns.

To understand the patterns, as I will explain in the following sections, we are obliged to go through the four zones one by one. Within the four-layer architectural structure of Liu Sheng's tomb, it makes better sense to begin with the innermost coffin and move outward to the outer layers of the tomb. Moving from inside out is also possible because the centrifugal process represented the ancient perspective implied in the *Book of Rites*: The tomb contains "the *guan* coffin all around the clothes (*yi* 衣); the *guo* casket all around the *guan* coffin; the earth all around the *guo* casket."[13] Moving in the outward direction, the deceased's "body" is constantly dissolving.

THE SOLID APPEARANCE OF THE KING

What sits in the very center of the nested coffins is the king's hardest "body," represented by the imperishable humanoid "jade suit" (or *yuyi* 玉衣), which is the conventional name for a special type of funerary outfit uniquely made during the Han period (fig. 1.2, no. 173).[14] The nature of jade suits hinges upon the metaphorical identity of body and clothing in Western Han China.

Worn by the corpse from head to toe, the jade suit, as its name implies, represents clothing. Perhaps to evoke the sense of using textiles, artists broke the hard material into 2,498 jade pieces and "sewed" them together with 1,100 grams of gold wire (fig. 1.3). The size of the pieces, which are mostly rectangular but occasionally circular, triangular, rectangular, or rhombic, varies in area from fifteen square centimeters to just one and a half square centimeters. The edges of the jade pieces are pierced by a series of small holes. Gold threads pass through these holes and suture the pieces into twelve individual sections, each covering a particular part of the body: the front and the back of the head, the front and the back of the torso, the two arms, the two hands, the two legs, and the two feet.[15] Once assembled, the twelve sections form an almost seamless human shape. Although no traces of silk or fabrics were discovered inside the jade suit, the excavators did uncover a jade belt hook and a jade seal, which further suggest the symbolic (if not actual) presence of clothing.[16]

The jade suit was not only a variation of traditional shrouds used to wrap a corpse. In fact, that purpose could have been fulfilled by the conventional method of covering the corpse tightly with multiple layers of clothes in order to isolate the physical remains from the corrosive natural forces of air, water, and earth, as well as flesh-eating insects.[17] By Liu Sheng's time, the belief in wrapping the body so as to preserve it had become so deeply rooted in people's minds that rejecting that custom might have triggered deep controversy. For example, a commoner named Yang Wangsun 楊王孫 (fl. late second century BCE) shocked his sons and friends by requesting that his body be buried naked without any clothes. His argument for this unusual request was based on the belief that wrapping his body with clothes would deter the natural transformation (i.e., the decay of the body) that, from the Daoist perspective, was part of a healthy process.[18] If the jade suit was a substitute for traditional shrouds, why did the Western Han designers bother to invent a new and far more costly covering that simply filled the same role as an existing burial device?

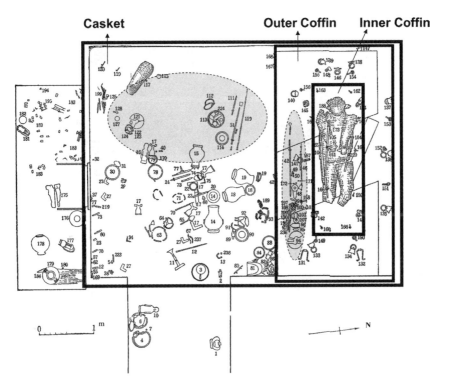

Casket   **Outer Coffin**   **Inner Coffin**

FIGURE 1.2 Plan and layout of rear chamber in Mancheng tomb no. 1, Mancheng, Hebei, ca. 113 BCE, with the location of the outfits highlighted. After Zhongguo shehui kexueyuan kaogu yanjiusuo, *Mancheng Han mu fajue baogao*, 1: 31, fig. 17. Courtesy of Wenwu Press.

1 Stone figurine; 2 Bronze crossbow trigger; 3 Bronze incense burner; 4 Lacquer platter; 5 Lacquer winged cup; 6 Lacquer platter; 7 Bronze ring; 10 Stone figurine; 11 Bronze lamp; 12 Iron stick; 13 Iron U-shaped object; 14 Bronze *hu* vessel; 15 Bronze *hu* vessel; 16 Stone figurine; 17 Bronze ornament of lacquer table; 18 Bronze *hu* vessel; 19 Bronze *hu* vessel; 20, 22 Bronze cauldrons; 23 Iron halberd; 24 Bronze sword; 27 Bronze ornament of lacquer table; 29 Bronze ornament; 30 Lacquer platter; 31 Lacquer winged cup; 32 Bronze fitting on lower end of ceremonial pole; 34 Bronze zoomorphic ornament; 35–37 Bronze zoomorphic masks; 38 Bronze coins; 40 Bronze belt hook; 42 Iron sword; 46 Bronze sword; 48 Jade disc; 49–50 Jade belt hooks; 51 Bronze sword; 54–55, 57 Bronze fittings on lower end of ceremonial pole; 60 Bronze ceremonial pole finial; 62 Bronze fitting on lower end of ceremonial pole; 63 Lacquer wine container; 64 Bronze tripod; 65 Bronze spoon; 67 Iron arrowhead; 70 Iron stick; 71 Lacquer platter; 73 Iron spear; 74 Bronze cauldron; 75 Bronze zoomorphic ornament; 77 Iron halberd; 78–79 Bronze cauldron; 80 Iron axle; 81 Bronze dustpan; 82 Bronze arrowhead; 84, 86–87, Bronze lamps; 88 Lacquer platter; 89 Bronze figurine; 90 Bronze incense burner; 91 Bronze zoomorphic ornament; 92 Iron heater; 93 Bronze coins; 94 Jade disc; 95–96 Jade tablets; 97 Bronze knife; 98 Jade disc; 99 Jade ring; 100 Jade pendant; 101 Jade hairpin; 103 Bronze zoomorphic mask; 104 Iron long knife; 105–106 Iron swords; 107 Jade disc; 108 Iron knife; 109 Iron short sword; 110 Iron sword; 111 Iron sword; 112 Lacquer box; 113 Lacquer toiletry box; 114 Lacquer platter; 115 Lacquer box; 117 Iron armor; 119–120 Silver shield ornaments; 121 Jade disc; 122–123 Glass winged cups; 124 Glass platter; 125 Iron hammer; 126 Painted lacquer fragment; 127 Lacquer box; 128 Bronze scoop-shaped object; 130 Carnelian bead; 131–132 Bronze pulley with iron bracket; 133–141 Bronze zoomorphic masks; 142–145 Bronze wheels; 146 Silver zoomorphic mask; 147–148 Bronze zoomorphic masks; 149–158 Large bronze coffin ring pulls; 159–166 Small bronze coffin ring pulls; 167 Bronze zoomorphic mask on a lacquerware; 168 Bronze hinge; 169 Iron baton; 170–171 Jade seals; 172 Jade figurine ("old jade man"); 173 Jade suit; 175 Stone figurine; 176 Bronze basin; 177 Bronze lamp; 178–179 Bronze *lei* wine jars; 180 Clay seal stamp; 181 Bronze lamp; 182 Bronze gilt incense burner; 183 Bronze fitting from object; 184 Rubbing stone; 188 Bronze pillow; 189 Gold bullion; 190 Bronze door security lock; 194 Bronze ceremonial pole finial; 195 Iron hinge; 196 Iron short sword; 197 Iron knife; 199 Iron bow handle; 219 Bronze fitting on lower end of ceremonial pole; 220 Gold belt buckle; 222 Iron arrowhead; 223 Jade cylinder ornament; 224 Bronze mirror; 236 Iron knife; 237 Iron handle; 238 Square iron object; 240–241 Jade half-rings

FIGURE 1.3 Jade suit from Mancheng tomb no. 1, Mancheng, Hebei, ca. 113 BCE. Courtesy of Hebei Museum, Shijiazhuang.

To answer this question, we must note some fundamental differences between a jade suit and traditional shrouds. The most obvious distinction is materiality. Regular cloth shrouds were soft and plastic, but the jade suit was hard and brittle. Hence, jade was unsuited for making clothing.

But jade, or nephrite, had the advantage of being so hard that it was considered immortal, while regular shrouds made of fabrics easily perished. For thousands of years, jade had been the primary "magic" material for the ancient Chinese, who believed it safeguarded the body from decay. Whereas the first use of jade in tombs occurred as early as the Neolithic period,[19] the practice of systematically covering corpses with jade ornaments dates directly back to the elaborate and coherent assemblage in the cemetery of the marquises of the Jin 晉 state at Tianma-Qucun, in present-day Houma, Shanxi.[20] A typical Zhou set of burial jades consisted of a face cover and chest ornaments. The face cover utilized a piece of cloth ornamented with a group of jade appliqués to sketch a fantastic human face, sometimes with stylized mustaches, eyebrows, hair, and even facial decorations.[21] The chest ornament consisted of a lavish group of jade pendants, including *bi* discs, *huan* rings, *huang* half-rings, and other small wearable ornaments such as beads that were strung together into a great "necklace."[22] It has been suggested that these jade body decorations were a probable origin of the Han jade suits.[23]

Unlike their Jin precedents, which were jade ornaments attached to textiles that might or might not possess magic powers, Han jade suits usually had no ornamentation and were totally independent of textiles. Rather, they formed a protective container; they completely encased the corpse unlike any regular clothing. This may be why jade suits were referred to in later Eastern Han texts as *yuxia* 玉匣 (jade caskets).[24] Although the word *xia* literally means "casket," a container meant for concealment and enclosure,[25] it could also be interpreted as "armor" because the archaic pronunciations

of the two words "casket" (*xia* 匣) and "armor" (*jia* 甲) are almost identical.[26] Perhaps because of this synonymous relationship, Wei Hong 衛宏
(fl. first century CE) made the following observation: "(The makers of jade
suits) transform the jade into a jacket which looks like a piece of armor
bound by gold wires."[27] Not coincidently, the small thin pieces of jade suits
and the way they are bound together recall the weapon-making technique of
scale armor, which is also found in the king's rear chamber.[28] Fragments of a
possible prototype of jade armor were recently brought to light in some late
Warring States royal tombs in Henan and Hebei,[29] but the best-known example of such stone armor was found in the First Emperor of Qin's necropolis.
In 1999, the discovery of a sacrificial pit in the mausoleum revealed dozens
of sets of heavy, brittle helmets and armor.[30] Like a jade suit, each suit of
armor was made of small stone plaques with holes around their edges so that
they could be bound together with bronze wires. The kinship of jade suits
to armor reinforces the former's magic protective power that is derived from
the imperishable materiality of jade.

But Liu Sheng's jade suit was more than armor because it not only clothed
and protected the human body but also accurately traced its entire shape.[31]
It was humanoid. The jade suit wrapped the whole corpse from head to toe,
while a real suit of armor and helmet (or their stone funerary counterparts)
only shielded certain critical parts of the body.[32] Even though some two
thousand years of natural erosion had reduced the royal remains to a two-
millimeter-thin layer of ash, the jade suit—once tightly wrapped around the
body—still preserved the king's disintegrated physical image on his coffin-
bed in the rear chamber. What's more, once assembled together, the head,
face, torso, limbs, hands, and feet added up to a full naturalistic body in
the round, characterized by saggy eyes and mouth, protruding nose, slightly
bulgy belly, fleshy butt cheeks, and precisely modeled thighs, calf muscles,
and fingers (fig. 1.3). Another jade suit excavated from the Shizishan royal
tomb in present-day Xuzhou, Jiangsu Province, even includes two nipples on
the front of the chest.[33]

The practice of making humanoid jade suits was not without conceptual
parallels. In late Eastern Zhou and Western Han literature, Chinese authors
used the phrase "jade body" (*yuti* 玉體) as a metaphor for the rulers' fragile
health.[34] A medical text excavated in an early second-century BCE burial at
present-day Zhangjiashan, Hubei, outlined the belief that leaving the five
organs empty would "benefit the jade body" and keep it healthy.[35] From
this perspective, the humanoid jade suit might have been the actualization

of this metaphysical concept. However, in another more likely theory, as I have suggested elsewhere, the jade suit in Mancheng tomb no. 1 probably was meant to represent a "jade man" (yuren 玉人) that was not only imperishable per se but also magically capable of granting life and extending the reign.[36] Even the less magic "stone men" (shiren 石人) had imperishable bodies and lived forever. According to Sima Qian, Empress Dowager Wang 王太后 (d. 125 BCE) once admitted that her son—Emperor Wu—could never live an eternal life like a "stone man."[37] If a stone man would never die, a jade man—made of what was the hardest and most beautiful stone known to the ancient Chinese—would certainly last forever. Furthermore, jade was believed to be a medium that connected the human and the spirit, a role that ordinary stones could not fulfill.[38] In the use of a "jade man" or a "stone man," there was no negative indication of jade or stone being fragile and brittle, such as in the concept of "jade body" (yuti); they fit in better with the funerary context at Mancheng, where preservation of the corpse was a primary concern.

Despite its undeniable naturalism, Liu Sheng's jade suit was by no means a perfectly faithful imitation of the human body. Although the jade head was fashioned in a naturalistic manner, the incisions for the eyes and mouth are so thin that they are barely recognizable; and, in fact, the ears are completely omitted. Also, the "jade man" is not entirely naked. For example, unlike the hands, where each finger was crafted in a realistic manner, the feet are represented as wearing shoes (fig. 1.3).[39] Furthermore, a group of small wearable items was found both inside and outside the jade suit. Within the jade suit, there were a group of bi discs, face covers, a necklace, a garment hook, and a seal; outside the jade suit, there were some swords and ritual jades. These objects were usually grouped together as an outfit to decorate the human body. If the jade suit only represented the human body, it would appear nonsensical for some of the personal items to be found inside the jade "body." Hence the placement implies the idea that the jade suit is part of a larger outfit that covered the deceased body.

Therefore, the jade suit was neither a mere representation of clothing nor that of a human body. It was not even a juxtaposition of the two archetypes. Instead, the complex jade suit merged the notions of body and clothing so that the two grew into each other and could not be easily separated. This inseparable intertwining testifies to the metaphorical relationship between the two. Clothes wrap, frame, and resemble the natural body within them. The twofold meaning of the jade suit perfectly embodies this relationship.

In early China, as demonstrated by the hybrid jade suit and the jade man described earlier, a noble person's costume and his or her appearance were metaphorically bound together. In the Eastern Zhou ethic, a cultivated gentleman could never put aside his clothing, which was considered a symbolic extension of his physical body. Even ghosts were always visualized as being clad in clothes rather than naked.[40] This is probably because, as a passage from the *Discourses of the States* (*Guoyu*) nicely puts it: "Clothing is the external pattern (*wen* 文) of the heart," the very core of the body.[41] According to an author of the *Luxuriant Dew of the Spring and Autumn Annals* (*Chunqiu fanlu* 春秋繁露, compiled in the second to first centuries BCE), while the human body was located at the center of the universe (between heaven and earth), the clothes upon it represented the gods of the four cardinal directions of the universe.[42] Hence the inseparable relationship between body and clothing resembles the relationship between the universe's center and its peripheries.[43]

The metaphorical relationship between body and clothing is by no means unique to early China. In many cultures of the world, clothing is not only a metaphor for the wearer's physical body but also the "social skin" that merges into his or her social body.[44] From a phenomenological point of view, clothing is a default part of the human experience of "the picture of our own body which we form in our own mind," which psychologist Paul Schilder called the "image of the body."[45]

Modern theorists have also realized that the metaphorical identity of body and clothing worked in death as well as it worked in life. Archaeologist Joanna Sofaer, ruminating on the ontological status of the corpse, has critiqued the view that biological death shifted the ontological perception of the body by turning it from a subject to an object and claimed that "the human skeleton may retain a social presence in death even though it becomes inanimate."[46] In fact, what modern archaeologists see as "human skeletons" might have been fleshy bodies clad in different clothing in the eyes of the ancient funeral participants. Nevertheless, the traditional divide between the living body as a cultural subject and the dead body as a natural object was untenable, for "bodies will always be both, albeit in different and changing configurations."[47] These contemporary theories, though not derived from a Chinese context, are an illuminating footnote to the metaphorical relationship between body and clothing in Western Han.

Indeed, this indisputable truth is clearly demonstrated in the social distinction of jade suits in Han China. Only emperors, kings, and marquises (and their principal wives) were eligible to receive jade suits, which were divided into three grades. According to the imperial norm during the Eastern Han dynasty, emperors could use gold wires to connect the jade plaques, kings could use silver wires, and marquises, only bronze wires.[48] If this rule also applied during the Western Han period, then the Zhongshan king and queen must have been given the exceptional imperial privilege by the emperor to use gold wiring. Because it was reserved exclusively for royalty, in this sense, a "jade man" also meant a royal person.

If the jade suit represented the perfect, incorruptible body, where was the soul in the inner coffin? It must be noted that besides the jade suit, Liu Sheng's corpse was also equipped with a group of jade pieces used to cover the so-called "nine orifices" (*jiuqiao* 九竅), including the two eyes, two nostrils, two ears, the mouth, the anus, and the genitalia. Fashioned into the right sizes and shapes to fit the different bodily parts, all these items appeared in the corresponding locations: the eyes, nostrils, ears, and mouth covers above the neck, and the anus and genital capsule below the belly. Some of these objects, such as the anus plug, were physically inserted into the human body. Jade was deliberately chosen as *the* proper material, for people in the Han dynasty might have generally believed that, as specified in a later statement by Ge Hong 葛洪 (285–343 CE), "when gold and jade are inserted into the nine orifices, corpses do not decay."[49] The reasoning behind this belief was that plugging the bodily orifices with magic jade would make the soul unable to leak from the body and thus keep the body in a "living" state.

Regardless of such artificial intervention, the body and the soul were imagined as being in a natural relationship. To explain the abstruse mechanism of body and soul, the philosopher Wang Chong 王充 (27–ca. 97 CE) made a lively analogy in his philosophical treatise titled *Balanced Discourses* (*Lunheng* 論衡):

Take a sack and fill it with millet or rice. When the millet or rice has been put into it, the sack will be full and sturdy and will stand up in clear view so that people looking at it from a distance can tell that it is a sack of millet or rice. Why? Because the shape of the sack bespeaks the contents. But if the sack has a hole in it and all the millet or rice runs out, then the sack collapses in a heap and people looking from a distance can no longer see it. The spirit of man is stored up in his bodily form like the millet or rice in the sack. When he dies and his body decays, his vital forces disperse like the grain running out of the sack. When the grain has run out, the sack no longer retains its shape. Then when the spirit of man has dispersed and disappeared, how could there still be a body to be seen by others?[50]

In Wang Chong's analogy, clothing frames the body, which in turn frames the soul. Put otherwise, the soul fills the body, which in turn fills the clothes. The three layers of things are hence metaphorically united. In light of this analogy, the orifices of the perfect human body ("jade suit") were plugged with pieces of jade to stop the soul (Wang Chong's "grains") from escaping from the body ("sack") and prevented the corpse from decaying (the "sack" collapsing and no longer visible).

In the funerary context, the apparently futile and paradoxical use of the jade suit (to pretend the body was incorruptible) and the jade plugs (to pretend the soul remained in the body without leaking) on the deceased king nonetheless demonstrate a wishful thinking, if not a magic technique, of keeping the royal tomb occupant immortal even in death.

However, the solid and seamless body of the royal subject lost its form in the outer coffin, while the plugged soul was no longer restricted.

THE INTANGIBLE APPEARANCE OF THE KING

The outer coffin was an important ritual component in early Chinese burial.[51] As part of a set of multilayer burial devices consisting of nested coffins (*guan* 棺) and caskets (*guo* 椁) used to conceal the dead, the outer coffin appeared in China as early as the Neolithic period as additional protection for the corpse.[52] During the Eastern Zhou period, with the theoretical justification of this practice, this simple protective device became a symbol of the social status of the deceased—the more layers one had, the higher his or her rank.[53] By the second century BCE, however, this rule was no longer strictly obeyed. Some layers could be reduced or omitted. Although in ritual codes it is prescribed that a king should have five layers of caskets and coffins,[54] Liu Sheng's horizontal tomb, strictly speaking, only consisted of one casket and two nested coffins.[55] If the use of nested coffins in Liu Sheng's tomb departed from pre-Han mortuary conventions and no longer appears to be a direct indicator of the deceased king's royal status,[56] for what reason was Liu Sheng's outer coffin added?

Answering this question requires us to examine the outer coffin more closely. Before the excavators opened Liu Sheng's outer coffin, they probably did not expect to see the variety of objects concentrated at the side of the inner coffin. With the inner coffin pushed to the northern side of the outer coffin, a long narrow area was cleared on the south side in which objects could be placed (fig. 1.2). All the objects in this area were small, portable,

FIGURE 1.4 Two jade seals from (*left*) Liu Sheng's *guo* casket and (*right*) outer coffin of Mancheng tomb no. 1, Mancheng, Hebei, ca. 113 BCE. Courtesy of Hebei Museum, Shijiazhuang.

jade or metal articles, including a hairpin (fig. 1.2, no. 101), a seal (fig. 1.2, no. 171), some swords and knives (fig. 1.2, nos. 42, 46, 97, 104–106), belt hooks (fig. 1.2, nos. 49–50), and ornamental pendants (fig. 1.2, nos. 98–100)—all designed to be part of a ceremonial outfit. The presence of such ritual props as *bi* discs and *gui* tablets, which were held in the hands, attests to the ritual function of this outfit.[57] Unlike the jade suit, which was an imperishable piece of work and remained almost intact upon discovery, many of these objects in the outer coffin were probably attached to a ritual robe, which did not survive. Because there is only one hairpin, one bead, two belt hooks, one seal, two long swords and two short swords, a few knives/tools, one *bi* disc, one *she* ring, and one *huan* ring, the ritual objects can form no more than one set, indicating that there might have been only one outfit and presumably one robe. No lacquer remains were reported in this area, suggesting these objects should have been laid out directly in the outer coffin, presumably on the ritual robe, without being contained in boxes.

This outfit was associated with Liu Sheng rather than any real or symbolic human attendant or sacrifice. The evidence is fourfold. First, the shape of the square jade seal (fig. 1.2, no. 171) ornamented with a freestanding roaming hornless dragon or tiger matches exactly the form of an imperial seal (fig. 1.4b).[58] Although this beautiful object was uninscribed and blank, its royal ownership is unquestionable.[59]

Second, the handheld *gui* tablets (fig. 1.2, nos. 95–96) were ritually entitled to male royal family members. Western Han emperors would hold jade tablets to attend the imperial heavenly cult.[60] The extensive presence of weapons further suggests the subject must be male because few weapons appear in women's tombs, a gender issue I will elaborate on in chapter 2.

(a) **(b)**

FIGURE 1.5 (a) Jade figure from the outer coffin of Mancheng tomb no. 1, Mancheng, Hebei, ca. 113 BCE. (b) Inscription on bottom of jade figure identifying it as "an old jade man." Courtesy of Hebei Museum, Shijiazhuang.

Third, among the ritual ornaments and props, the excavators also uncovered a jade figurine (fig. 1.2, no. 172; fig. 1.5a) presumably carried by the owner of the outfit for religious purposes.[61] The inscription carved on the base of the statuette claims: 維古/玉人/王公/延十/九年 (fig. 1.5b), or in English, "This is an old jade man [that possesses the power to] extend the prince's life by nineteen years."[62] Such prophetic texts for prolonging life were not uncommon in early China. Almost always associated with members of the ruling class, they usually begin with the explicit heavenly omen (e.g., the jade man or the movement of Mars) and end with the prophecy of extended life.[63]

Fourth and finally, a small carnelian bead (fig. 1.2, no. 130) uncovered beside the knives around the waist of the invisible person in the outer coffin is identical to the other beads of a necklace worn around Liu Sheng's neck inside the jade suit within the inner coffin, implying a shared identity.[64]

All the evidence supports the fact that the outfit should belong to a male king who shared his identity with Liu Sheng.[65] This also means the owner of the blank seal should also be the deceased king, who was yet to determine what his honorific title would be in the afterlife.[66]

The practice of placing empty outfits in the outer coffin to give the tomb occupant an extra layer of clothing was not exceptional during the second century BCE. A slightly earlier example was found in Fenghuangshan tomb no. 168 (dated early second century BCE), occupied by a fifth grandee (*Wudafu* 五大夫) (rank no. 9) aristocrat.[67] In this tomb, while the corpse in the inner coffin remained bareheaded, the outer coffin contained two silk hats in the east interstice between the two coffins, just above the head-level of the recumbent corpse. While the corpse wore a pair of linen shoes, another pair of silk shoes appeared in the west interstice between the two coffins, just below the foot level of the corpse. In addition, a wooden cane was placed on top of the outer coffin, approximately at the position of the arms.[68] In terms of position, all these items corresponded exactly to the affiliated parts of the deceased's body as if these objects, though detached from the corpse, formed an extra outfit for the human remains beyond the inner coffin. Although no silk or cloth has survived from Liu Sheng's outer coffin, in another Zhongshan royal tomb occupied by one of Liu Sheng's descendants, remains of such fragile materials were found on top of the outermost three coffins.[69]

However, the outfit in Liu Sheng's outer coffin was different from its precedents at Fenghuangshan or other sites in terms of placement. Most of the objects of the outfit were positioned as if they were worn by an invisible person lying in the same orientation as the corpse (fig. 1.2, marked gray area in the outer coffin). Texts, paintings, and archaeological remains from the Han period give us a clear idea of how various pendants usually appear on the body: (1) Belt hooks always define the level of the waist, from which all kinds of pendants are hung. In Liu Sheng's outer coffin, two belt hooks lie together (fig. 1.2, nos. 49–50). (2) A sword is usually attached to the waistband from a clasp on the scabbard. This clasp is located approximately at the midpoint of the entire sword, dividing the weapon into two equal halves. In Liu Sheng's outer coffin, the long swords precisely flank the two belt hooks, which divide the swords into two equal halves (fig. 1.2, no. 42). (3) Seals are often fastened to a ribbon that hangs slightly below the waist, sometimes contained in a leather purse suspended from the waistband.[70] In Liu Sheng's outer coffin, accordingly, between the long swords, the seal appears right below the belt hooks (fig. 1.2, no. 171). (4) Jade pendants including *bi* discs, *huan* rings, and *she* rings normally are suspended farther below the waist. In Liu Sheng's outer coffin, all the pendants appear below the belt hooks and the seal (fig. 1.2, nos. 98–100). (5) The small swords and knives usually appear right below the waist, and in the outer coffin, they do so below the long sword on the left. In Liu Sheng's outer coffin, all these objects are positioned as if they were worn by a person who lies in the same orientation as the corpse (fig. 1.2, marked gray area in the outer coffin).[71]

All these metal or jade objects in the outer coffin served as a suite of portable ritual paraphernalia. They were all physically associated with particular body parts: The hairpin was worn in the hair; the swords and knives, seal, ornament, and garment hooks decorated the waist; the discs and the tablets were held in the hands. Even with minor displacement or dislocation, many of the objects were arranged precisely as their counterparts in the inner coffin: The jade ornaments appeared in the center, and the weapons flanked the ornaments on both sides. This arrangement looks as if an invisible body inhabited the outfit.

The arrangement of the objects in the outer coffin was the result of great care. While in earlier or contemporary tombs the outer coffin was usually only slightly larger than the tightly encased inner coffin and was furnished with only a small number of ritual jades, such as *bi* discs or *gui* tablets, pendants, textiles, or cosmetics,[72] Liu Sheng's outer coffin contained a relatively spacious area, in which a large group of jades and metal objects was deposited to the south of the inner coffin (fig. 1.2, marked gray area in the outer coffin). This design was impractical because, with so much additional room, when the nested coffins were moved into position in the tomb, the unsecured inner coffin could easily slide or tip over, damaging the corpse and objects inside. This also suggests that people used extra care while transporting this nested burial device steadily and securely over the long distance from the royal home, where the funeral was usually held, to the cemetery. This additional cost of human energy spent in maintaining this open space attests to the importance of maintaining the unworn state of the outfit within it.

The carefully positioned and preserved outfit further recalls the metaphor of clothing and the body. The political philosophy of the same period furnished this metaphor with a special meaning. From this perspective, an ideal ruler, void of desire or ambition, takes no actions, and "his body is like a motionless, hung robe (*weiyi* 委衣)."[73] In the *Annals of Lü Buwei* text, the sage king Yao 堯, in the remote past is portrayed as one whose effective ruling cost him little effort: "Yao's appearance was like a hung robe, which means there were few (administrative) affairs."[74] Reflecting upon the end-less turbulence and power struggles of his own era, the scholar Jia Yi 賈誼 (201–169 BCE) lamented on the lost golden age of Chinese antiquity when, even in the absence of the king, the world remained in good order and minis-ters reported dutifully to the ruler's hung robe as if he were present in it.[75] In these texts, a ruler's empty clothing became a metaphor for the royal subject.

In the funerary context, the deceased's outfits were considered the most common symbol of his or her appearance during rituals. In the Eastern Zhou ritual, the presence of the ancestor was enacted by an impersonator (shi 尸)—another form of metaphor—who dressed up to imitate the departed spirit. However, during the Western Han period, the ancestor's empty cloth-ing replaced the human actor to evoke the supernatural presence. During the funeral, after the corpse had been put in the coffin, the deceased's clothes often took the place of and stood in for the concealed, invisible body. After the funeral, the ritual of the monthly parade of hats and robes (yue you yiguan 月遊衣冠) of the departed emperor demonstrated the metaphorical relationship between clothing and the wearer's physical appearance.[76] The procession started at the retiring chamber in the necropolis, where the cultic apparel and outfits were worshiped, then stopped at the ancestral temple to receive a sacrifice, and finally returned to the tomb. According to Michael Loewe, "Presumably the purpose for the conveyance of the imperial clothes was to symbolize a journey that was being undertaken by the emperor to a place where he would receive honors, i.e., from the ch'in (qin 寢), where he received four meals daily, to the miao 廟, where he was entertained with the more special offering that was presented only once monthly."[77]

Even in daily life, the clothing of the deceased could index his or her absent appearance. One touching episode took place in 78 CE, two hundred years after the death of Liu Sheng. Emperor Zhang 章帝 (r. 75–88 CE) of the Eastern Han dynasty sent a few clothes of his deceased grandmother to his uncle. In his enclosed letter, the emperor expressed his kind wish that his uncle would look respectfully at these clothes from time to time to visualize the appearance of his mother, whose physical remains had been forever hid-den in her mountain-like mausoleum.[78]

Rather than being distributed around the inner coffin, as seen in the Fen-ghuangshan case, the objects in Liu Sheng's outer coffin were arranged to simulate another invisible body lying next to the corpse in the inner coffin. In doing so, the furnisher of the coffins emphasized that the burial objects in the outer coffin were assigned not to the corpse, as was the case in the

Fenghuangshan tomb, but to another independent, invisible form of the king, existing outside the inner coffin.

Why did Liu Sheng have to possess a second form, albeit a metaphorical one, through the empty outfit, in addition to his unique physical form? The ontological state of this additional form is fourfold. First, it maintains a human shape; second, it is invisible; third, it is of a (dead) person; fourth and last, it exists outside the deceased's physical remains. While the first two conditions apply to all spirits,[79] to accord with the latter two conditions, the subject must be the soul of a deceased human subject. For a person about to die, his or her soul was imagined as lingering beyond and hovering above the body. And this was the moment when the ritual of "summoning the soul" (*zhaohun* 招魂 or *fupo* 復魄) took place. Because people in early China usually assumed that the departed soul would never remain naked without clothes,[80] a ritual specialist would ascend to the rooftop, waving a robe in his hands and calling the wandering soul to come back. At last, the soul was imagined as if it were in (or wearing) the robe, which was then brought down and put on the dying person, so as to introduce the escaping soul back into the body. When this effort of reuniting the body and soul failed, the person would be declared dead, and the dislodged soul would wander farther and fade away.[81]

The deceased's clothing, once attached to the soul, would assume certain agency and appear "alive." According to Ban Gu, the deceased Emperor Ai's 漢哀帝 (r. 7–1 BCE) spirit clothing originally concealed in a box once suddenly disappeared by itself:

On the day of *yiwei*, the "spirit outfit" (*shenyi* 神衣) at the Yi Mausoleum was concealed in the wooden case (*xia* 柙); in the morning of the day of *bingshen* [the next day], however, the outfit made its appearance on the outside bed (*waichuang* 外床).[82]

This incredible incident, which took place in 1 CE, was interpreted as the previous emperor's soul expressing his anger at the powerful minister Wang Mang 王莽 (45 BCE–23 CE), who was plotting to usurp the imperial throne. Located in the emperor's aboveground "funerary resting chamber" (*lingqin* 陵寝), this magic "spirit outfit" was surprisingly similar to the mysterious outfit in Liu Sheng's outer coffin as they were both concealed in a wooden case.

Because Liu Sheng's outer coffin surrounded the inner coffin from above and beside, the outfit in the outer coffin occupied an enclosed space that was both beyond and above the inner coffin, where a hovering soul was supposed

44

PART I

to linger. If the inner coffin held the perfectly undamaged (or rather, unbreakable) body—the jade suit that symbolically withheld the trapped soul, the outer coffin seems to have contained the almost intact soul that had wandered out of the body. In the outer coffin, despite the absence of the physical body, the invisible soul "wearing" the outfit without dispersing still maintained the form of the body.

However, as the soul began to dissipate, its integrity must rely on consuming the sacrifice. This is exactly what happens in Liu Sheng's casket—the stone house-shaped chamber.

THE DISSOLVING APPEARANCE OF THE KING

Encasing the outer coffin, Liu Sheng's *guo* casket contains another outfit in the west that registered the deceased's dissolving appearance (fig. 1.2, marked gray area in the casket), while a banquet of food and wine in the east arrests the soul and prevents it from dissipating completely.

Like the two previous outfits in the inner and outer coffins, this outfit also belongs to Liu Sheng. With the absence of sacrificed attendants in this chamber, all the life-sized objects can only be worn by the deceased, whereas miniaturized figurines were usually equipped with miniaturized artifacts.[83] Not coincidentally, this outfit includes an uninscribed jade seal that is almost identical to the one found in Liu Sheng's outer coffin, confirming the invisible master's royal identity (fig. 1.4a, fig. 1.2, no. 170).[84] In the aforementioned story of Emperor Ai's spirit outfit, it suddenly vanished from the secret case and appeared in the "outside bed." Such an "outside bed" corresponds well with Liu Sheng's stone casket.

However, in contrast to the elaborate, well-arranged ritual outfit in the outer coffin, the one found in the *guo* casket is much reduced and less organized in several aspects.

First, in typology, the pendants are reduced to the essential assemblage of a belt hook (fig. 1.2, no. 40), a seal (fig. 1.2, no. 170), a *bi* disc (fig. 1.2, no. 121), and three swords (fig. 1.2, nos. 51, 110, 111). Further, there are no decorative jade pendants, which are replaced by small lacquer toiletry cases for cosmetics. The different standard of dress suggests that the subject of this outfit was engaged more with such personal and relatively casual issues as beautification rather than with formal ceremonies.

Second, in terms of location, whereas the lavish outfit in the outer coffin was restricted to a narrow zone about thirty centimeters wide, the reduced outfit was loosely spread across an area three-and-a-half-times wider, even though the lengths of the two outfits are almost identical (approximately two meters).[85] It looks as if the deceased's form was spreading out. In accordance with the casual occasion, toward the east, a lavish banquet is centered on a large low dais surmounted by a small table. As in imperial rituals, the most honored figure usually took his or her position in the west. The outfit to the west of the table clearly represents such a figure facing toward the east.

Third, in terms of placement, the outfit no longer abides by an anthropomorphic form. Although the belt hook (fig. 1.2, no. 40) and the seal (fig. 1.2, no. 170) are located together in the middle of the spread-out area, the rest of the objects do not fall into the relative positions seen in the outfit of the outer coffin. Rather, they separate on the two sides. On the northwest side are a toiletry case set (fig. 1.2, no. 113), an individual lacquer box (fig. 1.2, no. 112), and the swords (fig. 1.2, nos. 51, 110, 111); on the southwest side are a *bi* disc and two individual lacquer boxes (fig. 1.2, nos. 115, 127).[86] As a result, even though the symbolic presence of the deceased is obvious, we are unable to recognize the shape of his body or its orientation.

In Liu Sheng's tomb, all these differences contribute to a progressively disintegrating state of clothing from inside to outside. More importantly, given the metaphorical relationship between man and clothing, as the outfit is breaking down, dispersing, and diminishing, so is the deceased's invisible appearance that is wrapped and framed by the outfit. The inner coffin contains Liu Sheng's jade suit, which encases the naked corpse with a jade *bi* disc, a belt hook, two seals, and three swords (the same essential pendant group as in the casket) and represent the concrete human body with a head, a torso, four limbs, and even facial features. The second outfit in the outer coffin frames the deceased's invisible and flexible body in a human form. The last outfit in the casket refers to the appearance of the deceased but rejects the anthropomorphic form. Beyond the deceased's physical body, his outfit gradually breaks down until it diminishes into a *bi* disc and a group of swords that are completely unrelated in space in the front chamber as I will demonstrate in the following section.

But why was the deceased's outfit that frames his body, which in turns frames his soul, gradually melting away? The concept of *xingjie* 形解 (literally, "body dissolution") may best capture the nature of this process. Although in medieval Daoism this term is often translated as "release from the form,"[87] in the Western Han religious context, its more literal translation, "body (*xing*) dissolution (*jie*)," seems more accurate. In the *Shiji* text,

Sima Qian reported that a few magicians from the Yan 燕 region "practiced the way of transcendence, broke and melted down their forms, and followed the affairs of ghosts and spirits."[88] After the topic word, *xing* (form), the author juxtaposed three synonymous verbs: *jie* 解, *xiao* 銷, and *hua* 化, to describe the magical changes to the body: The first verb, *jie*, literally means to break down (from whole to parts), the second verb, *xiao*, to melt down (from solid to liquid), and the third verb, *hua*, to ontologically transform (from human to divine). Although Sima Qian reduced the complex process to only these three abstract words, the material evidence in Liu Sheng's tomb visually simulated the same process with the gradual variation of the king's outfit.

This process of the devolving human appearance vividly echoes a theory of death seen in the writings of Wang Chong. To support his point that death was but a natural process and that belief in ghosts was a deceptive fantasy, he adopted a rhetoric that compared people with ice: "The vital force produces man just as water becomes ice. As water freezes into ice, so the vital force coagulates to form man. When ice melts it becomes water and when a man dies he becomes spirit again. He is called spirit just as ice which has melted changes its name to water."[89]

These and other related discussions of death paint a graphical picture of body and soul as different but mutually transformable states of matter. The body and the soul are essentially two different states of one and the same substance called "breath" (*qi* 氣). The less pure, heavier breath solidifies into a humanoid shell (*xing* 形) to hold the lighter, gaseous "purified breath" (*jingqi* 精氣, or the *hun* 魂) that inflates it. When death occurs, the no-longer-functioning (broken) shell immediately releases the pure breaths from within and slowly melts down to a fluid state (*po* 魄, perhaps) that is to be preserved underground.[90]

In Liu Sheng's tomb, from inside to outside, while the deceased's outfit gradually loses its solidity and anthropomorphic form, the deceased's humanoid appearance is becoming less and less concrete, just like solid ice slowly melting into liquid water, that is, it "becomes spirit again."

In Wang Chong's ice analogy, the process of *xingjie* is reversible because as naturally as ice melts into water, water freezes into ice. So if *xingjie* describes the passage of death, then its antithesis must describe that of birth. Indeed, reversing the process of *xingjie* is conceptualized as *liuxing* 流形 ("flowing into form"). In excavated texts from the Eastern Zhou and Han periods, the birth of people is imagined as *liuxing*.

In a bamboo manuscript titled *Ten Questions* (*Shiwen* 十問) excavated from Mawangdui tomb no. 3, the legendary ruler Huangdi 黃帝 asks the sage Rongchengshi 容成氏 a set of questions related to health preservation and life extension. The fourth question, which brings out the longest answer in the whole text, concerns the desirable secret of longevity. Huangdi inquires: "When people first dispense the purity that flows into the form, what is obtained so that life occurs? When flowing into the form produces a body, what is lost so that death occurs?"[91] In this text, an axiom is established: In the beginning, "people" are formless breath or water; later, they are flowing into an anthropomorphic form and become solid and complete "figures." In Rongchengshi's answer, the fluid vital elements only "flow into forms" when the subject takes in pure natural vapor and breath. In another manuscript from Mawangdui tomb no. 3, the related term *liuxing* 潘 (流) 形 was clearly interpreted as the first month of gestation. As Donald Harper has cogently explained, the question was about "how intercourse and conception lead to the production of a life."[92] Without doubt, those who believed in this theory of birth might easily imagine death as the opposite process of reducing the humanoid fetus back into formless semen.

This idea of humans flowing into the form was taken up and integrated into a number of philosophical treatises and acquired a political implication. In the "Water and Earth" (*Shuidi* 水地) chapter (dated by scholars to the fourth century BCE) of the *Guanzi* 管子 text, the author promotes a political philosophy grounded in ontology and ethics of water as the metaphor for good rulership.[93] One of the key arguments that support water's fundamental role in the world maintains that "human beings are made of water. As the semen and breath of men and women unite, water flows into form."[94] The belief that the human body is essentially a form filled with some fluid vital matter (semen, breath, or water) might find its root in the belief of water as the origin of the world and the true nature of the ultimate way (*Dao* 道).[95]

According to this theory of reversible transformation between body and spirit (soul), the dissolution of the body means the increasing leakage and diffusion of the spirit. As the *Book of Rites* claimed, once liberated from the body, "The soul in its energy can go everywhere," while "that the bones and flesh should return to earth is what is appointed."[96] This result of the natural process of death reveals the urgency to arrest the soul and stop it from wandering away. The stakes were high. If nothing was done to stop the soul from dispersing, the deceased's "pure breath" might lose its anchor in this world, vanish into the distant sky, and never return to the human world again.

The poet Sima Xiangru 司馬相如 (ca. 179–117 BCE), in one of his rhapsodies, precisely expressed such a horror brought forth by the incompetent Second Emperor of Qin 秦二世 (r. 210–207 BCE). This unwise ruler did not cultivate himself and listened to malicious words. As a result of his defeat, his ancestral temples were burnt to extinction and tombs were in ruins. "The souls lost their homes and had nothing to eat. They went dark, distant, and extinct without sacrifices. With time passing by, the souls became weaker and weaker, and the spirits diffused and flew up, scaling the Nine Heavens and vanished for good."[97]

As Sima Xiangru suggested, the soul must be fed to remain strong and stay together. While excavators found nothing but outfits in the coffins, the rear chamber was full of various ritual instruments, offering food, drinks, light, heat, and fragrance to the deceased's soul to arrest and nurture it.

In the center of the lavish banquet sits a low sacrificial dais and a smaller but taller table.[98] A group of large bronzes including five cauldrons (fig. 1.2, nos. 20, 22, 74, 78, 79), a tripod (fig. 1.2, no. 64), four beautifully inlaid wine *hu* vessels (fig. 1.2, nos. 14, 15, 18, 19), and a spoon (fig. 1.2, no. 65), are placed on or around the dais. They constitute a kitchen set. Lighter vessels including dishes and cups constitute the basic tableware. One platter (fig. 1.2, no. 71) originally contained a whole roast suckling pig.[99] Some other dishes identified by inscription as "royal ramie-cored lacquer plates for grains" (*yuzhu fanpan* 御褚[纻]飯盤) were used to hold rice.[100] All these vessels originally must have been filled with food or wine.

The function of these ritual instruments is simple: They present life-saving substances for the deceased's soul. Wine and food were believed to be the most important ways of nourishing and satisfying the ancestral spirit.[101] An inscription made on one of these bronze wine pots explicitly relates the activity of banqueting to the sustaining of the deceased's physical soundness (fig. 1.6): "With happy hearts [let us] gather in banquet. The occasion is grand and the fare sumptuous. Let delicacies fill the gates and increase the girth, and offer long life without illness for ten thousand years and more!"[102]

To increase the power of attraction, other instruments were added to the banquet. Four lamps (fig. 1.2, nos. 11, 84, 86, 87), two incense burners (fig. 1.2, nos. 3, 90), a heater (fig. 1.2, no. 92), and a bronze dustpan (fig. 1.2, no. 81)[103] flanking the couch to the east and the northeast sides supplied fragrance and heat. In this bright, aromatic, and warm atmosphere, figurines made of "deathless" stone or bronze are scattered here and there among the vessels to assist or entertain the soul. A unique bronze figurine (fig. 1.2, no. 89) amuses the banquet host. This disproportionate dwarf features a large head, a short

FIGURE 1.6 Inlaid bronze *hu* vessel bearing bird script inscriptions from the rear chamber of Mancheng tomb no. 1, Mancheng, Hebei, ca. 113 BCE. Courtesy of Hebei Museum, Shijiazhuang.

body, and puny legs.[104] These attendants "humanize" the static ritual setting into a lively scene of banqueting. In the minds of Western Han subjects, these ritual instruments could attract the deceased's soul like magnets attract iron.

In fact, this assemblage was not a Western Han invention but was developed from an earlier practice during the Eastern Zhou period. One of the best precedents of such banquets came from the well-known tomb of Marquis Yi of the Zeng state (dated to the early fifth century BCE) in present-day Suixian, Hubei. The eastern compartment of the tomb functioned as the casket, in which the deceased marquis's nested coffins were placed, and a seat, indicated by a bamboo mat and several mat weights, was set up to the east of the coffins. A few food vessels appeared nearby. The food in these vessels was supposed to be consumed by the deceased's soul, simulated by an outspreading group of a belt hook, three jade *bi* discs, two jade pendants, and two knives found next to the seat.[105] During the Western Han, the combination of an outfit and a set of banqueting vessels in the *guo* casket was not unique to the Mancheng site but spotted in at least one other intact royal tomb dated slightly later than the Mancheng counterparts and located in present-day Juye, Shandong. In it, the excavators found a small bamboo casket right below the feet of the deceased. Upon opening it, the archaeologists identified such basic outfit items as a bronze belt hook and jade pendants, as well as bronze ritual vessels.[106] This casket turned out to be a modest version of its lavish counterpart at the Mancheng site.

Like all these counterparts, Liu Sheng's stone house-shaped casket tomb was another effort to arrest the deceased king's volatile soul and prevent it from further diffusion. However, Liu Sheng's casket was also distinctive because it was encased by a fourth layer of the tomb structure—the front chamber.

THE EMPTY TENT OF THE KING

The front chamber, which is also the outermost zone of Liu Sheng's four-layer tomb, contains a few outfit items but also includes far more powerful sacrificial instruments to lure the further dissipated souls to come back. Visual and textual evidence jointly confirms that the souls of Liu Sheng and his wife were the expected recipients of the sacrifice.

Whereas Liu Sheng's casket is concealed behind a closed door, his front chamber remains open without gates or doors save for the outer doorway to the tomb.[107] Occupying the central position in the entire tomb plan, it is the tallest and largest apartment and is larger than all the other four chambers combined. The front chamber in tomb no. 1, for instance, measures 14.92 meters long, 12.6 meters wide, and 6.8 meters tall and is spacious enough to hold a huge party (figs. 0.3, 1.1).[108] In the original plan, a roofed structure was erected in this space with its interior divided into three parallel bays by two parallel grooves chiseled into the floor. These grooves, 0.3 to 0.4 meters wide and 0.2 meters deep, were probably the spots where wooden floor beams and pillars were initially installed to support the roof, which was covered by ceramic tiles. These two grooves shape the space into a standard Chinese hall, with a middle chamber flanked by two side chambers.[109] The intention to imitate a real house is evident.

Unlike the casket, in which the main furnished space is divided evenly into an outfit (representing the appearance of the king) and his banquet, the front chamber has a far more complex floor plan of distributed objects—mostly sacrificial instruments (fig. 1.7). Hundreds of objects surround the two tents installed in the central and southern bays. Although many of the

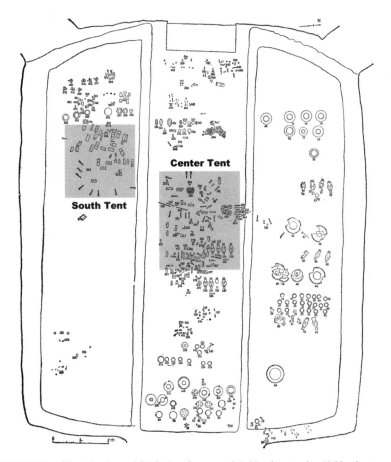

North (N) arrow shown at top right.

Center Tent

South Tent

0   1   2m

FIGURE 1.7 Plan of front chamber and distribution of grave goods in Mancheng tomb no. 1, Mancheng, Hebei, ca. 113 BCE. After Zhongguo shehui kexueyuan kaogu yanjiusuo, Mancheng *Han mu fajue baogao*, 1: 27, fig. 16. Courtesy of Wenwu Press.

1–10 Jade ornament; 11 Ceramic lamp; 12 Bronze ceremonial pole finial; 13 Bronze basin; 14–15 Ceramic figurines; 16 Three bronze miniature water buckets; 17 Two bronze miniature water buckets with handles; 18 Bronze dildo; 20 Bronze basin; 22–44 Ceramic lamps; 45–46 Ceramic basins; 47 Ivory carving; 48–59 Ceramic basins; 60–62 Ceramic figurines; 63 Ceramic basin; 64 Iron knife; 65 Ceramic basin; 70–74 Ceramic figurines; 75 Ceramic *hu* pot; 76–82 Ceramic jars; 83 Bronze decor; 84 Bronze canopy cap; 85 Bronze decor; 86 Bronze ceremonial pole finial; 88 Bronze decor; 89 Bronze crossbow; 90–92 Bronze ornaments of ceremonial pole finial; 93 Bronze basin; 94 Bronze cauldron; 95 Bronze basin; 96 Bronze scoop; 97 Bronze incense burner; 98 Bronze washbasin; 99–100 Bronze cauldrons; 101–102 Bronze tripods; 103 Bronze cauldron; 104 Bronze steamer; 106 Ceramic *hu* vessel; 107 Bronze *lei* pot; 108 Bronze *zhong* vessel; 109 Bronze chained *hu* vessel; 110 Bronze cauldron; 111 Bronze *lei* pot; 112–118 Bronze lamps; 120 Bronze lamp; 121–123 Ceramic lamps; 124 Jade disc; 125 Bronze zoomorphic ornament; 126–132 Jade ornaments; 133 Jade half-ring; 134–141 Jade ornaments; 142 Bronze tube; 143 Bronze ring; 144–145 Bronze plaques; 146 Vessel foot; 149–156 Ceramic figurines; 163–167 Bronze feline-shaped vessel feet; 168–169 Bronze human figurines; 170–171 Bronze deer-shaped ornaments; 172–173 Vessel feet; 174 Bronze zoomorphic mask (*pushou*); 175 Bronze ring; 176, 178 Bronze ornaments of lacquer table; 179 Bronze dildo; 180 Bronze stacked bowls; 181 Bronze tent fitting; 207 Bronze chained lid of incense burner; 208 Bronze bird-shaped ornament; 209 Iron axle; 219–220 Bronze daggers; 221 Bronze ornament of lacquer table; 222 Bronze ornament of lacquer winged cup; 223 Bronze vessel foot; 225 Iron axe; 226–227 Iron chisels; 246–249 Iron swords; 250 Iron saddle-shaped item; 263 Bronze cup; 264 Bronze ring; 274 Bronze lamp; 275–279 Bronze stacked cups; 280 Silver box; 281 Bronze disc-shaped vessel foot; 282–286 Oval cups; 292 Bronze hook; 293 Bronze disc-shaped vessel base; 294 Bronze bar-shaped ornament; 295 Bronze cup-like object; 296 Bronze hinge; 297 Bone fake horse tooth; 298–299 Bronze frontlets; 300 Bronze chariot wheel-axle cap; 301 Bronze chariot handle; 302–304 Bronze crossbow triggers; 305 Square iron object; 306 Iron hoe; 320 Bronze tent fitting; 322 Iron U-shaped object; 323 Bronze foot from lacquer vessel; 324 Stone figurine; 325 Bronze water clock; 326–327 Bronze *fang* vessels; 328 Bronze *juan* vessel; 330 Bronze cauldron; 331–332 Ceramic jars; 333 Iron hoe; 335 Bronze vessel foot; 336–343 Bronze crossbow triggers; 344 Iron arrowheads; 345 Bronze arrowheads; 346 Bronze tube-shaped object; 347 Bronze knife; 348 Bronze zoomorphic mask; 349 Bronze short sword; 350 Bronze ornament; 351 Bronze ring; 352 Bronze ornament of lacquer winged cup; 403–406 Bronze knives; 412 Iron chisel; 416–419: Iron chisels; 422, Iron chisel; 425 Iron saw; 432 Iron file; 440 Bronze horse bit; 444–445 Iron saw; 450 Bronze horse bit; 468 Bronze crossbow hanger types of objects look familiar, the front chamber gave little indication of the deceased's bodily appearance. Typical "outfit" articles including seals, garment hooks, and mirrors were totally absent in the two tents and the areas around them. Even remains of toiletry boxes were rare. The only portable items uncovered next to the center tent were four swords (fig. 1.7, nos. 246–249), but even they, mixed with long-range arms including dagger-spears (*ge* 戈) and crossbows, were originally fastened onto a wooden stand rather than being suspended from a waistband. Although some jades were spotted in front of the center tent, most of these jade plaques were only carved on one side, leaving the other side crude and unpolished.[110] They are most likely ornaments fitted on some disintegrated lacquerware rather than pendants, which are usually carved on both sides and suspended from ritual clothes. The large *bi* disc (fig. 1.7, no. 124) and the small *huang* half-ring (fig. 1.7, no. 133), and a group of gilt bronze plaques (fig. 1.7, nos. 144, 145) located before the center tent, were the only objects that might have possibly been attached to clothing. But isolated from one another across the tomb space, these items' association with an outfit, be it physical or conceptual, remains uncertain. This unique group of objects was more likely a sacrificial offering to the tomb occupant rather than a reference to the deceased subject's physical existence.

The absence of an outfit is strongly contrasted by the opulence of ritual instruments in the same space. Traditional sacrificial vessels, usually employed in the context of ancestral temples, surround the tents on both the front and back sides. On the east side of the tent, with all the traditional bronze ritual vessels such as *ding* 鼎, *yan* 甗, and *hu* 壺 lined up in rows on a lacquer offering table (fig. 1.7, nos. 93–96, 98–105, 107–111), the ritual scenario is unambiguous. On the west side of the center tent, despite the absence of traditional ritual vessels, a group of small cups of different scales was displayed successively from the largest to the smallest in two parallel rows (fig. 1.7, nos. 282–286), all with their handles pointing toward the tent, imitating the solemn and lavish display of tripods in a temple before the seats for the ancestral souls.[111]

These seats were set up in the center of the sacrificial hall, where also stood the two parallel tents, which were empty except for a table with a couple of wine cups. The central tent sat on the east-west central axis of the tomb in the central bay, which was the most richly furnished area among all three bays (fig. 1.7). This tent, presumably the highest and largest object in the center of the central bay, must have been the visual focus of the whole chamber. According to the distribution of surviving tent fittings on the floor, the central tent measured about 2 by 1.3 meters in area and about 1.84 meters high. A second tent once stood on the west side of the southern bay of the front chamber before it collapsed (fig. 1.7). After reconstruction, this house-shaped structure measured 1.8 by 1.8 meters in area and 1.8 meters tall.[112] These two tents are different in several aspects. Although the objects surrounding the two tents generally are similar, the tent to the south is smaller and was outfitted with fewer objects. It is also important to note that the two tents are not entirely parallel: the south tent is located slightly behind the central one.[113] Clearly, the two tents are of the same function but are different in status. Furthermore, there is also an obvious gender distinction: The central tent was accompanied by three swords, which were clear signs of the occupant's masculinity, while the south tent held none, implying femininity.

Scholars have assumed that the central tent was set up for Liu Sheng,[114] and the south one for his wife, Dou Wan.[115] I find evidence for this hypothesis in an Eastern Han textual record that describes two parallel tents in the ancestral temple in Chang'an, the capital of the Western Han. During the collective sacrifice held every three years, all imperial ancestors were jointly worshiped in the temple of Emperor Gao, the founder of the dynasty, and his empress:

In the Great Collective Sacrifice . . . Seats were set on the left and right sides. [The seat of] Emperor Gao faced towards the south in a sloping-roofed tent ornamented with embroidery . . . [The seat of] Empress Gao was on the right side, six *cun* (15 centimeters) further back, also in an embroidered sloping-roof tent.[116]

According to this passage, the imperial couple occupies two parallel empty tents, presiding over the whole ritual space. The husband "sits" on the left; the wife "sits" on the right, slightly behind him. This arrangement generally explains the relationship between the two tents in Liu Sheng's front chamber (fig. 1.7). The same practice of establishing a common "shrine" in the front of the tomb for the deceased couple while maintaining separate burials at the rear for husband and wife was repeated in many excavated Eastern Han burials.[117] This evidence demonstrates that the overwhelming number of sacrificial instruments were presented to the empty seats of the deceased king and queen.

The temple simulated in Liu Sheng's tomb is conceptually similar to the legendary Bright Hall (*mingtang* 明堂), which was one of the royal ritual sites for ancestral worship during the Western Han dynasty. Although the first explicit historical documentation of such a building dates to 110 BCE and the earliest known actual example was erected in 5 CE, similar structures likely had already been in existence since at least Emperor Wen's reign.[118] In Eastern Zhou texts, the *mingtang*, which was metonymous with ideal ruler-ship,[119] was described as an audience hall with a circular ceiling and square base, where the sovereign held ceremonial meetings with local vassals.[120] Liu Sheng's front chamber is precisely vaulted (as I will demonstrate in chapter 3—an unfinished dome) at the top and square at the base (fig. 1.1). The Bright Hall was called "bright" because, according to a Western Han text, its walls bore thirty-six doors and seventy-two windows, so that sunlight could easily penetrate the walls and illuminate the interior from all directions.[121] To emulate the brilliance of sunshine in the Bright Hall, an extraordinary number of lamps were displayed in the front chamber of Liu Sheng's tomb. In the central bay, the east side was illuminated by eight bronze (fig. 1.7, nos. 112–118, 120) and three ceramic lamps (fig. 1.7, nos. 121–123), all located to the west of the kitchenware. Each lamp had a circular base, a tall and slim stand, and a circular plate with oil and a wick in it. In the northern bay, twenty-three ceramic lamps (fig. 1.7, nos. 22–44) appeared in three parallel rows. Such a lavish display of lamps finds no parallel in any other early tomb. The lamps, which went beyond traditional ritual objects, deepened the religious mood in the ritual hall.

Four of the nine bronze lamps lined up in front of Liu Sheng's tent each bear an identical inscription, which identifies the device as a "bronze lamp of the Bright Hall of the Forest of Pepper Trees" (*Jiaolin mingtang tongdeng* 椒林明堂銅燈) (fig. 1.8).[122] Whereas the modifier *jiaolin* remains unknown, the key concept of *mingtang* carries a sacrificial meaning that was unmis-takable to well-educated Western Han kings.[123] According to the formula of Western Han bronze inscriptions, which I will analyze in chapter 4, this inscription suggests that before the entombment, these objects once had been in the possession of the official treasury of a certain Bright Hall. By being lit with these lamps, the sacrificial hall was somehow compared to the Bright Hall. In fact, inscriptional evidence has shown that by the second century CE, the concept of *mingtang* had been widely used to describe the front chamber of a tomb.[124]

The practice of simulating a temple in the tomb was against the tradition in which the tomb and the temple of the ancestor were built in separate loca-tions. The former was usually located in desolate suburban areas, and the latter remained in the city with the living. However, during the late Eastern Zhou period, with tombs gradually growing into a new center of sociopolitical

FIGURE 1.8 Bronze lamp with the inscription, "Bright Hall of the Forest of Pepper Trees" (*Jiaolin mingtang*), from Mancheng tomb no. 1, Mancheng, Hebei, ca. 113 BCE. Courtesy of Hebei Museum, Shijiazhuang.

and religious power, more and more ritual facilities developed in or near the cemetery.[125] This trend continued into the Western Han period with a simple purpose: to keep the soul near, if not in, the body so that the two vital elements of life could remain united as long as possible after death. In 191 BCE, Emperor Hui 惠帝 (r. 195–188 BCE) erected a duplicate temple (*yuanmiao* 原廟) for his deceased father, Emperor Gao, right next to the latter's mausoleum, located as far as twenty kilometers to the north of the capital city of Chang'an.[126] In 72 BCE, Emperor Xuan 宣帝 (r. 74–48 BCE) had an extra temple erected for each of his predecessors and himself next to their mausoleums.[127] But could the soul be drawn even closer to the body? The closest situation possible would be when a duplicate temple was erected in the tomb itself and directly embraced the corpse, as in the Mancheng site.

It is clear that there is a pronounced contrast between the scarcity of outfits and the abundance of instruments in the front chamber that simulated an ancestral temple. This phenomenon conveys two important meanings.

On the one hand, this suggests that the deceased's originally humanoid soul has almost entirely dissipated, with the near absence of the deceased's outfit. The bereft could only bemoan their beloved's departure. Emperor Wu of the Han clearly expressed such despair with the loss of his favorite lover, Lady Li 李夫人 (ca. second to first centuries BCE):

> All at once she was changed and does not turn back,
> her soul was set free, it flies away.
> Such a baffling blur are the hallowed spirits,
> I linger lamenting, I falter in distress.
> Her course carries her each day further from me,
> and I was bewildered as she took her leave.
> Going beyond in a journey westward,
> moving swiftly, now unseen.[128]

Facing this abysmal void, the emperor could only appeal to the magic power of sacrifice for making the absent present. A magician named Shaoweng 少翁 set up an empty tent at night, lit up candles, and dedicated wine and meat. Miraculously, from the distance, the emperor caught a glimpse of a beautiful lady who "appeared like Lady Li" showing up in the tent.[129]

On the other hand, and in accord with this literary passage, while the deceased's metaphorical body—the outfit—has almost been reduced to nothing in Liu Sheng's front chamber, the intensity of sacrifice reaches its peak in order to bring the dispersed soul back. This is exactly the antithesis of the situation in the double coffin, where the king has his firm physical presence but no sacrificial goods. Whereas the *guo* casket is fashioned into an intimate dining room for the deceased's soul behind a closed door, the front chamber was built on the model of an open magnificent imperial temple.

Turning the front chamber into a desirable Bright Hall—a compliment to the deceased soul as an ideal king—was one of the many baits used to lure the king's dispersed soul to return as an acknowledged worthy king. In the "Great Summoning" (*Dazhao* 大招) chapter of the *Song of the South* (Chuci 楚辭), the author enumerated all kinds of desirable things to attract a wandering soul to come back to its previous home. Among the various attractions, "ascend and descend in the hall" (*deng jiang tang zhi* 登降堂只) was one of the greatest worldly pleasures only a few noblemen could afford to enjoy.[130]

Once the soul had descended to the honorable hall, it would be further arrested by a variety of seductive, sensual experiences. The aroma emitted by two incense burners must have suffused the air of the front chamber. The fragrance of the incense would have mixed with the tempting odor released by the cooked food and aromatic wine. Because the soul remains invisible and ethereal, the people in early China imagined that the soul would only consume the vapor of the food and wine rather than the actual substance itself. As the *Guanzi* text relates, "Ghosts and spirits will absorb the breath (*qi* 氣) contained in them, whereas gentlemen will enjoy the taste."[131]

The enthralled soul would be satisfied by taking the privileged seat in the tent and consuming endless supplies of food and wine, stored physically and symbolically in more than six hundred ceramic containers crowded in the tomb's north side chamber. Representing the royal "warehouse," this space is directly connected to the front chamber. Among the vessels are sixteen giant jars each measuring sixty-six to seventy-six centimeters tall and about fifty centimeters in diameter, with a combined capacity of more than a thousand liters. Inscriptions on the shoulders of some of these jars list names of different kinds of alcohol.[132] Stains on the jar interiors verify that these containers were once filled with liquid. The extraordinary amount emphasized the irresistible power of enticement.

The tempting banquet was accompanied by amusing entertainment. Two little human figurines, both cast in bronze, were placed around the table before the primary tent (fig. 1.7, nos. 168, 169; fig. 1.9). Although initially manufactured as mat weights, the figurines were also vivid statuettes.[133] Fashioned to

FIGURE 1.9 Bronze storytellers from Mancheng tomb no. 1, Mancheng, Hebei, ca. 113 BCE. Courtesy of Hebei Museum, Shijiazhuang.

FIGURE 1.10 Bronze dildo and what may be stone "testicles" from Mancheng tomb no. 1, Mancheng, Hebei, ca. 113 BCE. Courtesy of Hebei Museum, Shijiazhuang.

the same scale and employing the same motif, these two objects clearly make a pair. Each man wears a circular pointed hat and a loose robe with half of his torso exposed. Compared with the ceramic figurines, the two half-naked men display non-Chinese physiognomy. Each face is particularly exaggerated with a prominent snout and bulging cheeks, while Han Chinese's visual depictions of themselves usually have a flat face and a low nose. One of the figures opens his mouth in a moment of speaking, chanting, or singing. In response, his companion holds his right palm upright close to his right ear and rests the other palm on his left knee as if he is attentively listening. This posture, reminiscent of the later Buddhist "fear not" mudra, might have impressed the Western Han viewer as exotic and even funny.[134] Watching such performances was surely an exclusive privilege for the noblest members of society.

Besides delicious food and wine and amusement, sex was another strong motivation for the king's disembodied soul to linger in the sacrificial hall. One of the most astonishing finds in front of the tent was a V-shaped bronze dildo representing two end-to-end joined penises (fig. 1.7, no. 179; fig. 1.10). Another similar bronze penis appears in the north bay of the chamber with two egg-shaped pebbles (fig. 1.7, no. 18), possibly representing testicles, and a third silver penis, whose exact original location remains unknown, also came from this chamber.[135] The placement of the phalli raises the question of the nature of the space. Although "closed tents" (*weibo* 帷薄) was a metonym for sex[136] during the Han dynasty because they were often used to shield sexual activities from public view, none of the dildos was found inside the tents.[137] Instead, one phallus was laid in front of the primary tent with wine cups and an incense burner next to the ceramic attendants. Another one in the northern bay was situated by the ceramic lamps in one of the brightest areas of the chamber. It seems these sexual instruments were not meant to be concealed but rather displayed. Identified as dildos made for female users during sexual games, these multiple sexual toys represent a randy revelry.[138] This lustful scenario contradicts, or at least complicates, the solemnity represented by the orderly arranged and dedicated ritual vessels. The place was no longer an ascetic religious one but a secularized occasion endorsing and celebrating the pleasures of the body. Robert van Gulik masterfully studied the shockingly brazen sadistic tendencies of some Western Han princes, who were entertained by open shows of sexual intercourse between palace ladies and male animals.[139] The existence of multiple sex toys reveals the carnival nature of the space, which might have been associated with Zhongshan's local culture, as I will analyze in chapter 3.[140]

In the aforementioned "Great Summoning" poem, to attract the wandering male soul to roam back to his previous home, the poet devoted a total of twenty-four lines—nearly a quarter of the entire piece—to a lengthy description of beautiful ladies as the greatest temptation:

> Ah, the vermeil lips and dazzling teeth, lovely and alluring!
> The uniformity of excellence, skillful and imposing!
> The well-rounded flesh and fine bones, elegant and pleasing!
> O Soul, come back to solacing and comfort![141]

Compared with the less sumptuous banquet in the rear chamber, the enhanced sensuous power in the front chamber was an urgent response to the largely diminishing soul, represented by the absence of the deceased's outfit. In the "Summoning the Soul" poem, the high thearch orders Shaman Yang to immediately summon back the poet's disembodied and scattered soul (*hunpo lisan* 魂魄离散) because it would be too late once the soul completely diffused and withered.[142] To borrow Wang Chong's fire analogy, no matter how feeble a fire is, as long as fuel is supplied, the flame will linger on; but once the fire has been extinguished, there is nothing left to save it.

Liu Sheng's tomb was not an isolated case. Similar sacrificial halls with abundant ritual instruments and few or no outfits also exist in Dou Wan's tomb and in the Hongtushan royal tomb, but the earliest known precursor for all three Western Han royal tombs can be found in the aforementioned Eastern Zhou tomb of Marquis Yi of Zeng. In this burial complex of four compartments, while the aforementioned eastern compartment housed a

modest banquet next to the marquis's nested coffin, the central compartment was fashioned into a glorious "ceremonial hall" mainly by two groups
of ritual vessels and musical instruments, including a set of nine tripods and
another set of bells and chimes, on the west and the east sides, respectively.[143]
And in the narrow space between them, the excavators uncovered an armrest covered by a folded mat.[144] This distinct combination of armrest and
mat makes an empty seat for the soul. Unlike the empty seat in his casket
with wearable articles, Marquis Yi's empty seat in the "ceremonial hall" was
not surrounded with remains of outfits, suggesting the general absence of
the deceased's soul. The almost identical visible pattern of *outfits* and *instruments* between Marquis Yi's and Liu Sheng's tombs suggests that the idea of a
varying soul as visualized in the Western Han royal tombs was deeply rooted
in early Chinese religious thought and ritual practice.

Liu Sheng's front chamber stands as the final stage of a four-step transformation beginning in the inner coffin: the total absence of the deceased
king's gradually dissolving outfit, which was a metaphor for his dissipating
soul that had previously filled the body.

THE EMBRACE OF BODY AND SOUL

In Liu Sheng's tomb, the desire for longevity could not be stronger because
the word *shou* 壽 (longevity) is the most frequently used concept in the
inscriptions found on a variety of interred objects. By attracting the soul to
surround the corpse in the iron-sealed, mountain-cut tomb, the deceased
king could unite his body and soul to secure a postmortem immortality.

Although in Liu Sheng's tomb the tomb space was divided evenly into two
halves, the rear and the front, the design still retained—deliberately—the
traditional practice of nested caskets and coffins. In this four-layer tomb,
the distribution of burial objects follows a two-track development from the
inside to the outside. On the one track, the king's outfit is gradually breaking down and diminishing, symbolizing his increasingly disintegrated soul.
On the other track, the number and types of sacrificial instruments keep
increasing, forming an ever-more-powerful means to arrest the soul and
prevent it from disintegrating completely.

The attempt to unite body and soul in the tomb was not new but already
in existence in the earlier Shang and Zhou tombs. In those tombs, people
designed a different model of juxtaposing body and soul vertically in a parallel relationship, with the former below and the latter above. For example, in

the tomb of Fu Hao 婦好 (one of King Wuding's 武丁 [fl. thirteenth century BCE] consorts), after the inner coffin had been settled into the casket, which rested on the bottom of the 7.5-meters-deep burial chamber, the deceased's soul was housed in an offering hall erected at ground level above the grave.[145] During the late Eastern Zhou period, similar dualistic structures with underground caskets and freestanding halls are seen in the royal cemeteries of the Zhongshan, Zhao, Wei, and Qin kingdoms.[146]

Keeping the harmony between body and soul was the key to personal immortality. In the *Zhuangzi* text (compiled in the third century BCE), Master Guangcheng 廣成子, one of the legendary sages of antiquity, claimed that he had been cultivating himself for twelve hundred years and his body had never withered. When asked for the secret, the master answered: "As for myself, I guard this unity, abide in this harmony, and therefore I have kept myself alive for twelve hundred years, and never has my body suffered any decay."[147] *The Master of Pheasant Hat* text (*Heguanzi* 鶡冠子, compiled ca. second century BCE) rendered the same idea in a slightly more abstract way: "When form and spirit are attuned/Life's principles are cultivated."[148] To such Confucians as Xun Yue 荀悅 (148–209 CE), the secret to living longer for those with benevolent minds lay in their ability to achieve a harmony between body and soul.[149]

However, in Liu Sheng's tomb, the same idea of uniting and harmonizing body and soul developed into a more complex and sophisticated graphical model—multilayer embracement. The gradually dispersing soul is artistically fixed around the corpse in a four-layer structure of containing and being contained. Wang Chong described such a model as "an embrace of the bodily breath and flesh and bones."[150] With the deceased king's soul in the peripheral zones surrounding his physical remains (corpse) in the center, the tomb designer established a repeated pattern of "soul embracing body." In the inner coffin, the jade suit metaphorically transformed the dead biological body into an incorruptible magic one, while the orifice plugs sealed the soul permanently within. This unity of body and soul was elaborated by two more middle layers: the outer wooden coffin and the stone house-shaped casket. In each of the two intermediary layers, the changing outfits represented the gradually dissipating soul of the departed king. In the outermost layer (the front chamber), even though the soul was absent, it was being called back by enhanced sacrifice as if in a temple setting.

The embrace of body and soul nonetheless ensures that the two basic vital ingredients hold fast to each other and never fully separate. It was believed that the means of achieving deathlessness was the permanent embrace of body and soul, *po* 魄 and *hun* 魂, or *xing* 形 and *shen* 神. In the *Laozi* text, it is claimed that "when the corporeal and the spiritual are held together in one embrace, they can be kept from separating."[151] In the *Zhuangzi* text, when the Yellow Emperor went to Master Guangcheng for the secret of longevity, the master answered: "Your spirit will protect your body, and the body will enjoy a long life."[152] A passage from the slightly later *Scripture of Great Peace* (*Taiping jing* 太平經), which was composed under the influence of *Laozi* and *Zhuangzi*, considered the mutual embracement of body and soul as "nature," and once "you have lost your nature, you will not live long."[153]

Hence, by repeating the embrace of body and soul four times, the unknown tomb planner(s) guaranteed the actualization of the absolute longevity of the deceased.

The phrase "longevity of the deceased" may sound like an oxymoron. A comparison with Egyptian ideas of the afterlife might shed some light on the problem. The practice of reintegrating various aspects of being after death to transform the deceased into an immortal being was perhaps a hallmark of ancient Egyptian civilization. The subject of an immortal afterlife was the multicomponent soul. A person, the Egyptians believed, consisted of a physical body and not one but two souls that lived on after his death: a *ka* (*kꜣ*) soul and a *ba* (*bꜣ*) soul. The *ka*, or life force, stayed in the tomb with the dead body and demanded nourishment from offerings of food, water, and incense, while the other soul, the *ba*, was believed to fly from the body with the last breath and held to be that part of man that enjoyed an eternal existence in heaven. The ancient Egyptians also trusted that the *ba* occasionally came back to "visit" the body in the tomb and to partake of the food and drink offerings there. Ideally, through ritual, all the parts of the person that had dispersed at death were reunited, and when the *ba* was rejoined with its *ka*, the soul was transformed into an *akh* (*ꜣḫ*), which was an eternal, perfected, or blessed being that had special powers. The key to the Egyptian practice was to ensure a smooth and successful transformation from this life to the afterlife, which had to pass the judgment of the gods.[154]

Although some of the Chinese practices, such as protecting the body and feeding the soul, expressed in the royal tombs at Mancheng apparently echo these Egyptian ideas, fundamental differences separate the two traditions. For the Chinese, as Wang Chong pointed out, body and soul were understood essentially as natural, homogeneous substances (*qi* breaths), like water and ice, rather than different ontologically distinct entities protected by gods as in the Egyptian context. Likewise, the transformation between life and death was considered a more natural rather than supernatural process. Living a long life was good because it was the result of respecting and following the way of nature. For Chinese rulers (especially those who modeled themselves after the ancient sages) during the late Eastern Zhou to early Western Han periods, the ruler's longevity became an important political issue because the stability of the society and the peace of the world hinged upon his personal health, as I will demonstrate in the following chapters. To avoid death and attain longevity, one must learn the techniques of "cultivating (fixing or managing) the self" (*xiushen* 修身 or *zhishen* 治身) as described in many early philosophical texts. The apparently paradoxical pursuit for postmortem immortality in the tomb could be best viewed as a mirror image of the persistent, albeit unsuccessful, striving for longevity in the mortal realm.

Chapter Two

THE UNION OF HUSBAND AND WIFE

Beyond the personal issue of immortality, the second crucial concern demonstrated in the Zhongshan royal tombs at Mancheng was family, and this concern was centered on the relationship between husband and wife. The two major tombs, namely tomb no. 1 and tomb no. 2, are not independent but interrelated.

According to a small bronze seal interred in the coffin, tomb no. 2 was the eternal home of a lady named Dou Wan, about whom no literary documents survive. She occupied the most privileged tomb of a female at the site. Furthermore, as I will discuss in chapter 4, an inscription impressed on a clay stamp in her tomb indicates that she was a royal house member. All scholars concur that because of her placement in the royal cemetery, this interred noble lady could only be the queen. The artifacts in the two tombs share a similar periodic style, indicating two very close dates of interment.[1] The most widely accepted theory suggests that Dou Wan might have been buried between 118 and 104 BCE.[2] Her husband, Liu Sheng, died in 113 BCE. The short duration between the two deaths suggests that both tombs were most likely designed and constructed around the same time. The fact that Dou Wan's tomb is more detailed might also suggest that although the tombs were constructed about the same time, the king died earlier than the queen (i.e., before his tomb was finished).

At first glance, Dou Wan's tomb appears almost like a generic copy of her husband's (fig. 2.1, comp. fig. 1.1), albeit slightly simplified.[3] Cut into the

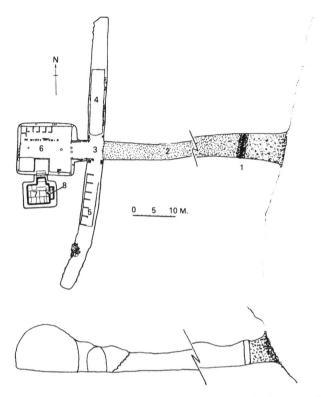

FIGURE 2.1 Plan and section (northward) of Mancheng tomb no. 2 showing the domes, Mancheng, Hebei. ca. 118–104 1BCE. After Wen Fong, *The Great Bronze Age of China*, p. 325, fig. 111. Courtesy of Metropolitan Museum of Art, New York City.
1 Sealed doorway; 2 Tomb passage filled with rubble; 3 Hallway (front section of front chamber); 4 Storage; 5 Stable or garage; 6 Front chamber; 7 Rear chamber (house-shaped stone *guo* casket); 8 Bathroom

same mountain slope, only one hundred and twenty meters to the north of Liu Sheng's tomb (on the right, when facing the entrances), the queen's tomb consists of four major chambers in a similar compact plan along a mostly east-west axis, including a front chamber representing a sacrificial space, two elongated side chambers simulating a kitchen and stable, and a rear chamber representing a bedroom for the deceased's body.

However, these external similarities constitute only one part of the story. The queen's burial conspicuously departs from the king's in the way in which burial objects are organized. For example, there were no tents installed in her front chamber, and her ritual vessels were fewer and smaller. How do we account for the similarities and the differences among various aspects of the two tombs? Were they simply the result of random decisions or were they the outcome of thoughtful planning? How do the similarities and differences relate to the concept and practice of gender during the Western Han dynasty?

We might have never been able to raise these questions, let alone hope to find their answers, had the tombs at the Mancheng site not remained undisturbed for so long. To understand these tombs as a holistic program, it is necessary to analyze not only the individual traits of each tomb but also the socially constructed gender relations between the royal husband and wife in the family cemetery.

The gender relations between husband and wife in Han China are a fascinating but puzzling topic. For example, the scholar Ban Gu tells us on one occasion that the word "wife" (*fu* 婦) means submission and, on another occasion, that "wife" (*qi* 妻) means equality with the husband.[4] Such an apparent contradiction might have been caused by the loss (or perhaps lack) of a systematic philosophical treatise on the topic. A few scattered and decontextualized sentences on gender here and there can be misleading.

However, at the Mancheng site, such a systematic articulation of the husband and wife relationship was miraculously preserved, albeit in a visual language. This chapter demonstrates that from inside to outside, from the inner coffin corresponding to the deceased's personal space to the outer caskets and burial chambers that alluded to their social space,[5] designer(s) used visual forms and material contents at the Mancheng site to negotiate gender relations between the royal subjects on three levels, each endowed with one identity, to formulate an idealized power dynamic. On the personal level, the two tomb occupants were male and female; on the sociopolitical level, they were king and queen; on the familial level, they were husband and wife. This book further argues that this multilevel gender ideology was a response to the new historical reality in the Western Han empire, which indicated an elevated political status for imperial women. This chapter closely details the architectural design and pattern of furnishings in the Mancheng tombs in light of both earlier and contemporary archaeological and textual materials and follows the sequence of the three levels of gender relations. We begin with a comparison of the jade suits and other decorations (outfits) that represented the everlasting bodies of the royal subjects in the two inner coffins. Then we will move on to another comparison of the ritual objects (instruments) in the rear and front chambers that marked the deceased individuals' social status. Finally, we will end with a discussion of the connections between the two tombs that forged the unity of one house.

CONSTRUCTING GENDER: NATURAL AND
CULTURAL DISTINCTIONS

In this first section, I argue that in the tombs at the Mancheng site, the visual and material decorations of the male and female bodies in their coffins express division, separation, and difference between the two genders. The gender distinction, physically inherent in the human body and manifested through primary and secondary sexual attributes, is represented in the outfits and paraphernalia of the body, which carry conventional gender implications.

Although the royals' flesh and bones had long since disintegrated before the site's excavation, the jade suits were well preserved upon discovery (fig. 1.3 and fig. 2.2). As discussed in chapter 1, each suit was made of thousands of small pieces of jade bound together by very thin gold wires through tiny holes pierced around the edges of the jade pieces. Western Han royalty wore jade suits in their tombs in the belief that jade and gold would keep the corpse incorruptible, ensuring postmortem immortality.[6] The jade suit had a twofold meaning: On the one hand, it was a suit of clothes, with shoes; on the other hand, it was a body with hands, ears, eyes, and so on. Although as clothing the two suits are almost indistinguishable in form and material, as bodies, they are fundamentally different in their sexual characteristics.

The treatment of the breast area varies between the two suits. The chest in the king's suit is formed by regular, small, rectangular jade pieces, each 5 centimeters by 2.5 centimeters in area (fig. 1.3); the queen's suit features four large rectangular jade plaques, each 12.9 centimeters by 10.5 centimeters in area, bound together to form a distinctive "shield" that covers her breasts (fig. 2.2). Even though they are entirely flat, these large jade plaques find no

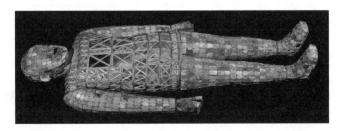

FIGURE 2.2 Jade suit of Dou Wan, Mancheng tomb no. 2, Mancheng, Hebei, ca. 118–104 BCE. Courtesy of Hebei Museum, Shijiazhuang.

Tablet

Queen

King

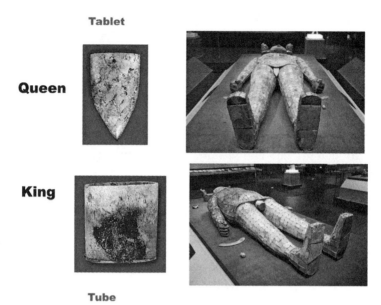

Tube

FIGURE 2.3 Genitalia in jade suits at Mancheng tombs no. 1 and no. 2, Mancheng, Hebei, ca. 118–104 BCE. Made by Jie Shi and courtesy of Hebei Museum, Shijiazhuang.

counterparts in any male jade suits discovered thus far.[7] This special design highlights a very feminine part of the royal lady's body, although it does not necessarily bear sexual implications.

But more explicit evidence about the gendered body comes from the groin area. In the queen's suit, a slim pointed jade tablet was positioned near the bottom of the torso to cover her sexual organ, the vulva (fig. 2.3).[8] In early Chinese rituals, such pointed tablets (*gui* 圭) were thought to imitate male genitalia.[9] In the king's jade suit, a unique genital capsule adapted from an ancient jade tube contained the male's phallus (fig. 2.3).[10] Such tubes (*cong* 琮) presumably resembled a receptacle for the penis (i.e., a vagina).

Despite the general function of these jade objects as genitalia covers, the choice of *cong* tubes and *gui* tablets was meaningful. It is worth noting that it was not at all necessary to make a cylindrical container to conceal the penis—or a pointed tablet to block the vagina—because anything as simple as a piece of cloth would have fulfilled the role equally well. So placing the phallic tablet near the bottom of the female's body and encapsulating the penis with the vaginal tube is full of sexual implications: The jade "vagina" held the king's real penis, and the jade "penis" symbolically penetrated into the queen's vagina. It is no coincidence that the dimensions of the two jade objects are similar. The king's modified *cong* tube is 6.8 centimeters long and 6.6 centimeters in diameter, and the queen's *gui* tablet measures 7.5 centimeters long and 1.3 centimeters thick, just long enough to hold the entire *cong* tube within it.

During the Western Han period, the practice of emphasizing genitalia was not unique to the jade suits at Mancheng. In the slightly later Dingxian tomb no. 40 (dated to the first century BCE), whose occupant was identified as Liu Xiu 劉修 (r. 69–54 BCE), the sixth Zhongshan king and a descendant of Liu Sheng, the excavators discovered an almost identical phallic penile sheath made of jade.[11] The parallel appearance of the male and female jade genitalia containers/covers indicates the enhanced importance of gender and sexuality, which would last into the afterlife.

Although it was uncommon in earlier tombs to visualize the deceased's genitalia, the practice of using ritual jades to mark the deceased's sex can be traced back some six centuries to the cemetery of the marquises of Jin at the Tianma-Qucun site. In the male tombs, archaeologists found jade *cong* tubes near the belly, and in at least one female tomb (tomb no. I11M31), a *gui* tablet.[12] It has been speculated that these objects might imply sexual intercourse.[13]

Emphasizing the sex organs might relate to early Chinese beliefs about reproduction. The major role for a couple was to produce children. In 715 BCE, Prince Hu 公子忽 of the Zheng 鄭 state made a trip to the Chen 陳 state to fetch his bride, but he reported the union to his ancestors only after the fact. The Chen minister who escorted the bride mounted a poignant criticism of the prince and questioned the legitimacy of the marriage: "They do not make for husband and wife. The ancestors have been deceived, and the rites have been violated." If the martial relationship was invalid, he asked, "How can they have heirs?"[14]

On a cosmological level, sexual intercourse is the essential mechanism of propagation in nature. In the eyes of an anonymous Western Han commentator in the *Book of Changes* (*Zhouyi* 周易), sexual activity initiated the creation of the world: "In a thick mist of heaven and earth the ten thousand things received their matter; man and woman joined their essence and the ten thousand things received their lives."[15]

Jade suits, as the imperishable bodies of the deceased, reflected the important role gender played in early Chinese thought. However, the Mancheng artists showed no interest in representing secondary sexual characteristics of male and female bodies (except for the special treatment of Dou Wan's breast area). In fact, it would be hard to distinguish between the two suits were it not for the sex organs (or primary sexual characteristics). In Liu Sheng's jade suit, although the eyes and mouth are marked out with thin, shallow incisions (fig. 1.3), there is no indication of the beard or mustache—characteristics often vividly depicted in many contemporaneous Western Han period jade, bronze, or clay figurines.

The absence of gendered features is even more obvious in Dou Wan's jade suit. Early Chinese literature was teeming with sensuous descriptions of eyes, eyebrows, lips, hair, waists, and feet as emblems of female beauty. For example, in the *Book of Poetry*, beautiful eyes (*meimu* 美目) and graceful feet (*qiaoqu* 巧趨) are two prominent feminine traits.[16] In the *Rhapsody on the Divine Lady* (*Shennü fu* 神女賦) attributed to Song Yu 宋玉 (fl. third century BCE), the poet describes the lady's face as "the jade face" (*yuyan* 玉顏) illuminated by "brilliant pupils," "high-flying eyebrows," and "vermillion lips."[17] Perhaps inspired by Song Yu, Sima Xiangru, a contemporary of Liu Sheng, added "lustrous cloud-like hair" to the list of lovely features in his *Rhapsody of the Beautiful Lady* (*Meiren fu* 美人賦).[18] Similarly, Western Han artists were very good at outlining sexual details of a female body. For example, in the rear and front tomb chambers of Liu Sheng and Dou Wan, the excavators uncovered a number of female figurines made of clay, bronze, or stone that feature white faces, red lips, slim waists, and elegant headdresses, as the texts had praised. In the hands of skillful artists, such efforts led to the creation of some of the most celebrated statuettes of dancers in ancient China, whose remarkably sensuous bodies display a balanced harmonious pose of *contrapposto*.[19] But Dou Wan's jade suit, in contrast, includes no renditions of such sexual details as eyes, eyebrows, mouth, or lips on her literal "jade face." Nor are there representations of her hair, waist, or feet. She remains almost faceless, bald, waistless, and her feet are concealed in shoes. In other words, her entire body remains totally gender neutral except for the sexual organs (and the unusual treatment of the breast area) (fig. 2.2).

Because sex is a biological concept and gender is a social and cultural concept, the jade suits representing sexual organs might seem to be expressing sex exclusively. However, featuring primary but lacking secondary sexual characteristics, the jade suits were not meant to depict the actual bodies of the male and female subjects. Instead, these are idealized, culturally encoded cosmological bodies of *yin* 陰 and *yang* 陽. In Western Han religion and philosophy, the polarity of *yin* (female) and *yang* (male) constitutes the two basic contradictory and complementary cosmic forces whose interactions give birth to every concrete being (including people) in the world.[20] Consequently, all things are attributed to these two forces. *Yin*, the negative force, is associated with coldness and darkness, which is correlated, in turn, with the north and winter. *Yang*, on the other hand, is a positive force related to warmth and brightness, which are characteristics of the south and summer. The bodies that are sexually distinguishable only by male and female genitalia should be regarded more accurately as cosmological bodies of *yang* and *yin*, which are contradictory yet equal, rather than as individual bodies.

Beyond the cosmological body, both the king and the queen carried a similar number of personal objects in their coffins, some of which were strongly gendered. Decorations of the body signify gender identity at the cultural level.

For example, the queen wore a necklace decorated with a small jade female dancer elegantly swirling her sleeves (fig. 2.4).[21] The king also wore a necklace, but his did not include a jade dancer. In excavated Western Han period tombs, as Lu Zhaoyin has noted, this humanoid motif appeared almost exclusively with female subjects.[22] Although the exact model for

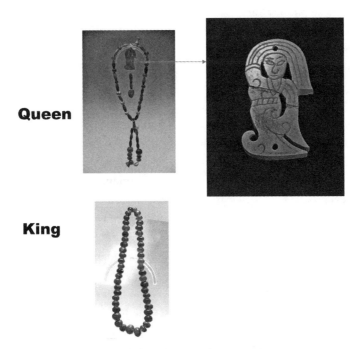

FIGURE 2.4 Necklaces at Mancheng tombs no. 1 and no. 2, Mancheng, Hebei, ca. 118–104 BCE. Made by Jie Shi and courtesy of Hebei Museum, Shijiazhuang.

such dancers remains unknown, it is possible that these beautiful jade ladies might more or less mirror their graceful female wearers, albeit in a generic and idealized sense.

In Han funerary art, probably few motifs carried a stronger feminine connotation than figures dancing with long sleeves.[23] During the Western Han, many imperial ladies who gained the favor of the emperors were excellent dancers, and some of them were trained professionals. For example, Lady Li, Emperor Wu's favorite consort, was a native of Zhongshan. When she was first presented to the emperor, according to the story in the *Hanshu*, she captured his majesty's attention immediately with her extraordinary beauty and charming dance.[24]

Another feminine object was the mirror. The queen held a small bronze mirror, only 4.8 centimeters in diameter, in her left hand as if she were anxious to check, even in the afterlife, whether her makeup looked perfect.[25] The king, in contrast, was supplied with no mirrors in his coffin. The fact that mirrors were granted a closer relationship to the female body than to the male body renders these objects as "feminine."

Although mirrors were used by men and women alike in everyday life, in early Chinese pictorial art, mirrors were associated almost exclusively with women. In extant murals and stone carvings dating from the Han dynasty, noble or wealthy ladies were portrayed as either sitting in front of a mirror or holding a mirror in their hands. One of the earliest known pictorial examples appeared in a stone carving at present-day Jiaxiang, Shandong, dated to the mid-second century CE. On the second floor of a two-story pavilion, an area considered the feminine space in a house, a group of ladies are adorning themselves in the boudoir. One lady is looking in a mirror held in her left hand.[26] It is not difficult to imagine placing Dou Wan as one such noble lady in her royal boudoir in Zhongshan. Although mirrors were used by men in everyday life as well, early Chinese artists almost never depicted such scenes. Mirrors were treated as a symbol of women's exceptional concern for their physical beauty and perhaps also as a metaphor for female vanity. An anonymous Eastern Han poet described how a nobleman wooed a beautiful lady by presenting her with a mirror as a gift: "He gives me a bronze mirror and ties it to my red silk skirt."[27]

Another similarly feminized object was the toiletry case set, a multilevel lacquer box encasing a group of smaller lacquer containers usually with beautification tools inside.[28] One of Dou Wan's toiletry cases was placed on top of her legs inside the coffin as if she were in the process of adorning her face or hair. In contrast, the king's inner and outer coffins (*guan*) were not provided with such objects, though one was found in his house-shaped stone casket.[29] Like the mirrors, the toiletry cases had a clear feminine connotation, even though they also were used by men in real life. The shining gold, silver, carnelian, turquoise, and jade inlays on the exterior face of these lacquer cases, which were originally wrapped in silk, indicate the power and wealth of their owner. Originally measuring twenty-five centimeters in diameter, the outer case of Dou Wan's toiletry set held a group of five smaller, square, rectangular, and circular containers of various sizes. In these little boxes lay one mirror and a cluster of small knives for beautification.[30] Brought into the royal lady's coffin, the toiletry case manifested an intimate relationship with the female subject and qualified as a feminine "outfit." Unlike the husband's toiletry case, which contained powder (probably facial cream), the wife's case contained no trace of makeup, presumably because such powder had already been applied to her face, thereby reinforcing the intimate relationship of the toiletry case set to the female subject.

Meanwhile, weapons represented masculinity, and they were totally absent from the queen's coffin. Whereas the queen remained totally unarmed, the king carried five swords in his coffin, including some of the most beautifully ornamented examples ever excavated from early China. Their exotic style will be closely examined in chapter 3.

These material decorations and equipment for the bodies in the coffins are sexually differentiated in cultural rather than natural terms. While the elegant jade dancer, the mirror, and the cosmetic cases were all symbols of female gentleness and beauty, the swords embodied masculine force. This symbolic contrast corresponds to a slightly later discourse on gender articulated in Han texts of the second century. Ban Zhao 班昭 (ca. 45–ca. 117 CE), one of the earliest known female authors in Chinese history, in her *Admonitions for Women* (*Nüjie* 女誡), listed a number of principles for women to follow in dealing with domestic relations in a patriarchal society. In the chapter "Respect and Prudence" (*Jingshen* 敬慎), she argued that the philosophical basis for men and women remaining respectful to one another was the natural difference between the two genders: "As *yin* and *yang* are not of the same nature, so man and woman have different characteristics. The distinctive quality of *yang* is rigidity; the function of *yin* is yielding. A man is honored for strength; a woman is beautiful on account of her gentleness."[31]

In the coffins of Liu Sheng and Dou Wan, the sexual organs alluded to by the jade suits were located closest to the body to indicate the natural and most fundamental difference between male and female. From this natural difference emerges various culturally determined differences displayed in artifacts such as the jade dancer ornaments, mirrors, cosmetic cases, and weapons.[32] These artificial/natural and cultural sexual characteristics defined the Mancheng bodies as living subjects clad to remain both naturally and culturally gendered.

HIERARCHY OF GENDER IN SOCIAL SPACE

Distinguishing *yin* from *yang* as equal and complimentary qualities is only the beginning of the narrative of gender in the tombs at the Mancheng site. All the differences I have demonstrated so far are found in the coffins, and these differences have expressed few hierarchical implications. The jade suits for the royal couple were made of the same materials, were approximately the same size, and were decorated with similar ornaments. In other words, the male and female bodies were fundamentally equal. However, when this sexual division extended beyond the personal body into the social space, that is, from the coffins to the external tomb chambers that represented the deceased's living realm, hierarchical implications between the two genders began to appear.

This change was perhaps most apparent in the shape of the tombs. Although the two separate tombs appear to be generic copies of each other, they were not structurally identical; the twisted placement of the queen's rear chamber sets them apart.

Dou Wan's tomb does not maintain the popular cruciform shape seen in Liu Sheng's and many other Western Han tombs. Instead, the queen's rear chamber mysteriously deviates from the central east-west axis of the tomb (figs. 1.1, 2.1). Instead of carving into the west (rear) wall of the front chamber, such as in Liu Sheng's case, the queen's rear chamber cuts into her front chamber's south wall. As a result, the plan of tomb no. 2 ends in an odd "L" shape.

Encountering this structural anomaly, Lu Zhaoyin, one of the leading excavators, made a keen observation in his diary:

At first, we suspected that the quality of the stone in the west of the front chamber was perhaps too poor to be cut into, but our later observation suggests no such quality problem. We then tried another theory. It should be intentional for the tomb builders to carve the rear chamber in the south, for the goal was to get closer to tomb no.1 to its south. This situation indicates that the two tombs were designed as a pair.[33]

According to Lu's observation, the intentional deviation of the wife's bedroom from its normal position resulted in its being closer to tomb no. 1,
thereby disrupting the otherwise strict parallel relationship between the two
tombs (fig. 2.5). Fifty years have passed, and we are now able to substantiate Lu's speculation that "the two tombs were designed as a pair" with more
recently excavated parallels.

This meaningful adjustment finds one of its best comparisons in the
famous tomb of the King (or Emperor Wen) of Nanyue, attributed to Zhao
Mo and excavated in present-day Guangzhou, Guangdong, in the 1980s.
Zhao Mo was the second ruler of the kingdom of Nanyue, which declared
its independence in 204 BCE following the fall of the Qin dynasty. Until its
conquest in 112 BCE by the Han imperial army, Nanyue was considered a
regional power rivaling the Han and the Xiongnu. Chinese records showed
Nanyue as being a satellite state of the Han since 179 BCE, which might
account for some of the similarities between the royal tombs of Nanyue and

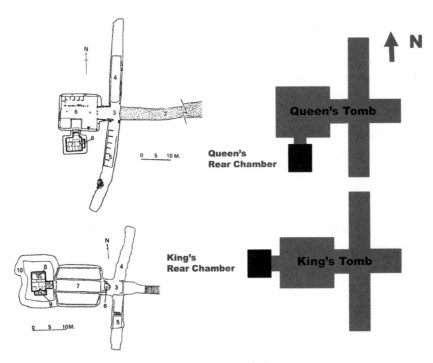

FIGURE 2.5 Diagram showing relationship between rear chambers in Mancheng tombs no. 1 and no. 2,
Mancheng, Hebei, ca. 113 BCE. Made by Jie Shi; courtesy of Metropolitan Museum of Art, New York City.

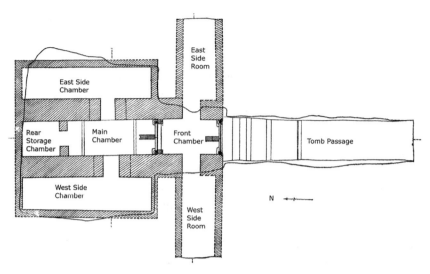

FIGURE 2.6 Plan of Zhao Mo's tomb, Guangzhou, Guangdong, late second century BCE. Made by Jie Shi and courtesy of Wenwu Press.

those of the Han.[34] Although the plan of Zhao Mo's tomb resembles that of the tombs at the Mancheng site, this male tomb was discovered without a female counterpart at its side. The rear section of the tomb was a nearly square architectural complex consisting of four interconnected chambers covered by a flat ceiling (fig. 2.6). Among the four chambers, the emperor's coffin compartment sat in the center, which was in turn surrounded on three sides by rooms on the east, west, and north. Besides the north chamber, which was used as storage for ritual vessels of the deceased king, the west chamber contained the physical remains of relatively low-status imperial attendants, and the east chamber housed the bodies of Zhao Mo's four lesser wives. Each of these noble ladies was buried with such daily paraphernalia as beautification tools as if she would continue to attend and please her husband in the afterlife.[35]

Regardless of the many differences between them, the designers of Zhao Mo's tomb and those of the Mancheng tombs faced a similar challenge: how to place husband and wife at one site. Their solutions are comparable in terms of the individuals' relative positions because the wives at both sites appeared on the left side of their husbands. Although Dou Wan's tomb was cut to the north of Liu's tomb, because the husband's head was oriented to the west and his feet to the east, the wife's body in the north appeared at his left side. In the tomb of Nanyue, although the imperial concubines were buried to the east of their husband, with the lord's head oriented to the north and his feet to the south, they again lay on his left side. This positioning was by no means a coincidence. During the early Western Han, the empresses and other lesser concubines were usually buried to the northeast or north-west of their emperors.[36] However, with tombs usually oriented to the east, the wives in the north would end up on the left side of the emperor. The model for this pattern might have come from the First Emperor of Qin's vast Lishan mausoleum, in which archaeologists have identified a group of small satellite burials tentatively attributed to his lesser wives on the north-east (left) side of the emperor's burial.[37] Understood in this broader cultural context, Dou Wan's position in the tomb is generally comparable to that of Zhao Mo's lesser wives.

The secondary status of Zhao Mo's lesser wives was evident in their marginal position in the entire tomb structure because the center is always more powerful than the periphery; but at the Mancheng site, a similar hierarchy was expressed through the deviation of Dou Wan's rear chamber toward her husband's. While this alteration apparently brought the couple closer to each other, the fact that the wife's burial tilts toward the husband's rather than the other way around suggests an unequal power relationship. It seems as if the husband's social gravity is pulling the wife's rear chamber, shifting its direction and deflecting it toward his tomb. It is not hard to imagine that had that gravitational force become strong enough, the wife's rear chamber would have merged into the husband's tomb, leading to a design like Zhao Mo's burial.

In addition to the hierarchical architectural plan, the king and queen's unequal burial objects apparently placed the male subject above the female subject in importance. More specifically, the ritual objects (perhaps the most important of all burial objects) that were displayed in the rear and front chambers of the king's tomb were superior in both quantity and size to those in the queen's tomb.[38]

First, the quantity of objects in the king's tomb was greater than that in the queen's. In terms of bronzes, the husband's tomb yielded 64 types totaling 419 pieces, while the wife's tomb yielded 40 types totaling 188 pieces.[39] Beyond the coffins, the king's rear chamber contained about twice as many objects as his wife's. The difference was even starker in the front chamber, in which the husband owned four times as many objects as the wife did. What is more, the husband's tomb featured two splendid life-sized carriages stationed at the entrance of the front chamber, while the wife's tomb contained none at the same location. In the traditional ritual context where "the multitude of things was the mark of distinction," this inequality unmistakably indicates male superiority.[40]

This numerical hierarchy was no coincidence but was derived from a tradition seen in earlier burials in the local region to the north of the Yellow River. During the Western Zhou period, even though—in theory—a deceased couple was entitled to the same social rank and privilege, the husband was usually buried with more objects than the wife.[41] For example, in the important Guo state cemetery located in present-day Sanmenxia, Henan, which dated from the eighth century BCE, Duke Ji 虢季 was buried with nearly half a ton of ritual bronzes, an amount three times heavier than those bronzes from his wife's (Lady Liang Ji 梁姬) burial.[42] In the Jin state cemetery at Tianma-Qucun, dating from about the same period, the situation was not very different.[43] With regard to the number of status-marking *ding* tripods, Lothar von Falkenhausen concludes that "wives systematically ranked one notch lower than their husbands."[44] The male superiority as it related to the number of ritual objects also applied to chariots in the tombs at the Mancheng site. While the husband's tomb contained six vehicles, the wife's only had four.

In terms of the scale of ritual vessels, Liu Sheng was again in a superior position to his wife. Some of the vessels in Dou Wan's tomb are significantly smaller than those in her husband's tomb. For example, while the husband's two *ding* tripods, each measuring between seventeen and eighteen centimeters tall, were cast to a regular scale, the wife's *ding* tripod is barely half that height—a mere 8.2 centimeters.[45] This difference also applies to some other ritual vessels, including *hu* or *yan* types. Although the excavators considered the lady's miniaturized objects as funerary surrogates or *mingqi* 明器 ("spirit objects") deprived of actual function,[46] those nearly half-size vessels from Dou's chamber were not as crude, deformed, or unusable as *mingqi*. Technically, they were all functional. The lid of each vessel could be freely removed and replaced; each leg or handle was meticulously cast so the vessel could firmly stand on its own or be lifted; and both the interior and exterior faces of the vessels were carefully polished. In fact, bronze ritual vessels cast on such a small scale were not uncommon. Some small *ding* tripods could be as little as ten centimeters tall.[47] Even if these small objects were surrogates, this still raises the question of why these surrogates for regular ritual objects did not appear in the husband's tomb.

In North China, associating small objects with female tomb occupants is a much older tradition than the second century BCE. In the famous tomb of the Shang royal consort Fu Hao, excavators found not only regular-size bronze ritual vessels but also a group of miniature *ding*, *gui*, and *fou* vessels, each no taller than ten centimeters.[48] Archaeologists have encountered more evidence of this phenomenon in several late Western Zhou royal cemeteries including those of the Guo, Jin, and Rui 芮 states.[49] For example, in the aforementioned Lady Liang Ji's tomb, the excavators found two miniaturized bronze vessels one-third the size of their regular counterparts. One of the two miniature bronze vessels measures 11.8 centimeters in height and 8.1 centimeters in diameter, and the other one is even smaller—8.4 centimeters in height and 6 centimeters in diameter.[50] Some scholars have speculated that these small objects were toys for female users[51] or were symbolic of the owner's cultural tradition (i.e., before marrying into the royal line of another state).[52] While in some places (e.g., tomb no. 63 at Tianma-Qucun) these small feminine objects were intermingled with regular ritual vessels, in other locations (e.g., tomb no. 26 at Liangdaicun), they were separated into two different groups: the miniaturized group was located in the east section of the *guo* casket, while the regular one was concentrated in the southwest corner of the casket.[53] Dou Wan's miniature bronzes followed the latter practice and were grouped together in an independent wooden box in her front chamber that was separate from the other regular vessels in her rear chamber.

This tradition of scaling down ritual objects persisted through the late Eastern Zhou period and continued into the Eastern Han era.[54] The closest known examples that are comparable to Dou Wan's miniature bronzes came from a hoard uncovered at Koudian in present-day Yanshi, Henan.[55] This cache, dated to the first century CE, concealed a group of gilt, miniaturized ritual bronzes that were stylistically almost identical with those found in Dou Wan's tomb, as well as some other gilt-bronze animal figurines. In another case, a miniaturized bronze *hu* vessel, similar to Dou Wan's, was interred in a small tomb attributed to an anonymous deceased child.[56] Dou Wan's miniature bronzes presumably fall into the same category as these so-called "toys."

Those petite ritual objects that only appeared in Dou Wan's tomb also included one small carriage in the side chamber. While the king's vehicles were all full-sized, the queen's tomb had one miniature carriage located at the northernmost end of the elongated chamber.[57] This special carriage was about half the regular size, with miniaturized carriage fittings. The vehicle was also drawn by smaller horses. Instead of regular horses that can be as tall as two meters, two ponies that could grow only up to one meter in height were killed and interred next to the small carriage.[58] The king's tomb, however, contained no such small horses.[59]

Dou Wan's singular small vehicle was similar to the local tradition in North China. While unearthing the cemetery of the marquises of the Jin state, excavators observed a notable difference between the male and female tombs in terms of the size of interred carriages. Whereas the marquises were buried with full-sized vehicles, whose wheels measured up to 150 centimeters in diameter, their wives' tombs were distinguished by one small, exquisite carriage with wheels only 95 centimeters in diameter, which was parked either on top of the casket or at the end of the tomb ramp.[60] These small vehicles were identified as entertaining instruments in the life of the elite,[61] but the fact that such vehicles were usually associated with women deserves further investigation.

The petite vessels, carriage, and ponies correspond with the smaller physical stature of their female user. Indeed, Dou Wan was physically shorter than her husband. While Liu Sheng's jade suit measures 1.88 meters in length, his wife's is only 1.72 meters (fig. 1.3, 2.2).[62] Even though the two jade suits showed few sexual characteristics other than the genitalia, as I have already demonstrated, the different physical statures of their male and female subjects were perhaps too important to dismiss.

But being small was not only a physical trait but also a sociological attribute of females in Han China. A discursive link clearly existed among "women," "small," and "lower status" in some early Chinese texts. In a controversial quote from the *Analects* (*Lunyu* 論語), Confucius (551–479 BCE) linked women to the "small people" (*xiaoren* 小人), namely, the poorly educated masses, and dismissed female souls as weaker, lower, and lesser than their (nobler) male counterparts.[63] Although this well-known comment has lost its original context, its gender overtone is undeniable. In Chinese, smallness (*xiao* 小) sometimes alludes to lowness (*bei* 卑) as well as scarcity (*shao* 少). That is perhaps why an entry in the third-century lexicon *Expanded Erya* (*Guangya* 廣雅) directly interpreted *bei* 椑 as connoting "small."[64]

POWER BALANCE BETWEEN KING AND QUEEN

It is too simplistic to consider the social space in the Mancheng tombs as entirely dominated by the male subject. It is worth noting that Dou Wan's disadvantages with regard to the quantity and scale of ritual objects was compensated by better artistic quality and by a larger architectural space.

Dou Wan displays an advantage over her husband in a number of aspects. First, in terms of architecture, her tomb is not only larger but is more complete. Occupying three thousand cubic meters, Dou Wan's tomb is more than 11 percent larger than her husband's.[65] According to the *Book of Rites*, "The greatness of size formed the mark. The dimensions of palaces and apartments; the measurements of dishes and (other) articles; the thickness of the inner and outer coffins; the greatness of eminences and mounds—these were cases in which the greatness of size was the nobler."[66] This suggests that greater size often signified greater power in ritual architecture. Indeed, it was unusual for the empress to overwhelm the emperor in terms of the scale of funerary monuments. In the Western Han imperial necropolises located in the suburbs of the capital, the tombs of most empresses displayed smaller tumuli than that of their husbands. Only Empress Lü Zhi 呂雉 (ca. 241–180 BCE), the first empress of the dynasty, was given the exclusive honor of having a tumulus as large as her husband's.[67] After her husband died, this ambitious lady successfully crushed her political opponents and became the de facto ruler of the empire, overseeing the court and issuing imperial orders for eight years.[68] Lü Zhi's exceptional tumulus is a great testimony to the political significance of size in Western Han royal funerary rites.

What is more, Dou Wan's tomb technically is finer in many respects. The interior face of her rock-cut cave is in a far more finished and polished condition than that of her husband's. In particular, her front chamber features a completed dome rather than the barely finished barrel-vaulted ceiling in her husband's burial (figs. 1.1, 2.1).

Second, in terms of buried objects, as excavators noted, the queen's jade suit demonstrates a finer level of craftsmanship.[69] Her jade-encrusted coffin—a wooden coffin covered with 192 pieces of jade on the interior and twenty-six jade *bi* discs on the exterior, humbled the king's regular wooden coffins, which were without such luxurious decoration.[70] Only four such precious jade coffins, all dating from the second century BCE, have been uncovered so far.[71] These rare, luxurious, burial devices were an unmistakable symbol of the occupants' prestigious social status. In a story from the *Shiji*, when King Zhuang of Chu 楚莊王 (r. 613–591 BCE) lost his favorite horse, he ordered the dead horse to be buried in a set of nested wooden coffins to which the grandee nobles (*dafu* 大夫) usually were entitled. Realizing the absurdity of the order, a clever actor named Meng 孟 went to the king and suggested that the dead horse deserved an even better coffin—a jade coffin—to which kings were exclusively entitled. Astounded, the king realized his mistake, changed his mind, and ordered the dead horse simply to be dumped.[72] The fact that Dou Wan, rather than Liu Sheng, was given the privileged jade coffin indicates the queen's special status.

Other objects also demonstrated the queen's advantage over the king. Among the ten thousand objects discovered in the two tombs, the most extraordinary one, a bronze lamp, conventionally known as the "lamp of the Palace of Lasting Trust," appeared as the only source of light in Dou Wan's otherwise pitch-black bedroom (fig. 2.7). Although excavators found a large number of lamps of various shapes in Liu Sheng's tomb, none of them demonstrates the same level of mechanical and artistic ingenuity as Dou Wan's. The superb design and aesthetics of this unique work has made it one of China's most famous national treasures.

First, the work stands out because of its impressive physical appearance. Standing forty-eight centimeters, it was the largest and tallest surviving object in the entire tomb; weighing nearly sixteen kilograms, it was almost immovable in the royal boudoir. Furthermore, this work's highly polished

FIGURE 2.7 Lamp of the Palace of Lasting Trust from the rear chamber of Mancheng tomb no. 2, Mancheng, Hebei, ca. 118–104 BCE. Courtesy of Hebei Museum, Shijiazhuang.

and thoroughly gilt surface made it one of the shiniest objects present, both emitting and reflecting light.

Second, the work distinguishes itself with its extraordinary artistic quality. The cylindrical lamp is held in the hands of a proportionally larger palace lady, who extends her left arm to grab the lamp from below and lays her right palm on top of the lamp to keep it stable.[73] She sat in the deceased queen's posthumous bedroom, prepared to provide light for the descending night that would supposedly last forever. The lady has long, sharp, and raised eyebrows, a little mouth with delicate lips, a flat and smooth forehead, a slim waist, and bare feet—all considered to be ideal secondary sexual characteristics of feminine beauty of this period. Such features demand primary visual attention, which is another sign of unparalleled significance. This large, extraordinary lamp carrier overwhelms the small, ordinary lamp, visually pushing the latter aside into a secondary role. It looks as though the work was designed primarily as a sculpture.

Third, the mechanical ingenuity of the lamp is exceptional. Both the lamp and the lady are hollow, with gilt all over the exterior face, and they were assembled from a number of separately cast bronze pieces. When used, the lamp's brightness and air flow are controlled through an adjustable opening on its side wall. More remarkably, the lady's right arm merges seamlessly with the lamp's cover, forming an integral conduit for unhealthy gas particles released from the burning fuel, which are vented into the lady's hollow body, where they would cool down and finally be deposited as ash.

Last but not least, the lady of the lamp distinguished herself from all other objects at Mancheng with her illustrious "social biography" as she traveled from hand to hand within the imperial house. A number of inscriptions on this object reveal how special it might have been in the eyes of its owners. According to the excavators' reconstruction, the lamp was made sometime between 173 and 159 BCE and then entered the collection of a marquis of the Yangxin family.[74] After the Yangxin family committed a crime, its properties were confiscated by the imperial court. As a result, the lamp passed into the hands of Grand Empress Dowager Dou, the most powerful woman in the empire who, after the death of her husband, maintained a strong influence on the court till her own death in 135 BCE. For some reason, the mighty empress sent this lamp as a gift to Dou Wan, who decided to keep it even in death. Having it placed next to her burial meant taking permanent possession of this imperial gift and proclaiming the favor the queen enjoyed from the supreme grand empress dowager.

The extraordinary weight, beauty, and luster, not to mention the social distinction, of this singular object constituted a power that rebalanced the otherwise male-dominated hierarchical relationship between husband and wife.[75] But what did this balance achieve?

It is almost certain that Dou Wan was related to Grand Empress Dowager Dou (Dou Yifang), the principal wife of Emperor Wen, mother of Emperor Jing, and grandmother of Liu Sheng and Emperor Wu.

Throughout the second century BCE, the power of the imperial consort's clan was dominant. After the death of Emperor Gao, as noted earlier, his principal wife, Grand Empress Dowager Lü (Lü Zhi), became the de facto ruler of the empire. To assist her, she relied on her father's lineage (the Lü lineage) by allowing her brothers and nephews to assume important government positions or even by making them regional kings. To further secure her control of the imperial throne, she arranged the marriage of her daughter's daughter, Empress Zhang 張皇后 (202–163 BCE), and Emperor Gao's son, Emperor Hui 惠帝 (r. 195–188 BCE). After Emperor Hui died, Lü Zhi arranged another marriage between her grandniece, Empress Lü 呂皇后 (possibly d. 180 BCE), and her grandson, the new Emperor Shao 少帝 (r. 184–180 BCE). This practice, known as a "double marital bond" (chongqin 重親), aimed to strengthen the kinship between the emperor and the grand empress dowager.[76] Later empress dowagers followed the same practice. Emperor Gao's consort, Grand Empress Dowager Bo 薄太后 (215–155 BCE), arranged the marriage between his grandson, Emperor Jing, and a woman from his father's family, Empress Bo 薄皇后 (d. 148 BCE). Emperor Wen's wife, Dou Yifang, did the same for her grandson, Emperor Wu, and her daughter's daughter, Empress Chen 陳皇后 (fl. late second century BCE).[77] It is unimaginable that Liu Sheng could have escaped from this powerful marital pattern and not succumb to the same fate as his grandfather, father, and brother: marrying a woman from his powerful grandmother's Dou clan, perhaps even a woman the grand empress dowager had handpicked. The consequence of even minor resistance could be fatal. According to a horrendous story, Liu You 劉友 (d. 180 BCE), King of Zhao refused to favor her queen, who was one of Lü Zhi's nieces. The resentful queen took revenge by accusing her husband of treason in front of her powerful aunt, who arrested the king and starved him to death.[78]

The power of grand empress dowagers during the Western Han era, particularly during the second century BCE, was not only derived from Lü Zhi's inspiring model but was also based upon administrative reality. In the first half of the Western Han period, the bureaucratic system's involvement in imperial decision-making was not fully established, and the family of the emperor (especially the grand empress dowager and her father's lineage) was able to intervene in politics and directly influence imperial policy.[79]

Dou Yifang's supreme power was best demonstrated by an event that took place in 140 BCE, after Emperor Wu ascended the throne. The grand empress dowager was a tough woman with strong ideological opinions. She imposed the so-called Huanglao 黃老 school of political philosophy (a topic substantially analyzed in chapter 5) on her grandsons, demanding that the princes study Huanglao works while dismissing other rival ideologies, particularly Confucianism, with contempt and harshness. Perhaps in an attempt to declare his independence, the new emperor was sympathetic to Confucianism and promoted Confucian scholars to high positions in the government, thereby heralding radical political reform. This action irritated the grand empress dowager, who furiously crushed the reform with an iron hand and executed its leaders. The emperor realized his lack of power and chose to submit.[80] Not until the death of his grandmother did the emperor dare to challenge her authority again. This episode demonstrates the unshakable influence of Dou Yifang over the imperial house.

If Dou Wan was indeed related to Dou Yifang, then in the kingdom of Zhongshan, Queen Dou Wan must have represented the powerful Dou lineage, which constituted what was called the "spousal branch" (*qizu* 妻族) in Liu Sheng's nine family branches (*jiuzu* 九族). During the Han dynasty, each person lived at the intersection of nine family branches, including four paternal branches (*fuzu* 父族), three maternal branches (*muzu* 母族), and two spousal branches, or in-laws.[81] Clearly, Dou Wan's special relationship with the dominant grand empress dowager must have been a powerful, perhaps also terrifying, political asset of her husband, Liu Sheng.

Liu Sheng's reliance on his wife's lineage is hinted at in a set of forty inscribed coins originally made for a drinker's wager game that were discovered in the southeast corner of the queen's front chamber (fig. 2.8).[82] The forty inscriptions together constitute twenty couplets of incantations. I will leave my detailed discussion of the inscriptions to chapter 5, but

FIGURE 2.8 Wager coins from Mancheng tomb no. 2, Mancheng, Hebei, ca. 118–104 BCE. Courtesy of Hebei Museum, Shijiazhuang.

here it suffices to focus on two inscriptions that contain explicit gender information:

畏妻鄙　　Awe-inspiring are my wife's fiefs!
壽夫王母　Long live the queen mother (or, live as long as the queen mother)!

The phrase *qibi* 妻鄙 in the first incantation most likely denotes the fiefs of the wife,[83] but the transcription of the first two graphs remains controversial. The excavators followed Guo Moruo's transcription and read the first two graphs as the two-syllable word, *tiantian* 田田, meaning "fields after fields," "many fields," or by extension, "many."[84] According to another paleographer, Qiu Xigui, however, these two graphs should be read as one single character: "wei" 畏, "to fear."[85] Regardless of which reading is correct, this line expresses the power of the spousal branches.

The second incantation refers to a "queen mother," whose identity remains ambiguous. The importance of this couplet is obvious because while each of the other nineteen incantations consists of three characters, this final one distinguishes itself with four graphs.[86] Here, it is necessary to offer two equally valid translations because of the tricky term *wangmu*. This two-syllable compound either means a "king's mother" (i.e., a royal mother or queen) or is used as an abridged title of the goddess "queen mother (of the west)" (*Xiwangmu* 西王母), who was the supreme goddess believed to reign on the sacred Mt. Kunlun in the remote west.

In transmitted texts from the Han period, *wangmu*, when used alone, most frequently refers to kings' mothers, who presided as matriarchs over the royal houses.[87] Furthermore, with the previous incantation placing Dou Wan at the top of the spousal branch, it is reasonable to read *wangmu* as an honorable title that compliments the noble lady—the king's mother. This scenario encourages the reading, "long live the queen mother!"

An inscription cast on a first-century BCE bronze mirror further bolsters this interpretation. In this long prayer, which likewise is composed of short rhymed couplets, the maker of the mirror included a similar auspicious wish for the longevity of a "queen mother" (*wangmu*): "The queen mother must forever extend her life" (*fu wangmu, yong yi shou* 夫王母, 永益壽).[88] Although the name of this "queen mother" on the coin remains unknown, she was presumably an aged royal woman who yearned for a prolonged life—either Dou Wan as the queen mother of the Zhongshan or Grand Empress Dowager Dou as the queen mother of the entire Western Han empire.

However, the other reading of *wangmu* works equally well. Although the title of the goddess often begins with her place of origin—the west (*Xi*), thus Xiwangmu—occasionally in bronze inscriptions, *wangmu* could be used as an abbreviated form of *Xiwangmu*, the divine Queen Mother of the West. In the popular imagination, this goddess resided in a rock cave on sacred Mt. Kunlun and possessed the secret of immortality.[89] She was so powerful, legend has it, that the Zhou king once traveled thousands of miles to visit her personally, bringing precious gifts.[90] Moreover, in funerary contexts and on bronze mirrors, *wangmu* usually refers to Xiwangmu. Thus, the incantation—so far the earliest excavated reference to the goddess—can be interpreted as "live as long as the queen mother!" A close comparison appears in an early first-century mirror inscription that hopes the owner will "live as long as the queen mother with the household possessions multiplied by a million times" (*Shouru wangmu jia wanbei* 壽如王母家萬倍).[91] Embodying the very notion of longevity, this goddess was presumably the role model for any woman who desired an unending life.

Despite the two different potential interpretations of the word *wangmu*, one "mortal" and one "immortal," they are not necessarily contradictory. The mortal matriarch of the royal family was often considered the earthly embodiment of the supreme goddess, in front of whom the son of heaven had to remain modest.[92] A well-known later example of this double identity was Grand Empress Dowager Wang Zhengjun 王政君 (71 BCE–13 CE). Her nephew, Wang Mang, compared this lady to the Queen Mother of the West and used her authority to help him usurp the emperorship and establish the Xin 新 dynasty (9–23 CE).[93] In either reading, the extraordinary scale and quality of objects in Dou Wan's tomb attest to the power of this imperial consort in the early Western Han period. Although it remains unknown whether this set of coins was made specifically for the tomb or was used before the deaths of the royal couple, their political implication remains unmistakable.

In sum, the equality established between the male and female bodies in the personal space (coffins) of the tombs at the Mancheng site was shattered by the male superiority in material properties in the tombs' social space (rear and front chambers). However, this was counterbalanced by the female subject's extra political capital that was gained due to her relationship with Grand Empress Dowager Dou's clan.

HUSBAND AND WIFE AS TWO HALVES OF ONE BODY

Negotiating power between a distinct man and woman in the social space was not intended to open up a competition between the two genders or a contradiction between masculinity and femininity. Instead, it aimed to establish an interdependent relationship between the two within a common body.

This fact is demonstrated by the complementary placement of the burial objects within the two tombs, which were arranged like mirror images. Although the architectural adjustment of Dou Wan's rear chamber toward the south disrupts the overall parallel relationship between the two rear chambers, the tomb designer nonetheless used the placement of the chambers' material contents to restore the lost symmetry. On more than one occasion, the distribution of objects was simply reversed, with the left transposed onto the right and the right onto the left.

The king's coffin was placed on the north side of his rear chamber, and the queen's coffin rested on the south side of hers (fig. 2.9a). Lying side by side but physically separated in two different burials, the husband and wife nonetheless remained as close as possible to each other. The husband's nested coffins were situated under the north wall rather than on the east-west central axis of the chamber. This positioning breaks the east-west symmetry of the tomb structure by allocating the most central content—the deceased's

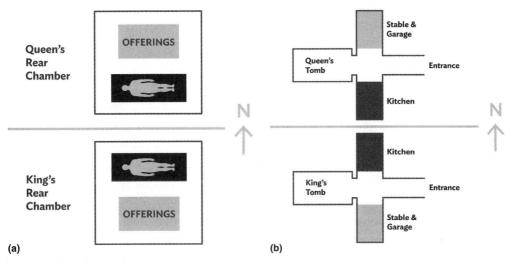

FIGURE 2.9 (a) Diagram of relative positional relationship between rear chambers in Mancheng tombs no. 1 and no. 2, Mancheng, Hebei, ca. 118–104 BCE; (b) Diagram of relative positional relationship between side chambers in Mancheng tombs no. 1 and no. 2, Mancheng, Hebei, ca. 118–104 BCE. Made by Jie Shi and Alex Brey.

body—to the north side. An intriguing suggestion to explain this abnormal modification is the necessity for the husband to remain on the side closest to his wife, whose separate burial was located to the north. Correspondingly, the wife's coffin was laid under the south wall of her rear chamber to stay adjacent to her husband's.

By the same token, the ritual offerings in the queen's rear chamber became a mirror image of the king's. First, the two groups of ritual objects fall into similar typological categories, including such ritual vessels as *hu* pots and such small personal items as a seal, a knife, and a toiletry case. The unique seal inscribed with the name "Dou Wan" on it was the only seal found in the tomb bearing the deceased's name, verifying that the invisible subject of the banquet was indeed Dou Wan's soul. A jade *bi* disc, formally identical to those scattered in Liu Sheng's tomb, was put on the north side of the queen's lamp. As the only such examples that appeared outside the queen's coffin, these intimate objects alluded to the royal lady's residence in the casket chamber.

Second, the two similar groups of offerings were in reversed positions in the two burials. In the husband's tomb, the objects were placed to the south of the coffin and, in the wife's tomb, to the north of the coffin. If we take the two tombs as one unified burial, the two bodies representing the occupants' physical presence occupy the center of the rear section of the unified burial and are flanked by two groups of ritual offerings on both sides, constituting yet another symmetrical plan along the east-west central axis between the two tombs.

The positional "inversion" between husband and wife in the rear chambers is unlikely to have been a coincidence. In fact, the same pattern extends into the side chambers. The husband's north side chamber housed food vessels and containers, and his south side chamber was reserved for horses and chariots. In the wife's tomb, the order was reversed, with the symbolic kitchen moved to the south side and the simulated stable switched to the north (fig. 2.9b).

The material contents of the two stables were almost identical except for their reversed orientation. The husband's stable contained four carriages and eleven horses, while the wife's held four carriages and thirteen horses. In the former, all but one vehicle was oriented to the north, while in the latter, all were directed to the south. In other words, most of the chariots were directed toward the entrance of the tombs, implying they were ready for an outing.[94] In both tombs, except for the singular miniaturized chariot in the wife's tomb, all vehicles were life-sized. Two to four harnessed steeds, acting as draught horses, were killed, and their bodies were laid on the tomb floor next to the chariots. Some of the vehicles were equipped with crossbows and arrows for hunting.[95] Excavators have associated these with the "princely blue canopied chariot" (wangqinggaiche 王青蓋車) documented in the "Treatise of Chariots and Costumes" included in the Book of the Latter Han (Hou Hanshu 後漢書).[96] Gao Chongwen, however, has related them to ritual chariots used specifically in funerary ceremonies.[97] Despite the disagreement in regard to the ritual function of the vehicles, there is no question that these magnificent vehicles were constructed as instruments for journeying and hunting, which were among the most entertaining activities of the royals.[98]

Like the two stables, the two kitchens of the two royal tombs were also furnished and indicated a mutually inverted relationship.

First, objects interred in the two symbolic kitchens were typologically similar. Other than a few lacquer vessels and an iron heater, most of the objects were wine and food containers made of fired clay, including jars, hu vessels, basins, pots, cauldrons, boxes, beakers, cups, and so on. Among them, the signature vessels were a number of giant jars used for the massive storage of grade A wine (shangzunjiu 上尊酒). These jars bear such inscriptions as "eleven shi [about 220 liters] of millet-brewed alcohol" (shujiu shiyi shi 黍酒十一石)

to mark their content.[99] The interior walls of the jars still carry wine stains. Liu Sheng was a notorious drinker.[100] As the wife of a notorious drinker, the queen's side chamber resembled her husband's in tomb no. 1 in the quantity and size of wine storage jars, although we do not know whether she herself was a heavy imbiber.[101] Unlike the other tomb chambers, both kitchens were similarly devoid of light, human agency, and sense of time; no lamps, figurines, or water clocks were found next to the vessels.

Second, the arrangement of these objects in the kitchens is also similar. Rather than being arrayed on the floor of the tomb chamber, which was divided horizontally by brick walls into six storage units, these objects were stacked, piled, or packed together, even though the chamber had no shortage of space. For example, in the deepest (sixth) unit of Liu Sheng's north side chamber, twelve basins lying on the bottom level were topped by a large number of pots, *hu* vessels, boxes, cauldrons, and cups on the upper level, while the first, third, and fourth units were left almost entirely empty.[102]

Despite all the similarities in content, the two kitchens displayed contradictory patterning in the density of their material contents. In Liu Sheng's north side chamber, most vessels were concentrated in the north (inner) end, but in Dou Wan's south side chamber, they were stacked and piled up in the south (inner) end.[103] The order of the vessels in the two side chambers had been physically reversed.

Because the two separate tombs are located at the same altitude, open in the same direction, are nearly parallel in structure, and are equal in scale, the inverted positions transform the husband and the wife into each other's reflection, thus uniting them into a common body.

One might wonder, however, if the deceased couple were interred in different years, how was this elaborate symmetry planned? How did the designer of the later tomb know the design of the earlier one? Such joint burials might have been planned together long before the deaths of the tomb occupants and their arrangement possibly preserved in diagrams such as those we see in King Cuo's cast bronze cemetery blueprint or in the painted silk examples found in Mawangdui tomb no. 3, which will be discussed in chapter 6.

In fact, arranging the coffins and burial objects of husband and wife into a mirrored relationship was not without precedent. The earliest known example was the joint burial of the lord of Fan (Fan Jun 樊君) and his wife, located in present-day Xinyang, Henan, and dated to the early Eastern Zhou period (ca. seventh century BCE).[104] In that case, the deceased husband and wife were buried in two parallel, equally deep, vertical pit graves—one in the north and one in the south. The husband's coffin was located on the south side of the tomb pit, while the wife's was on the northern side. The husband's burial objects were placed on an earthen ledge on the north side of his tomb pit, while the wife's were placed on a similar ledge on the southern side of her tomb pit. This symmetrical arrangement anticipated what we have seen in the rear chambers of the tombs at the Mancheng site. A similar but slightly later example (late first century BCE) was found in the joint burial of Shiqi Yao 侍其繇 and his wife at Haizhou, in present-day Lianyungang, Jiangsu.[105] In this tomb, the deceased husband and wife and their burial objects were similarly placed in parallel positions that mirrored each other. Perhaps with a similar motivation, the Han people tried other ways to display a husband and wife as being the two halves of one unit, such as breaking a mirror into two equal halves and interring one part with the husband and the other part with the wife[106] or turning the heads of the deceased couple to face each other across their coffins.[107]

As husband and wife, Liu Sheng and Dou Wan unite in one body as equals. As two halves of one unit, they transcended the hierarchical social and political relationship between king (lord) and queen (subject). This regained equality was reflected in the wedding ceremony described in the *Book of Rites*, where the husband and wife must eat at the same table and drink from the same cup, "thus showing that they now formed one body, were of equal rank, and pledged to mutual affection."[108] Marriage, regulated strictly by social norms, was the only legitimate, ethical, and therefore "safe" way of bringing the two sexes together without causing social disorder.

Such duality of male and female counterparts was most vividly portrayed in the first couple in Chinese mythology, Fuxi 伏羲 and Nüwa 女媧. During the first and second centuries CE, these two half-human and half-serpent deities usually were represented in pictorial art as a pair of mirror images. The male consort, Fuxi, usually depicted on the left, holds a carpenter's square in his right hand, while the female goddess, Nüwa, usually depicted on the right, holds a compass in her left hand.[109] Their lower serpentine tails remain intertwined as a visual metaphor for sexual intercourse.

This apparent complementary and mirrored structure has an even deeper root in the *yin-yang* polarity of Han cosmology and philosophy. First, like *yang* and *yin*, which are cosmic equals, the two burials are equal in orientation and altitude—and nearly so in form and structure. Second, like the two cosmic forces that were correlated with particular directions, the male burial of Liu Sheng was located in the south (i.e., the *yang* direction), and the female burial of Dou Wan was located in the north (i.e., the *yin* direction). In a marriage, the dominant husband is correlated with *yang*, while the submissive wife is correlated with *yin*.[110] Through this link, the husband is further correlated with the south, and the wife, with the north.

At the Mancheng site, the symmetry in the arrangement of burial devices and objects offsets the asymmetry caused by the architectural deviation of the queen's rear chamber because symmetry reoriented the queen's body in the same direction as the king's and juxtaposed the royal subjects literally as a proper "couple." Since the deviating architecture obviously was completed first, the inverted positioning of the material content restored the disrupted balance between the two royal subjects in the architectural framework. As a result, the balanced placement of the materials, which mirrors each other, reclaims the equal relationship between the couple.

TWO BURIALS AS ONE HOUSE

Unlike the complementary rear chambers, the front chambers of the two tombs at the Mancheng site were not furnished as simple mirror images of each other. They were counterparts united in another more sophisticated way—to simulate the inner (*nei* 内) and outer (*wai* 外) parts of a united royal house (figs. 1.7, 2.10). This observation is twofold: first, both chambers simulate real buildings, and second, they represent two different types of architecture that complement one another.

My first observation is that the designers shaped both front chambers into hall-like buildings. Artisans incorporated details that evoked a sense of realism. One example of such attentiveness is the three-layer floor of the front chambers and the two side chambers. The lowest layer of the floor was cut in rock, then covered by a middle layer made of charcoal and clay fragments, and then topped by another layer of earth. The upper two layers measure about thirty centimeters thick.[111] The purpose of this composite layering was not only to reduce humidity but also to simulate a real floor (which would not have been made of stone). Above the composite floor stood a timber-framed structure, whose basic function of defining an architectural interior would have been totally meaningless because the rock-cut limestone cave had already framed the interior. Directly on the hybrid floor of each tomb, a three-bay-wide wooden structure was erected. Such division of interior space was standard in a traditional Chinese building. The building's massive rooftop rested on top of a series of pillars anchored in four grooves cut

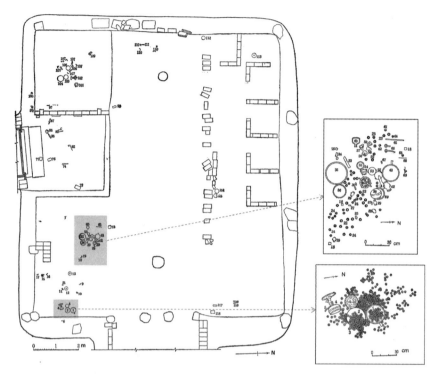

FIGURE 2.10 Distribution of burial objects in front chamber of Mancheng tomb no. 2. Mancheng, Hebei, ca. 118–104 BCE. After Zhongguo shehui kexueyuan kaogu yanjiusuo, *Mancheng Han mu fajue baogao*, p. 231, fig. 154. Courtesy of Wenwu Press.

1 Bronze cauldron; 2 Bronze bowl; 3 Bronze *wuzhu* coins; 4 Bronze incense burner; 5 Object with ivory handle; 6 Bone piece; 9 Bone material; 10–11 Bronze ornaments of ceremonial pole finial; 12–13 Jade *bi* discs; 15 Gold bullion; 16 Stone bullion; 17 Ceramic bullion; 18 Sealing clay; 19 Bronze *hu* vessel; 21 pear-shaped bone piece; 23 Bronze wager coins; 24 Bronze *wuzhu* coins; 25 Bronze miniature horseman; 27 Jade ornament; 28 Bronze winged-cup; 29 Bronze *fang* vessel; 30 Bronze miniature horseman; 31 Bronze heater; 33 Iron saw; 34 Bronze fitting on lower end of ceremonial pole; 35 Bronze basin; 36 Bronze tray; 37 Ivory bowl; 38 Bronze steamer; 39 Bronze cauldron; 41 Bronze scoop; 42 Bronze *hu* vessel; 43 Bronze cauldron; 52–54 Bronze tripods; 55 Bronze cauldron; 56–59 Bronze leopard-shaped mat weights; 60 Bronze *yi* cup; 61–63 Bronze vessel lids; 64 Bronze die; 65 Gold inlaid iron ruler; 66 Gold inlaid iron attachment; 67 Bronze miniature man; 68 Bone object; 69 Bronze ape-shaped hook; 72 Inner mold of iron hoe; 73 Lacquer rectangular box; 74 Iron poniard-shaped tool; 76–77 Inner mold of iron hoe; 82–83 Iron brackets; 85 Bronze steamer; 86–87 Bronze barrel-shaped object with a mushroom top; 93 Inner mold of iron hoe; 97 Iron; 99 Iron rake; 100 Bronze hoop; 101, 102 bronze lamps; 103 Lacquer *zun* container; 104 Bronze basin; 105 Lacquer platter; 106 Lacquer winged cup; 107 Lacquer table; 109 Bronze incense burner; 110 Lacquer circular box; 111 Iron saw; 112 Bronze cauldron; 113–115 Bronze bowls; 116 Iron harrow; 117 Inner mold of iron pickaxe; 118 Inner mold of iron hoe

in the floor. (In the cutaway diagram in fig. 0.3, however, only half of the structure is illustrated.)[112] Tiles were densely packed and carefully layered on the roof. The original function of the tiles (to protect the building from rain and snow) clearly is superfluous in the rock-cut cave. No traces of front doors were discovered, which again points to the function of the building as an open hall.

Such meticulously designed symbolic structures, which were costly and useless, have hitherto only been discovered in royal tombs from the Western Han period. For this reason, one may regard them as reduced, simplified palaces. The purpose of painstakingly constructing them could only have been to simulate a royal living environment suitable for the deceased's social status. Although the idea of symbolically transforming the royal tomb into a royal palace was by no means novel,[113] to the Western Han rulers, it represented a new challenge: how to modify traditional symbolism to express the familial bond between husband and wife.

This leads to my second observation. Despite their architectural similarity, the two front chambers at the Mancheng tomb site differed from and complemented each other in ritual function. To visualize this, some background about the spatial and functional division of a Chinese house or palace is necessary.

A standard Chinese house is oriented toward the south and consists of two units (fig. 2.11a). The front unit is a singular undivided space called a *tang* 堂 ("hall"); without a front wall, the semi-open hall represents the house's public zone. The rear unit is a group of connected rooms; the center one is called the *shi* 室 and the flanking ones are the *fang* 房 ("apartments"). Each space is entirely enclosed by walls, and this unit represents the private zone of the house. A royal palace in Han China was an upgraded version of the standard house (fig. 2.11b).[114] Textual evidence in the official history of the Han suggests that during the second century BCE, both the hall and the apartments hosted sacrificial rituals, but their purposes were different. The hall was reserved for those important events such as the great sacrifice of the ancestors (*xia* 祫), which was held every three or five years. For such major sacrifices, as I have explained in chapter 1, the male ancestor's soul was sheltered in a tent, and the female ancestor's soul was seated in another tent at her husband's side. In contrast, the apartments were reserved for relatively smaller and more intimate sacrificial rituals.

With this bipartite division in mind, I will move on to my third and most important observation. Although each of the two front chambers of the king and the queen contained a timber-structure building that architecturally resembled a hall, the two buildings were different from each other due to their material contents. The king's front chamber was modeled into a hall (*tang*) through interior decoration and furnishings, with two parallel tents for the king and queen's souls. The front chamber in the queen's tomb, on the other hand, simulated the inner apartments (*shi* or *fang*) that housed chamber rituals.

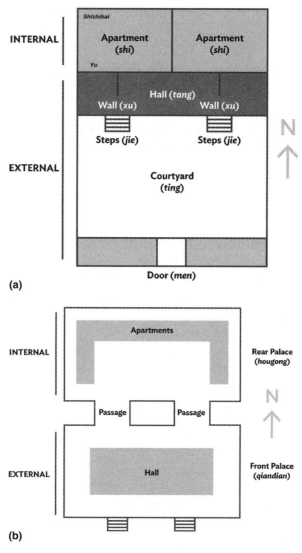

FIGURE 2.11 (a) Plan of standard house in Confucian classics. (b) Plan of palace in Western Han archaeology. Made by Jie Shi and Alex Brey.

Because the *tang* differed from the *shi* in terms of what type of rituals were held, we may distinguish a hall from an apartment based on the ritual function of the things it contained. As I have demonstrated in chapter 1, the king's front chamber was furnished in a way that resembled the hall of the imperial temple known as the "bright hall" where great sacrifices took place (fig. 1.7). In this brightly lit space, the king was the dominant subject, with his queen playing an affiliated role, as the placement of tents suggests. Various ritual bronzes such as *ding* tripods, *hu* vessels, and *yan* steamers were presented in an orderly fashion on both sides of the tents, calling the souls to come back and enjoy the offerings as if in the ancestral temple.

Whereas the king's front chamber simulates a grand auditorium, the queen's front chamber is comparable to the apartments (*shi* or *fang*) with different ritual functions. Supporting evidence comes from the material contents of her front chamber.

The first indication of a difference is the fact that the queen's front chamber was partially walled-off and hence separated into small cells, which contradicts the undivided space of the king's hall. The north side of the chamber was divided by a group of seventy-centimeter-tall brick walls into six separate cells, each measuring less than three square meters in area, with no grave goods housed within them (fig. 2.10). These spaces were clearly symbolic. The walls were not tall enough, and the cells were cramped and empty. They did not fit into the concept of an open, spacious, and accessible public hall (*tang*) but resembled apartments (*shi* or *fang*)—walled, small, and hidden in the rear with restricted access.

One of the best contemporary examples of the compartmented *shi* chamber as opposed to the undivided *tang* hall is found in the mausoleum of Liu Sheng's uncle, Liu Wu 劉武 (r. 178–144 BCE), King Xiao of the Liang kingdom, a site excavated in present-day Yongcheng in Henan. This is a well-preserved, aboveground, ritual complex presumably built next to the royal tombs to house sacrifices made to the deceased king and queen. Similar facilities might also have been built on the Mancheng site, but they did not survive. Like all royal palaces, the Liang complex, oriented to the south, consists of a front hall and a rear residential complex, or apartments (fig. 2.12). From the plan of the excavated foundations, it is easy to recognize the bipartite structure. One large rectangular platform stands in the south, on which timber-frame structures might have been erected to form a grand auditorium; to the north, a series of courtyards ends with a row of small rooms divided by walls at the very end, just like the walled cells to the north side of Queen Dou Wan's front chamber.[115] The Liang complex was one of many similar dual structures found in Western Han royal palaces and tombs, consisting of a hall sitting next to a cluster of apartments, whose direct model might be traced back to the First Emperor of Qin's Lishan mausoleum.[116]

In accordance with the bipartite structure of *tang* and *shi*, Liu Sheng's front chamber was furnished into a public ritual space exclusively for ancestral

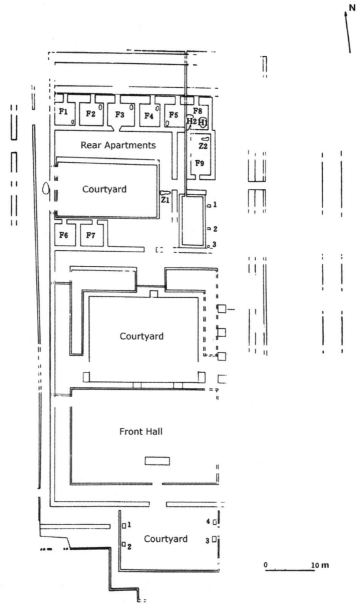

N

F1 F2 F3 F4 F5 F8
H2

Rear Apartments
Z2
F9
Courtyard
Z1
□ 1
□ 2
F6 F7
□ 3

Courtyard

Front Hall

□ 1
□ 2
Courtyard
4 □
3 □

0   10 m

FIGURE 2.12 Map of the residential complex of King Liu Wu's mausoleum at Mt. Baoan, Yongcheng, ca.
second half of second century BCE. After Henan sheng wenwu kaogu yanjiusuo 河南省文物考古研究所,
Yongcheng Xi Han Liangguo wangling yu qinyuan 永城西漢梁國王陵與寢園 (Zhengzhou: Zhongzhou guji
chubanshe, 1996), p. 26, fig.15. Courtesy of Henan Provincial Institute of Cultural Heritage and Archaeology,
Zhengzhou.

worship, while the queen's was organized into a royal residence (*gong* 宫 or *dian* 殿)—essentially an enlarged version of *shi* or *fang* apartments.

Besides the brick walls, more definitive evidence of the queen's chamber being a *shi* lies in the function and placement of ritual objects that reflected the kinds of sacrifices held traditionally in the apartments of a palace. These objects turned out to be very different from those displayed in the king's front hall.

First, there is no question about the sacrificial purpose of the queen's front chamber given the presence of "soul seats" to arrest the souls of deceased ancestors. In the southeast corner of the chamber, in addition to a group of banquet objects, a series of four leopard-shaped bronze mat weights (fig. 2.10, nos. 56–59) further confirm the expected presence of a soul who take part in the banquet. In the chamber's southwest corner, the group of ritual offerings was located on a square platform. Presumably, this was an offering altar as it was made of rammed earth and framed by bricks. This altar-like platform can be regarded as another form of "seat" to settle the soul in place.

This sacrificial role is verified by four square sealing clays uncovered in Dou Wan's front chamber that label the ritual vessels with the name of the government agency held accountable for their use. An identical inscription was impressed on each seal: "Ministry of Sacrifice of Zhongshan" (*Zhongshan cisi* 中山祠祀),[117] which was an office established under the Inner Lesser Treasury (*Zhongshanfu* 中少府) to take care of sacrifices held in royal palaces. These may have been similar to the "in-chamber sacrifices" (*fangzhongci* 房中祠) mentioned in Western Han literature.[118] The seals pronounce, unambiguously, that the purpose of the sealed objects was sacrifice.

The most direct evidence of the sacrificial use of Dou Wan's front chamber came from the ritual function of the sacrificial instruments. In the southeast corner of the chamber, excavators identified a wooden offering box, which contained such traditional sacrificial vessels as cauldrons (fig. 2.10, nos. 39, 43, 55), *ding* tripods (fig. 2.10, nos. 52–54), *hu* pots (fig. 2.10, nos. 19, 29), a *yan* steamer (fig. 2.10, no. 38), a winged cup (fig. 2.10, no. 28), a scoop (fig. 2.10, no. 41), and a *yi* cup (fig. 2.10, no. 60), as well as new types of ritual objects such as a heater (fig. 2.10, no. 31), a basin (fig. 2.10, no. 35), coins (fig. 2.10, nos. 23, 24), and figurines (fig. 2.10, nos. 25, 30, 67). To the southeast of the wooden box, there were a few more sacrificial objects including a bronze cauldron (fig. 2.10, no.1), a bowl (fig. 2.10, no. 2), and two jade *bi* discs (fig. 2.10, nos. 12–13), as well as an incense burner (fig. 2.10, no. 4) and some genuine and false cash (fig. 2.10, nos. 15–17). These items supplemented the previous encased group and enriched the content of the ritual offerings.

In the same chamber's southwest corner, excavators discovered another group of sacrificial vessels placed on a little lacquer table (fig. 2.10, no. 107), including a lacquer platter (fig. 2.10, no. 105) and a lacquer winged cup (fig. 2.10, no. 106) that occupied the center of this platform. One lacquer *zun* 樽 wine container (fig. 2.10, no. 103) and one bronze basin (fig. 2.10, no. 104)—probably for washing hands—appeared to the southeast of the table. The purpose of these ritual instruments, when placed next to altars or soul seats, can only be sacrificial in nature.

However, the sacrifices held in the queen's front chamber were fundamentally different from those that took place in the king's front chamber; they were not only smaller in scale but were also distinct in placement. In the early Chinese ritual tradition, the practice of concentrating a small group of ritual instruments at the southeast and southwest corners of an indoor space was almost exclusively associated with *shi* or *fang* apartments.

In orthodox rituals, including "the single beast offered in food to the ancestors" (*Shaolao* 少牢), "the smaller set of beasts offered as food to the ancestors" (*Tesheng kuishi* 特牲饋食), and "the assistant clears away" (*Yousiche* 有司徹), which were recorded in the *Book of Etiquette and Ceremonial* (*Yili*) text, some sacrifices were held behind closed doors at the northwest and the southwest corners in the *shi* or *fang*. In a traditional Chinese house, which is oriented to the south, windows are positioned relatively high in the south wall on the west side of the door. When light comes in through the windows at an angle, it hits the northwest corner of the room while leaving the room's southwest corner (under the shadow of the south wall) in relative darkness. Therefore, the southwest corner was designated "the dark (corner)" (*yu* 奧) and the northwest corner "the bright (corner) of the chamber" (*shizhibai* 室之白) (fig. 2.11a).[119] These dark and bright corners housed the special rituals called the "dark satisfying offering" (*yinyan* 陰厭) and the "bright satisfying offering" (*yangyan* 陽厭), respectively, which were centered in certain empty seats that had been prepared for the soul of the ancestor to receive offerings.[120] According to Zheng Xuan 鄭玄 (127–200 CE), an Eastern Han annotator of the *Book of Etiquette and Ceremonial* text, every nobleman who died in his adulthood should receive both offerings during a standard sacrificial ceremony.[121]

Corresponding to the southeast group of ritual objects in the queen's front chamber, the first sacrifice, *yinyan*, is held in the dark corner of the inner apartment (fig. 2.11a).[122] Lamps are intentionally excluded from this group of ritual objects. An empty soul seat, comprising a mat and an armrest (or a table), references the soul of the ancestor to whom the food and wine were offered.[123] A shaman presides over the ceremony during which the filial son enters the chamber, bows, kneels before the soul seat, and prays.[124]

While the *yinyan* sacrifice held in the dark corner of the inner apartment initiated the long ritual ceremony, the *yangyan* marked the end of it.[125] In this phase of the ritual, the offering moved to the brighter corner of the apartment, just like the southwest group of ritual objects in Dou Wan's front chamber (fig. 2.11a). Accordingly, two bronze lamps for lighting and a little incense burner to give off fragrance and warmth were added to the offerings. Like the earlier *yinyan*, *yangyan* was also dedicated to an empty soul seat rather than to an impersonator.[126] Food and wine were offered in front of an unoccupied mat and armrest.[127]

The *Book of Etiquette and Ceremonial* text, though composed during the late Eastern Zhou period, was one of the most important Confucian Classics studied during the Western Han period.[128] Although the popularity of this text is hard to assess before its canonization during Emperor Xuan's reign (74–48 BCE), performers of such (or similar) rituals had been directing imperial ceremonies since the beginning of the dynasty.[129] Thus, it should come as no surprise that certain elements of the Western Han royal ritual practice, as reflected at the Mancheng site, might echo some passages of the *Book of Etiquette and Ceremonial* text.

The contradictory layout of objects in the king and queen's front chambers at Mancheng reinforce the difference between the *tang* and the *shi* (*fang*) that I have previously observed in interior design. The two front chambers represented the public and private ritual spaces, even though both of them were related to sacrifice. While Liu Sheng's front chamber resembles the formal hall in the ancestral temple, in which soul seats for both male and female ancestors were set, Dou Wan's front chamber is similar to the inner apartment located behind (i.e., to the north of) the formal hall (fig. 2.13).[130]

Even though they were distinct and did not mirror each other, the two front chambers at the Mancheng site worked jointly to simulate the interdependent public and private zones in a united royal house, which conventionally consisted of a front hall and rear apartments. With this necropolis design, the separate male and female subjects were redefined as a unified couple who shared one house that encompassed both tombs, although the husband was the master of the hall (the public zone), and the wife was the mistress of the apartments (the private zone). Accordingly, two synonymous

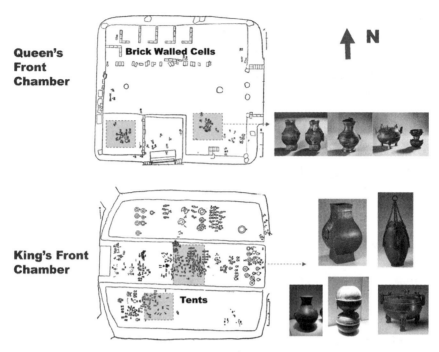

FIGURE 2.13 Hall (*tang*)-apartment (*shi*) relationship between front chambers of Mancheng tombs no. 1 and no. 2, Mancheng, ca. 118–104 BCE. Made by Jie Shi and courtesy of Wenwu Press.

sacrificial agencies (*Cisi* 祠祀) coexisted in the Western Han government. One of them, in charge of state rituals, reported to the emperor, and the other, responsible for palace rituals, reported to the empress.[131]

The Mancheng site was not alone in combining the male and female tombs as one unit. A similar intention of turning the husband's tomb into a hall and the wife's into apartments in one united architectural complex is even more obvious in the twin tombs at Mt. Baoan 保安 in the Liang royal cemetery.[132] Lying about twenty meters beneath the mountain's northern peak, the two royal tombs were cut side by side into the east slope and were situated only two hundred meters apart (fig. 2.14). Like their Mancheng counterparts, the Mt. Baoan tombs are both oriented to the east. The one to the south, dubbed Mt. Baoan tomb no. 1, has been attributed to Liu Wu, and the one to the north (tomb no. 2) has been identified as the tomb of Dowager Queen Li 李 (d. 123 BCE), Liu Wu's wife.[133] As was demonstrated elsewhere, the symmetrical plan, elevating section, and timber structure in Mt. Baoan tomb no.1 were all analogue of the imperial temples or the Bright Hall excavated near Xi'an, each with the main hall standing in the center surrounded by four identical

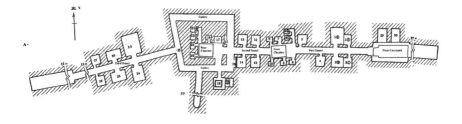

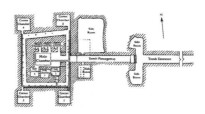

FIGURE 2.14 Plan of Mt. Baoan mausoleum, showing relative positions of tombs no. 1 (lower) and no. 2 (upper), Yongcheng, Hena, second half of second century BCE. Made by Jie Shi after Henan sheng Shangqiu shi wenwu guanli weiyuanhui 河南省商丘市文物管理委員會, *Xi Han Mangdangshan Liangwang* mudi 西漢芒碭山梁王墓地 (Beijing: Wenwu chubanshe, 2001), pp. 15, 44, figs. 3, 17. Courtesy of Wenwu Press.

side chambers.[134] The queen's tomb (Mt. Baoan tomb no. 2) was identified by inscriptions as a residential complex simulating "the eastern palace" (*donggong* 東宮) and "the western palace" (*xigong* 西宮). Mt. Baoan tomb no. 2's association with the inner private sector of a king's palace is confirmed by two inscriptions made on the north wall of an internal tunnel, which reads "east inner apartments" (*dongfang* 東旁[房]) and "northeast inner apartments" (*dongbeifang* 東北旁[房]).[135]

It is clear that the tombs at the Mancheng site were constructed not only as two parallel burials but also as two halves of a united house.

Although the practice of burying a deceased couple next to one another appeared much earlier in China,[136] until the late first century BCE, it had been uncommon for the deceased couple to be physically buried in one tomb. Before that, the couple were often buried in two parallel tomb pits, which shared approximately the same size, the same form, and primarily the same ritual objects with explicit gender implications, as demonstrated in the Tianma-Quncun cemetery of the Jin state.[137] This pattern did not change until the end of the early second century BCE.[138] The notion of husband and wife sharing a burial was voiced in early Eastern Zhou Chinese literature. One lyrist in the *Book of Poetry* (*Shijing*, ca. eighth to seventh centuries BCE) relates an oath a lady made to her lover: "In life, you shall have a different chamber (of your own); in death, you shall share my grave!"[139] At the Mancheng site and other locations, the royal houses put this idea into practice.

MULTILAYER GENDERED SPACE

Despite the hybrid nature of extant texts, there is no question that the relationship between the husband and wife was an essential issue in early Chinese political thought. In the *Lost Book of the Zhou Dynasty* (*Yizhoushu* 逸周書, compiled in first century BCE) text, the son of heaven must deal with eight political principles (*bazheng* 八政), among which the first and most important two are husband (*fu* 夫) and wife (*fu* 婦).[140] It was held that a wise king should adhere to these principles to correct the mistakes of the people. The author of the *Doctrine of the Mean* (*Zhongyong* 中庸, compiled ca. second century BCE) text, one of the essential Confucian writings, defined the principle of the Confucian superior man (*junzi* 君子) as based upon the way of married couples: "The way of the superior man may be found, in its simple elements, in the intercourse of common husbands and wives; but in its utmost reaches, it shines brightly through heaven and earth."[141] The relationship of husband and wife, compared to heaven and earth, was regarded as the first and also the most basic human relationship, which gave rise to such other connections—such as that of father and son or master and subject.

The excavated tombs at the Mancheng site offer a complex picture of how this most fundamental relationship was construed. The multilayer gender relations constructed in the tombs at the Mancheng site are like a complex unwritten discourse on gender that can be "read" indirectly through archaeological and topological analyses. In this case, the design(s) of the site expressed the gender relations through a sophisticated visual and material program, which was not necessarily a passive illustration of an already articulated thought but an active formulation of yet-to-be-expressed ideas. For example, the parallel placement of the two tombs at the Mancheng site expresses vividly the equal status of the deceased husband and wife.

My analysis of the tombs at the Mancheng site has shown a three-level ideology of gender relations in second-century BCE China.

The first level is manifested in the coffins, where the material contents—including the female and male bodies and their possessions—show different yet equal gendered status.

It is on the second level, as the gender difference extended further beyond the deceased's physical remains and into their social space, where inequality first appears. The husband possesses more items than his wife, and on a greater scale, yet the wife is compensated with finer artwork.

On the third level, the sexual difference and gender inequality are overcome by uniting the husband and wife in one body. In this unity, husband and wife are interdependent equals and work on a par. They share a common house of outer and inner spaces, and they form mirror images of each other.

The historical and ideological context of second century BCE China suggests that the designer(s) of tombs at the Mancheng site aimed ultimately at stability and peace.

The Western Han emperors, who still struggled to tighten their grip on the newly conquered lands in the eastern provinces, sent princes to rule these disorderly regions. In 154 BCE, only a few months before Liu Sheng was crowned, the empire had just crushed a rebellion in the eastern provinces, including the area that would later become the Zhongshan kingdom.[142] In the aftermath of this incident, the king's mission was to consolidate the empire's new frontier and effectively rule its people. As both the king of the local people and a representative of the imperial house, Liu Sheng successfully reigned over the state for forty-two years. When he died, the imperial court awarded him the posthumous title "the peaceful one" (*jing* 靖) to proclaim his achievements.

To maintain peace and stability, it was important for rulers to keep a healthy bond between husband and wife within the royal house (and by extension within all houses in the state). For some Western Han politicians, this idea was dear to their hearts. In 29 BCE, concerned by the ominous joint events of an earthquake and a solar eclipse, Gu Yong 谷永 (d. 8 BCE), sent this memorial to Emperor Cheng 成帝 (r. 33–7 BCE) to remind him of the importance of maintaining a proper family relationship: "The husband and wife relationship is the basic principle of kingship and the key to safety and danger. Sage kings are extremely cautious about it." Gu then concluded that, "There have never been cases in which families were in good order while the world under heaven was in turmoil."[143] This means that good government and world peace are rooted in and based upon the proper marital relationship, without which the basis of the empire could be shaken and the peace of the world could be thrown into turbulence. The tombs at the Mancheng site, with a repeated and thoughtful emphasis upon gender, portray Liu Sheng as one of those who dutifully followed the imperial political ideology.

Chapter Three

INTEGRATION OF ETHNIC HAN
AND NON-HAN

A Han-period tomb is not necessarily an ethnic-Han tomb because the word "Han," originally a name for a small region around the Han River in south Shaanxi, refers to both the dynastic title of the Liu family (and by extension, its multiethnic empire) as well as to the specific ethnic group commonly identified as Chinese. Since the day of their discovery, the tombs at the Mancheng site have been classified univocally as "ethnic-Han" Chinese tombs (*Han-mu* 漢墓) and have served as a standard for dating other Han-period tombs across China. Few have questioned this cultural attribution, which appears well grounded. The majority of material remains from the two tombs resemble those found in the metropolitan areas of Chang'an and Luoyang: The deceased couple decorated their clothes with such typical ethnic-Han Chinese jades as *bi* 璧 discs, *huang* 璜 half-rings, and *she* 韘 rings. They cooked and dined with ethnic-Han ritual bronzes including *ding*, *hu*, and *yan*. They defended themselves with ethnic-Han weapons such as long iron swords, extended *pi* 鈹 spears, and crossbows. They stored food and beverages in a large number of ethnic-Han pottery vessels—hard, gray ceramics fired at relatively high temperatures and characterized by outwardly turned lips.[1] The dominant ethnic-Han traits in these finds are not hard to explain. First, the tomb occupants, as shown in the official historiography of the period, were ethnically Han Chinese (*Han-ren* 漢人).[2] And second, conventional wisdom held that by the third century BCE, all the previous "barbarians" within the Chinese empire historiographically known as Rong-Di 戎狄 had been assimilated to ethnic-Han customs (*Han-su* 漢俗) and had thus been "sinicized."[3]

However, what has been missing from this traditional identification is a discussion of a number of funerary elements in the Mancheng tombs that do not easily fall into the typical categories of ethnic-Han material culture. For example, the decoration of the king's body with bead necklaces, short swords, and belt plaques ornamented with animal-combat motifs, and the use of domed vaults in the rock-cut architecture, all give the tombs a mysteriously exotic flavor. Comparative materials that could help scholars pinpoint the non-ethnic-Han origins of those unusual features and objects were still relatively scarce in 1980 when the excavation report of the Mancheng tombs was published, but the extensive archaeological work undertaken over the past four decades has yielded substantial new data that allow us to reevaluate the role of the overlooked non-ethnic-Han traits in the Mancheng tombs.

The existence of such non-ethnic-Han elements begs several serious questions that have never been asked before: If the Zhongshan region had been completely sinicized, how did these "barbaric" elements make their way into the tombs of an ethnically Han Chinese royal couple? If they were imported from beyond China, where did they come from? How did they interact with the ethnic-Han elements in the tombs, and why were they interred?

This chapter argues that these non-ethnic-Han elements, despite their minority status among all the objects placed in the tombs at the Mancheng site, were mixed with the ethnic-Han elements in style, motif, and placement in the spirit of "returning to antiquity" (*fugu* 復古) and the philosophy of "integrating customs" (*qisu* 齊俗) so that the Zhongshan rulers could effectively pacify their ethnically complex kingdom. In presenting this argument, this chapter deals with several problems one by one. It begins with a declaration that these non-ethnic-Han material remains—including objects as well as architecture—represented not only Han customs but also the largely faded traditions of the so-called Rong-Di people who lived on the northern, western, and northwestern frontiers of Huaxia 華夏 (Chinese) civilization during the pre-imperial period. Then this chapter shows that the practice of including these old-fashioned Rong-Di elements at the Mancheng site had a political implication deeply rooted in the history of the Zhongshan kingdom that referenced the incessant cross-cultural interaction between Huaxia and Rong-Di. This antiquarian practice, I will argue, was part of an effort to ensure the sagehood of the ruler and, ultimately the peace of the kingdom as prescribed by the dominant political philosophy of the time.

Most of our knowledge of Western Han history was established on the basis of several major texts, including the *Shiji* and the *Hanshu*. Whereas the value of these official histories should never be downplayed, it is also important for us to realize their limits. These texts were all from the hands of imperial authors and were more or less censored to suit the imperial political agenda. For example, Wei Hong reported that before they were allowed to circulate among the people, Sima Qian's original biographies were substantially edited or deleted because some accounts of the facts were politically unacceptable.[4] What is more, the censored imperial accounts were so dismissive of the histories of the regional kingdoms, including the Zhongshan, that little information on these potential rivals has passed down to us. Yet archaeologically discovered artifacts never lie, if their mute expression can be properly deciphered. My study takes this tenet as its point of departure.

THE "BARBARIC" DECORATION OF THE ROYAL BODY

Deeply concealed in the private zone of the royal couple's coffins were some of the most prominent non-ethnic-Han works at the Mancheng site. These works, which include jewelry and short swords that fall into the category of outfits, played an important role in defining the deceased's cultural identity by modifying their "social skin."

Perhaps the practice most alien to the ethnic-Han Chinese audience was decorating the king's chest with more than forty drum-shaped carnelian beads strung together to form a necklace (fig. 3.1a), which has been discussed in chapter 2 from the perspective of gender.[5] Found inside his jade suit, the necklace's beads each measure 1.2 to 1.6 centimeters in diameter and are pierced in the middle by a hole 0.2 to 0.4 centimeters wide. Queen Dou Wan wore an even more elaborate piece with thirty carnelian beads, five crystal beads, and nine stone beads in circular or oval shapes, as well as a few small jade ornaments (fig. 3.1b).[6]

Small as they might appear, pieces of jewelry can be some of the most culturally and ethnically defined artifacts found in China as well as in other parts of the world. Often made of shiny (semi)precious stones or rare metals, they instantly catch the viewer's attention and thus function as windows through which one presents the body and its cultural identity. In terms of placement, archaeology has shown that although beads were a common decoration in Western Zhou-period elite burials, during the late Eastern Zhou period,

(a) (b) (c)

FIGURE 3.1 (a) Beaded necklace from Mancheng tomb no. 1, Mancheng, Hebei, ca. 113 BCE. Courtesy of Hebei Museum; (b) Beaded necklace from Mancheng tomb no. 2, Mancheng, Hebei, ca. 118–104 BCE. Courtesy of Hebei Museum; (c) Beaded necklace from Jundushan cemeteries, Beijing, sixth to fifth centuries BCE. After Beijing shi wenwu yanjiusuo 北京市文物研究所, *Jundushan mudi: Yuhuangmiao* 軍都山墓地：玉皇廟, 4 vols. (Beijing: Wenwu chubanshe, 2007), 4: color pl. 69. Courtesy of Wenwu Press.

necklaces were no longer part of ritual paraphernalia among the Huaxia people,[7] the ethnic equivalent of Han in pre-imperial Chinese discourses.[8] The customary Huaxia ritual paraphernalia usually included only small jade pendants such as *bi* discs, *huang* half-rings, and *she* thumb rings, which were attached as body decorations to the wearer's waistband.[9] As for materiality, the Huaxia dressing decorum reported in received texts from the late Eastern Zhou to the Han period verified that men were supposed to wear jade pendants (*yu* 玉) rather than beads (*zhu* 珠), which were more closely associated with women. In a Western Han version of an Eastern Zhou story, recorded in the *Garden of Stories* (*Shuoyuan* 說苑, dated late first century BCE) collection, when Zichan 子產 (d. 522 BCE), the beloved chancellor of the Zheng state, died, every man in the country took off his jade pendant (*juepei* 玦佩) and every woman removed her beads and earrings (*zhuer* 珠珥) to express sorrow.[10] In the *Balanced Discourses* (Lunheng) text, Wang Chong summarized the contemporary custom with a simple sentence: "Men wear jades and women wear beads."[11]

So the practice for both men and women to wear bead necklaces was certainly unorthodox, if not heretical, in ethnic-Han eyes. Indeed, among more than seventy Western Han royal tombs excavated so far, archaeologists have reported only one similar example of another bead necklace and that also came from Hebei. When the excavators opened tomb no. 36 in Xianxian, whose occupant has been identified as the queen of Liu De 劉德

(r. 155–130 BCE), Liu Sheng's half-brother, they saw in this typical ethnic-Han wooden-structure pit grave that the deceased royal lady was wearing a bead necklace almost identical to the one found in Dou Wan's burial (map 4).[12] In addition, in Western Han-period murals, it was jade pendants rather than necklaces that adorned human bodies.[13] So where did these unconventional necklaces come from?

Field archaeological work during the past few decades points to China's frontier as the source. During the sixth to fourth centuries BCE, while the Huaxia people largely abandoned neck decoration in favor of waist decoration (such as jades suspended from the waistband), as seen in their tombs, the so-called Rong-Di people living along China's north, northwest, and west frontiers (basically, along the later Great Wall) continued to wear such necklaces in their tombs.[14]

The compound ethnonym Rong-Di was an umbrella term used by Eastern Zhou-period authors to denote the various non-Huaxia people that usually lived on the margins of the Zhou states and that shared many cultural elements among themselves but not with the Huaxia.[15] Traditional historiography sometimes specified that the Di were active in the north while the Rong were in the west, but such rigid distinction might be more of an ethnological than a historical fact. Perhaps because of their ethnic, cultural, and linguistic differences, the Huaxia and their Rong-Di neighbors naturally became competitors for land, natural resources, and ultimately, for political supremacy. While considering themselves civilized "metropolitans" (*zhong-guo* 中國), the former sometimes dismissed the latter as "barbarians" yet at the same time developed close social and political connections with them. The existence of these non-Huaxia or non-ethnic-Han cultures has been confirmed by Chinese archaeologists, who conventionally associate them with what is called the Iron Age (ninth to third centuries BCE) "Northern Zone culture" (*Beifang wenhua* 北方文化), which spread across a narrow crescent region along the frontier of Chinese civilization, ranging from Gansu in the west to Liaoning in the east and further broken down into four zones (map 4).[16]

Zone 1, located farthest to the west and represented by the Yanglang 楊郎 culture, was centered around Guyuan in Ningxia. To the north of Zone 1 lies Zone 2, best known as the Ordos area, which extended southward into northern Shaanxi. Further to the north, Zone 3, represented by the Maoqinggou 毛慶溝 site, covered the region to the north of the Yellow River. Zone 4, with its most famous site at Yuhuangmiao 玉皇廟 in Jundushan 軍都山,

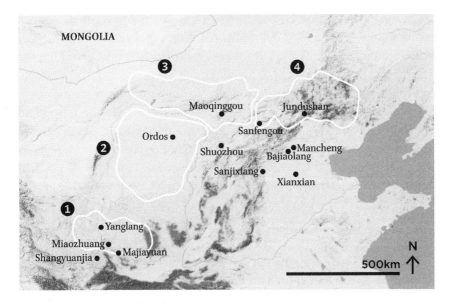

MAP 4 Northern Zones on China's frontiers from the fifth and second centuries BCE. Made by Jie Shi and Alex Brey.

was in the northeast, spread along northern Shanxi, Hebei, and Beijing, and extending to the Mancheng area in the south.[17]

Whereas similar bead necklaces are a rare species in thousands of burials excavated in the heartland of the Eastern Zhou cultural sphere, they have been found in all of the four frontier zones, most notably in Zone 4. In a large cemetery at the Jundushan site, about 160 kilometers to the north of the Mancheng site, archaeologists uncovered tens of thousands of such beads scattered next to the deceased's neck or chest in both male and female tombs because the strings used to bind them had disintegrated (fig. 3.1c).[18] At the Maoqinggou site (in Zone 3), 60 percent of fifty-three excavated burials contained such necklaces.[19] At the Yanglang site (in Zone 1), nearly two thousand carnelian and other semiprecious stone beads were recovered from the forty-nine tombs.[20] The statistics indisputably suggest the existence of a cultural connection between the Mancheng necklaces and their Eastern Zhou counterparts in north Hebei.

Besides the two carnelian bead necklaces, an ethnic-Han audience might also wonder about the two straight-bladed short swords suspended at the right side of Liu Sheng's ritual outfit in the outer coffin (attached to his "invisible body"). One of them measures 28.2 centimeters long, and the other one is 36.7 centimeters long; both are lavishly decorated (figs. 3.2a, 3.3a).[21]

Although both Huaxia and Rong-Di people used swords as combat weapons, they eventually developed two different preferences.[22] The Huaxia preferred longer swords; but swords cast in bronze have a technical limit to their length, for bronze is physically brittle and a long sword of bronze would easily break when struck by a hard object. To double or even triple the length of conventional swords to 80 to 140 centimeters, the Huaxia introduced tougher iron and steel to replace bronze around the third century BCE.[23] Consequently, short swords cast in bronze had become largely obsolete by Liu Sheng's time and were rarely seen either as real objects or in pictorial representations in Han-period tombs.[24] By contrast, the Rong-Di, even after having obtained the knowledge of iron and steel, proved to be persistent lovers of short swords, using them more frequently as cutting instruments as well as weapons on the battlefield.

Liu Sheng's two short swords faithfully preserve a Rong-Di flavor. The shorter piece was cast entirely in bronze with an oval knoblike pommel, a hilt featuring a spiral pattern on its front and back sides, and a small loop attached to the side, which probably was a hook for hanging the weapon (fig. 3.2a). To date, this hilt is distinct among weapons found in Western Han royal burials. While contemporary ethnic-Han swords are mostly plain with little ornamentation, the only comparable Western Han example I know of came from another Zhongshan royal tomb in Hebei. In the slightly later tomb no. 40 at Bajiaolang (dated 55 BCE) in present-day Dingzhou, only about eighteen kilometers to the south of the Mancheng site, the deceased king, one of Liu Sheng's descendants, was also buried with a short sword on the right side of his body (map 4).[25] This sword resembles Liu Sheng's bronze sword as it bears an ornate pattern of interlaced dragons on the hilt. Lacking the pommel and the loop on its hilt, even this sword looks less exotic than its counterpart from Mancheng.

Despite having few parallels in ethnic-Han tradition, like the bead necklaces, variants of such short swords were ubiquitous along China's western, northern, northwestern, and particularly northern frontiers in the early to mid-Eastern Zhou period.[26] Because of their popularity in burials in north Hebei, these weapons are referred to by some Chinese archaeologists as "Di-style swords" (Dishi jian 狄式劍).[27] Liu Sheng's exotic sword finds several almost identical counterparts in the Jundushan cemetery in north Hebei, dated three to four hundred years earlier.[28] These weapons all feature two unmistakable local markers: a loop attached to the side of the hilt and an open-worked knoblike pommel, almost exactly the same features seen on the

INTEGRATION OF ETHNIC HAN AND NON-HAN

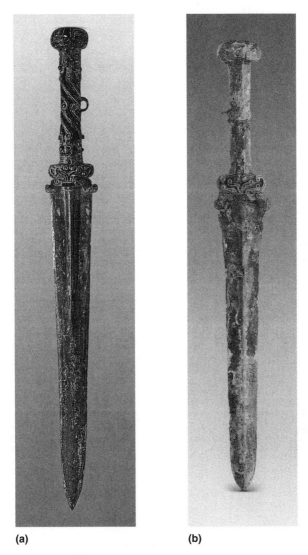

(a)   (b)

FIGURE 3.2 (a) Bronze short sword from Mancheng tomb no. 1, Mancheng, Hebei, ca. 113 BCE. Courtesy of Hebei Museum, Shijiazhuang; (b) Bronze short sword from Jundushan cemeteries, Beijing, sixth to fifth centuries BCE. After Beijing shi wenwu yanjiusuo, *Jundushan mudi: Yuhuangmiao*, 4: pl. 255.3. Courtesy of Wenwu Press.

sword in Liu Sheng's tomb (fig. 3.2b).[29] Since this style was no longer popular during Western Han, the parallel can only mean two possibilities: Liu Sheng's sword was either an authentic Eastern Zhou work or a very close replica.

The other iron sword from Liu Sheng's outer coffin largely falls into the same Rong-Di category linked to the Eurasian steppes (fig. 3.3a). This sword's

(a) **(b)**

FIGURE 3.3 (a) Iron short sword with gold guard, hilt, and foil, Mancheng tomb no. 1, Mancheng, Hebei, ca. 113 BCE. Courtesy of Hebei Museum, Shijiazhuang; (b) Iron sword from Arzhan tomb no. 2, Tuva, Russia, seventh century BCE. After Konstantin V. Čugunov, Hermann Parzinger, and Anatoli Nagler, *Der skythenzeitliche Fürstenkurgan Aržan 2 in Tuva* (Mainz: P. Von Zabern, 2010), pl. 40.1. Courtesy of German Archaeological Institute, Berlin.

strap-like hilt, shaped into two ribbed round bars flanking a sunken panel, finds its direct model in the Rong-Di remains in Hebei.[30] However, several other features of the sword were more likely Eurasian in inspiration.

First, in terms of craftsmanship, both the blade and the hilt are cast in iron, a technique popular in the so-called Scythian culture of Eurasia.[31] The guard and the pommel are made of a silver-based alloy and decorated with gold inlay and plating, another traditional steppe technique.[32] Similar examples include two iron short swords excavated from the seventh-century BCE Arzhan tomb no. 2 in a Scythian royal necropolis in Tuva, Southern Siberia (fig. 3.3b).[33]

Second, iconographically, in Liu Sheng's sword, each side of the blade is inlaid with two parallel rows of a flamboyant gold pattern, which resembles the enormous antlers of a male elk—a favorite motif for the nomads of the Eurasian steppes.[34] Similar iron blades decorated with "highly stylized heads of stags with antlers streaming behind them" have been excavated in magnificent kurgans at Filippovka on the south bank of the Ural River in eastern Russia.[35]

Third, as for style, the pommel and the guard on Liu Sheng's sword are fused with nomadic art motifs. Although the frontally posed zoomorphic mask featuring bulging eyes and C-shaped horns may bring to mind the well-known *taotie* 饕餮 motif in Shang bronze art, the comma-shaped ears are emblematic of the steppe "animal style."[36]

Finally, the ring-shaped pommel is made of two beasts that are joined head-to-head and tail-to-tail, each curving its body into a half-ring to face its opponent (fig. 3.3a). This motif of "confronted animals" was nomadic in origin and has been found on the pommels and guards of many swords from that region.[37]

It is clear that the bead necklaces and the short swords from the royal coffins represented an artistic and cultural tradition different from the ethnic-Han or Huaxia, even though the artists who crafted these items remain unknown. Did Liu Sheng understand the cultural differences between the Chinese and the "barbaric" styles in his own tomb? Even though the Western Han Empire managed to unify and assimilate many different regions that originally were not ethnically or culturally Han, some people in the frontier regions did recognize the distinction between their own tradition and that of the Han. For example, in a contemporary inventory of grave goods excavated from Luobowan tomb no. 1 (dated first half of second century BCE) in Guangxi, the author carefully distinguished the indigenous "Yue" 越 objects from those of the "Zhongtu" 中土 (literally, "central lands"), or territories of the ethnic-Han.[38] It was almost impossible to believe that Liu Sheng, deeply immersed in Chinese culture as a young prince, would wear a peculiar (at least from the Han point of view) necklace as the sole decoration on his chest in this most intimate funerary setting without understanding that object's ritual and cultural implications. The Rong-Di practice of decorating both men and women indistinguishably with beaded necklaces would seem totally alien to most Chinese observers.[39]

Were these objects meant to be exotica? Although Eurasian or "barbarian-style" objects found in many high-ranking tombs throughout China from the late Eastern Zhou to the early Western Han were probably included to show off the owner's wealth and social status, those Rong-Di elements found in the Mancheng tombs were of a different nature. Let us compare the Mancheng tombs with other Chinese royal tombs of the second century BCE. For example, one of the Chu kings interred near Xuzhou was buried with an outlandish silver box fashioned like a Persian phiale, a bowl with a flaring mouth and convex rays along the side. Also, Emperor Wen of Nanyue (Zhao Mo) carried into his tomb a luxurious West-Asian-style rhyton, a libation cup sculpted of jade, as well as another phiale-like silver box.[40] However, neither the Chu kingdom nor the Southern Yue was culturally related to Persia. In the Mancheng tombs, in contrast, the non-ethnic-Han decorations all cohere with the local cultural tradition in northern Hebei, especially that in Zhongshan, which had already embraced nomadic elements from the Eurasian steppes by the fourth century BCE. Some of the objects might have been deeply treasured heirlooms that eventually ended up in the king's outer coffin as his most intimate body decorations, culturally branding his burial with the marks of a Rong-Di ruler.[41]

It is worth noting that the royal couple did not store the bead necklaces and short swords in separate treasure boxes but wore them in an ethnically correct way as part of their ritual outfits. For example, just as at the Arzhan site, where the owner of tomb no. 2 carried his short sword with two small iron knives at the waist,[42] at Liu Sheng's waist, analogously, the iron sword was paired with two short iron knives, which, like their Arzhan counterparts, were similarly inlaid with gold on the blades.[43] It seems that incorporating the Eurasian manner of wearing small arms was a deliberate decision in Liu Sheng's tomb. The status of the objects as *being equipped* rather than *being stored* indicates the deceased's direct apprehension and appreciation of their cultural and ritual significance.

So, if introducing extra outfit objects might complicate the identity problem for the deceased, why did Liu Sheng and his wife don these emblematic non-ethnic-Han bead necklaces and short swords in their coffins? As was demonstrated in chapter 1, outfit objects represented the "social skin" of the wearer's body, which was a powerful symbol of identity (both cultural and social) in the eyes of Western Han observers. According to Sima Qian, Liu Bang 劉邦, the future Emperor Gao of the Han who disliked Confucian "pedants," refused to listen to a visitor named Shusun Tong 叔孫通 (fl. early second century BCE) because Shusun wore a scholar's robe. However, after taking off his robe and changing into a short dress in the "vulgar" Chu style, the visitor then delighted his host, who was also a native of Chu, and gained the latter's trust.[44] Liu Bang's assumption about clothing was similarly articulated in an anecdote recorded in the *Zhuangzi* text, in which Duke Ai of the Lu 魯哀公 (r. 495–486 BCE) acknowledged that he used to judge who were Confucians and who were not by the clothes they wore.[45] It seems many people in early China recognized that what they wore represented who they were. Putting on non-ethnic-Han objects modified the deceased's cultural identity as partially Rong-Di. Did Liu Sheng mind this modification or not?

Further investigations, presented in this chapter, demonstrate that it was an intentional decision to decorate Liu Sheng's body with these "barbaric" objects, along with ethnic-Han ritual jades, to portray him as both a king of the "barbarians" and as a member of the Chinese imperial house.

ANTIQUARIANISM AT MANCHENG: THE POWER OF THE PAST

Liu Sheng was not just any king but the new founder of the revived Zhongshan kingdom, one of the strongest footholds of Rong-Di culture in the Central Plains region, an area largely controlled by Huaxia kingdoms. By the time Liu Sheng ascended to the throne, the distinctive Rong-Di culture in Hebei had already been outmoded for more than a century and had dissolved into the multiethnic Han Empire. With the evocative memory of the past merging into the local identity, such typical Rong-Di artwork as the bead necklaces and short swords directly summoned the "barbaric" past, harking back to its Jundushan precedents as early as the sixth century BCE, when the power of Rong-Di culture was vigorously on the rise.

The previous incarnation of the Zhongshan kingdom during the Eastern Zhou period originated with a group of non-Huaxia people named in traditional Chinese historiography as the White Di (Baidi 白狄). The White Di, whose homeland was in present-day northern Shaanxi, were one of the many tribes generally known in historical texts as the Rong-Di barbarians, who were distributed widely throughout western and northern China as neighbors of the Zhou polities, or the Huaxia states.[46] The customs of the Rong-Di were different from those of the Zhou. While the Huaxia lived a sedentary life, practicing agriculture, the Rong-Di originally lived a half-nomadic and half-sedentary life, supporting themselves with herding, hunting, gathering, and some agriculture.[47]

The next episode in the history of the White Di witnessed the establishment of the Zhongshan kingdom in Hebei. It all started around the early Eastern Zhou period, as the power of the Zhou hegemony waned. The Di people migrated eastward, unhindered, bursting into northern Shanxi and Hebei, an area dotted by a number of Zhou fiefs. A group of Di invaded and conquered a land called Xianyu, initially ruled by a Zhou vassal, and settled down. From that time onward, they mixed with the local population and forged a new hybrid identity as the Xianyu people.[48] By the sixth to fifth centuries BCE, the new Xianyu polity had grown to become a regional power with which the neighboring Huaxia dukedoms, including those of Jin and Qin, had to contend. No later than 506 BCE, they established their own independent kingdom called Zhongshan, which literally meant "the land within the mountains."[49] This name reflects, as some scholars suggest, a cult of stone and possibly of mountains.[50] Claimed in the *Zhangguo ce* 戰國策 (third century BCE) text as being a "kingdom of a thousand chariots" (*qiansheng zhiguo* 千乘之國), the Warring States Zhongshan state claimed equal political status and rights along with its Chinese peers, which grew increasingly uneasy about this "barbaric" competitor.[51]

The wealth and power of this newly established kingdom is manifest in its royal cemeteries, which had remained veiled until the 1970s, when two major Warring States Zhongshan royal cemeteries were brought to light at Sanjixiang in present-day Pingshan, Hebei, 123 kilometers to the south of Mancheng (map 4). They were dug into a vast plateau located south of the twin mountains, Xiling 西陵 and Dongling 東陵.[52] The large burials held kings or queens; the more modest ones presumably interred aristocrats or royal concubines.[53] Of all these tombs, the best known is the suburban tomb no. 1, the burial complex of King Cuo, the next-to-last king of the Warring States-era Zhongshan (d. ca. 310 BCE).[54] A marvelous royal spectacle, it occupies an area 90 by 100 meters; the central tomb pit reaches as deep as 8.2 meters.

In these cemeteries, archaeologists unearthed many artifacts that exhibit an unmistakable Rong-Di style that separates these tombs from their Chinese counterparts to the south.

One distinctive type of "barbaric" object that furnished these Warring States Zhongshan burials was the previously discussed bead necklace, a string of round, tube- or drum-shaped beads made of the same carnelian, crystal, turquoise, or other precious or semiprecious stones, similar to those that were found in the Mancheng tombs. At the Sanjixiang cemetery, excavators retrieved an impressive 1,457 beads from three nearly emptied tombs (numbered as M3, M4, and M5) that were occupied by members of the Zhongshan royal household.[55] Completely a local product, the carnelian used to make these beads was mined less than two hundred kilometers away from Mancheng at Xinhe in Zhangjiakou in north Hebei.[56] The steady supply of the raw material from these mines gave rise to a long local tradition among these non-Chinese cultures of jewelry making and wearing that went back to the early Eastern Zhou period.[57]

Models for the short swords found in the Mancheng tombs can also be identified in the Warring States Zhongshan cemeteries, where there is evidence of a continuous local tradition lasting several centuries.[58] In the Sanjixiang royal cemeteries of Warring States-era Zhongshan, archaeologists uncovered several straight-bladed, bronze, short swords, whose hilts were decorated with a distinct, gridded, sometimes open-worked, pattern.[59]

Situated at the intersection between Huaxia and Rong-Di (who had closer cultural ties to the nomads on the Eurasian steppe), Zhongshan royalty embraced elements of Eurasian art that was characterized by its distinctive "animal style."[60] The remarkable discovery of the tomb of King Cuo surprised scholars with vivid animal motifs derived from the Eurasian steppes and even from West Asia.[61] The marriage between Western motifs and Chinese elements gave birth to a new figurative art in China that emphasized motion and realistic depiction of the body. In King Cuo's tomb, the east and west side pits yielded a group of bronze animal statuettes in the form of fantastic winged felines, perhaps originally used as mat weights.[62] Originating in West Asia, the motif of winged animals, identified as either chimeras or griffins, must have been introduced into China via Central Asia and the Eurasian steppe. These exotic animal figures, inlaid with gold or silver, are covered with ornamental patterns with a Chinese flavor: the motifs are of feather curls or cloud scrolls.[63] A sculptural decoration on a bronze stand of a disintegrated wooden object from King Cuo's tomb portrays a prowling tiger crushing a paralyzed deer with its teeth and claws (fig. 3.4). The tiger's powerful grip on the deer's leg in a movement of tearing it off shows a thrilling moment of dismemberment. Almost no previously excavated Zhou-period elite tombs yielded a comparably strong nomadic artistic flavor, a trait that also separates the later Zhongshan tombs at Mancheng from their contemporary Han Chinese counterparts.

Such a prominent and distinct Zhongshan past might have easily prompted an antiquarian impulse. As a well-educated prince, Liu Sheng revived the kingdom under imperial order. Effectively, he was not only a vassal of the Han Empire but also the legitimate heir of the Rong-Di "barbaric" kings, who were forced to assimilate to Huaxia culture for diplomatic expediency. Indeed, this antiquarian taste was further testified by artifacts usually associated with

FIGURE 3.4 Bronze feline crushing a deer, from King Cuo's tomb, Pingshan, Hebei, fourth century BCE. Courtesy of Hebei Museum, Shijiazhuang.

the ethnic-Han tradition but with a Rong-Di flavor. Whereas the beaded necklaces, short swords, and other artifacts were relatively authentic reproductions or evocations of Rong-Di culture, other ethnic-Han works were designed to include more or less traditional Rong-Di elements that were similarly old fashioned, if not obsolete, in the eyes of Liu Sheng's contemporaries.

Some of the ritual bronzes in the tombs at the Mancheng site are obviously out of date by the standards of the late second century BCE. The vessels with the finest artistry were the bronzes placed in the rear chambers, which assumed a more intimate relationship with the deceased.[64] These vessels with an archaic flavor, in both their Huaxia and Rong-Di components, were clearly different from the contemporary, more austere-looking artifacts produced in Luoyang and Hedong in the heartland of the ethnic-Han cultural sphere.[65] One such archaistic *hu* vessel (no. 4028), displayed in Dou Wan's rear chamber, features a slender body, a flaring mouth, a long neck, a downward sloping shoulder, and a bulging belly on top of a ring-shaped foot (fig. 3.5a).[66] Whereas the shape might have derived from models in South China,[67] two other features of the vessel reveal Rong-Di elements. First, the chain attached to the two sides of the vessel's shoulder that fastens a dragon-shaped handle was a popular component of *hu* vessels in the Eastern Zhou period, when chained *hu* vessels made in Zhongshan were collected and cherished as among the finest artwork.[68] A Chinese gentleman in the Yan state once carved a long inscription on a bronze *hu* vessel he acquired from the Zhongshan to extoll its "barbaric" Di provenance (fig. 3.5b).[69] Second, the body of the Mancheng *hu*

(a)   (b)

FIGURE 3.5 (a) Looped-handled bronze *hu* vessel with curled-up dragon and palm frond motifs from Mancheng tomb no. 2, Mancheng, Hebei, ca. 118–104 BCE. Courtesy of Hebei Museum, Shijiazhuang; (b) Bronze so-called *Ti shi hu* vessel, 475–221 BCE. Courtesy of Museum für Asiatische Kunst, Berlin.

vessel was ornamented with four parallel bands, and each band was formed of two parallel rows of identical rectangular "plaques" filled with low-relief, S-shaped dragons. Similar ornamental patterns have been identified on bronzes found in northern Shaanxi and Hebei, the traditional territory of the Rong-Di barbarians.[70]

More often, however, Western Han artists married archaistic Rong-Di décor with contemporary ethnic-Han vessel shapes. A notable example of this synthesis of old and new is another *hu* vessel in the king's rear chamber. The vessel (fig. 1.2, no. 19) boasts complex decoration using such precious materials as gold, silver, and glass (fig. 3.6a).[71] The shape of the vessel is characterized by a roundish belly bulging near the foot. Four horizontal bands divide the surface into three registers. The areas between these bands are ornamented with diagonal interlocking strips that divide the surface into identical lozenges with each intersection defined by a nipple. The strips are gilt, while the nipples are silvered. Green glass covers the interior of the lozenges in a grid pattern. While the shape of the vessel expresses a contemporary Han aesthetic, the ornament summons the taste of the Rong-Di. Almost identical ornaments that combine lozenges and nipples can be traced back to early Eastern Zhou-period bronze tripods in local Rong-Di cemeteries.[72]

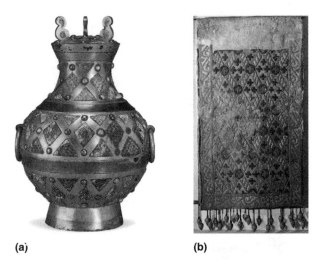

(a)   (b)

FIGURE 3.6 (a) Inlaid bronze *hu* vessel from the rear chamber of Mancheng tomb no. 1, Mancheng, Hebei, ca. 113 BCE. Courtesy of Hebei Museum, Shijiazhuang; (b) Wool saddlecloth, Pazyryk Kurgan V site, 252–238 BCE. Courtesy of the State Hermitage Museum, Saint Petersburg.

An almost identical pattern decorated a wool saddlecloth, a non-Chinese craft, found in a Scythian noble tomb at Pazyryk in South Siberia, which has been dated to about the fifth to fourth centuries BCE (fig. 3.6b).[73]

Iconographically, archaism at the Mancheng site is also evident in the "animal motifs" emblematic of the steppe art that had been popular at least three centuries earlier. Liu Sheng's tent in his front chamber, analyzed in chapter 1 as the ritual center for staging Han imperial sacrifices, was also the site of some traditional "barbaric" funerary motifs. To the south of the tent, excavators uncovered some small, cast-bronze animal figures. One group of animals includes two almost identical bronze elk with emblematic long antlers (fig. 1.7, nos. 170–171; fig. 3.7a). Although the two Mancheng elk were unquestionably Han Chinese products as evidenced by their style and casting technique, these three-dimensional bronze figures with hollowed torsos are reminiscent of those frequently found in burials in the Ordos region during the fourth to third centuries BCE. (Ordos was a buffer zone that separated the sedentary Chinese culture from the nomadic one later led by the Xiongnu.)[74] Such three-dimensional bronze animals as elk, horses, or ibexes usually stand, recline, or crouch on top of a square stand, with one or multiple holes pierced in the necks, bellies, or sides. A majority of these bronze figures have been identified as decorations that fit over a horizontal wooden yoke or the pole caps or finials of a wheeled funerary vehicle.[75] For example, two

(a)

(b)

FIGURE 3.7 (a) Two gilt bronze elks from Mancheng tomb no. 1, Mancheng, Hebei, ca. 113 BCE. Courtesy of Hebei Museum, Shijiazhuang; (b) Bronze finials of chariot poles with animal motifs from a tomb, Ordos, Inner Mongolia, fifth century BCE. After Emma C. Bunker, ed., *Ancient Bronzes of the Eastern Eurasian Steppes from the Arthur M. Sackler Collections* (New York: Harry N. Abrams, 1997), p. 230, ill. no. 181. Courtesy of the Arthur M. Sackler Foundation, New York City.

bronze finials, presumably from the Ordos, that form a pair and are currently in the collection of the Arthur M. Sackler Foundation (Washington, DC) are each surmounted by a standing ram on its four legs. Like the elk with side cavities from Mancheng, each ram has a small opening on its neck and is fastened to the upper end of a pole through the four hoofs (fig. 3.7b).[76] The round elk figures, each accented with a prominent slightly open mouth, find their closest precedents in Eastern Zhou-period Rong-Di cemeteries near present-day Beijing, which is dated to three centuries before the Mancheng site.[77]

Though some scholars have noted the old style and iconography of such individual animal figures, the archaic manner of placing these animal figures in the burial has remained entirely unnoticed. Unlike their excavated Ordos counterparts, these zoomorphic figures from Mancheng tomb no. 1 fail to form perfect, symmetrical sets. Both elk are pierced on the same side of the body without strictly mirroring each other. It seems as if these figures were randomly selected from a larger set and tossed into the tomb. Indeed, these two figures originally might have been attached through the side to some disintegrated wooden objects. With gilt over the entire exterior, each of the elk torsos reveals a cavity on the left side. Some core material still remained within the cavities upon discovery.[78] A small hole pierced the hoof of each beast, perhaps to fasten it to some unknown article.

The same observation could be made about a group of five figurines of crouching felines also found in the front of Liu Sheng's tent (fig. 1.7, nos. 163–167; fig. 3.8a). The felines were inscribed with texts identifying them as originally belonging to sets of four, each with a slot cut into the back of the animal to contain tenons. The slots might have been filled with some perishable material such as wood, indicating that the figures were probably attached to some larger wooden object(s) that disintegrated long ago. However, these beasts in Liu Sheng's tomb bear inscriptions on their abdomens that clearly refer to their original meaning (fig. 3.8b):

no. 167: "the left side horse" (*zuocan* 左驂)
no. 163: "the left side horse, right" (*zuocan you* 左驂右)
no. 164: "the right central horse, left" (*youfu zuo* 右服左)
no. 165: "the left central horse" (*zuofu* 左服)
no. 166: "the left central horse, right" (*zuofu you* 左服右)

The inscriptions probably refer to a type of carriage drawn by four horses, or *sima* 駟馬, who were supposed to align themselves side by side ahead of the carriage they pulled collectively.[79] Indeed, four of the five (fig. 1.7, nos. 164–167) were lined up approximately along the north-south axis, although the fifth one (fig. 1.7, no. 163) somehow made it over to the table (fig. 1.7, no. 178) to the east. The relative positions of the four aligned felines match the labels in their inscriptions: the left side "horse" (fig. 1.7, no. 167) to the far left (north), the left central horse (fig. 1.7, no. 166) on the near left, the right central horse (fig. 1.7, no. 164) on the near right, and the right side horse (fig. 1.7, no. 165, though labeled "the left central horse"), to the far right.[80]

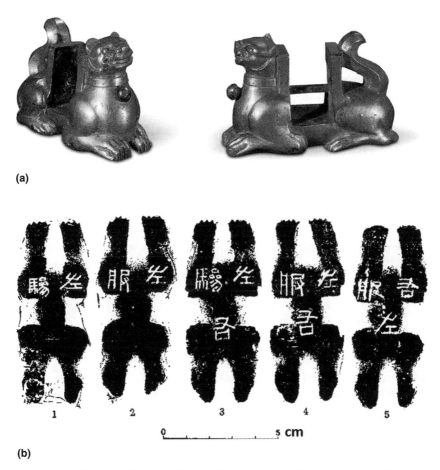

(a)

(b)

FIGURE 3.8 (a) Gilt bronze feline-shaped figures with inscriptions placed before the central tent in Mancheng tomb no. 1, Mancheng, Hebei, ca. 113 BCE. (3.8b) Inscriptions on bottoms of gilt bronze feline-shaped figures identifying them as chariot-drawing horses. Courtesy of Hebei Museum, Shijiazhuang.

The directional terms "left" and "right" in the inscription orient the whole group of felines toward the east, that is, in front of the tent.

Without any traces of carriages or carriage parts such as bronze axle end caps, we can only conclude that these felines were perhaps the draught team of a symbolic carriage, most likely the king's tent, which in form resembled the wheel-less sedan discovered in Hougudui tomb no. 1 at Gushi in Henan (dated to fifth century BCE).[81] It seems that these felines were removed from the objects they originally decorated and placed in front of the tent to represent the fantastic carriage team and effectively transform the king's soul into a royal traveler. The elk placed together with the felines might have functioned in a similar way to represent other draught animals or denizens of the land through which the travel was imagined to take place. The same theory might also apply to two gilt-bronze bear figures (fig. 1.7, nos. 146, 223) also found around the tent. Although bears often form a triplet to support a circular food or wine vessel, only two of the set were retrieved from the tomb. Moreover, instead of remaining close to each other as vessel legs would be expected to do upon decay, the two bears were found separated: one was located to the east of Liu Sheng's tent and the other was to the south of it. We might conclude that the bear figures were originally attached to and later removed from some larger wooden object and placed here to join in the collective representation of wildlife.

The incomplete or fragmentary condition of such assemblages was certainly not a result of carelessness or frugality, nor can it be explained by post-depositional disturbances such as earthquakes. A royal burial tolerated little carelessness, and a rich and powerful king who could afford priceless life-sized royal carriages for his burial would have no reason to spare some small wooden objects decorated with small figurines. There had to be a stronger motivation. The animal figures, such as the felines, the elk, and the bears, might have been deliberately removed from their original decorated objects and placed into the tomb for a ritual purpose.

Such a practice was by no means unheard of in the Rong-Di funerary tradition. When archaeologists opened a number of catacombs (dated to the fifth to fourth centuries BCE and belonging to the Rong people of the "Yanglang type" culture) in the Mazhuang cemetery in present-day Guyuan, Ningxia, they were surprised by a few zoomorphic carriage parts that were placed as stand-alone figurines scattered among sacrificed animal bones.[82] In a most remarkable case (tomb no. IIIM1), two deer-shaped bronze ornaments, which might have originally been mounted atop a carriage's yoke bar, were placed as a pair of freestanding sculptures flanking the tomb entrance (fig. 3.9a).[83] Each deer was fashioned in a plain, realistic style featuring a hollow body, which was reminiscent of the elk from Mancheng tomb no. 1 (fig. 3.9b). As new archaeological evidence has suggested, this special burial custom in western China was related to the Scythian culture of the Eurasian steppes. For example, a group of golden elk, probably originally used as carriage attachments but later employed as independent effigies, were unearthed in a burial at Filippovka in present-day southern Russia, dating from the fifth to fourth centuries BCE (fig. 3.9c).[84] Gernot Windfuhr has proposed that these deer were arranged in a meaningful pattern to convey some Mithraic ideas of death.[85] In light of this comparison, the unconventional practice of using detached animal figures in the tombs at the Mancheng site was almost surely an old Rong-Di ritual whose exact meaning is yet to be studied.

A large number of ethnic-Han-type artifacts interred in the Mancheng tombs were associated with the archaic Rong-Di tradition, be it through stylistic, iconographic, or positional allusion. This discovery should not surprise us because the history of Zhongshan was that of incessant interaction

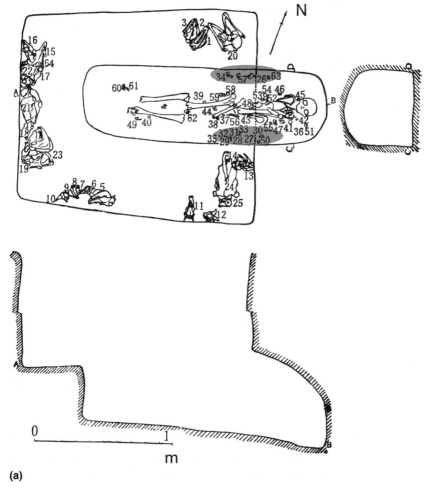

(a)

FIGURE 3.9 (a) Plan of tomb no. IIIM1 with bronze animal figures in Guyuan, Ningxia, fifth century BCE (nos. 26–35, 50, 57, 63, bronze animal figures, marked in gray), after Ningxia wenwu kaogu yanjiusuo 寧夏文物考古研究所 and Ningxia Guyuan bowuguan 寧夏固原博物館, "Ningxia Guyuan Yanglang qingtong wenhua mudi" 寧夏固原楊郎青銅文化墓地, *Kaogu xuebao* 1993.1: 24, fig. 12. Courtesy of *Acta Archaeologica Sinica* (*Kaogu xuebao*).

(b)   (c)

FIGURE 3.9 (*Cont.*) (b) Bronze animal figure, after Ningxia wenwu kaogu yanjiusuo and Ningxia Guyuan bowuguan, "Ningxia Guyuan Yanglang qingtong wenhua mudi," *Kaogu xuebao* 1993.1: 24, pl. 4.4. Courtesy of *Acta Archaeologica Sinica* (*Kaogu xuebao*). (c) Gold deer figures from a tomb at Filippovka, Ufa, Russia, third century BCE. Courtesy of the Museum of Archaeology and Ethnography, Ufa.

between the Rong-Di and Huaxia cultures. Although the Rong-Di elements represented in these objects had already declined in the archaeological record by the second century BCE and become largely a glory of the past, their symbolic power lived on in the new kingdom in Liu Sheng's hands.

However, finding old-fashioned objects in someone's tomb does not necessarily mean the tomb occupant consciously appreciated the age of the objects. Did Liu Sheng understand the archaism or antiquity of his vessels? Did he know that some of them were older than others?

Archaism in the Mancheng tombs appears to have been a conscious choice. The inscribed jade statuette placed in the outer coffin demonstrates a clear awareness of old styles (figs. 1.5a, 1.5b). As discussed in chapter 2, the inscription on the bottom of this statuette identified it as an "antique jade man" (*gu yuren*).[86] Although anthropomorphic jade figurines first emerged in tombs no later than the Shang period,[87] they became more and more realistic during the late Eastern Zhou period.[88] One of the closest comparisons comes from a royal tomb of the Han 韓 state, dated to about the mid-third century BCE. This gentleman stands nearly five centimeters tall and wears a Chinese robe and hat. He has a calm expression on his face, while holding his hands together before his stomach in a reverent manner.[89] Some other jade figurines were similarly found in the outer coffin on the right side of an Eastern Zhou corpse with a group of jade, stone, or glass ornaments.[90] Labeling Liu's statuette as an "antique jade man" rather than simply a "jade man" reveals that the maker was not only aware of but probably also proud of the work's archaism or ancient origin, and he was determined to make an announcement about it.

Being inspired by the glory of one's putative royal predecessors is one thing, but proclaiming that inspiration in the royal mausoleum as a public spectacle is another because the former might be a personal, psychological matter and the latter was a political action that needed ideological justification and endorsement. Liu Sheng's extensive adoption in his tomb of archaic elements of both Huaxia and Rong-Di traditions could be legitimated in the context of antiquarianism during the Western Han era.

The concept of "returning to antiquity" (fugu) can be traced back to the late Eastern Zhou period, when many philosophers, including Mozi and Xunzi, insisted on the importance of learning from the ancients; this was true particularly for rulers.[91] In the eyes of these thinkers, the ancients were more ethical, righteous, and wiser than contemporary men. But with their lives over, one of the ways to concretely visualize a ruler's world was through the material remains, including outfits and instruments that they left behind. Liu Sheng was certainly not alone among the Western Han elite in searching out the past and injecting it into the present. Many Western Han nobles, including the emperors, were fans of antique vessels and were sensitive to archaic styles. Emperor Wu "possessed antique bronzes" (shang you gu tongqi 上有故銅器) and was curious about their exact provenance. One vessel in his collection, according to legend, might date back to the age of Duke Huan of the Qi 齊桓公 (d. 643 BCE).[92] It appears that even abdicated emperors cherished ancient ritual vessels. Recently, archaeologists discovered a well-preserved elite tomb in present-day Nanchang, Jiangxi Province, occupied by the marquis of Haihun, Liu He 劉賀 (92–59 BCE), who was forced to abdicate the imperial throne only twenty-seven days into his reign. In this marvelous tomb, the excavators chanced upon a lavishly ornamented bronze wine container that dates back stylistically to the early Western Zhou period.[93] Such enthusiasm about ancient ritual bronzes even extended down to some of the lower elites.[94]

Old-fashioned ritual vessels were collected not only for aesthetic reasons but also for political symbolism. According to Sima Qian, King Zhaoxiang 昭襄王 of the Qin (r. 306–251 BCE) seized the ancient nine tripods, purportedly cast by the ancient sage king Yu 禹, as his booty from the defeated

Zhou king to justify his unparalleled authority over all under heaven, but he quickly lost them in the Si River. The First Emperor of Qin, King Zhaoxiang's great grandson, later attempted to retrieve them from the river but failed, an ominous sign of his loss of heaven's favor.[95] Emperor Wen of the Han, who was also eager to retrieve the lost tripods, was nearly tricked by a charlatan who claimed to see the "sacred breath" of the tripods rising from a river.[96] For a Chinese emperor, control of these sacred ritual vessels cast in the remote past symbolized the possession of a cultural legacy and legitimate power. Liu Sheng, who was tasked with reviving a lost kingdom, would have needed such tokens to legitimize his political agenda.

Besides providing political legitimacy, ancient outfits and instruments were able to transfer the moral power of the ancients to their later wearers or possessors. According to the *Xunzi* text, when asked about the method of governing the state, Confucius reportedly once answered: "To live in today's world but focus on one's intentions in the way of the ancients, to dwell in today's customs but dress in clothes of the ancients."[97] In other words, Confucius seems to be advising the rulers: Do you want to imitate the mind and spirit of the ancients? Then, go and put on their clothing! It seems these authentic objects held a secret power for moral purification and sagehood. As a king, Liu Sheng had to be aware of this teaching. His job would have demanded that he include traces of the past in his life.

THE PRESENCE OF RONG-DI ELEMENTS IN THE SOCIAL SPACE

Although the antiquarianism flourishing among the Western Han elite might have been a perfect incentive for the adoption of archaic outfits and other instruments in the tombs at the Mancheng site, how serious was this adoption? Did Liu Sheng dress up to identify with the "barbarians," or did he do so only for amusement or novelty? When we shift our attention from the coffins to the outside tomb chambers and look at some other non-ethnic-Han objects, it soon becomes clear that the "barbaric" side of the Zhongshan royal couple was real and serious.

In the burial chambers that represented the social realm of the deceased royal couple beyond the coffins, excavators uncovered various functional artifacts made in traditional "barbaric" fashion. Even though they are relatively few in number, in scope these works embody a full-scale style of life—represented by different clothing, and different ways of eating, traveling, and entertaining—that might not have entirely vanished by the time Liu Sheng died.

(a)

(b)

FIGURE 3.10 (a) Bronze belt plaque from the front chamber of Mancheng tomb no. 1, Hebei, ca. 113 BCE. Made by Alex Brey after Zhongguo shehui kexueyuan kaogu yanjiusuo, *Mancheng Han mu fajue baogao*, 2: pl. 58.3; (b) Openwork plaque with tiger and dragon, Ivolga tomb no. 100, first century CE. Made by Alex Brey after Bunker, *Ancient Bronzes of the Eastern Eurasian Steppes from the Arthur M. Sackler Collection*, p. 88, fig. A136.

First, regarding clothing, some outfit artifacts found in the front chambers exhibit non-ethnic-Han styles. These include four similar gilded bronze plaques (fig. 1.7, nos. 144, 145).[98] Used as decorations on a variety of objects, at Mancheng these rectangular plaques were most likely fastened to the exterior face of a leather belt that decorated the waist.[99] Each plaque bears an animal-combat motif on one side, while the other side is unpolished (fig. 3.10a). On the decorated side, a predator jumps upon its prey, opening its mouth to attack its victim's back. The prey, apparently a dragon, swings its long neck around in a beautiful C-shape in a desperate attempt to fight back. The Huaxia representations of animals during the Eastern Zhou through the early Western Han periods, on the other hand, were characterized by relatively abstract, ornamental patterns.

This traditional steppe animal-combat motif on the bronze plaques was unmistakably a Rong-Di legacy.[100] Chinese archaeologists have unearthed more than fifty similar belt plaques, or their earlier Eastern Zhou prototypes, from the Ordos and other parts of the Northern Zone.[101] Perhaps favored by Xiongnu noblemen, the same "swinging neck" motif is repeated on two plaques found in Ivolga and Szidorovka in modern-day Russia, deep in what formerly was Xiongnu territory (fig. 3.10b).[102] Another silver belt buckle (no. 4356) discovered in the front chamber also attests to this nomadic dressing style, though this object was not directly worn but laid in front of the king's tent; it may have been a special offering by funeral participants who may themselves have been Rong-Di descendants and powerful locals.[103] Unlike their counterparts in the coffins, these belt buckles instead represented the public image of the dead.

The Zhongshan royal couple also brought some traditional local crafts related to clothing into their tombs. Among the objects in Liu Sheng's tomb was a bronze, cylindrical, bamboo-shaped container (fig. 3.11a), a type of needle box popular in Jundushan and other earlier Rong-Di cemeteries (fig. 3.11b).[104] The queen was also interred with an unusual bone needle, perhaps used for sewing, in her burial chamber.[105] Small objects made of bone

(a)   (b)

FIGURE 3.11 (a) Bronze needle case from Mancheng tomb no. 1, Mancheng, Hebei, CA. 113 BCE. Courtesy of Hebei Museum, Shijiazhuang. (b) Bronze needle cases from Jundushan cemeteries, Beijing, sixth to fifth centuries BCE. After Beijing shi wenwu yanjiusuo, *Jundushan mudi: Yuhuangmiao* 4: color pl. 63.1. Courtesy of Wenwu Press.

(a)   (b)

FIGURE 3.12 (a) Glazed pot from Mancheng tomb no. 1, Mancheng, Hebei, ca. 113 BCE; (b) Ceramic pot with two loop-shaped ears from Mancheng tomb no. 1, Mancheng, Hebei, ca. 113 BCE. Courtesy of Hebei Museum, Shijiazhuang.

were rare in early Chinese tombs but were frequently spotted in Rong-Di burials during the Eastern Zhou period, including a number of them found in the Zhongshan polity region.[106]

Second, with regard to dining tools, some ceramic kitchenware in the Mancheng tombs was conspicuously non-ethnic-Han. Because pottery was usually mass-produced in nearby workshops, following generations of traditional craftsmanship, it served as a reliable index of the local culture. One of the most noticeable non-ethnic-Han ceramics in Liu Sheng's "warehouse" (northern side chamber) is a pot (no. 3220 in the 1980 excavation report) (fig. 3.12a). It features a flaring mouth, a long sloping neck, and two half-ring-shaped "ears" on its shoulder. Another exotic clay pot in Liu Sheng's tomb has a distinctive sagging belly and two half-ring-shaped ears at the belly of the vessel (fig. 3.12b). A typical ethnic-Han ceramic pot, however, would display none of these characteristics.[107]

The shapes of the two unusual ceramic pots resemble those of some pots excavated in Rong-Di cemeteries some five centuries earlier; clearly, they were most likely related.[108] The second pot (fig. 3.12b) appears to be related to a family of double-eared pots unique to the Rong-Di culture found in China's northern frontiers during the late Eastern Zhou period.[109]

Such an exotic style was not confined to "low-end" pottery but was applicable to some of the "high-end" bronzes from Liu Sheng's tomb as well. A special, legless bronze cauldron with upright walls, two erect, rectangular handles, and a flat bottom was found in Liu Sheng's rear chamber (fig. 3.13a; fig. 1.2, no. 20). This sort of vessel, often classified as a *fu* 鍑

(a)   (b)

FIGURE 3.13 (a) Bronze *fu* cauldron from Mancheng tomb no. 1, Mancheng, Hebei, ca. 113 BCE; (b) Bronze tripod from Mancheng tomb no. 1, Mancheng, Hebei, ca. 113 BCE. Courtesy of Hebei Museum, Shijiazhuang.

cauldron in Chinese archaeological literature, can be viewed as the Eurasian equivalent of a Chinese *ding* tripod.[110] As the favorite type of cooking vessel of the nomads, early *fu* cauldrons usually feature steep side walls, circular handles, circular bases, and no lids, whereas their Chinese counterparts have flaring side walls, rectangular handles, and pointed legs.[111] The bronze *fu* did not stand alone in tomb no. 1; Liu Sheng's tomb held another bronze cauldron that similarly followed the local tradition (fig. 3.13b; fig. 1.2, no. 64). It features a unique shape with a deep bowl and a pointed bottom supported by three short legs. Although excavators identified it as a *ding* tripod, this vessel's style is different from most of its ethnic-Han counterparts, which usually are characterized by a relatively shallow bowl and a flatter bottom.

Bronze vessels of these two types have been found extensively in Eastern Zhou-period Rong-Di sites in Hebei and beyond.[112] The distinct form of the second bronze vessel may be related to a special kind of three-legged cauldron noted in Chinese archaeological literature. Chinese archaeologists have associated these vessels with the non-Huaxia Northern Zone culture.[113]

Third, as a means for travel, Liu Sheng was supplied with carriages drawn by horses decorated with "barbaric" metal works. Among a number of silver and bronze horse frontlets found in tomb no. 1, two are so-called "horse face masks" (*mamian* 馬面) (fig. 3.14).[114] Cast into plaques that resemble a frontally posed horse head with two erect ears (and sometimes even eyes), these representational frontlets are starkly different from traditional Chinese horse frontlets, which usually have a simple geometric outline.[115]

Horse frontlets similar to the Mancheng example might have first appeared in the art of the Scythians, nomads for whom horses were of

FIGURE 3.14 "Horse-face" frontlet from Mancheng tomb no. 1, Mancheng, Hebei, ca. 113 BCE. Courtesy of Hebei Museum, Shijiazhuang.

primary importance.[116] Later they spread westward into the ancient Mediterranean world[117] and eastward into western China. Excavations of Eastern Zhou-period Rong-Di cemeteries have yielded mask-like frontlets almost identical to those found at Mancheng.[118]

Lastly, even in terms of entertainment, the deceased royal couple played games that also originated among nomadic cultures. In Dou Wan's front chamber, excavators found a set of tiny bronze figurines kept in a box. They represent an ox, a horse, three mounted riders (fig. 2.10, no. 25), and a stout man (fig. 2.10, no. 67), and they all measure between four and seven centimeters tall (fig. 3.15a). Among them, the most notable are the stout wrestler and the riders. The former displays an exotic and intimidating appearance with his bald head, handlebar mustache, bulging muscles, and clasped fists. With their short jackets, the three mounted riders with disheveled hair are all dressed in the non-Chinese "left lapel" (*zuoren* 左衽) style, in which the robe opens at the left side of the body.[119] The Chinese, however, were known for their "right lapel" (*youren* 右衽) dressing style. The riders each bear a spike below the

(a)   (b)

FIGURE 3.15 (a) Bronze figurines of dismountable rider and ox from Mancheng tomb no. 2, Mancheng, Hebei, ca. 118–104 BCE. Courtesy of Hebei Museum, Shijiazhuang; (b) Bronze die with gold and silver inlays from Mancheng tomb no. 2, Mancheng, Hebei, ca. 118–104 BCE. Courtesy of Hebei Museum, Shijiazhuang.

body, while the horse is pierced by a hole in its back. The correspondence between the nail and the hole allows the player to mount and dismount the rider at will. Although small, these figurines were not surrogates, or *mingqi*, because they appeared in a set, along with an eighteen-faceted die and the inscribed wager coins discussed in chapter 2 (and mentioned further in chapter 5). So, they were more likely gaming pieces. However, we can identify no form of gaming in the Huaxia tradition that could serve as a prototype.

Although the tiny horseback-rider gaming pieces and wrestler figurine were undoubtedly products made in China, their "barbarian" prototypes have been found in large numbers in the Ordos area and all over the entire Eurasian steppes.[120] The motif of mounted and unmounted riders along with animals also appeared in Kurgan V in the permanently frozen Siberian tundra at Pazyryk, Russia. In this barrow, dated to about the fifth to fourth centuries BCE, archaeologists unearthed a perfectly preserved square rug ornamented with colorful embroidered patterns (fig. 3.16). The composition consists of three concentric square zones. The inner zone contains twenty-four small squares, each ornamented with an eight-petal flower pattern, reminiscent of the decoration on the facets of Dou Wan's die (fig. 3.15b). Around the squares is a register of smaller squares of winged griffins. The middle zone comprises a sequence of clockwise roaming stags (fig. 3.16a) edged on all sides by a continuous floral pattern similar to that previously mentioned. The outer register holds a sequence of counterclockwise promenading horses and riders, with dismounted riders (standing beside their horses, on the left side) alternating with mounted ones (fig. 3.16b). Noting the initial markings (the two dice-like circles) at the bottom right-hand corner (fig. 3.16c), Joseph Wiesner was the first to speculate that this carpet was used as a game board, and later other scholars concurred.[121] In light of Dou Wan's small toys, we might surmise that the game was analogous to modern Ludo except for its hunting theme. At least two people could take part, probably one playing the hunter and one playing the hunted (beast). They might alternately throw the dice in the inner zone and move the game pieces (the figurines) along the middle and outer bands of the rug according to the roll of the dice.

The aforementioned eight examples from four different categories represent a small group of burial objects in the royal couple's public realm at the Mancheng site that cannot find their place among ethnic-Han material culture. As was demonstrated, these were later developments from older styles in the local Rong-Di culture in north Hebei (Zone No. 4), represented first by the Yuhuangmiao site and later by the Warring States Zhongshan

FIGURE 3.16 Wool carpet from Pazyryk Kurgan V, Russia, 252–238 BCE, and details: (a) roaming stag, (b) horseman, and (c) dice-like circles. Courtesy of the State Hermitage Museum, Saint Petersburg.

(a)

(b)

(c)

FIGURE 3.16 (*Cont.*)

remains.[122] Among the major types of grave goods characteristic of the local Di culture, about two-thirds of them also appear in the tombs at the Mancheng site.[123] But these functional objects also derived elements from other zones (nos. 1–3) of the Northern Zone culture and even received inspiration from the Eurasian steppe cultures (map 4).

Although these non-ethnic-Han artifacts constituted only a small fraction of the entire body of burial objects at the Mancheng site, they were sufficient to prove that the royal couple not only embraced Rong-Di and nomadic traditions symbolically but also more or less lived out aspects of these cultures. How?

First, with regard to dating, unlike the archaistic necklaces and short swords in the coffins, the bronzes and ceramics in the outside burial chambers were all fashioned in a more contemporary style that might have existed as late as the second century BCE. For example, the first bronze *fu* cauldron from Liu Sheng's tomb at Mancheng fits into the latest phase of this type of vessel (the third and second centuries BCE) (fig. 3.13a).[124] In other words, rather than exhibiting a heavy flavor of antiquarianism as seen in the bead necklaces or the short swords, some of these functional objects might have still been in service during Liu Sheng's reign.

Second, in terms of function, these objects covered all aspects of life. Unlike the visually stimulating bead necklaces and short swords, which functioned primarily as part of the deceased's ritual outfit and as decoration of the body, these exotic objects were made of less precious materials with less aesthetically charming forms. None bear inscriptions or stamps of provenance. Instead, they were meant to be practical tools of daily life. Moreover, some of these objects were present in the tombs in a more profound way than we might think. For example, the presence of the needle case suggests that what had been brought to the tomb included not only finished products but also craftsmanship or techniques that produced the products. It seems the Rong-Di culture was expected to continuously exert an enduring impact on the posthumous life of the royal tomb occupants.

Odd and eccentric as they may look, these living "barbaric" objects were mixed in with, rather than separated from, the majority of the Chinese objects in the tombs. In the inner coffin, the ethnic-Han jade suit was accompanied by the non-ethnic-Han necklace, and likewise in the outer coffin, the ethnic-Han ritual outfit was paired with the non-ethnic-Han short swords. The Rong-Di necklaces and short swords were put next to such Huaxia decorative jade items as *bi* discs, *huang* half-rings, *xi*, *jue* pendants, and humanoid figurines. Beyond the coffins, the bronze *ding* and the *fu* cauldrons from the Rong-Di tradition were juxtaposed with typical ethnic-Han vessels such as lacquer plates and eared-cups. It is also worthwhile to note that most of these Rong-Di objects were not deposited in the center of the ritual space near the soul seats but were scattered across the many burial chambers and swamped by the dominant ethnic-Han artifacts. For example, upon discovery, the four previously mentioned bronze plaques belonged to a group of objects that might initially have been placed in a disintegrated wooden box (fig. 1.7, nos. 144, 145).[125] Among the other objects were small rings that were usually coupled with plaques to attach to a belt hook or to hold pendants.[126] They appeared next to some jade sacrificial offerings, including a large *bi* disc and a series of jade ornaments of some perished lacquerware, which were quintessentially Huaxia objects.[127]

Mingled among an overwhelming number of ethnic-Han objects, these Rong-Di artifacts appear almost invisible. The practice of incorporating only some of these objects suggests three potential intentions: first, to preserve the authentic local tradition; second, to mix it in rather than separate it from the imperial mainstream Han culture; and lastly, to limit it to such an extent that it would not achieve a dominant status.

I return to the question posed at the beginning of this section: What prompted the inclusion of these functional non-ethnic-Han objects into the royal burials of the ethnic-Han royalty, if they held little aesthetic or symbolic value? As I will demonstrate next, this small group of artifacts was a faithful reflection of the non-Han tradition in Liu Sheng's Zhongshan kingdom, which was marginalized but not assimilated.

This reality was the result of centuries-long competition between Zhongshan and its neighbors. The close territorial relationship also heightened the tension between the Zhongshan people and their Huaxia neighbors, who were actively seeking new land. About 457 BCE, the Zhao kingdom to the north assaulted and defeated Zhongshan, seized its capital, and devastated the nation. Half a century later, between 408 and 406 BCE, the Wei kingdom in the south won a decisive victory over Zhongshan and annexed the entire country. In spite of these defeats, the Zhongshan people resisted with extraordinary tenacity and courage. It is believed that sometime between 380 and 378 BCE, while Wei was weakened in a battle against Chu and Zhao, the Zhongshan people, supported by the Qi kingdom, seized the opportunity to reclaim their state, though it remains unclear whether the previous ruling clan was restored.[128] Almost immediately, they began facing a new wave of attacks. The worst threat came from the Zhao kingdom, which considered the Zhongshan people as an enemy deep in its "belly and heart" (*fuxin* 腹心).[129] Eventually, in 299 BCE, after eight years of ceaseless bloody campaigns, the Zhao army crushed the defenses of Zhongshan and forced its king to flee to Qi. In the following year, the king of Zhao put a member of the Zhongshan royal house named Shang 尚 (or Sheng 勝), whose given name interestingly coincides with that of Liu Sheng, onto the throne and turned the hostile nation into a satellite state.[130] In 296 BCE, the victorious Zhao terminated the Zhongshan kingdom by sending the royal house of Zhongshan into exile at Fushi, later the prefecture seat of Shangjun, in present-day north Shaanxi (map 2).

In the aftermath of this tragic event, people of the Zhongshan kingdom were divided into two forces, each preserving a shadow of its glorious past. One group that migrated back to Fushi might have dissolved into the hybrid local population, which at that time was under the sway of the burgeoning power of the Xiongnu.[131] According to a historical source in the early second century BCE, the southern end of the Loufan 樓煩 tribe, which militarily aided the Zhao in the destruction of Zhongshan in 296 BCE, was only about 291 kilometers to the north of Chang'an, the imperial capital.[132] And, at that time, there was only one major city in northern Shaanxi that sat exactly at that distance from the Han capital—Fushi, where the Zhongshan royalty had been exiled. Loufan had remained independent until joining the Xiongnu Confederation during the early second century BCE and stiffly stood in the way of expanding Han power, only to be driven away by force in 127 BCE— that is, twenty-six years into Liu Sheng's reign.[133] It was not until 125 BCE that the Han Empire reestablished the Xihe Commandery to consolidate its control over this "new land."[134]

The other group of Zhongshan people did not leave their land and became subjects under the rule of Huaxia polities (first Zhao and later Qin and Han). After several hundred years of cultural synthesis, the Zhongshan population gradually lost its unique Rong-Di cultural association and forged distinct local customs that were at once highly sinicized but also "vulgar" to ethnic-Han eyes. More importantly, the memory of the Rong-Di tradition associated with the region still lived on and was integrated into the local identity. When Wang Mang usurped power from the Western Han dynasty in 9 CE, he renamed two commanderies previously under the control of the Rong-Di barbarians as "Zhendi" 鎮狄 and "Yandi" 厭狄, or "Suppressing the Di."[135] These auspicious and charm-like place-names chosen by Wang Mang betray the continuous influence of the Rong-Di "barbarians" on the north frontier.

The survival of the small number of functional non-ethnic-Han artifacts in the Mancheng site is a reflection of the cultural reality in north China during the late second century BCE, when the Western Han Empire was still in the process of digesting its various cultural components in order to forge a unified ethnic-Han identity, in which the modern concept of "Chinese" is grounded.

REINVENTING THE CATACOMB IN ZHONGSHAN

So far, we have examined two ways of mixing ethnic-Han elements with non-ethnic-Han elements: (1) preserving archaic Rong-Di artifacts with symbolic meanings and (2) including contemporary non-ethnic-Han artifacts that were still in daily use. However, there was a third, more creative way of synthesizing contemporary ethnic-Han and non-ethnic-Han artistic practices, and in this respect, nothing at the Mancheng site was more complex and sophisticated than the architecture of the tombs.

No matter how many ancient resources the designers of the Mancheng tombs could have drawn upon locally, the paradigmatic shift in tomb structure from verticality to horizontality has no answer in ancient Hebei but instead originated on China's west frontier nearly a thousand kilometers away. This inspiration spread to Hebei in Liu Sheng's day and became the contemporary inspiration for the tombs at Mancheng.

Although Chinese archaeologists recognized very early on the unique cliff-cut style of the tombs at the Mancheng site, they used to associate it with other similar tombs discovered in present-day Yongcheng (Liang kingdom) in the heartland of the Chinese Empire. These were usually called "cliff-cut cave tombs" (*yadongmu* 崖洞墓) in archaeological publications.[136] Indeed, in many aspects, the tombs at Mancheng appear like simplified versions of their counterparts at the Liang royal cemetery. While the Mancheng tombs are each approached by one tomb passage, Mt. Baoan tomb no. 2 boasts three. At Mancheng, the two main chambers (i.e., the front and the rear chambers) are directly connected, but at Mt. Baoan tomb no. 2, they are linked up with a long interior tunnel. Whereas the Mancheng tombs each include two side chambers, Mt. Baoan tomb no. 2 has a string of twenty symmetrically arranged side chambers flanking the ramps and interior tunnels. And while the front and rear chambers in the Mancheng tombs are devoid of side chambers, each of the two main chambers in Mt. Baoan tomb no. 2 is surrounded by seven affiliated smaller chambers clustered around the tomb's outer rim. These and other analogies recently led several archaeologists to conclude that the design of the Mancheng tombs might have referred to the earlier Mt. Baoan tombs as a blueprint.[137]

At the same time, the tombs at the Mancheng site are not merely an abridged and cruder version of their Mt. Baoan counterparts; they follow very different structural and conceptual models. Whereas the Chu and Liang royal tombs consisted of one layer of stone architecture that simulated a real palace,[138] the Mancheng burials featured two layers, including an outer rock "shell" that did not simulate real architecture but that enveloped an inner wooden or stone "core" that did.

To substantiate this point, we focus on the distinct outer shell of the Mancheng tombs: the simple round shape and unpolished face of the rock-cut interior.[139] Let us take the front chamber of Liu Sheng's Mancheng tomb no. 1, for example. Any visitor who walks into the tunnel and stands at the entrance to the front chamber will perceive a nearly hemispherical man-made cave, almost fifteen meters long and thirteen meters wide, with a height of 6.8 meters in the center, hollowed out of the body of the mountain (fig. 0.3). Whereas the chambers at Mt. Baoan are all dug in square plans with straight and upright walls, those at Mancheng are strikingly different. At Mancheng, although the chamber generally appears square, it is in fact rounded on all sides and at all the corners (fig. 1.1). The front (east) and the rear (west) sides of the rock chamber are conspicuously concave, and the other two sides are slightly curved, making the chamber look almost like a hemisphere.

The most impressive structure of the Mancheng tombs, the gigantic ceiling, generally resembles a vault in form, with the elevated center forming the apex of the space (figs. 1.1, 2.1). It is very likely that Liu Sheng's front chamber was originally designed to stand beneath a true dome but that somehow the work failed to be completed.[140] In his wife's tomb (no. 2), the ceiling of the front chamber was finished into a much more elegant dome (fig. 2.1).

This distinct hemispherical shape might have served a symbolic rather than a practical purpose. It should be noted that the space only needed to hold a rectangular wooden house-shaped structure (which I will analyze in detail later in this chapter). For that purpose, the designer(s) should have understood that a hemispherical cave was not the most efficient and economical option because it required a large amount of superfluous labor to chisel out practically useless gaps between the upright walls of the building and the concave sides of the chamber. None of the excavated Chu and Liang "prototypes" possess such superfluous domes. The apparent waste of energy spent on these unnecessary architectural features demands an explanation.

The Mancheng rock-cut chamber also differs from its Liang and Chu counterparts because it does not imitate a traditional Chinese timber-structure building, which featured straight, upright, and smooth, plastered walls. Whereas the walls in the earlier Liang and Chu cliff-cut tombs were all polished and painted like their palace counterparts, those in the Mancheng site only bear a crude treatment on their surface.[141]

It is clear that the idea embraced by the plan of the Mancheng site was different from that of the Liang or Chu royal cemeteries. For those marveling at the dazzling complexity of the earlier cliff-cut tombs, they might wonder about the minimalism in the style of the Mancheng tombs. But this contrast is only superficial. Despite the apparent analogies, the curve-walled and domed rock-cut chambers at the Mancheng site cannot be reduced to some simplified versions of their Liang and Chu forerunners at Yongcheng and Xuzhou, which directly simulated real buildings (palaces) in stone. The compact plan at Mancheng consists of only two major chambers whose tightly fitted wooden or stone structures denied any possibility of extra side chambers being added. Whereas the other cliff-cut tombs were direct architectural simulations, the Mancheng tombs had their simulated architecture encased in a seemingly amorphous rock shell, the meaning of which has remained unexplored. But where did this unusual idea come from?

New archaeological evidence suggests that the plan of the tombs at Mancheng was partly inspired by a fundamentally different model in the "barbaric" burials originating beyond the center of Chinese civilization. This model embraced a compact organic plan that was comprised of five basic elements. The model (A) cuts laterally into the ground or rock, (B) sits below vaulted or domed ceilings, (C) flanks the main chambers with two side chambers, (D) consists of two major horizontally connected chambers, and (E) includes a chamber or tunnel situated in the front part of the tomb for holding carriages or horses. Prior to the second century BCE, the majority of burials in the heartland of the Chinese cultural sphere were characterized by a vertically dug space, whereas tombs with more of the aforementioned elements were developed gradually on China's western borders.

Tombs with two or three of these elements appeared mostly in two types. One type combined (A) the horizontal burial space with (B) a vaulted or domed ceiling and was found extensively in western China from the pre-historic period onward (Type I-1) (fig. 3.17). These laterally cut or dug tombs, usually called "earthen cave burials" (*tudongmu* 土洞墓) or "cave-chamber burials" (*dongshimu* 洞室墓) in Chinese archaeological literature and equivalent to

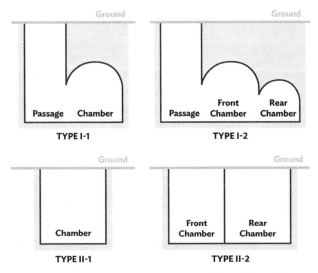

FIGURE 3.17 Diagram of two major burial types in early China. Made by Jie Shi and Alex Brey.

a "catacomb" in Western scholarship, normally consisted of a single vaulted or domed burial chamber, sometimes with a niche dug into a side wall of the chamber.[142] This burial style was first introduced by the indigenous Rong people. One of the most concentrated areas of vaulted catacombs in China was located at the Yanglang site (Zone 1 of the Northern Zone), identified by archaeologists as a typical Rong settlement that flourished between the fifth and third centuries BCE.[143] Around the mid-Warring States period, this style of burial was adopted by some of their Chinese (or sinicized non-Huaxia) neighbors in the Qin,[144] who enlarged the burial chamber and added a Chinese compartmentalized wooden casket.[145] Toward the late Warring States period, the niches became larger and turned into a pair of side chambers, thus adding (C) side chambers to the previous two-element combination.[146]

The second type of combination of elements (Type II-1) became popular during the late third century BCE. Perhaps inspired by the traditional Chinese vertical pit graves, (D) two horizontally connected burial chambers were merged with (E) a front garage in the Miaozhuang and Shangyuanjia cemeteries in Gansu (map 4).[147] Although these burials consisted of horizontally connected chambers, these chambers were constructed on the floor of a conventional vertical shaft rather than cutting laterally into the ground (Type II-2) (fig. 3.17).[148]

But examples that incorporated all five elements listed previously had remained unknown until an astonishing archaeological discovery was made at the Majiayuan site in Zhangjiachuan Hui Autonomous County, Gansu, in July 2006 (map 4).[149] In a cemetery dating from the late third century BCE, once probably on the western frontier of the Qin kingdom, archaeologists have by 2014 located sixty-nine burials accompanied by a number of sacrificial pits.[150] While bones of cows, sheep, or horses were uncovered in the sacrificial pits, and horses, chariots, and other grave goods were laid in the tomb passage and the burial chamber.[151] These objects surprised the discoverers with their shining gold and silver ornaments in the "animal style" popular across the Eurasian steppes during the seventh to third centuries BCE.[152] Studies of the material culture in the cemetery generally have identified the tomb occupants as a group of pastoral nomads referred to in traditional Chinese historiography as the "Xirong" 西戎, or "Western Rong Barbarians," who, much as the Di people, lived a half-nomadic and half-sedentary life on the western frontiers of the Qin kingdom.[153] Although the people buried in these tombs interred many items or objects fashioned in Huaxia styles, attesting to an active cultural interaction, they maintained a rather distinct cultural profile from their Huaxia neighbors to the east. The Majiayuan discovery has reshaped our understanding of the previously obscure "barbaric" culture, which might have served as the buffer zone and linking bridge between the steppes and Chinese civilization, during the late Eastern Zhou period.[154]

What is most striking about this rich cemetery is the fact that it yielded perhaps the earliest known combination of all the five elements I have singled out: (A) catacombs, under (B) vaulted or domed ceilings, sometimes with (C) side niches, divided into (D) two horizontally connected major chambers, and with (E) a front chamber housing carriages, just like in the tombs at the Mancheng site (Type I-2) (fig. 3.17). Almost all the burials at Majiayuan featured a perpendicular stepped tomb passage at the bottom of which one or two connected burial chambers were carved into the west wall to hold the deceased's coffin. Although the majority of burials in this cemetery consisted of only one burial chamber, three large examples, numbered as tomb nos. 1, 3, and 16, each held two horizontally connected chambers, with the larger one preceding the smaller one and anticipating the same plan as the tombs at the Mancheng site. In the largest one at the Majiayuan site, tomb no. 1, which was located at the center of the site, the front and rear chambers, totaling 6.64 meters in length, featured an unusual shape, with slightly rounded-out walls (fig. 3.18). Although the ceiling has since fallen, the two side walls as well as the ceiling of the chambers, which begin to curve at the level of 3.7 meters above the tomb floor, might have originally convened at the top to form a vault or dome.[155] In this way, the three elements characterizing the plan of the tombs at the Mancheng site were organically unified in these "barbaric" tombs.[156]

The recent discovery at Majiayuan has illuminated the fact that the tombs at the Mancheng site were related not only to the Chu and Liang cliff-cut royal burials but also to the Rong catacombs developed on China's western border through the third and second centuries BCE.

But how could the catacomb practice cross hundreds of kilometers to reach Mancheng? Although catacombs had almost never been part of the local mortuary tradition in Hebei prior to the second century BCE,[157] at that time, North China witnessed an increasing number of horizontally dug tombs that appropriated a Rong burial style. It was around the early second century BCE that simple catacombs started to appear in northern Shanxi and Hebei. By the time Liu Sheng ascended the throne, their shapes had developed into a plan with vaulted ceilings and side chambers.[158] In 1982, archaeologists unearthed an important cemetery that contained hundreds of Qin- and Han-period tombs at present-day Shuozhou, Shanxi, about 280 kilometers to the west of the Mancheng site, including a number of catacomb tombs (map 4).[159] Among these were tomb no. 6M158 and tomb no. 6M200, both dated to about the mid-second century BCE. The former featured a single burial chamber, preceded by two side chambers, and the latter consisted of a small front chamber and a major rear chamber (fig. 3.19a).[160] The basic cross-shaped structure of these tombs was similar to that of the Mancheng tombs.

As a step further toward Mancheng, another group of similar catacombs at the Sanfengou site in present-day Yangyuan, Hebei, about 160 kilometers to the east of Shuozhou and about 120 kilometers to the northwest of Mancheng, was brought to light in 1985 (map 4). In this distinctive cemetery, dated generally to the second to first centuries BCE, the horizontal burials dug into the earthen ground feature rectangular chambers with domed ceilings and wooden structures "not seen in any other places"[161] in North China but reminiscent of the Western Rong tombs at Majiayuan (fig. 3.19b). Beneath the dome, the rectangular tomb plan is slightly rounded at the corners, just like in the Mancheng tombs. The excavators recognized that, compared with the Shuozhou tombs, those at the Sanfengou site carried more "elements of Northern Zone (Eurasian) culture."[162] The existence of these

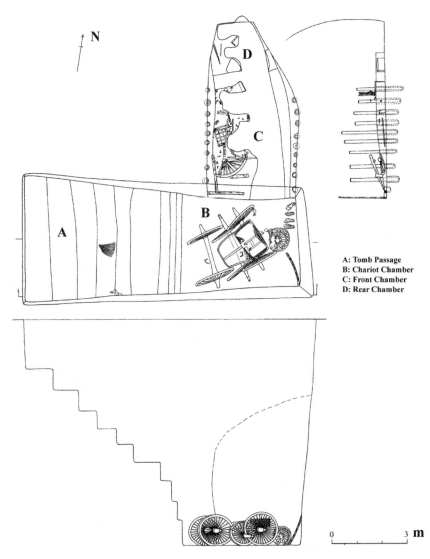

FIGURE 3.18 Plan and section of Majiayuan tomb no. 1, late third century BCE, Zhangjiachuan, Tianshui, Gansu province. After *Wenwu* 2008.9: 7, fig. 5. Courtesy of Wenwu Press.

developed catacombs in North Shanxi and Hebei suggests that the basic concept of a double-chamber horizontal tomb with a vaulted or domed ceiling, which had originated in the west, had almost reached the doorsteps of the Zhongshan kingdom by the late second century BCE.[163] The occupants of the Shuozhou and Sanfengou burials were probably descendants of the last of

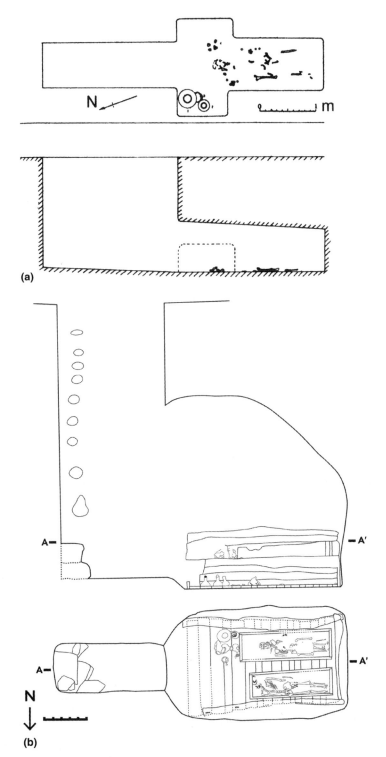

FIGURE 3.19 (a) Tomb no. 6M200, Shuozhou, Shanxi, second century BCE. After *Wenwu* 1987.6: 10, fig. 27. Courtesy of Wenwu Press; (b) Sanfengou tomb no. 2, Yangyuan, Hebei, second to first century BCE. After *Wenwu* 1990.1: 3, figs. 4–6. Courtesy of Wenwu Press.

the Rong-Di, if not the Eastern Zhou Zhongshan, who remained active in the middle Yellow River valley till the late second century BCE.

This cultural attribution has significant historical grounding. After the demise of the Eastern Zhou Zhongshan kingdom in 296 BCE, the defeated Zhongshan royal house was driven back to their ancestral land in north Shaanxi.[164] In the years that followed, they might have dissolved into the local population, which at that time was under the sway of the burgeoning power of the Xiongnu.[165] This "culturally most complex" area (Zone 2 of the Northern Zone complex) assimilated local and immigrant cultures and became a melting pot for the Rong and Di "barbarians."[166] Over time, "the gaps between their cultures were gradually diminishing and their burial customs merged into an inseparable unity."[167] Zhongshan was only one of the many Rong-Di tribes that had remained active through the late second century BCE in the middle Yellow River valley. The occupants of the vast cemeteries of catacombs in Shuozhou and Sanfengou were probably related to the last groups of Rong-Di in China before they vanished completely in the material record.

RULE BY INTEGRATING CUSTOMS (*QISU* 齊俗)

Even if the functional non-ethnic-Han artifacts in the Mancheng tombs were part of the cultural reality of Zhongshan at the end of the second century BCE, the tomb designer and occupant did not have to include them in the royal tomb. Why would Liu Sheng, a highly bred, cultivated Han Chinese prince, have to honor a conquered, defeated, and almost dead "barbaric" local culture? This question can only be answered by examining the branch of early Chinese political philosophy that dealt with how to rule as a good king, a path that the Western Han rulers ardently pursued in order not to repeat the disaster of the Qin dynasty.

In this discourse, the Chinese and non-Chinese people should be ruled under different standards. The philosopher Xunzi was one of the most eloquent proponents of this idea, which was developed in the tumultuous context of the Warring States period. Facing the lamentable reality that even the Chinese Huaxia states no longer followed identical Zhou institutions, Xunzi proposed the concept of "all under heaven in one body" (*tianxia yiti* 天下一體) to emphasize that all regional vassals must submit to the authority of the son of heaven, who represented the common interest of all under heaven.[168] However, Xunzi also stated that obeying the authority of the son of heaven was one issue, but following Chinese political institutions was another. In response to the claim that Tang 湯 and Wu 武, the two ancient sage kings, were incapable of effecting their prohibitions and commands because Chu and Yue, the major two southern "barbarian" polities of the time, "would not receive their ordinances," Xunzi argued that this was not the case. Instead, in Xunzi's eyes, "Tang and Wu were the most skillful men in the world at putting their prohibitions and commands in effect" because they knew how to rule different nations with different policies. Rather than making a historical argument, Xunzi used the past to promote his own political ideal:[169] "All the states of [Hua]-Xia Chinese have identical obligations for service to the king and have identical standards of conduct. The countries of the Man, Yi, Rong, and Di barbarians perform the same obligatory services to the king, but the regulations governing them are not the same."[170]

Why should these "barbarians" be treated differently? The author of the *Book of Rites* continued to elaborate on Xunzi's point: "The people of those five regions—the Middle states, and the Rong, Yi 夷, (and other wild tribes round them)—had all their several natures, which they could not be made to alter."[171]

To cope with this multicultural situation, back in the Western Zhou dynasty, when the Zhou king conferred land on Tang Shu 唐叔 to establish the Jin state near Taiyuan, which was adjacent to the Rong tribes, it was reported that the new vassal was advised to establish a government on the basis of local Huaxia custom but to curb the locals with the Rong "chains."[172] During Eastern Zhou times, the Chinese kings were advised to mobilize people via their own customs because it was the best way to achieve peace.[173] On another occasion, the *Rites of Zhou* repeated that, "Rites and customs can be used to administer the populace."[174] The *Book of Rites* included a similar caution: "Their training was varied, without changing their customs."[175] As a highly educated aristocrat, Liu Sheng must have been well-versed in these canonical teachings.

Xunzi deeply influenced many early Western Han thinkers, including Lu Jia 陸賈 (ca. 240–170 BCE), Jia Yi 賈誼 (200–168 BCE), and Dong Zhongshu 董仲舒 (179–104 BCE),[176] who maintained Xunzi's division between Chinese and non-Chinese. In the political discourse of Xunzi's time, people within the Chinese realm were called "inner subjects" (*neichen* 內臣) and those outside, "outer subjects" (*waichen* 外臣).[177] However, by the early Western Han period, the world in which Xunzi lived had profoundly changed. China was now a unified empire, and many of the "barbarians" had been conquered and brought under the imperial administration. The empire also constantly absorbed more non-ethnic-Han immigrants, particularly in the north.[178] The sharp distinction that Xunzi made between Huaxia and "barbarians" encountered difficulty when a large "barbarian" population that had not yet been fully assimilated or sinicized was under the direct administration of the Chinese Empire.

In particular, Zhongshan was an especially difficult case and was distinguished from all other Chinese kingdoms during the second century BCE by its ambiguous identity. In principle, the contemporary Zhongshan kingdom, which was created by the Chinese emperor himself to be ruled by his own son, should fall under the category of "inner subjects" (neichen). But no matter how sinicized Zhongshan was, many Chinese authors still dismissed its people as uncivilized.

This bias was rooted in Eastern Zhou-period classical texts. Chinese authors classified the people of Zhongshan as barbarians (Rong-Di) who, unlike Chinese Huaxia, lived an unethical life as "jackals and wolves" (chailang 豺狼).[179] One of their bad customs was severe enough to be considered criminal in Chinese eyes: their addiction to alcohol. According to the Zuozhuan text, the Jin state, one of the Chinese Huaxia polities, launched a military assault on the Rong-Di in 594 BCE. One of Jin's five justifications for the war was the latter's addiction to alcohol.[180] Indeed, according to some folk stories, the liquors of Zhongshan were deadly intoxicating. A legend recorded in the Six Dynasties (222–589 CE) text, In Search of the Supernatural (Soushen ji 搜神記), has it that a native of Zhongshan named Dixi 狄希 was able to brew a beverage that could cause the drinker to remain unconscious for a thousand days.[181] The surviving liquor preserved in King Cuo's tomb lends some credibility to this apparently fantastic account.[182]

Another moral failing of the Zhongshan that was pointed out by Chinese critics was the people's "shameless" indulgence in sex. In the Annals of Lü Buwei text, Tu Shu 屠黍, a legendary wise historian, ascribed the demise of Zhongshan to its lustful culture: "The customs of Zhongshan allow people to make the day into night, and the night to continue into the day. Men and women are always kissing and hugging and never want to stop. They indulge in pleasures, revel in debauchery."[183] The licentiousness of ordinary people was viewed as an impediment to orderly government and was said to be a characteristic of the Di barbarians.[184]

This prejudice was generally accepted in the Shiji as well. Sima Qian associated this excessive sexual drive of the Zhongshan with the decadent "leftover people" (*yindi yumin* 淫地餘民) at Shaqiu, which was believed to be the place where the notorious last king of the Shang dynasty, Zhou 紂 (d. 1046 BCE), dug "ponds of wine" and erected "forests of meat" for his debauched revelries.[185] With this bias, even ordinary hobbies of the Zhongshan people (which might have been shared with the Han Chinese) appeared suspiciously immoral. In the *Shiji*, the Zhongshan people were infamous for their idle hobbies of "gathering, touring, and playing games" (*xiangju youxi* 相聚游戲).[186] They were also good at staging dramas.[187] Lady Li, one of Emperor Wu's favorite lovers, was a dancer and a native of Zhongshan.[188]

Therefore, the Chinese attitude toward the Zhongshan area, at least as represented in the *Shiji*, can be summarized with the following paradox: Zhongshan was externally sinicized while remaining internally barbaric.

This paradoxical attitude of the Chinese toward the Zhongshan was best reflected in the imperial historiography of Liu Sheng's time. In his all-inclusive *Shiji*, Sima Qian composed a series of twelve chapters dubbed "Basic Annals" (*benji* 本紀) for all legitimate Chinese dynasties from the ancient Five Thearchs to the contemporary Han and another series of thirty chapters titled "Hereditary Houses" (*shijia* 世家) for the history of those lineages that "conducted the righteous way and served the Lord and Supreme" (i.e., the son of heaven). However, he excluded Zhongshan from both of the series. According to an inscription made on a bronze ax—a symbol of kingship—excavated from King Cuo's tomb, the Zhongshan kingdom was "conferred by the son of heaven" (*tianzi jianbang* 天子建邦) and thus should have qualified for inclusion as one of Sima Qian's "hereditary houses."[189] It must also be noted that Sima Qian did not exclude mention of Zhongshan throughout his work: The place name appears in his *Shiji* 186 times, and in his biographical postface to the *Shiji*, Sima Qian proudly announced that one of his ancestors once assumed the position of prime minister of Zhongshan.[190] Clearly, Sima Qian excluded Zhongshan from his table of contents not for personal reasons, but because the kingdom was not officially recognized as a legitimate member of the Chinese Huaxia club. At the same time, whereas Sima Qian composed "Arrayed Traditions" (*liezhuan* 列傳) to narrate the history of most major non-Chinese polities such as the Xiongnu and the Southern and Eastern Yue, Zhongshan was once again excluded. This leads us to wonder: What on earth was Zhongshan if it was neither Chinese nor "barbarian"?

Zhongshan's problematic identity, which was as much cultural as political, might have touched Liu Sheng as well. As the founder of the new Zhongshan kingdom, he inevitably confronted the question of how to properly rule his country, which had an ambiguous identity.

In Xunzi's teaching, for Liu Sheng to be an ideal ruler in the example of the ancient sage kings of Tang 湯 and Wu 武 (the founders of the Shang and Zhou Dynasties), he should make a distinction between Chinese and barbarians and treat them differently. But Liu Sheng would have found it difficult to execute this sagely doctrine because his (Western Han) Zhongshan kingdom was neither Chinese nor "barbaric," a new situation Xunzi had never anticipated. Liu Sheng faced many thorny questions: Should he rule the kingdom as an "inner subject" or an "outer subject" of the empire? Should he behave as a Chinese prince from the Han imperial family or as a traditional king of the Zhongshan? Although each Western Han king of the time would have faced similar challenges, this ambiguous cultural and political identity was unique to the Zhongshan kingdom.

Liu Sheng's response was to treat Zhongshan as Chinese *and* barbaric, united into one. Legally and politically, it was already predetermined that his kingdom must be defined as one of the empire's "inner subjects," that is, Chinese. Culturally and ideologically, however, he still had to keep the Rong-Di tradition on his agenda. The way in which the ethnic-Han and non-ethnic-Han elements interacted in the tombs at the Mancheng site visualizes Zhongshan's historical identity as an ancient Rong-Di polity not only surrounded by Chinese neighbors but also infiltrated, both actively and passively, by Chinese culture for centuries. Liu Sheng, who was charged with the political mission of reviving the Zhongshan kingdom and pacifying the northern border of the empire, could only succeed by negotiating between the imperial and the local, between the past and the present, as well as between the Chinese and Rong-Di barbarians. For this reason, Western Han imperial policies demanded that kings must honor and tolerate the local customs of their subjects.[191] Although the original imperial edict that conferred Liu Sheng's royal title is lost, three other surviving examples from 117 BCE included a relatively formulaic mission statement. In these edicts, the emperor "respectively warned [the kings] of their countries' customs." To rule their people, they must herd the local people, know their customs, and harness their habits.[192]

The political rationale of such warnings was articulated by Liu An 劉安 (179–122 BCE), one of Liu Sheng's uncles and ruler of the Huainan kingdom in present-day Jiangsu Province. Liu An commissioned a comprehensive volume titled the *Master of Huainan* (*Huainanzi* 淮南子, compiled in second century BCE), which blended various philosophic currents of the time. An entire lengthy chapter, titled "Integrating Customs" (*Qisu xun* 齊俗訓), was devoted to justifying non-Han customs. The text argues that there was no hierarchy among different customs and that Han Chinese ways were not morally or culturally superior to the ways of others. The author contended, in a polemical tone, that "arrogant falsehood that deludes the age and haughty conduct that separates one from the masses—these the sage does not take as customs for the people."[193] This injunction means that even though the king was more cultivated than his people, he should not isolate himself from the "vulgar" masses to claim cultural superiority. In fact, the "Integrating Customs" chapter went as far as to claim that it was normal for men and women to "touch shins and rub shoulders" in the busy streets of a contemporary metropolis, a practice forbidden in ancient times as immorally "barbaric."[194] Instead, a wise ruler should not attempt to unify the various customs under one standard but allow all of them to thrive.

Andrew Meyer correctly noted the historical context of Chinese imperialization in which the "Integrating Customs" chapter was conceived and composed: "Not only were the striking differences in ritual and customs among the Sinic people united under the empire but, with the expansion of the territorial boundaries into the non-Sinic world, imperial officials now had to face the challenge of governing people who had no knowledge of, or sense of participation in, the culture of the central court."[195] This was exactly the challenge that faced Liu Sheng in his Zhongshan kingdom, which stood between the Sinic and non-Sinic categories.

Although we cannot know whether Liu Sheng read the book that his uncle sponsored, he could not have ignored the same question that obsessed the author of the "Integrating Customs" chapter: How did a Chinese ruler effectively govern a people with "barbaric" customs? The Mancheng site gives us a clear answer. The three silver and bronze dildos, which were used for increasing sexual pleasure, make a perfect footnote to the Zhongshan's open attitude toward sex. The substantial quantity of liquor jars stored in Liu Sheng's and his wife's burials reflects, albeit symbolically, the excessive love of alcohol described in the transmitted texts.[196] The Ludo-like game placed in Dou Wan's burial was another example of Zhongshan's enthusiasm for games and play. As for the local passion for dramas, the two gilt-bronze storytellers in Liu Sheng's front chamber (fig. 1.7, nos. 168–169, fig. 1.9) and a bronze statuette of a dwarf (fig. 1.2, no. 89) in his rear chamber offer suggestive evidence. Fashioned in a rather comical style, the latter figure features a disproportionally large head and short legs, totally different from such gracefully proportioned figurines as the lady in the lamp of the palace of lasting trust. In the Western Han court culture, according to Sima Xiangru, storytellers, dwarfs, and foreign actors formed three important categories of entertainers.[197] The combination of all these materials demonstrates the lesson of the "Integrating Customs"—ruling the Zhongshan people by being one of them.

Eventually, the idea of "integrating customs" became united with the notion of "antiquarianism" in the practice of decorating Liu Sheng's and his wife's bodies with outfits in the traditional and local Rong-Di style. It seems that Liu Sheng's dress combined the two seemingly contradictory teachings: to wear ancient clothes (to express the sagely ancient mind) and to wear what local people wear (to follow the local customs). The Mancheng site, however, offers an insight into this dilemma. Liu Sheng used both contemporary sinicized styles and archaistic "barbaric" styles to portray his two identities in Zhongshan simultaneously. Instead of being separated from one another, the two identities were blended, mingled, overlain, or meshed together. This sophisticated use of styles resonates with the twofold political reality. On the one hand, Zhongshan was legally a vassal state of the Western Han Empire; it had a dominant Chinese present. As a vassal of the empire, Liu Sheng was obliged to execute the Han laws. On the other hand, Zhongshan was remembered as a Di country and was scoffed at as uncivilized; it had a "barbaric" past, which had not yet entirely vanished. As the legitimate heir of this Di past, Liu Sheng had to continue to honor that memory. Combining the two different practices offered a solution for imitating the sage kings. Indeed, the Mancheng site set all these political ideologies, as well as realistic concerns, permanently in stone.

PART II

Chapter Four

_____

THE PUBLIC KING

The first part of this book, largely based on the visual and material characteristics of royal tombs, focuses on the questions of how and why the tombs at the Mancheng site were planned as they were. My study has revealed three principles of organization with respect to the design of the architecture and the pattern of the furnishings: *embracing* (body and soul), *paralleling* (two genders), and *intermingling* (multiple cultures). The organizing principles of visual and material remains correspond to three fundamental religious, social, and political concerns of the royal tomb occupants: the harmony of body and soul, of husband and wife, and of Chinese and "barbarian." Taken as a whole, were these part of a deliberately unified program or merely three remarkable coincidences?

Considering its complexity, this question is difficult to answer directly. Instead, we can approach it via another more manageable question: Did the human subjects (or social institutions) in charge of or responsible for this funerary project share these three concerns in their totality? If the answer is affirmative, then we can reasonably infer that the organizational principles observed in different aspects of the burial site were not isolated but united. Yet, in order to probe into the intention of the subjects, the first priority is to solve the foremost question: Who planned this burial site and for whom?

Therefore, while the main purpose of the second part of this book is to understand the totality of the organizing principles in the royal tombs at Mancheng, this mission forces us to break our inquiry into three chapters

that investigate the three issues related to the agency of royal tombs in Western Han China: the patron, the master planners, and the (intended) viewers
of the royal tombs.

In this chapter, I will argue that a royal tomb from the Western Han period
usually was planned during a ruler's reign with their approval. However,
this was not a private decision but a public one because the ruler's life was
divided into two parallel and mutually exclusive spheres: public and private.
Royal tombs fell into the former category as official properties sponsored
and managed by the government. My analysis is focused on articulating the
political nature of royal tombs during the Western Han period. It was state
politics that ultimately defined the conceptual and institutional basis for all
royal burial projects, including the Mancheng site.

To do this, I will investigate historical records, ritual and administrative documents, excavated inscriptions and manuscripts, and philosophical
treatises associated with royal funerary practice during the Western Han
period. Four problems are dealt with in the next four sections of this chapter.
The first section clarifies the basic fact that Western Han rulers were usually the final decision-makers for their tombs. The next two sections delve
further into the political nature of royal decisions by showing the extensive governmental involvement in building and furnishing these structures.
The fourth section, shifting direction from history to discourse, examines
how the political nature of royal burials provoked public debates on the way
in which a good ruler should be buried.

THE RULER AS DECISION-MAKER FOR THE ROYAL TOMB PLAN

Due to the lack of written records, we do not know exactly who designed
the tombs at the Mancheng site, but it is almost certain that Liu Sheng was
informed of the final plan and undoubtedly approved it. This knowledge is
gained first by deduction because, administratively, rulers during the Western Han period were supposed to be the ultimate authority over their own
tomb plans, and second by extrapolation because a number of Han-period
rulers other than Liu Sheng were reported to have been directly involved in
the process of designing their tombs.

Although some nobles during the Eastern Zhou period might have
already personally planned their tombs, it is unclear how popular this practice was.[1] In late Eastern Zhou funerary rites, the kings' corpses ideally were
held aboveground for up to seven months, and the vassals, for up to five

months, before the final entombment.[2] This delay left enough time for plenty of mortuary preparation, including choosing the site of the grave, choosing the date of the interment, constructing the wooden *guo* casket in the tomb pit, and making the "spirit objects" (*mingqi* 明器) that had to be inspected outside of the house of mourning (*binmen* 殯門) on three occasions—as raw materials, as objects in the process of being made, and as finished products.[3]

In contrast, Western Han rulers had more control over their burials, which were designed and built throughout their reigns. The emperor or king, as head of state, was the one who had the final say over his tomb plan.

In fact, Western Han rulers often played a more active role than serving only as a passive endorser of the process. The model was probably set in the previous Qin period. A passage from the lost *Former Rituals of the Han* (*Han Jiuyi* 漢舊儀, dated first century CE) text specifies that the First Emperor of Qin gave specific orders to his chief minister, Li Si 李斯 (ca. 284–208 BCE), to extend his burial pit laterally for another three hundred *zhang* (approximately 693 meters).[4] This level of personal oversight might have set an example for the Western Han emperors. According to the Eastern Han scholar Ying Shao 應劭 (fl. late second century), Emperor Wu designed his mausoleum "for himself" (*ziwei ling* 自為陵).[5] When Emperor Cheng 成帝 (r. 33–7 BCE) took the throne, he soon began building his necropolis, which was called the Yan Mausoleum 延陵 and was located near Weicheng 渭城. Ten years into the construction, worried about the inauspicious geomancy of his mausoleum site, the emperor suddenly stopped the work halfway through and chose another location, at Xinfeng 新豐, for his new necropolis, the Chang Mausoleum 昌陵. But this construction did not go smoothly, either. Five years later, the emperor, amidst complaints and protests from his frustrated ministers, changed his mind once again, abandoned the second mausoleum site, and switched back to the previous Yan Mausoleum after a huge waste of public wealth. Needless to say, the emperor had the final say about how his mausoleum should look, even though his opinions, as Michael Loewe observed, might have been influenced by his trusted ministers or advisers.[6]

High officials emulated their emperors in planning their tombs in advance. Ban Gu related that Huo Guang 霍光 (d. 68 BCE), the powerful great marshall (*Da jiangjun* 大將軍), "designed [his tomb] for himself" (*zizao* 自造).[7]

Perhaps following the Western Han models, Eastern Han emperors were actively involved in designing their mausoleums, and this fact is explicitly stated in official historical records. Before planning a mausoleum for Emperor Guangwu 光武帝 (r. 25–57 CE), the minister in charge of the project requested specific instructions from the emperor himself about how to fill the cemetery with ritual structures: "Your Majesty's mausoleum is so vast that we were wondering how to make use of the space."[8] The emperor then responded with specific orders regarding the tomb mound and burial objects. Emperor Ming 明帝 (r. 58–75 CE) not only planned his mausoleum but also designed his own stone casket, which measured 25 *chi* (5.775 meters) long and 12 *chi* (2.772 meters) wide.[9] And all these decisions were not made in secrecy but announced publicly, sometimes in a "testamentary edict" (*yizhao* 遺詔). These later Eastern Han examples are not totally irrelevant because they may help us imagine the active role Western Han emperors played in planning their tombs.

In fact, even commoners could determine how they should be buried. Some ordinary people also injected their philosophical ideas into their tombs. Yang Wangsun, a contemporary of Liu Sheng, asked his sons to bury his body naked without clothes or caskets. A friend of Yang Wangsun's, terrified by this request, wrote him a letter in the hope of talking him out of his decision. Yang Wangsun rejected his friend's Confucian argument and insisted on the Daoist and Mohist definition of death as a good and natural process of returning to one's true origin.[10] Later, Zhao Qi 趙岐 (108–201 CE) even painted the portraits of four eminent Eastern Zhou politicians, including Ji Zha 季札, Zi Chan 子產, Yan Ying 晏嬰, and Shu Xiang 叔向, on the walls of his tomb as guests, while painting his own image as the host. In doing so, Zhao Qi expressed his personal political ideology.[11]

If ordinary people could make decisions about planning their tombs, it would be unimaginable that kings, who possessed much greater wealth and power, could have been denied the right to do the same.

THE ROYAL BURIAL AS POLITICAL SYMBOL

Rulers during the Western Han period made final decisions on their burials not as individual persons but as political leaders of state, of government, and of public affairs in general. A royal tomb was an embodiment of state politics rather than a piece of architecture reserved for the king's personal welfare in death and the afterlife. This fact legitimated the criticism of Emperor Cheng's reckless decisions in changing the site of his mausoleum, as I discussed in the previous section.

As the direct model for the Western Han rulers, the First Emperor of Qin upgraded, incorporated, and synthesized various architectural elements taken from the Eastern Zhou royal mausoleums in both the pre-imperial Qin and the eastern kingdoms he conquered to creatively forge his gigantic, multilayered, and all-inclusive necropolis.[12] As the most visible structure occupying the very center of the entire mausoleum, the towering tomb mound is, in some sense, the embodiment of the emperor's public persona and his understanding of the meaning of the encompassing empire.

From the very beginning of the dynasty, the Western Han emperors followed the Qin example in expressing ideas of order and hierarchy within the state and "all under heaven" through the planning of their tombs. The founder of the new dynasty, Emperor Gao, and his son, Emperor Hui, were buried in two parallel mausoleums in the northern outskirts of the capital, Chang'an. The names of the two mausoleums were carefully chosen: the father's was called the Chang Mausoleum 長陵 and the son's, the An Mausoleum 安陵. Thus, the two necropolises collectively formed a mirror image of the capital "Chang-An" across the Wei River, which also helped to express the separation of life from death.[13] Empress Lü Zhi, Emperor Gao's principal wife, made this arrangement to immortalize her own son, Emperor Hui, as the only legitimate heir of Emperor Gao, among other princes. This planning later forced Emperor Wen, another son of Emperor Gao, by Lady Bo 薄姬 (d. 155 BCE), to relocate his mausoleum away from the chosen imperial cemeteries to the southern outskirts of the capital, admitting his unorthodox place in the imperial lineage.[14]

In terms of the planning of individual mausoleums, Chinese archaeologists, including Liu Qingzhu, Zhao Huacheng, and others, all noticed the general intention of imitating imperial cities, palaces, or even government offices,[15] in other words, state facilities.

The idea that the royal cemetery was an image of the state can be traced back to the *Rites of Zhou* text, which prescribed that kings should be buried in the center of the "state cemetery" (*gongmu* 公墓); vassals should be buried in the south, and royal ministers in the north. And each group was buried with their families.[16] The Qin and Han imperial or royal cemeteries largely followed the same principle, except that each ruler would have a whole separate mausoleum complex to represent a specific reign.[17] For example, the Chang Mausoleum was centered on Emperor Gao's tomb, flanked by Empress Lü's parallel tomb, and further accompanied by sixty-three satellite burials of the dynasty's founding ministers such as Xiao He 蕭何 (ca. 257–193 BCE), Cao Shen 曹參 (d. 190 BCE), and Zhou Bo 周勃 (d. 169 BCE).[18]

The political profile of the ruler's burial should not be surprising given the fact that the "life" of the mausoleum was treated almost like the metaphorical life of the king. Whereas during the late Eastern Zhou period, the construction of a tomb ideally was conducted after the death of its occupant, according to a quotation from the *Former Rituals of the Han* text, the Western Han imperial norm was for each new emperor to start his mausoleum project one year into his reign.[19] This means a prince did (or should) not build his tomb until he officially had become head of the state and government after having buried his predecessor.[20] So, as the royal subject's political life continued, his tomb also grew, until death finally descended upon him. When that happened, even if the construction was not yet complete, the workers had to hastily bring it to an end.[21] This practice probably started with the First Emperor of Qin, who launched his mausoleum project shortly after his enthronement as king of Qin; the lengthy construction continued for thirty-seven years until the news of his death was suddenly announced.[22] Imitating the Qin model, the Western Han funerary custom required that the emperor's corpse must be interred in about a month, if not sooner, which was too short a time period to complete any major construction of funerary structures.[23] Liu Sheng's tomb as well as some other royal tombs indeed bear similar signs of incompletion, which suggests the sudden death of the king.[24] So the inception of a new reign coincided with the commencement of construction of the new king's tomb, and the demise of the reign signaled the end of tomb construction. If the ruler upgraded his political status during his life, such as in the case of the First Emperor of Qin, who was elevated from a regional king to emperor of China in 221 BCE, the mausoleum would also have to be upgraded, if not started all over again.[25]

Because royal tombs alluded to the rulers' political lives, desecrating them would symbolize the destruction of the dynasty.[26] Upon the fall of the Qin Empire, the First Emperor of Qin's all-inclusive necropolis was despoiled by General Xiang Yu 項羽 (232–202 BCE), the leader of the rebels. A descendant of an Eastern Zhou noble clan and a man who sought to restore feudalism, Xiang Yu set fire not only to the mausoleum's aboveground facilities but also to some of its underground structures to symbolically eliminate the First Emperor's political life and legacy. According to archaeologists, many symbolic underground buildings without economically valuable contents such as gold, silver, bronze, or jade—including part of the terra-cotta army pits—were burnt so severely that even bronze tripods in these pits completely melted.[27]

The political symbolism of the royal tombs extended to ritual facilities often enclosed in the same mausoleum. Most royal cemeteries during the Western Han dynasty included not only the ruler's own crypt but also sites that represented the government offices of his state. The earliest examples include a number of satellite pits in the First Emperor of Qin's mausoleum that were associated with various government agencies. For example, in a pit numbered K0006, excavators discovered a complex underground wooden structure made up of two chambers. The front chamber contained twelve life-sized terra-cotta figures, while the rear chamber yielded a group of horse bones.[28] Duan Qingbo, citing Sima Qian's account that the First Emperor of the Qin filled his mausoleum with "wondrous objects and precious rarities from palaces, observation towers, and a hundred government offices,"[29] identified the pit as representing an imperial judicial institution staffed with civil officials.[30] Western Han imperial mausoleums expressed an even clearer official implication. For example, in Emperor Jing's Yang Mausoleum, archaeologists have excavated a number of similar satellite pits full of goods labeled with various official stamps and seals.[31] One of the seals excavated from pit no. 16 to the east side of the mausoleum carries the inscription of "grand provision" (taiguan 太官), which was the directorate in charge of the emperor's meals. Although it is still debatable whether these pits actually represented government offices,[32] it seems indisputable that during both the Qin and Western Han periods, the government as the imperial political apparatus was actively involved in planning these royal tombs.

The political significance of royal tombs in Western Han China begs the question of the nature of these tombs: What justified the involvement of government in the ruler's tomb, which might appear to be a personal monument?

THE ROYAL BURIAL AS STATE PROJECT

The political nature of royal tombs, which was proclaimed by the government involvement in Western Han royal mausoleums, was forged in the reality that, administratively, it was the state rather than the ruler himself that funded the royal tomb project.

The significance of this fact is not easy for modern readers to appreciate. However, in many pre-modern civilizations all over the world, the monarch directly personified the state (L'Etat, c'est moi ["I am the state"], Louis XIV of France famously declared). The personal aspect of such a monarch is dissolved into his or her public image so that the monarch is no longer an individual person but a walking anthropomorphic symbol of the nation.[33] In contrast, in Western Han China, the ruler's public life was strictly separate from his private life, so he assumed two roles and lived two lives. In public, he functioned as if he were the highest administrator of the central government; in private, he acted like the most privileged nobleman in the country. In the public realm, the ruler held the highest office of the state, which was "appointed" (by heaven) with the mandate of heaven (*tianming* 天命) to govern the people. It was believed that the position of king was granted by heaven. As long as the mandate of heaven endured, the king would remain king. However, during the late Eastern Zhou period, when the traditional hereditary society was falling apart with the rise of a new bureaucratic society operated on the basis of meritocracy, the idea of an unchangeable mandate of heaven became problematic. Now that any official could be demoted or sacked if they failed in their government duty, one could reasonably assume their superior (the ruler) must also obey the same set of rules: When he did his job well, heaven would keep his position and reward him; when the ruler failed, heaven must punish him and even take back the mandate. This implication that the ruler was a government official who must perform his public duty well enough to keep his job was radical.

This administrative separation was grounded in the conceptual polarity of *si* 私 (private, personal, or individual) and *gong* 公 (public, official, or collective) that was rooted in the changing institutional reality of the late Warring States period when China started to develop a bureaucratic system based on merit rather than on aristocratic lineage.[34] With this development, administrative power began to be concentrated in the hands of the ruler, who reigned over a government that was allegedly charged with taking care of the people (*min* 民). Many intellectuals devoted their thoughts to the question of what constituted good rulership and efficient government. As Yuri Pines has written, during the late Eastern Zhou period, philosophers demonstrated an "ever-stronger pro-centralization and ruler-centered tendency."[35] A centralized government headed by the ruler and run by selected officials was the solution to prevent powerful and wealthy individuals from infringing on the rest of society for private benefit. The ruler, in this picture, was no more than a protector of the public welfare. As is stated in the *Annals of Lü Buwei* text, "The all under heaven is not the all under heaven of one man, but that of all under heaven."[36] But how could the people safely entrust all public power to the ruler without the danger of becoming private slaves of one man? An important part of their argument hinged upon the paradox of *gong*, based on the neutral laws of heaven and earth, and *si*, a subject's private interest. While the fundamental contradiction between the two concepts is unresolvable, the proper way to manage the conflict of interest was to suppress the private in favor of the public. Although for commoners not holding government office, it was a relatively easy job to separate the *si* from the *gong*, for the ruler, who was head of the government and represented the public interest, this required that he must always resist the temptation to satisfy his own private desires, which should be forsaken or sacrificed. Those rulers who were able to do so were admired as sage kings who managed to create a public state (*gongguo* 公國) or even a public world (*tianxia weigong* 天下為公) that was totally just, fair, and harmonious.[37]

Within this philosophical setting, the ruling class of the Western Han, understanding the importance of *gong*, while also recognizing the ruler's undeniable prerogatives for *si*, created a bipartite system that separated the two realms, so that the latter would not intervene into and encroach upon the former. While in the previous Warring States period, the ruler did not distinguish his person (*wang* 王) and house from the state (*guo* 國) and the government, during the Western Han period, the identity of the ruler and the state split into two parts. The ruler's private life was institutionally and legally recognized as separate from his public life.

The Western Han financial system directly reflected this new institutional and legal reality. During the Qin dynasty, capitation taxes (*koufu* 口賦) and land taxes (*tianzu* 田租), the two most important taxes, went into the emperor's private purse—the "lesser treasury" (*Shaofu* 少府) to pay for such public expenses as military and administrative activities, the two major expenses of the government.[38] This made the Qin State function almost like the emperor's household, as Shusun Tong commented, "all under heaven as one family" (*tianxia yijia* 天下一家).[39] Yamada Katsuyoshi recently argued that the separation between *gong* and *si* finances had already been implicit in the Qin dynasty, although the split was not formally established.[40] Although the first three Western Han emperors followed the Qin convention, Liu Sheng's father, Emperor Jing, presumably in the aftermath of the Rebellion of the Seven States in 154 BCE, split the unitary state-family structure into a dualistic structure of state *versus* family that operated under two separate budgets. All expenses of the emperor—including those for meals, clothing, utensils, carriages, medicine, entertainment, dependents (royal concubines and children), coinage, gifts, and other miscellaneous fees—were paid by his majesty's privy purse (*Shaofu* or *Shuiheng duwei*

水衡都尉), but the bills for running the government went to the state treasury, the grand minister for agriculture (*Da sinong* 大司農[41]), who collected land and capitation taxes and spent those funds on public projects such as irrigation and on the military on the people's behalf.[42]

During the Eastern Han period, however, the bipartite system, which had been based on a realistic appreciation of a ruler's human weakness and political duty, was once again replaced by a unitary system, which pretended that the ruler had eliminated his selfishness (like the ancient sages) once and for all.[43] All expenses of the emperor, henceforth, were paid by the state treasury. This "selfless ruler," of course, was an idealized illusion and could not stop the monarch's surging personal desire from eating away at the public welfare. Hans Bielenstein lamented about this as an institutional "retrograding."[44]

From the Eastern Zhou to the Western Han periods, royal tombs gradually transformed their nature from *si* (private) to *gong* (public) in the context of radical social and political reforms.[45] It is within this changing ideological and institutional context that the Western Han royal tombs were defined as "public" rather than "private" projects. Three facts support this view.

First, since the late Warring States period, the construction of royal tombs had fallen into the hands of the state government, which during the Western Han period was separate from the imperial purse and household that only handled the emperor's private matters.[46] For instance, in the tomb of King Cuo of Zhongshan, excavated at the Sanjixiang site, archaeologists discovered a bronze tablet cast with a blueprint of the royal mausoleum. On this tablet, an inscription asserts that the king ordered the state chancellor (*Xiangbang* 相邦), the chief official of the government, to draw a plan of the dimensions of the mausoleum.[47] Similarly, Li Si, the chief minister (*Chengxiang* 丞相) leading the government of the First Emperor of Qin, oversaw the construction of the emperor's necropolis, while the great craftsman (*Dajiang* 大匠), the chief architect of the realm, took care of the technical details.[48] The public role in royal tomb projects deepened during the Western Han. This is because during the Qin dynasty, the office of the great craftsman was probably still under the ruler's own lesser treasury, which was responsible for the monarch's private projects. But during Emperor Jing's reign (157–141 BCE), the descendant office, now called the minister for imperial palace buildings (*Jiangzuo dajiang* 將作大匠), which was in charge of building royal tombs as well as some other major public construction projects such as dams, was transferred to the public sector of the government.[49]

Second, a Western Han imperial or royal mausoleum was probably viewed as public because it was funded by the public revenue of the state rather than the emperor's private purse. Whereas the emperor's own treasury paid most of his expenses, only the costs for building his palaces and tombs were covered by the state treasury.[50] According to Suo Lin 索琳 (fl. early fourth century CE), the budget for constructing (and probably also maintaining) a Western Han mausoleum consumed one-third of the total (public) revenue from "all under heaven"[51] Although the accuracy of this oft-cited account is questionable, it nevertheless acknowledges the expense was taken from the public treasury. The regional kingdoms ran a similar bipartite financial system.[52]

It must be noted that funding such huge projects as royal mausoleums with public funds was not due to a shortage of cash in the ruler's private purse. On the contrary, the emperor's purse was sometimes richer than the state treasury.[53] Therefore, the reason for having the state pay for the mausoleum was political rather than economic. When Emperor Xuan used his own money to pay for the tomb of his nominal predecessor, Emperor Zhao 昭帝 (r. 87–74 BCE), he was later denounced by the Eastern Han scholar Ying Shao 應邵 (fl. late second century CE) for carrying out an "unorthodox policy" (*yizheng* 異政) that confused the public and private sectors.[54] The public funding defines a Western Han mausoleum as a state project for the common good rather than as a private construction only serving the interests of the monarch.[55]

The third and final piece of evidence that the royal tomb was considered public was that the government maintained and administered the royal tomb as a functioning ritual organism consisting of various facilities such as offices, dorms, and kitchens, along with food and water supplies that were staffed by government employees receiving salaries from the state. The First Emperor of Qin further expanded his necropolis at Mt. Li into a bustling "mausoleum town" (*lingyi* 陵邑) for the living, called Liyi 驪邑, which was populated by about thirty thousand households that "attended" or "served" (*feng* 奉) the departed emperor.[56] The residents of the town were neither forced laborers nor paid employees of the government but regular citizens who were granted exemption from regular government labor service for up to ten years.[57] The Western Han emperors and kings creatively embraced such a mausoleum model.[58] Their mausoleum towns were sited next to their funerary parks and grew into local administrative units. Each of these parks was literally a self-sufficient mini-town. Governed by an officially appointed administrator (*ling* 令), each was staffed with full government personnel, including officials, servants, cooks, entertainers, and guards, and even had cemeteries for those who worked there.[59] Some grew so large that their population became greater than that of the capital city of Chang'an itself.[60]

Perhaps because of the three reasons outlined here, the concepts of royal burial and the state became conceptually correlated in Western Han dictionaries. The lexicographer Yang Xiong 揚雄 (53 BCE–18 CE) recorded this in his dictionary titled *The Dialects* (*Fangyan* 方言): "As for the word 'tumulus' (*zhong* 塚) . . . some refer to it as a 'fief' (*cai* 采/寀)."[61] Tall tumuli, whose form might have been derived from the *kurgan* in southern Siberia and the Eurasian steppes during the first millennia BCE,[62] began to appear in Chinese high-ranking cemeteries during the fifth century BCE.[63] The towering tumulus in the public view could easily have become a compelling index, if not a synonym, for the invisible burial hiding beneath it. Yang Xiong further explained: "Because ancient feudal lords possessed fiefs, and upon death, they were buried therein, thus the name [i.e., that a tomb could be called a *cai* 'fief']."[64] In other words, the royal tomb symbolized the king's realm.

BURIAL OBJECTS FROM STATE TREASURIES

While the building of royal tombs was funded directly by the state, the burial objects were of a more complex nature. Despite the fact that many of the objects came from treasuries that served the private sector of the ruler's life, they were nevertheless possessed (if not owned) and managed by government agencies, which further revealed the public side of the royal mausoleum. Excavated seals and inscriptional texts from the tombs at Mancheng and other royal sites support this point.

Almost all seals found in the tombs at Mancheng were official ones.[65] Among them, the two most prominent state offices involved in the preparation of the burial were "minister (or ministry) of state sacrifices of Zhongshan" (*Zhongshan cisi* 中山祠祀) and "vice-director of the palace wardrobe of the Zhongshan State" (*Zhongshan yucheng* 中山御丞).[66]

The first official name, "minister (or ministry) of state sacrifices of Zhongshan" was imprinted on four sealing clays (no. 19) in the front chamber of Dou Wan's tomb. Each clay block measured 2.7 centimeters by 2.6 centimeters and was one centimeter in thickness.[67] The clay was perforated to allow threads to pass through it. Based on their shape and placement, the blocks were presumably sealing clays for some disintegrated lacquer boxes containing the ritual offerings I have analyzed in chapter 2.[68] During the Western Han period, both the emperor and the empress had their own parallel offices of state sacrifices. In the imperial government, that office reported to the chamberlain for ceremonials (*Taichang* 太常), one of the nine ministries (*jiuqing* 九卿) and that was in charge of state sacrifices.[69] In the empress's palace, a synonymous office of state sacrifices was established under the inner lesser treasury (*Zhongshaofu* 中少府) to take care of palace sacrifices.[70] At the Mancheng site, because the seal of the "minister of state sacrifices of Zhongshan" was present only in Dou Wan's tomb, it seems that an affiliation with a parallel inner lesser treasury in Zhongshan may be appropriate, though an affiliation with a chamberlain for ceremonials in Zhongshan cannot be entirely ruled out.[71]

The meaning of the second stamp, "Zhongshan yucheng" is obscure, for this title does not appear in any received text. It has been speculated that this office was probably in charge of the kingdom's treasury, including cash and silk.[72] However, considering the fact that Western Han seals often shorten the official titles by omitting some Chinese characters, Zhao Ping'an argued, I believe correctly, that the phrase "Yucheng" 御丞 might be an abbreviation for "Yufu cheng" 御府丞, or, "vice-director of the palace wardrobe," which reported to the lesser treasury in the parallel Han government.[73] These official stamps indicate that government offices of the Zhongshan kingdom directly handled many of the ritual objects during the royal couple's funerary ceremony.

In addition to the limited number of sealing clays, a larger number of inscriptions made on bronze vessels reiterated the agency of government on the burial objects.

Because of the relative complexity of these inscriptions in comparison with the sealing clays, to pin down the governmental relationship with these objects, it is necessary to first introduce the basic formula for Western Han inscriptions with some concrete examples. An inscription made on an object during the Western Han period usually included the basic information of ownership, medium, type, number, date, and provenance of the inscribed object. In the rear chamber of tomb no. 1, excavators discovered a few lacquer plates laid out on top of a wooden table next to the king's body. Disintegrated as it was, one of these vessels with refined silver inlays contained a whole roast suckling pig.[74] An inscription made on the bottom of the plate identifies this object as the king's food platter.[75]

御。褚飯盤，一。卅七年十月，趙獻。

For royal use. Ramie-cored food platter, one. In the tenth month of the thirty-seventh year, Zhao presented it.

Inscriptions on bronzes from this period followed the same formula except that they often provided the dimensions or weight of the inscribed objects. For example, one bronze vessel entered the same collection together with the previous lacquer food platter:

御。銅金雍甒盆，一。容十斗，盆備。卅七年十月，趙獻。[76]

For royal use. Bronze *pen* basin [as part of] the *yan* steamer, one. Capacity ten *dou*. The *pen* basin is prepared. In the tenth month of the thirty-seventh year, Zhao presented it.

All such inscriptions share a relatively fixed formula: Each begins with the name of the possessor, then goes on to describe the medium, type, and serial number of the object, and finally concludes with the date and the provenance of the acquirement.[77] If the object was made locally rather than purchased from elsewhere, the name of the local artisan or workshop was also specified.

When objects changed hands, the new possessor usually would re-measure and re-number them before putting his or her name or title on them. For example, before entering the empress dowager's palace, the lamp of the palace of lasting trust's first possessor was an aristocrat, a marquis of Yangxin (*Yangxin jia* 陽信家). He started his inscription with the name of his hereditary house:

陽信家。并重二鈞十二斤。七年，第一。[78]

The house of Yangxin. In all it weighs two *jun* and twelve *jin*. In the seventh year, no. 1.

Another bronze *ding* tripod from tomb no. 1 was engraved with the name "Liang family from Mali" 馬里梁氏, indicating its former possessor was a commoner.[79]

In these inscriptions, the most valued information is undoubtedly the possessor because the name of the possessor not only occupied the most privileged position (the beginning) in the inscription but also was the last information to be omitted. Indeed, many other bronze inscriptions from the Mancheng site followed the same formula except with omissions of certain parts. For example, on the lamp of the palace of lasting trust, the aforementioned longer inscription also had its shorter version, which only included the name of one of its possessors: the house of the marquis of Yangxin. This name was repeated six times to reassert its importance, while the artist who ingeniously designed this work was not even mentioned once.

Considering this formula, it is not difficult to determine that, despite a few objects labeled "for royal use" in the king's tomb, the majority of inscribed bronze objects in Mancheng tombs no. 1 and no. 2 were identified as being possessed by the inner treasury of Zhongshan (*Zhongshan neifu* 中山內府), occasionally seen as "treasury of Zhongshan" (*Zhongshan fu* 中山府). A bronze basin dedicated in front of the king's tent in the front chamber of tomb no. 1 has an inscription that reads:

中山內府。銅盆。容二斗，重六斤六兩。第六。卅四年，中郎柳買雒陽。

The inner treasury of Zhongshan. Bronze *pen* basin. Capacity two *dou*, weighing six *jin* and six *liang*. No. 6. In the thirty-fourth year, Liu, gentleman of the palace, bought it in Luoyang.

In another case, a bronze *huo* cauldron entered the same palace treasury five years later:

中山內府。銅鑊，容十斗，重卅一斤。卅九年九月乙酉，工丙造。[80]

The inner treasury of Zhongshan. Bronze *huo* cauldron. Capacity ten *dou*, weighing thirty-one *jin*. On the day of *yiyou* (the twenty-second day) of the ninth month in the thirty-ninth year, craftsman Bing made it.

The meaning of *neifu* in the title *Zhongshan neifu* 中山內府 is unclear.[81] The term appears in extant Western Han texts only twice. In the *Shiji*, it is described as a storehouse for grain.[82] In the *Discourses on Salt and Iron* (*Yantielun* 鹽鐵輪, dated first century BCE) text, *neifu* refers to a storehouse for precious goods.[83] In both instances, it seems the word was a general designation for state treasuries rather than a specific reference to a particular office.

Despite the lack of textual references, the institution of *Zhongshan neifu* was undoubtedly a government agency of the Zhongshan kingdom. The name *neifu* was probably related to a synonymous government agency during the Warring States period, as recorded in the *Rites of Zhou* (*Zhouli* 周禮) text. As one of the three treasuries, the Zhou "inner treasury" (*neifu*) was in charge of various tributes, gifts, fine weapons, and ritual vessels for "the great uses of the state," namely, warfare and sacrifice.[84] Not surprisingly, some of the vessels from the *neifu* in Mancheng tomb no. 1 were indeed gifts or tribute. The aforementioned lacquer plate and bronze *yan* 甗 steamer set that ended up in the inner treasury of Zhongshan (*Zhongshan neifu*) were a gift from Zhao, probably referring to the neighboring kingdom to the south of Zhongshan.[85] Another bronze basin came from Zhongshan's own Lunu 盧奴 County, whose local authorities presented this vessel as a tribute to the central government of Zhongshan.

In the bipartite imperial financial system, as discussed in the previous section, the grand ministry for agriculture (*Da sinong*) managed the empire's public expenses, and the lesser treasury (*Shaofu* 少府) was in charge of the imperial house's private expenses. It was not clear, however, whether the Zhongshan *neifu* was subject to the former or latter's parallel financial institution in the Zhongshan state.

What remains certain, however, is the fact that the inner treasury of Zhongshan, which handled burial objects in both the king and queen's tombs, was in charge of objects unambiguously reserved as the ruler's private expenses. On several bronze lamps, the title "for royal use" and *neifu* coexisted in the inscription, indicating the two institutions might have been closely related:

御銅卮錠一。中山內府。第鵲。[86]

For royal use. Bronze goblet-shaped lamp, one. Inner treasury of Zhongshan. No. Jia.

This overlap suggests that the office of *neifu* might have been similar under the lesser treasury and possibly a local variation of its imperial counterpart, *Zhongfu* 中府 or *Sifu* 私府, reported in imperial annals, which was a government agency that managed the ruler's private expenses.[87]

It is true that only a small portion of burial objects in the Mancheng site were inscribed, and it is also true that not every person in the Han period declared their rights to their possessions by inscribing on them because many objects that remained uninscribed must have had proper owners. However, it is clear that when someone (either an individual or group) did so, the intention to claim their rights was indisputable. Among these inscribed objects, when one was labelled with a personal name or title that did not belong to the maker of the object, the object was probably a private possession; when the object was inscribed with the name of a governmental agency, the object was declared as having official ownership or supervision.

If the inner treasury of Zhongshan was a public treasury like the grand minister for agriculture, then objects inscribed with its name should be public property. But, if this institution functioned like the lesser treasury, which was more likely, then the owner of the objects could possibly be the ruler himself. But, even in this scenario, the way the ruler's property was managed would render the property semipublic during the Western Han period.

In the Western Han era, the properties of the ruler (emperor or king) normally included the mountains, seas, lakes, and rivers within his country. All revenues generated from these sources, in addition to the industrial and commercial taxes, constituted the regular income of the ruler. However, unlike lesser aristocrats and commoners, the ruler—as the head of the central or local government—had to entrust his assets and private income to the lesser treasury for management, which was not a private institution but a public one that operated under imperial laws and statutes. In fact, the *Shaofu* (or lesser treasury) was one of the nine ministries of the government, and its officials received salaries from the grand ministry for agriculture, which was in charge of the empire's public budget.[88] Moreover, as an operating government office, the lesser treasury also had its own public possessions, which were separate from the ruler's private property that it managed. The nature of the lesser treasury as a public institution in charge of the ruler's private property resulted in the ambiguous ownership of the institution's possessions.

The complex nature of the ruler's belongings sometimes even caused confusion among imperial family members. Empress Xu 許 (d. 8 BCE), the principal wife of Emperor Cheng, was the occupant of the Jiaofang Palace (*Jiaofang Dian* 椒房殿), or Inner Palace (*Zhonggong* 中宮). But the emperor issued an edict (*zhao* 詔), which was a legal executive order, to restrict her access to the treasury of her own Jiaofang Palace. Empress Xu wrote a resentful letter to the emperor in protest:

今言無得發取諸官，殆謂未央宮不屬妾，不宜獨取也。言妾家府亦不當得，妾竊惑焉。幸得賜湯沐邑以自奉養，亦小發取其中，何害於誼而不可哉？[89]

Now the edict demands that I must not request and take things from government offices. It was said that I should not take [things] from the Weiyang Palace, because it does not belong to me; but saying I cannot take things even from my household treasury confuses me. I am fortunate to have been awarded a fief of hot water and washing to support myself, and modestly requested things from its inner treasury. So what righteousness would it hurt (for me to do the same to the treasury of the Jiaofang Palace)?

Empress Xu was angry with the imperial edict because she thought of the Jiaofang Palace as her private property and confused the nature of two totally different properties: the Jiafang Palace and her fief. While the latter, funded by taxes on the lands and people, was a property granted legally to her as an individual, the former was essentially a government agency (*guan* 官) assigned to the current empress. The personnel in the Jiaofang Palace were not Ms. Xu's private servants but government employees that received salaries to serve the empress. Unsurprisingly, upon receiving the edict, they "dutifully executed the order" and showed no personal loyalty to Empress Xu. In legal terms, Empress Xu *owned* her fief but only temporarily *possessed* the Jiaofang Palace. If Ms. Xu ceased to be the empress, she would immediately lose her rights to it, as later she did.

Therefore, in the eyes of the commoners, even the ruler's private wealth, in the hands of a government office such as the lesser treasury, might be seen as public property. No wonder some rulers, perhaps unhappy with the restricted power, desired real private wealth for themselves. Emperor Cheng, for one, used his own money to hire a personal entourage and to purchase private vehicles and real estate from private hands. Although this conduct incurred vehement criticism from government officials who blamed him for "behaving like a commoner," the emperor simply ignored the protests.[90] This story demonstrates that a ruler during the Western Han practically had two different financial accounts related to his personal expenses: a state fund managed by the government and a private one under his majesty's direct control. The latter might have originated from personal gifts to the emperor, which after investment, grew into an independent source of income.[91]

These stories inform us that during the Western Han era, emperors, kings, and other members of the ruling house might have financed their daily lives both officially and personally. Bronze inscriptions from the Mancheng site suggest that those objects were from the official account of the ruler, if the inner treasury of Zhongshan was a lesser treasury-affiliated office managing the ruler's private wealth. This means they were not entirely private assets in the modern sense but were of a semipublic nature.

Among royal burials, as far as we can tell from inscriptions, the tombs at the Mancheng site were not isolated cases that were predominantly furnished with official possessions. In fact, in most excavated Western Han royal tombs, as well as in their imperial counterparts near Xi'an, seals and inscriptions suggest a similarly non-private nature for interred objects. For example, in the slightly earlier royal tomb at Shizishan in present-day

Xuzhou, built for a ruler of the Chu kingdom who died in the early second century BCE, excavators encountered a staggering number of more than eighty sealing clays and two hundred actual seals, attesting to the wide involvement of both the central and local Chu government offices (of both civilian and military types) in provisioning the royal tomb.[92] In the Shizishan tomb, whereas some grave goods came from the "great granary of the Chu state" (*Chu taicang* 楚太倉) of the central government, many of them were gifts from the local governments of the kingdom. The government agencies participating in preparing for the royal burial included not only the state's top civilian minister, the "governor of the capital area" (*Neishi* 內史), but also its highest military officer, the "commandant of capital security" (*Zhongwei* 中尉), who belonged unambiguously to the non-private sector of the ruler's life.[93] The ritual and logistical departments were also involved. The Shizishan tomb also contained a seal of the "bureau of Chu state sacrifices" (*Chu cisi* 楚祠祀), the counterpart of the "Zhongshan cisi," and "[director] of the palace wardrobe of Chu" (*Chu yufu* 楚御府), whose position was equivalent to the senior partner of the vice-director of the palace wardrobe [of Zhongshan] mentioned earlier.[94]

Only in rare cases did archaeologists encounter entirely private objects in a royal tomb. For example, a bronze basin for hair washing and another *zhong* 鍾 jar came from another almost contemporary Chu royal tomb at Dongdongshan in Xuzhou. An inscribed label identified this vessel's possessor as Lady Zhao (Zhao Ji 趙姬), a person, rather than a state institution.[95]

During the late Eastern Zhou period, the nature of the material contents in royal tombs shifted from private to public. Before this shift, from the Shang through the early Eastern Zhou periods, most inscribed bronzes mentioned individual names as the makers or owners of the objects. For example, the heaviest bronze tripod ever excavated in China, as well as another 108 bronzes from the same tomb, was labeled with the title of a royal consort—Fu 婦, and her personal name (Hao 好), who was identified as the owner of the vessel.[96] In the tomb of Marquis Yi of Zeng, dated to the early fifth century BCE, 109 bronze objects featured not only the noble title but also the given name (Yi 乙) of the marquis, which was repeated 208 times.[97] On a lavishly ornamented *pan* vessel, which Yi inherited from his ancestor, he scraped his grandfather's name off the inscription and replaced it with his own name.[98] This updating demonstrates the utter importance of identifying an object as one's own possession, separate from that of an ancestor.

178

PART II

However, beginning during the late Eastern Zhou period, personal names of the noble patrons and recipients (usually also the possessors) of bronze vessels disappeared almost entirely from inscriptions. Instead, more and more bronzes were labeled with the names of certain government bureaus that possessed the objects. For example, in King Cuo's tomb at Zhongshan, constructed about two centuries later than that of Marquis Yi, even though the name of the royal deceased was still preserved in a long inscription that commemorated his achievements, his name was absent from most of the objects and was replaced by such government offices as the left state warehouse (*Zuo shi ku* 左使庫) and the right state warehouse (*You shi ku* 右使庫), which might have been either the workshops who produced the objects or the possessors of the objects.[99]

This new trend of de-personalization of burial objects, many of which were possessed by the government, further reinforced the non-private nature of royal or imperial mausoleums, which were not only funded—but also built and administered—by the government.

LAVISH BURIAL AS "THE WAY OF THE SAGES"

The practice of using public revenue and resources to build lavish structures that apparently served but one person (the ruler) and his principal wife was the subject of a now famous debate between two influential Warring States philosophical schools on what justified the ruler making such an astronomical expenditure. Both Mozi and Xunzi shared the common belief that royal burial must essentially be a public matter. And this basic agreement laid the conceptual foundation for the Western Han's institutionalization of royal tombs as a public enterprise separate from the ruler's private business.

Traditionally viewed as a spokesman for the people, particularly the craftsmen, Mozi was morally motivated to raise the question of whether taxes collected from the people were being spent wisely for the benefit of the country. Therefore, his argument was centered on whether lavish burial could bring well-being to individual lives, to the family, and to the state. Xunzi, too, must have felt obliged to defend any righteous public expense that would eventually benefit everyone. In his argument in support of lavish royal expenditure, he never paid any attention to the personal welfare of the rulers themselves but only to the common good for the people and the world.

The three harmonizations of the self, the family, and the state, as represented in the design of the Mancheng site, were the most basic standards by

which a royal tomb was evaluated in the political discourse of the late Warring States to the early Western Han period.

By Mozi's standards, the tombs at the Mancheng site would undoubtedly
fall into the category of "lavish burial" (*houzang* 厚葬) because the material
contents of these tombs, including nested coffins, carriages, and other precious metals, matched Mozi's descriptions of such burials perfectly:

此存乎王公大人有喪者，曰棺槨必重，葬埋必厚，衣衾必多，文繡必繁，丘
隴必巨；存乎匹夫賤人死者，殆竭家室； 存乎諸侯死者，虛車府，然後金玉
珠璣比乎身，綸組節約，車馬藏乎壙，又必多為屋幕。鼎鼓几梴壺濫，戈劍
羽旄齒革，挾而埋之，滿意。

The funeral of a king or high ministers will require several inner and outer coffins,
a deep grave, numerous grave clothes, a large amount of embroidery for decorating the coffins, and a large grave mound. If the family of the deceased happen to be
humble commoners the wealth of the family will be exhausted, and if they are feudal
lords their treasuries will be emptied. After the above articles have been supplied, one
still needs gold, jewels, and pearls to adorn the corpse, and bundles of silk, carriages,
and horses to inter in the grave. In addition, there must be draperies and hangings,
tripods, baskets, tables, mats, vessels, basins, spears, swords, feathers banners, and
articles of ivory and hide to bury with the dead before the requirements are fulfilled.[100]

Mozi told us that these kings, dukes, and other nobles were encouraged
to have lavish burials because many gentlemen during this period argued
that such practices could "benefit the country and the family" (*weishihu guo
jia* 為事乎國家), "manage all under heaven well" (*zhi tianxia* 治天下), and
therefore embodied "the way of the sage kings." Those who practiced lavish
burials proudly claimed: "I am following the way handed down from antiquity by Yao, Shun, Yu, Tang, Wen, and Wu."[101]

When Mozi launched a harsh criticism of the practice of lavish burials,
he built his argument on three levels: the self, the family, and the state (along
with all under heaven). Mozi argued that lavish burials could not enrich the
family (*fujia* 富家), increase the population (*zhong renmin* 眾人民), manage
the government (*zhi xingzheng* 治刑政), or pacify the world (*jin daguo gong
xiaoguo* 禁大國攻小國) (lit. "stop big states from attacking small states").
Condemning the extremely ascetic privations practiced by people during the
mourning period that followed lavish burial rites, Mozi argued that engaging
in luxurious burials could hurt an individual's bodily health, causing "his
ears and eyes to appear dull, his hands and feet lacking in strength, as though

he had lost the use of them," and could make them "sicken and die." With such weakened people, who could hardly perform the duty of bearing children, how was it possible to enrich the family and increase the population? With families poor and the number of people decreasing, it would become even more impossible to govern the state and stop wars. If a practice would not lead to the good of the self, the family, the state, and the world, how could it qualify as "the way of the sage kings"?[102]

The "gentlemen" that the authors of the *Mozi* text confronted were almost surely followers of Confucius. The most radical Confucian defender of lavish burial was arguably Xunzi. Although Xunzi, unlike Mozi, did not directly address the three issues of self, family, and state in his argument, he implied all of them by associating the exhaustive preparation for burials with the "way of the sages":

喪禮者，以生者飾死者也，大象其生以送其死也。故事死如生，事亡如存，終始一也。......事生，飾始也；送死，飾終也；終始具，而孝子之事畢，聖人之道備矣。

The funeral rites use life to ornament death—they make abundant use of semblances of the person's life to send him off in death. Thus, one treats the dead as if still alive, and one treats the departed as if they survive, in order that end and beginning be given one and the same care . . . To serve the living is to ornament the beginning, and to send off the dead is to ornament the end. When end and beginning are both properly arranged, then the tasks of a filial son are fully realized, and the way of the sage is complete.[103]

Xunzi made two major points in the previously quoted passage. First, funerary rites (including burial) were the mirror image of everyday life; second, funerary rites were concrete "ornaments" (*shi* 飾) for the abstract idea of *zhong* 終 (the end), which was then the mirror image of the idea of *shi* 始 (the beginning). Here, he used one of his most important philosophical concepts, "ornament" (*shi*, or in some other contexts, *wen* 文), to describe the funerary rites. Scholars have observed that this concept is peppered throughout Xunzi's text and is used far more frequently in his works than in any other philosophical text of the time. The word *shi*, according to Eastern Han exegetes including Zheng Xuan, refers to the external visual manifestation (*zhangbiao* 章表) of the internal abstract nature.[104] To Xunzi, such visual externalizations had a meaning beyond superficial utility because they were "auspicious" to the overall welfare of the state and people—the ultimate concern of wise rulers, including kings, dukes, and nobles. As a means to maintain good social and political order, ornament was worth the cost.[105] If the peace of all under heaven was in jeopardy, then what was the point of saving money? (Waiting for it to be squandered on warfare?) In fact, Xunzi believed that within the perfected form of the exalted rites hid "explanations that provided for everything."[106]

The same argument about nonpractical but auspicious ornament also applies to burial, an essential part of the funerary rites. From Xunzi's viewpoint, these seemingly useless ornaments were utterly essential to the practice of the way of the sages because burial was a meaningful and symbolic continuation of life, with a general purpose "to match what is fitting and turns out well and good."[107] To Xunzi, the ways of the sages (*shengren* 聖人) and that of sage kings (*shengwang* 聖王) were one and the same, both serving to acquire order in society and "unify the world."[108] While Mozi considered the ascetic requirement to starve one's body during the funerary rites irrational and harmful, Xunzi took it as the utmost ornament of humanity, "something in which the hundred kings are identical."[109] Thus, unlike Mozi, who measured the effect of lavish burial by material benefits, Xunzi measured it by its moral or didactic results.

But how did Xunzi answer the question Mozi raised: By what means could funerary art, as an ornament of death (and, by extension, life), exert its moral impact on the people and manifest the way of the sages? Xunzi laid down a general principle, resemblance (*xiang* 象), and gave a few examples that were popular during his time:

故壙壟、其貌象室屋也；棺槨、其貌象版蓋斯象拂也；無帾絲歶縷翣，其貌以象菲帷幬尉也。抗折，其貌以象槾茨番閼也。

The appearance of the tomb resembles a home and dwelling. The inner and outer coffins resemble the front, back, sides, and covering of a chariot. The coverings and decorations for the coffins and funerary cart resemble curtains and canopy. The bracing for the burial pit resembles walls, roofing, fencing, and door and window coverings.[110]

The word *xiang* means not only physical resemblance but also all kinds of metaphorical and metonymical similitude. More importantly, Xunzi emphasized that in addition to these detailed resemblances, the burial must in general "greatly resemble the deceased's life" (*daxiang qishi* 大象其生) to send him off for death. But what did he mean by "great resemblance"? Did the emphatic modifier "great" (*da*) in the phrase imply the negation of smallness (*xiao* 小)? Mengzi 孟子 (ca. 372–289 BCE), for example, frequently distinguished "great men" (*daren* 大人), the rulers, from "small men" (*xiaoren* 小人), the ruled. The former should constantly be responsible for the "great" business of the state welfare, while the latter might worry only about the "small" issue of their bodily benefits.[111] In the *Laozi* text, otherwise known as the *Dao De Jing*, the same phrase *daxiang* is glossed as "the great way" (*dadao* 大道) of governing a country.[112] If this interpretation stands equally for Xunzi's concept of "great resemblance," then what aspect of life was considered "great" and worth imitating?

As a critical reader of the Daoist works, Xunzi would not have ignored the distinctive phrasing of "daxiang" as the greatest form that "has no shape" with the power of pacifying all under heaven in the *Laozi*, one of the most influential philosophical texts during the late Eastern Zhou period. According to the *Laozi* text, "Grasp the great image and the world will come; coming and encountering no harm, it will settle in great peace."[113] The Xiang'er 想尔 commentary offered a political interpretation of this passage: "The king upholds the righteous law and imitates the great way. All under heaven comes to follow him."[114]

Although it remains unclear whether Xunzi had these meanings in mind when he borrowed the *Laozi* phrasing, it is nonetheless clear that Xunzi used this term to refer to an overall image of the deceased that ultimately corresponded with the way of the sages, rather than only to specific forms in the deceased's daily life.

Xunzi criticized Mozi for his failure to grasp the significance of *xiang* or *daxiang* in the burial, which translates death ritual into daily ritual, a visible ornament of the invisible way of the sage kings. Mozi only saw the value of burials exclusively on a material and economic level, but Xunzi understood burials on a moral and political level, where they were invaluable. To Xunzi, since human nature was basically bad, material wealth would only corrupt people further if it was not used as a means of self-salvation by educating people to go against their wayward nature and pursue good deeds. Such edification was only possible through rituals (*li* 禮) created by the sages. So, it is understandable why Xunzi paid no attention to the high material cost of implementing the rituals Mozi worried about. Compared with the ultimate order and harmony of the world, such material cost was trivial.

"The way of the sages" (*shengren zhidao* 聖人之道), or "the way of the sage kings" (*shengwang zhidao* 聖王之道), was one of the most important

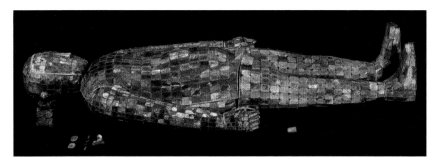

FIGURE 1.3 Jade suit from Mancheng tomb no. 1, Mancheng, Hebei, ca. 113 BCE. Courtesy of Hebei Museum, Shijiazhuang.

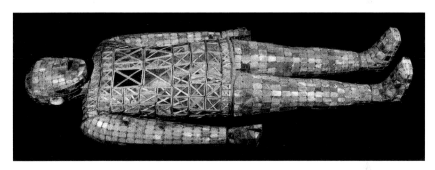

FIGURE 2.2 Jade suit of Dou Wan, Mancheng tomb no. 2, Mancheng, Hebei, ca. 118–104 BCE. Courtesy of Hebei Museum, Shijiazhuang.

FIGURE 2.7 Lamp of the Palace of Lasting Trust from the rear chamber of Mancheng tomb no. 2, Mancheng, Hebei, ca. 118–104 BCE. Courtesy of Hebei Museum, Shijiazhuang.

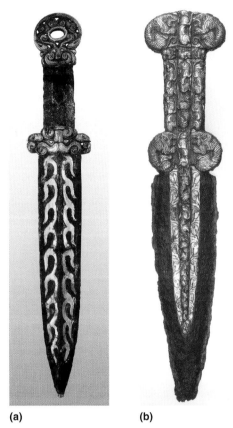

(a)   **(b)**

FIGURE 3.3 (a) Iron short sword with gold guard, hilt, and foil, Mancheng tomb no. 1, Mancheng, Hebei, ca. 113 BCE. Courtesy of Hebei Museum, Shijiazhuang; (b) Iron sword from Arzhan tomb no. 2, Tuva, Russia, seventh century BCE. After Konstantin V. Čugunov, Hermann Parzinger, and Anatoli Nagler, *Der skythenzeitliche Fürstenkurgan Aržan 2 in Tuva* (Mainz: P. Von Zabern, 2010), pl. 40.1. Courtesy of German Archaeological Institute, Berlin.

(a)

(b)

FIGURE 3.16 Wool carpet from Pazyryk Kurgan V, Russia, 252–238 BCE, and details: (a) roaming stag, (b) horseman.

topics among philosophers in early China.[115] The roles of a sage king, as agreed upon among the philosophers of various schools, generally would include cultivating the self, taking no deliberate action, and following the way of heaven, which is connected to the ultimate goal of bringing peace to the world.[116] An ideal king was required to have pacified his own self before extending that pacification to others—first to the family, then to the state, and eventually, to all under heaven. As we have discussed, this perfectly sums up the three major ideological issues present in the Mancheng tombs.

In reality, both Mozi and Xunzi won supporters for their positions. Emperor Wen, Liu Sheng's grandfather, chose to be buried in a stone casket and instructed that his tomb must be furnished in a thrifty manner.[117] This example was imitated by King Xiang of Chu 楚襄王 (d. 113 BCE), who left an epitaph carved on a stone cube that blocked the entry into his monumental cliff-cut tomb at Xuzhou. The inscription directly addresses the future visitor:

楚古尸王通於天，述："葬，棺郭不布瓦鼎盛器，令群臣已葬去服，毋金玉器。後世賢大夫幸視此書，如目君也。仁者悲之。"

The departed King Yi of the Chu who has reached heaven had related: "Do not put ceramic tripods or food containers in the burial. Let the ministers remove their mourning costumes right after the entombment. There is neither gold nor jade. If a virtuous gentleman in the future happens to see these words, it shall be like seeing the Lord himself. Beneficent people, grieve for him![118]

In accordance with this, in the sole un-robbed chamber of this largely plundered tomb, excavators spotted only a handful of simple ceramic vessels and figurines.

However, these thrifty burials constituted only a minority of royal and noble burials. It seems that most Eastern Zhou, Qin, and Western Han rulers were buried in lavish tombs just as Mozi had cited his opponents' proud claim, "The gentlemen of the central states are continuing to practice them (lavish burials) and not giving them up."[119] Furthermore, archaeologists have discovered that the practice of lavish burials actually increased during the Qin and Han periods. The First Emperor of Qin built a vast mausoleum larger than fifty-six square kilometers, nearly twice the size of the lower capital of the Yan State, the largest city in existence from the Warring States period so far unearthed.[120] In this as yet to be fully explored tomb, archaeologists have made numerous findings, including the renowned terra-cotta army pits, not to mention those unknown treasures still hiding in the emperor's secret tomb chamber thirty meters deep in the ground.[121] Emulating the Qin example, the Western Han emperors planned enormous mausoleums for themselves and spent about a third of the entire imperial revenue, by one estimate, on constructing and maintaining them. Emperor Wen, whose frugal tomb was mentioned previously and who was the only Western Han emperor with a will recorded in our sources, was perhaps too eccentric for Sima Qian to ignore. Archaeological work in the past few decades has largely confirmed the fact that the practice of luxurious royal and noble burials was pervasive throughout the Qin and Western Han periods.

During the early Western Han period, the debate between Mozi and Xunzi over lavish burial was interpreted as an ideological battle between the Mohists and Daoists on one side and the Confucians on the other. The authors of the *Huainanzi* assert:

夫弦歌鼓舞以為樂，盤旋揖讓以修禮，厚葬久喪以送死，孔子之所立也，而墨子非之。

Singing to stringed instruments and dancing to drums so as to make music; turning, bestowing, diminishing, yielding so as to practice the rites; having lavish burials and lengthy mourning so as to send off the dead. These were established by Confucius, but Mozi opposed them.[122]

In another story in the same book, Mozi is portrayed as a rebellious student of Confucius, but the contradiction remains the same:

墨子學儒者之業，受孔子之術，以為其禮煩擾而不說，厚葬靡財而貧民，服傷生而害事，故背周道而行夏政。

Master Mo studied the work of Confucians and received the techniques of Confucius. [However,] he regarded their rituals to be worrisome and inappropriate, their lavish funerals to be wasteful of resources, impoverishing the people, while their lengthy mourning periods harmed life and impeded undertakings. Thus Master Mo rejected the Way of the Zhou dynasty and used the regulations of the Xia dynasty.[123]

During the later Western Han period, the fight over lavish burial continued between what Michael Loewe has called the "Modernists" and the "Reformers," with the former criticizing the latter just as Mozi criticized the Confucians.[124]

The public debate about lavish burial during late Eastern Zhou times was in part stimulated by the increasingly public nature of the royal tombs, a phenomenon that fully matured during the Western Han. Had the tomb simply been the ruler's private property supported by the ruler's own funds, it would have been inappropriate for Mozi and Xunzi to intervene. During the Western Han period, with stricter divisions between the public and private zones of the ruler's life, and with the royal burial allocated to the public zone just like palaces or government buildings, any decisions the ruler made about the tomb had to be made public. Understandably, this publicly sponsored architectural space had to comply with the ruler's public persona. As I will continue to explore in chapter 5, the ideas expressed in the tombs at the Mancheng site match up coherently with Liu Sheng's political ideology and image, as reported in his official biographies and tomb inscriptions.

Chapter Five

THE KING OF PEACE

Although royal tombs during the Western Han period were state projects, it is not yet known how deeply Liu Sheng—the head of the Zhongshan state—was involved in planning the tombs at the Mancheng site. To what extent did the king influence the design of the tombs? Did he introduce (or authorize the introduction of) his ideas into the tombs at the Mancheng site? These are difficult questions to answer because Liu Sheng's original instructions to the officials in charge of the project no longer survive. However, we can investigate whether any comparisons can be made between the deceased's ideas, recorded in various textual materials, and those expressed in the tomb designs preserved in the archaeological site. If we can find a plausible link, then we might be able to tackle the original questions and make an informed assessment of Liu Sheng's role in and contribution to the tomb project.

In this chapter, I argue that Liu Sheng's political ideology, epitomized by his official posthumous title, "Jing Wang" 靖王 (king of peace), is in accord with the organizing principles of royal tombs—harmonizing the self, the family, and the state—that I have analyzed earlier in this book. Liu Sheng's political thought, preserved piecemeal in the transmitted texts and entombed inscriptions at the Mancheng site, mingled Huang-Lao and Confucian teachings, both of which generally emphasized peace and harmony. This suggests that Liu Sheng not only might have overseen the construction of his own tomb as a state project but also might have identified ideologically with its design.

To support this argument, it is first necessary to reconstruct Liu Sheng's political ideology. Fragmentary as they are, extant textual sources, both received and excavated, jointly paint a picture of Liu Sheng as a deft and successful ruler and politician, recognized as a peacemaker who held his country together. He was a practitioner of two seemingly contradictory political ideologies: Huang-Lao, a school of political thought that advocated "rule through taking no deliberate action" (*wuwei erzhi* 無為而治), and Confucianism, which urged rulers to take an active role in governance.

In reconstructing Liu Sheng's public image, obscured by the passage of time, it is necessary to closely read relative textual sources, including his two biographies in the received versions of the *Shiji* and the *Hanshu* and a group of bronze inscriptions interred in Mancheng tomb no. 2. These texts were not from the same source or by the same author. The biographies were written by two official historians, Sima Qian and Ban Gu, but the authors of the inscriptions are anonymous. Nor were the texts written to reflect the thoughts of one individual or one particular philosophic school. Sima Qian and Ban Gu each highlighted different aspects of Liu Sheng's life and career that mirrored their own philosophical or ideological agendas, while the bronze inscriptions synthesized contemporary doctrines of different schools of thought. However, a comparison of all these different sources may free us from the danger of prioritizing one narrative over another and allow us to acquire a variety of different perspectives that might eventually lead us as close as possible to the truth.

THE PACIFIER AND THE PACIFIED: LIU SHENG AS A HUANG-LAO RULER

Liu Sheng's identification with Huang-Lao philosophy is implied in his official records. Upon his death, the imperial court awarded him the posthumous honorific title "Jing Wang" (literally, "the pacified king" or "the king who pacifies," or more lyrically, "the king of peace"). The operative word *jing* 靖 (pacified, pacifier, or peace) in Liu Sheng's posthumous title represents the ultimate standard of rulership in the eyes of Huang-Lao ideology.

The school of Huang-Lao 黃老, an abbreviated compound of Huangdi 黃帝 (the yellow emperor) and Laozi 老子, influenced imperial ideology during the early Western Han period.[1] As Sima Qian describes in the *Shiji*, Huang-Lao (otherwise known as Daojia 道家) was a synthesis of many existing schools of thought: "They follow the general tendency of the Naturalists (i.e., Daoists), select the best from the Confucians and Mohists, and adopt the essentials of the Terminologists and the Legalists."[2] This school claimed that because the natural way (*dao* 道) gave rise to natural law (*fa* 法), which further defined human order, a good ruler must respect and obey natural law without meddling with it.[3] A breakthrough in understanding the nature of Huang-Lao thought came when a silk manuscript identified by scholars as the *Four Classics of the Yellow Emperor* (*Huangdi sijing* 黃帝四經) was excavated from Mawangdui tomb no. 3 in 1973.[4] If, as Tang Lan argued, these books had already obtained the status of classics by the reign of Emperor Jing, it is very likely that Liu Sheng was familiar with them.[5] In addition to the Mawangdui silk manuscript, a number of transmitted texts that originated during the late Eastern Zhou period, including the *Guanzi, Hanfeizi, Shenzi* 申子, and the *Annals of Lü Buwei* were associated with or influenced by this school of thought. During the Western Han period, the *Huainanzi* text that Liu An edited sometime before 139 BCE was believed to be the most important Huang-Lao work.[6]

Huang-Lao ideology was crystallized in the word *jing* 靖 in Liu Sheng's honorific posthumous title, which had relatively fixed definitions. In the *Rules for Posthumous Titles* (*Shifa* 諡法 or *Shifa jie* 諡法解, dated to the third to first centuries BCE)—a text for selecting (or at least explaining) the posthumous titles given to rulers (now incorporated as part of the *Lost Book of Zhou*, or *Yizhoushu* 逸周書, text)—Liu Sheng's title, *jing*, possessed three definitions related to the discourse of Huang-Lao philosophy.[7]

The first meaning describes the pliancy of governing strategies: "pacifying the masses by gentle virtue." Unlike other apparently synonymous titles in the manual, including *ping* 平 ("placating [without inner virtue]"), *yi* 夷 ("suppressing by force"), or *ding* 定 ("settling [through the use of schemes]"), *jing* emphasizes sincere and benevolent rule of the people rather than a forcible approach. Furthermore, in transmitted texts, the word *jing* has a connotation of bringing turmoil to an end (Table 5.1).

The other two meanings of the word *jing* listed in the manual describe the tranquility and serenity of the ruler's mind. In both cases, the character 靖 can be written alternatively as *jing* 静 (quiet or silent) or *qing* 清 (clear and clean).[8] The second definition found in the manual, "practicing self-restraint and seldom speaking," suggests a state of "taking no action," as would be required of a Huang-Lao sage. Only sages were worthy of the praise of *gongji* 恭己, "practicing self-restraint," which refers to the political philosophy of ruling without intervening in anything beyond the ruler's own person.[9] The third definition found in the manual, "being tolerant and happy with a good end (i.e., until a

TABLE 5.1
Some posthumous titles in the *Rules for Posthumous Titles* text

Title	Meaning
Jing 靖 (the one who pacifies)	柔德安眾曰靖
	Pacifying the masses by gentle virtue
	恭己鮮言曰靖
	Practicing self-restraint and seldom speaking
	寬樂令終曰靖
	Being tolerant and happy with a good end (i.e., until a good death)
Ping 平 (the who one placates)	治而無眚曰平
	Ruling without errors
	執事有制曰平
	Administering through regulations
Yi 夷 (the one who suppresses)	剋殺秉政曰夷
	Holding power through conquering and killing
	安心好静曰夷
	Calming the mind and being fond of quietude
Ding 定 (the one who settles)	大慮静民曰定
	Pacifying the people through great schemes
	安民大慮曰定
	Calming the people through great schemes
	純行不爽曰定
	Being pure of conduct without error
	安民法古曰定
	Pacifying the people by modeling oneself on antiquity
Jing 敬 (the one who respects)	夙夜警戒曰敬
	Being alert day and night
	合善典法曰敬
	Harmonizing and refining the canons and statutes
Su 肅 (the one who is serious)	剛德克就曰肅
	Being tough and virtuous for success and achievement
	執心決斷曰肅
	Being uncompromising and decisive

good death)," in a similar way, highlights a natural, easy demeanor—a readily forgiving altitude toward the self and others. In all, the concept of *jing* describes a quiet ruler who brought peace to his people in a gentle way.

Regarding the state and the self, the three meanings of *jing* presented in the *Rules for Posthumous Titles* text are united in the philosophy of the Huang-Lao school. In the opening chapter of the *Huainanzi* text, "Originating in the Way" (*Yuandao* 原道), the three definitions of *jing*—pliancy, tranquility, and serenity—are brought together in one sentence to describe the essential state of nature without violence, harshness, or agitation:

是故清靜者，德之至也；而柔弱者，道之要也; 虛無恬愉者，萬物之用也。

Clarity and tranquility (*jing* 靜) are the perfections of Potency; pliancy (*rou* 柔) and suppleness are the essentials of the Way; empty Nonexistence and calm serenity (*tianyu* 恬愉) are the ancestors of the myriad things.[10]

The three natural qualities of being tranquil, pliant, and serene (imagine a deep, peaceful lake as an appropriate metaphor) are the common characteristics of not only the universe but also of the sage kings. In the *Guanzi* text, the sage kings cultivated themselves to imitate the natural way and law and became the embodiment of the natural way (*dao*) and potency (*de*): "Tranquil as they are, they maintained good order; serene as they are, they gained respect."[11] By imitating nature, the sage must first be pacified internally (mentally) before he could pacify the external world and other people.

The Western Han authority was aware of the Huang-Lao implications of the word *jing* as discussed in the *Huainanzi*. Liu An, a loyal follower of Huang-Lao, presented the *Huainanzi* text to Emperor Wu in 139 BCE, shortly after the latter had ascended the imperial throne, in an attempt to indoctrinate the new emperor to the ideas of Huang-Lao. The emperor fell in love with this text and secretly hid it under his pillow.[12] This historical episode suggests that Emperor Wu, the endorser of Liu Sheng's posthumous title, must have understood what it meant to call someone *jing* 靖/靜 (or *qing* 清) in Huang-Lao thought.

But how does this posthumous title objectively reflect Liu Sheng's own deeds and thoughts? Selecting an official posthumous title for a departed emperor, king, or high-ranking official was a very serious political event during the Western Han period. First introduced during the Western Zhou period, a posthumous honorific title was the official evaluation of a nobleman's lifelong political performance. In the literature of the Han dynasty, a posthumous title, usually composed of one to two words, was supposed to sum up the deceased's reputation during his or her lifetime.[13] In his commentary to the *Book of Poetry*, the exegete Zheng Xuan further emphasized that this designation ought to be a meticulous and thorough summary of the recipient's "every deed from beginning to end."[14] Once decided, no further alteration was usually allowed. For better or worse, those one or two words constituted the final judgment of the deceased's life and would forever describe him or her in historical archives, ancestral rituals, court ceremonials, or on other formal occasions. Therefore, the title often was selected to reflect the opinions of the highest government officials. For example, three days after the burial of Liu Bang, the first emperor of the Western Han, the new emperor ascended the throne and summoned a meeting in the imperial ancestral temple to make a decision on the departed emperor's posthumous title. At this meeting, the ministers collectively chose "Gao" 高 (meaning "the highest") to crystalize the lofty deeds of the dynasty founder.[15] In Liu Sheng's day, the procedure for selecting a posthumous title for a departed ruler or noble was standardized: After a regional king had died, the grand herald (*Da honglu* 大鴻臚) in charge of imperial ceremonies would check the deceased's conduct against the many potential titles listed in such manuals as the extant *Rules for Posthumous Titles* text. When different opinions were expressed, high ministers were called in for discussion until the final decision was made. Although many posthumous titles focus on the merits rather than the faults of the deceased person, the fact that these titles were selected based on a fixed procedure—a book of rules—and sometimes open discussions demanded that they be politically appropriate and reasonable.

Indeed, awarding the title Jing to Liu Sheng was more or less grounded in the king's political deeds as recorded in the *Shiji* and *Hanshu*. One of the three definitions of the posthumous title, "pacifying the masses by gentle virtue," directly matches Liu Sheng's historical mission and achievement in governing the Zhongshan region.

From the very beginning, Liu Sheng's mission was to maintain peace in a frontier region close to the northern border of the Han Empire. It was a remarkable feat for Liu Sheng to successfully rule his kingdom for forty-two years because it was not an easy task being up against two major enemies: the bellicose Xiongnu beyond the frontier and an uncurbed local population within the boundaries of the kingdom. The latter posed an even more serious threat than the former. One of the largest rebellions during the Western Han period started in the first month of 154 BCE, when seven of the most powerful regional kingdoms launched a coordinated military insurgence (historiographically known as the Rebellion of Seven Kingdoms or *qiguo zhiluan* 七國之亂), with the fate of the empire hanging in the balance.[16] Although the rebels were soon crushed and the empire rescued, Emperor Jing's shock and resentment over the overt betrayal did not easily heal.

In the immediate aftermath of this event, the emperor dismembered one of the largest rebellious states, the Zhao 趙 Kingdom (located in what is now Hebei in North China), into six much smaller kingdoms.[17] The harshest and most ironic revenge the emperor took against the rebels, however, was his plan of hammering out a new kingdom of Zhongshan, right in the heartland of Zhao—the namesake of the old Warring States polity that had destroyed the original Zhongshan, its irreconcilable foe, in 296 BCE (maps 2–3). With this strategy, the emperor hoped to forge a reliable and strong ally in this hostile territory by "restoring" his enemy's bitterest foe. The revival of Zhongshan was part of the emperor's greater political scheme of securing imperial control of the rebellious region and its people once and for all.

But behind Emperor Jing's strategic restoration of Zhongshan was a greater fear that China might slip back into the old age of division and civil war seen during the Eastern Zhou dynasty. This was a period when, in Sima Qian's lament, "Rituals were discarded and music was ruined" (*lifei yuehuai* 禮廢樂壞).[18] Although the chaos ended in 221 BCE with the First Emperor of Qin using military force to crush the other six rival states and unify China into the first bureaucratic empire, the First Emperor's iron-fist policy proved to be unsustainable. Only three years after the emperor's death, the peace was shattered by a series of rebellions in the eastern commanderies. In 207 BCE, the rebels took the Qin capital and ended once and for all the dream of "great peace" (*taiping* 太平) that the First Emperor had proclaimed.[19]

The job of restoring peace in Zhongshan fell to Liu Sheng who, by all measures, succeeded. Some evidence suggests that he closely cooperated with the imperial government to defend the empire's northern frontier. In 135 BCE, after Emperor Wu settled a military conflict between the Minyue 閩越 and Nanyue 南越 kingdoms in the south, subjugating both, he was free to turn his attention to the north. Immediately after this policy change, Liu Sheng uncharacteristically increased the frequency of his visits to the imperial court (*chaoqing* 朝請), a practice usually scheduled for the beginning (tenth) month of the year.[20] Before 138 BCE, Liu Sheng visited every eight years; but during 133 and 132 BCE, Liu Sheng personally reported to Emperor Wu in two consecutive years, each time making a two-thousand-kilometer round-trip journey.[21] This suddenly intensified communication between the emperor and the king was most likely due to preparations for war against the Xiongnu. The conflict began in the spring of 133 BCE, just three months after Liu Sheng's report. This military action was partially launched from the Dai 代 commandery, located between the Xiongnu confederation and the

Zhongshan kingdom.[22] It would have been Liu Sheng's responsibility to offer logistical support for the Han imperial army.[23]

Another aspect of Liu Sheng's posthumous title, "being tolerant and happy with a good end," also matches Sima Qian's biographical summation of Liu Sheng as a person—a man who enjoyed life and cared little about government affairs. This fits with teachings from the Huang-Lao school that encouraged rulers to "take no deliberate actions" (*wuwei* 無為 or *buwei* 不為).[24] Although Sima Qian did not directly mention Huang-Lao in his biographical record of Liu Sheng, the historian nevertheless implied as much by placing him in contrast with his brother, Liu Pengzu 劉彭祖, King of Zhao (r. 154–92 BCE):

勝為人樂酒好內，有子枝屬百二十餘人。常與兄趙王相非，曰：「兄為王，專代吏治事。王者當日聽音樂聲色。」趙王亦非之，曰：「中山王徒日淫，不佐天子拊循百姓，何以稱為藩臣！」

As a person, Liu Sheng was fond of alcohol and sex and had more than 120 descendants. He and his older brother, [Liu] Pengzu, King of Zhao, often criticized each other. He (Liu Sheng) said, "Elder brother, as a king, you rule by handling administrative affairs for your officials. As kings, we should listen to music and enjoy women every day!" The King of Zhao rebutted this, saying, "You, the King of Zhongshan, only lead a lustful life without assisting the son of heaven to comfort and nurture the people. How can you deserve the title of 'vassal'?"[25]

At first glance, this description does not seem to match the lofty image of Liu Sheng represented by his honorific title and seems almost like a caricature of a licentious and irresponsible ruler, a king who brazenly indulged in excessive daily drinking and sex without the slightest interest in the serious work of governing. In addition, he even shamelessly justified his "misconduct" to his royal peers. But, in fact, this superficial reading is a misinterpretation. Sima Qian actually was commenting on the king's Huang-Lao philosophy, which held that kings should enjoy music and women instead of meddling in the business of bureaucrats; namely, they should "act through taking no deliberate action" (*wuwei wei* 無為為).[26] By lining up the four concepts of "melodies" (*yin* 音), "music" (*yue* 樂), "sounds" (*sheng* 聲), and "women" (*se* 色), Liu Sheng's statement in the debate with his brother recalled a familiar passage titled "Stressing the Self" (*Zhong ji* 重己) in the *Annals of Lü Buwei* text, in which the author articulated the importance of the ruler cherishing his life: "Now my life is something that I possess, and the benefits

I enjoy from it are indeed supreme." One of the secrets the sage kings had for prolonging their lives was following life's natural course without falling into the trap of desire. This included the enjoyment of sounds, women, melodies, and music (*sheng se yin yue*) to the extent that it was "sufficient to give repose to their inborn natures and to amuse."[27]

Liu Sheng's criticism of Liu Pengzu's "handling administrative affairs" for his officials reflects another principle in his political philosophy. Huang-Lao thought held that "sovereign and subject are divided in their differing responsibilities."[28] The former selects capable ministers and "clarifies the principles," while the latter "attend to their tasks" by laboring with their minds and bodies. This division of labor was a result of rational calculation rather than classism. According to the *Guanzi* text, "If the prince exercises his own skills, he will lack good judgment."[29] Why? The author of the *Annals of Lü Buwei* text offered the answer: "If the ruler of men enjoys performing the tasks of government himself, those charged with the responsibilities will ignore them and simply agree with what the ruler does. Since they agree with what the ruler does, should he be in error, the ruler would have no means to criticize what was done."[30] When the ruler lacks good judgment, his authority will be weakened and the administration will end up in disorder and disaster.

This teaching was closely related to the meaning of Liu Sheng's posthumous title, *jing*, in the Huang-Lao context. In the "Art of Rulership" (*Zhushu xun* 主術訓) chapter of the *Huainanzi* text, a ruler who lets his ministers take the workload is one that is mentally "clear and quiet" (*qingjing* 清静): "The ruler's techniques [consist of] establishing non-active management and carrying out wordless instructions. Quiet and tranquil, he does not move; by [even] one degree, he does not waver; adaptive and compliant, he relies on his underlings; dutiful and accomplished, he does not labor."[31] This passage would be a perfect footnote to Liu Sheng's posthumous title.

Thus, it is clear that Liu Sheng's indulgence in drinking and sex was not a sign of moral decadence but marked his practice of the Huang-Lao teaching, "taking no actions." The same practice was common among many of the most powerful politicians of the early Western Han period, who followed the Huang-Lao teachings wholeheartedly. When Cao Shen 曹参 (d. 190 BCE), a faithful student of Huang-Lao, succeeded Xiao He 蕭何 (ca. 257–193 BCE) and became the chief minister of the empire, he maintained the old way of administration and followed Xiao He's regulations in every respect.[32] What is more, Cao Shen "drank alcohol day and night." When his staff or guests tried to stop him, he treated them to alcohol until the visitors got drunk and could not speak either.[33] According to Sima Qian, Cao's successor, Chen Ping 陳平 (d. 178 BCE), indulged in exactly the same manner as his predecessor.[34] Instead of dealing with administrative affairs, Chen Ping "drank alcohol during the day and had sex with women at night."[35] These descriptions could apply to Liu Sheng as well. The archaeological discovery of dozens of large wine jars and pots and three life-sized silver or bronze replicas of the male phallus (possibly sexual toys) in Liu Sheng's tomb are a perfect footnote to these stories of drinking and sex.[36]

Therefore, rather than quarreling with his brother about personal habits, Liu Sheng actually was making a philosophical argument from the Huang-Lao perspective while blaming his brother for not executing rulership in the right way and for confusing his duty with that of the ministers.

Equally well-educated, Liu Pengzu acted from the philosophical perspective of Confucianism. "Loving to perform clerkship" (*hao wei li shi* 好為 吏事), this king of Zhao believed that a good ruler should personally execute his office rather than entrusting it to his staff.[37] He blamed Liu Sheng for "not assisting the son of heaven to comfort and nurture the people" and for not performing his duty as a "vassal." These two accusations remind us of some arguments presented in the *Xunzi* text. In the "Correct Judgment" (*Zhenglun* 正論) chapter, Xunzi expressed a similar idea when he insisted that, whereas the son of heaven was entitled to an easy, comfortable life without laboring, the vassals, instead, should "walk rapidly below the hall" as servants wrestling with concrete government affairs.[38] In the "Enriching the State" (*Fuguo* 富國) chapter, Xunzi used the same phrase, *fuxun* 拊循 ("comfort and nurture"), as Liu Pengzu did to show the ruler's attention to the people.[39] Unlike an actionless ruler of the Huang-Lao school, a Confucian ruler should always offer active and passionate service, as was suggested in a couplet in the *Book of Poetry*, "When among any of the people there was a death, I crawled on my knees to help them."[40]

Not coincidentally, upon his death, Liu Pengzu received a posthumous honorific title, "Jing-Su" 敬肅, which held a far different meaning from Liu Sheng's. In the *Rules for Posthumous Titles*, the title *jing* 敬 (the one who respects) denotes "being alert day and night" and "harmonizing and refining the canons and statutes"; the definitions of *su* (the one who is serious) include: "being tough and virtuous for success and achievement" and "being uncompromising and decisive." In his biography, Liu Pengzu is described as a character who personally led squads patrolling the streets at night, studied laws, and who never hesitated to use all possible means to achieve his political objectives.⁴¹

Therefore, in Sima Qian's account, Liu Sheng personified the Huang-Lao ideology, while Liu Pengzu opposed it. The former followed Huang-Lao teachings and identified himself as an independent "master" (*zhu* 主) or regional "lord" (*jun* 君). The latter, while identifying himself as a minister or vassal of the son of heaven (i.e., the Han emperor), was closer to the position of Confucianism (*Ru* 儒), which advised the ruler to take active personal actions (*youwei* 有為) to serve the people, even if those efforts might be in vain. The seemingly trivial quarrel between the two brothers reflects the ideological battle between these two different schools of thought during the early Western Han period. According to Hans van Ess, "The bulk of biographies of persons living in the second century B.C., as transmitted by *Shiji* and *Hanshu*, can be neatly divided into two groups. One group contains the members of the Huang-Lao faction, the other one those of the 'Ru,' the so-called 'Confucians,' and also of the 'Legalists' ('Fa')."⁴²

It is possible that Liu Sheng's dramatic pose—as a Huang-Lao champion against Liu Pengzu's Confucian ideology in the *Shiji*—might be partially caused by his biographer's personal sympathy with the Huang-Lao faction and his dislike of Confucianism. Through his father's mouth, Sima Qian enthusiastically praised Huang-Lao thought as being "adequate," "concise," and "easy":

道家使人精神專一，動合無形，澹足萬物，其為術也，因陰陽之大順，采儒墨之善，撮名法之要，與時遷徙，應物變化，立俗施事，無所不宜，指約而易操，事少而功多。

The Daoists (Huang-Lao) enable the numinous essence within people to be concentrated and unified. They move in unison with the Formless and provide adequately for all living things. In deriving their techniques, they follow the grand compliances of the Naturalists, select the best of the Confucians and Mohists, and extract the essentials of the Terminologists and Legalists. They shift [their policies] in accordance with the seasons and respond to the transformations of things. In establishing customs and promulgating policies, they do nothing unsuitable. Their tenets are concise and easy to grasp; their policies are few, but their achievements are many.⁴³

Immediately following this passage, the author abruptly changes his tone, following the aforementioned *Guanzi* and *Annals of Lü Buwei* texts, and criticizes Confucianism for inverting the proper relationship between the lord and the minister:

儒者則不然。以為人主天下之儀表也，主倡而臣和，主先而臣隨。如此則主勞而臣逸。

The Confucians are not like this [the Daoists]. They maintain that the ruler is the exemplar for all under heaven. For them, the ruler guides and the officials harmonize with him; the ruler initiates and the officials follow. Proceeding in this manner, the ruler labors hard and the officials sit idle.[44]

It seems as if Sima Qian was not only reaffirming Liu Sheng's criticism of Liu Pengzu but also defending the former from the latter's attack. According to Sima Qian, the Confucian practice that "the ruler guides and the officials harmonize with him" would result in the ruination of rulership, as the *Guanzi* and *Annals of Lü Buwei* texts had predicted.

However, Sima Qian's personal philosophical inclination does not necessarily invalidate Liu Sheng's Huang-Lao association, which was implied not only in Liu Sheng's official posthumous title but also in his marriage to Dou Wan, whose personal seals were found in her coffin. Despite the absence of direct historical records about Dou Wan's relationship to the Grand Empress Dowager Dou (Dou Yifang), the unique culture of the "double marital bond" during the early Western Han renders Liu Sheng's marital link to the Dou family almost certain, as I discussed in chapter 2. Dou Wan's possession of the bronze lamp that was once in the grand empress dowager's palace of lasting trust reinforces the premise that the Zhongshan queen was related to that powerful lady.

By marrying Dou Wan, Liu Sheng could not have escaped the dominant influence of the powerful Grand Empress Dowager Dou, who actively promoted Huang-Lao ideology. She was said to push her sons and grandsons (the emperors and princes) and members of her own Dou clan to read works attributed to Huangdi and Laozi and to honor the Huang-Lao methodology of ruling.[45] In the meantime, she despised Confucians as irrelevant bureaucrats who only labored on trivial paperwork (exactly what interested Liu Pengzu). The story goes that the imperial lady once summoned Yuan Gu 轅固 (fl. second century BCE), a leading Confucian scholar of the *Book of Poetry*, to lecture her on the *Laozi* text. Yuan refused, dismissing the *Laozi* as "commoners' words." Feeling insulted, the imperial mother furiously scorched the Confucian Classics as being no more than bureaucratic manuals on how to punish criminals.[46] To punish this arrogant scholar, she threw Yuan Gu into a pen to confront a ferocious boar. Until her death, this lady's influence on the imperial court remained unshakable.

Through a combined, critical examination of various textual and archaeological sources, I have demonstrated Liu Sheng's association with Huang-Lao ideology. However, Liu Sheng might not have been as dogmatic with regard to Huang-Lao tradition as Sima Qian characterized him in the *Shiji*. He may have taken a more nuanced position, as the changing political climate of the second century BCE might have dictated.

ETHICS AND ADMONITION:
LIU SHENG AS A CONFUCIAN RULER

Whereas Sima Qian portrayed Liu Sheng as an unswerving practitioner of the Huang-Lao tradition, another historian, Ban Gu, added more details to the historical and literary image of the king and represented him as a practitioner of Confucianism. Ban Gu reported a historical episode, not recorded in the current *Shiji* text, that describes Liu Sheng as an erudite Confucian gentleman and skillful rhetorician capable of using classical poetry to teach the emperor about Confucian values.

In 138 BCE, according to an episode apparently first recorded in the *Hanshu*, the emperor hosted a party for his brother kings who came to report on their duties. When everyone was in high spirits and the atmosphere was in perfect harmony, Liu Sheng suddenly wept. After the emperor wondered what had gone wrong, Liu Sheng translated his literary talent into a heartwarming speech, later titled "Response Upon Hearing Music" (*Wenyue dui* 聞樂對), that expressed his deep sorrow and sadness upon being vilified by unrelated imperial officials and mistrusted by his own brother—the emperor.[47]

The historical background of this episode was Emperor Wu's dismissal at court of "the hundred schools" (*baijia* 百家), including the Huang-Lao school, in favor of Confucianism exclusively. Emperor Wu was educated and indoctrinated by Confucian scholars as a young prince. After he had ascended to the imperial throne, he immediately began to appoint Confucian scholars, including Zhao Guan 趙綰 and Wang Zang 王臧, to be his top ministers in the central government. But this radical action infuriated the old party; the Huang-Lao faction rallied around the aging yet still powerful Grand Empress Dowager Dou, who forced the new emperor to sack his favorite ministers.[48] It was only after the death of his mother that the emperor finally enjoyed the freedom to embrace Confucianism.

Liu Sheng must have known that the new emperor was a devotee of Confucianism, so he framed the aforementioned speech with the Confucian theme of "kindred affinity for one's kin" (*qinqin* 親親) and elaborated upon it with quotes and anecdotes from Confucian rather than Huang-Lao texts. His "politically correct" performance proved to be successful.

Liu Sheng began his speech with a description of his deep sadness and his sympathy with several ancient heroes who similarly responded to music with an expression of sorrow:

I, your servant, once heard that sad persons should not sigh repeatedly and contemplating people should not make long deep breaths. So upon hearing Gao Jianli's 高漸離 beating the *zhu* zither on the bank of the Yi river, Jing Ke 荆軻 dropped his head and stopped eating; upon hearing Yongmen Zi's (Yongmen Zhou 雍門周) low-pitched chant, Lord Mengchang 孟嘗君 turned melancholic. Now my heart has been knotted for a while. Every time I hear sentimental music, I cannot control my tears and snot from shedding together on my face.

And then Liu Sheng went on to explain the reason for his unhappiness: He was wrongly defamed by malicious officials. Once accumulated, such slander could be so destructive that even such stainless saints as King Wen of the Zhou 周文王 and Confucius could not escape being wronged because once a lie has been repeated a thousand times, it becomes the truth: "Numerous gusts of wind can move a mountain and aggregated mosquito hums sound like thunder. A gang or party can capture a tiger; ten men can bend an iron hammer." Liu Sheng referred to the current emperor as the great mountain, which was shielded from sight by dusts and clouds—a metaphor for maligners. These lines echo the poet Qu Yuan's 屈原 (ca. 340–ca. 278 BCE) famous work "encountering sorrow" (*Li Sao* 離騷), in which the virtuous protagonist complained of being wronged by evil officials who badmouthed him before the king.[49]

While they both faced vilification, Qu Yuan maintained his own uncompromising moral integrity by committing suicide, whereas Liu Sheng fought back by appealing to the Confucian principle of honoring blood ties. Like the philosopher Han Fei 韓非 (ca. 281–233 BCE), Liu Sheng warned the emperor that a minister "does not have a kinship of flesh and bones with him (*gu rou zhi qin* 骨肉之親)." These temporary employees hired by the ruler were trying to break the permanent brotherhood within the imperial house and to estrange the emperor from his royal relatives.[50] To reinforce his point, Liu Sheng made reference to historical examples. He advised the emperor not to repeat the mistakes of Yin Jifu 尹吉甫, a Zhou-dynasty minister who sent his virtuous son Bo Qi 伯奇 into exile, or King Zhou, the last king of the Shang dynasty, who executed his loyal uncle, Bigan 比干.[51] In the end, Liu Sheng elegantly quoted the *Xiao Bian* 小弁 poem from the *Book of Poetry*—one of the Five Confucian Classics, to sum up his feelings:

我心憂傷，怒焉如擣。假寐永歎，唯憂用老。心之憂矣，疢如疾首。

> My heart is wounded with sorrow,
> And I think till I feel as if pounded [all over].
> I lie down undressed, and sigh continually;
> Through my grief I am growing old.
> My heart is sad;—
> It puts me in pain like a headache.[52]

Emperor Wu, who was well versed in the Confucian Classics and was making an effort to replace Huang-Lao teachings with Confucianism as his imperial ideology, must have understood that in the orthodox exegesis, this poem was interpreted as a criticism of King You 幽王 of the Zhou dynasty (r. 782–771 BCE), who listened to slanderous words from outsiders and wronged his own righteous son.[53] Hearing these complaints at the imperial banquet, the emperor, who was playing his role as a benign host and brother, was forced into a situation in which he could not say "no" to Liu Sheng's plea. As a result, Liu Sheng cleverly achieved his objective: The emperor dismissed the critical officials and rewarded his uncles, brothers, and cousins generously.[54]

Sima Qian neither mentioned this banquet nor recorded the speech, although he should have known if it actually occurred. Ban Gu, while copying Sima Qian's short biographical note on Liu Sheng (totaling 138 words) almost in its entirety, diluted the Huang-Lao flavor of the original account by adding this lengthy story (totaling 662 words) and thereby set up a new and compelling Confucian image for Liu Sheng. The reason for this repainting is obvious. Liu Sheng's biographers, Sima Qian and Ban Gu, were not ideologically neutral historians.[55] The former, as demonstrated earlier, was sympathetic with Huang-Lao teachings but critical of Confucianism, while the latter was a Confucian scholar who did not trust the Huang-Lao ideology.[56] While Sima Qian highlighted Liu Sheng as a Huang-Lao practitioner, Ban Gu downplayed his Huang-Lao identity and emphasized his Confucian training instead.[57]

It is impossible to understand this ideological fight between imperial officials and relatives as recorded in the *Hanshu* without looking into the historical context of the second century BCE, when the contradiction between state law and personal kinship was embedded in the basic structure of the empire. When Emperor Gao founded the Western Han dynasty, to keep his dynasty stable, he established fifteen commanderies in the west under the control of his directly appointed governors.[58] Meanwhile, in order to exert imperial influence in the administrative affairs of the semiautonomous kingdoms to the east and south, Liu Bang made it a rule that the imperial government must hold the power to appoint chief ministers for these kings. During Emperor Wen's reign, this power extended to the appointment of high-ranking officials of "two-thousand-bushels" (*erqianshi* 二千石) in the kingdoms, which included all the major ministers below the chief minister. However, the kings still enjoyed great power and authority within their territories, and they still posed a great threat to the imperial throne.[59] Emperor Jing adopted a more radical policy of "weakening the vassals" (*xuefan* 削藩), proposed by his minister, Chao Cuo 鼂錯 (200–154 BCE). Rather than strengthening the loyal kingdoms, he was advised to reduce the size of those states that were considered as threatening.[60] But this policy backfired; it caused panic and resentment among the kings that directly triggered the Rebellion of the Seven Kingdoms in 154 BCE.

After crushing the rebellion, the imperial court continued to cautiously enhance its control over the regional kingdoms. But the battle was not yet won. Although Emperor Jing issued a famous edict in 144 BCE that banned the kings from handling government affairs, historians have noted that this administrative order was not thoroughly enforced, and at least some kings still ruled as before.[61] In 141 BCE, Emperor Wu ascended the imperial throne and was anxious to take new and more effective measures to consolidate his power. Some of his ministers consulted Chao Cuo's policy and frequently searched for excuses to prosecute regional kings in front of the emperor, who loved to exploit any chance to weaken his sibling rivals.[62] In fact, from 135 BCE onward, with the death of Grand Dowager Empress Dou, the kings were required to report their duties more frequently to the unchallenged emperor, who was embracing a more aggressive hands-on policy in the name of Confucianism.[63]

It was during this intensified political struggle between the empire and the regional kingdoms that Liu Sheng stood up and spoke to Emperor Wu at the imperial banquet. Although the accuracy of the story is an issue for debate,[64] Ban Gu clearly intended to overwrite Sima Qian's account and portray Liu Sheng as a Confucian instead of follower of Huang-Lao teachings. Throughout the speech, Liu Sheng carefully avoided all Huang-Lao terminology and closely stuck to one of the central teachings of Confucius: love between brothers, or the principle of fraternity (*ti* 悌).

According to the basic doctrine of the *Classic of Filial Piety* (*Xiaojing* 孝經), the younger brother (in this context, Emperor Wu) was supposed to find pleasure in respecting the elder brother (Liu Sheng).[65] In addition, by denouncing the officials as non-relatives, Liu Sheng was promoting the Confucian tenet of "kindred affinity for one's kin (*qinqin*)." How could the emperor, who was elevating Confucianism to replace Huang-Lao as the state ideology and promoting his own image as Confucianism's champion, reject these essential teachings of the master? If Ban Gu's story can be trusted, then it confirms Liu Sheng's political wisdom: he knew exactly how to gain his brother's favor by playing to the emperor's philosophical tendencies.

If the apparently contradictory pictures of Liu Sheng in the *Shiji* and *Hanshu* are not total literary fabrications but accurate reflections of two different aspects of the king of Zhongshan, then Liu Sheng's skillful engagement with both Huang-Lao thought and Confucianism might explain his success in the drastically changing political and ideological climate of the latter half of the second century BCE, in which Huang-Lao doctrines and Confucianism competed for court dominance. Being familiar with both the Huang-Lao and Confucian classics, Liu Sheng expressed his opinions appropriately, depending on his audience. Facing the new Confucian emperor in the court, he spoke out like a Confucian scholar, while back in his kingdom in Hebei, he preached the Huang-Lao doctrine. Liu Sheng's eclectic, multivalent political ideology left a legacy among his descendants. In the royal Dingxian tomb no. 40, excavated in 1973 and occupied by Liu Xiu, the sixth King of Zhongshan, the excavators found manuscripts with both Huang-Lao and Confucian contents.[66]

The royal tombs at the Mancheng site thus crystallized the two major currents of thinking in the historical context of the second century BCE, when the royal court was struggling to consolidate imperial order across the provinces. This result finds support in excavated bronze inscriptions as well as in the design of the Mancheng royal tombs, as I will demonstrate next.

PLAYING FOR PEACE: WAGER COINS AND POLITICAL IDEOLOGY

A number of bronze inscriptions made on the various burial objects in the royal couple's tombs echo the image of Liu Sheng painted in the transmitted texts as a royal practitioner of both Huang-Lao and Confucian teachings.

The longest inscription was cast on the set of forty wager coins, which I initially examined in chapter 2 (fig. 2.8).[67] The excavators believe that these coins were used by the royal couple during a banquet to entertain their guests.[68] Two to four characters were cast on one side of each of these 3.3-centimeter diameter coins. Twenty of the forty bear a numbered inscription, beginning with "no.1" (*diyi* 第一) and ending with "no. 20" (*dinian* 第廿), and the other twenty carry wishful incantations, each composed of three to four characters. Perhaps by observing the rhyme scheme and semantic connection (e.g., nos. 17 and 18) among these incantations, Guo Moruo assumed that the forty inscriptions formed a uniform text. So, he first paired each of the numbered coins with one of the incantation coins to form one clause, and then he repeated this practice to retrieve a total of twenty individual clauses before he finally linked them up to make one rhymed text. Hypothetical as it is, Guo's reconstruction generally has held up:[69]

第一，聖主佐	no. 1, May the sage ruler be assisted,
第二，得佳士	no. 2, and obtain wise officials.
第三，常毋苛	no. 3, May you always be non-harsh,
第四，驕次[恣]已	no. 4, and pride and arrogance cease.
第五，府庫實	no. 5, May the treasuries and storehouses be full;
第六，五穀成	no. 6, and the five grains ripen.
第七，金錢施	no. 7, May gold and cash be disbursed;
第八，珠玉行	no. 8, and pearls and jades circulate.
第九，貴富壽	no. 9, May you be noble, rich, and long-lived,
第十，壽毋病	no. 10, a longevity without sickness.
第十一，萬民番	no. 11, May the myriad people prosper[70];
第十二，天下安	no. 12, and the world reside in peace.
第十三，起行酒	no. 13, Get up and have a drink;
第十四，樂無憂	no. 14, May you be joyous without care.
第十五，飲酒歌	no. 15, Sing as you drink;
第十六，飲其右	no. 16, and let the one on your right drink.[71]
第十七，自飲止	no. 17, When the drinking is over,
第十八，樂乃始	no. 18, let the music begin.
第十九，畏妻鄙	no. 19, Awe-inspiring are my wife's branches!
第廿，壽夫王母	no. 20, Long live the queen mother (or, Live as long as the queen mother)!

Although at first glance, these phrases appear no more than auspicious wishes for such things as fortune, health, joy, and longevity, upon further scrutiny, they express ideas similar to those implied in Liu Sheng's biography and posthumous title. Three themes dominate the reconstructed wager-coin text inscriptions.

The first theme, consisting of six lines (line nos. 13–18), is alcohol and music, essential for a merry banquet. The drinker stands up and makes toasts; he drinks as he sings and bids his company to drink as well. The music starts once the drinking is over. That seems to be a perfect description of the kind of life Liu Sheng promoted in his *Shiji* biography: a king should always remain at leisure rather than bothering with state affairs. The purpose of drinking is to attain longevity without sickness (line nos. 9–10), the very basis of the Huang-Lao philosophy. This wish was so essential that it was repeated on several other elements in the tomb. A bronze mirror found in Dou Wan's coffin is inscribed with this fervent wish: "For tens of thousands of years, extend [her] years and prolong [her] life!" (*qianqiu wansui, yannian yishou* 千秋萬歲, 延年益壽). The exterior of two bronze *hu* wine pots from Liu Sheng's tomb bear elaborate bird script inscriptions that even suggest a method for achieving longevity (see fig. 1.6).[72] Among the words:

盛兄盛味，於心佳都。淥於口味，延壽卻病，萬年有餘。

> With happy hearts [let us] gather in banquet.
> The occasion is grand and the fare sumptuous.
> Let delicacies fill the gates and increase our girth,
> And give us long life without illness for ten thousand years and more.[73]

Once inscribed on the vessels, these lines blessing the health of the honorable user would serve as magic spells and transform the wine in the vessels into a potion that offered the drinker a "long life without illness for ten thousand years and more."[74] The same desire for longevity is also voiced in the short inscription made on the jade figurine interred in Liu Sheng's outer coffin, which, as discussed in chapter 2, promises nineteen more years of life to its bearer, the king.

Sensuous pleasures were not necessarily against the Huang-Lao teachings. The "Six Divisions" (*Liufen* 六分) chapter in the excavated *Four Classics of the Yellow Emperor* text from Mawangdui tomb no. 3 asserts that a ruler who knows the "technique of kingship" (*wangshu* 王術) will stay immune to the potential harm of self-indulgence because "though he may urge his horses to a gallop in the hunt, yet he will not go so far as the abandoned wastelands and, though he may drink and eat and enjoy entertainment, yet he will not go so far as to be dissipated in drink and reckless trinkets and seductive girls, his heart will not be deluded."[75] In other words, if the ruler was wise, material extravagance never did him any harm. However, as the author continued to assert, if the ruler was blind to the techniques of kingship, the same activities would cause disaster.

The second, though less elaborated, theme in the inscriptions is family. The two lines (nos. 19–20) that I have thoroughly examined in chapter 2 praise the power of the wife's branches and pray for the longevity of the king's mother. Although Confucian ethics embraced filial piety and family harmony more than the Huang-Lao tradition did, the latter never rejected it, as I will show in the next section of this chapter.

But the third and most dominant theme in the wager-coin inscriptions is related to governance of the state and all under heaven. The author devoted an overwhelming total of ten lines to this concern. Lines nos. 1–2 in this reconstructed text focus on ruling without deliberate action, the main idea of Huang-Lao thought. These two lines address the need to find capable and sensible officials (de jiashi) to help the sage ruler (shengzhu zuo) deal with state affairs. By juxtaposing these two lines, the author implied that kings should not deal with administrative affairs but find capable officials to do the job. This idea exactly matches Liu Sheng's "actionless" practice described in his Shiji biography.

With the ruler being assisted by capable officials, line nos. 3–4 continue Huang-Lao teachings by warning the ruler to constantly remain tolerant (chang wuke 常毋苛) and to put an end to arrogance and self-indulgence (jiaozi yi 驕次[恣]已). The wording here matters. In the Shiji, Liu Sheng's near-contemporary, Sima Qian, consistently used the exact word, jiaozi 驕恣 ("arrogant and self-indulgent"), to describe those rebellious kings who died pathetic deaths.[76] Casting this phrase on the wager coins might show Liu Sheng's constant awareness of not repeating their mistake. The word wuke ("do not be harsh [in it]" 毋苛), in contrast, was used in the Shiji to convey a meaning that was the opposite of jiaozi. Sima Qian contrasted the two words in his biography of Yuan Ang 爰盎 (ca. 200–150 BCE). As the chief minister of the Wu state, Yuan Ang remained "non-harsh" (wuke) but was pushed aside in the government by his "arrogant and self-indulgent" (jiaozi) king, Liu Pi 劉濞 (216–154 BCE). In the end, the reckless king went so far as to rebel against the emperor but only got himself killed,[77] whereas Yuan Ang's life was spared.

In fact, in the Huang-Lao teachings, being and acting "non-harsh" (written variously as *wuke* 毋苛, 無苛, or *buke* 不苛) was an essential quality for a wise ruler. In fact, it is one of the three meanings of the posthumous title *jing* accorded to Liu Sheng: "being tolerant and happy with a good end." In the *Guanzi* text, the author compares a good ruler to a deep well that all life can draw upon for support because "the ruler is one to whom men look for their livelihood. If he is capable of leniency and sincerity without oppression, the people will attach themselves to him."[78] The same principle also applied to officials. In the Qin-period Shuihudi tomb no. 11, excavated in Yunmeng, Hubei, in 1975, the tomb occupant, a local official named Xi 喜, was buried with a number of legal and administrative texts written on bamboo slips. One of them focuses on "the way of being an official" (Wei li zhi dao 為吏之道) and describes a good official as "calm, quiet, and non-harsh" (*anjing wuke* 安静毋苛).[79]

In contrast, "arrogance" (*jiaozi*) was one of the most condemned faults of a ruler. The *Annals of Lü Buwei* text contained an entire section with this designation ("On Arrogance and Self-Indulgence") and discussed its harm to the state. In the opening remarks of the section, the author claims that any ruler that lost his country must have made the mistake of being arrogant, for such rulers tended to despise others.[80]

Another trait of wise rulers referred to in the combined inscription on the wager coins is paying sufficient attention to the preparation of material goods. This is the teaching of line nos. 5–8 in the reconstructed text, which emphasize that the state storehouses must be full of utensils, the harvest should be abundant with the five grains, and plentiful wealth needs to circulate. These phrases recall a very similar passage in the *Spring and Autumn Annals of Wu and Yue* (*Wu-Yue chunqiu* 吳越春秋, dated second century CE) text, in which Gou Jian 勾踐 (497–465 BCE), the wise king of the Yue kingdom, successfully "filled the storehouses and opened up agricultural fields," creating a wealthy nation and a strong country.[81] Although the original author of this passage is unknown, the text is unmistakably related to the Huang-Lao tradition because the king's secret to success was his practicing "no deliberate action": "The ruler did not talk about instruction; the ministers did not talk about planning; the people did not talk about employment; the officials did not talk about government affairs. Within the country, far and wide, there were no government ordinances."[82]

Not coincidently, an inscription cast on one of the bronze mirrors from Liu Sheng's tomb wishes for "lasting wealth and nobility and happiness without troubles" (*chang fugui, le wushi* 長富貴, 樂毌事).[83] The outcome of "no deliberate action" is summed up in line nos. 11–12 of the wager-coin text: "May the myriad people prosper and the world reside in peace," that is, *jing* 靖, or, pacification, Liu Sheng's posthumous name. With the rulership of the kingdom in good condition, the final fruits, as line nos. 11–12 state, are the prosperity of the people and a peaceful world.

It can be safely concluded that the political philosophy of the Huang-Lao doctrine permeates almost every line of the entombed inscriptions from the Mancheng site.

Meanwhile, the material extravagance of the royal tombs, which apparently contradicts the largely ascetic doctrine of the Huang-Lao school, registers another influential impact from Xunzi, arguably the greatest Confucian teacher in the late third century BCE, who defended the material elaboration of ritual (with the burial being one of the most important rituals) as the necessary external ornament (*shi* 飾 or *wen* 文) of the invisible way of the sage kings. Ban Gu's description of Liu Sheng as a cultivated gentleman who skillfully quoted and interpreted the *Book of Poetry* to promote Confucian values attests to his training in the exegetical tradition of that text, which was almost single-handedly passed down through Xunzi.[84]

EMBODYING POLITICAL IDEOLOGY AT MANCHENG

As the decision-maker and final authority on his mausoleum project, Liu Sheng possessed both the power and the motivation to implant his political ideology—a fusion of Huang-Lao thought and Confucianism—into the design of the tomb. Within the ideology of both Huang-Lao and Confucianism that Liu Sheng might have practiced, the fundamental task for the ruler was to imitate ancient sage kings in attaining personal well-being and extending it to the realization of the well-being of the world. However, no one believed this extension could be achieved in one quick step. Instead, it required a process, beginning with the cultivation of the self, passing through the harmony of the family and local communities, and eventually ending in the peace of the country (and further, "all under heaven"). Although it remains uncertain how definitively Liu Sheng, as the final authority on his burial project, requested the implementation of his personal political ideology, the multistepped process of pacification of the self, the family, and the state was certainly deeply embedded in the design of the Mancheng tombs.

At the Mancheng site, the union between the body and the soul was constructed through several nested coffins and caskets. The Mancheng designer furnished these zones as if a gradual natural transformation was occurring between a solid body in the center and an ethereal soul that surrounded the body. Across these layers, a multilayer "union" ensured the everlasting embrace of the body and the soul, which further ensured the longevity of the deceased subjects (see chapter 1).

Whereas the *embracing* principle linked up the body and the soul through a succession of transitional phases, the *paralleling* principle held the husband and the wife together by turning their tombs into each other's mirror image, be it physically or symbolically. It appears as if the deceased couple were conceived as one unity, or as the *Book of Etiquette and Ceremonial* relates, "united in one body"[85] (see chapter 2). The *paralleling* principle might have also encompassed the extended family as well, which consisted of other subordinate family members, as eighteen satellite burials with stone pyramids dot the lower mountain slopes at the site.[86]

The third principle, *intermingling*, encompassed the ethnic-Han and non-ethnic-Han elements in the tombs. A relatively small number of non-ethnic-Han elements, both symbolically and functionally, permeated the tomb space in all major aspects of living, including clothing, cooking, building, and transportation, and were mixed and integrated among the dominant ethnic-Han elements. More importantly, these non-ethnic-Han remains were not exotica that boasted of the owner's social status, wealth, and distinction, but rather, they were associated specifically with the local Rong-Di cultural tradition in north Hebei (see chapter 3).

The three organizing principles in the tombs of the Mancheng site represent a special variation on the influential political discourse of a pacified ruler pacifying the world in second-century BCE China.[87]

In Huang-Lao teachings, personal longevity formed the foundation of good rulership. The opposite of longevity was death, which meant breaking the union of body and soul and resulting in the failure to cultivate the self. The most basic design in the Mancheng tombs was to secure an inseparable relationship between body and soul. Meanwhile, public welfare stood at the apex of the political mission of the Western Han rulers—above the self. All under heaven (*tianxia*), after all, was made up not only of the Chinese "central kingdoms" (*zhongguo* 中國) but also "barbarians" living on the peripheries of the Huaxia civilization.[88] One of the most hotly debated issues in the study of political thought in the ancient world concerned the wise handling of the relationship between "us" and "the other," or the foreigners,[89] and early China was certainly engaged in this discourse.[90] In the tombs at the Mancheng site, one of the most pervasive characteristics in the pattern of furnishings was the integration of the ethnic-non-Han custom into the ethnic-Han custom.

In terms of the relationship between personal longevity and worldly peace, the former was certainly a condition for the latter. According to Sima Tan's summary, uniting the body (*xing* 形) and the spirit (*shen* 神) assured the personal longevity of the ruler, who was able to bring peace and harmony to the world by following the natural laws (*yinxun* 因循) and taking no actions (*buwei* 不為):

凡人所生者神也，所託者形也。神大用則竭，形大勞則敝，形神離則死。死者不可復生，離者不可復反，故聖人重之。由是觀之，神者生之本也，形者生之具也。不先定其神〔形〕，而曰「我有以治天下」，何由哉？

What gives life to all human beings is the numen (*shen*), and what they rely upon is the body (*xing*). When the numen is used excessively it becomes depleted; when the body toils excessively it wears out. When the body and numen separate we die; when we die we cannot return to life; what separates cannot return to how it was. Therefore, the sage attaches great importance to this. From this we observe that the numen is the foundation of life, and the physical form is the vessel of life. How could anyone say, "I possess the means to rule all under heaven" without first stabilizing the numen?[91]

In alignment with this persuasive point, the authors of the *Annals of Lü Buwei* text lamented that many contemporary rulers harried themselves to benefit other people at the cost of their own health: "The ordinary ruler diminishes his own life to supply the men of the world," just like "a wine-cup from which many drink always quickly emptied." Although the ruler may have achieved great things externally, (within) his life force has been depleted.[92] Therefore, the author advised these mistaken rulers to learn from the ancients by modeling themselves after the natural laws of heaven and earth in order to maintain an enduring, healthy life, both physically and mentally. Indeed, one of the reasons given by historians such as Derk Bodde for the triumph of the Qin kingdom over all the six rival states was the general "longevity of rulers," which provided "political continuity and stability."[93]

Although Sima Tan omitted a discussion of family, in the *Four Classics of the Yellow Emperor* text, the problem of maintaining good order within the royal household (*jia* 家) was indeed a concern. The warning was serious: if the husband (king) and wife (queen) contended (*zheng* 爭) for authority rather than harmonized with each other, then the whole state would be torn apart and end up in chaos.[94] Furthermore, the *Laozi* text did pay attention to the relationship between men and women, or more generally, between male and female, noting that "It is only by knowing the Male and maintaining the Female that one can reach the pure state of being 'the ravine of the world.'"[95]

The idea that the ruler should cultivate the self before cultivating the world was not only accepted by Huang-Lao doctrine but also by some other schools of political philosophy from the Eastern Zhou to the Western Han periods. In Confucianism, a similar idea was rendered as "fixing the self, putting the family in order, managing the state, and pacifying all under heaven" (*xiushen, qijia, zhiguo, pingtianxia*), as famously expressed in the "Great Learning" (*Daxue* 大學) chapter of the *Book of Rites*:

古之欲明明德於天下者，先治其國；欲治其國者，先齊其家；欲齊其家者，先修其身。

The ancients who wished to illustrate illustrious virtue throughout the kingdom, first ordered well their own states. Wishing to order well their states, they first regulated their families. Wishing to regulate their families, they first cultivated their persons.[96]

The deceased's three identities as an immortal, as part of a reunited family, and as state peacemaker correspond with the ideal king's tripartite obligations: to correct the self (*xiushen* 修身), to put one's family in order (*qijia* 齊家), and to manage the state (*zhiguo* 治國), in addition to his obligation to help the emperor pacify the world (*ping tianxia* 平天下), following the example of the ancient sage kings.

However, the Confucian agenda differed from that of the Huang-Lao in putting more emphasis on the value of family, with husband and wife standing at the heart of it. An early Western Han commentator on the *Book of Changes* text, one of the Confucian Classics, considered husband and wife the very first social relationship for mankind after the creation of the world. And only with that in place did everything else start to take shape:

有天地然後有萬物，有萬物然後有男女，有男女然後有夫婦，有夫婦然後有
父子，有父子然後有君臣，有君臣然後有上下，有上下然後禮義有所錯。

Heaven and earth existing, all (material) things then got their existence. All (material) things having existence, afterward there came male and female. From the existence of male and female there came afterward husband and wife. From husband and wife there came father and son. From father and son there came ruler and minister. From ruler and minister there came high and low. When (the distinction of) high and low had existence, afterward came the arrangements of propriety and righteousness.[97]

This view can be traced back to a fourth-century BCE manuscript, attributed to some early Confucian authors, excavated from a tomb in present-day Guodian 郭店 in Hubei.[98] The author of the "Cultivation of Political Power" (*Quanxiu* 權修) chapter in the *Guanzi* text took up this idea and emphasized the hierarchy among these steps. If a ruler cannot manage his self well, he surely cannot manage his family properly; if he fails to manage his family, he can hardly manage the state and all under heaven.[99] The same idea was repeated in a bamboo manuscript excavated from present-day Yinqueshan 銀雀山 in Linyi, Shandong, and dating from the early second century BCE.[100] This precisely reverses the logic in the aforementioned "Great Learning." A notable difference is that to the Confucians, the interpretation of self-cultivation (*xiushen* 修身) was more of a moral than a physical issue. If, for Huang-Lao believers, the harmony of body and soul was the key to longevity, for the Confucians, the secret of successfully cultivating the person (self) was to rectify the "heart" (*xin* 心), the "mind" (*yi* 意), and the "intelligence" (*zhi* 知).[101]

In the tombs at the Mancheng site, the three major domains for a ruler to fulfill his mission—the self, the family, and the state (all under heaven)—were clearly "cultivated" by visual and material means to show harmonious states: embracing, paralleling, and intermingling. Even a sort of sequence or hierarchy among the three states was clearly visible in the design: The self was physically "contained" by the family because the two individual tombs were encompassed by the joint cemetery of the royal couple. But the state, which contained both the family and the self, was the most pervasive element because the practice of integrating customs (i.e., the Han and the non-Han) permeated almost every chamber and section of the tombs.

Chapter Six

THE KING UNDER THE GAZE

After the funeral, an early Chinese tomb would be closed and transformed into a forbidden zone that denied all physical access. It would be impossible for someone to lawfully reopen it as one might do with a catacomb in ancient Rome or to tour the tomb as if visiting a modern museum. Yet the fact that the tombs eventually were shut in darkness does not necessarily contradict or invalidate various kinds of observation (or "gaze") in the tombs but signals an important change in the early Chinese concept of funerary ritual and art. Throughout this book, I contend that the worldly scrutiny of a ruler continued in the underground world of his tomb and that the ruler would still be subject to the opinions of spectators who were constantly weighing his significance to this world, even in his afterlife. This chapter will demonstrate that Western Han royal tombs fell under three types of gazes: first, the direct gaze of spectators during the funeral ceremony; second, the gaze of ancestral spirits in the underground world; and lastly, the gaze of authorities from government agencies. All these different gazes stimulated the increasing tendency to turn a royal tomb's interior into a visual spectacle that displayed not only various installations of objects but also the ideology (in essence, the mind and image) of the deceased ruler.

THE ROYAL TOMB AS THE OBJECT OF THE GAZE

As far as visuality is concerned, there is always the inherent question of viewership. As I have shown in earlier chapters, various visual patterns were established among the numerous objects in the Mancheng tombs as a response to the epistemological quest for an understandable, meaningful death. But then, for whom was the way of the sages visualized and displayed in the tombs? This question is particularly thorny because by the late second century BCE, Chinese burials were always hidden permanently from the living world after entombment (unlike contemporaneous Roman catacombs that could be reopened multiple times). After the closure of the tomb, no viewer would have access to its concealed space; nothing in the interior of tombs was meant to be inspected by any living person. In fact, anyone who might see it one day was expected to see it in ruination.[1] It has been assumed that because a viewer did not exist for Chinese tombs, current art historical theories based on viewing do not apply to this totally restricted space.[2] However, as we have already seen through the chapters of this book, there was an undeniable emphasis on visuality in Western Han royal tombs; burial objects were arranged and displayed in artificial light provided by real lamps to facilitate seeing them in an accessible house-like structure.

So, what does such a display mean in tombs? If we assume that such a tableau was on display *for* someone, who, then, was the intended viewer?

It should be noted that for the tomb designer, the intended audience did not have to be physically present but could just be a psychological construct. From a religious perspective, this seemingly futile display in a dark, inaccessible burial site would indicate only one possible group of viewers who might appreciate the concealed royal spectacle: the souls of the deceased, including Liu Sheng and Dou Wan, and more importantly, their ancestors and the gods.

Beginning during the Qin and Han period, some more elaborate representations of the spirit realm described an underground world ruled by departed emperors. A story recorded in the *Hanshu* text has it that after Wang Mang's usurpation of the Western Han dynasty, the former emperor Wen, who had died more than 160 years before, became "angry" and "called up an army underground" to fight this traitor.[3] Perhaps to simulate such spirit armies, miniaturized figurines of soldiers and war horses fashioned in terra-cotta were buried in several royal cemeteries and accompanied the main grave of the deceased king or marquis. These included sites such as Shizishan 獅子山 (Jiangsu), Weishan 危山 (Shandong), Xiangshan 香山 (Shandong), Yangjiawan 楊家灣 (Shaanxi), and Shanwangcun 山王村 (Shandong), which all date to the second century BCE.[4] In these sites, thousands of miniaturized troops were grouped in battle formations, equipped with weapons, and were ready to engage any enemies.

Related to this imagination of the underworld, there was a popular belief that deceased spirits not only "lived" but also acted "under the ground" (*dixia* 地下)—a phrase synonymous with tombs—in response to the events in the living world.[5] It seems that when people imagined themselves as dead spirits, they often expected to see their deceased lords under the ground. In the *Shiji*, when Wang Ling 王陵 (d. 180 BCE) accused his fellow ministers of betraying the oath they had sworn to the previous emperor, he bitterly said, "How will you face Emperor Gao under the ground?"[6] In other stories, it was the dying king who was ashamed to confront his loyal ministers beneath the ground. Legend has it that after a decisive victory over the Yue, General Wu Zixu 伍子胥 (d. 484 BCE) advised his king, Fuchai 夫差 (d. 473 BCE) of the Wu, to eliminate this bitter foe once and for all, but the arrogant king not only rejected this advice and allowed the Yue to survive but also forced Wu Zixu to commit suicide. Later, when the tide changed, and the revitalized Yue army defeated the Wu, Fuchai sighed "How can I face Wu Zixu under the ground?" and then killed himself.[7] If Liu Sheng also believed that he would become a spirit upon his death, he should have expected to see his father, Emperor Jing, under the ground, reporting on his duty to pacify Zhongshan. Perhaps he also would see his fearsome grandmother, Grand Empress Dowager Dou, and would tell her about his faithful practice of the Huang-Lao political philosophy that she ordered him and his brothers to study as young princes.

During the Han period, people felt that they were constantly being watched by ghosts and gods. Xu Gan 徐幹 (171–217 or 218 CE) described this experience in his book, *Balanced Discourses* (*Zhonglun* 中論). To emphasize the importance of people being aware of themselves at all times, he noted that "the gentleman is cautious when alone and vigilant when in obscurity" because in spite of the absence of people, ghosts and spirits are always watching.[8] No location is more obscure than the inside of a burial.

However, the psychologically constructed viewer in the concealed tomb did not necessarily have to be ancestral spirits or ghosts. For those who did not believe in the existence of such supernatural beings, an invisible "other" was sufficient to inspire a feeling of being watched.

Even with the absence of actual viewers, many people shared the perception of being peered at by an invisible eye. For the author of the *Huainanzi* text, the eagerness to look beyond one's self was part of human nature: "Now if you lock them in a dark room," such as in a burial, "though you nourish them with fine delicacies, though you clothe them with embroidered garments, they will be incapable of joy because their eyes have nothing to look upon . . . If they were to peek through a narrow crack and see [even] rain and fog, they would laugh happily."[9]

This inherent desire to see others can easily prompt one's equally keen awareness of being looked back upon by those "others." In the *Book of Poetry*, one poet warned the ruler: "Our sovereign should not lightly utter his words, lest an ear be laid close to the wall." The *Guanzi* text confessed that the fear that "the walls have ears" was felt by everyone.[10] What applies to the ear also applies to the eye. Jean-Paul Sartre and other contemporary thinkers see this experience as grounded in the reversible relationship between subject and object and that it applies to everyone. In the fundamental relation that Sartre calls "being-seen-by-another," the "other" who looks back does not have to be physically present.[11] As Janne Seppänen has written, "The sense of being looked at does not require a definite certainty that some specific physical human being sees me. However, 'a look' directed toward me gives me cause to pay heed to my behavior."[12] In other words, the experience of being watched by others does not necessarily posit a natural viewer.[13] As long as this other subject is sensed, the psychological phenomenon of the "gaze" means nothing more than the experience of being looked at from outside— the feeling of constantly being watched and monitored by others.

Although Sartre articulated the universal feeling of "being-seen-by-another" in the context of mid-twentieth-century Europe, his analysis provides a useful perspective for understanding the paradox of viewership in the dark, forbidden, royal tombs of Western Han China. If, as Sartre articulates, the sense of being watched does not require an actual gaze from a specific human presence, the true beholder of the visual spectacle in the tombs at the Mancheng site could be imaginary rather than physical. This suggests that the hidden space with its obscure content might have been visualized and presented to an assumed viewer as a rational design. Only after having distinguished the natural viewer from the phenomenological viewer can we explain the newly developed interest in display in Western Han royal tombs.

Historical evidence endorses the validity of Sartre's theory in Western Han-period Chinese tombs. Besides his ministers, the people (the ruled), were the emperor or king's direct and most relevant "other" because they constituted the polar opposite of the power structure. In early China, people were constantly assessing political leaders and their behavior, with positive or negative reactions. The *Guanzi* text, perhaps, best summarizes the basic motivation: "The ruler is one to whom people look for livelihood."[14]

From the Zhou period on, with the death of a ruler, his ministers would submit suggestions for positive or negative posthumous titles that summed up their views of the deceased lord. The First Emperor of Qin, who probably dreaded this practice as much as any other ruler, was the only one that dared to abolish it, but it was quickly reinstated after the fall of the Qin.[15] The practice of giving posthumous titles to departed rulers as an evaluation of their public performance was like keeping an invisible eye on them even after their death. Beginning with Sima Qian's *Shiji*, historiographic tradition was another instance where rulers could be ruthlessly judged. Wei Hong, the second-century CE historian, reported that Sima Qian so infuriated his then-emperor (Emperor Wu) with his honest portrayal of his sovereign's behavior, that Wu reportedly ordered certain chapters to be deleted.[16]

Constantly being judged and evaluated under such ubiquitous observation, a ruler—as the head of the government—was not free to act recklessly or willfully but had to behave appropriately to meet his audience's expectations. In the fifty-fourth chapter of the *Laozi* text, it is said that just as a person who is good at building would never tear things down and one who is good at holding things would never let them go, a wise person (meaning a ruler) would seize all opportunities to build up rather than undo his or her own virtue. To that end, one's virtue should be cultivated not only by one's self but also in relation to the family, the hamlet, the state, and all under heaven because one can benefit from looking at external models. In the last sentence of that section, however, the meaning becomes somewhat obscure:

故以身觀身，以家觀家，以鄉觀鄉，以國觀國，以天下觀天下。吾何以知天下然哉？以此。

Therefore, look at the person through the person; look at the family through the family; look at the hamlet through the hamlet; look at the state through the state; look at all under heaven through all under heaven. How do I know that all under heaven is like that? By means of this.[17]

What the philosopher is really saying behind the obscure phrasing is that in order to judge how well the world is being governed, one only has to look at the conditions of the self, the family, the state, and the world during the current ruler's administration and measure them against similar conditions under the governance of other rulers (presumably the sage kings). If the conditions match, the current ruler is performing well; if not, something in the government has gone wrong.

A ruler always must have felt he was constantly being watched and measured. He could not get away from this feeling—even in his dark burial, which was not a secret but public knowledge and, in many ways, a public spectacle. It must be stressed that the practice of hiding architecture and objects in a royal tomb was different from locking up personal items such as old pictures, letters, or diaries in our basement. Whereas concealing personal objects in a personal space results in a total lack of public exposure, the royal practice of hiding objects in a burial was only the climactic stage of a lengthy public spectacle during the funeral ceremony, which was anything but secret. If, in ancient Rome, the burning of the emperor's corpse and paraphernalia on a pyre in the public forum marked the end of the funeral (and the apotheosis of the deceased ruler's life),[18] in ancient China, it was the interment (*xia* 下, literally "descending") of the royal body and grave goods, which "vanished" right before the onlookers' eyes, that signaled the end of the funerary rite. Thus, it is impossible to grasp the meaning of the practice of hiding without understanding its relationship to the practice of displaying. Such hiding was only ritually meaningful when it was performed under the gaze of a large audience. This was the paradoxical nature of an early Chinese royal burial—hiding was a public spectacle.

Like their counterparts in ancient Egypt, the Near East, and Rome, early Chinese royal funerals from the late Eastern Zhou to the Han period were meant to be public spectacles. Although extant ancient texts have left no systematic documentation of a Western Han funeral ceremony, it is possible to form a general picture by comparing two nearly contemporaneous texts—one slightly earlier and one later than the Western Han—to appreciate certain persistent elements over the centuries.[19] One text is the *Book of Etiquette and Ceremonial* (*Yili*), a third-century BCE ritual manual circulated and studied as one of the most important Confucian classics during the Western Han.[20] The other text is part of the "Continuation of Han Treatises" (*Xu Han zhi* 續漢志), which was a firsthand record of Eastern Han imperial rituals compiled by historian Sima Biao 司馬彪 (d. 306 CE).[21] Although the Western Han funerary ritual did not necessarily match exactly the Eastern Zhou or the Eastern Han protocols recorded in these texts, and using either of the two texts to explain Western Han ritual practice can be methodologically risky, a prudent comparison of Eastern Zhou and Eastern Han rituals can help us understand Western Han archaeological materials. The goal, to be clear, is not to reconstruct a "Western Han funerary ritual," which might never have been based on a fixed set of unchanging rules. Rather, the more relevant issue concerns the structure of the ritual process and the key elements of the practice because the larger steps involved in the funeral ritual show far more continuity than the minute details.[22]

In the first stage of both the Eastern Zhou and Eastern Han funerary rituals, an ostentatious ceremonial procession consisting of chariots moving from the royal residence to the royal cemetery occurred prior to the entombment—all under the eyes of funeral participants.

In the *Book of Etiquette and Ceremonial* text, the ceremony took place at the residence of the deceased and lasted for days.[23] On the day chosen for the interment (determined by divination), the deceased's coffin was sent to the ancestral temple to bid farewell to the ancestors and was then driven toward the cemetery.[24] In the center of the funerary procession, three soul carriages (called *shengche* 乘車, *daoche* 導車, and *gauche* 藁車), loaded with the deceased's three different sets of clothes, preceded the hearse.[25] Whereas the soul carriages were horse-drawn, people pulled the hearse by hand.

Despite some variation, the basic structure of the Eastern Han funerary ritual remained largely the same as its Eastern Zhou precedent. The imperial funerary ceremony lasted for a few weeks at the emperor's residence—the imperial palace.[26] On the day of entombment, the deceased emperor was "duplicated" on two ritual vehicles: a four-wheeled carriage (*silunzhou* 四輪輈), the hearse (*binche* 賓車), held the coffined body and a two-wheeled soul carriage (*rongche* 容車, or *ronggenche* 容根車) held the emperor's clothes.[27] Both were ornamented in the same way and shared the same imperial cortège; the hearse was pulled by three hundred men and the soul carriage was drawn by six horses.[28] After arriving at the cemetery, the hearse was parked temporarily on the tomb passage to the south of the grave, and the soul carriage was stationed right before a tent (the "spirit seat") to the west of the tomb passage, facing south.

In the second stage of both the Eastern Zhou and Eastern Han rites, after the spectacular processions, the ritual of interment was performed under the gaze of a crowd made up of the deceased's relatives and guests, who were gathered at the cemetery.

In the late Eastern Zhou ritual, after the coffin arrived at the graveyard, the burial objects were displayed on the east and west sides of the tomb passage. The relatives of the deceased gathered to witness the process of entombment: First, the coffin was lowered down into the grave, then the ritual specialists circled the coffin with various grave goods, and finally, the casket (*guo*) was covered with a heavy lid lowered from overhead. This procedure was designed for the vertical pit graves of the era, around which a crowd might have stood and watched from above.[29]

In the Eastern Han rite, although the plan of the tomb had changed from a vertical pit to a chamber-like space, the whole process of entombment was still under constant observation. When the interment began, the hearse moved forward along the ramp into the underground tomb chamber. Grave goods followed. After the corpse and the burial objects had been laid down, a number of honorable guests—usually top officials in the imperial government—walked into the tomb chamber (*fang* 房) to perform the ritual of cry (*ku* 哭) and to bid farewell to the departed emperor. When the ritual ended, every living person present in the tomb chamber retreated back aboveground. But even after this evacuation, the tomb chamber still remained open temporarily because the ritual of interment had not yet ended. Still contained within the soul carriage, the deceased emperor's clothes then were sent to the "hall of ease" (*biandian* 便殿) in the aboveground ritual compound. A wine offering was presented to the ritual outfits as soon as they had been enshrined in the hall. Then, the whole interment ceremony—described in Sima Biao's account as "descent" or "sending down" and taking ten "quarters" of time (about two-and-half hours)—finally came to an end. The grave was sealed and then covered by a tumulus.[30]

For both the Eastern Zhou and the Eastern Han, the entire process of the funeral ceremony was conducted as a visual spectacle until the very last minute (the "sending down") and the greatest monitor of this ritual was the government.

It seems that nothing escaped the surveillance of the government. According to Sima Qian, the son of General Zhou Yafu 周亞夫 (d. 143 BCE) bought five hundred sets of surrogate armor from the imperial workshop for his father's tomb. When Zhou was accused of committing treason, this purchase became proof of his guilt. The legal officials berated him, "Even if you did not plan to use the armor to rebel above the ground, you can still do so under the ground!"[31] The general was finally convicted. In this story, the personal act of acquiring grave goods was not really private but was monitored by the government, and the underworld (burial) was not a safe haven where people could hide from political persecution.

Even after someone had been buried, the government still reserved the right to open and inspect the tomb to make necessary alterations, though such instances usually happened when the deceased's political status changed posthumously. For example, when Grand Marshal (*Dasima* 大司馬)

Dong Xian 董賢 (22–1 BCE) lost his power and committed suicide, Dong's father hurriedly and secretly interred his son's body at night, hoping to hide the excessiveness of the burial goods. But his attempt was in vain. The government ordered the tomb to be exhumed for inspection and found the deceased wearing a jade suit, pearls, and *bi* discs in a lavishly ornamented coffin painted with images of the sun, the moon, and the four directional gods and fashioned with precious cinnabar, gold, and silver pigments, which the disgraced Dong Xian no longer merited. After stripping off the inappropriate material extravagance, Dong was reburied in a prison, with his body totally naked.[32]

What was concealed from public view in a burial was not forgotten by worldly authorities, even many years after the entombment. In 5 CE, the imperial government, under the direction of Wang Mang, prosecuted Empress Dowager Fu 傅 (d. 2 BCE) and Empress Dowager Ding 丁 (d. 5 BCE), both of whom had died years earlier. In addition to stripping them of their honored titles, officials ordered their bodies exhumed from the imperial cemetery, smashed their seals, removed their jewelry and jades, downgraded their coffins, and banished their burials from the royal mausoleum to the local principality of Dingtao 定陶 where they were from originally.[33] Clearly, the imperial government had never forgotten what was concealed in the royal ladies' hidden tombs. It is very likely that all burial information was written down and kept on file, so that it could be checked at any time during a new political situation.

But why did the Han Chinese not opt to abandon the traditional practice of permanently hiding the burial and make it completely open and accessible to the public like their Roman counterparts? Why was it necessary to keep the burial a secret—albeit an open secret—at the conclusion of a public spectacle?

Han-period exegetes interpreted tombs as signifying "concealment" (*cang* 藏), a broader concept that usually applied to those state possessions (*fucang* 府藏) that had restricted access.[34] Interpreting the tomb as signifying "concealment" elevated the value of the tomb and associated its contents—the most important of which was the deceased's body—with power and authority.

Like the encoffined tomb occupants, sacred rulers were supposed to be concealed from ordinary people. This idea is advanced in the *Zhuangzi* text, which argued that the godly "true man" (*zhenren* 真人 or *zhiren* 至人) must remain hidden from others. The First Emperor of Qin was a faithful practitioner of this principle. According to Sima Qian, the emperor insisted that he must travel on secret roads that were shielded on both sides by tall walls, so nobody beyond the walls could see his carriage. On one occasion, when information about his whereabouts leaked out, the emperor immediately identified and executed all those in attendance upon him that day.[35]

Besides the ruler's body, another thing that was often concealed in early China was knowledge about governance. These included techniques for cultivating personal longevity and ruling the state, which, as I have argued, were united in Huang-Lao thought. After Liu An presented the *Huainanzi* to Emperor Wu, the emperor "cherished and hid" this "secret book" (*mishu* 秘書) in his personal collection. [36] Likewise, a secret "bronze casket" and "stone chamber" (*jinkui shishi* 金匱石室) located in the deepest niche of the imperial ancestral temple concealed the most important texts concerning the welfare of the royal family and the state.[37] In the *Elder Dai's Record of Ritual* (*Dadai liji* 大戴禮記) text, one of the Confucian canons compiled no later than the second century CE, the sacred "Way of Prenatal Teachings" (*taijiao zidao* 胎教之道) was inscribed on jade tablets and hidden in a bronze casket placed in the ancestral temple.[38] In a similar manner, Emperor Gao made "vermilion documents" (*zhushu* 朱書) and "iron contracts" (*tiequan* 鐵券) with his dynasty-founding ministers and generals and sealed them up in a bronze casket and stone chamber in the ancestral temple to ensure these agreements would never expire.[39] If anyone dared to steal such secret knowledge and give it to outsiders without the emperor's permission, he or she would be punished;[40] as the *Master Yin Wen* (*Yin Wenzi* 尹文子) text states, "Rulers must use the art of rulership in secrecy, and those of the lower ranks must not look at them without permission."[41]

The reason for keeping the burial inaccessible seems to be similar. The tomb was designed intentionally as a permanently closed space to render its contents (including both the corpse and the grave goods) sacred. Restricted access signified the sacredness of the hidden object, and the burial's absolute inaccessibility meant unsurpassed sacredness. However, people in early China clearly understood that no burial could escape tomb robbery forever. In the *Annals of Lü Buwei* text, the authors confessed that, "From antiquity until now, there has never been an imperishable state. Since there are no imperishable states, there are no impregnable tombs."[42] But making all efforts to deter break-ins was not so much a measure used to avoid plundering as it was an effort to keep the contents of a tomb as restricted as possible, and thus, as sacred as possible. In this case, even when a tomb's many defenses were eventually breached, the arduous process of trying to overcome them attested to the extraordinary value of the pursued contents.

Therefore, it is not that concealment was the nature of tombs, but that tombs exemplified the essence of concealment, a concept that existed in other sociopolitical domains. In light of the metaphorical parallel between the concealed tomb (itself a casket) and the concealed "bronze caskets" and "stone chamber" used to store state secrets, we might assume that the contents of the former were conceptually comparable to the contents of the latter—the sacred ruler and the secret of ruling techniques.

This culture of concealment may help us better understand why the entrances to the richly furnished tombs at the Mancheng site were concealed behind stone and earth coverings that imitated the exterior face of the natural mountain (fig. 0.2). This was fundamentally different from the ancient Persian royal cliff-cut burials at Naqsh-e Rustam (in what is now Iran) that dated to the Achaemenid Empire (550–330 BCE). Here, locations and entrances had lavishly decorated, flamboyant facades that simulated the front view of a royal building (while the interior of the tomb was much simpler).[43] Conversely, only a few privileged people might have been admitted into the spacious house-like Han royal tombs and allowed a glimpse at what were called "secret objects" (*miqi* 秘器) by Han authors.[44] Indeed, the same practice applied to other items, such as the clandestine ritual offerings to heaven made during Feng and Shan 封禪 ceremonies. Emperor Wu reportedly held such "secret sacrifices" (*mici* 祕祠) to heavenly gods at the top of Mt. Tai, and no one was allowed to witness or document these events.[45] At the Mancheng site, it is possible that the concealed sacrificial space in the front chambers of the tombs cut into Mt. Ling might have shared a similar consecrated meaning.

In short, while it was true that royal tombs in Western Han China were meant to be permanently shut and sealed up after the final entombment, this fact does not negate viewership in the forbidden structures. For the tomb designer, the intended viewers were more likely the ancestral spirits or a psychological construct (such as the imaginary "other") because the ruler's experience of being watched did not require the physical presence of an actual viewer. What might have amplified the experience of being watched was the fact that the concealed royal burial was the conclusion of a public spectacle, the funeral ceremony, which was intended to be viewed by spectators. It was under the latter's gaze that the burial was finally closed and the tomb kept secret to ensure the sacredness of its contents—including the physical remains of the deceased ruler and his political ideology—as among the state's most guarded assets.

THE ROYAL TOMB AS A DISPLAY OF OBJECTS

Concealed deeply underground, the order of things in a Chinese tomb evolved over time till it reached a turning point in the second century BCE. The much-enlarged interior space of Western Han royal tombs was the result of a consistent practice of "unzipping" and "unpacking" earlier burial spaces.[46] This practice turned what used to be a closed burial space into an open one, a dense space into a loose one, a wrapped space into an unfolded one, and a shapeless space into a shaped one. The logic behind tomb design was manifested so thoroughly that spatial order is lucid enough to be sensed, observed, and deciphered. Two important new changes characterized Western Han royal tombs.

First, the burial was reoriented from vertical to horizontal, which redefined how the tomb was accessed. Whereas the early Shang and Zhou shaft graves imposed a bird's-eye view on the viewer (fig. 0.1), Western Han royal tombs, such as those at the Mancheng site, each contained a door that shaped the space into *front* and *rear* (fig. 0.3). It should be noted that not every opening qualifies as a door. A skylight piercing a roof is not a door, even if it can be used as an entry into a house. Rather, a door, as the Chinese pictograph 門 shows, is a vertical installation of two leaves that marks a border where front meets rear, inside meets outside.[47] A door must also open and close, thus connecting and separating spaces. With doors that could open laterally (sometimes symbolically), people actually could walk into burial chambers via sloping ramps. Therefore, a tomb's space was measured by its horizontal rather than its vertical depth.

This spatial transformation was accompanied by increased sacrificial activities in the tomb, particularly in the front area, which imitated a temple setting. Light, pleasant aromas, and delightful sounds were emitted physically or symbolically from the objects that were interwoven across the unfolded and expanded space, which constituted a sensuous world. The body retreated to the rear of the burial space and no longer formed the sole center of the tomb. Instead, what dominated the tomb was a dual structure of corporeal and incorporeal existence, each bound to the other in a harmonious unity. The corpse's spiritual companion was housed, seated, and worshipped in a visual and material setting. Here, the polarity of body and soul, which baffled many scholars of Chinese religion and philosophy, finds its most vivid illustration. Action was simulated by the staging of banqueting, traveling, and hunting, each attended by servants. All these formal, structural, and compositional changes marked a significant shift in the relationship between the other world (represented by the tomb) and this world. Once temple sacrifices were duplicated in the tomb chamber, this buried sacrificial space gained a double identity as burial and temple, concealed and open, dead and alive.

Second, the way in which the burial was furnished also changed from substance-oriented (*typological*) to organization-oriented (*topological*). The obscure, dense chunk of ritual materials packed up in a stereotypical wooden casket in a vertical pit tomb was transformed into an intelligible material composition in a house-like architectural space simulating a daily-living environment.

In typical Shang- and Zhou-period vertical pit graves, many low-profile vessels such as cups or basins were stacked up.[48] Small objects were often put inside larger vessels. Some round vessels that could not be stacked, such as pots, were often piled together. The purpose of such an arrangement was more to emphasize sheer material abundance rather than to represent a dining scene.

Western Han royal tombs were different from those Zhou precedents in how space was assigned to objects contained within. As the architectural setting shifted from the vertical casket (*guo* 椁) to the horizontal chamber (*shi* 室), the burial objects acquired new spatial dimensions and potential. From the viewpoint of archaeologist Huang Xiaofen, the two morphological characteristics that distinguish the horizontal chamber from the casket are connectivity and openness, rather than isolation and inaccessibility.[49] Needless to say, the closed casket assumed much less physical and visual access than the open horizontal chamber. As a result, the horizontal tomb was no longer a tightly filled container packed with grave goods.[50] It became an organic space endowed with intuitive or habitual qualities (such as directions) that characterized a daily environment. Rather than being stacked on different levels, the burial objects were laid out on a common flat floor. Like images scattered across a canvas, they coalesced to form a "picture" in the burial space; yet somehow they mirrored, albeit in more or less distorted forms, those familiar scenes and scenarios from daily life. Objects across space then acquired directions, orientations, and relations, unfolding into a topological network.

These new features of Western Han royal tombs subverted the conventions of earlier Shang and Zhou designs. So, what is the nature of this transformation? How do we understand the rational impetus that forged a new look for these tombs during this period? What is the "first cause" of this transformation? Was it the architecture, the burial objects, the deceased's subjectivity, or the ritual?

Since all these elements changed simultaneously, none of them can be regarded as logically conditioning the others. These individual transformations were not causes but were consequences of a new situation and a new desire that could no longer be satisfied by the old mortuary conventions. I will argue that what essentially drove the external changes in these tombs was a "visual turn," which was the result of an impetus to create visible formations among burial objects that could "show" ideas and let them be seen. Eventually, this new trend would give birth to the widespread use of murals in Chinese tombs during the late Western Han (ca. first century BCE), an important issue that will be explained in the next section.

Whereas the Western Han royal tombs are "visual," earlier Shang and Zhou vertical shaft tombs may be described as predominantly "substantial." Here, the term substantial emphasizes two dominant concerns expressed in traditional vertical pit graves. First, the pit burial demonstrates an obsession with the content (the material, number, and combination) of ritual grave goods, which measured and registered the tomb occupant's social status. For instance, during the Eastern Zhou, a lord could own seven *ding* tripods, while a *shi* gentleman could only possess one; this numerical difference was more crucial than how these tripods were handled or arranged. Second, the hierarchical material content was not meant to be displayed to any audience in the tomb but was more likely just a deposit, a hidden bulk of ritual vessels packed in a large or small space. Not coincidently, in the *Book of Etiquette and Ceremonial*, the author described what grave goods were included but did not specify how they should be arranged in the tomb.[51] In the excavated inventories of burial objects (conventionally called *qiance* 遣冊) interred in a number of well-preserved tombs in South China, scholars have identified only lists of names and quantities of objects without any indication of their spatial arrangement or relationship in the tombs.[52]

While Eastern Zhou authors seem to have been quite comfortable with the notion of obscurity in death, they were more focused on constructing good order in life. In the *Book of Etiquette and Ceremonial*, the placement of ritual vessels was specified in great detail for sacrificial occasions in above-ground temples; the ritual canon always painstakingly dictates how many and what types of vessels should be placed at what locations and in what formations in the temple. For example, on the evening before the "single beast offering rite" (*Tesheng kuishi* 特牲饋食),

[The tripods must be set] outside the door, facing north, and graded from the west . . .
The trencher is to the south of them, with its edge adjusted squarely south. On it are
laid the dried game, with their heads to the east. The beast is to the west of this, with
its head to the north, and its feet to the east. The used-jar is set to the southeast of
the eastern steps, and a jar on a stand against the east inner wall. The wooden and
splint holders and the tureen are laid in the east chamber, graded from the south. The
body-rest, mat, and two jars of grain are in the west side-hall . . .[53]

If this was a description of an ideal ritual occasion, then the amount of
attention the reporter paid to the positional detail is nearly excessive (for
instance, the edge of trencher has to be "squarely south" rather than just
south). Noting the stark difference in how life and death interested his contemporaries, Confucius is said to have remarked, "We have not yet learned
to know life. How can we know death?"[54] The master probably spoke about
a general view of death at that time. In fact, few Eastern Zhou texts discussed
such unknowns as what the underworld might look like, what deity might
manage it, and how it could relate to the living world—issues that were of
utmost importance in Egyptian texts and depictions.[55]

The visual turn I have identified indicates that Western Han subjects were
no longer content with the previous darkness attributed to death; a similar care once lavished on the placement of objects in aboveground temples
now also appeared in burials. This remarkable deed, to borrow Mark Lewis's
phrasing, created "space out of chaos" through "technical, moral, and intellectual innovations" that only cultural heroes and sages could undertake.[56]
This, as I will argue later, was precisely what demanded the royal attention
to and passion for planning mausoleums, especially hidden, subterranean
burials. This visual turn attested to an effort made to unzip, unravel, and illuminate the inaccessible, packed, and dark casket—in other words, to visualize the world of the dead. This paradigmatic shift thus describes the creation
of an order of things by visual means. Subsequently, the extremely orderly
sacrifices, which used to be held only aboveground, moved down into the
tomb, as we see in the two front chambers at the Mancheng site.

It is important to note that the word "turn" in "visual turn" means "shift of
focus" rather than "invention." To be more explicit, earlier vertical pit graves
did contain order, and the substantiality of grave goods continued to be a
concern in tombs. However, there was a critical shift of focus away from the
tomb's contents (i.e., their quantity and material quality) and onto the visual
order of the contents. Chinese tombs were in a constant state of evolution

characterized by a subtle tension between continuity and discontinuity, as Alain Thote has noted in non-elite Chu tombs during the late Eastern Zhou period.[57] However, it was not until the second century BCE, and notably in royal tombs, that the tension intensified into a critical turning point, where discontinuity burst forth, breaking the balance and shifting the paradigm toward a radically different mode.

As a result of this visual turn, the tomb designer would have to impose some cognitive or interpretative order on the opened tomb structure and its unpacked contents—the type of order that in W. J. T. Mitchell's words, "holds the world together" with "figures of knowledge."[58] Among the cognitive efforts, the projection of daily scenes (as abstract structures, models, or concrete scenes) onto the burial objects attested to an attempt to domesticate the sacred space and turn it into a familiar place. Under the gaze of an ideal viewer, this visual shift in early Chinese royal tombs brought a lucid order to the previously forbidden area that no mourners were supposed to enter during or after the funeral. The elucidation of the burial space is essentially an epistemological project of making sense of what was previously unexpressed or inexpressible.

What determined the placement of burial objects during the Western Han period? Whereas the tomb pits, burial devices (*guan* 棺 and *guo* 槨, coffins and caskets), and the types of objects were often generic, the pattern of arranging grave goods varied from case to case. This should come as no surprise because early Western Han laws seemed to be relatively flexible regarding what objects should be interred with the tomb occupant and how they should be arranged. In the recently discovered "Statutes on Burial" (*Zanglü* 葬律) from Shuihudi tomb no. 77—the only surviving law from the second century BCE regulating elite burials in detail—the published statute text is devoted to specificities of the coffins, sacrificed animals, and ritual structures, without any restrictions on objects buried with the dead:[59]

徹侯衣衾毋過盈棺，衣衾斂束。（荒）所用次也。其殺：小斂用一特牛，棺、開各一大牢，祖一特牛，遣一大牢。棺中之廣毋過三尺二寸，深三尺一寸，表丈一尺，厚七寸。椁二，其一厚尺一八寸；臧椁一，厚五寸，得用炭。（墼）、斗、羡深淵上六丈，坟大方十三丈，高三丈。荣（茔）東西四十五丈，北南四十二丈，重圍（？）垣之，高丈。祠（？）舍盖，盖地方六丈。中垣为門，外為闕，垣四陬為不（罘）思（罳）。

The number of clothes and quilts for a Penetrating Lord [i.e., a marquis] should not exceed the capacity of the coffin. The clothes and quilts must be packed with ropes into bundles. The fabric used for the coffin cover should not be finer than that used for clothes and quilts. As for animal killing [i.e., sacrifice], at the time of the lesser dressing, one singular bull is used. At the times of the major dressing and coffining, a bull, a ram, and a boar. At the sacrifice of departure, a singular bull. When sending the coffin away to the grave, a bull, a ram, and a boar. The width of the coffin should not exceed three *chi* and two *cun* [approximately 0.74 meters], the height, three *chi* and one *cun* [approximately 0.72 meters], the length, eleven *chi* [approximately 2.541 meters], thickness, seven *cun* [approximately 0.16 meters]. There should be two outer coffins [*guo*]. One of them [for the corpse] should measure one *chi* and eighteen *cun* [approximately 0.65 meters] thick, and the other one for grave goods is five *cun* thick [approximately 0.12 meters]. Charcoal may be applied [to encase the outer coffins]. The floor of the tomb pit, the shaft, and the ramp goes six *zhang* [approximately 13.86 meters] down below the ground. The square tumulus measures thirteen *zhang* [approximately 30 meters] on each side and three *zhang* [approximately 6.93 meters] in height. The graveyard measures 45 *zhang* [approximately 103.95 meters] from east to west, and 42 *zhang* [approximately 97.02 meters] from north to south. The graveyard is enclosed by two walls, each of which stands one *zhang* [approximately 2.31 meters] in height. The funerary shrine is sheltered by a square roof, six *zhang* [approximately 13.86 meters] on each side. For the inner wall construct gates, and for the outer wall build gate-pillars. At the four corners of the outer wall construct watch towers.[60]

Although the law speaks to those holding the rank of penetrating lord (*Chehou* 徹侯), or marquis, who were one level below the kings (*Zhuhou Wang* 諸侯王) on the social ladder,[61] it reveals that the early Western Han legal authority was more interested in the dimensions of funerary spaces (coffins, tomb pits, graveyards, and so on) rather than the material contents (bronzes, lacquerware, ceramics, and so on) that filled them. Likewise, in this passage, there is no indication of the geography or the topography of the cemetery; the surviving law did not prescribe where one should situate his or her grave. Although the Shuihudi material is yet to be fully published, and we have no idea whether the aforementioned section constituted the entire original statute, the current silence on the regulation of burial objects is not an isolated phenomenon. Transmitted texts only include a few fragments of Han laws that regulate the height of tumulus and the number of people who participated in the funeral of a marquis.[62] Discovered in King Cuo's tomb in Pingshan and dated to the late fourth century BCE, the cast bronze blueprint of the king's tomb was similarly marked with the dimensions of the coffins, walls of the mausoleum, and affiliated ritual facilities without any specification about grave goods.[63] The same interest and disinterest were vividly illustrated in a small painting on silk, identified as a map, from Mawangdui tomb no. 3.[64] This simple ink sketch consists of two parts. The upper part features the plan of a mounded tomb, consisting of a square tomb pit approached by a short ramp, and the lower part features another plan of a walled courtyard complex, most likely representing a funerary shrine erected to the south of the grave.[65] However, the painter excluded information about the grave's contents from this map.

The similar omission of burial objects from both the surviving law and the map of an elite burial might suggest there was more freedom in selecting grave goods during the Han period. In fact, the thrifty Emperor Wen ordered only simple ceramics to be interred in his tomb, but his extravagant grandson, Emperor Wu, filled his tomb in the Mao Mausoleum with so many precious treasures that even before his death the originally spacious burial was already full.[66]

The reduced regulation concerning grave goods left ample room for innovation, probably based on the patron's special request. Around this period time, Chinese people began to pay more attention to the arrangement of things in tombs. It was reported in the *Former Rituals of the Han* (Han Jiuyi) text (ca. first century CE) that in Emperor Wu's Mao Mausoleum, various burial objects were placed in the center of the "inner chamber" (*neifang* 內方) and then encircled by carriages and horses, which were in turn surrounded by weapons installed in the "outer chamber" (*waifang* 外方).[67] A similar awareness about placement can be observed in other imperial tombs as well. A third-century CE text, *Readings for the Emperor* (*Huanglan* 皇覽), relates:

漢家之葬，方中百步，已穿築為方城。其中開四門，四通，足放六馬，然後錯渾雜物，抒漆繒綺金寶米穀，及埋車馬虎豹禽獸。

The burial of a Han imperial house member measures a hundred footsteps on each side of the central chamber [approximately 138.6 meters]. After excavating down and building up a square [retaining] wall, four gates were opened in the four directions. The gates were broad enough to contain six horses. Afterward, [they interred] various miscellaneous goods including lacquer, silk, embroidery, gold treasures, rice, and grains. And later, [they] interred carriages, horses, tigers, leopards, birds, and beasts.[68]

The author used a series of adverbs governing time (*yi* 已, *ranhou* 然後, and *ji* 及) to outline the imperial ritual process: After constructing the tomb architecture, people first brought in various utensils and provisions, which were supposed to fill the inner zone of the tomb. Then they placed carriages and horses for traveling and animals for hunting in the outer zone of the tomb.

These transmitted texts, succinct as they are, expressed a new appreciation for the burial as a space of objects that emerged during the Western Han dynasty. During the second century BCE, such an epistemological quest for a lucid order of things in a forbidden burial was not isolated from other cultural innovations of this period. It was not until the Qin and Han, as Donald Harper, Poo Mou-chou, and other scholars have demonstrated, that Chinese people attempted to systematically explain the world after death through various religious or philosophical discourses on the forms of otherworldly lands.[69]

THE ROYAL TOMB AS A LATENT PICTORIAL NARRATIVE

One of the direct consequences of the visual turn in Chinese tombs was the introduction of murals. This increased visual lucidity at Mancheng and other royal burial sites fostered the development of pictorial wall paintings in tombs. Although the popularity of mural painting occurred in China much later than in ancient Egypt, Crete, or Italy, this new art medium quickly grew into an influential artistic tradition in the first century BCE and fundamentally reshaped the way in which royal tombs were designed in the post-Han period. Throughout the Western Han dynasty, however, these murals—commissioned mainly by officials and rich commoners—rarely aroused the interest of royalty. In the tombs at the Mancheng site, for instance, not even an inch of the walls was found covered with paintings. This was not due to the ignorance of the mural as an artistic medium or to a lack of skilled painters. On the contrary, archaeological evidence has proven that Chinese painters had been decorating the walls of imperial palaces since at least the late Eastern Zhou period.[70] So what kept murals out of the royal tombs at the Mancheng site?

In this last section, I will argue that this overt rejection of the mural form was not a rejection of pictorialization itself but rather the adoption of a different form of pictorialization through object installations. For instance, many of the most popular pictorial motifs seen in carved or painted murals in tombs, including banquets and chariot processions, were latent and sometimes even were made visible through the object installations at the Mancheng site. As Martin Powers has argued, it may be that royal subjects during the Han period rejected explicit pictorial representations as more suited for ruled subjects or commoners.[71]

So how did the installation of objects form a picture or even a picto-rial narrative? One of the most "pictorial" scenes in royal tombs is found in Liu Sheng's front chamber, which depicted a dining event similar to those portrayed in numerous tomb murals from the early Eastern Han and later periods. The offering of food was one of the most important rituals in the social life of the early Chinese.[72] This was just as true in Han royal tombs where kitchen and tableware constituted the majority of all burial objects.

Recognizing the latent theme of dining within Liu Sheng's front chamber is not easy because the installation consisted of two groups of three-dimensional objects rather than flat pictorial images. The first group portrayed a kitchen, and the second, a banquet. Because the objects were made individually and assembled together in the tomb to form a unit, they did not possess the interactive postures or gestures from one to another that we normally would see among figures in a picture.[73] Therefore, it is necessary for the viewer's imagination to turn the installation of objects into a meaningful pictorial scene or narrative.

A kitchen scene can be identified in the northern bay of the structure in Liu Sheng's front chamber, which was filled with common functional ceram-ics instead of precious ceremonial metal objects, usually staged in or around tents or tables. Besides the lamps set on the eastern side, from east to west, there were a series of basins (fig. 1.7, nos. 45–46, 48–59, 63, 65), a *hu* vessel (fig. 1.7, no. 75), and jars (fig. 1.7, nos. 76–82). These ceramic vessels consisted of two types: wine or food containers (including the *hu* vessels and the jars) and washbowls for food preparation, which were the hallmarks of a kitchen. The five, shallow, round-bottomed bowls, the only ones in this tomb, were water containers and cannot be mistaken for the deep flat-bottomed jars that usually served as food containers.[74]

What clinches the kitchen theme in this assemblage is a group of five small bronze vessels—three identical vessels without handles (fig. 1.7, no. 16) and two identical vessels with handles (fig. 1.7, no. 17)—that were located in the east section next to the basins. Measuring 5.3 centimeters tall and 2.3 centimeters in diameter, each of these miniature vessels has a flat mouth and a pointed bottom (fig. 6.1a). Two of them bear little holes in the bottom. The jars measure 6.2 centimeters by 2.8 centimeters and stand 5.7 centimeters tall, each with a round bottom and a handle.[75] The identical material and similar scale make the vases and jars a perfect set. These were obviously

(a)

(b)

FIGURE 6.1 (a) Miniature bronze buckets from Mancheng tomb no. 1, Mancheng, Hebei, ca. 113 BCE. Courtesy of Hebei Museum, Shijiazhuang; (b) One miniature ceramic well model, height: 26 cm, Luoyang, Henan, first to second centuries CE. Courtesy of Henan Museum, Zhengzhou.

too small to be functional utensils. Miniature devices that usually consist of a ceramic model of a shaft (represented by a square or circular basin or bucket) and small containers that hold water have been uncovered in many contemporary tombs (fig. 6.1b).[76] In the light of this evidence, we can confidently identify these tiny bronze vessels found in the front chamber of Liu Sheng's tomb as suspended buckets for drawing water from a well.[77] These containers might have been paired with the ceramic basins to symbolize wells and water resources, indispensable elements for a kitchen.

What really enlivened this installation of kitchenware, turning it into a pictorial narrative of food preparation activities, was the presence of figurines. Two arrayed assemblages of female figures (fig. 1.7, nos. 60–62, 70–74) stood among the ceramic lamps, food and wine containers, washbowls, and water buckets, as though they were busy using these instruments to make meals.

Using figurines to evoke narratives in a spatial context was an invention of the Western Han period. Western Han figurines were essentially different from their Eastern Zhou counterparts—not in representation but in their relationship to the space around them. In Chu tombs of the late Eastern Zhou period, figurines populated the burial compartments along with various objects such as musical instruments, food vessels, and other utensils of daily life.[78] They may have represented keepers or watchers of these household items, but in such busy compartments crammed with tightly packed grave goods, this meaningful association was never lucidly defined but only vaguely implied. In Changtaiguan tomb no. 2, dating to the late fourth century BCE, for example, ten wooden figures were literally "buried" among multiple layers of objects and were barely visible in the compartment.[79] In contrast, figurines in Liu Sheng's tomb demonstrate a completely different method of presentation. As Machida Akira has observed in the First Emperor of Qin's mausoleum, the upright stance of the terra-cotta soldiers in the satellite pits redefined the vertical pit as a new type of lived space.[80] Likewise, in Liu Sheng's tomb, the change of architecture was synchronic with the transformed role of figurines in the space. It is hard to determine which preceded which in triggering the paradigmatic shift of the tomb space and its meaning.

Standing or sitting, and oriented in various directions, these figurines generated an inter-bodily space with one another and coordinated the household environment. Situated in a tall and spacious horizontal tomb chamber, burial objects also reclaimed their concrete bonds with these figurines as their subjects. Figurines obtained a spatial dimension that both linked objects and modified space. The location, orientation, and arrangement of these figurines conveyed rich information that otherwise would have been unknown. For example, around Liu Sheng's tent in the front chamber of Mancheng tomb no. 1, two rows of standing figurines (fig. 1.7, nos. 149–156) were placed on the east side of the tent facing toward it. This placement defines not only the tent's orientation as facing eastward but also the figurines as attending to the tent (and its occupant). Without the human figurines in the royal hall, the structure of the space would have become less lucid and intelligible because a standing human torso automatically defines a three-dimensional space (and the potential for a pictorial narrative), dividing the front from the back and the top from the bottom. The figurines dressed and positioned as attendants implied a direct face-to-face meeting with their master. Although there were multiple tables and at least one more seat in front of the tent, the direction of the figurines clearly excluded them from being the focus of this assemblage and marked them as being affiliated with the central focus.

This distinct characteristic made the Western Han figurines both *object* and *subject* at the same time. As an object, they lost all human nature and became part of the grave goods listed in tomb inventories as property of the tomb occupant. But as subject, they coordinated (rather than just filling) a household space—not just as mere things but as potentially dynamic "bodies." In their capacity as subjects, the figurines turn the static sites of kitchen and dining room into lively events of preparing and eating food.

Representing a kitchen, the clay lamps, figurines, jars, washbowls, and water buckets formed a generic combination repeated in many early and mid-Western Han period tombs that were sometimes supplemented with other representations of daily-use objects such as grindstones, food containers, or stoves.[81] In many of these lesser tombs, however, the ceramic utensils and figurines were often mixed with traditional ritual vessels including *ding* tripods, *hu* or *fang* pots, and *he* boxes.[82] Yet with all the artifacts mingling together in a small pit grave, it is difficult to determine the relationships among them. What makes Liu Sheng's tomb special is the fact that these two groups of objects were clearly separate. While the ritual assemblage was located at the eastern end of the central bay of Liu Sheng's front chamber, the ceramic utensils and figurines lay in the northern bay (fig. 1.7). This implies a hierarchy between the two groups because the ritual assemblage, mostly fashioned of bronze, occupied the center while the clay objects were pushed to the periphery; this also indicates that these objects, all associated with eating, had been distributed in multiple locations across space with a more lucid distinction between the two scenes of preparing the food and serving the meal.

In the central and southern bays of Liu Sheng's front chamber, however, the dominant theme clearly shifted from cooking to dining.

Various vessels used for banqueting were found around the two tents set up in the two bays. Whereas in the Shang and Western Zhou periods, the deceased usually was buried with a set of ritual vessels placed near the corpse, in Western Han tombs, such ritual vessels were mixed up with other daily-use utensils to represent the tomb occupant's consumption of food. Perhaps aware of this change, Jessica Rawson compared Liu Sheng's front chamber with wall paintings of banqueting in Eastern Han decorated tombs and concluded "for the time being, that there was no difference between everyday banqueting utensils, employed to nourish the tomb occupant, and those that in life were used for offerings for ancestors."[83] This, of course, does not mean the ritual scenario had entirely vanished in the tomb but rather demonstrates that the conventional "ritual" (i.e., cultic) instruments in Shang and Zhou tombs acquired a narrative meaning and now represented dining in Han period tombs.

This change gave rise to two interconnected parallel sections in the tomb space: on the one side, kitchen and cooking (producing), and on the other side, banquet and eating (consuming). Sometimes the divide between the two sections was implicit. Around the second tent in Liu Sheng's front chamber, for instance, cooking and dining wares were combined and "squeezed" into a compact space. Such mixing was commonly practiced in many lesser Han tombs where space was limited.

The narrative of making, serving, and consuming a meal was still implicit in Mancheng tomb no. 1 because it lacked a pictorial approach. However, in a lavish mural tomb at Dahuting (tomb no. 1) in present-day Mixian, Henan, dated nearly three centuries later, a series of elaborate wall engravings rendered the relationship between cooking and banqueting explicitly. Murals in the east side chamber represent a busy kitchen, in which chefs are shown handling cauldrons, pots, washbasins, steamers, and much kitchenware—similar to items displayed in Liu Sheng's front chamber (fig. 6.2a). On the walls of the passageway of the north side chamber, a few female servants, reminiscent of the figurines in Liu Sheng's tomb, are transporting cooked dishes (fig. 6.2b). They are heading toward the north side chamber in which a grand banquet is taking place inside a lavish tent, one that resembles the actual tent in Mancheng tomb no. 1. Many ladies sit behind tables, holding cups and plates in their hands (fig. 6.2c).[84] The east side chamber housed a kitchen, and the north side chamber hosted the banquet. These two chambers and scenes were simultaneously separated and connected in the middle

(a)

(b)

(c)

FIGURE 6.2 (a) Preparing food in kitchen at Dahuting tomb no. 1, line drawing of bas-relief, Mixian, Henan, second century CE. After An Jinhuai 安金槐, *Mixian dahuting Han mu* 密縣打虎亭漢墓 (Beijing: Wenwu chubanshe, 1993), fig. 105. Courtesy of Wenwu Press; (b) Transporting food at Dahuting tomb no. 1, line drawing of bas-relief, Mixian, Henan, second century CE. After An Jinhuai *Mixian dahuting Han mu*, fig. 109. Courtesy of Wenwu Press; (c) Banqueting at Dahuting tomb no. 1, line drawing of bas-relief, Mixian, Henan, second century CE. After An Jinhuai *Mixian dahuting Han mu*, fig. 127. Courtesy of Wenwu Press.

by the passageway. This is a perfect pictorial companion to the central bay of Liu Sheng's front chamber in which the tent hosted a banquet and the east side of the chamber held kitchen instruments.[85]

In both the Mancheng and Dahuting sites, despite the differences in artistic mediums, the sequence between scenes implies a narrative. In Liu Sheng's tomb, narrative elements including the characters, the plot, and the setting were available in the form of arranged objects. This was an entirely new development in Chinese funerary art. During the Shang and Zhou periods, objects—rather than the relationships among them—formed the major contents of a tomb; during the Western Han period, when tombs displayed an architectural context that more intuitively simulated the daily environment, things began to interact with one another to simulate day-to-day happenings or events. That is why scholars are able to identify the scene in Liu Sheng's front chamber as a banquet rather than merely a food offering, and they are able to identify the act of hunting, instead of just a chariot dedication. This significant change suggests that the tomb designer must have had several connected scenes taken from daily life in mind while furnishing the tomb. The mural genre that emerged during the first century BCE was a much stronger tool for representing such narratives.

However, Western Han rulers and top aristocrats showed a common indifference toward the extensive use of murals (such as stamped bricks, bas-reliefs, or wall paintings). Although murals (as an aboveground phenomenon) appeared in China long before the completion of the tombs at Mancheng,[86] most of the excavated Western Han royal tombs rejected wall paintings (or stone carvings with narrative content) even after such images had become popular in some lesser tombs around the metropolitan areas near Luoyang and Chang'an.[87] Why did Han royalty reject painting—a more effective tool for constructing a narrative—in their tombs?

The narrative implication in the Mancheng and other Western Han royal tombs does not mean that scenes formed by objects, such as cooking and dining, were merely rudimentary forms of later sophisticated pictorial displays evidenced by the murals at Dahuting. We must reject this teleological illusion of a gradual development of narrative representation from Western Han to Eastern Han without considering the differences across social strata.

It is important to realize that murals grew into a newer and, in some sense, more radical artistic fashion mainly in the hands of the commoners. In Martin Powers's opinion, the critical nature of pictorial art, which questioned the authority of the royals, was welcomed by the commoners.[88]

For Michael Nylan, however, "presumably most of those of mid-ranking wealth or status would have found it more difficult to supply the tomb with a complete set of sumptuous grave furnishings" so they used texts and paintings as substitutes.[89] If either of these theories is true, then the royalty clearly did not want or need murals.

A fundamental difference also stands between the two artistic media, painting and objects. Unlike images that *substitute* for objects, burial artifacts *are* objects.[90] Material, size, shape, decoration, and placement are equally important in determining a particular object's meaning in a tomb. Some grave goods such as figurines carry substitutive value, but most others— including functional utensils or daily-use items—are not substitutions at all. In no circumstances do objects present meanings in the same way as pictures.[91] The former are things themselves and therefore instances of presence, but the latter substitute for other things and are thus images.

The Western Han royal patrons understood the ontological difference between things and images, and their preference for objects over images is not a coincidence. For them, an image (*xiang* 象) was never a real thing (*shi* 實).[92] In Liu Sheng's front chamber, a full-scale representation of a banquet was carefully avoided. Unlike the busy scenes illustrated in the murals at Dahuting, some pieces of bronze kitchenware displayed in Liu Sheng's front chamber were ordered in alignment directly facing the "soul seats" (see fig. 1.7). These vessels, consisting of many traditional ritual styles (such as *ding* tripods), were organized more as being "dedicated" than as being "used." And no figurines were placed next to these large bronzes to highlight narrative relations. The same observation also applies to the chariots in the tomb tunnel. These meticulous details demonstrate the continuity of the traditional idea of ritual presentation, inherited from Shang and Zhou mortuary practices, in the Western Han royal tombs despite the dramatic change in the placement of burial objects. The rejection of pictures in favor of installations of objects conveys this message: As rulers, we do not need substitutes for things because we only display the real things that others do not possess and therefore must paint.

The latent narrative in the innovative installation of traditional burial objects sums up the most radical aspect of the royal tombs at Mancheng and other contemporaneous royal burial sites in the history of Chinese funerary art. The paradox can only be explained in the nature of the royal tombs during the Western Han period in which objects were intended to be concealed, displayed, and understood.

CONCLUSION

Chinese tombs are rich books that we are only beginning to learn how to read. Through the previous chapters, I have scrutinized an individual site—the twin tombs at Mancheng—to reveal the visual and material expression of political ideology associated with a particular subject—King Liu Sheng—in second century BCE Zhongshan, a kingdom struggling to achieve and maintain peace near the northern border of the Western Han Empire.

This book combines material, visual, and historical perspectives by studying the design of the Mancheng tombs, including architecture and objects, as a total work that embodies Liu Sheng's basic sociopolitical concerns. Following the norm of the Western Han period, the massive tombs at the Mancheng site were designed and built during Liu Sheng's reign and were funded by the state of Zhongshan. With Liu Sheng presumably presiding over the tomb plan as the final authority, the royal burials were designed to illuminate the proper order of the living world and to portray Liu Sheng's public image as the "king of peace." In this sense, the tombs at the Mancheng site functioned as an objective "model" of ideal rulership from the dual perspectives of Huang-Lao and Confucianism, both of which Liu Sheng practiced.[1] The design of the tomb architecture and furnishings visually articulates the political–philosophical idea of "pacifying" the world by reconciling body with soul, husband with wife, and Han Chinese with Rong-Di barbarians (*zhishen, zhijia, zhiguo* 治身, 治家, 治國). I argue that this tripartite model was a response to the political situation in the Zhongshan kingdom during the second century BCE. Liu Sheng externally supported the empire's goal to bring peace to the northern border, which was under the threat of the Xiongnu, and internally negotiated between the Dou family (his spousal branch) and the new Emperor Wu (his brother), who championed Huang-Lao thought and Confucianism, respectively. It seems that Liu Sheng deftly handled both challenges by reigning peacefully over Zhongshan for more than four decades. This achievement fully justified his official honorific title, "king of peace," which epitomizes an ideal of rulership in early Chinese political discourse.

If we extend our view beyond this particular site, how much can we learn about other royal tombs from this case study? How universally true are the observations we have made?

In the introduction to this book, I claimed that the Mancheng site is both a generic and a special case among Western Han royal tombs. Now that we have completed our exploration, it is clear that the Mancheng tombs are indeed comparable—in terms of design—to many other contemporary royal tombs, such as those in the Juye, Xuzhou, Yongcheng, and Guangzhou sites, during the Western Han period.

On the most basic level, all these tombs were physically labor-intensive projects, substantially furnished with official objects, and visually organized to evoke scenes from daily life. These generic features were projections of the public's image of a king. The tombs were planned during the reigns of their eventual occupants, sponsored by the state government, and intended as spectacles to behold.

On a higher level, these other contemporary tombs shared similar types of objects (such as ritual outfits, sacrificial instruments, and vehicles) arranged in similar ways (such as embracing, paralleling, and intermingling), following the modes I detected at Mancheng. Regarding the embrace of body and soul, the tomb designs were similarly divided into realms for the body and the soul, which were dominated by outfits and instruments, respectively. At the Hongtushan tomb, the sharpness of the dualism reached an extreme. The entire front chamber did not yield a single outfit object and the entire space was furnished solely by ritual instruments, particularly cooking and food vessels, which were centered in an offering table with a lacquer wine container placed on it.[2] As the distance from the corpse increased, burial objects shifted from outfits toward instruments in a manner similar to the displays at the Mancheng site. This shift can therefore be viewed as a process of disembodiment of the deceased and represents an effort to keep the increasingly disintegrating soul close to the well-protected body.

As for the relationship between husband and wife, most royal cemeteries included two parallel tombs—one for the king and one for the queen—oriented in the same direction. In some cases, these tombs were physically connected to each other by a short tunnel cut between the rear sections of both burials, where coffins were usually located. For example, a Chu royal cemetery dug into a low hill called Mt. Gui at Xuzhou consisted of two parallel burials both oriented to the west. While the two burials remained separate in the front, they were physically connected to each other through a short tunnel cut between chambers III and VII in the rear sections of both burials. In the Liang royal cemetery at Mt. Baoan with two parallel tombs, tomb no. 2 featured a tunnel hiding entirely in the mountain and extending straightly towards the south where tomb no. 1 is situated, though it never physically reaches the other tomb.[3] The scenario cannot be clearer: the deceased husband and his wife would stay in their bedrooms, forever connected.

The integration of various cultures was also a popular and notable phenomenon in royal tombs during the Western Han. At the tomb of the king (Emperor Wen) of Nanyue at Guangzhou, for example, archaeologists discovered two types of artifacts—some in Huaxia styles and others in the indigenous Yue style. Some objects found in the tomb, such as a bronze mirror, were directly imported from the neighboring Han.[4] Other objects, including a set of bronze bells, were local imitations based on Han models.[5] On the other hand, a set of bronze barrels was identified as a traditional ritual vessel typical of the Yue people.[6] The ornamentation on the barrels is reminiscent of the style of another non-ethnic-Han people called the Dian, who resided in what is now Yunnan, located west of the Yue.[7] Such examples of cultural mixtures seem to suggest an ideology similar to that in evidence at the Mancheng site: integration of customs.

These more advanced similarities are in accord with the comparable historical backgrounds and with the political and ideological climates in which these tombs were planned and built. During the period between 150 and 50 BCE, the young empire was still struggling at its frontiers to tighten its grip on newly conquered lands and populations, to fight the Xiongnu, and to prevent domestic rebellion. As recorded in historical texts, the predominant goal of maintaining local peace was firmly established as the primary political motivation for Emperor Wu's edicts bestowing fiefs to his sons.

This same time period was also when Huang-Lao thought and Confucianism were competing for dominance at the imperial court. In fact, it was not until Emperor Yuan's reign (r. 49–33 BCE) that Confucianism eventually prevailed in this contest.[8] Because of such broadly shared trends, it is not surprising that the Huang-Laoist and Confucian cultivation of the self, the family, and the state, which were among Liu Sheng's concerns, were also reflected at a number of other royal funerary sites.

The results from my study of the royal tombs challenge the well-received assumption that Chinese tombs at all social levels were built mainly to serve the deceased's private interest in enjoying a happy afterlife in a permanently shut and sealed underground "home." A close reading and contextualization of the tombs at Mancheng and other comparable royal sites demonstrates that in the Western Han royal cemeteries, the design of the tombs addressed issues far beyond personal welfare. Other dominant themes included the harmony and stabilization of family and state. The desire for longevity, which was apparently a personal interest, also served as the basis for other higher purposes in the king's political agenda.

Tombs were constructed in a particular manner (wooden-chambered, cliff-cut, or other forms) for a particular client (a king or a queen) to meet a particular goal (materializing and visualizing royal ideology). In this sense, each tomb was a work—or more generally, a thing or object—always associated with certain royal subjects.[9]

This basic fact leads to another obviously true proposition: the designer and the intention behind the design—rather than the actual occupant of the tomb—were what mattered in determining the tomb's meaning, even though the two subjects could possibly be one and the same under certain social circumstances. Because of this fact, in our research, a tomb must always be understood as associated with a living agent.

This living agent carried two levels of being: psychological and historical. On the psychological level, a tomb might be called a "dream-work" that gave shape to a vision of an ideal life, which could evoke anything denied, impossible, unfulfilled, or unperfected in this world, such as a longer, nobler, richer, or a more righteous and respected life. This vision was usually in accord with prevailing sociopolitical ideology. As discussed earlier, a royal tomb was a metaphor for a ruler's political life because a Western Han ruler usually launched his tomb project shortly after ascending the throne and the construction continued until his death. Liu Sheng's tomb was such an example. In this sense, a Western Han royal tomb thus can be read as a mirror image of a royal subject with the king who oversaw the tomb project officially identifying with his monumental burial.[10]

At the historical level, the living agent must comply with his social reality, which was constructed on the basis of his multiple roles in the society. The Zhongshan king was the head of state and a member of the imperial Han house who also sat at the intersection of two different realms—one public and one private. He was at once a son of Emperor Jing, a grandson of Grand Dowager Empress Dou, and a brother of Emperor Wu. My study of the Mancheng site has been conducted on both the psychological and historical levels.

This also means that any study of tombs should eventually become a study of the agendas of the living agents of the tombs, who were active decision-makers in that society. But because a royal subject (particularly during the Western Han) always had personal and public agendas, it is important that we differentiate between the concept of "a royal tomb" and that of "a tomb of X (who used to be king or queen)." A royal tomb is part of a greater royal agenda and involves more social actors, such as the government. A king's or queen's tomb merely implies a burial that contains the physical remains of a singular privileged person. For one thing, the designations of "Liu Sheng's tomb" and "King of Zhongshan's tomb" mean differently, even though Liu Sheng was once the king of Zhongshan. Many tombs, including Liu Sheng's, did not contain any seals, stamps, or labels with his personal names. Even though the tomb occupants' personal identities can still be pinned down with stylistic and chronological evidence, the absence of direct mentions of the persons seems to suggest that such tombs were more likely designed to be royal tombs rather than tombs of individuals.

As the inquiry of tombs advancing from the object to the subject, our study can go beyond archaeology or art history and make a greater contribution to a broader understanding of a particular living society, including its philosophy, politics, social institutions, and religion. For example, my study of the Mancheng site provides a glimpse into Liu Sheng's religious notions about the body and soul, his ethics concerning the family, and his political strategy for harmonizing ethnic-Han and non-ethnic-Han cultures—topics that are totally obscure in extant received texts. These results not only deepen our understanding of Liu Sheng's political ideology, but also offer a prism through which we can obtain a fuller picture of early Chinese society and thought.

Meanwhile, we must acknowledge that even during the same period, each royal tomb in that region was more or less different from the others. For example, many royal tombs had a simpler structure, with fewer layers of coffins and caskets than in Liu Sheng's tomb. This might indicate more of a duality (of body and spirit) than the "melting" transformation between the body and soul seen at the Mancheng site. Most tombs also were different from those at Mancheng in maintaining the husband's superiority over the wife in almost all aspects of the design, including tomb architecture and furnishings, despite their close connection. The King of Nanyue's tomb, for example, appeared to be more international in character than those at Mancheng and included exotic imitations of Persian rhyta and lobed omphalos bowls that did not bear any cultural association with the local regime.[11] These kinds of differences are easy to understand because each kingdom was in the more or less unique historical situation of facing different cultural and social problems that dictated different political agendas. Each tomb deserves careful study on a case-by-case basis.

Methodologically, to explore such individual cases requires a coordinated analysis of two different types of evidence: object and text. In my introduction, I outlined the possibility and necessity of reading "mute" visual materials; here, I wish to briefly sum up the relationship between visual and textual analysis. How do we use both to study cultural relics? Should we use them separately or jointly? Reviewing the chapters of this book, we see that no significant result is possible without properly coordinating the information from both types of evidence. Archaeologically excavated visual remains and inscriptions enable us to delve into the immediate intention of each tomb's designer and the unconcealed meaning of each tomb. Meanwhile, transmitted texts allow us to understand the encrypted ideas encoded into the plans. These interdependent relationships between archaeology and history, artifact and text, and object and subject, best capture the basic relationship between the two parts of this study.

However, mutual dependence does not necessarily mean that archaeological and transmitted materials are equal in status. An excavated artifact is always primary and authentic when studying cultural relics in the sense that an artifact was made directly by a creator (its patron, artist, or artisan). In comparison, a text, even when its content is more or less objective, remains secondary in the sense that it is a description or an interpretation by a contemporary (or later) observer, who might or might not have direct connection with that artifact's creator. The difference between the visual and textual material, in my view, is not so much about the medium (non-written versus written) as it is about the perspective (creator versus interpreter). Indeed, to a well-trained art historian, an object can be as transparent and legible as a text is to a skillful literary critic. There is nothing mysterious about attentive study, which unveils the intuitive meaning of visual materials. Art historians often render their principle metaphorically as "objects never lie," though they are apparently "mute." Part I of this book includes examples supporting this approach, which is grounded in intuitive facts. For example, in chapter 2, we do not need any textual justification to comprehend the parallel placement of the two Mancheng tombs as a statement of the equal status of the deceased husband and wife. On such occasions, isolated citations of discrete texts by different authors in different contexts might even threaten to mislead the interpreter, guiding him or her off track.

Yet the fact that material remains from the past have an active voice of their own does not mean that text is unnecessary because not all of the meaning encoded in a historical object is apparent to the innocent eye, even the best trained one—as Erwin Panofsky argued.[12] Panofsky identified three levels of meaning that coexist in one work of art. Whereas the first level refers to simple identification through familiarity, or "primary or natural subject matter," that is self-evident to all viewers throughout time and across cultures,[13] the second and third levels are only understood by those who possess knowledge of specific texts or cultural norms. For such encoded meaning, the material and its visual interpreter must resort to those texts produced in the same context—not as direct answers (unless we identify the very text where the artist's plan was recorded) but as coordinates for adjusting one's interpretation of the archaeological facts. For example, as noted in chapter two, without knowledge of the *Book of Etiquette and Ceremonial* text, Queen Dou Wan's front chamber might have appeared to be simply a sacrificial space. But the ancient author of the *Book of Etiquette and Ceremonial* tells us that different sacrifices were held in different types of sacrificial spaces, and because of what was staged in Dou Wan's front chamber that space was closer to a *shi* apartment than to a *tang* hall. That special meaning is deeply lodged in the historical context and is totally invisible to uninformed eyes. More importantly, part II of this study is entirely devoted to exploring the historical purpose of the tomb design at the Mancheng site, which is not— and cannot be—intuitive to the modern audience. Unless we choose to give up the search for these meanings, we cannot dismiss ancient texts, even if they apparently are not directly related to an object in question.

However, even Panofsky himself warned his readers to be cautious in using the iconological method he advocated because it could be easily abused.[14] In response, while Ernst Gombrich insisted that the meaning of a work should be confined only to what the author intended,[15] Umberto Eco's limits of "interpretation" were set by the intention of the text rather than by the intention of the author or the interpreter.[16] "Over-interpretation," meaning "limitless, uncheckable flow of 'readings' " to Eco, is often exacerbated by a lack of direct evidence and an abundance of indirect texts. The practice of using a text that is not directly related to an object to interpret that object is extrapolation. Extrapolation, though not necessarily wrong, is logically insufficient and potentially flawed. What complicates this issue is the fact that the relationship of a text to an object in question, even if it is contemporary, is hard to pin down. For example, we do not know if the designer of the tombs at the Mancheng site actually read or even knew of such classical texts as the *Huainanzi*, *Annals of Lü Buwei*, or *Guanzi*. Even if the designer read these texts, we cannot know to what extent he agreed with the views expressed within them. However, given that (1) Liu Sheng would be the final decision-maker regarding the design; (2) these texts are in accord with Huang-Lao thought; (3) Liu Sheng was a well-educated prince and a grandson of Grand Empress Dowager Dou; (4) Empress Dowager Dou pushed her sons and grandsons (the "Liu princes") to study Huang-Lao writings; and (5) Liu Sheng was portrayed in texts such as the *Shiji* as a Huang-Lao sympathizer, then we are able to validate the possible link between the tomb and the Huang-Lao ideas preached in those texts. The absence of any one of these five facts would have significantly weakened (though not necessarily cancelled out) the likelihood of a link. Of course, these five facts can only establish the possibility of a link; to further substantiate this link requires a careful comparison of the discourse in the text and the logic of an object, which is possible only after a visual analysis of that object has been conducted independently. This is a synopsis of the kind of coordination of visual and textual analysis that has been practiced throughout this book.

My interest in the object–text relationship is not to repeat or revive the old debate of "art history or sinology"[17] but centers on the fundamental question of how to get as close to the original meaning of ancient artwork as possible. Should we do so by dissecting the object itself or by understanding the object's subject and his or her world? My study of the Mancheng site suggests that, on the one hand, the object should be prioritized as the basis and point of departure of our research, and, on the other hand, the subject's story cannot be dismissed as insignificant because it fills in the gap in our knowledge left by the object itself.

My final note, based on research of the Mancheng site, is about the value of cross-cultural comparison. I saved this issue for last because it is relatively uncharted territory. The Western Han royal tombs, though crystalizing the highest artistic and technological ingenuity in the local Chinese context, were not unique or unprecedented in every aspect of the broader global context. Many other civilizations, including but not limited to those of ancient Egypt, Mesopotamia, Persia, and Rome, developed sophisticated state institutions and constructed spectacular royal mausoleums similar to those of the Han Chinese of the second century BCE.[18] This fact, however, is often ignored in the conventional culture-centered scholarship. The common ground for all these royal spectacles is the shared challenge of achieving effective governance, which is a political science question that must be considered above all cultural and historical division. An Egyptian pharaoh or a Roman emperor must have faced the same basic question of how to utilize all the resources at his disposal to consolidate and expand his rule. History shows that these options were limited. For example, the Egyptians were similarly obsessed with securing personal posthumous immortality as a way of assuring political stability.[19] They also invested in the monumentality of mausoleums (such as pyramids and obelisks) as a method of visual persuasion, and they also furnished the royal tombs with jewelry, furniture, and other valuables, as well as pottery and stone vessels, and figurines.[20] Do these similarities suggest a universal humanity or some fixed structures ("laws") of thinking or practice across cultures and civilizations? Perhaps. But it is more likely that a shared political identity and a shared duty pushed royal tomb designers around the world in the same direction—toward a limited number of solutions to the common challenge of effective rulership, albeit from the standpoint of different cultural traditions and different historical circumstances.

In this book, my reference to the burial practices of ancient Egypt, Persia, and Rome mainly serves to distinguish the unconventional aspects of the Chinese practice or the different solutions the Chinese used to address universal concerns, problems, or challenges that all rulers faced. For example, why did the Chinese choose to hide their royal spectacles in mountains or underground? Why did they refuse to attribute royal tombs to each ruler's private rather than public domain, which were clearly separate? Hopefully, using the current study, we will be able to advance our understanding of such important questions from a more global perspective in future inquiries.

NOTES

INTRODUCTION

1. I will elaborate on my definition of "royal" in the later chapters. Suffice it to say here that although the actual role of the king changed over time in China as in many other civilizations (for example, a Shang-period king did not demonstrate power and authority in the same way as a Han-period king), such concrete historical differences do not change the fact that all these kings (and later emperors) were regarded as rulers (*jun* 君) as opposed to the ruled (*chen* 臣). On formal occasions, an aristocrat below the rank of vassal (*zhuhou* 諸侯) was rarely considered *jun*, which was a title only reserved for kings or vassals, who owned or were bestowed land to establish and govern a state. For concepts of "royalty" and "kingship" in traditional China, see Julia Ching, *Mysticism and Kingship in China: The Heart of Chinese Wisdom* (Cambridge: Cambridge University Press, 1997).

2. Liang Siyong 梁思永 and Gao Quxun 高去尋, *Houjiazhuang: Henan Anyang Houjiazhuang Yin dai mudi* 侯家莊: 河南安陽侯家莊殷代墓地, 5 vols. (Taipei: Zhongyang yanjiuyuan lishi yuyan yanjiusuo, 1962); Guo Baojun 郭寶鈞, "1950 nian chun Yinxu fajue baogao" 一九五零年春殷墟發掘報告, *Zhongguo kaogu xuebao* 中國考古學報 5 (1951): 1–62. See also Li Chi, *Anyang* (Seattle: University of Washington Press, 1977).

3. Yang Baocheng 楊寶成, *Yinxu wenhua yanjiu* 殷墟文化研究 (Taipei: Taiwan guji chuban youxian gongsi, 2004), 121. For the excavation report, see Liang Siyong and Gao Quxun, *Houjiazhuang*, vol. 2.

4. Kwang-chih Chang, *Shang Civilization* (New Haven, CT: Yale University Press, 1980), 114–17; Robert Bagley, "Shang Archaeology," in *Cambridge History of Ancient China: From the Origins of Civilisation to 221 B.C.*, ed. Michael Loewe and Edward Shaughnessy (Cambridge: Cambridge University Press, 1999), 185–94; Robert Thorp, *China in the Early Bronze Age: Shang Civilization* (Philadelphia: University of Pennsylvania Press, 2006), 117–72.

5. These include: 2 Yan 燕, 2 Yu 彊, 19 Jin 晉, 2 Ying 應, 3 Guo 虢, 5 Wei 衛, 5 Xing 邢, 8 Guo, 1 Song 宋, 1 Yi 宜, 2 Hei 㵎, 2 Ge 戈, 2 Rui 芮, 2 Peng 倗, and 8 Zeng 曾 burials. See Zhongguo shehui kexueyuan kaogu yanjiusuo 中國社會科學院考古研究所, *Zhongguo kaoguxue Liangzhou juan* 中國考古學兩周卷 (Beijing: Zhongguo shehui kexueyuan chubanshe, 2004), 78–128. For important excavation reports, see Zhongguo kexueyuan kaogu yanjiusuo 中國科學院考古研究所, *Shangcunling Guoguo mudi* 上村嶺虢國墓地 (Beijing: Kexue chubanshe, 1959); Henan sheng wenwu kaogu yanjiusuo 河南省文物考古研究所 and Sanmenxia shi wenwu gongzuodui 三門峽市文物工作隊, *Sanmenxia Guo guo mudi* 三門峽虢國墓地, 2 vols. (Beijing: Wenwu chubanshe, 1999); Shaanxi sheng kaogu yanjiyuan 陝西省考古研究院, et al., *Liangdaicun Rui guo mudi—2007 niandu fajue baogao* 梁帶村芮國墓地—2007年度發掘報告, 2 vols. (Beijing: Wenwu chubanshe, 2010); Hubei sheng wenwu kaogu yanjiusuo 湖北省文物考古研究所 and Suizhou shi bowuguan 隨州市博物館, "Hubei Suizhou Yejiashan Xi Zhou mudi fajue jianbao" 湖北隨州葉家山西周墓地發掘簡報, *Wenwu* 2011.11: 4–60; idem, "Hubei Suizhou Yejiashan M28 fajue baogao" 湖北隨州葉家山M28發掘報告, *Jianghan kaogu* 江漢考古 2013.4: 3–57; idem, "Hubei Suizhou Yejiashan M107 fajue jianbao" 湖北隨州葉家山M107 發掘簡報, *Jianghan kaogu* 2016.3: 3–40; Guo Baojun 郭寶鈞, *Junxian Xingcun* 濬縣辛村 (Beijing: Kexue chubanshe, 1964); Henan sheng wenwu kaogu yanjiusuo and Pingdingshan shi wenwu guanliju 平頂山市文物管理局, *Pingdingshan Ying guo mudi* 平頂山應國墓地, 2 vols. (Zhengzhou: Daxiang chubanshe, 2012); Lu Liancheng 盧連成 and Hu Zhisheng 胡智生, *Baoji Yu guo mudi* 寶雞𢀝國墓地, 2 vols. (Beijing: Wenwu chubanshe, 1988); Shanxi sheng kaogu yanjiusuo 山西省考古研究所 and Beijing daxue kaogu xi 北京大學考古系, "Tianma-Qucun yizhi—Beizhao Jin hou mudi dierci fajue" 天馬—曲村遺址——北趙晉侯墓地第二次發掘, *Wenwu* 1994.1: 4–28; idem, "Tianma-Qucun yizhi—Beizhao Jin hou mudi disanci fajue" 天馬—曲村遺址——北趙晉侯墓地第三次發掘, *Wenwu* 1994.8: 22–33, 68; idem, "Tianma-Qucun yizhi—Beizhao Jin hou mudi disici fajue" 天馬—曲村遺址——北趙晉侯墓地第四次發掘, *Wenwu* 1994.8: 4–21; idem, "Tianma-Qucun yizhi—Beizhao Jin hou mudi diwuci fajue" 天馬—曲村遺址——北趙晉侯墓地第五次發掘, *Wenwu* 1995.7: 4–39; Beijing daxue kaogu wenbo xueyuan 北京大學考古文博學院 and Shanxi sheng kaogu yanjiusuo, "Tianma-Qucun yizhi—Beizhao Jin hou mudi diliuci fajue" 天馬—曲村遺址——北趙晉侯墓地第六次發掘, *Wenwu* 2001.8: 4–21, 55; Shanxi sheng kaogu yanjiusuo et al. "Shanxi Jiangxian Hengshui Xi Zhou mu fajue jianbao" 山西絳縣橫水西周墓發掘簡報, *Wenwu* 2006.8: 4–18.

6. Jay Xu, "The Cemetery of the Western Zhou Lords of Jin," *Artibus Asiae* 56.3/4 (1996): 193–231; Jessica Rawson, "Western Zhou Archaeology," in *Cambridge History of Ancient China*, 440–46; Feng Li, *Landscape and Power in Early China: The Crisis and Fall of the Western Zhou, 1045–771 BC* (Cambridge: Cambridge University Press, 2006), 84–87.

7. Wang Longzheng 王龍正 and Jiang Tao 姜濤, "Chutu qiwu zuiduo de Xi Zhou guojun mu" 出土器物最多的西周國君墓, in *Zhongguo shinian baida kaogu xinfaxian* 中國十年百大考古新發現, ed. Li Wenru 李文儒 (Beijing: Wenwu chubanshe, 2002), 337–41. It must be noted that the statistics in the archaeological reports may not necessarily reflect the original quantity of the burial objects. Two factors should be considered. First, the definition of "objects" (*qiwu* 器物) in archaeological context is broad and includes not only large vessels but also small artifacts such as individual beads, which might originally have been part of a larger object like a necklace.

Second, perishable objects such as fabrics and wooden objects rarely survive and cannot be counted.

8. Zhongguo shehui kexueyuan kaogu yanjiusuo, *Zhongguo kaoguxue Liangzhou juan*, 275–405. For important excavation reports, see Shaanxi sheng Yongcheng kaogudui 陝西省雍城考古隊, "Fengxiang Qingong lingyuan zuantan yu shijue jianbao" 鳳翔秦公陵園鑽探與試掘簡報, *Wenwu* 1983.7: 30–37; Shaanxi sheng Yongcheng kaogudui, "Fengxiang Qingong lingyuan dierci zuantan baogao" 鳳翔秦公陵園第二次鑽探報告, *Wenwu* 1987.5: 55–65; Shaanxi sheng kaogu yanjiusuo 陝西省考古研究所 and Lintong xian wenguanhui 臨潼縣文管會, "Qin Dongling diyihao lingyuan kanchaji" 秦東陵第一號陵園勘察記, *Kaogu yu wenwu* 考古與文物 1987.4: 19–28; Cheng Xuehua 程學華 and Lin Bo 林泊, "Qin Dongling dierhao lingyuan diaocha zuantan jianbao" 秦東陵第二號陵園調查鑽探報告, *Kaogu yu wenwu* 1990.4: 22–30; Shaanxi sheng kaogu yanjiusuo Qinling gongzuozhan, "Qin Dongling disihao lingyuan diaocha zuantan jianbao" 秦東陵第四號陵園調查鑽探簡報, *Kaogu yu wenwu* 1993.3: 48–51; Hebei sheng wenwu yanjiusuo 河北省文物研究所, *Yan Xiadu* 燕下都, 2 vols. (Beijing: Wenwu chubanshe, 1996); Henan sheng wenwu kaogu yanjiusuo 河南省文物考古研究所, "Henan Xinzheng Huzhuang Han wangling kaogu faxian gaishu" 河南新鄭胡莊韓王陵考古發現概述, *Huaxia kaogu* 華夏考古2009.3: 14–18; Hebei sheng wenguanchu 河北省文管處 et al., "Hebei Handan Zhao wangling" 河北邯鄲趙王陵, *Kaogu* 考古 1982.6: 597–604, 564; Shandong sheng wenwu kaogu yanjiusuo 山東省文物考古研究所, *Linzi Qi mu* 臨淄齊墓, vol. 1 (Beijing: Wenwu chubanshe, 2007); Zhongguo kexueyuan kaogu yanjiusuo 中國科學院考古研究所, *Huixian fajue baogao* 輝縣發掘報告 (Beijing: Kexue chubanshe, 1956); Hebei sheng wenwu yanjiusuo, *Cuo mu: Zhanguo Zhongshanguo guowang zhi mu* 響墓：戰國中山國國王之墓, 2 vols. (Beijing: Wenwu chubanshe, 1996). Hebei sheng wenwu yanjiusuo, *Zhanguo Zhongshanguo Lingshou cheng: 1975–1993 nian kaogu fajue baogao* 戰國中山國靈壽城1975–1993年考古發掘報告 (Beijing: Wenwu chubanshe, 2005). Zhejiang sheng wenwu kaogu yanjiusuo 浙江省文物考古研究所 and Shaoxing xian wenwu baohu guanliju 紹興縣文物保護管理局, *Yinshan Yuewang ling* 印山越王陵 (Beijing: Wenwu chubanshe, 2002).

9. Ma Zhenzhi 馬振智, "Shi tan Qingong yihao damu de guozhi" 試談秦公一號大墓的槨制, *Kaogu yu wenwu* 2002.5: 56–59.

10. Alain Thote, "Burial Practices as Seen in Rulers' Tombs of the Eastern Zhou Period: Patterns and Regional Traditions," in *Religion and Chinese Society: A Centennial Conference of the Ecole francaise d'Extreme-Orient*, 2 vols., ed. John Lagerwey (Paris: École française d'Extrême-Orient, 2004), 1: 65–107.

11. Shaanxi sheng kaogu yanjiusuo and Qin Shihuang bingmayong bowuguan 秦始皇兵馬俑博物館, *Qin Shihuangdi lingyuan fajue baogao 1999* 秦始皇帝陵園發掘報告1999 (Beijing: Kexue chubanshe, 2000), 7. Note that this measurement dates from 1962.

12. Liu Qingzhu 劉慶柱 and Li Yufang 李毓芳, *Xi Han shiyi ling* 西漢十一陵 (Xi'an: Shaanxi renmin chubanshe, 1987); Xianyang shi wenwu kaogu yanjiusuo 咸陽市文物考古研究所, *Xi Han diling zuantan diaocha baogao* 西漢帝陵鑽探調查報告 (Beijing: Wenwu chubanshe, 2010).

13. Henan sheng wenwu kaogu yanjiusuo, *Yongcheng Xi Han Liangguo wangling yu qinyuan* 永城西漢梁國王陵與寢園 (Zhengzhou: Zhongzhou guji chubanshe, 1996); Yan Genqi 閻根齊, *Mangdangshan Xi Han Liangwang mudi* 芒碭山西漢梁王墓地 (Beijing: Wenwu chubanshe, 2001).

14. Guangzhou shi wenwu guanli weiyuanhui 廣州市文物管理委員會 et al., *Xi Han Nanyue wang mu* 西漢南越王墓, 2 vols. (Beijing: Wenwu chubanshe, 1991). According to the excavation report, whereas the tomb's total "building area" (*jianzhu mianji* 建築面積) is about a hundred square meters, my calculation shows that the furnished areas of the tomb add up to about 68.74 square meters.

15. Wang Yongbo 王永波, *Changqing Xi Han Jibei wang ling* 長清西漢濟北王陵 (Beijing: Sanlian shudian, 2005); Shandong Heze diqu Han mu fajue xiaozu 山東菏澤地區漢墓發掘小組, "Juye Hongtushan Xi Han mu" 巨野紅土山西漢墓, *Kaogu xuebao* 1983.5: 471–500. The date and attribution of the Hongtushan tomb has been disputed. Here, I follow the latest study by Liu Rui 劉瑞 and Liu Tao 劉濤, *Xi Han zhuhouwang lingmu zhidu yanjiu* 西漢諸侯王陵墓制度研究 (Beijing: Zhongguo shehui kexue chubanshe, 2010), 259.

16. To name a few, Liu Rui and Liu Tao, *Xi Han zhuhouwang lingmu zhidu yanjiu*; Alison Miller, "Politics, and the Emergence of Rock-Cut Tombs in Early Han China" (PhD diss., Harvard University, 2011); Jie Shi, "The Mancheng Tombs: Shaping the Afterlife of the 'Kingdom within the Mountains'" (PhD diss., University of Chicago, 2017).

17. It is impossible to list all the excavation reports here. An up-to-date survey of these royal tombs with a comprehensive bibliography in Chinese, however, can be found in Liu Rui and Liu Tao, *Xi Han zhuhouwang lingmu zhidu yanjiu*.

18. Lothar von Falkenhausen, *Chinese Society in the Age of Confucius (1000–250 BC): The Archaeological Evidence* (Los Angeles, CA: Cotsen Institute of Archaeology, UCLA, 2006), 326.

19. My calculation is based on the figures provided in Zheng Shaozong 鄭紹宗, *Mancheng Han mu* 滿城漢墓 (Beijing: Wenwu chubanshe, 2003), 68.

20. Lin Yun 林澐, "Shuo Wang" 說王, *Kaogu* 1965.6: 311–12.

21. Kong Yingda 孔穎達, *Maoshi zhengyi* 毛詩正義, 13.195, in *Shisanjing zhushu* 十三經注疏, ed. Ruan Yuan 阮元 (Beijing: Zhonghua shuju, 1980), 463; English translation by Bernard Karlgren, *The Book of Odes* (Stockholm: Museum of Far Eastern Antiquities, 1950), 157–58.

22. Mark Lewis, "Warring States: Political History," in *Cambridge History of Ancient China*, 602–3.

23. Yang Kuan 楊寬, *Zhongguo gudai lingqin zhidushi yanjiu* 中國古代陵寢制度史研究 (Shanghai: Shanghai guji chubanshe, 1985), 12–14.

24. Yang Kuan, *Zhongguo gudai lingqin zhidushi yanjiu*, 12.

25. Sima Qian 司馬遷, *Shiji* 史記 (Beijing: Zhonghua shuju, 1959), 5.218, 6.289.

26. Yang Kuan, *Zhongguo gudai lingqin zhidushi yanjiu*, 13.

27. Miao Wenyuan 繆文遠, *Zhanguo ce xin jiaozhu* 戰國策新校注 (Chengdu: Bashu shushe, 1987), 770–72.

28. Ban Gu 班固, *Hanshu* 漢書 (Beijing: Zhonghua shuju, 1962), 27.1335, 18.703, 97.3998, 98.4028.

29. Lothar von Falkenhausen, "Mortuary Behavior in Pre-Imperial Qin: A Religious Interpretation," in *Religion and Chinese Society*, 1: 109–72; Constance Cook, *Death in Ancient China: The Tale of One Man's Journey* (Leiden: Brill, 2006); Alice Yao, *The Ancient Highlands of Southwest China: From the Bronze Age to the Han Empire* (Oxford: Oxford University Press, 2015); Guolong Lai, *Excavating the Afterlife: The Archaeology of Early Chinese Religion* (Seattle: University of Washington Press, 2015); Xiaolong Wu, *Material Culture, Power, and Identity in Ancient China* (Cambridge: Cambridge University Press, 2017).

30. Jessica Rawson, "The First Emperor's Tomb: The Afterlife Universe," in *The First Emperor: China's Terracotta Army*, ed. Jane Portal (London: British Museum, 2007), 120–24. See also her "Ewige Wohnstätten: Die Gräber des Königs von Nan Yue und der kaiserlichen Prinzen in Ostchina," in *Schätze für König Zhao Mo: Das Grab von Nan Yue*, ed. Margarete Prüch (Heidelberg: Braus, 1998), 80–95, esp. 92; "The Eternal Palaces of the Western Han: A New View of the Universe," *Artibus Asiae* 59.1/2 (1999): 5–58.

31. Wu Hung, *The Art of the Yellow Springs: Understanding Chinese Tombs* (London: Reaktion Books, 2009), 34–62.

32. Kwang-chih Chang, *Art, Myth and Ritual: The Path to Political Authority in Ancient China* (Cambridge, MA: Harvard University Press, 1983). This theory is in alignment with Michel Ragon's study in non-Chinese contexts, *The Space of Death: A Study of Funerary Architecture, Decoration, and Urbanism* (Charlottesville, VA: University of Virginia Press, 1983).

33. James D. Sellmann, *Timing and Rulership in* Master Lü's Spring and Autumn Annals (Lüshi chunqiu) (Albany, NY: SUNY Press, 2002), 101.

34. For a theory of common religion, see Donald Harper, "Chinese Religions—The State of the Field, Part I Early Religious Traditions: The Neolithic Period through the Han Dynasty, ca. 4000 B.C.E. to 220 C.E, Warring States, Ch'in, and Han Periods," *Journal of Asian Studies* 54.1(1995): 152–60.

35. Poo Mu-chou, *In Search of Personal Welfare: A View of Ancient Chinese Religion* (Albany, NY: SUNY Press, 1998), 3.

36. Martin J. Powers, *Art and Political Expressions in Early China* (New Haven, CT: Yale University Press, 1991).

37. For the excavation report, see Lianyungang shi bowuguan 連雲港市博物館, "Jiangsu Donghai xian Yinwan Han muqun fajue jianbao" 江蘇東海縣尹灣漢墓群發掘簡報, *Wenwu* 1996.8: 4–25. For the manuscripts, see Lianyungang shi bowuguan et al., *Yinwan Han mu jiandu* 尹灣漢墓簡牘 (Beijing: Wenwu chubanshe, 1997).

38. Von Falkenhausen, *Chinese Society in the Age of Confucius (1000–250 BC): The Archaeological Evidence*, 398.

39. Rawson, "The First Emperor's Tomb: The Afterlife Universe," 119.

40. Xing Yitian 邢義田, *Tianxia yijia: Huangdi, guanliao yu shehui* 天下一家：皇帝、官僚與社會 (Beijing: Zhonghua shuju, 2008), 53.

41. Duan Qingbo 段清波, *Qin Shi Huangdi lingyuan kaogu yanjiu* 秦始皇帝陵園考古研究 (Beijing: Beijing daxue chubanshe, 2011), 176.

42. Robert K. Yin, *Case Study Research: Design and Methods* (Newbury Park, CA: Sage, 1984), 23.

43. Zheng Shaozong 鄭紹宗 and Zheng Luanming 鄭灤明, "Mancheng Han mu fajue rizhi" 滿城漢墓發掘日誌, *Wenwu chunqiu* 文物春秋, 2002.5: 55–65. Usually, as close relatives of the emperor, these provincial vassals occupied the summit of the Han social hierarchy. They cumulatively numbered in the hundreds, each ruling a small state for a certain period of time; see Michael Loewe and Denis Twitchett, eds., *The Cambridge History of China*, vol. 1, "The Ch'in and Han Empires" (Cambridge: Cambridge University Press, 1986), 136–49. For a survey of these kingdoms, see Zhou Zhenhe 周振鶴, *Xi Han zhengqu dili* 西漢政區地理 (Beijing: Renmin chubanshe, 1987); Wang Hui 王恢, *Han wangguo yu houguo zhi yanbian* 漢王國與侯國之演變 (Taipei: Zhonghua shuju, 1984); for their arts, see Michéle Pirazzoli t'Serstevens, *The Han Dynasty*, trans. Janet Seligman (New York: Rizzoli, 1982); Wang Zhongshu, *Han Civilization*,

trans. K. C. Chang et al. (New Haven, CT: Yale University Press, 1982); Michael Nylan and Michael Loewe, eds., *China's Early Empires: A Re-Appraisal* (Cambridge: Cambridge University Press, 2010).

44. Zhongguo shehui kexueyuan kaogu yanjiusuo, *Mancheng Han mu fajue baogao* 滿城漢墓發掘報告, 2 vols. (Beijing: Wenwu chubanshe, 1980), 1: 337.

45. Zhongguo shehui kexueyuan kaogu yanjiusuo, *Mancheng Han mu fajue baogao*, 1: 337.

46. Zhongguo shehui kexueyuan kaogu yanjiusuo, *Mancheng Han mu fajue baogao*, 1: 7–9.

47. Zhongguo shehui kexueyuan kaogu yanjiusuo, *Mancheng Han mu fajue baogao*, 1: 7.

48. Although the archaeological report often calls it the "central chamber" (*zhongshi* 中室), as opposed to the "main chamber" (*zhushi* 主室), which is the rear chamber, Wang Zhongshu 王仲殊 identified it as the "front chamber" (*qianshi* 前室), which I believe is more reasonable. See Wang Zhongshu, *Han Civilization*, 176.

49. Zhongguo shehui kexueyuan kaogu yanjiusuo, *Mancheng Han mu fajue baogao*, 1: 10–23.

50. For a list and survey of these royal tombs as of 2010, see Liu Rui and Liu Tao, *Xi Han zhuhouwang lingmu zhidu yanjiu*; for new archaeological data after 2010, see Lilian Lan-ying Tseng, "Princely Tombs in Han China: New Discoveries from Dayunshan and Nanchang," *Orientations* 48.2 (2017): 103–9.

51. As a norm, these kings ruled "east of the mountain (*Shandong* 山東)," that is, east of Mt. Taihang 太行 in present-day Shanxi Province, while the emperor who granted the lands ruled "inside of the pass (*Guanzhong* 關中)," or to the west of the Hangu 函谷 Pass. For geopolitical circumstances, see Loewe and Twitchett, *The Cambridge History of China*, vol. 1, 136–49.

52. The other unplundered tombs include the Hongtushan Tomb at Juye, a Southern Yue royal tomb at Guangzhou, and a Jibei royal tomb at Changqing. See Shandong Heze diqu Han mu fajue xiaozu, "Juye Hongtushan Xi Han mu"; Guangzhou shi wenwu guanli weiyuanhui, *Xi Han Nanyue wang mu*; Wang Yongbo, *Changqing Xi Han Jibei wang ling*.

53. Lu Zhaoyin 盧兆蔭, *Mancheng Han mu* 滿城漢墓 (Beijing: Sanlian shudian, 2005); Zhongguo shehui kexueyuan kaogu yanjiusuo and Beijing yiqichang gongren lilunzu 北京儀器廠工人理論組, *Mancheng Han mu* 滿城漢墓 (Beijing: Wenwu chubanshe, 1978).

54. Yu Weichao 俞偉超, "Handai zhuhouwang yu liehou muzang de xingzhi fenxi—jian lun 'Zhou zhi,' 'Han zhi' yu 'Jin zhi'de sanjieduan xing," 漢代諸侯王與列侯墓葬的性質分析—兼論"周制"、"漢制"和"晉制"的三階段性 in *Zhongguo kaoguxuehui diyici nianhui lunwenji* 中國考古學會第一次年會論文集, ed. Zhongguo kaogu xuehui (Beijing: Wenwu chubanshe, 1979), 332–37.

55. Bent Flyvbjerg, "Five Misunderstandings About Case-Study Research," *Qualitative Inquiry*, 12.2 (2006): 219–45.

56. John Gerring, *Case Study Research: Principles and Practices* (Cambridge: Cambridge University Press, 2007), 88.

57. Roger B. Nelsen, *Proofs Without Words: Exercises in Visual Thinking—Volume 1* (Mathematical Association of America, 1993), vi.

58. For a historiography, see Amiria Henare, Martin Holbraad, and Sari Wastell, "Introduction," in *Thinking Through Things: Theorising Artefacts Ethnographically*, ed. Amiria Henare, Martin Holbraad, and Sari Wastell (London: Routledge, 2007), 1–31.

59. Daniel Miller, *A Theory of Shopping* (Ithaca, NY: Cornell University Press, 1998); George Kubler, *The Shape of Time: Remarks on the History of Things* (New Haven, CT: Yale University Press, 1962); Claude Lévi-Strauss, *Structural Anthropology*, trans. Claire Jacobson and Brooke Grundfest Schoepf (New York: Basic Books, 1968).

60. David N. Keightley, "The Religious Commitment: Shang Theology and the Genesis of Chinese Political Culture," *History of Religions*, 17 (1978): 213.

61. Among recent cultural studies are the aforementioned Xiaolong Wu's book on Eastern Zhou Zhongshan (2017); Guolong Lai's work on Chu (2015), Alice Yao's book on Dian (2015), as well as Erika Brindley's book on Yue, *Ancient China and the Yue: Perceptions and Identities on the Southern Frontier, c. 400 BCE–50 CE* (Cambridge: Cambridge University Press, 2015), and Sophia-Karin Psarras's book on Han, *Han Material Culture: An Archaeological Analysis and Vessel Typology* (Cambridge: Cambridge University Press, 2015).

62. Johann Joachim Winckelmann, *History of the Art of Antiquity*, trans. Harry Francis Mallgrave (Los Angeles, CA: Getty Publications, 2006). In this work, Winckelmann associates the naturalistic style of Greek and Roman sculptures with political freedom in Greco-Roman culture during this period.

63. Rudolf Arnheim, *The Power of the Center: A Study of Composition in the Visual Arts*, revised edition (Berkeley: University of California Press, 1982), xi.

64. Norman Bryson, *Word and Image: French Painting of the Ancient Regime* (Cambridge: Cambridge University Press, 1981), 5.

65. Edward Shaughnessy, "Once Again on Ideographs and Iconolatry," in *Shijie hanzi tongbao* 世界漢字通報 2.1 (2016): 1–31; Yang Xiaoneng 楊曉能, *Ling yizhong gushi: Qingtongqi wenshi, tuxing wenzi yu tuxiang mingwen de jiedu* 另一種古史：青銅器文飾、圖形文字與圖像銘文的解讀 (Beijing: Sanlian shudian, 2008).

66. This effort reached its climax in Alois Riegl's 1901 monograph on the late Roman art industry, which showed "the way (through Kunstwollen) to these 'central formative principles' (or 'higher structural principles') that underlie surface appearance and in an essential way expose the cognitive structure of a group of individuals." See Jaś Elsner, "From Empirical Evidence to the Big Picture: Some Reflections on Riegl's Concept of Kunstwollen," *Critical Inquiry* 32. 4 (Summer 2006): 741–66.

67. Christopher Wood, "Introduction," in *The Vienna School Reader*, ed. Christopher Wood (New York: Zone Books, 2000), 14.

68. For example, Powers argued that the fluid cloud patterns ubiquitous in Western Han art expressed a sense of, and therefore became a "graphical model" of, a type of social mobility impossible in China until the new meritocratic society replaced the old hereditary one around about the same period; see Martin J. Powers, *Pattern and Person: Ornament, Society, and Self in Classical China* (Cambridge, MA: Harvard University Asia Center, 2006).

69. Erwin Panofsky, *Studies in Iconology; Humanistic Themes in the Art of the Renaissance* (New York: Oxford University Press, 1939).

70. Lillian Lan-ying Tseng, *Picturing Heaven in Early China* (Cambridge, MA: Harvard University Asia Center, 2011). Wu Hung was undoubtedly under the sway of Panofsky when he attempted to link up Confucian scholar Wu Liang's classical learning with the decorative program in his funerary shrine in his book, *The Wu Liang Shrine: The Ideology of Early Chinese Pictorial Art* (Stanford, CA: Stanford University Press, 1989).

71. Anke Hein, "The Problem of Typology in Chinese Archaeology," *Early China* 39 (2016): 21–52.

256

INTRODUCTION

72. *Merriam-Webster's Collegiate Dictionary.* Springfield, MA: Merriam-Webster at http://www.merriam-webster.com.
73. Formal taxonomy is basic in both art history and archaeology. In art history, the idea is best articulated in Kubler, *The Shape of Time.* For a summary of the "typology debate" in archaeology between the 1930s and 1950s, see Alison Wylie, *Thinking from Things: Essays in the Philosophy of Archaeology* (Berkeley: University of California Press, 2002), 42–56.
74. Ernst Mayr, *The Growth of Biological Thought* (Cambridge, MA: Harvard University Press, 1982), 147–208.
75. David Scott Richeson, *Euler's Gem: The Polyhedron Formula and the Birth of Topology* (Princeton, NJ: Princeton University Press, 2008); Ioan Mackenzie James, *History of Topology* (Amsterdam: Elsevier B.V., 1999).
76. Gaston Bachelard, *The Poetics of Space,* trans. M. Jolas (Boston: Beacon Press, 1994), 8.

1. THE EMBRACE OF BODY AND SOUL

1. Kwang-chih Chang, *Rethinking Archaeology* (New York: Random House, 1967), 4.
2. Chinese archaeologists conventionally classify burial objects first by media into metal, clay, or stone, and then, under each category, further by function and form into different types (such as weapons) and subtypes (such as swords and spears). See the excavation report, *Mancheng Han mu fajue baogao.* My classification from a different perspective is primarily based on morphology and function rather than on materiality.
3. Xu Yuangao 徐元誥, *Guoyu jijie* 國語集解 (Beijing: Zhonghua shuju, 2002), 513.
4. Kong Yingda, *Liji zhengyi* 禮記正義, 35.284, in *Shisanjing zhushu,* 1512.
5. He Ning 何寧, *Chunqiu gongyangzhuan zhushu* 春秋公羊傳註疏, 24.135, in *Shisanjing zhushu,* 2329.
6. As I will discuss later, some swords and jades found in the front chamber were more likely ritual gifts dedicated to the deceased's soul rather than a reference to the physical body.
7. For example, the Hongtushan tomb at Juye, Shandong; see Shandong Heze diqu Han mu fajue xiaozu, "Juye Hongtushan Xi Han mu."
8. For a detailed study of the typological transformation of vertical casket burial to horizontal chamber burial, see Huang Xiaofen 黃曉芬, *Han mu de kaoguxue yanjiu* 漢墓的考古學研究 (Changsha: Yuelu shuyuan, 2002), esp. 92–93. Her terminology was derived from the Japanese art historian Sekino Tadashi, who was the first to observe that the tomb space in these Han tombs could be divided into two major types: the vertical pit (*jūkō* 縱壙) and the horizontal pit (*ōkō* 橫壙); Sekino Tadashi 関野貞, "Rikuchō izen no bojō ni tsuite" 六朝以前の墓壙に就いて, *Kōkogaku zasshi* 考古學雜誌 6.11(1916): 605–24.
9. Zhongguo shehui kexueyuan kaogu yanjiusuo, *Mancheng Han mu fajue baogao,* 1: 11, fig. 4.
10. Zhongguo shehui kexueyuan kaogu yanjiusuo, *Mancheng Han mu fajue baogao,* 1: 225.
11. For a survey of such mortuary practices in the Zhou, see Tian Wei 田偉, "Shi lun liang Zhou de jishi jitan mu" 試論兩周的積石積炭墓, *Zhongguo lishi wenwu* 中國歷史文物 2009.2: 59–67; for the original text, see Chen Qiyou 陳奇猷, *Lüshi Chunqiu xin jiaoshi* 呂氏春秋新校釋 (Shanghai: Shanghai guji chubanshe, 2002), 532.

12. For the transitional role of the second-level ledge (*ercengtai* 二層臺) in smaller cata-combs during the late Warring States period, see Li Rusen 李如森, "Lüelun Luoyang diqu Zhanguo Xi Han Dongshimu de yuanliu" 略論洛陽地區戰國西漢洞室墓的源流, *Shehui kexue zhanxian* 社會科學戰線 1988.3: 206.

13. Kong Yingda, *Liji zhengyi*, 8.64, in *Shisanjing zhushu*, 1292; James Legge, trans., *Li Chi: The Book of Rites*, 2 vols. (New York: Columbia University Press, 1967), 1: 155–56.

14. Lu Zhaoyin, "Shi lun liang Han de yuyi" 試論兩漢的玉衣, *Kaogu* 1981.1: 51–58; Lu Zhaoyin, "Zai lun liang Han de yuyi" 再論兩漢的玉衣, *Wenwu* 1989.10: 60–67; Jeffrey Kao and Yang Zuosheng, "On Jade Suits and Han Archaeology," *Archaeology* 36.6 (1983): 30–33.

15. Zhongguo shehui kexueyuan kaogu yanjiusuo, *Mancheng Han mu fajue baogao*, 1: 348.

16. Zhongguo shehui kexuan kaogu yanjiusuo, *Mancheng Han mu fajue baogao*, 1: 37. Although the excavators thought the body was naked in the jade suit, and indeed in some cases (such as the king of Nanyue's tomb in Guangzhou, which I will discuss in chapter 2), archaeologists found definite evidence of a naked body, in the case of the Mancheng site, because few fabrics survived, the possibility of actual clothing cannot be entirely ruled out.

17. In the ritual manual *The Book of Etiquette and Ceremonial* (*Yili* 儀禮) (dated ca. fourth century BCE), a deceased nobleman (*shi* 士), the lowest rank of the aristocracy, could be shrouded in up to thirty sets of clothes; according to the Tang commentator, a vassal could have up to 100 sets of clothes; Jia Gongyan 賈公彥, *Yili zhushu* 儀禮注疏, 37.195, in *Shisanjing zhushu*, 1139. For marquises, a recently unearthed statute from Shuihudi tomb no. 77 in present-day Jiangling, Hubei, dated only decades prior to the Mancheng site, dictated that the amount of clothing worn by the corpse should not exceed the capacity of the coffin; Peng Hao 彭浩, "Du Yunmeng Shuihudi M77 Han jian zanglü" 讀雲夢睡虎地M77漢簡葬律, *Jianghan kaogu* 2009.4: 130–34. Many early Western Han tombs followed this traditional mortuary practice. Among them the best-known is Mawangdui tomb no. 1 (dated slightly after 168 BCE) in present-day Changsha, Hunan, featuring seven nested coffins and caskets, one of the most elaborate of that kind ever discovered in ancient China. The perfect condition of the corpse of the old Lady Dai 軑 lying in the center of the burial might have been aided by the seamless protection of her twenty-layer shrouds as well as to the waterproof white sticky clay; Hunan sheng bowuguan and Zhongguo kexueyuan kaogu yanjiusuo, *Changsha Mawangdui yihao Han mu* 長沙馬王堆一號漢墓, 2 vols. (Beijing: Wenwu chubanshe, 1972), 1: 28–31.

18. Ban Gu, *Hanshu*, 67.2908.

19. The traditional jade-accompanied burial became popular as early as the Neolithic period, most notably in wealthy tombs in the coastal culture called Liangzhu 良渚. In these burials, the head and chest of the corpse were covered by a layer of ritual jades, including perforated discs (*bi* 璧) and tubes (*cong* 琮), along with other jade ornaments. Wang Zunguo 汪遵國, "Liangzhu wenhua 'yulianzang' shulüe" 良渚文化玉斂葬述略, *Wenwu* 1984.2: 23–35. For a general study of the jade culture at Liangzhu, see Jason Sun, "The Liangzhu Culture: Its Discovery and Its Jades," *Early China* 18 (1993): 1–40.

20. Lin Lanying 林蘭英, "Shixi Zhou dai de zangyu dui Han dai yuyi de yingxiang" 試析周代的葬玉對漢代玉衣的影響, *Dongnan wenhua* 東南文化 1998.2: 127–31; Michael Loewe, "State Funerals of the Han Empire," *Bulletin of the Museum of Far*

Eastern Antiquities 71 (1999): 18. For an example, see Shanxi sheng wenwuju 山西省文物局, et al., *Jin guo qi zhen: Shanxi Jin hou muqun chutu wenwu jing pin* 晉國奇珍: 山西晉侯墓群出土文物精品 (Shanghai: Shanghai renmin meishu chubanshe, 2002), 70.

21. Ma Sha 馬沙, "Woguo gudai 'fumian' yanjiu'" 我國古代 "覆面" 研究, *Jianghan kaogu* 1999.1: 66–74; Yuan Shengwen 袁勝文 and Shi Wenjia 石文嘉, "Yushi fumian yanjiu" 玉石覆面研究, *Zhongyuan wenwu* 中原文物 2009.3: 76–81, 108.

22. Hayashi Minao 林巳奈夫, *Chūgoku kogyoku no kenkyū* 中國古玉の研究 (Tokyo: Yoshikawa Kōbunkan, 1991), 141–72.

23. Sun Qingwei 孫慶偉, "Jinhou mudi chutu yuqi zhaji" 晉侯墓地出土玉器札記, *Huaxia kaogu* 1999.1: 60–71, esp. 62–63.

24. Fan Ye 范曄, *Hou Hanshu* 後漢書 (Beijing: Zhonghua shuju, 1965), 10.446, 11.484, 16.615, 34.1174, 43.1470, 49.1637, 65.2143, 85.2811.

25. Duan Yucai 段玉裁, *Shuowen jiezi zhu* 説文解字注 (Hangzhou: Zhejiang guji chubanshe, 1999), 637.

26. Duan Yucai, *Shuowen jiezi zhu*, 637. The archaic pronunciations are reconstructed by Baxter and Sagart as *[g]ˤr[a]p and *[k]ˤr[a]p, respectively; see Baxter-Sagart Old Chinese reconstruction, version 1.1, http://ocbaxtersagart.lsait.lsa.umich.edu/Baxter SagartOCbyMandarinMC2014-09-20.pdf. For the principles of reconstruction, see William H. Baxter and Laurent Sagart, *Old Chinese: A New Reconstruction* (New York: Oxford University Press, 2014). See also Lu Zhaoyin, "Shilun Liang Han de yuyi," 56.

27. Cited from Wei Hong 衛宏, *Han jiuyi* 漢舊儀, see Sun Xingyan 孫星衍 et al., *Han guan liuzhong* 漢官六种 (Beijing: Zhonghua shuju, 1990), 105.

28. Lu Zhaoyin, "Shilun liang Han de yuyi," 55–56; James Lin, "Jade Suits and Iron Armour," *East Asia Journal: Studies in Material Culture* 1.2 (2003): 20–43.

29. The excavation of a tomb (M4) in the royal cemetery of the Han 韓 state, dating from the late third century BCE yielded ninety-eight jade pieces pierced by small holes around each piece; see Wang Shuping 王叔平, "Xinzheng fajue Xugang damu" 新鄭發掘許崗大墓, in *Henan wenhua wenwu nianjian* 河南文化文物年鑑 (Zhengzhou: Henan sheng wuhuating & wenwuju, 2004), 97. In 1997, a group of 179 jade pieces, mostly square or rectangular, with identical small holes on the edges, were stolen from royal tomb no. 2 of the Zhao kingdom, dating from the mid-third century BCE. Although the exact function of these jade pieces remains a question for debate, some scholars have suggested that they might have been parts of a jade suit of armor; see Zhao Jianchao 趙建朝 and Li Haixiang 李海祥, "Hebei Handan Zhaowangling erhaoling chutu de Zhanguo wenwu" 河北邯鄲趙王陵二號陵出土的戰國文物, *Wenwu* 2009.3: 90; Chen Bin 陳斌, "Shi lun Zhanguo Zhao wangling yupian de xingzhi" 試論戰國趙王陵玉片的性質, *Handan zhiye jishu xueyuan xuebao* 邯鄲職業技術學院學報 18.2 (2005):12–15.

30. The finds unearthed during the excavation of 1998 include eighty-seven armor suits and forty-three helmets. Shaanxi sheng kaogu yanjiusuo and Qin Shihuang bingmayong bowuguan, *Qin Shihuangdi lingyuan fajue baogao* 1999, 144. As the excavators have suggested, such stone armor and helmets were too heavy and brittle for soldiers to wear during a real battle; see Shaanxi sheng kaogu yanjiusuo, *Qin Shihuangdi lingyuan fajue baogao* 1999, 144; James Lin, "Armor for the Afterlife," in *The First Emperor: China's Terracotta Army*, 181–91.

31. Zhongguo shehui kexueyuan kaogu yanjiusuo, *Mancheng Han mu fajue baogao*, 1: 348.

32. Occasionally, archaeologists have found incomplete jade suits that only covered part of the body. One such example was found in an aristocrat's tomb at Linyi, which only consists of a head, two hands, and two feet. Each unit is made in a similar manner as Liu Sheng's jade suit. Because these five parts represent the five "ends" of the body, covering them probably symbolizes sealing the entire body. An almost identical example appeared in Hanshan tomb no. 1, indicating such minimalism was not a singular occurrence. See Linyi diqu wenwuzu 臨沂地區文物組, "Shandong Linyi Xi Han Liu Ci mu" 山東臨沂西漢劉疵墓, *Kaogu* 1980.6: 493–95. Xuzhou Bowuguan 徐州博物館, "Xuzhou Hanshan Xi Han mu" 徐州韓山西漢墓, *Wenwu* 1997.2: 26–43; Xuzhou bowuguan, "Xuzhou diqu de Handai yuyi jiqi xiangguan weni" 徐州地區的漢代玉衣及其相關問題, *Dongnan wenwu* 1996.1: 26–32, esp. 30. Some scholars such as Lu Zhaoyin believe this minimal style, which predated the later complete style, was perhaps an immature prototype. Lu Zhaoyin, "Shilun Liang Han de yuyi," 55. An extreme example of such minimization recently was found in Xiaochangshan tomb no.1, which yielded one jade device with only the front and back sides of the deceased's head. See Xuzhou bowuguan, "Jiangsu Xuzhou Xiaochangshan Han mu M4 fajue jianbao" 江蘇徐州小長山漢墓M4發掘簡報, *Zhongyuan wenwu* 2010.6: 4–9. It is also possible that these reduced jade suits followed a sumptuary regulation for those not entitled to a whole suit.

33. Zhongguo guojia bowuguan 中國國家博物館 and Xuzhou bowuguan 徐州博物館, *Da Han Chu wang: Xuzhou Xi Han Chu wang ling mu wenwu ji cui* 大漢楚王：徐州西漢楚王陵墓文物輯萃 (Beijing: Zhongguo shehui kexue chubanshe, 2005), 312.

34. This phrase was usually used in this context when the ruler's health was a concern; see Miao Wenyuan, *Zhanguo ce xin jiaozhu*, 767; Ban Gu, *Hanshu*, 72.3059.

35. Zhangjiashan Han mu zhujian zhengli xiaozu 張家山漢墓竹簡整理小組, *Zhangjiashan Han mu zhujian ersiqi hao mu (shiwen xiudingben)* 張家山漢墓竹簡247號墓 (釋文修訂本) (Beijing: Wenwu chubanshe, 2006), 124. I would like to thank Professor Donald Harper for kindly directing me to this source. The concept of *yuti* also appeared once in the *Zhanguo ce* text to describe an empress dowager's body; see Gao Dalun 高大倫, *Zhangjiashan Hanjian Maishu jiaoshi* 張家山漢簡脈書校釋 (Chengdu: Chengdu chubanshe, 1992), 94–95; Miao Wenyuan, *Zhanguo ce xin jiaozhu*, 767. Wu Hung once discussed Liu Sheng's "jade suit" and noted its being as a "jade body." See Wu Hung, "The Prince of Jade Revisited: Material Symbolism of Jade as Observed in the Mancheng Tomb," in *Chinese Jade, Colloquies on Art and Archaeology in Asia* 18, ed. Rosemary E. Scott (London: Percival David Foundation of Chinese Art, 1997), 147–70. Although this observation confirms the finding in the excavation report, Wu did not mention another fact noted in the excavation report that the object was not just an imitation of the body but also an imitation of clothing; see Zhongguo shehui kexueyuan kaogu yanjiusuo, *Mancheng Han mu fajue baogao*, 1: 349, 351.

36. Jie Shi, "Revisiting the 'Old Jade Man' at Mancheng Tomb No. 1 in Western Han China," a paper presented at the symposium, *Age of Empires: Chinese Art from the Qin and Han Dynasties*, organized by the Metropolitan Museum of Art, New York, April 2017.

37. Sima Qian, *Shiji*, 107.2852.

38. For the symbolism of jade in the traditional Chinese culture, see Berthold Laufer, *Jade: A Study in Chinese Archaeology and Religion* (Chicago: Field Museum of Natural History, 1912), 80–103.

39. The terra-cotta soldiers in the First Emperor's mausoleum at Lishan wear similar shoes featuring a square front and a round rear. Shaanxi sheng kaogu yanjiusuo 陝西省考古研究所 and Shihuang ling Qin yongkeng kaogu fajuedui 始皇陵秦俑坑考古發掘隊, *Qin Shihuang ling bingmayongkeng—yihao keng fajue baogao 1974–1984* 秦始皇陵兵馬俑坑——一號坑發掘報告 1974–1984 (Beijing: Wenwu chubanshe, 1988), 1: 164–68.

40. Huang Hui 黃暉, *Lunheng jiaoshi* 論衡校釋 (Beijing: Zhonghua shuju, 1991), 3: 874.

41. Xu Yuangao, *Guoyu jijie*, 187.

42. For a study of these four directional cosmological powers (*sishen* 四神), see Ni Run'an 倪潤安, "Lun liang Han siling de yuanliu" 論兩漢四靈的源流, *Zhongyuan wenwu* 1999.1: 83–91; Ogata Toru 大形徹, "Shishin kō: Zenkan Gokan ki no shiryō o chūshin toshite" 四神考: 前漢、後漢期の資料を中心として, *Jinbengaku ronshū* 人文學論集 15 (1997): 127–43.

43. "The swords are [worn] on the left to represent the Blue Dragon; the knives are [worn] on the right to represent the White Tiger; the knee hide covers the front to represent the Red Bird; the hat is [worn] on the head to represent the Black Warrior. These four objects are magnificent decorations of a gentleman." Su Yu 蘇輿, *Chunqiu fanlu yizheng* 春秋繁露義證 (Beijing: Zhonghua shuju, 1992), 151. Translations are mine; see also Michael Loewe, *Dong Zhongshu, a "Confucian" Heritage and the Chunqiu Fanlu* (Leiden: Brill, 2011), 233.

44. Anthropologist Terence Turner beautifully documented this in his ethnographic study of the Kayapo tribe in the Amazon rain forest in South America. See Terence Turner, "The Social Skin," in *Not Work Alone: A Cross-Cultural View of Activities Superfluous to Survival*, ed. Jeremy Cherfas and Roger Lewin (London: Temple Smith, 1980), 112–40.

45. Paul Schilder, *The Image and Appearance of the Human Body* (New York: International University Press, 1935/1950), 11. For an updated introduction to this concept, see Thomas Pruzinsky and Thomas F. Cash, "Understanding Body Images: Historical and Contemporary Perspectives," in *Body Image: A Handbook of Theory, Research, and Clinical Practice*, ed. Thomas Pruzinsky and Thomas F. Cash (New York: Guilford, 2004), 3–12.

46. Joanna R. Sofaer, *The Body as Material Culture: A Theoretical Osteoarchaeology* (Cambridge: Cambridge University Press, 2006), 62.

47. Sofaer, *The Body as Material Culture*, 62.

48. Fan Ye, *Hou Hanshu*, 3156.

49. Wang Ming 王明, *Baopuzi neipian jiaoshi* 抱朴子內篇校釋 (Beijing: Zhonghua shushu, 1985), 51; also see Joseph Needham, *Science and Civilisation in China*, vol. 5, part 2, *Spagyrical Discovery and Invention: Magisteries of Gold and Immortality* (Cambridge: Cambridge University Press, 1974), 284.

50. Huang Hui, *Lunheng jiaoshi*, 872; English translation by Burton Watson in Cyril Birch, *Anthology of Chinese Literature: From Early Times to the Fourteenth Century*, 2 vols. (New York: Grove, 1965), 1: 88–89.

51. Chen Gongrou 陳公柔, "Shisangli, Jixili zhong suo jizai de sangzang zhidu" 士喪禮, 既夕禮中記載的喪葬制度, *Kaogu xuebao* 1956.4: 67–84, esp. 77–80.

52. Luan Fengshi 欒豐實, "Shiqian guanguo de chansheng, fazhan, he guanguo zhidu de xingcheng" 史前棺槨的產生、發展和棺槨制度的形成, *Wenwu* 2006.6: 49–55. Yuan Shengwen 袁勝文, "Guanguo zhidu de chansheng yu yanbian lunshu" 棺槨制度的產生與演變論述, *Nankai xuebao* 南開學報 2014.3: 94–101.

53. Zhao Huacheng 趙化成, "Zhou dai guanguo duochong zhidu yanjiu" 周代棺槨多重制度研究, *Guoxue yanjiu* 國學研究 5(1998): 27–74.

54. "Hence the inner and outer coffins of the son of heaven consist of seven layers; those of the feudal lords consist of five layers; those of the high ministers, three layers; and those of the officials, two layers." See Burton Watson, trans., *Hsun Tzu: Basic Writings* (New York: Columbia University Press, 1963), 97.

55. That might also explain why the gallery around the rear chamber was shaped into a form that looks like an extension of the front chamber that "embraces" the rear chamber as I have demonstrated in the previous section. But even from this perspective, Liu Sheng's tomb features only four nested coffins and caskets.

56. Wang Zhongshu, *Han Civilization*, 177.

57. Hayashi Minao, *Chūgoku kogyoku no kenkyū*, 1–80, 119–26.

58. Zhongguo shehui kexueyuan kaogu yanjiusuo, *Mancheng Han mu fajue baogao*, 1: 140. According to Wei Hong, the emperor owned six official jade seals, each with its superstructure shaped into "a hornless dragon or tiger," Fan Ye, *Hou Hanshu*, 3672.

59. In Zhao Mo's tomb at Guangzhou, a group of jade or gold seals bearing the inscriptions of "the crown prince" (*taizi* 太子), "Zhao Mo", "the emperor's seal" (*diyin* 帝印), and "Emperor Wen's emissary seal" (*Wendi xing xi* 文帝行璽) were found next to his jade suit; Guangzhou shi wenwu guanli weiyuanhui, *Xi Han Nanyue wang mu*, 1: 199–202.

60. Ban Gu, *Hanshu*, 4.126.

61. Zhongguo shehui kexueyuan kaogu yanjiusuo, *Mancheng Han mu fajue baogao*, 1: 140.

62. Zhongguo shehui kexueyuan kaogu yanjiusuo, *Mancheng Han mu fajue baogao*, 1: 140. Jeffrey Riegel has provided the following translation: "Verily this old jade man, the royal sire, will extend life by nineteen years." Jeffrey Riegel, "Kou-mang and Ju-shou," *Cahiers d'Extrême-Asie* 5(1989): 55–83, esp. 81. Professor Anthony Barbieri-Low, in a personal note to me, translated the inscription as "This old jade man is the king father of the east. May he grant nineteen more years of life." Their work has been very illuminating. However, one of the major revisions I have to make to these translations is to treat "wanggong" as the subject of "extending nineteen years of life" rather than as the predicate of "this old jade man." My argument is based on the fact that all extant textual parallels specify the subject of the extra life. For example, Wu Yujiang 吳毓江, *Mozi jiaozhu* 墨子校注 (Beijing: Zhonghua shuju, 1993), 338; Sima Qian, *Shiji*, 10.430; Huang Hui, *Lunheng jiaoshi*, 1:203, 205.

63. For a detailed study of this inscription and jade figurine, see Jie Shi, "Revisiting the 'Old Jade Man' at Mancheng Tomb No. 1 in Western Han China."

64. Zhongguo shehui kexueyuan kaogu yanjiusuo, *Mancheng Han mu fajue baogao*, 1: 143.

65. One might wonder why the outfit can't belong to a son of Liu Sheng or other inferior members of the royal house who died prematurely. Whereas a royal burial chamber might indeed contain coffins of lesser people (e.g., the king of Nanyue's tomb in Guangzhou and the Shizishan tomb in Xuzhou), these affiliated coffins were usually located outside the major tomb occupants' coffins and in external burial chambers built on-site. The practice of burying another person directly in the king's outer coffin was extremely rare.

66. Such blank seals were not unique to the Mancheng tombs; they also appeared in Zhao Mo's coffin together with those that were inscribed. This coexistence suggests that at least in Zhao Mo's tomb, likewise, the blank and the inscribed seals all belonged to

the same owner—the deceased king; see Guangzhou shi wenwu guanli weiyuanhui, *Xi Han Nanyue wang mu*, 1: 199–202.

67. Jinan cheng Fenghuangshan yiliuba hao Han mu fajue zhenglizu 紀南城鳳凰山一六八號漢墓發掘整理組, "Hubei Jiangling Fenghuangshan yiliuba hao Han mu fajue jianbao" 湖北江陵鳳凰山一六八號漢墓發掘簡報, *Wenwu* 1975.9: 1–22.

68. Hubei sheng wenwu kaogu yanjiusuo 湖北省考文物古研究所, "Jiangling Fenghuangshan yiliuba hao Han mu" 江陵鳳凰山一六八號漢墓, *Kaogu xuebao* 1993.4: 455–512, esp. 463, fig. 6.

69. Hebei sheng wenwu yanjiusuo, "Hebei Dingxian 40 hao Han mu fajue jianbao" 河北定縣40號漢墓發掘簡報, *Wenwu* 1981.8: 1–10, esp. 2.

70. For such leather purses, see Sun Ji 孫機, *Handai wuzhi wenhua ziliao tushuo* 漢代物質文化資料圖說 (Beijing: Wenwu chubanshe, 1991), 248.

71. The hairpin is the only object of this group that was found not in the supposed place but was near the waist. This might suggest that all the other objects were originally attached to a robe that later disintegrated and that the hairpin was later put on the robe.

72. In the royal cemetery of the Guo State, dating from the late Western Zhou or early Eastern Zhou, archaeologists discovered ritual jades and pendants placed on top of the inner coffin inside the outer coffin in tomb no. 2001. In tomb no. 2012, they found two bronze containers and a bronze toiletry box; see Henan sheng wenwu kaogu yanjiusuo and Sanmenxia shi wenwu gongzuodui, *Sanmenxia Guoguo mudi*, 1: 26, 238, 251. In Marquis Yi's outer coffin (early fifth century BCE), there were jades, objects made of animal horns and bones, silks, and linen objects; see Hubei sheng bowuguan, *Zeng hou Yi mu* 曾侯乙墓, 2 vols. (Beijing: Wenwu chubanshe, 1989), 1: 60. In Tianxingguan tomb no. 2 (fourth century BCE), the badly damaged outer coffin still contained jade *bi* discs and stone *gui* tablets upon discovery; see Hubei sheng Jingzhou bowuguan, *Jingzhou Tianxingguan erhao Chu mu* 荊州天星觀二號楚墓 (Beijing: Wenwu chubanshe, 2003), 29. In the three nested coffins at Baoshan tomb no. 2, seven layers of ornaments were placed on top of the middle coffin; see Hubei sheng Jing Sha tielu kaogudui 湖北省荊沙铁路考古队, *Baoshan Chu mu* 包山楚墓, 2 vols. (Beijing: Wenwu chubanshe, 1991), 1: 65.

73. Su Yu, *Chunqiu fanlu yizheng*, 166.

74. Chen Qiyou, *Lüshi Chunqiu xin jiaoshi*, 1451; John Knoblock and Jeffrey Riegel, trans., *The Annals of Lü Buwei* (Stanford, CA: Stanford University Press, 2000), 553. The translation should be corrected as "Yao's appearance is like a hanging fur cloak."

75. Ban Gu, *Hanshu*, 48.2238.

76. Ban Gu, *Hanshu*, 73.3116. According to Wang Su 王肅 (195–256 CE), these robes and headdresses were called "appearance robes" (*rongyi* 容衣). See Du You 杜佑, *Tongdian* 通典 (Beijing: Zhonghua shuju, 1988), 2142.

77. Michael Loewe, *Divination, Mythology and Monarchy in Han China* (Cambridge: Cambridge University Press, 1994), 283–84.

78. Wu Shuping 吳樹平, *Dongguan Hanji jiaozhu* 東觀漢紀校注 (Beijing: Zhonghua shuju, 2008), 240.

79. That spirits were invisible but more or less behaved like human beings was not a paradoxical idea in the popular imagination during the Western Han period. A story in the *Shiji* relates that Emperor Wu once set up a tent for his meeting with the invisible spiritual lords (*shenjun* 神君), who spoke, sat, and ate like humans but came and went from time to time accompanied by a whirl of wind; Sima Qian, *Shiji*, 12.460; Ban Gu, *Hanshu*, 25.1220.

80. This popular idea was preserved in Wang Chong's criticism of it. In his chapter "Discussion of Death," Wang argued: "Now people say that ghosts are the spirits of the dead. If this were true, then when men see them they ought to appear completely naked and not clothed in robes and sashes. Why? Because clothes have no spirits. When a man dies they all rot away along with his bodily form, so how could he put them on again?" See Huang Hui, *Lunheng jiaoshi*, 874. English translation by Watson in Birch, *Anthology of Chinese Literature*, 1: 89. In fact, the very fact that the ghosts were always visualized as being clad in clothes precisely shows clothes' inherent relationship to the human body.

81. Ying-shih Yu, "'O Soul, Come Back!': A Study in the Changing Conceptions of the Soul and Afterlife in Pre-Buddhist China," *Harvard Journal of Asiatic Studies* 27 (1987): 363–95.

82. Ban Gu, *Hanshu*, 12.351.

83. For contemporary examples of sacrificed human attendants and their equipment, see Guangzhou shi wenwu guanli weiyuanhui, *Xi Han Nanyue wang mu*, 1: 254–58; for examples of miniaturized figurines, see Yan Genqi 閻根齊, *Mangdangshan Xi Han Liangwang mudi* 芒碭山西漢梁王墓地 (Beijing: Wenwu chubanshe, 2001), 232.

84. Zhongguo shehui kexueyuan kaogu yanjiusuo, *Mancheng Han mu fajue baogao*, 1: 140.

85. Measurements taken from Zhongguo shehui kexueyuan kaogu yanjiusuo, *Mancheng Han mu fajue baogao*, 1: 31, fig. 17.

86. Zhongguo shehui kexueyuan kaogu yanjiusuo, *Mancheng Han mu fajue baogao*, 1: 148–49. The function of these small (one of them measures 7.5 centimeters in diameter), light (cloth-cored) individual lacquer boxes is not specified but presumably they were used for cosmetic purposes.

87. Fabrizio Pregadio, *The Encyclopedia of Taoism*, 2 vols. (London: Routledge, 2008), 896–97.

88. Sima Qian, *Shiji*, 28.1368.

89. English translation by Watson in Birch, *Anthology of Chinese Literature*, 1: 88. Wang Chong repeated the same idea twice in one chapter to emphasize his firm reception of this theory. Huang Hui, *Lunheng jiaoshi*, 877.

90. Besides Yu's 1987 article cited earlier, another important discussion of *hun-po* can be found in Kenneth E. Brashier, "Han Thanatology and the Division of 'Souls,'" *Early China* 21 (1996): 125–58. My reconstruction, however, is based more on the graphical imagination of *xingjie* than on purely intellectual concepts.

91. Donald Harper, *Early Chinese Medical Literature* (New York: Routledge, 2009), 393.

92. Harper, *Early Chinese Medical Literature*, 393. The character 流 was often written as 溜 in Han manuscripts; for example, see Yinqueshan Han mu zhujian zhengli xiaozu 銀雀山漢墓竹簡整理小組 *Yinqueshan Han mu zhujian* 銀雀山漢墓竹簡, 2 vols. (Beijing: Wenwu chubanshe, 1985–2010), 1:61.

93. Huang Jian 黃劍 dates the content of this chapter to 376–355 BCE; see his "Guanzi Shuidi pian kao lun" 管子·水地篇考論, in *Daojia wenhua yanjiu* 道家文化研究, issue 2 (Shanghai: Shanghai guji chubanshe, 1992), 336–46; for a discussion, see Chen Guying 陳鼓應, "*Guanzi* Xingshi, Zhouhe, Shuyan, Shuidi zhupian de Huanglao sixiang" 管子形勢宙合樞言水地諸篇的黃老思想, *Hanxue yanjiu* 漢學研究 20.1 (2002): 1–26.

94. W. Allyn Rickett, *Guanzi: Political, Economic, and Philosophical Essays from Early China*, 2 vols. (Princeton, NJ: Princeton University Press, 1998), 1: 103.

95. Sarah Allan, *The Way of Water and Sprouts of Virtue* (Albany, NY: SUNY Press, 1997).
96. Kong Yingda, *Liji zhengyi*, 10.86, in *Shisanjing zhushu*, 1314; Legge, *Li Chi: The Book of Rites*, 1: 193.
97. Sima Xiangru, "Ai Qin Ershi fu" 哀秦二世賦, in *Quan Han fu* 全漢賦, ed. Fei Zhengang 費振剛 (Beijing: Beijing daxue chubanshe, 1993), 89. English translation mine.
98. Upon discovery, it was found that only bronze legs of the couch survived. Such dragon-shaped bronze objects were also found in Xuzhou as supporters of a jade pillow. See Zhongguo guojia bowuguan and Xuzhou bowuguan, *Da Han Chu wang: Xuzhou Xi Han Chu wang ling mu wenwu ji cui*, 332–39. Another similar example is published in Umehara Sueji 梅原末治, *Rakuyō Kin-son kobo shūei* 洛陽金村古墓聚英 (Kyoto: Kobayashi Shashin Seihanjo Shuppanbu 1937), 40–41, and pl. LXVII.
99. Zhongguo shehui kexueyuan kaogu yanjiusuo, *Mancheng Han mu fajue baogao*, 1: 30.
100. Zhongguo shehui kexueyuan kaogu yanjiusuo, *Mancheng Han mu fajue baogao*, 1: 150.
101. Roel Sterckx, *Food, Sacrifice, and Sagehood in Early China* (Cambridge: Cambridge University Press, 2011), 83–121.
102. Zhongguo shehui kexueyuan kaogu yanjiusuo, *Mancheng Han mu fajue baogao*, 1: 43. English translation is from Wen Fong, ed., *The Great Bronze Age of China* (New York: Metropolitan Museum of Art, 1980), 331.
103. Such dustpan-shaped objects appeared as early as in the Shang tombs. A good example was from Lady Fu Hao's tomb at Anyang. See Zhongguo shehui kexueyuan kaogu yanjiusuo, *Yinxu Fu Hao mu* 殷墟婦好墓 (Beijing: Wenwu chubanshe, 1980), 92–94. These instruments normally were positioned with bronze ritual vessels around the coffin, but as the author of the report remarks, their exact function "is not clear." This puzzle seems to have been resolved with the excavation of Marquis Yi's tomb at Leigudun, in which a bronze dustpan was placed on a charcoal heater. Hubei sheng bowuguan, *Zeng hou Yi mu*, 1: 246–47.
104. Zhongguo shehui kexueyuan kaogu yanjiusuo, *Mancheng Han mu fajue baogao*, 1: 100.
105. Hubei sheng bowuguan, *Zeng hou Yi mu*, 1: 61–62, figs. 32–33.
106. Shandong Heze diqu Han mu fajue xiaozu, "Juye Hongtushan Xi Han mu," 476.
107. It should be noted that the iron-sealed door is not a real door (though it might impress us as such) but a wall that was built after the ritual activities had ended.
108. Zhongguo shehui kexueyuan kaogu yanjiusuo, *Mancheng Han mu fajue baogao*, 1: 15–16.
109. See Zheng Liangshu 鄭良樹, *Yili gongshi kao* 儀禮宮室考 (Taipei: Zhonghua shuju, 1971).
110. Zhongguo shehui kexueyuan kaogu yanjiusuo, *Mancheng Han mu fajue baogao*, 1: 141.
111. Lothar von Falkenhausen, "Archaeological Perspectives on the Philosophicization of Royal Zhou Ritual," in *Perceptions of Antiquity in Chinese Civilization*, ed. Dieter Kuhn and Helga Stahl (Heidelberg: Edition Forum, 2008), 135–75.
112. Zhongguo shehui kexueyuan kaogu yanjiusuo, *Mancheng Han mu fajue baogao*, 1: 178.
113. Due to the collapse and disintegration of the two tents, it is hard to know their precise positions. It seems the smaller tent was located about 50 centimeters to 100 centimeters to the west of the larger tent.

114. Lu Zhaoyin, *Mancheng Han mu*, 71.

115. Wu Hung, "The King of Jade Revisited: Material Symbolism of Jade as Observed in the Mancheng Tomb," 152. Wu, however, did not provide evidence.

116. Wei Hong, *Han jiuyi*, in Sun Xingyan et al., *Han guan liuzhong*, 100.

117. For example, see Jie Shi, "Rolling Between Burial and Shrine: A Tale of Two Chariot Processions at Chulan Tomb No. 2 in Eastern Han China (171 CE)," *Journal of American Oriental Society* 135.3(2015): 433–52.

118. Sima Qian, *Shiji*, 28.1382. Tang Jinyu 唐金裕, "Xi'an xijiao Han dai jianzhu yizhi fajue baogao," 西安西郊漢代建築遺址發掘報告 *Kaogu xuebao* 1959.2: 45–55. An abridged version is reprinted in Huang Zhanyue 黃展嶽, *Xi Han lizhi jianzhu yizhi* 西漢禮制建築遺址 (Beijing: Wenwu chubanshe, 2003), 197–207; Yang Hongxun 楊鴻勳, "Cong yizhi kan Xi Han Chang'an Mingtang (Biyong) xing zhi" 從遺址看西漢長安明堂（辟雍）形制, in *Jianzhu kaoguxue lunwen ji* 建築考古學論文集 (Beijing: Wenwu chubanshe, 1987), 169–200. See also Shi Jie 施傑, "Jiaotong youming: Xi Han zhuhouwangmu zhong de jisi kongjian" 交通幽冥：西漢諸侯王墓中的祭祀空間, in *Gudai muzang meishu yanjiu* 古代墓葬美術研究, vol. 2, ed. Wu Hung, Zheng Yan, and Zhu Qingsheng (Changsha: Hunan meishu chubanshe, 2013), 72–93.

119. Mengzi 孟子 (ca. 372–289 BCE) once advised King Hui of the Liang Kingdom that, "The Bright Hall is the hall of kings. If your majesty wishes to practice the true kingly governance, then do not pull it down!" James Legge, trans., *The Works of Menfucius* (New York: Dover, 1990), 161.

120. "If it should do all this, then even if it should construct a Bright Hall and summon the feudal lords to pay court there, it would almost be proper." John Knoblock, *Xunzi: A Translation and Study of the Complete Works*, 3 vols. (Stanford, CA: Stanford University Press, 1994), 2: 246; see also Henry Maspero, "Le Ming-t'ang et la crise religieuse Chinoise avant les Han," *Mélanges chinois et bouddhiques* 9(1948–1951): 1–71.

121. Wang Guowei 王國維, "Mingtang miao qin tongkao" 明堂廟寢通考, in *Guantang ji lin* 觀堂集林 (Shijiazhuang: Hebei jiaoyu, 2003), 58–68.

122. Zhongguo shehui kexueyuan kaogu yanjiusuo, *Mancheng Han mu fajue baogao*, 1: 74.

123. Zhou Jun 周筠 and Chen Jing 陳靜, "Mancheng Han mu chutu tongqi mingwen yanjiu" 滿城漢墓出土銅器銘文研究, *Wenwu chunqiu* 2010.3: 54.

124. An Eastern Han scholar named Fan Ran 范冉 (112–185 CE) made a will prescribing that after his death, the offerings in his "Mingtang" should include nothing but dry rice and cold water and any food or beverage should not be brought into his tomb (其明堂之奠，干飯寒水，飲食之物，勿有所下). Fan Ye, *Hou Hanshu*, 2690. An Eastern Han grave-quelling text also refers to the central hall of the tomb as a Mingtang (中央明堂，皆有尺六桃券、錢、布、鉛人). From Zhang Xunliao 張勛燎 and Bai Bing 白彬, *Zhongguo daojiao kaogu* 中國道教考古, 6 vols. (Beijing: Xianzhuang shuju, 2006), 1: 230. Miao Yu's 繆紆 (84–155 CE) tomb inscription, found near Xuzhou, also mentions a "Mingtang." The text is barely legible due to damage, but there is no question that this "Mingtang" must be associated with the tomb; see Zhou Xiaolu 周曉路, "Miao Yu muzhi dukao" 繆紆墓誌讀考, *Wenwu* 1995.4: 83–87.

125. Yang Kuan, *Zhongguo gudai lingqin zhidushi yanjiu*, 14–33.

126. Sima Qian, *Shiji*, 99.2725–26.

127. Ban Gu, *Hanshu*, 73.3115. See also Kimura Yoshikazu 北村良和, "Zenkan matsu no kōrei ni tsuite" 前漢末の改禮について, *Nihon Chūgoku Gakkai hō* 日本中國學會報 33(1981): 43–57.

128. Ban Gu, *Hanshu*, 97.3953. Translation by Stephen Owen in his "One Sight: The Han shu Biography of Lady Li," in *Rhetoric and the Discourses of Power in Court Culture: China, Europe, and Japan*, ed. David R. Knechtges and Eugene Vance (Seattle: University of Washington Press, 2005), 242.

129. Owen, "One Sight," 239–59.

130. David Hawkes, trans., *The Songs of the South: An Ancient Chinese Anthology of Poems by Qu Yuan and Other Poets* (Harmondsworth: Penguin, 1985), 238.

131. Li Xiangfeng 黎翔鳳, *Guanzi jiaozhu* 管子校注 (Beijing: Zhonghua shuju, 2004), 2: 876. A translation and discussion can be found in Sterckx, *Food, Sacrifice, and Sagehood in Early China*, 84–85; see also Rickett, *Guanzi: Political, Economic, and Philosophical Essays from Early China*, 2: 126.

132. Zhongguo shehui kexueyuan kaogu yanjiusuo, *Mancheng Han mu fajue baogao*, 1: 126–27.

133. Sun Ji, "Han zhen yishu" 漢鎮藝術, *Wenwu* 1983.6: 69–72. Early mat weights appeared in the Eastern Zhou tombs. See Sun Hua 孫華, "Banqiuxing qi yongtu lüe kao" 半球形器用途略考, *Nanfang wenwu* 1995.10: 107–10. For a recent exhibition catalogue of such mat weights, see Michelle C. Wang et al., *A Bronze Menagerie: Mat Weights of Early China* (Boston, MA: Isabella Stewart Gardner Museum, 2006). A group of four similar bronze figurines was uncovered in Xin Shiqu tomb no. 5 at Yima. They were just slightly smaller than the two counterparts in Liu Sheng's front chamber and less elaborate in decoration. See Li Hong 李虹, "Yima Xinshiqu wu hao Xi Han mu fajue jianbao" 義馬新市區5號西漢墓發掘簡報, *Wenwu* 1995.11: 20–23. Another four-piece set was recently unearthed at Dayunshan tomb no. 1 in 2010; see Nanjing bowuyuan and Xuyi xian wenguang xinju 盱眙縣文廣新局, "Jiangsu Xuyi xian Dayunshan Xi Han Jiangdu wangling yihao mu" 江蘇盱眙縣大雲山西漢江都王陵一號墓, *Kaogu* 2013.10: 36.

134. Zhongguo shehui kexueyuan kaogu yanjiusuo, *Mancheng Han mu fajue baogao*, 1: 100.

135. Zhongguo shehui kexueyuan kaogu yanjiusuo, *Mancheng Han mu fajue baogao*, 1: 100, 120.

136. For example, see Ban Gu, *Hanshu*, 48.2257.

137. Nylan and Loewe, *China's Early Empires: A Re-Appraisal*, 80.

138. Li Ling 李零, *Zhongguo fangshu kao* 中國方術考 (Shanghai: Dongfang chubanshe, 2001), 450.

139. Robert van Gulik, *Sexual Life in Ancient China: A Preliminary Survey of Chinese Sex and Society from ca. 1500 B.C. till 1644 A.D.* (Leiden: E. J. Brill, 1961), 55–72.

140. An alternative explanation might be that they represent fertility symbols, which are related to the theme of longevity. But this theory does not satisfactorily explain why these dildos appeared only in the public space—the front chamber that represents the sacrificial hall, rather than in other spaces such as the coffins. It seems that part of the intention was probably to intensify the seductive power where it was most needed.

141. Hawkes, *The Songs of the South*, 235–36.

142. Hawkes, *The Songs of the South*, 224.

143. Robert L. Thorp, "The Sui Xian Tomb: Re-Thinking the Fifth Century," *Artibus Asiae* 43. 1/2 (1981): 67–110. Citation on p. 76.

144. Hubei sheng bowuguan, *Zeng hou Yi mu*, 1: 68–69.

145. Zhongguo shehui kexueyuan kaogu yanjiusuo, *Yinxu Fu Hao mu*, 9–11. Fu Hao's shaft was not an isolated case. In the ramps of Xibeigang tomb no. 1001, perhaps

belonging to a Shang king, archaeologists discovered a horrifying ritual practice of laying mutilated human sacrifices on multiple levels; see Liang Siyong and Gao Quxun, *Houjiazhuang: Henan Anyang Houjiazhuang Yindai mudi*, 2: 37–48. Scholars usually identify such structures as offering halls (*xiangtang* 享堂) dedicated to the posthumous soul hovering above the burial. Yang Hongxun 楊鴻勳, "Guanyu Qindai yiqian mushang jianzhu de wenti" 關於秦代以前墓上建築的問題, *Kaogu* 1982.4: 38–42. Historian Yang Kuan believes that these pre-Qin buildings erected upon the grave were not temple-like shrines but resting chambers called *qin* meant to serve the deceaseds' souls; see Yang Kuan, *Zhongguo gudai lingqin zhidushi yanjiu*, 32–33, 103–6.

146. For excavation reports, see Hebei sheng wenguanchu et al., "Hebei Handan Zhao wang ling"; Zhongguo kexueyuan kaogu yanjiusuo, *Huixian fajue baogao*, 70, 88, 97; Shaanxi sheng Yongcheng kaogudui, "Fengxiang Qingong lingyuan zuantan yu shijue jianbao"; Shaanxi sheng Yongcheng kaogudui, "Fengxiang Qingong lingyuan dierci zuantan jianbao."

147. Guo Qingfan 郭慶藩, *Zhuangzi jishi* 莊子集釋 (Beijing: Zhonghua shuju, 1961), 351; Translation from Burton Watson, trans., *The Complete Works of Zhuangzi* (New York: Columbia University Press, 2013), 79.

148. Huang Huaixin 黃懷信, *Heguanzi jiaozhu* 鶡冠子校注 (Beijing: Zhonghua shuju, 2014), 136. Translation from Marnix Wells, *The Pheasant Cap Master and the End of History: Linking Religion to Philosophy in Early China* (St. Petersburg, FL.: Three Pines, 2013), 131.

149. Xun Yue 荀悦, *Shen jian* 申鑒 (Shanghai: Shangwu yinshuguan, 1925), Hanwei congshu 漢魏叢書 edition (1592), 3.6.

150. Huang Hui, *Lunheng jiaoshi*, 1: 59.

151. Zhu Qianzhi 朱謙之, *Laozi jiaoshi* 老子校釋 (Beijing: Zhonghua shuju, 1984), 37. Translation from James Legge trans. *Tao Te Ching* (Mineola, NY: Dover, 1997), 7, modified.

152. Guo Qingfan, *Zhuangzi jishi*, 381; Translation from Burton, *The Complete Works of Zhuangzi*, 78.

153. Wang Ming 王明, *Taipingjing hejiao* 太平經合校 (Beijing: Zhonghua shuju, 1979), 330.

154. John H. Taylor, *Death and the Afterlife in Ancient Egypt* (Chicago: University of Chicago Press, 2001).

2. THE UNION OF HUSBAND AND WIFE

1. Zhongguo shehui kexueyuan kaogu yanjiusuo, *Mancheng Han mu fajue baogao*, 1: 337–38.

2. Some other scholars proposed an even more precise dating, arguing Dou Wan might have died before Liu Sheng, between 118 and 113 BCE; see Li Jianli 李建麗 and Zhao Weiping 趙衛平, "Dou Wan zang yu heshi" 竇綰葬於何時? *Wenwu chunqiu* 1991.1: 54–57; Jiang Ruoshi 蔣若是, "Junguo, chize, he sanguan wuzhuqian zhi kaoguxue yanzheng" 郡國，赤仄與三官五銖錢之考古學驗證, *Wenwu* 1989.4: 84–91.

3. For example, Dou Wan's tomb lacks the gallery around the rear chamber and the outer coffin, which suggests the lack of two layers in the multilayered tomb space. Hence, in terms of structure, her tomb is simpler than her husband's. Robert Thorp,

"Mountain Tombs and Jade Burial Suits: Preparations for Eternity in the Western Han," in *Ancient Mortuary Traditions of China: Papers on Chinese Ceramic Funerary Sculptures*, ed. George Kuwayama (Los Angeles: Los Angeles County Museum of Art, 1991), 26–39.

4. Thus states *Comprehensive Meanings Held in the White Tiger [Hall]* (Baihutong 白虎通), the official exegetic canon of the Eastern Han Dynasty: "The word *fu* 婦 (women) means *fu* 服, or, to be obedient according to the ritual and etiquette" 婦者, 服也, 以 禮屈服. Chen Li 陳立, *Baihutong shuzheng* 白虎通疏證, 2 vols. (Beijing: Zhonghua shuju, 1994), 376. At the same time, Ban Gu also states: "Wife (*qi* 妻) means being equal (to husband)" 妻者, 齊也, 與夫齊體. Chen Li, *Baihutong shuzheng*, 490. In legal terminology, *fu* (consort) is a more general term for all types of wives, concubines, and consorts, while *qi* is specifically the legal primary wife, who is indeed equal to her husband in rank. See Anthony J. Barbieri-Low and Robin D. S. Yates, *Law, State, and Society in Early Imperial China: A Study With Critical Edition and Translation of the Legal Texts from Zhangjiashan Tomb No. 247* (Leiden: Brill, 2015), 2: 446, note 173. I thank Professor Barbieri-Low for directing me to this information.

5. The separation between the inner coffin (*guan*) and the outer casket (*guo*) as private and public realms might have existed in the Western Zhou period; see Yu Jiang, "Ritual Practice, Status, and Gender Identity: Western Zhou Tombs at Baoji," in *Gender and Chinese Archaeology*, ed. Katheryn M. Linduff, Yan Sun (New York: Altamira Press, 2004), 117–36.

6. Joseph Needham, *Science and Civilisation in China: Spagyrical Discovery and Invention: Magisteries of Gold and Immortality*, vol. 5, part 2, 284.

7. So far, about ten jade suits sewn with gold threads have been excavated and restored. See Lu Zhaoyin, "Shilun liang Han de yuyi"; Lu Zhaoyin, "Zai lun liang Han de yuyi"; James Lin, "Jade Suits and Iron Armour," *East Asia Journal: Studies in Material Culture* 1.2 (2003): 20–43. For two recent discoveries at Dayunshan, see Nanjing bowuyuan and Yuyi wenguang xinju, "Jiangsu Xuyi xian Dayunshan Xi Han Jiangdu wangling yihao mu," 45–47. Nanjing bowuyuan and Yuyi wenguang xinju, "Jiangsu Xuyi Dayunshan Xi Han Jiangdu wangling erhao mu fajue jianbao" 江蘇盱眙大 雲山西漢江都王陵二號墓發掘簡報, *Wenwu* 2013.1: 42–47. One of them has been reconstructed and restored; see Wang Wei 王瑋 and Wang Jinchao 王金潮, "Dayunshan Han mu jinlü yuyi xiufu baogao" 大雲山漢墓金縷玉衣修復報告, *Jianghan kaogu* 2014.1: 113–18.

8. Zhongguo shehui kexueyuan kaogu yanjiusuo, *Mancheng Han mu fajue baogao*, 1: 350.

9. Eduard Erkes, "Some Remarks on Karlgren's 'Fecundity Symbols in Ancient China,'" *Bulletin of the Museum of Far Eastern Antiquities* 3 (1931): 63–68; Ling Chunsheng 凌純聲, "Zhonggu gudai shenzhu yu yinyang xingqi chongbai" 中國古代神主與陰 陽性器崇拜, *Zhongyang yanjiuyuan minzuxue yanjiu jikan* 中央研究院民族學研 究集刊 8 (1959): 1–46. Other scholars who agree with *cong*'s femininity include Nan Zhiliang 那志良, Feng Hanji 馮漢驥, Tong Enzheng 童恩正, Shi Zhilian 石志廉, and Zhou Nanquan 周南泉; see Zang Zheng 臧振, "Yucong gongneng yanjiu shuping" 玉琮功能研究述評, *Wenbo* 1993.5: 61–66, 20.

10. Zhongguo shehui kexueyuan kaogu yanjiusuo, *Mancheng Han mu fajue baogao*, 1: 295, 348.

11. Hebei sheng bowuguan et al., "Dingxian sishi hao Han mu chutu de jinlü yuyi" 定縣 40 號漢墓出土的金縷玉衣, *Wenwu* 1976.7: 56–59, 98. For excavation reports,

see Hebei sheng wenwu yanjiusuo, "Hebei Dingxian 40 hao Han mu fajue jianbao." It remains a question whether this practice was unique to the region of Zhongshan or Hebei.

12. Shanxi sheng kaogu yanjiusuo and Beijing daxue kaoguxuexi, "Tianma-Qucun yizhi—Beizhao Jinhou mudi disanci fajue jianbao."

13. For a study of the genitalia capsule, see Jenny So (Su Fangshu 蘇芳淑), "Guren cungu—Yucong zai gudai muzang zhong de zhu yiyi" 古人存古—玉琮在古代墓葬中的諸意義, in *Gudai muzang meishu yanjiu*, 1–18.

14. Kong Yingda, *Chunqiu zuozhuan zhengyi* 春秋左傳正義, 4.31, in *Shisanjing zhushu*, 1733.

15. Kong Yingda, *Zhouyi zhengyi* 周易正義, in *Shisanjing zhushu*, 88.

16. Kong Yingda, *Maoshi zhengyi*, 5:2.87, in *Shisanjing zhushu*, 355. Bernhard Karlgren, trans., *The Book of Odes* (Stockholm: Museum of Far Eastern Antiquities, 1950), 68.

17. Wu Guangping 吳廣平, *Song Yu ji* 宋玉集 (Changsha: Yuelu shuyuan, 2001), 67–78.

18. Fei Zhengang, *Quan Han fu*, 97.

19. For examples, see Shaanxi sheng kaogu yanjiusuo Han ling kaogudui 陝西省考古研究所漢陵考古隊, *Zhongguo Han Yangling caiyong* 中國漢陽陵彩俑 (Xi'an: Shaanxi lüyou chubanshe, 1992); Zhongguo guojia bowuguan and Xuzhou bowuguan, *Da Han Chu wang: Xuzhou Xi Han Chu wang ling mu wenwu ji cui*, 151–77.

20. For the *yin-yang* cosmology and its role in early Chinese art and philosophy, see Cheng Te-k'un, "Yin-Yang Wu-Hsing and Han Art," *Harvard Journal of Asiatic Studies* 20.1/2 (1957): 162–86; Julian F. Pas, "Yin-Yang Polarity: A Binocular Vision of the World," *Asian Thought and Society* 8 (1983): 188–201.

21. Zhongguo shehui kexueyuan kaogu yanjiusuo, *Mancheng Han mu fajue baogao*, 1: 245.

22. Lu Zhaoyin, "Handai guizu funü xiai de peiyu—yuwuren" 漢代貴族婦女喜愛的珮玉—玉舞人, *Shoucangjia* 收藏家 1996.3: 4–7; Liu Yunhui 劉雲輝 and Liu Sizhe 劉思哲, "Han Duling lingqu xin chutu de yubei he yuwuren" 漢杜陵陵區新出土的玉盃與玉舞人, *Wenwu* 2012.12: 73–79. Susan N. Erickson, " 'Twirling Their Long Sleeves, They Dance Again and Again . . .': Jade Plaque Sleeve Dancers of the Western Han Dynasty," *Ars Orientalis* 24 (1994): 39–63. One remarkable example was recently found in Marquis Liu He's 劉賀 (92–59 BCE) tomb in present-day Nanchang, Jiangxi, but it was not worn by the male deceased but deposited in a lacquer box with other "entertaining objects" in one of the west storage chamber of the tomb; see Jiangxi sheng wenwu kaogu yanjiuyuan 江西省文物考古研究院 and Xiamen daxue lishixi 廈門大學歷史系, "Jiangxi Nanchang Xi Han Haihunhou Liu He mu chutu yuqi" 江西南昌西漢海昏侯劉賀墓出土玉器, *Wenwu* 2018.11: 57.

23. Kenneth J. DeWoskin, "Music and Voices from the Han Tombs: Music, Dance, and Entertainments during the Han," in *Stories from China's Past: Han Dynasty Pictorial Tomb Reliefs and Archaeological Objects from Sichuan Province, People's Republic of China*, ed. Lucy Lim (San Francisco, CA: Chinese Culture Foundation of San Francisco, 1987), 64–71.

24. Ban Gu, *Hanshu*, 97.3951.

25. Zhongguo shehui kexueyuan kaogu yanjiusuo, *Mancheng Han mu fajue baogao*, 1: 265.

26. Zhongguo huaxiangshi quanji bianji weiyuanhui 中國畫像石全集編輯委員會, *Zhongguo huaxiangshi quanji* 中國畫像石全集, 8 vols. (Ji'nan: Shandong meishu chubanshe, 2000), 2: pl. 105.

27. Yu Guanying 余冠英, *Han Wei Liuchao shixuan* 漢魏六朝詩選 (Beijing: Renmin wenxue chubanshe, 1987), 21. Sheri Lullo raised a different theory that mirrors and toiletry cases in Western Han were equally used by both male and female subjects in tombs and were not feminine objects, but that theory is based on data from a number of lesser tombs preserved in south China; see Sheri A. Lullo, "Making up Status and Authority: Practices of Beautification in Warring States through Han Dynasty China (Fourth Century BCE–Third Century CE)," *Fashion Theory* 20.4 (2016): 415–40.

28. For a survey of early Chinese toiletry cases and their forms, functions, and placement in tombs, see Sheri A. Lullo, "Toiletry Case-Sets Across Life and Death in Early China (fifth century BCE to third century CE)" (PhD diss., University of Pittsburgh, 2009).

29. Liu Sheng's only toiletry case (fig. 1.2, no. 113) appeared on the floor of the *guo* casket outside his coffins; see Zhongguo shehui kexueyuan kaogu yanjiusuo, *Mancheng Han mu fajue baogao*, 1: 148.

30. Zhongguo shehui kexueyuan kaogu yanjiusuo, *Mancheng Han mu fajue baogao*, 1: 300–2.

31. Qiu Yufang 裘毓芳, *Nüjie zhushi* 女誡註釋 (Shanghai: Shanghai yixue shuji, 1916), 7. Translation in Robin Wang, *Images of Women in Chinese Thought and Culture: Writings from the Pre-Qin* (Indianapolis, IN: Hackett, 2003), 181.

32. Another gendered item was the ruler. The excavators found a gold inlaid iron ruler in Dou Wan's front chamber, while none was found in Liu Sheng's tomb. It has been noted that rulers were feminine in Han tombs; see Bai Yunxiang 白雲翔, "Handai chidu de kaogu faxian ji xianguan wenti yanjiu" 漢代尺度的考古發現及相關問題研究, *Dongnan wenhua* 2014.2: 85–93, esp. 90.

33. Lu Zhaoyin, *Mancheng Han mu*, 116.

34. Brindley, *Ancient China and the Yue*, 85–112.

35. Guangzhou shi wenwu guanli weiyuanhui, *Xi Han Nanyue wang mu*, 1: 249.

36. This is true in the case of Emperors Hui, Wen, Jing, and Wu, Yuan, Ai; see Liu Qingzhu and Li Yufang, *Xi Han shiyi ling*; Xianyang shi wenwu kaogu yanjiusuo, *Xi Han diling zuantan baogao*.

37. Jiao Nanfeng 焦南峰, "Xi Han diling furen zangzhi chutan" 西漢帝陵夫人葬制初探, *Kaogu* 2014.1: 77–83.

38. Zhongguo shehui kexueyuan kaogu yanjiusuo, *Mancheng Han mu fajue baogao*, 1: 337.

39. Zhongguo shehui kexueyuan kaogu yanjiusuo, *Mancheng Han mu fajue baogao*, 1: 38, 246.

40. Legge, *Li Chi: The Book of Rites*, 1: 397.

41. Chen Zhaorong 陳昭容, "Xingbie, shenfen yu caifu—cong Shang Zhou qingtongqi yu muzang yiwu suozuo de guancha" 性別、身份與財富—從商周青銅器與墓葬遺物所做的觀察, in *Zhongguoshi xinlun—xingbie shi fence* 中國史新論—性別史分冊 (Taipei: Lianjing, 2009), 54–55.

42. Henan sheng wenwu kaogu yanjiusuo and Sanmenxia wenwu gongzuodui, *Sanmenxia Guoguo mudi (diyijuan)*, 1: 30, 241. Similar observations were also made in Zhao Peng 趙鵬, "Shangcunling Guoguo mudi M2001, M2012 suo fanying de liangxing guanxi" 上村嶺虢國墓地M2001, M2012所反映的兩性關係, *Dongfang cangpin* 東方藏品 2018.7: 199–200.

43. Cao Wei 曹瑋, "Guanyu Jinhou mu suizang qiyong zhidu de sikao" 關於晉侯墓隨葬器用制度的思考, in *Yuanwang ji* 遠望集, ed. Yuanwangji bianji weiyuanhui (Xi'an: Shaanxi renmin meishu chubanshe, 1998), 294–301.

44. Von Falkenhausen, *Chinese Society in the Age of Confucius (1000–250 BC): The Archaeological Evidence*, 122.

45. Zhongguo shehui kexueyuan kaogu yanjiusuo, *Mancheng Han mu fajue baogao*, 1: 51–52, 249.

46. Zhongguo shehui kexueyuan kaogu yanjiusuo, *Mancheng Han mu fajue baogao*, 1: 249. According to Xunzi's classic definition, "Spirit objects resemble lived objects but bear no function." Burton Watson, trans., *Hsün Tzu: Basic Writings* (New York: Columbia University Press, 1963), 104.

47. Shandong Heze diqu Han mu fajue xiaozu, "Juye Hongtushan Xi Han mu," 478.

48. Zhongguo shehui kexueyuan kaogu yanjiusuo, *Yinxu Fu Hao mu*, 38, 43–44, 49, 67.

49. For a summary, see Fang Hui 方輝, "Shi lun Zhoudai de tongkui" 試論周代的銅匱, in *Haidai diqu qingtong shidai kaogu* 海岱地區青銅時代考古 (Ji'nan: Shandong daxue chubanshe, 2007), 483–98; Chen Zhaorong, "Xingbie, shenfen yu caifu—cong Shang Zhou qingtongqi yu muzang yiwu suozuo de guancha," 41–50; Li Ling, "Shuo kui—Zhongguo zaoqi de funü yongpin: shoushihe, huazhuanghe he xianghe" 說匱—中國早期的婦女用品：首飾盒、化妝盒和香盒,*Gugongbowuyuanyuankan* 2009.3: 69–86.

50. Shaanxi sheng kaogu yanjiusuo 陝西省考古研究所et al., "Shaanxi Hancheng Liangdaicun yizhi M26 fajue jianbao" 陝西韓城梁帶村遺址M26發掘簡報, *Wenwu* 2008.1: 4–21.

51. On the concept of *nongqi* 弄器, see Huang Mingchong 黃銘崇, "Yindai yu Dong Zhou zhi 'nongqi' jiqi yiyi" 殷代與東周之弄器及其意義, *Gujin lunheng* 古今論衡 6 (2001): 66–88.

52. Chen Fangmei 陳芳妹, "Jinhou mudi suojian xingbie yanjiu de xin xiansuo" 晉侯墓地所見性別研究的新線索, in *Jinhou mudi chutu qingtongqi guoji xueshu yantaohui lunwenji* 晉侯墓地出土青銅器國際學術研討會論文集, ed. Shanghai bowuguan (Shanghai: Shanghai shuhua chubanshe, 2002), 164.

53. Wang Yang 王洋, "Liangdaicun Rui Huangong fufu mu suizang qingtongqi de xingbie guancha" 梁帶村芮桓公夫婦墓隨葬青銅器的性別觀察, *Kaogyu yu wenwu* 2013.2: 69–77; for the preliminary excavation report, also see Shaanxi sheng kaogu yanjiusuo et al., "Shaanxi Hancheng Liangdaicun yizhi M26 fajue jianbao," 5.

54. At Jiuliandun tomb no. 2 in present-day Jingzhou in South China, dated to the fourth century BCE, which was occupied by a noble lady, the excavators discovered a set of miniature bronzes reminiscent of the late Western Zhou bronzes in the north; see Qin Yu 秦玉, "Jiuliandun Zhanguo gumuqun: zhenjing guoneiwai de Chu wenhua faxian" 九連墩戰國古墓群：震驚國內外的楚文化發現, in *Dalian ribao* 大連日報, July 24, 2013, http://roll.sohu.com/20130724/n382399916.shtml.

55. Yanshi Shangcheng bowuguan 偃師商城博物館, "Henan Yanshi Koudian faxian Dong Han tongqi jiaocang" 河南偃師寇店發現東漢銅器窖藏, *Kaogu* 1992.9: 803–5.

56. Li Shaonan 李少南, "Shandong Boxing xian chutu tongjing he huobi" 山東博興縣出土銅鏡和貨幣, *Kaogu* 1984.11: 1041–44.

57. Zhongguo shehui kexueyuan kaogu yanjiusuo, *Mancheng Han mu fajue baogao*, 1: 319.

58. Zhongguo shehui kexueyuan kaogu yanjiusuo, *Mancheng Han mu fajue baogao*, 1: 320.

59. Zhongguo shehui kexueyuan kaogu yanjiusuo, *Mancheng Han mu fajue baogao*, 1: 179–81.

60. Wu Xiaojun 吳曉筠, *Shang Zhou shiqi chema maizang yanjiu* 商周時期車馬埋葬研究 (Beijing: Kexue chubanshe, 2009), 77.

61. Liu Xu 劉緒 and Xu Tianjin 徐天進, "Guanyu Tianma-Qucun yizhi Jinguo muzang de jige wenti" 關於天馬—曲村遺址晉國墓葬的幾個問題, in *Jinhou mudi chutu qingtongqi guoji xueshu yantaohui lunwenji* 晉侯墓地出土青銅器國際學術研討會論文集 (Shanghai: Shanghai shuhua chubanshe, 2002), 47–48.

62. Zhongguo shehui kexueyuan kaogu yanjiusuo, *Mancheng Han mu fajue baogao*, 1: 37, 244.

63. Wang, *Images of Women in Chinese Thought and Culture*, 66.

64. Wang Niansun 王念孫, *Guangya shuzheng* 廣雅疏證 (Nanjing: Jiangsu guji chubanshe, 1984), 53.

65. Mancheng tomb no. 2 measures 3,000 cubic meters in size, and Mancheng tomb no. 1, 2,700 cubic meters; Zhongguo shehui kexueyuan kaogu yanjiusuo, *Mancheng Han mu fajue baogao*, 1: 10, 216.

66. Kong Yingda, *Liji zhengyi*, 23.205, in *Shisanjing zhushu*, 1433; Legge, *Li Chi: The Book of Rites*, 1: 399, slightly modified.

67. Liu Qingzhu and Li Yufang, *Xi Han shiyi ling*, 161–62.

68. Lisa Ann Raphals, *Sharing the Light: Representations of Women and Virtue in Early China* (Albany, NY: SUNY Press, 1998), 70–77.

69. Zhongguo shehui kexueyuan kaogu yanjiusuo, *Mancheng Han mu fajue baogao*, 1: 353.

70. Zhongguo shehui kexueyuan kaogu yanjiusuo, *Mancheng Han mu fajue baogao*, 1: 234–42. In addition to the *bi* discs, there are eight rhombic jade wedges fastened to the exterior of the coffin.

71. Among the other three examples, one comes from the Shizishan tomb (dated to the early second century BCE) and the two others from Dayunshan tombs nos. 1 and 2 (dated ca. 128 BCE). For the Shizishan coffin, see Li Chunlei 李春雷, "Jiangsu Xuzhou Shizishan Chu wangling chutu xiangyu qiguan de tuili fuyuan yanjiu" 江蘇徐州獅子山楚王陵出土鑲玉漆棺的推理復原研究, *Kaogu yu wenwu* 1999.1: 56–71. This theory of reconstruction has been challenged by Ge Mingyu 葛明宇, "Shizishan Chuwang ling chutu biyu guanpian ying wei guanti neishi kao" 獅子山楚王陵出土碧玉棺片應為棺體內飾考, *Jianghan kaogu* 2018.1: 80–88. The Dayunshan coffins were reported in Nanjing bowuyuan and Yuyi wenguang xinju, "Jiangsu Xuyi xian Dayunshan Xi Han Jiangdu wangling yihao mu," 43–45; Nanjing bowuyuan and Yuyi wenguang xinju, "Jiangsu Xuyi xian Dayunshan Xi Han Jiangdu wangling erhao mu fajue jianbao," 47–61.

72. Sima Qian, *Shiji*, 126. 3200; see also Lu Zhaoyin, *Mancheng Han mu*, 149–50.

73. Zheng Shaozong, *Mancheng Han mu*, 154–56.

74. Zhongguo shehui kexueyuan kaogu yanjiusuo, *Mancheng Han mu fajue baogao*, 1: 258. Anthony Barbieri-Low offers a translation and discussion of the inscriptions on this lamp in Anthony J. Barbieri-Low, *Artisans in Early Imperial China* (Seattle: University of Washington Press, 2007), 10–15.

75. Chen Zhaorong has speculated that in Western Zhou tombs, the political power of the female deceased's paternal clan might have increased the richness of the material content in her tomb; see Chen Zhaorong, "Xingbie, shenfen yu caifu," 64–65.

76. Ban Gu, *Hanshu*, 97.3940.

77. Yang Shuda 楊樹達, *Han dai hunsang lisu kao* 漢代婚喪禮俗考 (Shanghai: Shanghai guji chubanshe, 2000), 20–27.

78. Sima Qian, *Shiji*, 9.403.

79. Taniguchi Yasuyo 谷口やすよ, "Kandai no 'taigō rinchō'" 漢代の太后臨朝, *Rekishi hyōron* 歴史評論159 (1980): 86–98.

80. Sima Qian, *Shiji*, 12.425.

81. For consort families in Han society, see Qu Tongzu, *Han Social Structure*, ed. Jack L. Dull (Seattle: University of Washington Press, 1972), 168–74.

82. Zhongguo shehui kexueyuan kaogu yanjiusuo, *Mancheng Han mu fajue baogao*, 1: 271–72.

83. Lu Zhaoyin thinks *qibi* 妻鄙 refers to *qidang* 妻黨 (wife's fraction, or Liu Sheng's spousal branch), see *Mancheng Han mu*, 162.

84. Lu Zhaoyin, *Mancheng Han mu*, 161–62. Xu Zhengkao 徐正考 follows the *tiantian* reading in his *Han dai tongqi mingwen wenzibian* 漢代銅器銘文文字編 (Changchun: Jilin daxue chubanshe, 2005), 53.

85. Qiu Xigui 裘錫圭, "Du kaogu fajue suode wenzi ziliao biji (yi)" 讀考古發掘所得文字資料筆記（一）, *Renwen zazhi* 人文雜誌 1981.6: 97–99.

86. Qiu Xigui reads the prayer as "shou wu du" 壽無壽, which is based on the assumption that the vertical stroke in the graph 王 actually emerges above the top horizontal stroke and therefore invalidates the reading of the graph as 王; see Qiu Xigui, "Du kaogu fajue suode wenzi ziliao biji (yi)." However, a high-quality photograph of the coin published afterward clearly shows that the graph is unmistakably 王 because the vertical stroke never reaches beyond the top horizontal stroke (see fig. 2.8).

87. For such examples, see Ban Gu, *Hanshu*, 9.277, 55.2480, 97.4000; more often, *wangmu* was modified by the posthumous title of the king.

88. Chūgoku kokyō no kenkyuhan 中國古鏡の研究班, "Zen-Kan kyōmei shakuchū" 前漢鏡銘集釋, *Tōhō gakuhō* 東方學報 84 (2009): 172, inscription no. 403.

89. For studies of Xiwangmu, see Jean M. James, "An Iconographic Study of Xiwangmu During the Han Dynasty," *Artibus Asiae* 55.1/2 (1995): 17–41; Li Song 李凇, *Lun Handai yishu zhong de Xiwangmu tuxiang* 論漢代藝術中的西王母圖像 (Changsha: Hunan jiaoyu chubanshe, 2000).

90. Wang Yiliang 王貽樑, *Mutianzi zhuan huijiao jishi* 穆天子傳滙校集釋 (Shanghai: Huadong shifan daxue chubanshe, 1994), 161.

91. This mirror inscription is published in Wang Ganghuai 王綱懷, *Zhishui ji: Wang Ganghuai tongjing yanjiu lunji* 止水集: 王綱懷銅鏡研究論集 (Shanghai: Shanghai guji chubanshe, 2010), 77.

92. A good example was the legendary westward journey of King Mu, or *Mutianzi* 穆天子, of the Western Zhou dynasty, who became a guest in the court of the queen mother of the west; see Deborah Lynn Porter, *From Deluge to Discourse: Myth, History, and the Generation of Chinese Fiction* (Albany, NY: SUNY Press, 1996), 86–104.

93. Ban Gu, *Hanshu*, 11.342. Yan Shigu 顏師古 (581–645 CE), while annotating this passage, noted that the queen mother of the west "was the image of the long-living Empress Dowager Wang."

94. Zhongguo shehui kexueyuan kaogu yanjiusuo, *Mancheng Han mu fajue baogao*, 1: 179–81, 311–20. In tomb no. 1, the only vehicle oriented to the south was carriage no. 4. The anomaly is very puzzling.

95. Zhongguo shehui kexueyuan kaogu yanjiusuo, *Mancheng Han mu fajue baogao*, 179–81, 311–20.

96. Zhongguo shehui kexueyuan kaogu yanjiusuo, *Mancheng Han mu fajue baogao*, 1: 204.

97. Gao Chongwen 高崇文, "Xi Han zhuhouwang mu chema xunzang zhidu tantao" 西漢諸侯王墓車馬殉葬制度探討, *Wenwu* 1992.2: 37–43.

98. An emperor's ceremonial travel to the remote provinces to visit his local governors, a tradition traceable to the pre-dynastic age, was called "inspection and hunting" (*xunshou* 巡狩); He Pingli 何平立, *Xunshou yu fengshan: Fengjian zhengzhi de wenhua guiji* 巡狩與封禪：封建政治的文化軌跡 (Ji'nan: Qilu shushe, 2003), 7–13. During the Qin and Han periods, a recently dead emperor was given the title *Daxing* 大行, which literally means "a great journey" and implies "going to heaven." According to Tosaki Tetsuhiko, the doctrine of interpreting *Daxing* as "a great journey" was established at the time of the First Emperor with his inspectional journeys. It is not surprising that Western Han princes would have followed this imperial practice by demonstrating their political privilege. Tosaki Tetsuhiko 戶崎哲彦, "Chūgoku kodai no taisō ni okeru taikō shōni tsuite" 中国古代の大喪における「大行」称について, *Shigaku zasshi* 史學雜誌 100.9 (1991): 1546–68.

99. Zhongguo shehui kexueyuan kaogu yanjiusuo, *Mancheng Han mu fajue baogao*, 1: 126.

100. Sima Qian, *Shiji*, 59.2099.

101. Zhongguo shehui kexueyuan kaogu yanjiusuo, *Mancheng Han mu fajue baogao*, 1: 288–89.

102. Zhongguo shehui kexueyuan kaogu yanjiusuo, *Mancheng Han mu fajue baogao*, 1: 25, fig. 15.

103. Zhongguo shehui kexueyuan kaogu yanjiusuo, *Mancheng Han mu fajue baogao*, 1: 229, fig. 153.

104. Henan sheng bowuguan et al., "Henan Xinyang shi Pingqiao Chunqiu mu fajue jianbao" 河南信陽市平橋春秋墓發掘簡報, *Wenwu* 1981.1: 9–12.

105. Nan Bo 南波, "Jiangsu Lianyungang shi Haizhou Xi Han Shiqi Yao mu" 江蘇連雲港市海州西漢侍其繇墓, *Kaogu* 1975.3: 169–77.

106. For two late Western Han examples, see Zhongguo kexueyuan kaogu yanjiusuo, *Luoyang Shaogou Han mu* 洛陽燒溝漢墓 (Beijing: Kexue chubanshe, 1959), 33, 160, 165, pl. 43; and Guangzhou wenwu guanli weiyuanhui and Guangzhou shi bowuguan, *Guangzhou Han mu* 廣州漢墓, 2 vols. (Beijing: Wenwu chubanshe, 1981), 1: 301.

107. For example, Yinwan tomb no. 6, see Lianyungang shi bowuguan 連雲港市博物館, "Jiangsu Donghai xian Yinwan Han muqun fajue jianbao" 江蘇東海縣尹灣漢墓群發掘簡報, *Wenwu* 1996.8: 4–25, esp. fig. 2.

108. Kong Yingda, *Liji zhengyi*, 61.452, in *Shisanjing zhushu*, 1680. Legge, *Li Chi: The Book of Rites*, 2: 429–30.

109. Hayashi Minao, *Kandai no kamigami* 漢代の神神 (Kyoto: Rinsen Shoten, 1989), 287–98.

110. Raphals, *Sharing the Light*, 139–68; Bret Hinsch, *Women in Early Imperial China* (Plymouth: Rowman and Littlefield, 2011), 162ff; Alison H. Black, "Gender and Cosmology in Chinese Correlative Thinking," in Caroline Walker Bynum et al., ed. *Gender and Religion: On the Complexity of Symbols* (Boston: Beacon, 1986), 166–95.

111. Zhongguo shehui kexueyuan kaogu yanjiusuo, *Mancheng Han mu fajue baogao*, 1: 15–16; 219–20.

112. These grooves carved in the floor could not have served as drainage, as the excavator suggests, because they did not connect with the ditches around the front chamber; see Lu Zhaoyin, *Mancheng Han mu*, 24. Unlike the deep and narrow ditches, the

grooves were shallow, wide, and evenly spaced, with a different function; see Zhongguo shehui kexueyuan kaogu yanjiusuo, *Mancheng Han mu fajue baogao*, 1: 16.

113. This palace symbolism was perhaps in existence as early as the Shang period; its
archetype was found in the Shang royal cemetery at Anyang, dating from the thirteenth century; see Li, *Anyang*, 86; Chang, *Shang Civilization*, 114; for Eastern Zhou
examples, see Von Falkenhausen, *Chinese Society in the Age of Confucius*, 308.

114. Zheng Liangshu 鄭良樹, *Yili gongshi kao* 儀禮宮室考 (Taipei: Zhonghua shuju,
1971).

115. Henan sheng wenwu kaogu yanjiusuo, *Yongcheng Xi Han Liangguo wangling yu qinyuan*, 26, fig. 15.

116. For another well-preserved and published Western Han example, see Zhongguo shehui kexueyuan kaogu yanjiusuo, *Han Duling lingyuan yizhi* 漢杜陵陵園遺址 (Beijing: Wenwu chubanshe, 1993), 23–42; for the Qin model, see Shaanxi sheng kaogu
yanjiusuo and Qin Shihuang bingmayong bowuguan, *Qin Shihuangdi lingyuan
kaogu baogao* (1999), 10–12.

117. Zhongguo shehui kexueyuan kaogu yanjiusuo, *Mancheng Han mu fajue baogao*, 1:
228, 335.

118. For Emperor Gaozu's seventeen ancestral hymns of the "Anshi fangzhongge" 安世房
中歌 (songs of a pacified age for the inner chamber), see Martin Kern, *Die Hymnen
der chinesischen Staatsopfer: Literatur und Ritual in der politischen Repräsentation
von der Han-Zeit bis zu den Sechs Dynastien* (Stuttgart, Germany: Franz Steiner Verlag, 1999), 100–173; Xu Yunhe 許雲和, "Han Fangzhongci yue yu Anshi fangzhongge
shiqi zhang" 漢房中祠樂與安世房中歌十七章, *Zhongshan daxue xuebao* 中山大
學學報 2010.2:33–44. Zhang Shuguo 張樹國, "Lun Anshi fangzhong ge yu Han chu
zongmiao jiyue de chuangzhi" 論安世房中歌與漢初宗廟祭樂的創制, *Hangzhou
shifan daxue xuebao* 杭州師範大學學報 2010.5: 70–77.

119. Zheng Liangshu, *Yili gongshi kao*, 46–49.

120. The reason for having multiple offerings is explained in the *Book of Rites* as: "They
knew not whether the soul were here, or whether it were there, or far off, away from
all men." Kong Yingda, *Liji zhengyi*, 26.229, in *Shisanjing zhushu*, 1457; Legge, *Li Chi:
The Book of Rites*, 1: 444. The word *yan* 厭 (literally, "to feed") refers to a particular
type of offering set up in the absence of the impersonator, who dressed like and
played the role of ancestor during the ritual; Kong Yingda, *Liji zhengyi*, 19.171, in
Shisanjing zhushu, 1399.

121. Zheng Xuan annotates: "To hold sacrifice to an adult, offerings are first dedicated
at the southeast corner before the impersonator is received. This is called the 'dark
satisfying offering.' After the impersonator has risen (to leave), the offerings are
switched to the northwest corner. This is called the 'bright satisfying offering.'" 祭成
人始設奠於奧, 迎尸之前, 謂之陰厭. 尸謖之後, 改饌於西北隅. 謂之陽厭. Kong
Yingda, *Liji zhengyi*, 19.171, in *Shisanjing zhushu*, 1399.

122. Jia Gongyan, *Yili zhushu*, 46.247, in *Shisanjing zhushu*, 1191. The *Book of Rites* offers
an interpretation of this offering: "Confucius said, 'When the oldest son, who would
take the father's place, dies prematurely, no brother by an inferior wife can be his
successor. At the auspicious sacrifice to him, there is a single bullock; but the service
being to one who died prematurely, there is no presentation (of the lungs), no stand
with the heart and tongue, no dark-coloured spirits, no announcement of the nourishment being completed. This is what is called the dark satisfying offering.'" Legge,
Li Chi: The Book of Rites, 1: 338.

123. Jia Gongyan, *Yili zhushu*, 45.239, in *Shisanjing zhushu*, 1183. See also Yang Fu 楊復, *Yilitu* 儀禮圖, in *Yingyin Wenyuange siku quanshu* 景印文淵閣四庫全書, 1500 vols. (Taipei: Xinwenfeng, 1986), 104.265.

124. Jia Gongyan, *Yili zhushu*, 48.257, in *Shisanjing zhushu*, 1201; John Steele trans., *The I-li or Book of Etiquette and Ceremonial*, 2 vols. (London: Probsthain, 1917), 2: 167.

125. Between the two sacrifices was the "formal sacrifice" (*zhengji* 正祭), which also took place in the *shi* apartment. During this ritual, the recipient of the offering was not an empty "spirit seat" but an impersonator, acting as the ancestor, who entered the door of the temple, crossed the courtyard, and stepped into the inner chamber for a meeting with the hosts and guests of the ritual event. During the sacrificial ceremony, the dedicators (hosts) exchanged toasts with the dedicatee (impersonator) for multiple rounds. See Jia Gongyan, *Yili zhushu*, 45.239–46.247, in *Shisanjing zhushu*, 1183–191; Steele, *The I-li or Book of Etiquette and Ceremonial* 2: 135–52. See also Yang Fu, *Yilitu*, in *Yingyin Wenyuange siku quanshu*, 104.267–78.

126. The most detailed explanation of *yinyan* and *yangyan* can be found in Kong Yingda, *Liji zhengyi*, 19.172, in *Shisanjing zhushu*, 1400. "In regard to all others who have died prematurely and have left no offspring, the sacrifice is offered to them in the house of the oldest son, where the apartment is most light, with the vases in the chamber on the east. This is what is called the bright satisfying offering." Legge, *Li Chi: The Book of Rites*, 1: 338.

127. Jia Gongyan, *Yili zhushu*, 46.247, in *Shisanjing zhushu*, 1191. "The waiter removes the relishes and stand and the grain jars used by the impersonator, and places them in the north-west corner, with the body-rest to the south of them. He covers all with a mat, and sets a jar of wine along with them. The waiter closes the window and door, and descends the steps." Steele, *The I-li or Book of Etiquette and Ceremonial*, 2: 153. See also Yang Fu, *Yilitu*, in *Yingyin Wenyuange siku quanshu*, 104.279.

128. For the dating, see William Boltz, "Yili," in *Early Chinese Texts: A Bibliographical Guide*, ed. William Boltz (Berkeley, CA: Society for the Study of Early China, 1993), 237–39.

129. Ban Gu, *Hanshu*, 88.3615, 3621.

130. The only modification to this bipartite hall-apartment unity concerns the orientation. In real life, a temple complex should face to the south, but at the Mancheng site, the sacrificial space of the "formal hall," represented by the wooden structure in Liu Sheng's front chamber, was turned 90 degrees counterclockwise to face to the east because the main axis of the tomb was east to west. This revision literally places the deceased in the west and the living worshipper in the east. This puzzling alteration might have resulted from the popular belief that "the tomb of the spirit is in the west and the house of the spirit is in the east." Sima Qian, *Shiji*, 28.1382. Or, it was just necessitated by the desire to use this particular mountain location and this face of the mountain.

131. For a discussion on the office of *Cisi*, see chapter 4.

132. For a latest introduction to this cemetery, see Liu Rui and Liu Tao, *Xi Han zhuhouwang lingmu zhidu yanjiu*, 497–98.

133. Henan sheng wenwu kaogu yanjiusuo, *Yongcheng Xi Han Liangguo wangling yu qinyuan*, 91–226.

134. Shi, "Jiaotong youming: Xi Han zhuhouwangmu zhong de jisi kongjian," 85–90.

135. Henan sheng wenwu kaogu yanjiusuo, *Yongcheng Xi Han Liangguo wangling yu qinyuan*, 104–10, 116, 148, 222.

136. In the Shang capital near present-day Anyang, archaeologists have identified some lesser adjacent burials with male and female occupants; see Meng Xianwu 孟憲武, "Yinxu nanqu muzang fajue zongshu—jian tan jige xiangguan wenti" 殷墟南區墓葬發掘綜述—兼談幾個相關問題, *Zhongyuan wenwu* 1986.3: 78–83; Tang Jigen 唐際根, "Yinxu jiazu mudi chutan" 殷墟家族墓地初探, in *Zhongguo Shang wenhua guoji xueshu taolunhui lunwenji* 中國商文化國際學術討論會論文集, ed. Zhongguo shehui kexueyuan kaogu yanjiusuo (Beijing: Zhongguo dabaike quanshu chubanshe, 1998), 201–7. By the end of the Western Zhou period, the practice of interring husband and wife in two adjacent burials had gained popularity in elite cemeteries; see Li Boqian 李伯謙, "Cong Jinhou mudi kan Xi Zhou gongmu mudi zhidu de jige wenti" 從晉侯墓地看西周公墓墓地制度的幾個問題, *Kaogu* 1997.11: 51–60.

137. Xu, "The Cemetery of the Western Zhou Lords of Jin"; Geng Chao 耿超, "Jinhou mudi de xingbie kaocha" 晉侯墓地的性別考察, *Zhongyuan wenwu* 2014.3: 36–43, 84.

138. Toward the end of the Eastern Zhou period, tombs of deceased kings and queens appeared increasingly equal, though still distinct in design. And this evolution in the burial tradition of royal husbands and wives is most obvious in the royal cemeteries of the Qin kingdom during the late Eastern Zhou period. Before the fourth century BCE, the Qin royal couples were buried in separate sites, with the king's burial notably larger than the queen's, but from the mid-Warring States period onward, the royal couple's burials moved closer to each other in a parallel relationship with similar sizes. Ding Yan 丁岩, "Qin wanghou de hezang yu feizi de fuzang—yi Xianyangyuan Zhanguo Qin lingyuan de faxian wei zhongxin" 秦王后的合葬與妃子的祔葬—以咸陽原戰國秦陵園的發現為中心, *Xianyang shifan xueyuan xuebao* 咸陽師範學院學報 2014. 1: 1–5.

139. Kong Yingda, *Maoshi zhengyi*, 4:1.65, in *Shisanjing zhushu*, 333; Karlgren, *The Book of Odes*, 48–50.

140. Huang Huaixin, Zhang Maorong 張懋容, and Tian Xudong 田旭東, *Yi Zhou shu huijiao jizhu* 逸周書匯校集註, 2 vols. (Shanghai: Shanghai guji chubanshe, 2007), 1: 53.

141. Kong Yingda, *Liji zhengyi*, 52.398, in *Shisanjing zhushu*, 1626. James Legge, trans., *The Four Books* (New York: Paragon, 1966), 363.

142. A. F. P. Hulsewé, "Royal Rebels," *Bulletin de l'Ecole Française d'Extrême-Orient* 69 (1981): 315–25.

143. Ban Gu, *Hanshu*, 85.3446.

3. INTEGRATION OF ETHNIC HAN AND NON-HAN

1. For a recent survey of Han material culture, see Psarras, *Han Material Culture: An Archaeological Analysis and Vessel Typology*.

2. The term "Han ren" first appears in Sima Qian's works, denoting the Han people as opposed to the Xiongnu; Sima Qian, *Shiji*, 111. 2933.

3. Ge Jianxiong 葛劍雄, *Zhongguo yiminshi* 中國移民史, 6 vols. (Fuzhou: Fujian renmin chubanhe, 1997), 2: 42. Lin Yun 林澐, "Rong-Di fei hu lun" 戎狄非胡論, in his *Lin Yun xueshu lunwenji (er)* 林澐學術論文集 (二) (Beijing: Kexue chubanshe, 2009), 6. Shan Yueying 單月英, "Dong Zhou Qindai Zhongguo beifang diqu kaoguxue wenhua geju—jianlun Rong, Di, Hu yu Huaxia zhijian de hudong"

東周秦代中國北方地區考古學文化格局—兼論戎狄胡與華夏之間的互動, *Kaogu xuebao* 2015.3: 319.

4. See Pei Yin's 裴駰 annotation on Sima Qian, *Shiji*, 130.3320. See also Lü Shihao 呂世浩, *Cong Shiji dao Hanshu—zhuanzhe guocheng yu lishi yiyi* 從史記到漢書—轉折過程 與歷史意義 (Taipei: Taida chuban zhongxin, 2009), 147.

5. Zhongguo shehui kexueyuan kaogu yanjiusuo, *Mancheng Han mu fajue baogao*, 1: 143.

6. Zhongguo shehui kexueyuan kaogu yanjiusuo, *Mancheng Han mu fajue baogao*, 1: 298.

7. Jessica Rawson, *Chinese Jade from the Neolithic to the Qing* (London: British Museum Press, 1995), 44–60. Sun Ji, "Zhoudai de zuyupei" 周代的組玉佩, *Wenwu* 1998.4: 4–14.

8. In transmitted texts, the earliest use of the concept "Huaxia" can be found in the *Zuo Commentary to the Spring and Autumn Annals*, Kong Yingda, *Chunqiu zuozhuan zhengyi* 56.446, in *Shisanjing zhushu*, 2148. The text was largely completed during the fourth century BCE; see Stephen Durrant, Li Wai-yee, and David Schaberg trans., *Zuo Tradition (Zuozhuan): Commentary on the "Spring and Autumn Annals,"* 3 vols. (Seattle: University of Washington, 2016), 1:xxx.

9. Hayashi Minao, *Chūgoku kogyoku no kenkyū*, 141–65.

10. Xiang Zonglu 向宗魯, *Shuoyuan jiaozheng* 說苑校證 (Beijing: Zhonghua shuju, 1987), 106.

11. Huang Hui, *Lunheng jiaoshi*, 376.

12. Hebei sheng wenwu yanjiusuo et al., "Xianxian di sanshiliu hao Han mu fajue baogao" 獻縣第36號漢墓發掘報告, in *Hebei sheng kaogu wenji* 河北省考古文集, ed. Hebei sheng wenwu yanjiusuo (Shanghai: Dongfang chubanshe, 1998), 241–60, esp. 257.

13. See Shen Congwen 沈從文, *Zhongguo gudai fushi yanjiu* 中國古代服飾研究 (Hong Kong: Shangwu yinshuguan, 1992), 107–59.

14. Sun Ji, "Zhoudai de zuyupei."

15. Shi Nianhai 史念海, "Xi Zhou yu Chunqiu shiqi huazu yu fei huazu de zaju jiqi dili fenbu (shangpian)" 西周與春秋時期華族與非華族的雜居及其地理分佈 (上篇), *Zhongguo lishi dili luncong* 中國歷史地理論叢, 1990.1: 27–40.

16. Katherine Linduff, "An Archaeological Overview," in *Ancient Bronzes of the Eastern Eurasian Steppes from the Arthur M. Sackler Collections*, ed. Emma C. Bunker (New York: Harry N. Abrams, 1997), 33. However, Linduff actually adds a fifth zone to her discussion, referring to the northeastern area in Eastern Mongolia and Western Liaoning, centering on the Upper Xiajiadian culture.

17. Han Jianye 韓建業, *Beijing xian Qin kaogu* 北京先秦考古 (Beijing: Wenwu chua- banshe, 2011), 166.

18. Beijing shi wenwu yanjiusuo 北京市文物研究所, *Jundushan mudi: Yuhuangmiao* 軍都山墓地：玉皇廟, 4 vols. (Beijing: Wenwu chubanshe, 2007), 3: 1328, 1131, 1344. Beijing shi wenwu yanjiusuo, *Jundushan mudi: Hulugou yu Xiliangguang* 军都山墓 地：葫蘆溝與西梁洸, 2 vols (Beijing: Wenwu chubanshe, 2009), 1: 311, 524.

19. Tian Guangjin 田廣金 and Guo Suxin 郭素新, *E'erduosi shi qingtongqi* 鄂爾多斯式 青銅器 (Beijing: Wenwu chubanshe, 1986), 205, 264.

20. Ningxia wenwu kaogu yanjiusuo 寧夏文物考古研究所 and Ningxia Guyuan bowu- guan 寧夏固原博物館, "Ningxia Guyuan Yanglang qingtong wenhua mudi" 寧夏 固原楊郎青銅文化墓地, *Kaogu xuebao* 1993.1: 49.

21. Zhongguo shehui kexueyuan kaogu yanjiusuo, *Mancheng Han mu fajue baogao*, 1: 83, 105.

22. Yang Hong 楊泓, *Zhongguo gudai bingqi luncong* 中國古代兵器論叢 (Beijing: Wenwu chubanshe, 1980), 116–17. Lin Meicun 林梅村, "Shang Zhou qingtongjian yuanyuan kao" 商周青銅劍淵源考, in his *Han Tang xiyu yu Zhongguo wenming* 漢唐西域與中國文明 (Beijing: Wenwu chubanshe, 1998), 39–63.

23. Yang Hong, *Zhongguo gudai bingqi luncong*, 121–23.

24. Wu En 烏恩, "Guanyu woguo beifang de qingtong duanjian" 關於我國北方的青銅 短劍, *Kaogu* 1978.5: 324–33, 360.

25. Hebei sheng wenwu yanjiusuo, "Hebei Dingxian 40 hao Han mu fajue jianbao" 河 北定縣40號漢墓發掘簡報, *Wenwu* 1981.8: 1–10, esp. 3. This sword, 59.5 centimeters long, is currently in the collection of Hebei Provincial Institute for Studies of Cultural Relics (Hebei sheng wenwu yanjiusuo 河北省文物研究所).

26. Yang Jianhua 楊建華, "Lüe lun Qin wenhua yu beifang wenhua de guanxi" 略論秦 文化與北方文化的關係, *Kaogu yu wenwu* 2013.1: 46.

27. Chen Ping 陳平, "Shi lun Baoji Yimen erhao mu duanjian ji youguan wenti" 試論寶 雞益門二號墓短劍及有關問題, *Kaogu* 1995.4: 370.

28. About 21.5 percent of the excavated burials in the Yuhuangmiao cemetery, all occupied by males, included bronze short swords; see Beijing shi wenwu yanjiusuo, *Jundushan mudi: Yuhuangmiao*, 2: 915.

29. Beijing shi wenwu yanjiusuo, *Jundushan mudi: Yuhuangmiao*, 2: 925–26, type IV. See also Shao Huiqiu 邵會秋 and Xiong Zenglong 熊增瓏, "Jibei diqu Dong Zhou shiqi beifang wenhua qingtong duanjian yanjiu" 冀北地區東周時期北方文化青銅器短 劍研究, *Wenwu chunqiu* 2005.4: 7–22, 51, type Bb. A similar example is catalogued in Bunker, *Ancient Bronzes of the Eastern Eurasian Steppes*, 180, pl. 95.

30. Bunker, *Ancient Bronzes of the Eastern Eurasian Steppes*, 181.

31. Jenny F. So, "The Inlaid Bronzes of the Warring States Period," in *Great Bronze Age of China*, ed. Wen Fong (New York: Metropolitan Museum of Art, 1980), 305–11. For comparable examples, see Joan Aruz et al., ed., *The Golden Deer of Eurasia* (New York: Metropolitian Museum of Art, 2000), 80–81, pls. 5–6; Leonid Teodorovich Yablonsky, "New Excavations of the Early Nomadic Burial Ground at Filippovka (Southern Ural Region, Russia)," *American Journal of Archaeology* 114.1 (2010): 129–43.

32. B. R. Armbruster, "Technologische Aspekte der Goldschmiedekunst aus Arzan 2," in *Der skythenzeitlichen Fürstenkurgan Arzan 2 in Tuva*, ed. K. V. Chugunov, H. Parzinger, and A. Nagle (Berlin: Archäologie in Eurasien, 2010), 183–99; Marina Shemakhanskaya, Mikhail Treister, and Leonid Yablonsky, "The Technique of Gold Inlaid Decoration in the 5th–4th Centuries BC: Silver and Iron Finds from the Early Sarmatian Barrows of Filippovka, Southern Urals," *ArchéoSciences* 33 (2009): 211–20.

33. K. Chugunov, H. Parzinger, and A. Nagler, "Arzhan 2: La Tombe d'un Prince Scythe en Sibérie du Sud Rapport préliminaire des Fouilles Russo-Allemandes de 2000–2002," *Arts Asiatiques*, 59 (2004): 5–29.

34. Compare, for example, Mikhail P. Gryaznov, *The Ancient Civilization of Southern Siberia: An Archaeological Adventure*, trans. James Horgarth (New York: Cowles, 1969), figs. 56–58. For a stylistic study of the stag motif, see Esther Jacobson, "Siberian Roots of the Scythian Stag Image," *Journal of Asian History* 17 (1983): 68–120. And for a more thorough exploration of the meaning of this motif, see Esther Jacobson-Tepfer, *The Hunter, the Stag, and the Mother of Animals: Image, Monument, and Landscape in Ancient North Asia* (Oxford: Oxford University Press, 2015).

35. Aruz et al., *The Golden Deer of Eurasia*, 80, pl. 5.

36. Chinese archaeologists call this motif the "recessed leaf-like decor" (*aoru yezhuan-gwen* 凹入葉狀紋) or "water drops decor" (*shuidiwen* 水滴紋); Zhongguo shehui kexueyuan kaogu yanjiusuo, *Mancheng Han mu fajue baogao*, 1: 105; see Tian and Guo, *E'erduosi shi qingtongqi*, 72.

37. This zoomorphic motif was a popular decoration on short swords during the sixth to fifth centuries BCE in China's western frontier and beyond; Zhang Tian'en 張天恩, "Zai lun Qin shi duanjian" 再論秦式短劍, *Kaogu* 1995.9: 841–53, esp. 848.

38. Guangxi zhuangzu zizhiqu bowuguan 廣西壯族自治區博物館, *Guangxi Guix-ian Luobowan Han mu* 廣西貴縣羅伯灣漢墓 (Beijing: Wenwu chubanshe, 1988), 79–85, pl. 41.

39. Male necklaces were alien not only to the Chinese but also to the Greeks. Esther Jacobson was surprised by the alien custom of adorning men with necklaces in the Scythian tombs, for in the Greco-Roman culture, only women wore such jewelry; see Esther Jacobson, *The Art of the Scythians* (Leiden: Brill, 1995), 108.

40. Zhao Deyun 趙德雲, "Tubanwen yin tonghe santi" 凸瓣紋銀銅盒三題, *Wenwu* 2007.3: 81–88; Jessica Rawson, "The Han Empire and its Northern Neighbours: The Fascination of the Exotic," in *The Search for Immortality, Tomb Treasures of Han China*, ed. James Lin (New Haven, CT: Yale University Press, 2012), 23–36.

41. Jing Zhonwei 井中偉 and Li Liandi 李連娣, "Zhongguo beifangxi qintong 'huagejian' yanjiu yu tansuo" 中國北方系青銅'花格劍'研究與探索, *Bianjiang kaogu yanjiu* 邊疆考古研究 10 (2013): 176.

42. Chugunov, Parzinger, and Nagler, "Arzhan 2."

43. Zhongguo shehui kexueyuan kaogu yanjiusuo, *Mancheng Han mu fajue baogao*, 2: B/W pl. 68.1.

44. Sima Qian, *Shiji*, 99.2721.

45. Guo Qingfan, *Zhuangzi jishi*, 717; James Legge, trans., *The Texts of Taoism* (New York: Dover, 1962), 2: 50.

46. Shi Nianhai, "Xi Zhou yu Chunqiu shiqi huazu yu fei huazu de zaju jiqi dili fenbu (shangpian)."

47. Owen Lattimore, *Inner Asian Frontiers of China* (Oxford: Oxford University Press, 1988), 347–49. Unlike Lattimore, who considered the mounted nomads living on the fringe of the Chinese civilization "probably the same people" as the old un-mounted barbarians, Egami Namio made a cultural and ethnic distinction between "nomads" and "horseriders," who also practiced some agriculture; see Egami Namio 江上波夫, *Yūrashia hoppō bunka no kenkyū* ユウラシア北方文化の研究 (Tokyo: Yamakawa Shuppansha, 1951), 294–95; Egami Namio, *Kiba minzoku kokka: Nihon kodaishi e no apurōchi* 騎馬民族国家: 日本古代史へのアプローチ (Tokyo: Chūo Kōronsha, 1968), 1–10. In alignment with Egami's distinction, Lin Yun holds that the old un-mounted barbarians were historiographically known as Rong-Di and the new "horseriders" were Hu; see Lin Yun, "Rongdi fei hu lun," 3–6. Nicola Di Cosmo associates these people with "pastoral nomadism" or "pre-nomadic pastoral or agro-pastoral society." See his book, *Ancient China and its Enemies: The Rise of Nomadic Power in East Asian History* (Cambridge: Cambridge University Press, 2002), 74–75.

48. Meng Wentong 蒙文通, *Zhou Qin shaoshu minzu yanjiu* 周秦少數民族研究 (Shanghai: Shanghai Longmen lianhe shuju, 1958), 81–85. He Yanjie 何艷傑 et al., *Xianyu Zhongshanguo shi* 鮮虞中山國史 (Beijing: Kexue chubanshe, 2011), 19–22.

49. He Yanjie et al., *Xianyu Zhongshanguo shi*, 58.

50. Hu Jinhua 胡金華 observes the relationship between mountain veneration of the Zhongshan people and their stone burials; see "Heibei diqu shigoumu zangzhi de chubu yanjiu" 河北地區石構墓葬制度的初步研究, in *Heibei sheng kaogu wenji* 河北省考古文集, ed. Hebei sheng wenwu yanjiusuo (Shanghai: East Press, 1998), 428–35, esp. 433.

51. Miao Wenyuan, *Zhanguo ce xin jiaozhu*, 1149. See also James I. Crump, Jr., *Chan-kuo ts'e* (Oxford: Clarendon, 1970), 525. For monographs on the history of Zhong-shan, see Duan Lianqin 段連勤, *Bei Di zu yu Zhongshanguo* 北狄族與中山國 (Shijiazhuang: Hebei renmin chubanshe, 1982) and He Yanjie et al., *Xianyu Zhong-shanguo shi*.

52. Hebei sheng wenwu guanlichu, "Hebei sheng Pingshan xian Zhanguo shiqi Zhong-shanguo muzang fajue jianbao" 河北省平山縣戰國時期中山國墓葬發掘簡報, *Wenwu* 1979.1: 1–26.

53. Among them, tomb no. 1 and no. 6 have been published and tomb no. 7 has been briefly reported. Tomb no. 2 has no literature whatsoever; Hebei sheng wenwu yan-jiusuo, *Zhanguo Zhongshanguo Lingshou cheng: 1975–1993 nian kaogu fajue baogao* 戰國中山國靈壽城: 1975–1993 年考古發掘報告 (Beijing: Wenwu chubanshe, 2005), 119.

54. King Cuo's exact death date remains a matter of debate. The archaeological report gives it as 313 BCE. See Hebei sheng wenwu yanjiusuo, *Cuo mu*, 1: 533. Li Xueqin 李學勤 and Li Ling hold to 309 BCE, "Pingshan sanqi yu Zhongshanguo shi de ruogan wenti" 平山三器與中山國史的若干問題, *Kaogu xuebao* 1979.2: 147–69.

55. Hebei sheng wenwu yanjiusuo, *Zhanguo Zhongshanguo Lingshou cheng*, 228.

56. Zhou Nanquan 周南泉, "Zhongshan guo de yuqi" 中山國的玉器, *Gugong bowuyuan yuankan* 故宮博物院院刊 1979.2: 95–96.

57. For example, in a large cemetery at Jundushan in present-day Beijing, predating the Sanjixiang cemetery by two to three centuries, nearly half (42.5 percent) of more than 400 excavated burials were furnished with almost identical beads at around the same position relative to the human bodies; see Beijing shi wenwu yanjiusuo, *Jundushan mudi: Yuhuangmiao* 1:237–40.

58. Yang Jianhua, *Chunqiu Zhanguo shiqi Zhongguo beifang wenhuadai de xingcheng*, 80–82.

59. Hebei sheng wenwu yanjiusuo, *Zhanguo Zhongshanguo Lingshou cheng*, 283.

60. Max Loehr, "Weapons and Tools from Anyang, and Siberian Analogies," *American Journal of Archaeology* 53. 2 (1949): 126–44.

61. So, "The Inlaid Bronzes of the Warring States Period," 309–11; Robert Bagley, "Orna-ment, Representation, and Imaginary Animals in Bronze Age China," *Arts Asiatiques* 61 (2006): 17–29.

62. Hebei sheng wenwu yanjiusuo, *Cuo mu*, 1: 139–43. For a discussion of these objects in the archaeological and intercultural context, see Xiaolong Wu, *Material Culture, Power, and Identity in Ancient China*, 93–107.

63. So, "The Inlaid Bronzes of the Warring States Period," 310–11.

64. Jessica Rawson, "Chu Influences on the Development of Han Bronze Vessels," *Arts Asiatiques* 44 (1989): 84–99.

65. Zhongguo shehui kexueyuan kaogu yanjiusuo, *Mancheng Han mu fajue baogao*, 1: 49–57.

66. Zhongguo shehui kexueyuan kaogu yanjiusuo, *Mancheng Han mu fajue baogao*, 1: 247.

67. Rawson, "Chu Influences on the Development of Han Bronze Vessels." There is an almost identical unprovenanced vessel in the Baoli collection; see Baoli cang jin bianji weiyuanhui 保利藏金編輯委員會, *Baoli cang jin: Baoli yishu bowuguan jingpin xuan* 保利藏金：保利藝術博物館精品選 (Guangzhou: Lingnan meishu chubanshe, 1999), 194.

68. Yang Jianhua, "Zhongguo beifang Dong Zhou shiqi liangzhong wenhua yicun bianxi—jianlun *rongdi* yu *hu* de guanxi" 中國北方東周時期兩種文化遺存辨析—兼論戎狄与胡的關係, *Kaogu xuebao* 2009.2: 156–63; a similar view is proposed in Shan Yueying, "Dong Zhou Qindai Zhongguo beifang diqu kaoguxue wenhua geju," 311–14.

69. For this so-called "Di Lineage *Hu*" 杕氏壺, see Guo Moruo 郭沫若, *Liang Zhou jinwenci daxi kaoshi* 兩周金文辭大系考釋 (Beijing: Kexue chubanshe, 1958), 227.

70. Sophia-Karin Psarras has noted that this type of ornamentation on vessels was more popular in the north; see her *Han Material Culture*, 87. Examples can also be found in Cao Wei, ed., *Shaanbei chutu qingtongqi* 陝北出土青銅器, 5 vols. (Chengdu: Bashu shushe, 2009), 2: 190–93. Another very similar *hu* vessel was collected in Beijing during the 1950s; see Beijing shi wenwu guanlichu 北京市文物管理處, "Beijing shi xin zhengji de Shang Zhou qingtongqi" 北京市新徵集的商周青銅器, *Wenwu ziliao congkan* 文物資料叢刊2 (1978): 14–21, fig. 8.

71. Zhongguo shehui kexueyuan kaogu yanjiusuo, *Mancheng Han mu fajue baogao*, 1: 38–41.

72. Wang Wuyu 王武鈺 and Wang Ce 王策, "Longqingxia bieshu gongcheng zhong faxian de Chunqiu shiqi muzang" 龍慶峽別墅工程中發現的春秋時期墓葬, *Beijing wenwu yu kaogu* 北京文物與考古 1994.2: 32–45, fig. 8. Following this example, information about a very similar bronze vessel dated to the late Eastern Zhou period is published in Umehara Sueji 梅原末治, *Rakuyō Kin-son kobo shūei* 洛陽金村古墓聚英 (Kyoto: Kobayashi Shashin Seihanjo Shuppanbu 1937), App. pls. V and VI; Psarras, *Han Material Culture*, 96–97.

73. Gryaznov, *The Ancient Civilization of Southern Siberia*, 117.

74. Neimenggu bowuguan 內蒙古博物館 and Neimenggu wenwu gongzuodui 內蒙古文物工作隊, "Neimenggu Zhunge'erqi Yulongtai de Xiongnu mu" 內蒙古准格爾旗玉隆太的匈奴墓, *Kaogu* 1977.2: 111–14; Neimenggu wenwu gongzuodui, "Neimenggu Zizhiqu Zhunge'erqi Sujigou chutu yipi tongqi" 內蒙古自治區准格爾旗速機溝出土一批銅器, *Wenwu* 1965.2: 44–46. Tian and Guo, *E'erduosi shi qingtongqi*, 156–58. However, prototypes of such yoke ornaments may date back to the late Shang period in the twelfth century BCE. At chariot pit no. 40 at Meiyuanzhuang, archaeologists found a pair of bronze ornaments, each with two rabbits crouching on the top of a tube. Like the late Ordos bronze figures, the bodies of these rabbits were all hollowed out; see Zhongguo shehui kexueyuan kaogu yanjiusuo, "Henan Anyang shi Meiyuanzhuang dongnan de Yindai chenmakeng" 河南安陽市梅園莊東南的殷代車馬坑, *Kaogu* 1998.10: 48–65, esp. 53, fig. 3.2. See also Yang Baocheng 楊寶成, *Yinxu wenhua yanjiu* 殷墟文化研究 (Wuhan: Wuhan daxue chubanshe, 2002), 130.

75. Bunker, *Ancient Bronzes of the Eastern Eurasian Steppes*, 53–55.

76. Bunker, *Ancient Bronzes of the Eastern Eurasian Steppes*, 230–31. See also Jessica Rawson and Emma C. Bunker, *Ancient Chinese and Ordos Bronzes* (Hong Kong: Oriental Ceramic Society of Hong Kong, 1990), 322. Another similar pair of deer is now in the Metropolitan Museum of Art, New York; see Maxwell K. Hearn, *Ancient*

Chinese Art: The Ernest Erickson Collection in the Metropolitan Museum of Art (New York: The Metropolitan Museum of Art, 1987), 63.

77. A number of round bronze statuettes of deer, probably decorations for belts, were uncovered in the Jundushan cemeteries, dating from the fifth century BCE; see Beijing shi wenwu yanjiusuo, *Jundushan mudi: Yuhuangmiao*, 3:1239.

78. Zhongguo shehui kexueyuan kaogu yanjiusuo, *Mancheng Han mu fajue baogao*, 1: 97.

79. Sun Ji, *Zhongguo gu yufu luncong* 中國古輿服論叢 (Beijing: Wenwu chubanshe, 2001), 16.

80. Various parts, including frontlets, reins, belts, and even horse hooves, of the half-life-sized bronze horses and chariots excavated in the First Emperor's mausoleum at Lishan bear similar positional inscriptions, which reinforces the Mancheng figures' connection with horses or carriages; see Qin Shihuang binmayong bowuguan 秦始皇兵馬俑博物館 and Shaanxi sheng kaogu yanjiusuo 陝西省考古研究所, *Qin Shihuang ling tongchema fajue baogao* 秦始皇陵銅車馬發掘報告 (Beijing: Wenwu chubanshe, 1998).

81. Henan sheng wenwu kaogu yanjiusuo, *Gushi Hougudui yihaomu* 固始侯古堆一號墓 (Zhengzhou: Daxiang chubanshe, 2004), 73–79. See also Guo Jianbang 郭建邦, "Shilun Gushi Hougudui damu peizangkeng chutu de daibu gongju—jianyu" 試論固始侯古堆大墓陪葬坑出土的代步工具—肩輿, *Zhongyuan wenwu* 1981.1: 43–47.

82. Ningxia wenwu kaogu yanjiusuo, "Ningxia Guyuan Yanglang qingtong wenhua mudi."

83. Ningxia wenwu kaogu yanjiusuo, "Ningxia Guyuan Yanglang qingtong wenhua mudi," 17.

84. Aruz et al., *The Golden Deer of Eurasia*, 69–71.

85. Gernot Windfuhr, "The Stags of Filippovka: Mithraic Coding on the South Ural Steppes," in *The Golden Deer of Eurasia: Perspectives on the Steppe Nomads of the Ancient World*, ed. Joan Aruz et al. (New York: Metropolitan Museum of Art, 2006), 46–81.

86. Zhongguo shehui kexueyuan kaogu yanjiusuo, *Mancheng Han mu fajue baogao*, 1: 140.

87. Chêng Tê-K'un, "Some Standing Jade Figurines of the Shang-Chou Period," *Artibus Asiae* 28.1 (1966): 39–52; Rawson, *Chinese Jade from the Neolithic to the Qing*, 281–85.

88. Hayashi Minao, *Sengoku jidai shutsudo bunbutsu no kenkyū* 戰國時代出土文物の研究 (Kyoto: Kyōto Daigaku Jinbun Kagaku Kenkyūjo, 1985), 57–145.

89. Wang Shuping 王叔平, "Xinzheng fajue Xugang damu" 新鄭發掘許崗大墓, in *Henan wenhua wenwu nianjian* 河南文化文物年鑑 (Zhengzhou: Henan sheng wuhuating & wenwuju, 2004), 97.

90. Luoyang shi wenwu gongzuodui 洛陽市文物工作隊, "Luoyang zhenzhichang Dong Zhou mu (C1M5269) de qingli" 洛陽市針織廠東周墓 (C1M5269) 的清理, *Wenwu* 2001.12: 41–59, 64.

91. Sun Yirang 孫詒讓, *Mozi jiangu* 墨子閒詁 (Beijing: Zhonghua shuju, 2001), 78; Wang Xianqian 王先謙, *Xunzi jijie* 荀子集解 (Beiijng: Zhonghua shuju, 1988), 159.

92. Ban Gu, *Hanshu*, 59.1216.

93. Chen Zhi 陳致, "Haihunhou mu suojian zi yun fu yi you shishi" 海昏侯墓所見子畎父乙卣試釋, *Jiangxi shifan daxue xuebao* 江西師範大學學報 49.5 (2016): 7–15. For the excavation report, see Jiangxi sheng wenwu kaogu yanjiuyuan and Zhongguo renmin daxue lishi xueyuan kaogu wenboxi 中國人民大學歷史學院考古文博系, "Jiangxi Nanchang Xi Han Haihun hou Liu He mu chutu tongqi" 江西南昌西漢海昏侯劉賀墓出土銅器, *Wenwu* 2018.11: 4–26, esp. 6.

94. Zhu Jieyuan 朱捷元 and Li Yuzheng 李域錚, "Xi'an dongjiao Sandiancun Xi Han mu" 西安東郊三店村西漢墓, *Kaogu yu wenwu* 1983.2: 22–25.

95. Sima Qian, *Shiji*, 6.248, 28.1392.

96. Sima Qian, *Shiji*, 28.1382.

97. Wang Xianqian, *Xunzi jijie*, 537; Eric Hutton, trans., *Xunzi: The Complete Text* (Princeton, NJ: Princeton University Press, 2014), 333.

98. Zhongguo shehui kexueyuan kaogu yanjiusuo, *Mancheng Han mu fajue baogao*, 1: 98–100.

99. Sun Ji, *Zhongguo gu yufu luncong*, 253–92; Lu Yan 盧岩 and Shan Yueying 單月英, "Xi Han muzang chutu de dongwuwen yaoshipai" 西漢墓葬出土的動物紋腰飾牌, *Kaogu yu wenwu* 2007.4: 45–55.

100. Some scholars have argued that these plaques were made by Rong-Di descendants; see Shan Yueying and Lu Yan, "Xiongnu yaoshipai ji xiangguan wenti yanjiu" 匈奴腰飾牌及相關問題研究, *Gugong bowuyuan yuankan* 2008.2: 147.

101. Tian and Guo, *E'erduosi shi qingtongqi*, 71–103.

102. Tian and Guo, *E'erduosi shi qingtongqi*, 80, fig. 47.4. Katherine Linduff, "An Archaeological Overview," in Bunker, *Ancient Bronzes of the Eastern Eurasian Steppes*, 87–88. Ursula Brosseder, "Belt Plaques as an Indicator of East-West Relations," in *Xiongnu Archaeology: Multidisciplinary Perspectives of the First Steppe Empire in Inner Asia*, ed. Ursula Brosseder et al. (Bonn: Vor-und Frühgeschichtliche Archäologie, Rheinische Friedrich-Wilhelms-Universität Bonn, 2011), 372–78. Although dating of the plaque varies from the third century BCE to the fourth century CE, the object's similarity to the Mancheng piece suggests the late second century BCE.

103. I would like to thank Professor Anthony Barbieri-Low for this suggestion.

104. Zhongguo shehui kexueyuan kaogu yanjiusuo, *Mancheng Han mu fajue baogao*, 2: pl. 59.3.2; compare Beijing shi wenwu yanjiusuo, *Jundushan mudi: Yuhuangmiao*, 4: pl. 329, color pl. 63.

105. Zhongguo shehui kexueyuan kaogu yanjiusuo, *Mancheng Han mu fajue baogao*, 1: 214, 335.

106. Wuen Yuesitu 烏恩岳斯圖, *Beifang caoyuan kaoguxue wenhua yanjiu—qingtong shidai zhi zaoqi tieqi shidai* 北方草原考古學文化研究—青銅時代至早期鐵器時代 (Beijing: Kexue chubanshe, 2007), 375.

107. For a typical Han pottery typology in northern China during the Western Han including Hebei, see Jiang Lu 蔣璐, "Zhongguo beifang diqu Han mu yanjiu" 中國北方地區漢墓研究 (PhD diss., Jilin University, 2008), 166, fig. 15.5.

108. Beijing shi wenwu yanjiusuo, *Jundushan mudi: Yuhuangmiao*, 2: 808, fig. 529.2. As Yang Zhefeng first discovered, the glazed surface reminds us of some southern-style Eastern Zhou pottery found in present-day Zhejiang or Jiangsu; Yang Zhefeng 楊哲峰, "Beifeng diqu Han mu chutu de nanfang leixing taociqi" 北方地區漢墓出土的南方類型陶瓷器, in *Han Chang'an cheng kaogu yu Han wenhua* 漢長安城考古與漢文化 (Beijing: Kexue chubanshe, 2008), 507–42.

109. Xu Yongjie 許永傑, "Changcheng yanxian Zhou Qin shiqi shuanger taoqi de chubu kaocha" 長城沿線周秦時期雙耳陶器的初步考察, *Beifang wenwu* 北方文物 1992.2: 3–11, esp. figs 2, 5; it seems this vessel belongs in the so-called "double-belly-eared pot with curved neck" (*shuang fu er hu ling hu* 雙腹耳弧領壺) that was popular in north Hebei during the Warring States and Qin period.

110. Elena E. Kuz'mina, *The Origin of the Indo-Iranians*, ed. J. P. Mallory (Leiden: Brill, 2007), 404–7.

111. Teng Mingyu 滕銘予, "Zhongguo beifang diqu liang Zhou shiqi tongfu de zai tan-tao" 中國北方地區兩周時期銅鍑的再探討, *Bianjiang kaogu yanjiu* 1(2002): 34–54. Guo Wu 郭物, "Dierqun tong(tie) fu yanjiu" 第二群銅（鐵）鍑研究, *Kaogu xue-bao* 2007.1: 61–96.

112. For example, see Beijing shi wenwu yanjiusuo, *Jundushan mudi: Yuhuangmiao*, 908–13.

113. Yang Jianhua, "Shaanxi Qingjian Lijiaya Dong Zhou mu yu 'Hexi Baidi' " 陝西清澗李家崖東周墓與"河西白狄", *Kaogu yu wenwu* 2008.5: 35–36.

114. Zhongguo shehui kexueyuan kaogu yanjiusuo, *Mancheng Han mu fajue baogao*, 2: pl. 138.

115. Wu Xiaojun, "Shang zhi Chunqiu shiqi zhongyuan diqu qingtong chemaqi xingshi yanjiu" 商至春秋時期中原地區青銅車馬器形式研究, *Gudai wenming* 古代文明 1(2002): 180–277.

116. Jacobson, *The Art of the Scythians*, figs. 141–43; Jeannne Davis-Kimball et al., *Nomads of the Eurasian Steppes in the Early Iron Age* (Berkeley, CA: Zinat, 1995), 39, fig. 14.

117. Komai Kazuchika 駒井和愛, "Xian-Qin shidai mamian jiqi yuanshi" 先秦時代馬面及其源始, trans., Sun Zuoyun, *Beiping Yanjing daxue kaogu xueshe shekan* 北平燕京大學考古學社社刊 5 (1936): 320–24.

118. Wuen Yuesitu, *Beifang caoyuan kaoguxue wenhua bijiao yanjiu—qingtong shidai zhi zaoqi tieqi shidai*, 370, 373.

119. Zhongguo shehui kexueyuan kaogu yanjiusuo, *Mancheng Han mu fajue baogao*, 1: 228, 275. Similar figurines, including a 4-centimeter-tall tin mounted rider and a 3.3-centimeter-tall sturdy clay figurine, were found in another bamboo case at another slightly later royal tomb at Hongtushan, Juye, Shandong Province; see Shandong Heze diqu Han mu fajue xiaozu, "Juye Hongtushan Xi Han mu," 471–500.

120. Tianjin and Guo, *E'erduosi shi qingtongqi*, 134–36.

121. Karl Jettmar, *Art of the Steppes* (London: Methuen, 1967), 137. According to Renate Rolle, "We have no idea how the game started or whether they played with dice or with small bones taken from sheep's ankle-joints, popular objects resembling pol-ished ivory which are found in many graves. We do not know how the game was won or lost, or whether only one game could be played on the carpet or several (as draughts and chess can be played on the same board today)." Renate Rolle, *The World of the Scythians*, trans. Gayna Walls (London: B.T. Batsford, 1989), 97–98.

122. Yang Jianhua, "Zhongguo beifang Dong Zhou shiqi liangzhong wenhua yicun bianxi—jianlun *rongdi* yu *hu* de guanxi," 156–61.

123. These include bronze *fu* cauldrons, low-bottom tripods, short swords, small knives, necklaces, and tiger-shaped plaques. See Yang Jianhua, "Baidi dongqian kao—cong Baidi jianli de Zhongshanguo tanqi" 白狄東遷考—從白狄建立的中山國談起, in *E'erduosi qingtongqi guoji xueshu yantaohui lunwenji* 鄂爾多斯青銅器國際學術研討會論文集 (Beijing: Kexue chubanshe, 2009), 283–94.

124. Guo Wu, "Dierqun tong(tie) fu yanjiu," 67–68. Tian and Guo, *E'erduosi shi qing-tongqi*, 145–49.

125. Zhongguo shehui kexueyuan kaogu yanjiusuo, *Mancheng Han mu fajue baogao*, 1: 98–100.

126. For parallels in the Northern Zone, see Tian and Guo, *E'erduosi shi qingtongqi*, 108–9, 268.

127. Zhongguo shehui kexueyuan kaogu yanjiusuo, *Mancheng Han mu fajue baogao*, 1: 141. There was another group of jade pieces (fig. 1.7, nos. 1–10) found in the northeast

end of the groove of the front chamber. Along with them were lacquer fragments. They were clearly attached to some perished wooden wares. The excavator suggested these pieces probably fell into the groove and drifted into this place. Their initial location remains uncertain. See Zhongguo shehui kexueyuan kaogu yanjiusuo, *Mancheng Han mu fajue baogao*, 1: 29, 141–43.

128. Though not dramatically different, there are varying opinions regarding the year of the kingdom's reestablishment. Yang Kuan believed it to be 380 BCE, and Meng Wentong 蒙文通 held it to be 378 BCE. While Yang's view was shared by Duan Lianqin, Meng's theory was supported by Li Xueqin and Li Ling. See Yang Kuan, *Zhanguo shi* 戰國史 (Shanghai: Shanghai renmin chubanshe, 2003), 299; Meng Wentong, *Zhou Qin shaoshu minzu yanjiu*, 87; Duan Lianqin, *Bei Di zu yu Zhongshanguo*, 105–9; Li Xueqin and Li Ling, "Pingshan sanqi yu Zhongshanguo shi de ruogan wenti," 166. See also He Yanjie et al., *Xianyu Zhongshanguo shi*, 72–73.

129. Sima Qian, *Shiji*, 43.1806.

130. Sima Qian, *Shiji*, 5.210.

131. Di Cosmo, *Ancient China and its Enemies*, 83–87.

132. According to *Shiji*, 99.2719, the closest Loufan was only 700 Chinese miles (*li*) away from Chang'an.

133. Sima Qian, *Shiji*, 110.2889–890, 111.2923.

134. Ban Gu, *Hanshu*, 28. 1618.

135. Ban Gu, *Hanshu*, 28. 1621, 1622.

136. Huang Zhanyue 黃展嶽, "Handai zhuhouwang mu lunshu" 漢代諸侯王墓論述, *Kaogu xuebao* 1998.1: 11–34.

137. Yan Genqi, *Mangdangshan Xi Han Liangwang mudi*, 311; Huang Xiaofen, *Han mu de kaoguxue yanjiu*, 89, fig. 28; Liu Rui and Liu Tao, *Xi Han zhuhouwang lingmu zhidu yanjiu*, 497–98.

138. At Xuzhou, beginning in the late second century BCE, some tombs also began to develop a two-layer structure, containing house-shaped wooden structures in the rock shell, which also simulated real architecture. It was not until the first century BCE that the outer shell lost its architectural semblance; see Zhou Baoping 周保平 and Liu Zhaojian 劉照建, "Xi Han Chu wang lingmu xingzhi yanjiu" 西漢楚王陵墓形制研究, *Zhongguo lishi wenwu* 2005.6: 66–79, esp. 72.

139. Though perhaps among the earliest examples, the Mancheng tombs were not the only Western Han royal burials with vaults or domes. Other analogous cases include Nandongshan tomb no. 2 at Xuzhou and Huangtushan tomb no. 2 at Yongcheng, dating from the late second to first centuries BCE, which feature a similar dome in the main chamber; one side chamber in Jiulongshan tomb no. 3, possibly a contemporary of the Mancheng tombs, is also vaulted; see Zhou Xueying 周学鹰, *Xuzhou Han mu jianzhu—Zhongguo Handai Chu(Pengcheng)guo muzang jianzhu kao* 徐州漢墓建筑—中國漢代楚(彭城)國墓葬建筑考 (Beijing: Zhongguo jianzhu gongye chubanshe, 2001), 131–32; Yan Genqi, *Mangdangshan Xi Han Liangwang mudi*, 306–8. And it was not until the latter half of the first century BCE that vaulted or domed burials became popular among low-ranking brick tombs in metropolitan areas including Chang'an and Luoyang; see Huang Xiaofen, *Han mu de kaoguxue yanjiu*, 130ff.

140. In Hebei, such a vaulted or domed shape was later followed in the Sanfengou cemetery at Yangyuan in present-day Zhangjiakou, Hebei Province, about the first century BCE; see Hebei sheng wenwu yanjiusuo and Zhangjiakou diqu wenhuaju, "Hebei

Yangyuan Sanfengou Hanmuqun fajue baogao." It seems the Mancheng tombs were probably the direct origin of this new, distinct burial shape.

141. A royal tomb at Shiyuan, for example, was even painted with a polychrome mural on the ceiling of the main chamber; see Yan Genqi, *Mangdangshan Xi Han Liangwang mudi*, 115–20. In Xuzhou, the same occurred in those tombs cut during the early and middle Western Han period; see Liu Zhaojian, "Xuzhou diqu daxing yadong mu chubu yanjiu" 徐州地區大型崖洞墓初步研究, *Dongnan wenhua* 2004.5: 29–30; Liu Zun-zhi 劉尊志, "Xuzhou liang Han zhuhouwang mu yanjiu" 徐州兩漢諸侯王墓研究, *Kaogu xuebao* 2011.1: 62.

142. Han Jianye 韓建業, "Zhongguo Xian-Qin dongshimu puxi chutan" 中國先秦洞室墓譜系初探, *Zhongguo lishi wenwu* 2007.4:16–25; Xie Duanju 謝端琚, "Shilun woguo zaoqi tudongmu" 試論我國早期土洞墓, *Kaogu* 1987.12: 1097–104.

143. Han Jianye, "Zhongguo Xian Qin dongshimu puxi chutan," 21.

144. Yu Weichao, "Gudai Xirong he Qiang Hu kaoguxue wenhua guishu de tantao" 古代西戎和羌胡考古學文化歸屬的探討, in his *Xian-Qin Liang Han kaoguxue lunji* 先秦兩漢考古學論集 (Beijing: Wenwu chubanshe, 1985), 188.

145. Teng Mingyu 滕銘予, "Lun Guanzhong Qin mu zhong dongshimu de niandai" 論關中秦墓中洞室墓的年代, *Huaxia kaogu* 1993.2: 90–97; see for example, Shangjiaocun tombs no. 11 and no. 18, in Qinyong kaogudui 秦俑考古隊, "Lintong Shangjiaocun Qin mu qingli jianbao" 臨潼上焦村秦墓清理簡報, *Kaogu yu wenwu* 1980.2: 42–50.

146. Li Rusen, "Lüe lun Luoyang diqu Zhanguo Xi-Han dongshimu de yuanliu", *Kexue shehui zhanxian* 1988.3: 206.

147. Gansu sheng wenwu kaogu yanjiusuo 甘肅省文物考古研究所, "Gansu Qin'an Shangyuanjia Qin Han muzang fajue" 甘肅秦安上袁家秦漢墓葬發掘, *Kaogu xuebao* 1997.1: 57–79; Gansu sheng bowuguan, "Gansu Pingliang Miaozhuang de liangzuo Zhanguo mu" 甘肅平涼廟莊的兩座戰國墓, *Kaogu yu wenwu* 1982. 5: 21–33.

148. It must be noted that such a lateral structure was occasionally found in high-ranking tombs that date back to the sixth century BCE, but it was not until the late third century BCE that it became popular. For an early example, see the Duke Jing of Qin's tomb, and for an example in the Central Plain area, see Guweicun tomb no. 1 (fourth to third century BCE); Han Wei 韓偉 and Jiao Nanfeng 焦南峰, "Qin du Yongcheng kaogu fajue yanjiu zongshu" 秦都雍城考古發掘研究綜述, *Kaogu yu wenwu* 1988.5–6: 111–26; Ma Zhenzhi, "Shi tan Qin gong yihao damu de guozhi"; Zhongguo kexueyuan kaogu yanjiusuo, *Huixian fajue baogao*, 70.

149. Gansu sheng wenwu kaogu yanjiusuo 甘肅省文物考古研究所 and Zhangjiazhuang Huizu zizhixian bowuguan 張家川回族自治縣博物館, "2006 niandu Gansu Zhangjiachuan Huizu zizhixian Majiayuan Zhanguo mudi fajue jianbao" 2006年度甘肅張家川回族自治縣馬家塬戰國墓地發掘簡報, *Wenwu* 2008.9: 4–28. Gansu sheng wenwu kaogu yanjiusuo, *Xirong yizhen* 西戎遺珍 (Beijing: Wenwu chuban-she, 2014), 10–31.

150. Zaoqi Qin wenhua lianhe kaogudui 早期秦文化聯合考古隊and Zhangjiachuan Huizu zizhixian bowuguan, "Gansu Zhangjiachuan Majiayuan Zhanguo mudi 2012–2014 nian fajue jianbao" 甘肅張家川馬家塬戰國墓地2012–2014年發掘簡報, *Wenwu* 2018.3: 4–25.

151. Wang Hui 王輝, "Zhangjiachuan Majiayuan mudi xiangguan wenti chutan" 張家川馬家塬墓地相關問題初探, *Wenwu* 2009.10: 70–77.

152. Hou Yubin 侯煜斌, "Qianyi Majiayuan Zhanguo mudi chutu de dongwuwen huangjin shijian" 淺議馬家塬戰國墓地出土的動物紋黃金飾件, *Sichou zhilu* 絲綢之路 2012.12: 54–55.

153. For an anthropological perspective on Rong and Xirong, see Wang Mingke 王明珂, *Huaxia bianyuan: lishi jiyi yu zuqun rentong* 華夏邊緣—歷史際遇與族群認同 (Taipei: Yunchen, 1997), 214–17. For a historical perspective, see Shi Nianhai 史念海, "Xi Zhou yu Chunqiu shiqi huazu yu fei huazu de zaju jiqi dili fenbu (xiapian)" 西周與春秋時期華族與非華族的雜居及其地理分佈 （下篇）, *Zhongguo lishi dili luncong* 1990.2: 71–76. See also Di Cosmo, *Ancient China and Its Enemies*, 93–126. Archaeologist Lin Yun suggests that, like the Di, the Rong people were also ethnically East Asian Mongoloids and spoke the same language as the Chinese (Hua or Xia); see "Rong-Di fei hu lun," 6. But Edwin Pulleyblank thought the Xirong might speak a Tibeto-Burman language; see Edwin Pullyblank, "The Chinese and their Neighbors in Prehistoric and Early Historic Times," in *The Origins of Chinese Civilization*, ed. David N. Keightley (Berkeley: University of California Press, 1983), 419.

154. Nicola Di Cosmo, "The Northern Frontier in Pre-Imperial China," in *Cambridge History of Ancient China*, 885–966. See also Di Cosmo's *Ancient China and Its Enemies: The Rise of Nomadic Power in East Asian History*, 44–92; Lin Yun, "Zhongguo beifang changcheng didai youmu wenhuadai de xingcheng guocheng" 中國北方長城地帶遊牧文化帶的形成過程, in his *Lin Yun xueshu lunwenji (er)*, 39–76.

155. Gansu sheng wenwu kaogu yanjiusuo and Zhangjiazhuang Huizu zizhixian bowuguan, "2006 niandu Gansu Zhangjiachuan Huizu zizhixian Majiayuan Zhanguo mudi fajue jianbao", 5.

156. Although the question of the origin of the Majiayuan catacombs lies beyond the scope of this study, it should be noted that these "barbarian" tombs were very similar to those catacombs found on the Eurasian steppe, which were often identified as Scythian in Greek historiography. A typical Scythian catacomb, according to Renate Rolle, consisted of "a descent, usually leading steeply down from the original surface, with a corridor or short passage below opening into a cave-like burial chamber," which was often vaulted or domed; Rolle, *The World of the Scythians*, 21. See also Renate Rolle, *Totenkult der Skythen, Teil I. Das Steppengebiet* (Berlin: De Gruyter, 1979), 6–11.

157. Oddly, even Liu Sheng's descendants, the later kings of Zhongshan, did not follow his example. Instead, all the four later Zhongshan royal tombs excavated in present-day Dingzhou, Hebei, just about seventy kilometers south of the Mancheng site, returned to the conventional form of large-scale vertical pit graves dug into the earth. One is located at Bajiaolang (numbered as M40), the other three are at Sanpanshan (numbered as M120, 121, and 122). All these tombs have been attributed to three other Zhongshan kings or their wives, postdating Liu Sheng, the occupant of Mancheng tomb no. 1. For excavation reports, see Hebei sheng wenwu yanjiusuo, "Hebei Dingxian 40 hao Han mu fajue jianbao;" Wenwu bianji weiyuanhui 文物編輯委員會, *Wenwu kaogu gongzuo sanshinian* 文物考古工作三十年 (Beijing: Wenwu chubanshe, 1979), 46.

158. Huang Xiaofen, *Han mu de kaoguxue yanjiu*, 107.

159. Pingshuo kaogudui 平朔考古隊, "Shanxi Shuoxian Qin Han mu fajue jianbao" 山西朔縣秦漢墓發掘簡報, *Wenwu* 1987.6: 1–52.

160. Pingshuo kaogudui, "Shanxi Shuoxian Qin Han mu fajue jianbao," 10–11.

161. Jiang Lu, "Zhongguo beifang diqu Han mu yanjiu," 25.

162. Hebei sheng wenwu yanjiusuo and Zhangjiakou diqu wenhuaju 張家口地區文化局, "Hebei Yangyuan Sanfengou Han mu qun fajue baogao" 河北陽原三汾溝漢墓群發掘報告, *Wenwu* 1990.1: 1–18.

163. Catacomb tombs can also be seen sporadically in north Hebei in the early second century BCE. Archaeologists spotted a small number of single-chamber catacombs cut into the ground in the Guanzhuang cemetery in Huailai, in north Hebei, about 280 kilometers to the northeast of Mancheng. Whereas the excavators dated these tombs to no earlier than the first century BCE, recently Jiang Lu proposed an earlier date from the early Western Han, i.e., the early second century BCE; see Jiang Lu, "Beifang diqu Xi Han zaoqi muzang yanjiu" 北方地區西漢早期墓葬研究, *Bianjiang kaogu yanjiu* 邊疆考古研究 9 (2010): 126–37, as well as her "Zhongguo beifang diqu Han mu yanjiu," 55.

164. Sima Qian, *Shiji*, 43.1813.

165. Di Cosmo, *Ancient China and its Enemies: The Rise of Nomadic Power in East Asian History*, 83–87.

166. Yang Jianhua, *Chunqiu Zhanguo shiqi Zhongguo beifang wenhuadai de xingcheng* 春秋戰國時期中國北方文化帶的形成 (Beijing: Kexue chubanshe, 2004), 104.

167. Xu Cheng 許成 and Li Jinzeng 李進增, "Dong Zhou shiqi de rongdi qingtong wenhua" 東周時期的戎狄青銅文化, *Kaogu xuebao* 1993.1: 1–11, esp. p. 9.

168. One of the most important advocates of "great unification" was Dong Zhongshu. See Loewe, *Dong Zhongshu, a "Confucian" Heritage and the* Chunqiu fanlu, 177–81.

169. Antonio S. Cua, "Ethical Uses of the Past," in his *Human Nature, Ritual, and History: Studies in Xunzi and Chinese Philosophy* (Washington, DC: Catholic University of America Press, 2005), 73–98.

170. Wang Xianqian, *Xunzi jijie*, 329; John Knoblock, *Xunzi: A Translation and Study of the Complete Works*, 3 vols. (Stanford, CA: Stanford University Press, 1994), 3: 38. For an alternative translation, see Hutton, *Xunzi: The Complete Text*, 189.

171. Kong Yingda, *Liji zhengyi*, 12.110, in *Shisanjing zhushu*, 1338; Legge, *Li Chi: The Book of Rites*, 1: 187–88.

172. Kong Yingda, *Chunqiu zuozhuan zhengyi* 春秋左傳正義, 54.433, in *Shisanjing zhushu*, 2135; see also Yang Kuan, *Xi Zhou shi* 西周史 (Shanghai: Shanghai renmin chubanshe, 2008), 383–84.

173. Jia Gongyan, *Zhouli zhushu* 周禮注疏, 10.65, in *Shisanjing zhushu*, 703.

174. Jia Gongyan, *Zhouli zhushu*, 2.8, in *Shisanjing zhushu*, 646.

175. Kong Yingda, *Liji zhengyi*, in *Shisanjing zhushu*, 1338; Legge, *Li Chi: The Book of Rites*, 1: 229.

176. For the Huang-lao elements in Xunzi, see Yu Mingguang, "Xunzi's Philosophy and the School of Huang-Lao: On the Renewal and Development of Early Confucianism," *Contemporary Chinese Thought* 34.1 (2002): 37–60. For Xunzi's influence in early Han, see Paul Goldin, "Xunzi and Early Han Philosophy," *Harvard Journal of Asiatic Studies* 67.1 (2007): 135–66.

177. For a discussion of "inner" and "outer" subjects, see Kurihara Tomonobu 栗原朋信, *Shin Kan shi no kenkyū* 秦漢史の研究 (Tokyo: Yoshikawa Kōbunkan, 1961); Abe Yukinobu 阿部幸信, "Zen Kan jidai ni okeru naigai kan no henken—insei no shiten kara" 前漢時代における内外觀の變遷—印制の視點から, *Chūgoku shikagu* 中国史学 18 (2008): 121–40. For the general political discourse of space and geography in early China, see Aihe Wang, *Cosmology and Political Culture in Early China* (Cambridge: Cambridge University Press, 2000), 23–74.

178. Ge Jianxiong, *Xi Han renkou dili* 西漢人口地理 (Beijing: Renmin chubanshe, 1986), 164–205.

179. Kong Yingda, *Chunqiu zuozhuan zhengyi*, 11.84, in *Shisanjing zhushu*, 1786.

180. Kong Yingda, *Chunqiu zuozhuan zhengyi*, 24.185, in *Shisanjing zhushu*, 1887.

181. Gan Bao 干寶, *Soushen ji* 搜神記, collated by Wang Shaoying (Beijing: Zhonghua shuju, 1979), 235.

182. Hebei sheng wenwu yanjiusuo, *Cuo mu*, 1: 124.

183. Chen Qiyou, *Lüshi chunqiu xin jiaoshi*, 956; Knoblock and Riegel, *The Annals of Lü Buwei*, 374–76.

184. Paul R. Goldin, *The Culture of Sex in Ancient China* (Honolulu: University of Hawaii Press, 2002), 60–61, 93.

185. Sima Qian, *Shiji*, 129.3263.

186. Sima Qian, *Shiji*, 129.3263.

187. Sima Qian, *Shiji*, 129.3263.

188. Ban Gu, *Hanshu*, 97.3950.

189. Hebei sheng wenwu yanjiusuo, *Cuo mu*, 1: 396–98.

190. Sima Qian, *Shiji*, 70: 3286.

191. Chen Suzhen 陳蘇鎮, "Hanchu wangguo zhidu kaoshu" 漢初王國制度考述, *Zhongguoshi yanjiu* 中國史研究 2004.3: 27–40.

192. Ban Gu, *Hanshu*, 63.2749, 2759.

193. Zhang Shuangdi 張雙棣, *Huainanzi jiaoshi* 淮南子校釋 (Beijing: Beijing daxue chubanshe, 1997), 1116; John S. Major et al., *The Huainanzi: A Guide to the Theory and Practice of Government in Early Han China* (New York: Columbia University Press, 2010), 400.

194. Zhang Shuangdi, *Huainanzi jiaoshi*, 1137; Major et al., *The Huainanzi*, 406. Remarking on "nan nü qieyi" 男女切倚, this passage echoes the *Lüshi chunqiu* text about the Zhongshan custom in note 183, this chapter.

195. Major et al., *The Huainanzi*, 393.

196. Zhongguo shehui kexueyuan kaogu yanjiusuo, *Mancheng Han mu fajue baogao*, 1: 24; similar contents of wine can also be found in the Eastern Zhou Zhongshan tombs; see Hebei sheng wenwu yanjiusuo, *Cuo mu*, 1: 509–10.

197. Sima Qian, *Shiji*, 117.3038. For dwarfs, see also *Shiji*, 24.1222, 47.1915, 126.3202. Cai Yong 蔡邕 (133–192 CE) left a rhapsody titled "Rhapsody of Dwarfs" (*Duanren fu* 短人賦) portraying these popular entertainers; see Fei Zhengang, *Quan Han fu*, 576.

4. THE PUBLIC KING

1. For example, in the *Zuozhuan* text, it is related that Huan Tui 桓魋, a minister of the Song state, made a stone casket for himself and did not complete it in three years; Legge, *Li Chi: The Book of Rites*, 1: 149. In the inscriptions made on the Zhongshan bronze tablet, the king demanded that the scale of the mausoleum could only be enlarged rather than reduced. However, in this example, it remains uncertain whether the royal endorser of the plan was the departed king or the new king. See Hebei sheng wenwu yanjiusuo, *Cuo mu*, 1: 399.

2. Wang Xianqian, *Xunzi jijie*, 375. Watson, *Hsunzi, Basic Writings*, 113.

3. Jia Gongyan, *Yili zhushu*, 37.199, in *Shisanjing zhushu*, 1: 1143; Steele, *The I-li or Book of Etiquette and Ceremonial*, 2: 72.

4. Ma Duanlin 馬端臨, *Wenxian tongkao* 文獻通考 (Shenduzhai 慎獨齋 edition, 1521), 124.1b, quoting a lost passage from the *Former Rituals of the Han* (Han jiuyi). The figure might have been exaggerated.

5. Ban Gu, *Hanshu*, 6.158, commentary.

6. Michael Loewe, "The Tombs Built for Han Chengdi and Migrations of Population," in *Chang'an 26 BCE: An Augustan Age in China*, ed. Michael Nylan and Griet Vankeeberghen (Seattle: University of Washington Press, 2015), 201–28. The same idea was expressed in Xianyang shi wenwu kaogu yanjiusuo, *Xi Han diling zuantan diaocha baogao*, 177.

7. Ban Gu, *Hanshu*, 68.2950; Burton Watson, *Courtier and Commoner: Selections of the History of the Former Han by Pan Ku* (New York: Columbia University Press, 1974), 141.

8. Wu Shuping, *Dongguan Han ji jiaozhu*, 11–12. See also Fan Ye, *Hou Hanshu*, 1.77.

9. Wu Shuping, *Dongguan Han ji jiaozhu*, 58.

10. Ban Gu, *Hanshu*, 67.2907–8.

11. Fan Ye, *Hou Hanshu*, 64.2124.

12. Jie Shi, "Incorporating All for One: The First Emperor's Tomb Mound," *Early China*, 37 (2014): 359–91.

13. Liu Qingzhu and Li Yufang, *Xi Han shiyi ling*, 27.

14. Xianyang shi wenwu kaogu yanjiusuo, *Xi Han diling zuantan diaocha baogao*, 176.

15. Liu Qingzhu and Li Yufang, "Guanyu Xi Han diling xingzhi zhu wenti de tantao" 關於西漢帝陵形制諸問題的探討, *Kaogu yu wenwu* 1985.5: 102–9; Zhao Huacheng, "Qin Shihuang lingyuan buju jiegou de zai renshi" 秦始皇陵園佈局結構的再認識, in *Yuanwangji* 遠望集 (Xi'an: Shaanxi renmin meishu chubanshe, 1998), 501–8; Jiao Nanfeng, "Shilun Xi Han diling de jianshe linian" 試論西漢帝陵的建設理念, *Kaogu* 2007.11: 78–87.

16. Jia Gongyan, *Zhouli zhushu*, 22.148, in *Shisanjing zhushu*, 786.

17. Zhao Huacheng, "Cong Shang Zhou jizhong gongmuzhi dao Qin Han duli lingyuan zhi de yanhua guiji" 從商周集中公墓制到秦漢獨立陵園制的演化軌跡, *Wenwu* 2006.7: 41–48.

18. Liu Qingzhu and Li Yufang, *Xi Han shiyi ling*, 11–15; Xianyang shi wenwu kaogu yanjiusuo, *Xi Han diling zuantan diaocha baogao*, 11–17.

19. The passage is preserved in Fan Ye, *Hou Hanshu*, 3144.

20. Evidence, both textual and archaeological, indicates that regional kingdoms generally imitated the imperial administrative and institutional system (*tong zhi jingshi* 同制京師) with slight variations; see Ban Gu, *Hanshu*, 14.394; for a detailed study, see Kamata Shigeo 鎌田重雄, *Shin, Kan seiji seido no kenkyū* 秦漢政治制度の研究 (Tokyo: Nihon Gakujutsu Shinkōkai, 1962), 152–64; Kamiya Masakazu 紙屋正和, "Zen Kan shōko ōkoku no kansei—Naishi o chūshin ni shite" 前漢諸侯王国の官制—内史を中心にして, *Kyūshū Daigaku Tōyōshi ronshū* 九州大学東洋史論集 3(1974): 17–35; Wu Rongzeng 吳榮曾, "Xi Han wangguo guanzhi kaoshi" 西漢王國官制考實, *Beijing daxue xuebao (zhexue shehui kexue ban)* 北京大學學報（哲學社會科學版） 1990.3: 110–122, 109.

21. Sun Xingyan et al., *Han guan liuzhong*, 106. See also Liu Rui 劉瑞, "Xi Han zhuhouwang mu zhidu san ti" 西漢諸侯王墓制度三題, in *Handai kaogu yu Han wenhua guoji xueshu taolunhui lunwenji* 漢代考古與漢文化國際學術討論會論文集 (Ji'nan: Qilu shushe, 2006), 157–71, esp. 157–59. Yang Aiguo 楊愛國, "Handai de yuzuo shoucang" 漢代的預作壽藏, in *Handai kaogu yu Han wenhua guoji xueshu taolunhui lunwenji*, 271–81.

22. Sima Qian, *Shiji*, 6.265.

23. For the number of days between death and entombment, Emperor Gaozu, 23 days; Emperor Hui, 24 days; Emperor Wen, 7 days; Emperor Jing, 10 days; Emperor Wu, 18 days; Emperor Zhao, 50 days; Emperor Xuan, 28 days; Emperor Yuan, 55 days; Emperor Cheng, 54 days; Emperor Ai, 105 days; and Emperor Ping, unreported; see Sima Qian, *Shiji, juan* 8, 10, 11. Yang Shuda, *Han dai hunsang lisu kao*, 87–97. Toward the end of the Western Han, as Yang noted, people tended to prolong the period of lying in state, during which they might have stored the corpse at a temporary location.

24. For example, in the Shizishan tomb at Xuzhou, archaeologists were surprised to find that the tomb was actually unfinished at the time of the hasty entombment, see Wang Kai 王愷 and Ge Mingyu 葛明宇, *Xuzhou Shizishan Xi Han Chuwang ling* 徐州獅子山西漢楚王陵 (Beijing: Sanlian, 2005), 139; the same also happened to Mt. Baoan tomb no. 2, in which a tunnel was unfinished; see Henan sheng wenwu kaogu yanjiusuo, *Yongcheng Xi Han Liangguo wangling yu qinyuan*, 134.

25. Duan Qingbo, *Qin Shi Huangdi lingyuan kaogu yanjiu*, 56–76, and his "Guanyu Shengheyuan damu ji xiangguan wenti de taolun" 關於神禾原大墓及相關問題的討論, *Kaogu yu wenwu* 2009.4: 53–61, esp. 59.

26. Desecrating a ruler's tomb was not unique to China. In fact, wherever tombs were political symbols, destroying them was politically symbolic, too. In ancient Egypt, for example, the most desecrated royal tomb is that of Akhenaten, whose ideology was heretical to those who came after him; see Cyril Aldred and A. T. Sandison, "The Tomb of Akhenaten at Thebes [and Appendix]," *The Journal of Egyptian Archaeology*, 47 (1961): 41–65; see also Aidan Dodson, *Amarna Sunset: Nefertiti, Tutankhamun, Ay, Horemheb, and the Egyptian Counter-Reformation* (Oxford: Oxford University Press, 2009).

27. Shaanxi sheng kaogu yanjiusuo and Qin Shihuang bingmayong bowuguan, *Qin Shihuangdi lingyuan fajue baogao 1999*, 195.

28. Shaanxi sheng kaogu yanjiusuo and Qin Shihuang bingmayong bowuguan, *Qin Shihuangdi lingyuan kaogu baogao 2000* 秦始皇帝陵園考古報告 2000 (Beijing: Wenwu chubanshe, 2006), 259–65.

29. Sima Qian, *Shiji*, 6.265.

30. Duan Qingbo, "Qin Shihuangdi lingyuan K0006 peizangkeng xingzhi chuyi" 秦始皇帝陵園K0006陪葬坑性質芻議, *Zhongguo lishi wenwu* 2002.2: 59–66.

31. Shaanxi sheng kaogu yanjiusuo Hanling kaogudui 陝西省考古研究所漢陵考古隊, "Han Jingdi Yangling nanqu congzangkeng fajue diyihao jianbao" 漢景帝陽陵南區從葬坑發掘第一號簡報, *Wenwu* 1992.4: 1–13; Shaanxi sheng kaogu yanjiusuo Hanling kaogudui, "Han Jingdi Yangling nanqu congzang keng fajue dierhao jianbao" 漢景帝陽陵南區從葬坑發掘第二號簡報, *Wenwu* 1994.6: 4–23; Shaanxi sheng kaogu yanjiuyuan, "Han Yangling diling dongce shiyi—ershiyi hao waicangkeng fajue jianbao" 漢陽陵帝陵東側11–21號外藏坑發掘簡報, *Kaogu yu wenwu* 2008.3: 3–32.

32. To Ma Yongying 馬永贏, Jiao Nanfeng 焦南峰, and some other archeologists, these official labels indicate the presence of imperial government agencies that would continue to serve the emperor in the afterlife; see Ma Yongying, "'Daguan zhi yin' yu Xi Han de Taiguan" 大官之印" 與西漢的太官, *Kaogu yu wenwu* 2006.5: 77–79; Jiao Nanfeng, "Han Yangling congzangkeng chutan" 漢陽陵從葬坑初探, *Wenwu* 2006.7: 51–57. Zhao Huacheng, however, argues against Duan, Ma, and Jiao in his "Qin Han diling waicang xitong (congzangkeng) de xingzhi wenti" 秦漢帝陵外藏

系統(從葬坑)的性質問題, *Qin Shihuang diling bowuyuan* 秦始皇帝陵博物院 1 (2011): 119–30.

33. Jürgen Habermas, *The Structural Transformation of the Public Sphere: An Inquiry into a Category of Bourgeois Society* (Cambridge: Polity, 1989), 5–13.

34. Yang Kuan, *Zhanguo shi*, 236.

35. Yuri Pines, *Envisioning Eternal Empire: Chinese Political Thought of the Warring States* (Honolulu: University of Hawaii Press, 2009), 27.

36. Chen Qiyou, *Lüshi chunqiu xin jiaoshi*, 1: 45; Knoblock and Riegel, *The Annals of Lü Buwei*, 71.

37. Liu Zehua 劉澤華, "Chunqiu Zhanguo de 'ligong miesi' guannian yu shehui zhenghe" 春秋戰國的" 立公滅私" 觀念與社會整合, in *Gongsi guannian yu Zhongguo shehui* 公私觀念與中國社會 (Beijing: Zhongguo renmin daxue chubanshe, 2003), 1–39, esp. 18, 24.

38. Japanese historians designate this financial system as "state as family property" (*kasan kokka sei* 家產國家制); Ochi Shigeaki 越智重明, "Shin no kokka saisei seido" 秦の国家財政制度, *Kyūshū Daigaku Tōyōshi ronshū* 九州大学東洋史論集 15 (1986): 1–21.

39. Sima Qian, *Shiji*, 99.2720, 夫天下合為一家. This metaphorical expression, however, cannot be taken at face value because the concept of *jia* 家 was clearly defined in Qin and Han legal texts as a social unit whose members shared blood kinship and common wealth and usually lived together. Zhang Wenjiang 張文江, *Qin Han jia, hu falü yanjiu—yi jia, hu falü gouzao wei shijiao* 秦漢家戶法律研究—以家戶法律構造為視角 (Beijing: Renmin ribao chubanshe, 2016).

40. Yamada Katsuyoshi 山田勝芳, "Qin Han shiqi de caizheng wenti" 秦漢時期的財政問題, in *Yin Zhou Qin Han shixue de jiben wenti* 殷周秦漢史學的基本問題, ed. Satake Yasuhiko (Beijing: Zhonghua shuju, 2008), 204–23, esp. notes 41, 42.

41. The name of the office changed over time. During the early Han, it was the *Zhisu neishi* 治粟內史 (scribe of the capital area for grain), then in 144 BCE, *Da nong ling* 大農令 (grand prefect of agriculture), then *Da sinong* in 104 BCE. Hereafter, I will use *Da sinong* throughout to represent the state treasury.

42. Katō Shigeshi 加藤繁, *Shina keizaishi kōshō* 支那經濟史考證 (Tokyo: Tōyō Bunko, 1952), 1: 36–40. Ochi Shigeaki, "Zen Kan no zaisei ni tsuite" 前漢の財政につい て, *Kyūshū Daigaku Tōyōshi ronshū* 10 (1982): 1–21. For *Da sinong* and *Shaofu*, see Michael Loewe, *The Government of the Qin and Han Empires: 221 BCE–220 CE* (Indianapolis: Hackett, 2006), 29–34; Hans Bielenstein, *The Bureaucracy of Han Times* (Cambridge: Cambridge University Press, 1980), 43–7, 47–68.

43. Katō Shigeshi, *Shina keizaishi kōshō*, 1: 150.

44. Hans Bielenstein, *The Bureaucracy of Han Times*, 46.

45. Erica Brindley, "The Polarization of the Concepts 'Si' (Private Interest) and 'Gong' (Public Interest) in Early Chinese Thought," *Asia Major* third series, 26.2 (2013): 1–31. It must be noted, however, that the Chinese concepts *gong* and *si* do not have strict English equivalents. The conventional English translation of "public" and "private" may not always be accurate in different contexts. See Mark E. Lewis, "Public Spaces in Cities in the Roman and Han Empires," in *State Power in Ancient China and Rome*, ed. Walter Scheider (Oxford: Oxford University Press, 2015), 204–29.

46. Zhao Dingxin, "The Han Bureaucracy: Its Origin, Nature, and Development," in *State Power in Ancient China and Rome*, 64–65.

47. Hebei sheng wenwu yanjiusuo, *Cuo mu*, 1: 399. For a description of this tablet in English, see Xiaolong Wu, *Material Culture, Power, and Identity in Ancient China*, 171–79.

48. Liu Rui, "Qin Han shiqi de jiangzuo dajiang" 秦漢時期的將作大匠, *Zhongguo shi yanjiu* 1998.4: 168–70. An Zuozhang 安作璋 and Xiong Tieji 熊鐵基, *Qin Han guanzhi shigao* 秦漢官制史稿 (Ji'nan: Qilu shushe, 2007), 224–29.

49. Ma Yongying 馬永贏, "Cong *Jiangzuo dajiang* kan Xi Han diling de bianhua" 從將作大匠看西漢帝陵的變化, *Kaogu yu wenwu* 2009.4: 72–76. It was called *Dajiang guansikong* 大匠官司空 in early Han legal texts; see Zhangjiashan Han mu zhujian zhengli xiaozu, *Zhangjiashan Han mu zhujian ersiqi hao mu (shiwen xiudingben)*, 74. Most scholars now read this Zhangjiashan line as representing two titles. See Barbieri-Low and Yates, *Law, State, and Society in Early Imperial China*, 2: 976.

50. Katō Shigeshi, *Shina keizaishi kōshō*, 1: 212–25.

51. Fang Xuanling 房玄齡, *Jinshu* 晉書 (Beijing: Zhonghua shuju, 1974), 60.1651.

52. Zhong Yiming 鐘一鳴, "Xi Han zhuhouwang zhi caiquan kaoshu" 西漢諸侯王之財權考述, *Yiyang shizhuan xuebao* 益陽師專學報 1987.3: 9–13.

53. An Zuozhang and Xiong Tieji, *Qin Han guanzhi shigao*, 180–1.

54. Ban Gu, *Hanshu*, 8.242.

55. Bu Xianqun 卜憲群, *Qin Han guanliao zhidu* 秦漢官僚制度 (Beijing: Shehui kexue wenxian chubanshe, 2002), 136.

56. Liu Rongqing 劉榮慶, "Qin zhi Liyi kao bian" 秦置驪邑考辨, *Wenbo* 1990.5: 235; Sun Weigang 孫偉剛, "Xi, Liyi, yu Lishanyuan—jian lun Qin Shihuangdi Liyi de gongneng yu zuoyong" 戲, 驪邑與驪山園—兼論秦始皇帝驪邑的功能與作用, *Kaogu yu wenwu* 2009.4: 61–71.

57. Sima Qian, *Shiji*, 6.256.

58. Wang Xueli 王學理, "Qin Han xiang cheng, diwang tongzhi—lüe lun Qin Han huangdi he Han zhuhouwang lingyuan de jicheng yu yanbian" 秦漢相承 帝王同制—略論秦漢皇帝和漢諸侯王陵園制度的繼承與演變, *Kaogu yu wenwu* 2000.6: 60–66, 79.

59. For the meanings of *qin* and *biandian*, see Yang Kuan, *Zhongguo gudai lingqin zhidushi yanjiu*, 14–33; Liu Qingzhu and Li Yufang, *Xi Han shiyi ling*, 184–95; Michael Loewe, "The Imperial Tombs of the Former Han Dynasty and their Shrines," *T'oung Pao* 78.4/5(1992): 302–40.

60. For example, the mausoleum town of Maoling had a population of 277,277, more than that of the city of Chang'an, which was inhabited by 246,200 people; see Ge Jianxiong, *Xi Han renkou dili*, 138.

61. Hua Xuecheng 華學誠, *Yang Xiong Fangyan jiaoshi huizheng* 揚雄方言校釋匯證 (Beijing: Zhonghua shuju, 2005), 997. In the *Book of Rites*, it is stated that, "The son of heaven has his domain that he may settle there his sons and grandsons; and the feudal princes have their states; and great officers their appanages that they may do the same for theirs. This constitutes 'the statutory arrangement.'" Kong Yingda, *Liji zhengyi*, 21.190, in *Shisanjing zhushu*, 1418.

62. Sekino Takeshi 關野雄, *Chūgoku kōkogaku kenkyū* 中國考古學研究 (Tokyo: Tōkyō Daigaku Shuppankai, 1963), 563–91.

63. Hu Fangping 胡方平, "Zhongguo fengtu mu de chansheng he liuxing" 中國封土墓的產生和流行, *Kaogu* 1994: 6: 556–58. Lothar von Falkenhausen, however, believes it was an indigenous invention: "At the present state of research, it seems safest to consider them as an early fifth-century innovation, completely

independent of mound-building in contemporaneous cultures of neighboring areas such as the Lower Yangzi region and the Central Eurasian steppes." Lothar von Falkenhausen, *Chinese Society in the Age of Confucius (1000–250 BC): The Archaeological Evidence*, 336.

64. Hua Xuecheng, *Yang Xiong Fangyan jiaoshi huizheng*, 997.

65. The only exception came from Dou Wan's coffin; see Zhongguo shehui kexueyuan kaogu yanjiusuo, *Mancheng Han mu fajue baogao*, 1: 274–75.

66. Guo Zheng 郭錚, "Mancheng Han mu chutu fengni shitan" 滿城漢墓出土封泥試探, *Wenwu chunqiu* 1992.1: 35–37.

67. Zhongguo shehui kexueyuan kaogu yanjiusuo, *Mancheng Han mu fajue baogao*, 1: 335.

68. Zhongguo shehui kexueyuan kaogu yanjiusuo, *Mancheng Han mu fajue baogao*, 1: 228.

69. According to the excavators, the "bureau of sacrifice" in charge of the imperial sacrifices was a branch of the imperial bureau of "the ministry of ceremonies" (*Taichang* 太常). First titled "the great supplicant" (*Taizhu* 太祝), this office changed its name to "bureau of sacrifice" (*Cisi* 祠祀) in 144 BCE, and forty years later, switched it again to *Miaosi* 廟祀 (still, "bureau of sacrifice"); Ban Gu, *Hanshu*, 726.

70. An Zuozhang and Xiong Tieji, *Qin Han guanzhi shigao*, 337–39.

71. Ban Gu, *Hanshu*, 726. Zhangjiashan Han mu zhujian zhengli xiaozu, *Zhangjiashan Han mu zhujian ersiqi hao mu (shiwen xiudingben)*, 74.

72. Guo Zheng, "Mancheng Han mu chutu fengni shitan," 35.

73. Zhao Ping'an 趙平安, *Qin Xi Han yinzhang yanjiu* 秦西漢印章研究 (Shanghai: Shanghai guji chubanshe, 2013), 65.

74. Zhongguo shehui kexueyuan kaogu yanjiusuo, *Mancheng Han mu fajue baogao*, 1: 30.

75. Zhongguo shehui kexueyuan kaogu yanjiusuo, *Mancheng Han mu fajue baogao*, 1: 150.

76. Zhongguo shehui kexueyuan kaogu yanjiusuo, *Mancheng Han mu fajue baogao*, 1: 52.

77. For a detailed study of the formula, see Xu Zhengkao 徐正考, *Handai tongqi mingwen zonghe yanjiu* 漢代銅器銘文綜合研究 (Beijing: Zuojia chubanshe, 2007). It is hard to determine, however, whether the name usually appearing in the beginning of the inscription denotes the possessor or owner of the object. The two concepts are different: Although someone who possesses an object may well be its owner, some things legally belong to their owner but are merely in the hands of a possessor. Nothing in the inscriptions specifies the ownership of the inscribed objects. In some cases when the object changed hands and the new possessor left an inscription on the object, it seems the possessor was also the owner, but in many other cases, especially when the possessor was a palace or government office, it is hard to be sure. Perhaps because of this difficulty, in his book, on pages 185–206, Xu Zhengkao shifts between "the users" (*shiyongzhe* 使用者) and "the masters of the objects" (*qizhu* 器主) in describing the possessors without addressing the problem of ownership.

78. Zhongguo shehui kexueyuan kaogu yanjiusuo, *Mancheng Han mu fajue baogao*, 1: 258.

79. Zhongguo shehui kexueyuan kaogu yanjiusuo, *Mancheng Han mu fajue baogao*, 1: 56, fig. 36.2. This time the name can also possibly denote the maker of the vessel.

80. Zhongguo shehui kexueyuan kaogu yanjiusuo, *Mancheng Han mu fajue baogao*, 1: 56.

81. Wu Rongzeng, "Xi Han wangguo guanzhi kaoshi," 119–20.

82. Sima Qian, *Shiji*, 92.2623.

83. Wang Liqi 王利器, *Yantielun jiaozhu* 鹽鐵輪校注 (Beijing: Zhonghua shuju, 1992), 28

84. Jia Gongyan, *Zhouli zhushu*, 6.40; in *Shisanjing zhushu*, 678.

85. Zhongguo shehui kexueyuan kaogu yanjiusuo, *Mancheng Han mu fajue baogao*, 1: 52, 58.

86. Zhongguo shehui kexueyuan kaogu yanjiusuo, *Mancheng Han mu fajue baogao*, 1: 71.

87. An Zuozhang and Xiong Tieji, *Qin Han guanzhi shigao*, 1: 335–36.

88. To better understand the paradox, it might be helpful to imagine that the president of the United States entrusts a government agency paid by taxpayers to manage his private properties and living costs. This would surely be a violation of property rights in modern society.

89. Ban Gu, *Hanshu*, 97.3975.

90. Ban Gu, *Hanshu*, 27.1368.

91. In another episode, Emperor Wu's aunt, Princess Guantao 館陶公主, once presented his nephew with her private garden of Changmen as a gift, which greatly pleased the emperor, who in return upgraded the status of her residence; see Ban Gu, *Hanshu*, 65.2853.

92. Shizishan Chuwangling kaogu fajuedui, "Xuzhou Shizishan Xi Han Chuwangling fajue jianbao" 徐州獅子山西漢楚王陵發掘簡報, *Wenwu* 1998.8: 4–33.

93. Zhao Ping'an, "Dui Shizishan Chuwangling suochu yinzhang fengni de zairenshi" 對獅子山楚王陵所出印章封泥的再認識, *Wenwu* 1999.1: 52–55.

94. Geng Jianjun 耿建軍, "Shixi Xuzhou Xi Han Chuwang mu chutu guanyin ji fengni de xingzhi" 試析徐州西漢楚王墓出土官印及封泥的性質, *Kaogu* 2000.9: 79–85.

95. Xuzhou bowuguan, "Xuzhou Shiqiao Han mu qingli baogao" 徐州石橋漢墓清理簡報, *Wenwu* 1984.11: 22–40; Zhongguo guojia bowuguan and Xuzhou bowuguan, *Da Han Chu wang: Xuzhou Xi Han Chu wang ling mu wenwu ji cui*, 224.

96. Zhongguo shehui kexueyuan kaogu yanjiusuo, *Yinxu Fu Hao mu*, 95. It must be noted that from the same tomb, bronzes marked Si Mu Xin 司母辛 (Fu Hao's posthumous temple title) were made after Fu Hao's death, specifically for burial, so the bronzes inscribed with the name Fu Hao were possessions in life.

97. Hubei sheng bowuguan, *Zeng hou Yi mu*, 1: 459.

98. Hubei sheng bowuguan, *Zeng hou Yi mu*, 1: 229.

99. Hebei sheng wenwu yanjiusuo, *Cuo mu*, 1: 111–55.

100. Sun Yirang, *Mozi jiangu*, 171–72. Burton Watson, trans., *Mozi: Basic Writings* (New York: Columbia University Press, 2003), 71.

101. Sun Yirang, *Mozi jiangu*, 170; Watson, *Mozi: Basic Writings*, 71.

102. Sun Yirang, *Mozi jiangu*, 187; Watson, *Mozi: Basic Writings*, 76–77.

103. Wang Xianqian, *Xunzi jijie*, 366; Hutton, *Xunzi, The Complete Text*, 212.

104. Zheng Xuan annotated: "Ornament is the manifestation of feelings" (*shi, qing zhi zhang biao ye* 飾, 情之章表也); Kong Yingda, *Liji zhengyi*, 58.435, in *Shisanjing zhushu*, 1663.

105. Hui-chieh Loy, "Xunzi contra Mozi," in *Dao Companion to the Philosophy of Xunzi*, ed. Eric L. Hutton (Dordrecht: Springer, 2016), 356–58.

106. Wang Xianqian, *Xunzi jijie*, 355; Hutton, *Xunzi, The Complete Text*, 204.

107. Wang Xianqian, *Xunzi jijie*, 372; Hutton, *Xunzi, The Complete Text*, 213.

108. Knoblock, *Xunzi: A Translation and Study of the Complete Works*, 2: 158.

109. Wang Xianqian, *Xunzi jijie*, 374; Hutton, *Xunzi, The Complete Text*, 214.

110. Wang Xianqian, *Xunzi jijie*, 369; Hutton, *Xunzi, The Complete Text*, 212.

111. Sun Shi 孫奭, *Mengzi zhushu* 孟子注疏, 5.41, in *Shisanjing zhushu*, 2705; James Legge, trans. *The Book of Mencius* (Raleigh, NC: Hayes Barton, 2006), 53. Similar distinctions between *daren* and *xiaoren* can also be found in *Lunyu* and *Mozi*.

112. Zhu Qianzhi, *Laozi jiaoshi*, 140. Robert Eno, trans. *Dao de jing*, 2010, version 1.1, http://www.indiana.edu/~p374/Daodejing.pdf, 20. Heshanggong 河上公 annotates, "*xiang* means *dao* (Way). The sage remains faithful to the great way, and the ten thousand people changed their minds and came over and pledged allegiance to him."

113. Zhu Qianzhi, *Laozi jiaoshi*, 140; Eno, *Dao de jing*, 20.

114. Rao Zongyi 饒宗頤, *Laozi Xiang'er zhu jiaozheng* 老子想爾注校證 (Hong Kong: Zhonghua shuju, 2015), 52.

115. Ho Ping-Ti 何炳棣, "Cong Zhuangzi Tianxia pian jiexi Xian Qin sixiang zhong de jiben guanhuai" 從莊子天下篇首解析先秦思想中的基本關懷, in *He Bingdi sixiang zhidushi lun* 何炳棣思想制度史論 (Taipei: Lianjing chuban gongsi, 2013), 285–330.

116. Pines, *Envisioning Eternal Empire: Chinese Political Thought of the Warring States*, 26.

117. Sima Qian, *Shiji*, 120.2753; Ban Gu, *Hanshu*, 36.1951, 50.2309; Xun Yue 荀悅, *Qian Han ji* 前漢紀, Sibu congkan edition (1919–1936), 8.3.

118. This is my own transcription and translation. I personally visited the site and checked the inscription in the summer of 2007. The transcription provided in the excavation report, which is slightly different from mine, identifies the last two lines as as "視此書□目此(？)也仁者悲之," which have been blurred over time. Nevertheless, it is still clear that there is a character following "shu" 書. I read it as "ru" 如. Moreover, the character after "mu" 目 does not resemble "ci" 此, as the excavation report suggests, but looks similar to "jun" 君. Although I examined the original stone, the reading of these two characters is difficult to be conclusive. For a focused study, see Yokota Kiozo 横田恭三, "Kameyama Kanbo no saiseki kokuji ni tsuite" 龜山漢墓の塞石刻字について, *Atomi Gakuen Joshi Daigaku kiyō* 跡見学園女子大学紀要 33 (2000): 83–95. For the excavation report, see Nanjing bowuyuan and Tongshan xian wenhuaguan 銅山縣文化館, "Tongshan Guishan erhao Xi Han yadong mu" 銅山龜山二號西漢崖洞墓, *Kaogu xuebao* 1985.1: 119–33.

119. Sun Yirang, *Mozi jiangu*, 1: 187. Watson, *Mozi: Basic Writings*, 76–77.

120. For the physical dimensions of the Qin mausoleum, see Shaanxi sheng kaogu yanjiusuo and Qin Shihuang bingmayong bowuguan, *Qin Shihuangdi lingyuan fajue baogao 1999*, 6; for those of the Yan capital, see Hebei sheng wenwu yanjiusuo, *Yan Xiadu*, 1: 13–19.

121. Shaanxi sheng kaogu yanjiuyuan 陝西省考古研究院 and Qin Shihuang bingmayong bowuguan, *Qin Shihuangdi lingyuan kaogu baogao 2001–2003* 秦始皇帝陵園考古報告 2001–2003 (Beijing: Wenwu chubanshe, 2007), 102.

122. Zhang Shuangdi, *Huainanzi jiaoshi* 2: 1380; Major et al., *The Huainanzi*, 500–1.

123. Zhang Shuangdi, *Huainanzi jiaoshi* 2: 2150; Major et al., *The Huainanzi*, 846.

124. Wang Liqi, *Yantielun jiaozhu*, 1: 299; Michael Loewe, *Crisis and Conflict in Han China* (London: Routledge, 1974), 11–12.

5. THE KING OF PEACE

1. Mark Csikszentmihalyi, "Emulating the Yellow Emperor: The Theory and Practice of Huang-Lao, 180–141 B.C.E." (PhD dissertation, Stanford University, 1994), 8–9.

2. Sima Qian, *Shiji*, 130.3289.

3. Randall P. Peerenboom, *Law and Morality in Ancient China: The Silk Manuscripts of Huang-Lao* (Albany, NY: SUNY Press, 1993), 27–102.

4. The four classics of this lost Huang-Lao canon include "The Constancy of Laws" (*Jingfa* 經法), "The Sixteen Classics" (*Shiliu jing* 十六經), "Aphorisms" (*Chen* 稱), and "On Dao the Fundamental" (*Yuan dao* 原道). For a historiographical review, see Paola Carrozza, "A Critical Review of the Principal Studies on the Four Manuscripts Preceding the B Version of the Mawangdui Laozi," *Asian Review* 13 (2002): 49–69.

5. Tang Lan 唐蘭, "Mawangdui chutu Laozi yiben juanqian gu yishu de yanjiu—jian-lun qi yu Han chu ru fa douzheng de guanxi" 馬王堆出土老子乙本卷前古軼書的研究—兼論其與漢初儒法鬥爭的關係, *Kaogu xuebao* 1975. 1: 8–38.

6. Peerenboom, *Law and Morality in Ancient China*, 3.

7. The *Shifa* text was included in the *Yizhoushu* (*I Chou shu*) sometime between the third and first centuries BCE; see Edward Shaughnessy, "I Chou shu," in *Early Chinese Texts: A Bibliographical Guide*, 229–33. I mainly refer to Zhang Shoujie's 張守節 edition in his annotation to the *Shiji* (Beijing: Zhonghua shuju 1959), 18–31.

8. Shen Bingzhen 沈炳震, *Jiujing bian zi du meng* 九經辨字瀆蒙, 7.26, in *Yingyin Wenyuange siku quanshu*, 194. 224.

9. Burton Watson trans., *The Analects of Confucius* (New York: Columbia University Press, 2007), 15.4.

10. Major et al., *The Huainanzi*, 64. My punctuation is slightly different from the afore-mentioned translation and renders the passage as one single sentence with three parallel sections.

11. Li Xiangfeng 黎翔鳳, *Guanzi jiaozhu* 管子校註, 3 vols. (Beijing: Zhonghua shuju, 2004), 1: 282; W. Allyn Rickett, trans., *Guanzi: Political, Economic, and Philosophical Essays from Early China*, 2 vols. (Princeton, NJ: Princeton University Press, 1998), 1: 242.

12. Ban Gu, *Hanshu*, 24.1250.

13. Ban Gu, *Hanshu*, 63.2748.

14. Kong Yingda *Maoshi zhengyi*, 16.235, in *Shisanjing zhushu*, 503.

15. Sima Qian, *Shiji*, 8.392; Ban Gu, *Hanshu*, 1.80.

16. For a historical background of this rebellion, see A. F. P. Hulsewé, "Royal Rebels."

17. Zhou Zhenhe, *Xi Han zhengqu dili*, 79–97; Wang Hui, *Han wangguo yu houguo zhi yanbian*, 55–61.

18. Sima Qian, *Shiji*, 23.1159.

19. The victorious Qin king declared himself "August-Thearch" (*huangdi*) and issued a famous edict across the empire to commemorate his greatest achievement of bring-ing the desired peace to the world: "In the twenty-sixth year, the emperor annexed all vassals in all under heaven; people are enjoying great peace." See Qin Shihuang jinshi keci zhu zhushizu 秦始皇金石刻辭注註釋組, *Qin Shihuang jinshi keci zhu* 秦始皇金石刻辭註 (Shanghai: Shanghai renmin chubanshe, 1975); Martin Kern, *The Stele Inscriptions of Ch'in Shih-huang: Text and Ritual in Early Chinese Imperial Representation* (New Haven, CT: American Oriental Society, 2000).

20. For a general study of *chaoqing* during the Western Han, see Sigimura Shinji 杉村 伸二, "Kan sho no gunkokubyō to nyūchō seido ni tsuite: Kan sho gunkokusei to ketsuen teki chūtai" 漢初の郡国廟と入朝制度について：漢初郡国制と血縁的 紐帯, *Kyūshū Daigaku Tōyōshi ronshū* 37 (2009): 1–23, esp. 8–15.

21. Wang Hui, *Han wangguo yu houguo zhi yanbian*, 93–104.

22. Sima Qian, *Shiji*, 108. 2861–863.

23. During the Eastern Han period, Zhongshan still played a role in defending the empire's northern border; see Fan Ye, *Hou Hanshu*, 22.779.

24. For a summary of the ideal politics of the Huang-Lao school, see Asano Yūichi 浅野 裕一, *Kō-Rō-dō no seiritsu to tenkai* 黄老道の成立と展開 (Tokyo: Sōbunsha 1992), 463.

25. Sima Qian, *Shiji*, 59.2099. The later *Hanshu* version is almost identical except for a couple of minor differences.

26. For the concept *wuwei* ("take no deliberate actions"), see Roger Ames, *The Art of Rulership: A Study of Ancient Chinese Political Thought* (Albany, NY: SUNY Press, 1994), 28–64. See also Edward Slingerland, *Effortless Action: Wu-Wei as Conceptual Metaphor and Spiritual Ideal in Early China* (Oxford: Oxford University Press, 2003).

27. Chen Qiyou, *Lüshi chunqiu xin jiaoshi*, 35–36; Knoblock and Riegel, *The Annals of Lü Buwei*, 69–70.

28. Li Xiangfeng, *Guanzi jiaozhu*, 2: 553; Rickett, *Guanzi*, 1: 406.

29. Li Xiangfeng, *Guanzi jiaozhu*, 2: 554; Rickett, *Guanzi*, 1: 407.

30. Knoblock and Riegel, *The Annals of Lü Buwei*, 412–13.

31. Zhang Shuandi, *Huainanzi jiaoshi*, 1:559; Major et al., *The Huainanzi*, 295.

32. Sima Qian told us that Cao Shen was from the scholarly lineage of Huang-Lao teachings beginning from the late Warring States period. Sima Qian, *Shiji*, 80.2436.

33. Sima Qian, *Shiji*, 54.2029.

34. Sima Qian, *Shiji*, 56.2062.

35. Sima Qian, *Shiji*, 56.2060.

36. In chapter 1, I argued that these pleasurable things were put there to attract and keep the dispersing souls. But one might also ask: Since there might be a variety of ways to attract the souls, why were dildos and wine not only chosen but also highlighted? For example, why were there three dildos, while only one was found in the more recently excavated Dayunshan tomb in Jiangsu? The wine jars were also much larger than any known wine containers in other tombs of the time. I believe our interpretation should deal not only with "why X makes sense" in this context but also "why X and not other alternatives." So, in chapter 1, I mostly concentrated on the first question, but in chapters 3 and 5, I responded to the second question by zooming in on the special historical and ideological context of Liu Sheng and Zhongshan.

37. Sima Qian, *Shiji*, 59.2098.

38. Wang Xianqian, *Xunzi jijie*, 1: 334. Hutton, *Xunzi: The Complete Text*, 193.

39. Wang Xianqian, *Xunzi jijie*, 1: 188; Hutton, *Xunzi: The Complete Text*, 91.

40. Kong Yingda, *Maoshi zhengyi*, 2–2: 36, in *Shisanjing zhushu*, 304. Legge, *Li Chi: The Book of Rites*, 2:279.

41. Sima Qian, *Shiji*, 59.2098.

42. Hans van Ess, "The Meaning of Huang-Lao in the *Shiji* and *Hanshu*," *Études chinoises* 12.2 (1993): 161–77.

43. Sima Qian, *Shiji*, 130.3289.

44. Sima Qian, *Shiji*, 130.3289. English translation in William Theodore De Bary, *Sources of East Asian Tradition: Premodern Asia*, Vol. 1 (New York: Columbia University Press, 2008), 150.

45. Sima Qian, *Shiji*, 49.1975.

46. Sima Qian, *Shiji*, 121.3123.

47. Ban Gu, *Hanshu*, 53.2422.

48. Sima Qian, *Shiji*, 12.452.

49. Hawkes, *The Songs of the South*, 67.

50. Chen Qiyou, *Hanfeizi xin jiaozhu* 韓非子新校注 (Shanghai: Shanghai guji chuban-she, 2000), 321–22.

51. Sima Qian, *Shiji*, 3.108. Ban Gu, *Hanshu*, 53.2425.

52. Kong Yingda, *Maoshi zhengyi*, 12–3. 184, in *Shisanjing zhushu*, 452. The only difference between the citation in the *Hanshu* and the current edition of the *Book of Poetry* is the auxiliary adverb *wei*, with the former written as 唯 and the latter as 維.

53. Wang Xianqian, *Shi sanjia yi jishu* 詩三家義集疏 (Beijing: Zhonghua shuju, 1987), 697–98.

54. Ban Gu, *Hanshu*, 53.2422.

55. For the problem of subjectivity in the writing of the *Shiji*, see Stephen W. Durrant, *The Cloudy Mirror: Tension and Conflict in the Writings of Sima Qian* (Albany, NY: SUNY Press, 1995), especially chapter 6, "Ideologue versus Narrator." For the *Hanshu*, see Anthony E. Clark, "Praise and Blame: Ruist Historiography in Ban Gu's *Hanshu*," *The Chinese Historical Review* 18.1 (2011): 1–24, and his *Ban Gu's History of Early China* (Amherst, NY: Cambria, 2008).

56. Ban Gu, *Hanshu*, 62.2737.

57. For differences between the *Shiji* and the *Hanshu*, see Hans van Ess, "Praise and Slander: The Evocation of Empress Lü in the *Shiji* and the *Hanshu*," *Nannü* 8.2 (2006): 221–54, as well as his *Politik und Geschichtsschreibung im alten China: Pan-ma i-t'ung* 班馬異同, 2 vols. (Wiesbaden: Harrassowitz, 2014).

58. Loewe and Twitchett, *The Cambridge History of China*, vol. 1, 136–49.

59. Xu Zhuoyun 許倬雲, "Xi Han zhengquan yu shehui shili de jiaohu zuoyong" 西漢政權與社會勢力的交互作用, *Zhongyang yanjiuyuan lishi yuyan yanjiusuo jikan* 中央研究院歷史語言研究所集刊 35 (1964): 261–81.

60. Sigimura Shinji 杉村伸二, "Zen Kan Keiteiki kokusei tankan no haikei" 前漢景帝期國制轉換の背景, *Tōyōshi kenkyū* 東洋史研究67.2 (2008): 161–93.

61. Yamada Katsuyoshi in his review of Kamiya Masakazu's 紙屋正和 "Zen Kan shokōō no saisei to Butei no sazei zōshū" 前漢諸侯王國の財政と武帝の財政增收, has noted that Liu Pengzu (r. 154–92 BCE), the king of the Zhao State, had "considerable administrative power" till his death. See *Hōseishiki kenkyū* 法制史研究 29(1979): 234. Recently, Yasunaga Tomoaki 安永知晃 elaborated on this view in his "Zen Kan zenhanki no tai shokōō seisaku: Keitei chūgonen kaikaku no igi no saikentō" 前漢前半期の対諸侯王政策: 景帝中五年改革の意義の再檢討, *Jinbun ronkyū* 人文論究64/65 (2015): 79–95.

62. Ban Gu, *Hanshu*, 53.2422.

63. Loewe and Twitchett, *The Cambridge History of China*, vol. 1, 152–60.

64. For example, historian Sugimura Shinji has noted that the *Tui'en* (extension of grace) decree mentioned in this episode was issued eleven years later and therefore suggested that this passage was an anachronistic record; see Sugimra Shinji, "Kan

sho no gunkokubyō to nyūchō seido ni tsuite: Kan sho gunkokusei to ketsuen teki chūtai," 15.

65. Xing Bing 邢昺, *Xiaojing zhushu* 孝經注疏, 7.19, in *Shisanjing zhushu*, 2557. Henry Rosemont and Roger T. Ames, trans., *The Chinese Classic of Family Reverence: A Philosophical Translation of the Xiaojing* (Honolulu: University of Hawaii Press, 2009), 112.

66. Li Xueqin 李學勤, "Dingxian Bajiaolang Hanjian Rushu xiaoyi" 定縣八角廊漢簡儒書小議, *Jianbo yanjiu* 簡帛研究 1 (1993): 257–65; Li Xueqin, "Shilun Bajiaolang jian *Wenzi*" 試論八角廊簡〈文子〉, *Wenwu* 1996.1: 36–40.

67. Zhongguo shehui kexueyuan kaogu yanjiusuo, *Mancheng Han mu fajue baogao*, 1: 271–72. Lu Zhaoyin, *Mancheng Han mu*, 161–64. Zhao Shaozong, *Mancheng Han mu*, 164–65. For the so-called "colorful coins" (*huaqian* 花錢), see Liu Yuli 劉餘力 and Xu Bainian 徐柏年, "Luoyang Han mu chutu de jicidi huaqian ji xiangguan wenti" 洛陽漢墓出土的紀次第花錢及相關問題, *Luoyang daxue xuebao* 洛陽大學學報 2006.1: 11–13.

68. Lu Zhaoyin, *Mancheng Han mu*, 162.

69. Lu Zhaoyin, *Mancheng Han mu*, 161–62.

70. Qiu Xigui reads the second character as *pi* 匹; see his "Du kaogu fajue suode wenzi ziliao biji (yi)," 97–99.

71. The excavation report transcribes it as "yin qi jia" 飲其加, but Qiu Xigui suggests that the last character should be "you" 右; see his "Du kaogu fajue suode wenzi ziliao biji (yi)."

72. Bird script first appeared during the Eastern Zhou period. See W. Perceval Yetts, "'Bird Script' on Ancient Chinese Swords," *The Journal of the Royal Asiatic Society of Great Britain and Ireland* 3 (1934): 547–52. For a recent survey and study, see Cao Jinyan 曹錦炎, *Niaochongshu tongkao* 鳥蟲書通考 (Shanghai: Shanghai shuhua chubanshe, 1999).

73. Zhongguo shehui kexueyuan kaogu yanjiusuo, *Mancheng Han mu fajue baogao*, 1: 43. See also Zhang Zhenglang 張政烺 (=Xiao Yun 肖蘊), "Mancheng Han mu chutu de cuo jinyin niaochongshu tonghu" 滿城漢墓出土的錯金銀鳥蟲書銅壺, *Kaogu* 1972.5: 49–52; Zhang Zhenglang, "Guanyu Mancheng Han mu tonghu niaozhuan shiwen de taolun (sanpian)" 關於滿城漢墓銅壺鳥篆釋文的討論 (三篇), *Kaogu* 1979.4: 356–59. A slightly different transcription is found in Zhou Jun and Chen Jing, "Mancheng Han mu chutu tongqi mingwen yanjiu," 52. The English transla-tion is from Wen Fong, *The Great Bronze Age of China*, 331; see also François Louis, "Written Ornament—Ornamental Writing: Birdscript of the early Han Dynasty and the Art of Enchanting," *Ars Orientalis* 33 (2003): 10–31.

74. In 2014, scholars discovered a similar *hu* vessel with similar bird inscriptions in the previous collection of Paul Pelliot that dates from the same mid-Western Han period. This suggests that such inscriptions emphasizing longevity might not be unique to the Mancheng tombs. See Cao Jinyan, "Faguo Boxihe jiucang Xi Han niaochongshu tonghu mingwen yanjiu" 法國伯希和舊藏西漢鳥蟲書銅壺銘文研究, *Wenwu* 2015.11: 57–61.

75. Robin Yates, *Five Lost Classics: Tao, Huang-Lao, and Yin-Yang in Han China* (New York: Ballantine, 1997), 68–71; Yu Mingguang 于明光, *Huangdi sijing yu Huang-Lao sixiang* 黃帝四經與黃老思想 (Harbing: Heilongjiang renmin chubanshe, 1989), 255.

76. Sima Qian, *Shiji*, 118.3076, 130.3303.

77. Sima Qian, *Shiji*, 111.2741.

78. Li Xiangfeng, *Guanzi jiaozhu*, 3: 1166; Rickett, *Guanzi*, 1: 63.

79. Shuihudi Qin mu zhujian zhengli xiaozu 睡虎地秦墓竹簡整理小組, *Shuihudi Qin mu zhujian* 睡虎地秦墓竹簡 (Beijing: Wenwu chubanshe, 1990), 167.

80. Chen Qiyou, *Lüshi chunqiu xin jiaoshi*, 1413; Knoblock and Riegel, *The Annals of Lü Buwei*, 536.

81. Zhao Ye 趙曄, *Wu Yue chunqiu* 吳越春秋 (Nanjing: Jiangsu guji chubanshe, 1999), 131.

82. Zhao Ye, *Wu Yue chunqiu*, 131.

83. Zhongguo shehui kexueyuan kaogu yanjiusuo, *Mancheng Han mu fajue baogao*, 1: 81.

84. Pei Puyan 裴溥言, "Xunzi yu Shijing" 荀子與詩經, *Taiwan daxue wenshi zhexue bao* 台灣大學文史哲學報 17(1968): 180.

85. Jia Gongyan, *Yili zhushu* 30.161, in *Shisanjing zhushu*, 1105. John Steele's translation is "husband and wife . . . are of one flesh," Steele, *The I-Li or Book of Etiquette and Ceremonial*, 2: 17.

86. Zheng Shaozong, *Mancheng Han mu*, 65–69.

87. Liu Wenxing 劉文星, *Jun ren nanmian zhi shu: Xian Qin zhi Xi Han zhongye Huang Lao sichao yingxiang xia de xiushen sixiang yu zhiguo xueshuo* 君人南面之術：先秦至西漢中葉黃老思潮影響下的修身思想與治國學說 (Taipei: Zhongguo wenhua daxue huagang chubanbu, 2006).

88. For the concept of *tianxia*, see Yuri Pines, "Changing Views of Tianxia in Pre-Imperial Discourse," *Oriens Extremus* 43.1–2 (2002): 101–16. For Sarah Allan's comment, see her *Buried Ideas: Legends of Abdication and Ideal Government in Early Chinese Bamboo-Slip Manuscripts*, second edition (Albany, NY: SUNY Press, 2015), 13, note 7. See also Watanabe Shin'ichirō 渡辺信一郎, *Chūgoku kodai no ōken to tenka chitsujo: Nitchū hikakushi no shiten kara* 中国古代の王権と天下秩序: 日中比較史の視点から (Tokyo: Azekura Shobō, 2003).

89. Bonnie Honig, *Democracy and the Foreigner* (Princeton, NJ: Princeton University Press, 2001).

90. Poo Mu-chou, *Enemies of Civilization: Attitudes Toward Foreigners in Ancient Mesopotamia, Egypt, and China* (Albany, NY: SUNY Series in Chinese Philosophy and Culture, 2005); Hyun Jin Kim, *Ethnicity and Foreigners in Ancient Greece and China* (London: Gerald Duckworth, 2009).

91. Sima Qian, *Shiji*, 130.3292. William Theodore de Bary and Irene Bloom, trans., *Sources of Chinese Tradition: Volume 1: From Earliest Times to 1600* (New York: Columbia University Press, 1999), 282. Although both the *Shiji* and the *Hanshu* contain this passage, the two versions are not exactly the same. In the *Shiji* version, the character *xing* 形 appears before the character *shen* 神, whereas in the *Hanshu* version, the character *xing* is missing (see Ban Gu, *Hanshu*, 62.2714). So, in the collated *Shiji* edition published by Zhonghua shuju in 1959, the missing character 形 is added in brackets.

92. Chen Qiyou, *Lüshi chunqiu xin jiaoshi*, 87; Knoblock and Riegel, *The Annals of Lü Buwei*, 86.

93. Loewe and Twitchett, *The Cambridge History of China*, vol. 1, 48.

94. Yates, *Five Lost Classics*, 66–67; Yu Mingguang, *Huangdi sijing yu Huang-Lao sixiang*, 252.

95. Paul Goldin, *The Culture of Sex in Ancient China* (Honolulu: University of Hawaii Press, 2001), 71.

96. Kong Yingda, *Liji zhengyi*, 60.445, in *Shisanjing zhushu*; 2: 1673; Legge, *Li Chi: The Book of Rites*, 1: 411.

97. Kong Yingda, *Zhouyi zhengyi* 周易正義, 9.84, in *Shisanjing zhushu*, 96; Z. D. Sung, ed., *The Text of Yi King and its Appendixes* (Taipei: Ch'eng Wen, 1971), 350.

98. Jingmen shi bowuguan 荊門市博物館. *Guodian Chu mu zhujian* 郭店楚墓竹简 (Beijing: Wenwu chubanshe, 1998), 188.

99. Li Xiangfeng, *Guanzi jiaozhu*, 1: 52; Rickett, *Guanzi*, 1: 96.

100. The text reads: "If the self is not managed well, one cannot save himself; if the family is not managed well, family members cannot gather together; if the government is not managed well, functionaries cannot be dispatched; if the state is not managed well, the country will not belong to the ruler." (身不治，不能自保。家不治，不能相聚。官不治，不能相使。國不治，非其主之有也。) Yinqueshan Han mu zhujian zhengli xiaozu 銀雀山漢墓竹簡整理小組, *Yinqueshan Han mu zhujian* 銀雀山漢墓竹簡, 2 vols. (Beijing: Wenwu chubanshe, 1985–2010), 1: 132–33.

101. Kong Yingda, *Liji zhengyi*, 60.445, in *Shisanjing zhushu*, 2: 1673; Legge, *Li Chi: The Book of Rites*, 1: 411.

6. THE KING UNDER THE GAZE

1. Xuzhou bowuguan, "Jiangsu Tongshan xian Xi Han erhao yadongmu cailiao de zai buchong" 江蘇銅山縣西漢二號崖洞墓材料的再補充, *Kaogu* 1997.2: 36–46.

2. Wu Hung, "Rethinking East Asian Tombs: A Methodological Proposal," in *Dialogues in Art History, from Mesopotamian to Modern: Readings for a New Century*, ed. Elizabeth Cropper (Washington, DC: National Gallery of Art, 2009), 139–65.

3. Ban Gu, *Hanshu*, 99.4166.

4. Xuzhou bowuguan, "Xuzhou Shizishan bingmayong keng diyici fajue jianbao" 徐州獅子山兵馬俑坑第一次發掘簡報, *Wenwu* 1986. 12: 1–12; Shandong sheng kaogu yanjiusuo, "Zhangqiu shi Weishan Han mu peizangkeng" 章丘市危山漢墓陪葬坑, *Zhongguo kaoguxue nianjian* (2003) 中國考古學年鑑 (2003), 216–18; Cui Shengkuan 崔聖寬 and Hao Daohua 郝導華, "Qingzhou shi Xiangshan Han mu peizangkeng" 青州市香山漢墓陪葬坑, *Zhongguo kaoguxue nianjian* (2007), 269–72; Yangjiawan Han mu fajue xiaozu 楊家灣漢墓發掘小組, "Xianyang Yangjiawan Han mu fajue jianbao" 咸陽楊家灣漢墓發掘簡報, *Wenwu* 1977.10: 10–16. In the recently discovered mid-Western Han pit at Shanwangcun in Zibo, which has been attributed to Liu Hong 劉閎 (d. 110 BCE), King Huai of the Qi state, the underground army was situated in an underground manor; see Shandong sheng wenwu kaogu yanjiusuo and Linzi shi Linzi qu wenwu guanliju 臨淄市臨淄區文物管理局, "Shandong Linzi Shanwangcun Han dai bingmayong keng fajue jianbao" 山東臨淄山王村漢代兵馬俑坑發掘簡報, *Wenwu* 2016.6: 5–29; Shandong sheng wenwu kaogu yanjiusuo, Linzi shi Linzi qu wenwu guanliju, Han Weidong 韓偉東, Wei Chengmin 魏成敏, and Wang Huitian 王會田, *Linzi Shanwangcun Han dai bingmayong* 臨淄山王村漢代兵馬俑 (Beijing: Wenwu chubanshe, 2017).

5. Poo Mu-chou, *In Search of Personal Welfare: A View of Ancient Chinese Religion*, 41–68. For a case study, see Donald Harper, "A Chinese Demonology of the Third Century B.C.," *Harvard Journal of Asiatic Studies* 45.2 (1985): 459–98. This complexity might be understood as a common religion that transcends the boundary of the elite and the vulgar.

6. Sima Qian, *Shiji*, 9.400.

7. Knoblock and Riegel, *The Annals of Lü Buwei*, 595.

8. Xu Gan, *Balanced Discourses*, trans. John Makeham (New Haven, CT: Yale University Press, 2002), 20–21.

9. Zhang Shuandi, *Huainanzi jiaoshi*, 2: 2098. Major et al., *The Huainanzi*, 828.

10. Li Xiangfeng, *Guanzi jiao zhu*, 578; Rickett, *Guanzi*, 1: 416.

11. Jean-Paul Sartre, *Being and Nothingness: An Essay on Phenomenological Ontology*, trans. Hazel E. Barnes (London: Methuen, 1958), 256–57. Maurice Merleau-Ponty offers a similar view in his book *The Visible and the Invisible*, where he describes perception as a "chiasmus." See *The Visible and the Invisible* (Evanston, IL: Northwestern University Press, 1968).

12. Janne Seppänen, *The Power of the Gaze: An Introduction to Visual Literacy*, trans. Aijaleena Ahonen and Kris Clarke (New York: Peter Lang, 2006), 70.

13. Jacques Lacan, *Four Fundamental Concepts of Psychoanalysis*, trans. Alan Sheridan (London: Hogarth, 1977), 67–122.

14. Li Xiangfeng, *Guanzi jiaozhu*, 3: 1166. For the English translation, see Rickett, *Guanzi*, 1: 63.

15. Sima Qian, *Shiji*, 6.236.

16. Xu Fuguan 徐復觀, *Liang Han sixiangshi* 兩漢思想史, 3 vols. (Shanghai: Huadong shifan chubanshe, 2001), 3: 217–18.

17. Zhu Qianzhi, *Laozi jiaoshi*, 214–18; for the English translation, see D.C. Lau, trans., *Tao Te Ching* (New York: Columbia University Press, 1989), 79, slightly modified. For a comment on this passage, see Robert Moss, trans., *Dao De Jing: The Book of the Way* (Berkeley: University of California Press, 2001), 139–40.

18. Penelope J. E. Davies, *Death and the Emperor: Roman Imperial Funerary Monuments, from Augustus to Marcus Aurelius* (Austin: University of Texas Press, 2004), 9–10.

19. In the *Outer Commentary to the Book of Songs by Master Han* (*Hanshi waizhuan* 韓詩外傳), edited approximately in the mid-second century BCE, there was one brief yet important account of the funeral ritual procedure: "After the body was put into the coffin, and that put into the outer coffin, vessels are set out for the sacrifice." (既斂而槨，布器而祭。) James R. Hightower, *Han Shih Wai Chuan: Han Ying's Illustration of the Didactic Application of the Classic Songs* (Cambridge, MA: Harvard University Press, 1952), 307. Although the exact location for the sacrifice is not specified in this short passage, it seems plausible that a standard Western Han funeral usually ended with a sacrifice. Some sacrifices were even performed as the grave was being filled. See Li Rusen 李如森, *Han dai sangzang zhidu* 漢代喪葬制度 (Changchun: Jilin renmin chubanshe, 1995), 71–72.

20. In 1959, Chinese archaeologists discovered a late Western Han manuscript of the *Book Etiquette and Ceremonial* from Mozuizi tomb 6 at Wuwei, which included 469 bamboo strips and 27,298 characters. This finding is evidence of the text's reception and circulation during the Western Han period. See Gansu Sheng bo wu guan 甘肅省博物館, Zhongguo kexueyuan kaogu yanjiusuo 中國科學院考古研究所, *Wuwei Han jian* 武威漢簡 (Beijing: Wenwu chubanshe, 1964).

21. Fan Ye, *Hou Hanshu*, 3144ff.

22. Arnold Van Gennep, *The Rites of Passage* (Chicago: The University of Chicago Press, 1960), 146–65. Richard Huntington and Peter Metcalf, *Celebrations of Death: The Anthropology of Mortuary Ritual* (Cambridge: Cambridge University Press, 1979).

In the Chinese context, see James L. Watson and Evelyn S. Rawski, *Death Ritual in Late Imperial and Modern China* (Berkeley: University of California Press, 1988).

23. Jia Gongyan, *Yili zhu shu*, 35.184ff, in *Shisanjing zhushu*, 1128ff. For a complete English translation, see Steele, *The I-li or Book of Etiquette and Ceremonial*, 2: 45ff. See also Joy Beckman, "Layers of Being: Bodies, Objects and Spaces in Warring States Burials," PhD diss., University of Chicago, 2006, 52–137.

24. Jia Gongyan, *Yili zhushu*, 38.202, in *Shisanjing zhushu*, 1146. Steele, *The I-li or Book of Etiquette and Ceremonial*, 2: 78–81.

25. Jia Gongyan, *Yili zhushu*, 41.219, in *Shisanjing zhushu*, 1163. Steele, *The I-li or Book of Etiquette and Ceremonial*, 2: 102–3.

26. It is recorded that when Emperor Wu of the Western Han died, his bier was laid in the main hall (*Qian Dian* 前殿) of the Weiyang Palace. See Ban Gu, *Hanshu*, 6.212.

27. "The soul carriage (*rongche* 容車) is the chariot of appearance and ornament representing the living situations" (容車, 容飾之車, 象生時也。), Fan Ye, *Hou Hanshu*, 742.

28. Fan Ye, *Hou Hanshu*, 3650.

29. It was reported that Confucius himself once went to watch Ji Zha burying his son; Legge, *Li Chi: Book of Rites*, 1: 192–93.

30. Fan Ye, *Hou Hanshu*, 3148; Du You, *Tongdian*, 2135–140. Kirimoto Tota 桐本東太, "Go Kan ōchō no shisha girei—Go Kanjo gireisho genhen yakuchūkō (2)" 後漢王朝の死者儀禮 —『後漢書』禮儀志・下篇譯注稿(2), *Shigaku* 58.1 (1988): 73–90, esp. 88. See also Michael Loewe, "The Imperial Way of Death in Han China," in *State and Court Ritual in China*, ed. Joseph P. McDermott (Cambridge: Cambridge University Press, 1999), 81–111.

31. Ban Gu, *Hanshu*, 40.2062.

32. Ban Gu, *Hanshu*, 93.3739.

33. Ban Gu, *Hanshu*, 97.4003.

34. Duan Yucai 段玉裁, *Shuowen jiezi zhu* 說文解字註 (Hangzhou: Zhejiang guji chubanshe, 1999), 48. Xu Shen 許慎 actually quoted the *The Book of Rites* in which Guo-zi gao said, "Burying means hiding away." James Legge, *Li Chi: The Book of Rites*, 1: 155.

35. Sima Qian, *Shiji*, 6.257.

36. Ban Gu, *Hanshu*, 44.2145.

37. This phrase might actually refer to a bronze casket (inside) a stone chamber, for two layers of secrecy. I thank Professor Barbieri-Low for this insight.

38. Wang Pinzhen 王聘珍, *Da Dai liji jiegu* 大戴禮記解詁 (Beijing: Zhonghua shuju, 1983), 59.

39. Ban Gu, *Hanshu*, 1.81.

40. Ban Gu, *Hanshu*, 19.796.

41. Wang Kailuan 王愷鑾, *Yin Wenzi jiaozheng* 尹文子校正, *Minguo congshu* 民國叢書 edition, vol. 05009, no. 1, 3. The current *Yinwen zi* 尹文子 text is dated to the fourth to sixth centuries CE.

42. Chen Qiyou, *Lüshi chunqiu xin jiaoshi*, 543; Knoblock and Riegel, *The Annals of Lü Buwei*, 231.

43. E. F. Schmidt, *Persepolis III: The Royal Tombs and Other Monuments* (Chicago: University of Chicago Press, 1970). A recent discussion can be found in Matthew P. Canepa, "Topographies of Power, Theorizing the Visual, Spatial and Ritual Contexts of Rock Reliefs in Ancient Iran," in *Of Rocks and Water: Towards an Archaeology of Place*, ed. Omur Harmanşah (Oxford: Oxbow, 2014), 53–92.

44. Fan Ye, *Hou Hanshu*, 41.1402, 45.1523.

45. Sima Qian, *Shiji*, 12.480.

46. Jie Shi, "The Mancheng Tombs: Shaping the Afterlife of the 'Kingdom within the Mountains.'"

47. Duan Yucai, *Shuowen jiezi zhu*, 587.

48. Shanxi sheng kaogusuo and Taiyuan shi wenwu guanli weiyuanhui, *Taiyuan Jin guo Zhao qing mu* 太原晉國趙卿墓 (Beijing: Wenwu chubanshe, 1996)

49. Huang Xiaofen, *Han mu de kaoguxue yanjiu*, 16, 20.

50. Guolong Lai, "Death and the Otherworldly Journey in Early China as Seen through Tomb Texts, Travel Paraphernalia, and Road Rituals," *Asia Major* 18.1 (2005): 1–44.

51. The only description is "the spirit vessels are laid at the side of the coffin" 藏器於旁. Jia Gongyan, *Yili zhushu*, 40.213, in *Shisanjing zhushu*, 1157. Steele, *The I-li or Book of Etiquette and Ceremonial*, 2: 91.

52. Tian He 田河, "Chutu Zhanguo qiance suoji mingwu fenlei huishi" 出土戰國遣冊所記名物分類彙釋 (PhD dissertation, Jilin University, 2007). Rarely, the inventory only lists the compartments that burial objects were supposed to fill. In the case of Baoshan tomb no. 2, the "tail (west) compartment" (*xiangwei* 廂尾) was reserved for traveling paraphernalia, and some bronze food vessels were interred in the "dining room" (*shishi* 食室); see Hubei sheng Jingsha tielu kaogudui, *Baoshan Chu mu*, 1: 369. Chen Wei read *xiangwei* as "the west and north compartments"; see Chen Wei 陳偉, *Baoshan Chu jian chutan* 包山楚簡初探 (Wuhan: Wuhan daxue chubanshe, 1996), 192–97.

53. Jia Gongyan, *Yili zhushu*, 44.236, in *Shisanjing zhushu*, 1180. Steele, *The I-li or Book of Etiquette and Ceremonial*, 2: 130.

54. Xing Bing, *Lunyu zhushu* 論語注疏, 11.43, in *Shisanjing zhushu*, 2498. James Legge, *The Life and Teachings of Confucius: With Explanatory Notes* (London: Trübner, 1867), 185. Scholars of Chinese philosophy or religion have extensively interpreted this statement from various perspectives; see Donald N. Blakeley, "The *Analects* on Death," *Journal of Chinese Philosophy* 37.3 (2010): 397–416.

55. Hayashi Minao 林巳奈夫 once argued that Eastern Zhou bronzes were buried in the tombs to serve the deceased in the "underworld" (*xiatu* 下土), a term inscribed on one bronze tripod made on behalf of Aicheng Shu 哀成叔. Hayashi's argument is largely based on his reading of the sentence, "shi yu xiatu" 尸於下土, which is translated as "Though Ai Chengshu is in the underground realm." See Hayashi Minao, "Concerning the Inscription 'May Sons and Grandsons Eternally Use This Vessel,'" trans. Elizabeth Childs-Johnson, *Artibus Asiae* 53.1/2 (1993): 51–58. Li Xueqin and Zhang Zhenglang expresses a similar ideas; see Zhang Zhenglang 張政烺, "Ai Chengshu ding shiwen" 哀成叔鼎釋文, in his *Jiagu jiwen yu Shang Zhou shi yanjiu* 甲骨金文與商周史研究 (Beijing: Zhonghua shuju, 2012), 266, and Li Xueqin, "Zheng ren jinwen liangzhong duidu" 鄭人金文兩種對讀, in *Tongxiang wenming zhilu* 通向文明之路 (Beijing: Shangwu yinshuguan, 2010), 166. However, there are two questions about this theory. First, whether the term *xiatu* means "underworld" or simply "the earthly world" still remains unclear. See Huang Tingqi 黃庭頎, "Ai Chengshu mingwen xinkao" 哀成叔銘文新考, *Zhongguo wenxue yanjiu* 中國文學研究 41(2016): 41–66, esp. 20. Second, even if the deceased's performance of temple sacrifice was truly implied in Eastern Zhou vertical pit tombs, as Hayashi argued, then the fact that most interred ritual vessels were not displayed in such neat fashions as prescribed in the *Book of Etiquette and Ceremonial* text demonstrates that there was little interest in making this underground

"sacrifice" simulate the well-ordered ones aboveground. Instead, the arrangement of grave goods is reminiscent of the concealed sacrificial pits as those discovered in Xinzheng, Henan; see Henan sheng wenwu kaogu yanjiusuo, *Xinzheng Zheng guo jisi yizhi* 新鄭鄭國祭祀遺址, 2 vols. (Zhengzhou: Daxiang chubanshe, 2006). For the Egyptian view of the underworld, see John H. Taylor, *Journey Through the Afterlife: Ancient Egyptian Book of the Dead* (Cambridge, MA: Harvard University Press, 2010).

56. Mark E. Lewis, *The Construction of Space in Early China* (Albany, NY: SUNY Press, 2005), 2.

57. Alain Thote, "Continuities and Discontinuities: Chu Burials during the Eastern Zhou Period," in *Exploring China's Past: New Discoveries and Studies in Archaeology and Art*, ed. R. Whitfield and Wang Tao (London: Saffron International Series in Chinese Archaeology and Art, 2000), 189–204.

58. W. J. T. Mitchell, *Iconology: Image, Text, Ideology* (Chicago: University of Chicago Press, 1986), 11; Michel Foucault, *The Order of Things: An Archaeology of the Human Sciences* (London: Routledge, 2002), 19.

59. The text was excavated from Shuihudi tomb no. 77 (dated ca. 157–140 BCE) in present-day Yunmeng, Hubei; see Hubei sheng wenwu kaogu yanjiusuo and Yunmeng xian bowuguan 雲夢縣博物館, "Hubei Yunmeng Shuihudi M77 fajue jianbao" 湖北雲夢睡虎地M77發掘簡報, *Jianghan kaogu* 2008.4: 31–37; Xiong Beisheng 熊北生, Chen Wei 陳偉, and Cai Dan 蔡丹, "Hubei Yunmeng Shuihudi 77 hao Han mu chutu jiandu gaishu" 湖北雲夢睡虎地77號漢墓出土簡牘概述, *Wenwu* 2018.3: 43–53.

60. Peng Hao 彭浩, "Du Yunmeng Shuihudi M77 Han jian zanglü" 讀雲夢睡虎地M77漢簡葬律, *Jianghan kaogu* 2009.4: 130–34.

61. Marquises (*hou* 侯) and kings (*wang* 王) were often juxtaposed in Western Han texts. While the former's fief was institutionally parallel to the county (*xian* 縣), the latter was equal to the commandery (*jun* 郡). See Tang Qiling 湯其領, "Yinwan Han mu jiandu zhong youguan junxian houguo lizhi de jige wenti" 尹灣漢墓簡牘中有關郡縣侯國吏治的幾個問題, *Shixue yuekan* 史學月刊 2005.11: 16–9.

62. These include one comment made by Zheng Xuan when he annotated the *Rites of Zhou*, and one record in Ban Gu's *History of Han*; see Kong Yingda, *Zhouli zhengyi*, 23.148, in *Shisanjing zhushu*, 786; Ban Gu, *Hanshu*, 5.145. See also Du Guichi 杜貴墀, *Han lü jizheng* 漢律輯證, Xiuding falüguan 修訂法律館 edition (1897), 5.7.

63. Hebei sheng wenwu yanjiusuo, *Cuo mu*, 1: 104–10.

64. It was initially identified as a diagram of city (*Chengyitu* 城邑圖) in He Jiejun 何介鈞, *Mawangdui er san hao Han mu* 馬王堆二三號漢墓 (Beijing: Wenwu chubanshe, 2003), 90, and later it was re-identified as a diagram of burial in Qiu Xigui 裘錫圭, *Changsha Mawangdui Han mu jianbo jicheng* 長沙馬王堆漢墓簡帛集成, 7 vols. (Beijing: Zhonghua shuju, 2014), vols. 2, 7.

65. Cao Lüning 曹旅寧, "Han chu zanglü yu Mawangdui sanhao mu zhu Li Xi" 漢初葬律與馬王堆三號墓主利豨, in *Jinian Mawangdui Han mu fajue sishi zhounian guoji xueshu yantaohui lunwenji* 紀念馬王堆漢墓發掘四十週年國際學術研討會論文集, ed. Hunan sheng bowuguan (Changsha: Yuelu shuyuan, 2016), 52–55. Dong Shan 董珊 argues that the building in the lower part of the diagram represents the former residence of the deceased, see his "Mawangdui sanhao Han mu chutu de Juzangtu" 馬王堆三號漢墓出土的居葬圖, in his *Jianbo wenxian kaoshi luncong* 簡帛文獻考釋論叢 (Shanghai: Shanghai guji chubanshe, 2014), 244–50. This possibility cannot be ruled out, either.

66. Ban Gu, *Hanshu*, 72.3070. Liu Xu 劉煦, *Jiu Tangshu* 舊唐書 (Beijing: Zhonghua shuju, 1975), 72.2568.

67. Sun Xingyan et al., *Han guan liuzhong*, 106.

68. This information is preserved in a commentary in Fan Ye, *Hou Hanshu*, 3144. Edited for the emperor during the Three Kingdoms period (220–280 CE) as a reference, *Huanglan* was lost during the Tang (618–907 CE). The current edition was a compilation of excerpts that survived in other books edited during the pre-Tang period.

69. See note 5.

70. The earliest mural in China was found in one of the palaces of the Qin at Xianyang during the late Eastern Zhou period, about the third century BCE; see Shaanxi sheng kaogu yanjiusuo, *Qindu Xianyang kaogu baogao* 秦都咸陽考古報告 (Beijing: Kexue chubanshe, 2004).

71. Powers, *Art and Political Expression in Early China*.

72. Sarah M. Nelson, "Feasting the Ancestors in Early China," in *The Archaeology and Politics of Food and Feasting in Early States and Empires*, ed. Tamara L. Bray (New York: Kluwer Academic/Plenum, 2003), 65–90; Roel Sterckx, "Food and Philosophy in Early China," in *Of Tripod and Palate: Food, Politics, and Religion in Traditional China*, ed. Roel Sterckx (New York: Palgrave Macmillan, 2005), 34–61.

73. An early example of such narrative pictures can be found in pictorial bronzes during the Eastern Zhou period; see Esther Jacobson, "The Structure of Narrative in Early Chinese Pictorial Vessels," *Representations* 8 (1984): 61–83.

74. Sun Ji, *Handai wuzhi wenhua ziliao tushuo*, 259.

75. Zhongguo shehui kexueyuan kaogu yanjiusuo, *Mancheng Han mu fajue baogao*, 1: 78.

76. Sun Ji, *Handai wuzhi wenhua ziliao tushuo*, 13–17, esp. 15, illus. 4–4, 4–5. For examples, see Henan Bowuyuan 河南博物院, *Henan chutu Handai jianzhu mingqi* 河南出土漢代建築明器 (Zhengzhou: Daxiang chubanshe, 2002), 99–103. In general, a vessel with a pointed or round bottom does not seem to be typically Chinese. One similar example was uncovered in an Eastern Han princely tomb at Dingxian. Also having a flat mouth and a pointed bottom, this small bronze object is about twice as large as the vases found in Liu Sheng's tomb yet having no holes but with a handle. See Dingxian bowuguan, "Hebei Dingxian 43 hao Han mu fajue jianbao," *Wenwu* 1973.11: 8–20. Sun Ji identifies this object as a suspended bucket to hold water. See Sun Ji, *Handai wuzhi wenhua ziliao tushuo*, 259.

77. Remarkably, similar sets of bronze miniaturized vessels with pointed bottoms were found in a Western Zhou cemetery at Zhuyuangou 竹園溝 in Baoji. The excavation report problematically identifies them as "drinking cups." See Lu Liancheng and Hu Zhisheng, *Baoji Yu guo mudi*, 1: 78, 2: pl. 30. There were also ceramic versions of such small vessels excavated from the same cemetery, see 1: 91, 2: pl. 41.

78. Lai, *Excavating the Afterlife: The Archaeology of Early Chinese Religion*.

79. Henan sheng wenwu yanjiusuo 河南省文物研究所. *Xinyang Chu mu* 信陽楚墓 (Beijing: Wenwu chubanshe, 1986), 84, fig. 58.

80. Machida Akira 町田章, "Kahoku chihō ni okeru Kanbo no kōzō" 華北地方における漢墓の構造, *Tōhō gakuhō* 49 (1977): 1–66, esp. 3–6.

81. For the Xi'an region, see Han Baoquan 韓保全 et al., *Xi'an Longshouyuan Han mu* 西安龍首原漢墓 (Lanzhou: Xibei daxue chubanshe, 1999), 222–28; for the Luoyang region, see Zhongguo kexueyuan kaogu yanjiusuo, *Luoyang Shaogou Han mu*, fig.101; for the Guangzhou region, see Guangzhou shi wenwu guanli weiyuanhui and Guangzhou shi bowuguan, *Guangzhou Han mu*, 1: 223–27; however, the Xuzhou

region was perhaps the first to adopt this everyday ceramic assemblage, including the well. See Zhou Xueying, "Handai jianzhu mingqi tanyuan" 漢代建筑明器探源, in *Jianzhushi lunwenji* 建築史論文集 17 (2003): 12–24, esp. 22–23. For the Xuzhou region, see Song Rong 宋蓉, "Xuzhou diqu Xi Han muzang de fenqi he wenhua yinsu fenxi" 徐州地區西漢墓葬的分期和文化因素分析, *Huaxia kaogu* 2010. 4: 101–13.

82. Examples are ample. One such example is the Mishan 米山 tomb no. 1 near Xuzhou, dating to the early Western Han. Mixed with the assemblage of the ritual vessel set of *ding, hu, fang*, and *he*, a miniature well, a basin, and a standing figurine were buried next to one another. Xuzhou bowuguan, "Jiangsu Xuzhou Mishan Han mu," 江蘇徐州米山漢墓 *Kaogu* 1996.4: 36–37, 44.

83. Jessica Rawson, "Ritual Vessel Changes in the Warring States, Qin and Han Periods," in *Regional Culture, Religion, and Arts Before the Seventh Century* 中世紀以前的地域文化、宗教與藝術, papers from the Third International Conference on Sinology, History Section, ed. Hsing I-tien (Taipei: Academia Sinica, 2002), 36–37.

84. An Jinhuai 安金槐, *Mixian Dahuting Han mu* 密縣打虎亭漢墓 (Beijing: Wenwu chubanshe, 1993), 120–184. See also Michèle Pirazolli-t'Serstevens, "Two Eastern Han Sites: Dahuting and Houshiguo," in *China's Early Empires: A Re-Appraisal*, ed. Michael Nylan and Michael Loewe (Cambridge: Cambridge University Press, 2010), 83–113.

85. In Hebei, tomb murals during the Eastern Han dynasty show a similar narrative; for a detailed study, see Hsin-mei Agnes Hsu, "Pictorial Eulogies in Three Eastern Han Tombs" (PhD dissertation, University of Pennsylvania, 2004).

86. One of the earliest known murals decorated the Xianyang Palace of the Qin dynasty and is dated to the third century BCE; see Shaanxi sheng kaogu yanjiusuo, *Qin du Xianyang kaogu baogao.*

87. Among the seventy excavated princely tombs, only two were painted. Besides Zhao Mo's tomb, there was a wall painting of fantastic animals in the front chamber of the tomb at Shiyuan but without narrative content. See Yan Genqi, *Mangdangshan Xi Han Liangwang mudi*, 115–19.

88. Powers, *Art and Political Expression in Early China.*

89. Michael Nylan, "Toward an Archaeology of Writing: Text, Ritual, and the Culture of Public Display in the Classical Period (475 B.C.E–220 C.E.)," in *Text and Ritual in Early China*, ed. Martin Kern (Seattle: University of Washington Press, 2005), 3–49, esp. 35–36.

90. One opinion holds that images can generate both representational and presentational seeing. See Richard Wollheim, "Seeing-As, Seeing-In, and Pictorial Representation," in his *Art and Its Objects: With Six Supplementary Essays* (Cambridge: Cambridge University Press, 1980), 205–26. Another theory regards object as image in a broad semiotic view. For example, D. Hebdige, "Object as Image: The Italian Scooter Cycle," in *Material Culture: Critical Concepts in the Social Sciences*, ed. Victor Buchli (London: Routledge, 2004), 2: 121–59. But these interesting observations do not dismiss the difference between image and object in broader terms, particularly phenomenological.

91. The following simple intuition can prove this point. If one looks at a painted chariot, one will identify it immediately as a *chariot* proper no matter how small it is. But if one looks at a freestanding miniature chariot, he or she will see a model instead of a chariot.

92. As Wang Chong succinctly remarked: "The presence of an empty and fictional image does not necessarily guarantee the existence of the real thing." (*kongxu zhi xiang, bubi shiyou* 空虛之象,不必實有.) See Huang Hui, *Lunheng jiaoshi*, 162.

CONCLUSION

1. In this instance, modeling is a scientific activity, the aim of which is to make a particular part or feature of the world easier to understand, define, quantify, visualize, or simulate by referencing it to existing and (usually) commonly accepted knowledge. One of the best examples of such scientific modeling in ancient China is perhaps the cosmological model of *Gaitian* 蓋天 theory, which compares the shape of the universe to a carriage.

2. Shandong Heze diqu Han mu fajue xiaozu, "Juye Hongtushan Xi Han mu."

3. For these two examples, see Nanjing bowuyuan and Tongshan xian wenhuaguan, "Tongshan Guishan erhao Xihan Yadong mu"; Henan sheng wenwu kaogu yanjiusuo, *Yongcheng Xi Han Liangguo wangling yu qinyuan*, 93, fig. 64.

4. Guangzhou shi wenwu guanli weiyuanhui et al., *Xi Han Nanyue wang mu*, 1: 406–7.

5. Qu Yongxin 曲用心, "Lüelun Lingnan diqu Xi Han zaoqi qingtongqi de tezheng ji chengyin" 略論嶺南地區西漢早期青銅器的特徵及成因, *Dongnan wenhua* 2009.4: 65.

6. Jiang Yingyu 蔣廷瑜, "Xi Han Nanyue guo shiqi de tongtong" 西漢南越國時期的銅桶, *Dongnan wenhua* 2002.12: 38–43.

7. Guangzhou shi wenwu guanli weiyuanhui et al., *Xi Han Nanyue wang mu*, 1: fig. 38.

8. As the Qing classist Pi Xirui (1850–1908) already noted, Confucianism reached its peak between the late Western Han and the Eastern Han periods; Pi Xirui 皮錫瑞, *Jingxue lishi* 經學歷史 (Beijing: Zhonghua shuju, 1959), 101.

9. The word "thing" basically means entity, matter, or body, and the word "object" is derived from the Medieval Latin *objectum*, which denotes "things put before." These two concepts generally are used as synonyms, though not without philosophic reflections. For example, Martin Heidegger suggests that the two terms have very different meanings. While the term *object* assumes its opposition—subject—is epistemological, the term *thing* has an ontological meaning of being in the world. For a general survey of theories on things, see Bill Brown, "Thing Theory," *Critical Inquiry* 28.1 (2001): 1–22.

10. A similar mechanism was described by the French thinker Jacques Lacan as the "mirror stage," in which the ego is formed via the process of identifying with one's own specular image. But the image of a unified body is a fantasy that does not correspond with the vulnerable and uncoordinated body experience of the infant. However, the mirror stage does not represent merely a moment in the life of an infant; as a mechanism for structuring subjectivity, it keeps functioning throughout a person's life as it shapes the subject's ego with distorted mirror images. By the early 1950s, Lacan no longer regards the mirror stage simply as a moment in the life of the infant but sees it as also representing a permanent structure of subjectivity, the paradigm of the imaginary order; it is a stadium (stade) in which the subject is permanently caught and captivated by his own image: "[The mirror stage is] a phenomenon to which I assign a twofold value. In the first place, it has historical value as it marks a decisive turning-point in the mental development of the child. In the second place,

it typifies an essential libidinal relationship with the body-image." Jacques Lacan, "Some Reflections on the Ego," *International Journal of Psycho-Analysis* 34 (1953): 11–17.

11. Guangzhou shi wenwu guanli weiyuanhui et al., *Xi Han Nanyue wang mu*, 1:202, 209–10.

12. Erwin Panofsky, *Studies in Iconology: Humanistic Themes in the Art of the Renaissance*.

13. Although this concept was denounced by many scholars, including Earnest Gombrich, Nelson Goodman, Norman Bryson, and Miekel Bal among others, as Branko Mitrović has recently reminded us, "Scholars in the humanities are often not aware how obsolete the view that there is no innocent eye has become." See Mitrović, "A Defence of Light: Ernst Gombrich, the Innocent Eye and Seeing in Perspective," *Journal of Art Historiography* 3 (2010): 4. The psychologist Zenon Pylyshin has demonstrated that perception is impervious to the direct influence of conceptual thinking. The intuitive grasp of space, unpolluted by subsequent conceptual thinking, is independent of any prior interpretation. Zenon Pylyshyn, *Seeing and Visualizing* (Cambridge, MA: MIT Press, 2003), 64–68.

14. Erwin Panofsky, foreword to the second German edition of his *Idea: Ein Beitrag zur Begriffsgeschichte der älteren Kunsttheorie* (Berlin: Wissenschaftsverlag Volker Spiess, 1993), ii (preface to 1959 edition). For a discussion, see Georges Didi-Huberman, *Confronting Images: Questioning the Ends of a Certain History of Art* (University Park: Pennsylvania State University, 2005), xvi.

15. Ernst Gombrich, *Symbolic Images: Studies in the Art of the Renaissance* (London: Phaidon, 1972), introduction.

16. Umberto Eco, *The Limits of Interpretation* (Bloomington: Indiana University Press, 1990); Umberto Eco, *Interpretation and Overinterpretation* (Cambridge: Cambridge University Press, 1992).

17. John A. Pope, "Sinology or Art History: Notes on Method in the Study of Chinese Art," *Harvard Journal of Asiatic Studies* 10.3/4 (1947): 388–417.

18. For Egyptian tombs, see Salima Ikram, *Death and Burial in Ancient Egypt* (Cairo: American University in Cairo Press, 2015), and Aidan Dodson and Salima Ikram, *The Tomb in Ancient Egypt: Royal and Private Sepulchres from the Early Dynastic Period to the Romans* (London: Thames & Hudson, 2008); for Mesopotamian tombs, see Andrew C. Cohen, *Death Rituals, Ideology, and the Development of Early Mesopotamian Kingship: Towards a New Understanding of Iraq's Royal Cemetery of Ur* (Leiden: Brill Styx, 2005); for Persian tombs, see Matthew Canepa, *The Iranian Expanse: Transforming Royal Identity through Architecture, Landscape, and the Built Environment, 550 BCE–642 CE* (Berkeley: University of California Press, 2018), 211–32; for Roman tombs, see Davies, *Death and the Emperor: Roman Imperial Funerary Monuments from Augustus to Marcus Aurelius*.

19. Etim E. Okon, "Religion and Politics in Ancient Egypt," *The American Journal of Social and Management Sciences* 3.3 (2012): 93–98.

20. See Ikram, *Death and Burial in Ancient Egypt*, and Dodson and Ikram, *The Tomb in Ancient Egypt*.

BIBLIOGRAPHY

Abe, Yukinobu 阿部幸信. "Zen Kan jidai ni okeru naigai no henken—insei no shiten kara" 前漢時代における内外觀の變遷—印制の視點から. *Chugokū shikagu*中国史学 18 (2008): 121–40.

Akikawa, Mitsuhiko 秋川光彦. "Zen-Kan buntei no taishōkoō satsu: Go sō shiichi koku no ran no ichi haikei toshite" 前漢文帝の対諸侯王策: 呉楚七国の乱の一背景として. *Taishō Daigaku Daigakuin kenkyū ronshū* 大正大學大學院研究論集 25 (2001): 119–32.

Aldred, Cyril and A. T. Sandison. "The Tomb of Akhenaten at Thebes [and Appendix]." *The Journal of Egyptian Archaeology* 47 (1961): 41–65.

Allan, Sarah. *Buried Ideas: Legends of Abdication and Ideal Government in Early Chinese Bamboo-Slip Manuscripts.* 2nd ed. Albany, NY: SUNY Press, 2015.

——. *The Way of Water and Sprouts of Virtue.* Albany, NY: SUNY Press, 1997.

Ames, Roger. *The Art of Rulership: A Study of Ancient Chinese Political Thought.* Albany, NY: SUNY, 1994.

An, Jinhuai 安金槐. *Mixian Dahuting Han mu* 密縣打虎亭漢墓. Beijing: Wenwu chubanshe, 1994.

An, Zuozhang 安作璋 and Xiong Tieji 熊鐵基. *Qin Han guanzhi shigao* 秦漢官制史稿. Ji'nan: Qilu shushe, 2007.

Armbruster, B. R. "Technologische Aspekte der Goldschmiedekunst aus Arzan 2." In *Der skythenzeitlichen Fürstenkurgan Arzan 2 in Tuva*, ed. Chugunov, K.V., H. Parzinger, and A. Nagler, 183–99. Berlin: Archäologie in Eurasien, 2010.

Armheim, Rudolf. *The Power of the Center: A Study of Composition in the Visual Arts*, Revised edition. Berkeley: University of California Press, 1982.

Aruz, Joan. *The Golden Deer of Eurasia.* New York: Metropolitian Museum of Art, 2000.

Asano, Yūichi 浅野裕一. *Kō-Rō-dō no seiritsu to tenkai* 黄老道の成立と展開. Tokyo: Sōbunsha, 1992.

Bachelard, Gaston. *The Poetics of Space.* Trans. M. Jolas. Boston: Beacon, 1994.

Bagley, Robert. "Ornament, Representation, and Imaginary Animals in Bronze Age China." *Arts Asiatiques* 61 (2006): 17–29.

——. "Shang Archaeology." In *Cambridge History of Ancient China: From the Origins of Civilisation to 221 B.C.*, ed. Michael Loewe and Edward Shaughnessy, 185–94. Cambridge: Cambridge University Press, 1999.

Bai, Yunxiang 白雲翔. "Handai chidu de kaogu faxian ji xiangguan wenti yanjiu" 漢代尺度的考古發現及相關問題研究. *Dongnan wenhua* 東南文化 2014.2: 85–93.

Ban, Gu 班固. *Hanshu* 漢書. Beijing: Zhonghua shuju, 1962.

Baoli cang jin bianji weiyuanhui 保利藏金編輯委員會, *Baoli cang jin: Baoli ishu bowuguan jingpin xuan* 保利藏金: 保利藝術博物館精品選. Guangzhou: Lingnan meishu chubanshe, 1999.

Barbieri-Low, Anthony J. *Artisans in Early Imperial China*. Seattle: University of Washington Press, 2007.

Barbieri-Low, Anthony J. and Robin D. S. Yates. *Law, State, and Society in Early Imperial China (2 vols): A Study with Critical Edition and Translation of the Legal Texts from Zhangjiashan Tomb no. 247*. Leiden: Brill, 2015.

Bary, William Theodore De. *Sources of East Asian Tradition: Premodern Asia, Volume 1*. New York: Columbia University Press, 2008.

Bary, William Theodore de and Irene Bloom. *Sources of Chinese Tradition: Volume 1: From Earliest Times to 1600*. New York: Columbia University Press, 1999.

Baxter, William and Laurent Sagart. Baxter-Sagart Old Chinese Reconstruction, version 1.1, 2014, http://ocbaxtersagart.lsait.lsa.umich.edu/BaxterSagartOCbyMandarinMC2014 -09-20.pdf.

Beckman, Joy. "Layers of Being: Bodies, Objects and Spaces in Warring States Burials." PhD diss., University of Chicago, 2006.

Beijing shi wenwu guanlichu 北京市文物管理處. "Beijing shi xin shouji de Shang Zhou qingtongqi" 北京市新徵集的商周青銅器. *Wenwu ziliao congkan* 文物資料叢刊2 (1978): 14–21.

Beijing shi wenwu yanjiusuo 北京市文物研究所. *Jundushan mudi: Hulugou yu Xiliangguang* 军都山墓地：葫蘆溝與西梁洸. Two volumes. Beijing: Wenwu chubanshe, 2009.

——. *Jundushan mudi: Yuhuangmiao* 軍都山墓地：玉皇廟. Four volumes. Beijing: Wenwu chubanshe, 2007.

Bielenstein, Hans. *The Bureaucracy of Han Times*. Cambridge: Cambridge University Press, 1980.

Birch, Cyril Brich. *Anthology of Chinese Literature: From Early Times to the Fourteenth Century*. Two volumes. New York: Grove, 1965.

Black, Alison H. "Gender and Cosmology in Chinese Correlative Thinking." In *Gender and Religion: On the Complexity of Symbols*, ed. Caroline Walker Bynum et al., 166–95. Boston: Beacon, 1986.

Blakeley, Donald N. "The *Analects* on Death." *Journal of Chinese Philosophy* 37.3 (2010): 397–416.

Boltz, William. "Yili." In *Early Chinese Texts: A Bibliographical Guide*, ed. William Boltz, 237–39. Berkeley, CA: Society for the Study of Early China, 1993.

Brashier, Kenneth E. "Han Thanatology and the Division of 'Souls.'" *Early China* 21 (1996): 125–58.

Brindley, Erica Brindley. *Ancient China and the Yue: Perceptions and Identities on the Southern Frontier, c. 400 BCE–50 CE*. Cambridge: Cambridge University Press, 2015.

——. "The Polarization of the Concepts 'Si' (Private Interest) and 'Gong' (Public Interest) in Early Chinese Thought." *Asia Major* third series 26.2 (2013): 1–31.

Brosseder, Ursula. "Belt Plaques as an Indicator of East-West Relations." In *Xiongnu Archaeology: Multidisciplinary Perspectives of the First Steppe Empire in Inner Asia*, ed. Ursula Brosseder et al., 349–424. Bonn: Vor- und Frühgeschichtliche Archäologie, Rheinische Friedrich-Wilhelms-Universität Bonn, 2011.

Brown, Bill. "Thing Theory." *Critical Inquiry* 28.1 (2001): 1–22.

Bryson, Norman. *Word and Image: French Painting of the Ancient Regime*. Cambridge: Cambridge University Press, 1981.

Bu, Xianqun 卜憲群. *Qin Han guanliao zhidu* 秦漢官僚制度. Beijing: Shehui kexue wenxian chubanshe, 2002.

Bunker, Emma C. *Ancient Bronzes of the Eastern Eurasian Steppes from the Arthur M. Sackler Collection*. New York: Arthur M. Sackler Museum, 1997.

Canepa, Matthew P. "Topographies of Power, Theorizing the Visual, Spatial and Ritual Contexts of Rock Reliefs in Ancient Iran." In *Of Rocks and Water: Towards an Archaeology of* Place, ed. Omur Harmanşah, 53–92. Oxford: Oxbow Books, 2014.

——. *The Iranian Expanse: Transforming Royal Identity through Architecture, Landscape, and the Built Environment, 550 BCE–642 CE*. Berkeley: University of California Press, 2018.

Cao, Jinyan 曹錦炎. "Faguo Boxihe jiucang Xi Han niaochongshu tonghu mingwen yanjiu" 法國伯希和舊藏西漢鳥蟲書銅壺銘文研究. *Wenwu* 文物 2015.11: 57–61.

——. *Niaochongshu tongkao* 鳥蟲書通考. Shanghai: Shanghai shuhua chubanshe, 1999.

Cao, Lüning 曹旅寧. "Han chu Zanglü yu Mawangdui boshu Juzangtu" 漢初《葬律》與馬王堆帛書《居葬圖》. In *Jinian Mawangdui Han mu fajue sishi zhounian guoji xueshu yantaohui lunwenji* 紀念馬王堆漢墓發掘四十週年國際學術研討會論文集, ed. Hunan sheng bowuguan, 52–55. Changsha: Yuelu shuyuan, 2016.

Cao, Wei 曹偉. "Guanyu Jinhou mu suizang qiyong zhidu de sikao" 關於晉侯墓隨葬器用制度的思考. In *Yuanwang ji* 遠望集, ed. Yuanwangji bianji weiyuanhui, 294–301. Xi'an: Shaanxi renmin meishu chubanshe, 1998.

——. *Shaanbei chutu qingtongqi* 陝北出土青銅器. Five volumes. Chengdu: Bashu shushe, 2009.

Chang, Kwang-chih. *Rethinking Archaeology*. New York: Random House, 1967.

——. *Shang Civilization*. New Haven, CT: Yale University Press, 1980.

——. *Art, Myth and Ritual: The Path to Political Authority in Ancient China*. Cambridge, MA: Harvard University Press, 1983.

Chen, Bin 陳斌. "Shi lun Zhanguo Zhao wangling yupian de xingzhi" 試論戰國趙王陵玉片的性質. *Handan zhiye jishu xueyuan xuebao* 邯鄲職業技術學院學報 18.2 (2005): 12–15.

Chen, Fangmei 陳芳妹. "Jinhou mudi suojian xingbie yanjiu de xin xiansuo" 晉侯墓地所見性別研究的新線索. In *Jinhou mudi chutu qingtongqi guoji xueshu yantaohui lunwenji* 晉侯墓地出土青銅器國際學術研討會論文集, ed. Shanghai bowuguan, 157–96. Shanghai: Shanghai shuhua chubanshe, 2002.

Chen, Gongrou 陳公柔. "Shisangli, Jixili zhong suo jizai de sangzang zhidu" 士喪禮, 既夕禮中記載的喪葬制度. *Kaogu xuebao* 考古學報 1956.4: 67–84.

Chen, Guying 陳鼓應. "*Guanzi* Xingshi, Zhouhe, Shuyan, Shuidi zhupian de Huanglao sixiang" 管子形勢宙合樞言水地諸篇的黃老思想. *Hanxue yanjiu* 漢學研究 20.1 (2002): 1–26.

Chen, Li 陳立. *Baihutong shuzheng* 白虎通疏證. Beijing: Zhonghua shuju, 1994.

Chen, Ping 陳平. "Shi lun Baoji Yimen erhao mu duanjian ji youguan wenti" 試論寶雞益門二號墓短劍及有關問題. *Kaogu* 考古1995.4: 361–75.

Chen, Qiyou 陳其猷. *Hanfeizi xin jiaozhu* 韓非子新校注. Shanghai: Shanghai guji chubanshe, 2000.

——. *Lüshi Chunqiu xin jiaoshi* 呂氏春秋新校釋. Shanghai: Shanghai guji chubanshe, 2002.

Chen, Suzhen 陳蘇鎮. "Hanchu wangguo zhidu kaoshu" 漢初王國制度考述. *Zhongguoshi yanjiu* 2004.3: 27–40.

Chen, Wei 陳偉. *Baoshan Chu jian chutan* 包山楚簡初探. Wuhan: Wuhan daxue chubanshe, 1996.

Chen, Zhaorong 陳昭容. "Xingbie, shenfen yu caifu—cong Shang Zhou qingtongqi yu muzang yiwu suozuo de guancha" 性別、身份與財富—從商周青銅器與墓葬遺物所做的觀察. In *Zhongguoshi xinlun—xingbie shi fence* 中國史新論—性別史分冊, ed. Li Zhende, 1–53. Taipei: Lianjing, 2009.

Chen, Zhi 陳致. "Haihunhou mu suojian zi yun fu yi you shishi" 海昏侯墓所見子畩父乙卣試釋. *Jiangxi shifan daxue xuebao* 江西師範大學學報 49.5 (2016): 7–15.

Cheng, Te-k'un. "Some Standing Jade Figurines of the Shang-Chou Period." *Artibus Asiae* 28.1 (1966): 39–52.

——. "Yin-Yang Wu-Hsing and Han Art." *Harvard Journal of Asiatic Studies* 20.1/2 (1957): 162–86.

Cheng, Xuehua 程學華 and Lin Bo 林泊. "Qin Dongling dierhao lingyuan diaocha zuantan jianbao" 秦東陵第二號陵園調查鑽探報告. *Kaogu yu wenwu* 考古與文物 1990.4: 22–30.

Ching, Julia. *Mysticism and Kingship in China: The Heart of Chinese Wisdom.* Cambridge: Cambridge University Press, 1997.

Chūgoku kokyō no kenkyuhan 中國古鏡の研究班. "Zen-Kan kyōmei shakuchū" 前漢鏡銘集釋. *Tōhō gakuhō* 84 (2009): 139–209.

Chugunov, K., H. Parzinger, and A. Nagler. "Arzhan 2: la tombe d'un prince scythe en Sibérie du Sud Rapport préliminaire des fouilles russo-allemandes de 2000-2002." *Arts Asiatiques* 59 (2004): 5–29.

Clark, Anthony E. *Ban Gu's History of Early China.* Amherst, NY: Cambria, 2008.

——. "Praise and Blame: Ruist Historiography in Ban Gu's *Hanshu.*" *The Chinese Historical Review* 18.1 (2011): 1–24.

Cohen, Andrew C. *Death Rituals, Ideology, and the Development of Early Mesopotamian Kingship: Towards a New Understanding of Iraq's Royal Cemetery of Ur.* Leiden: Brill Styx, 2005.

Cook, Constance. *Death in Ancient China: The Tale of One Man's Journey.* Leiden: Brill, 2006.

Cosmo, Nicole Di. *Ancient China and its Enemies: The Rise of Nomadic Power in East Asian History.* Cambridge: Cambridge University Press, 2004.

——. "The Northern Frontier in Pre-imperial China." In *Cambridge History of Ancient China*, ed. Michael Loewe and Edward Shaughnessy, 885–966. Cambridge: Cambridge University Press, 1999.

Crump, James I. Jr. *Chan-kuo ts'e.* Oxford: Clarendon Press, 1970.

Csikszentmihalyi, Mark. "Emulating the Yellow Emperor: The Theory and Practice of HuangLao, 180–141 B.C.E." PhD diss., Stanford University, 1994.

Cua, Antonio S. "Ethical Uses of the Past." In *Human Nature, Ritual, and History: Studies in Xunzi and Chinese Philosophy*, ed. Antonio S. Cuo, 73–98. Washington, DC: Catholic University of America Press, 2005.

Cui, Shengkuan 崔聖寬 and Hao Daohua 郝導華. "Qingzhou shi Xiangshan Han mu peizangkeng" 青州市香山漢墓陪葬坑. In *Zhongguo kaoguxue nianjian (2007)* 中國考古學年鑑 (2007), ed. Zhongguo kaogu xuehui, 269–72. Beijing: Zhongguo shehui kexue chubanshe, 2008.

Davies, Penelope J. E. *Death and the Emperor: Roman Imperial Funerary Monuments, from Augustus to Marcus Aurelius.* Austin: University of Texas Press, 2004.

Davis-Kimball, Jeannne. *Nomads of the Eurasian Steppes in the Early Iron Age.* Berkeley, CA: Zinat Press, 1995.

DeWoskin, Kenneth J. "Music and Voices from the Han Tombs: Music, Dance, and Entertainments during the Han." In *Stories from China's past: Han Dynasty Pictorial Tomb Reliefs and Archaeological Bbjects from Sichuan Province, People's Republic of China*, ed. Lucy Lim, 64–71. San Francisco, CA: Chinese Culture Foundation of San Francisco, 1987.

Didi-Huberman, Georges. *Confronting Images: Questioning the Ends of a Certain History of Art.* University Park: Pennsylvania State University, 2005.

Ding, Yan 丁岩. "Qin wanghou de hezang yu feizi de fuzang—yi Xianyangyuan Zhanguo Qin lingyuan de faxian wei zhongxin" 秦王后的合葬與妃子的祔葬—以咸陽原戰國秦陵園的發現為中心. *Xianyang shifan xueyuan xuebao* 咸陽師範學院學報 2014. 1: 1–5.

Dingxian bowuguan 定縣博物館. "Hebei Dingxian 43 hao Han mu fajue jianbao" 河北定縣43號漢墓發掘簡報. *Wenwu* 1973.11: 8–20.

Dodson, Aidan. *Amarna Sunset: Nefertiti, Tutankhamun, Ay, Horemheb, and the Egyptian Counter-Reformation.* Oxford: Oxford University Press, 2009.

Dodson, Aidan and Salima Ikram, *The Tomb in Ancient Egypt: Royal and Private Sepulchres from the Early Dynastic Period to the Romans.* London: Thames & Hudson, 2008.

Dong, Shan 董珊. "Mawangdui sanhao Han mu chutu de Juzangtu" 馬王堆三號漢墓出土的居葬圖. In *Jianbo wenian kaoshi luncong* 簡帛文獻考釋論叢, ed. Dong Shan, 244–50. Shanghai: Shanghai guji chubanshe, 2014.

Du, Guichi 杜貴墀. *Han lu jizheng* 漢律輯證, Xiuding falüguan 修訂法律館 edition (1897).

Du, You 杜佑. *Tongdian* 通典. Beijing: Zhonghua shuju, 1988.

Duan, Lianqin 段連勤. *Bei Di zu yu Zhongshanguo* 北狄族與中山國. Shijiazhuang: Hebei renmin chubanshe, 1982.

Duan, Qingbo 段清波. "Guanyu Shengheyuan damu ji xiangguan wenti de taolun" 關於神禾原大墓及相關問題的討論. *Kaogu yu wenwu* 2009.4: 53–61.

——. *Qin Shi Huangdi lingyuan kaogu yanjiu* 秦始皇帝陵園考古研究. Beijing: Beijing daxue chubanshe, 2011.

——. "Qin Shihuangdi lingyuan K0006 peizangkeng xingzhi chuyi" 秦始皇帝陵園 K0006 陪葬坑性質芻議. *Zhongguo lishi wenwu* 中國歷史文物 2002.2: 59–66.

Duan, Yucai 段玉裁. *Shuowen jiezi zhu* 說文解字注. Hangzhou: Zhejiang guji chubanshe, 1999.

Durrant, Stephen W. *The Cloudy Mirror: Tension and Conflict in the Writings of Sima Qian.* Albany, NY: SUNY, 1995.

Durrant, Stephen, Li Wai-yee, and David Schaberg. *Zuo Tradition (Zuozhuan): Commentary on the "Spring and Autumn Annals."* Three volumes. Seattle: University of Washington, 2016.

Eco, Umberto. *Interpretation and Overinterpretation.* Cambridge: Cambridge University Press, 1992.

——. *The Limits of Interpretation.* Bloomington: Indiana University Press, 1990.

Egami, Namio 江上波夫. *Kiba minzoku kokka: Nihon kodaishi e no apurōchi* 騎馬民族国家: 日本古代史へのアプローチ. Tokyo: Chūo Kōronsha, 1968.

——. *Yūrashia hoppō bunka no kenkyū* ユウラシア北方文化の研究. Tokyo: Yamakawa Shuppansha, 1951.

Elsner, Jaś. "From Empirical Evidence to the Big Picture: Some Reflections on Riegl's Concept of Kunstwollen." *Critical Inquiry* 32.4 (2006): 741–66.

Eno, Robert. *Dao de jing*, 2010, version 1.1, http://www.indiana.edu/~p374/Daodejing.pdf.

Erickson, Susan. "'Twirling Their Long Sleeves, They Dance Again and Again . . .': Jade Plaque Sleeve Dancers of the Western Han Dynasty." *Ars Orientalis* 24 (1994): 39–63.

Erkes, Eduard. "Some Remarks on Karlgren's 'Fecundity Symbols in Ancient China.'" *Bulletin of the Museum of Far Eastern Antiquities* 3 (1931): 63–68.

Ess, Hans van. *Politik und Geschichtsschreibung im alten China: Pan-ma i-t'ung* 班馬異同. Two volumes. Lun Wen 18. Wiesbaden: Harrassowitz, 2014.

——. "Praise and Slander: The Evocation of Empress Lü in the *Shiji* and the *Hanshu*." *Nannü* 8.2 (2006): 221–54.

——. "The Meaning of Huang-Lao in the *Shiji* and *Hanshu*." *Études chinoises* 12.2 (1993): 161–77.

Falkenhausen, Lothar von. "Archaeological Perspectives on the Philosophicization of Royal Zhou Ritual." In *Perceptions of Antiquity in Chinese Civilization*, ed. Dieter Kuhn and Helga Stahl, 135–75. Heidelberg: Edition Forum, 2008.

——. *Chinese Society in the Age of Confucius (1000–250 BC): The Archaeological Evidence.* Los Angeles: Cotsen Institute of Archaeology, UCLA, 2006.

——. "Mortuary Behavior in Pre-Imperial Qin: A Religious Interpretation." In *Religion and Chinese Society: A Centennial Conference of the École française d'Extrême-Orient.* Two volumes, ed. John Lagerway, 1:109–72. Paris: École française d'Extrême-Orient, 2004.

Fan, Ye 范曄. *Hou Hanshu* 後漢書. Beijing: Zhonghua shuju, 1965.

Fang, Xuanling 房玄齡. *Jinshu* 晉書. Beijing: Zhonghua shuju, 1974.

Fang, Hui 方輝. "Shi lun Zhoudai de tongkui" 試論周代的銅匱. In *Haidai diqu qingtong shidai kaogu* 海岱地區青銅時代考古, ed. Fang Hui, 483–98. Ji'nan: Shandong daxue chubanshe, 2007.

Fei, Zhengang 費振綱. *Quan Han fu* 全漢賦. Beijing: Beijing daxue chubanshe, 1993.

Foucault, Michel. *The Order of Things: An Archaeology of the Human Sciences.* London: Routledge, 2002.

Lyvbjerg, Bent. "Five Misunderstandings about Case-Study Research." *Qualitative Inquiry* 12.2 (2006): 219–45.

Fong, Wen. *The Great Bronze Age of China.* New York: Metropolitan Museum of Art, 1980.

Foucault 2002. Michel Foucault. *The Order of Things.* London: Routledge, 2002.

Fraser, Chris. "Mohism." Stanford Encyclopedia of Philosophy. http://plato.stanford.edu/entries/mohism/ (revised 2015).

Freedberg, David. *The Power of Images.* Chicago: University of Chicago Press, 1989.

Fu, Xinian 傅熹年. "Zhangguo Zhongshanwang Cuo mu chutu de Zhaoyutu jiqi lingyuan guizhi de yanjiu" 戰國中山王嚳墓出土的兆域圖及其陵園規制的研究. *Kaogu xuebao* 1980.1: 97–118.

Gan, Bao 干寶. *Soushen ji* 搜神記. Collated by Wang Shaoying. Beijing: Zhonghua shuju, 1979.

Gansu sheng bowuguan 甘肅省博物館. "Gansu Pingliang Miaozhuang de liangzuo Zhanguo mu" 甘肅平涼廟莊的兩座戰國墓. *Kaogu yu wenwu* 1982. 5: 21–33.

Gansu Sheng bo wu guan and Zhongguo kexueyuan kaogu yanjiusuo 中國科學院考古研究所. *Wuwei Han jian* 武威漢簡. Beijing: Wenwu chubanshe, 1964.

Gansu sheng wenwu kaogu yanjiusuo 甘肅省文物考古研究所. "Gansu Qin'an Shangyuanjia Qin Han muzang fajue" 甘肅秦安上袁家秦漢墓葬發掘. *Kaogu xuebao* 1997.1: 57–79.

Gansu sheng wenwu kaogu yanjiusuo. *Xirong yizhen* 西戎遺珍. Beijing: Wenwu chubanshe, 2014.

Gansu sheng wenwu kaogu yanjiusuo and Zhangjiazhuang Huizu zizhixian bowuguan 張家川回族自治縣博物館. "2006 niandu Gansu Zhangjiachuan Huizu zizhixian Majiayuan Zhanguo mudi fajue jianbao" 2006年度甘肅張家川回族自治縣馬家塬戰國墓地發掘簡報. *Wenwu* 2008.9: 4–28.

Gao, Chongwen 高崇文. "Xi Han zhuhouwang mu chema xunzang zhidu tantao" 西漢諸侯王墓車馬殉葬制度探討. *Wenwu* 1992.2: 37–43.

Gao, Dalun 高大倫. *Zhangjiashan Hanjian maishu jiaoshi* 張家山漢簡脈書校釋. Chengdu: Chengdu chubanshe, 1992.

Ge, Jianxiong 葛劍雄. *Xi Han renkou dili* 西漢人口地理. Beijing: Renmin chubanshe, 1986.

——. *Zhongguo yiminshi* 中國移民史. Six volumes. Fuzhou: Fujian renmin chubanhe, 1997.

Ge, Mingyu 葛明宇. "Shizishan Chuwang ling chutu biyu guanpian ying wei guanti neishi kao" 獅子山楚王陵出土碧玉棺片應為棺體內飾考. *Jianghan kaogu* 江漢考古 2018.1: 80–88.

Geng, Chao 耿超. "Jinhou mudi de xingbie kaocha" 晉侯墓地的性別考察. *Zhongyuan wenwu* 中原文物 2014.3: 36–43, 84.

Geng, Jianjun 耿建軍. "Shixi Xuzhou Xi Han Chuwang mu chutu guanyin ji fengni de xingzhi" 試析徐州西漢楚王墓出土官印及封泥的性質. *Kaogu* 2000.9: 79–85.

Gennep, Arnold Van. *The Rites of Passage*. Chicago: University of Chicago Press, 1960.

Gerring, John. *Case Study Research: Principles and Practices*. Cambridge: Cambridge University Press, 2007.

Goldin, Paul R. *The Culture of Sex in Ancient China*. Honolulu: University of Hawaii Press, 2002.

——. "Xunzi and Early Han Philosophy." *Harvard Journal of Asiatic Studies* 67.1 (2007): 135–66.

Gombrich, Ernst. *Symbolic Images: Studies in the Art of the Renaissance*. London: Phaidon, 1972.

Gryaznov, Mikhail P. *The Ancient Civilization of Southern Siberia: An Archaeological Adventure*. trans. James Horgarth. New York: Cowles, 1969.

Gu, Donggao 顧棟高. *Chunqiu dashi biao* 春秋大事表. Beijing: Zhonghua shuju, 1993.

Guangxi zhuangzu zizhiqu bowuguan 廣西壯族自治區博物館. *Guangxi Guixian Luobowan Han mu* 廣西貴縣羅灣漢墓. Beijing: Wenw chubanshe, 1988.

Guangzhou wenwu guanli weiyuanhui 廣州文物管理委員會and Guangzhou shi bowuguan. *Guangzhou Han mu* 廣州漢墓. Two volumes. Beijing: Wenwu chubanshe, 1981.

Guangzhou shi wenwu guanli weiyuanhui 廣州市文物管理委員會 et al. *Xi Han Nanyue wang mu* 西漢南越王墓. Two volumes. Beijing: Wenwu chubanshe, 1991.

Gulik, Robert Van. *Sexual Life in Ancient China: A Preliminary Survey of Chinese Sex and Society from ca. 1500 B.C. till 1644 A.D.* Leiden: E. J. Brill, 1961.

Guo, Baojun 郭寶鈞. *Junxian Xingcun* 浚縣辛村. Beijing: Kexue chubanshe, 1964.

——. "1950 nian chun Yinxu fajue baogao" 一九五零年春殷墟發掘報告. *Zhongguo kaogu xuebao* 中國考古學報 5 (1951): 1–62.

Guo, Jianbang 郭建邦. "Shilun Gushi Hougudui damu peizangkeng chutu de daibu gongju—jianyu" 試論固始侯古堆大墓陪葬坑出土的代步工具—肩輿. *Zhongyuan wenwu* 1981.1: 43–47.

Guo, Moruo 郭沫若. *Liang Zhou jinwenci daxi kaoshi* 兩周金文辭大系考釋. Beijing: Kexue chubanshe, 1958.

Guo, Qingfan 郭慶藩. *Zhuangzi jishi* 莊子集釋. Beijing: Zhonghua shuju, 1961.

Guo, Wu 郭物. "Dierqun tong(tie) fu yanjiu" 第二群銅（鐵）鍑研究. *Kaogu xuebao* 2007.1: 61–96.

Guo, Zheng 郭錚. "Mancheng Han mu chutu fengni shitan" 滿城漢墓出土封泥試探. *Wenwu chunqiu* 文物春秋 1992.1: 35–37.

Habermas, Jürgen. *The Structural Transformation of the Public Sphere: An Inquiry into a category of Bourgeois Society*. Cambridge: Polity, 1989.

Han, Baoquan 韓保全 et al. *Xi'an Longshouyuan Han mu* 西安龍首原漢墓. Lanzhou: Xibei daxue chubanshe, 1999.

Han, Jianye 韓建業. *Beijing Xian Qin kaogu* 北京先秦考古. Beijing: Wenwu chuabanshe, 2011.

——. "Zhongguo Xian Qin dongshimu puxi chutan" 中國先秦洞室墓譜系初探. *Zhongguo lishi wenwu* 2007.4:16–25.

Han, Wei 韓偉 and Jiao Nanfeng 焦南峰. "Qin du Yongcheng kaogu fajue yanjiu zongshu" 秦都雍城考古發掘研究綜述. *Kaogu yu wenwu* 1988.5–6: 111–26.

Harper, Donald. "A Chinese Demonology of the Third Century B.C." *Harvard Journal of Asiatic Studies* 45.2 (1985): 459–98.

——. "Chinese Religions—The State of the Field, Part I Early Religious Traditions: The Neolithic Period through the Han Dynasty, ca. 4000 B.C.E. to 220 C.E, Warring States, Ch'in, and Han Periods." *Journal of Asian Studies* 54.1 (1995): 152–60.

——. *Early Chinese Medical Literature*. New York: Routledge, 2009.

Hawks, David. *The Songs of the South: An Anthology of Ancient Chinese Poems by Qu Yuan and Other Poets*. Harmondsworth: Penguin, 1985.

Hayashi, Minao 林巳奈夫. *Chūgoku kogyoku no kenkyū* 中國古玉の研究. Tokyo: Yoshikawa Kōbunkan, 1991.

——. "Concerning the Inscription 'May Sons and Grandsons Eternally Use This Vessel].'" Trans. Elizabeth Childs-Johnson. *Artibus Asiae* 53.1/2 (1993): 51–58.

——. *Kandai no kamigami* 漢代の神神. Kyoto: Rinsen Shoten, 1989.

——. *Sengoku jidai shutsudo bunbutsu no kenkyū* 戰國時代出土文物の研究. Kyoto: Kyōto Daigaku Jinbun Kagaku Kenkyūjo, 1985.

He, Jiejun 何介鈞. *Mawangdui er san hao Han mu* 馬王堆二三號漢墓. Beijing: Wenwu chubanshe, 2003.

He, Pingli 何平立. *Xunshou yu fengshan: Fengjian zhengzhi de wenhua guiji* 巡狩與封禪：封建政治的文化軌跡. Ji'nan: Qilu shushe, 2003.

He, Yanjie 何艷傑 et al. *Xianyu Zhongshanguo shi* 鮮虞中山國史. Beijing: Kexue chubanshe, 2011.

Hearn, Maxwell K. *Ancient Chinese Art: The Ernest Erickson Collection in the Metropolitan Museum of Art*. New York: The Metropolitan Museum of Art, 1987.

Hebdige, Dick. "Object as Image: The Italian Scooter Cycle." In *Material Culture: Critical Concepts in the Social Sciences*. Two volumes, ed. Victor Buchli, 2: 121–59. London: Routledge, 2004.

Hebei sheng bowuguan et al. "Dingxian sishi hao Han mu chutu de jinlü yuyi" 定縣 40 號漢墓出土的金縷玉衣. *Wenwu* 1976.7: 56–59, 98.

Hebei sheng wenhuaju wenwu gongzuodui 河北省文化局文物工作隊. "Hebei Dingxian Beizhuang Han mu fajue baogao" 河北定縣北莊漢墓發掘報告. *Kaogu xuebao* 1964.2: 26–45.

Hebei sheng wenwu guanlichu. "Hebei sheng Pingshan xian Zhanguo shiqi Zhongshanguo muzang fajue jianbao" 河北省平山縣戰國時期中山國墓葬發掘簡報. *Wenwu* 1979.1: 1–26.

Hebei sheng wenwu yanjiusuo 河北省文物研究所. *Cuo mu: Zhanguo Zhongshanguo guowang zhi mu* 𰯲墓：戰國中山國國王之墓. Two volumes. Beijing: Wenwu chubanshe, 1996.

——. "Hebei Dingxian 40 hao Han mu fajue jianbao" 河北定縣40號漢墓發掘簡報. *Wenwu* 1981.8: 1–10.

——. *Yan Xiadu* 燕下都. Two volumes. Beijing: Wenwu chubanshe, 1996.

——. *Zhanguo Zhongshanguo Lingshou cheng: 1975–1993 nian kaogu fajue baogao* 戰國中山國靈壽城: 1975–1993 年發掘報告. Beijing: Wenwu chubanshe, 2005.

Hebei sheng wenwu yanjiusuo et al. "Xianxian di sanshiliu hao Han mu fajue baogao" 獻縣第36號漢墓發掘報告. In *Hebei sheng kaogu wenji* 河北省考古文集, ed. Hebei sheng wenwu yanjiusuo 河北省文物研究所, 241–60. Shanghai: Dongfang chubanshe, 1998.

Hebei sheng wenwu yanjiusuo and Zhangjiakou diqu wenhuaju 張家口地區文化局. "Hebei Yangyuan Sanfengou Han mu qun fajue baogao" 河北陽原三汾溝漢墓群發掘報告. *Wenwu* 1990.1: 1–18.

Hein, Anke. "The Problem of Typology in Chinese Archaeology." *Early China* 39 (2016): 21–52.

Henan bowuyuan 河南博物院. *Henan chutu Handai jianzhu mingqi* 河南出土漢代建筑明器. Zhengzhou: Daxiang chubanshe, 2002.

Henan sheng bowuguan 河南省博物館 et al. "Henan Xinyang shi Pingqiao Chunqiu mu fajue jianbao" 河南信陽市平橋春秋墓發掘簡報. *Wenwu* 1981.1: 9–12.

Henan sheng wenwu kaogu yanjiusuo 河南省文物考古研究所. *Gushi Hougudui yihaomu* 固始侯古堆一號墓. Zhengzhou: Daxiang chubanshe, 2004.

——. "Henan Xinzheng Huzhuang Han wangling kaogu faxian gaishu" 河南新鄭胡莊韓王陵考古發現概述. *Huaxia kaogu* 華夏考古 2009.3: 14–18.

——. *Xinzheng Zheng guo jisi yizhi* 新鄭鄭國祭祀遺址. Two volumes. Zhengzhou: Daxiang chubanshe, 2006.

——. *Yongcheng Xi Han Liangguo wangling yu qinyuan* 永城西漢梁國王陵與寢園. Zhengzhou: Zhongzhou guji chubanshe, 1996.

Henan sheng wenwu kaogu yanjiusuo and Pingdingshan shi wenwu guanliju 平頂山市文物管理局. *Pingdingshan Ying guo mudi* 平頂山應國墓地. Two volumes. Zhengzhou: Daxiang chubanshe, 2012.

Henan sheng wenwu kaogu yanjiusuo and Xiamenxia shi wenwu gongzuodui 三門峽市文物工作隊. *Sanmenxia Guoguo mudi* 三門峽虢國墓地. Two volumes. Beijing: Wenwu chubanshe, 1999.

Henan sheng wenwu yanjiusuo 河南省文物研究所. *Xinyang Chu mu* 信陽楚墓. Beijing: Wenwu chubanshe, 1986.

Henare, Amiria, Martin Holbraad, and Sari Wastell. "Introduction." In *Thinking through Things: Theorising Artefacts Ethnographically*, ed. Amiria Henare, Martin Holbraad, and Sari Wastell, 1–31. London: Routledge, 2007.

Hightower, James R. *Han Shih Wai Chuan: Han Ying's Illustration of the Didactic Application of the Classic Songs*. Cambridge, MA: Harvard University Press, 1952.

Hinsch, Bret. *Women in Early Imperial China*. Plymouth: Rowman and Littlefield, 2011.

Ho, Ping-Ti 何炳棣. "Cong Zhuangzi Tianxia pian jiexi Xian Qin sixiang zhong de jiben guanhuai" 從莊子天下篇首解析先秦思想中的基本關懷. In *He Bingdi sixiang zhidushi lun* 何炳棣思想制度史論, ed. Ho Ping-Ti, 285–330. Taipei: Lianjing chuban gongsi, 2013.

Honig, Bonnie. *Democracy and the Foreigner*. Princeton: Princeton University Press, 2001.

Hou, Yubin 侯煜斌. "Qianyi Majiayuan Zhanguo mudi chutu de dongwuwen huangjin shijian" 淺議馬家塬戰國墓地出土的動物紋黃金飾件. *Sichou zhilu* 絲綢之路 2012.12: 54–55.

Hsu, Chuo-yun 許倬雲. "Xi Han zhengquan yu shehui shili de jiaohu zuoyong" 西漢政權與社會勢力的交互作用. *Zhongyang yanjiuyuan lishi yuyan yanjiusuo jikan* 中央研究院歷史語言研究所集刊 35 (1964): 261–81.

Hsu, Hsin-Mei Agnes. "Pictorial eulogies in three Eastern Han tombs." PhD diss., University of Pennsylvania, 2004.

Hu, Fangping 胡方平. "Zhongguo fengtu mu de chansheng he liuxing" 中國封土墓的產生和流行. *Kaogu* 6 (1994): 556–68.

Hu, Jinhua 胡金華. "Heibei diqu shigoumu zangzhi de chubu yanjiu" 河北地區石構墓葬制度的初步研究. In *Heibei sheng Kaogu Wenji* 河北省考古文集, ed. Hebei sheng wenwu yanjiusuo, 428–35. Shanghai: East Press, 1998.

Huang, Huaixin 黃懷信. *Heguanzi jiaozhu* 鶡冠子校注. Beijing: Zhonghua shuju, 2014.

Huang, Huaixin, Zhang Maorong 張懋容, and Tian Xudong 田旭東. *Yi Zhou shu huijiao jizhu* 逸周書匯校集註. Two volumes. Shanghai: Shanghai guji chubanshe, 2007.

Huang, Hui 黃暉. *Lunheng jiaoshi* 論衡校釋. Beijing: Zhonghua shuju, 1990.

Huang, Jian 黃劍. Guanzi Shuidi pian kao lun" 管子·水地篇考論. In *Daojia wenhua yanjiu* 道家文化研究, issue 2, ed. Xianggang daoxueyuan, 336–46. Shanghai: Shanghai guji chubanshe, 1992.

Huang, Mingchong 黃銘崇. "Yindai yu Dong Zhou zhi 'nongqi' jiqi yiyi" 殷代與東周之弄器及其意義. *Gujin lunheng* 古今論衡 6 (2001): 66–88.

Huang, Tingqi 黃庭頎. "Ai Chengshu mingwen xinkao" 哀成叔銘文新考. *Zhongguo wenxue yanjiu* 中國文學研究 41 (2016): 41–66.

Huang, Xiaofen黃曉芬. *Han mu de kaoguxue yanjiu* 漢墓的考古學研究. Changsha: Yuelu shuyuan, 2002.

Huang, Zhanyue 黃展嶽. "Handai zhuhouwang mu lunshu" 漢代諸侯王墓論述. *Kaogu xuebao* 1998.1: 11–34.

——. *Xi Han lizhi jianzhu yizhi* 西漢禮制建築遺址. Beijing: Wenwu chubanshe, 2003.

Hubei sheng bowuguan 湖北省博物館. *Zeng hou Yi mu* 曾侯乙墓. Two volumes. Beijing: Wenwu chubanshe, 1989.

Hubei sheng Jing Sha tielu kaogudui 湖北省荊沙鐵路考古隊. *Baoshan Chu mu* 包山楚墓. Beijing: Wenwu chubanshe, 1991.

Hubei sheng Jingzhou bowuguan. *Jingzhou Tianxinggui erhao Chu mu* 荊州天星觀二號楚墓. Beijing: Wenwu chubanshe, 2003.

Hubei sheng wenwu kaogu yanjiusuo 湖北省文物考古研究所. "Jiangling Fenghuangshan yiliuba hao Han mu" 江陵鳳凰山一六八號漢墓. *Kaogu xuebao* 1993.4: 455–512.

Hubei sheng wenwu kaogu yanjiusuo and Yunmeng xian bowuguan 雲夢縣博物館. "Hubei Yunmeng Shuihudi M77 fajue jianbao" 湖北雲夢睡虎地M77發掘簡報. *Jianghan kaogu* 2008.4: 31–37.

Hubei sheng wenwu kaogu yanjiusuo and Suizhou shi bowuguan 隨州市博物館. "Hubei Suizhou Yejiashan M28 fajue baogao" 湖北隨州葉家山M28發掘報告. *Jianghan kaogu* 2013.4: 3–57.

——. "Hubei Suizhou Yejiashan M107 fajue jianbao" 湖北隨州葉家山M107發掘簡報. *Jianghan kaogu* 2016.3: 3–40.

——. "Hubei Suizhou Yejiashan Xi Zhou mu mudi fajue jianbao" 湖北隨州葉家山西周墓地發掘簡報. *Wenwu* 2011.11: 4–60.

Hulsewé, A.F.P. "Royal Rebels." *Bulletin de l'Ecole Française d'Extrême-Orient* 69 (1981): 315–25.

Hunan sheng bowuguan 湖南省博物館. "Changsha Shazitang Xi Han mu fajue jianbao" 湖南砂子塘西漢墓發掘簡報. *Wenwu* 1963.2: 13–24.

Hunan sheng bowuguan and Zhongguo kexueyuan kaogu yanjiusuo. *Changsha Mawang-dui yihao Han mu* 長沙馬王堆一號漢墓. Two volumes. Beijing: Wenwu chubanshe, 1972.

Huntington, Richard and Peter Metcalf. *Celebrations of Death: The Anthropology of Mortuary Ritual*. Cambridge: Cambridge University Press, 1979.

Hutton, Eric. *Xunzi: The Complete Text*. Princeton: Princeton University Press, 2014.

Ikram, Salima. *Death and Burial in Ancient Egypt*. Cairo: American University in Cairo Press, 2015.

Jacobson, Esther. "Siberian Roots of the Scythian Stag Image." *Journal of Asian History* 17 (1983): 68–120.

——. *The Art of the Scythians*. Leiden: Brill, 1995.

——. "The Structure of Narrative in Early Chinese Pictorial Vessels." *Representations* 8 (1984): 61–83.

Jacobson-Tepfer, Esther. *The Hunter, the Stag, and the Mother of Animals: Image, Monument, and Landscape in Ancient North Asia*. Oxford: Oxford University Press, 2015.

James, Ioan Mackenzie. *History of Topology*. Amsterdam: Elsevier B.V., 1999.

James, Jean M. "An Iconographic Study of Xiwangmu During the Han Dynasty." *Artibus Asiae* 55.1/2 (1995): 17–41.

Jettmar, Karl. *Art of the Steppes*. London: Methuen, 1967.

Jiang, Lu 蔣璐. "Beifang diqu Xi Han zaoqi muzang yanjiu" 北方地區西漢早期墓葬研究. *Bianjiang kaogu yanjiu* 邊疆考古研究 9 (2010): 126–37.

——. "Zhongguo beifang diqu Han mu yanjiu" 中國北方地區漢墓研究. PhD diss., Jilin University, 2008.

Jiang, Ruoshi 蔣若是. "Junguo, chize, he sanguan wuzhuqian zhi kaoguxue yanzheng" 郡國，赤仄與三官五銖錢之考古學驗證. *Wenwu* 1989.4: 84–90.

Jiang, Yingyu 蔣廷瑜. "Xi Han Nanyue guo shiqi de tongtong" 西漢南越國時期的銅桶. *Dongnan wenhua* 2002.12: 38–43.

Jiang, Yu. "Ritual Practice, Status, and Gender Identity: Western Zhou Tombs at Baoji." In *Gender and Chinese Archaeology*, ed. Katheryn M. Linduff and Yan Sun, 117–36. New York: Altamira Press, 2004.

Jiangxi sheng wenwu kaogu yanjiuyuan 江西省文物考古研究院 and Xiamen daxue lishixi 廈門大學歷史系. "Jiangxi Nanchang Xi Han Haihunhou Liu He mu chutu yuqi" 江西南昌西漢海昏侯劉賀墓出土玉器. *Wenwu* 2018.11: 57–72.

Jiangxi sheng wenwu kaogu yanjiuyuan and Zhongguo renmin daxue lishi xueyuan kaogu wenboxi 中國人民大學歷史學院考古文博系. "Jiangxi Nanchang Xi Han Haihun hou Liu He mu chutu tongqi" 江西南昌西漢海昏侯劉賀墓出土銅器. *Wenwu* 2018.11: 4–26.

Jiao, Nanfeng 焦南峰. "Han Yangling congzangkeng chutan" 漢陽陵從葬坑初探. *Wenwu* 2006.7: 51–57.

——. "Shilun Xi Han diling de jianshe linian" 試論西漢帝陵的建設理念. *Kaogu* 2007.11: 78–87.

——. "Xi Han diling furen zangzhi chutan" 西漢帝陵夫人葬制初探. *Kaogu* 2014.1: 77–83.

Jinan cheng Fenghuangshan yiliuba hao Han mu fajue zhenglizu 紀南城鳳凰山一六八號漢墓發掘整理組. "Hubei Jiangling Fenghuangshan yiliuba hao Han mu fajue jianbao" 湖北江陵鳳凰山一六八號漢墓發掘簡報. *Wenwu* 1975.9: 1–22.

Jing, Zhonwei 井中偉 and Li Liandi 李連娣. "Zhongguo beifangxi qintong 'huagejian'yanjiu yu tansuo" 中國北方系青銅'花格劍'研究與探索. *Bianjiang kaogu yanjiu* 邊疆考古研究 10 (2013): 163–79.

Jingmen shi bowuguan 荊門市博物館. *Guodian Chumu zhujian* 郭店楚墓竹简. Beijing: Wenwu chubanshe, 1998.

Kamata, Shigeo 鎌田重雄. *Shin, Kan seiji seido no kenkyū* 秦漢政治制度の研究. Tokyo: Nihon Gakujutsu Shinkōkai, 1962.

Kamiya, Masakazu 紙屋正和. "Zen Kan shōko ōkoku no kansei—Naishi o chūshin ni shite" 前漢諸侯王国の官制—内史を中心にして. *Kyūshū Daigaku Toyōshi ronshū* 九州大学東洋史論集 3 (1974): 17–35.

Kao, Jeffrey and Yang Zuosheng. "On jade suits and Han archaeology." *Archaeology* 36.6 (1983): 30–37.

Karlgren, Bernhard. *The Book of Odes*. Stockholm: Museum of Far Eastern Antiquities, 1950.

Katō, Shigeshi 加藤繁. *Shina keizaishi kōshō* 支那經濟史考證. Tokyo: Tōyō Bunko, 1952.

Keightley, David N. "The Religious Commitment: Shang Theology and the Genesis of Chinese Political Culture." *History of Religions* 17 (1978): 211–24.

Kern, Martin. *Die Hymnen der chinesischen Staatsopfer: Literatur und Ritual in der politischen Repräsentation von der Han-Zeit bis zu den Sechs Dynastien*. Stuttgart, Germany: Franz Steiner Verlag, 1999.

——. *The Stele Inscriptions of Ch'in Shih-huang: Text and Ritual in Early Chinese Imperial Representation*. New Haven, CT: American Oriental Society, 2000.

Kim, Hyun Jin. *Ethnicity and Foreigners in Ancient Greece and China*. London: Gerald Duckworth, 2009.

Kimura, Yoshikazu 北村良和. "Zenkan matsu no kōrei ni tsuite" 前漢末の改禮について, *Nihon Chūgoku Gakkai hō* 日本中國學會報 33 (1981): 43–57.

Kirimoto, Tota 桐本東太. "Go Kan ōchō no shishya girei—*Go Kanjo gireisho genhen yakuchūkō I*" 後漢王朝の死者儀禮—『後漢書』禮儀志・下篇譯注稿(2). *Shigaku* 史學 58.1 (1988): 73–90.

Knoblock, John. *Xunzi: A Translation and Study of the Complete Works*. Two volumes. Stanford, CA: Stanford University Press, 1994.

Knoblock, John and Jeffrey Riegel. *Mozi: A Study and Translation of the Ethical and Political Writings*. Berkeley: University of California Press, 2013.

——. *The Annals of Lü Buwei*. Stanford, CA: Stanford University Press, 2000.

Komai, Kazuchika 駒井和愛. "Xian-Qin shidai mamian jiqi yuanshi" 先秦時代馬面及其源始. trans. Sun Zuoyun. *Beiping Yanjing daxue kaogu xueshe shekan* 北平燕京大學考古學社社刊 5 (1936): 320–24.

Kubler, George. *The Shape of Time: Remarks on the History of Things*. New Haven, CT: Yale University Press, 1962.

Kurihara, Tomonobu 栗原朋信. *Shin Kan shi no kenkyū* 秦漢史の研究. Tokyo: Yoshikawa Kōbunkan, 1961.

Kuz'mina, Elena E. *The Origin of the Indo-Iranians*, ed. Mallory J. P. Leiden: Brill, 2007.

Lacan, Jacques. *Four Fundamental Concepts of Psychoanalysis*. trans. Alan Sheridan. London: Hogarth, 1977.

——. "Some Reflections on the Ego." *International Journal of Psycho-Analysis* 34 (1953): 11–17.

Lai, Guolong. "Death and the Otherworldly Journey in Early China as Seen through Tomb Texts, Travel Paraphernalia, and Road Rituals." *Asia Major* 18.1 (2005): 1–44.

——. *Excavating the Afterlife: The Archaeology of Early Chinese Religion*. Seattle: University of Washington Press, 2015.

Lattimore, Owen. *Inner Asian Frontiers of China*. Oxford: Oxford University Press, 1988.

Lau, D.C. *Tao Te Ching*. New York: Columbia University Press, 1989.

Laufer, Berthold. *Jade: A Study in Chinese Archaeology and Religion*. Chicago: Field Museum of Natural History, 1912.

Legge, James. *Li Chi: Book of Rites*. Two volumes. New York: Columbia University Press, 1967.

——. *Lao Tzu, Tao Te Ching*. Mineola, NY: Dover, 1997.

——. *The Four Books*. New York: Paragon, 1966.

——. *The Texts of Taoism*. New York: Dover, 1962.

——. *The Book of Mencius*. Raleigh, NC: Hayes Barton, 2006.

Lévi-Strauss, Claude. *Structural Anthropology*. Trans. Claire Jacobson and Brooke Grundfest Schoepf. New York: Basic Books, 1968.

Lewis, Mark E. "Public Spaces in Cities in the Roman and Han Empires." In *State Power in Ancient China and Rome*, ed. Walter Scheider, 204–29. Oxford: Oxford University Press, 2015.

——. *The Construction of Space in Early China*. Albany, NY: SUNY Press, 2005.

——. "Warring States: Political History." In *Cambridge History of Ancient China: From the Origin of Civilization to 221 B.C.*, ed. Michael Loewe and Edward Shaughnessy, 587–650. Cambridge: Cambridge University Press, 1999.

Li, Boqian 李伯謙. "Cong Jinhou mudi kan Xi Zhou gongmu mudi zhidu de jige wenti" 從晉侯墓地看西周公墓地制度的幾個問題. *Kaogu* 1997.11: 51–60.

Li, Chi. *Anyang*. Seattle: University of Washington Press, 1977.

Li, Chunlei 李春雷. "Jiangsu Xuzhou Shizishan Chu wangling chutu xiangyu qiguan de tuili fuyaun yanjiu" 江蘇徐州獅子山楚王陵出土鑲玉漆棺的推理復原研究. *Kaogu yu wenwu* 1999.1: 56–71.

Li, Feng. *Landscape and Power in Early China: The Crisis and Fall of the Western Zhou, 1045–771 BC*. Cambridge: Cambridge University Press, 2006.

Li, Hong 李虹. "Yima Xinshiqu wu hao Xi Han mu fajue jianbao" 義馬新市區5號西漢墓發掘簡報. *Wenwu* 1995.11: 20–23.

Li, Jianli 李建麗 and Zhao Weiping 趙衛平. "Dou Wan zangyu heshi" 竇綰葬於何時? *Wenwu chunqiu* 1991.1: 54–57.

Li, Ling 李零. "Shuo kui—Zhongguo zaoqi de funü yongpin: Shoushihe, huazhuanghe he xianghe" 說匵—中國早期的婦女用品：首飾盒、化妝盒和香盒. *Gugongbowuyuan yuankan* 故宮博物院院刊 2009.3: 69–86.

——. *Zhongguo fangshu kao* 中國方術考. Shanghai: Dongfang chubanshe, 2001.

Li, Rusen 李如森. *Han dai sangzang zhidu* 漢代喪葬制度. Changchun: Jilin renmin chubanshe, 1995.

——. "Lüe lun Luoyang diqu Zhanguo Xi-Han dongshimu de yuanliu" 略論洛陽地區戰國西漢洞室墓的源流. *Kexue shehui zhanxian* 科學社會戰線 1988.3: 205–7.

Li, Song 李凇. *Lun Handai yishu zhong de Xiwangmu tuxiang* 論漢代藝術中的西王母圖像. Changsha: Hunan jiaoyu chubanshe, 2000.

Li, Shaonan 李少南. "Shandong Boxing xian chutu tongjing he huobi" 山東博興縣出土銅鏡和貨幣. *Kaogu* 1984.11: 1041–44.

Li Xueqin 李學勤. "Dingxian Bajiaolang Hanjian Rushu xiaoyi" 定縣八角廊漢簡儒書小議. *Jianbo yanjiu* 簡帛研究 1 (1993): 257–65.

———. "Shilun Bajiaolang jian Wenzi" 試論八角廊簡〈文子〉. *Wenwu* 1996.1: 36–40.

———. "Zheng ren jinwen liangzhong duidu" 鄭人金文兩種對讀. In *Tongxiang wenming zhilu* 通向文明之路, ed. Li Xueqin, 166–70. Beijing: Shangwu yinshuguan, 2010.

Li, Xueqin and Li Ling 李零. "Pingshan sanqi yu Zhongshanguo shi de ruogan wenti" 平山三器與中山國史的若干問題. *Kaogu xuebao* 1979.2: 147–69.

Li, Xiangfeng 黎翔鳳. *Guanzi jiaozhu* 管子校注. Beijing: Zhonghua shuju, 2004.

Liang, Siyong 梁思永 and Gao Quxun 高去尋. *Houjiazhuang: Henan Anyang Houjiazhuang Yin dai mudi* 侯家莊: 河南安陽侯家莊殷代墓地. Five volumes. Taipei: Zhongyang yanjiuyuan lishi yuyan yanjiusuo, 1962.

Lianyungang shi bowuguan 連雲港市博物館. "Jiangsu Donghai xian Yinwan Han muqun fajue jianbao" 江蘇東海縣尹灣漢墓群發掘簡報. *Wenwu* 1996.8: 4–25.

———. Lianyungang shi bowuguan et al., *Yinwan Han mu jiandu* 尹灣漢墓簡牘. Beijing: Wenwu chubanshe, 1997.

Lin, Lanying 林蘭英. "Shixi Zhou dai de zangyu dui Han dai yuyi de yingxiang" 試析周代的葬玉對漢代玉衣的影響. *Dongnan wenhua* 東南文化 1998.2: 127–31.

Lin, James. "Armor for the Afterlife." In *The First Emperor: China's Terracotta Army*, ed. Jane Portal, 181–91. Cambridge: Harvard University Press, 2007.

———. "Jade Suits and Iron Armour." *East Asia Journal: Studies in Material Culture* 1.2 (2003): 20–43.

Lin, Meicun 林梅村. "Shang Zhou qingtongjian yuanyuankao" 商周青銅劍淵源考. In *Han Tang xiyu yu Zhongguo wenming* 漢唐西域與中國文明, ed. Lin Meicun, 39–63. Beijing: Wenwu chubanshe, 1998.

Lin, Yun 林澐. "Rongdi fei hu lun" 戎狄非胡論. In *Lin Yun xueshu lunwenji (er)* 林澐學術論文集 (二), ed. Lin Yun, 3–6. Beijing: Kexue chubanshe, 2009.

———. "Shuo Wang" 說王. *Kaogu* 1965.6: 311–12.

———. "Zhongguo beifang changcheng didai youmu wenhuadai de xingcheng guocheng" 中國北方長城地帶遊牧文化帶的形成過程. In *Lin Yun xueshu lunwenji (er)* 林沄學術論文集 (二), ed. Lin Yun, 39–76. Beijing: Kexue chubanshe, 2009.

Linduff, Katherine. "An Archaeological Overview." In *Ancient Bronzes of the Eastern Eurasian Steppes from the Arthur M. Sackler Collection*, ed. Emma C. Bunker, 18–98. New York: Arthur M. Sackler Museum, 1997.

Ling, Chunsheng 凌純聲. "Zhonggu gudai shenzhu yu yinyang xingqi chongbai" 中國古代神主與陰陽性器崇拜. *Zhongyang yanjiuyuan minzuxue yanjiu jikan* 中央研究院民族學研究集刊 8 (1959): 1–46.

Linyi diqu wenwuzu 臨沂地區文物組. "Shandong Linyi Xi Han Liu Ci mu" 山東臨沂西漢劉疵墓. *Kaogu* 1980.6: 493–35.

Liu, Qingzhu 劉慶柱 and Li Yufang 李毓芳. *Xi Han shiyi ling* 西漢十一陵. Xi'an: Shaanxi Renmin, 1987.

———. "Guanyu Xi Han diling xingzhi zhu wenti de tantao" 關於西漢帝陵形制諸問題的探討. *Kaogu yu wenwu* 1985.5: 102–9.

Liu, Rongqing 劉榮慶. "Qin zhi Liyi kao bian" 秦置驪邑考辨. *Wenbo* 文博 1990.5: 232–35, 168.

Liu, Rui 劉瑞. "Qin Han shiqi de jiangzuo dajiang" 秦漢時期的將作大匠. *Zhongguoshi yanjiu* 中國史研究 1998.4: 168–70.

——. "Xi Han zhuhouwang mu zhidu san ti" 西漢諸侯王墓制度三題. In *Handai kaogu yu Han wenhua guoji xueshu taolunhui lunwenji* 漢代考古與漢文化國際學術討論會論文集, ed. Bianweihui, 157–71. Ji'nan: Qilu shushe, 2006.

Liu, Rui and Liu Tao 劉濤. *Xi Han zhuhouwang lingmu zhidu yanjiu* 西漢諸侯王陵墓制度研究. Beijing: Zhongguo shehui kexue chubanshe, 2010.

Liu, Wenxing 劉文星. *Jun ren nanmian zhi shu: Xian Qin zhi Xi Han zhongye huanglao sichao yingxiang xia de xiushen sixiang yu zhiguo xueshuo* 君人南面之術：先秦至西漢中葉黃老思潮影響下的修身思想與治國學說. Taipei: Zhongguo wenhua daxue huagang chubanbu, 2006.

Liu, Xu 劉煦. *Jiu Tangshu* 舊唐書. Beijing: Zhonghua shuju, 1975.

Liu, Zehua 劉澤華. "Chunqiu Zhanguo de 'ligong miesi' guannian yu shehui zhenghe" 春秋戰國的 "立公滅私" 觀念與社會整合. In *Gongsi guannian yu Zhongguo shehui* 公私觀念與中國社會, ed. Liu Zehua, 1–39. Beijing: Zhongguo renmin daxue chubanshe, 2003.

Liu, Zhaojian 劉照建. "Xuzhou diqu daxing yadong mu yanjiu" 徐州地區大型崖洞墓研究. *Dongnan wenhua* 2004.5: 25–31.

Liu, Zunzhi 劉尊志. "Xuzhou liang Han zhuhouwang mu yanjiu" 徐州兩漢諸侯王墓研究. *Kaogu xuebao* 2011.1: 57–96.

Liu, Xu 劉緒 and Xu Tianjin 徐天進. "Guanyu Tianma-Qucun yizhi Jinguo muzang de jige wenti" 關於天馬—曲村遺址晉國墓葬的幾個問題. In *Jinhou mudi chutu qingtongqi guoji xueshu yantaohui lunwenji* 晉侯墓地出土青銅器國際學術研討會論文集, ed. Shanghai bowuguan, 41–52. Shanghai: Shanghai shuhua chubanshe, 2002.

Liu, Yuli 劉餘力 and Xu Bainian 徐柏年. "Luoyang Han mu chutu de jicidi huaqian ji xiangguan wenti" 洛陽漢墓出土的紀次第花錢及相關問題. *Luoyang daxue xuebao* 洛陽大學學報 2006.1: 11–13.

Liu, Yunhui 劉雲輝 and Liu Sizhe 劉思哲. "Han Duling lingqu xin chutu de yubei he yuwuren" 漢杜陵陵區新出土的玉盃與玉舞人. *Wenwu* 2012.12: 73–79.

Loehr, Max. "Weapons and Tools from Anyang, and Siberian Analogies." *American Journal of Archaeology* 53.2 (1949): 126–44.

Loewe, Michael. *Dong Zhongshu, a "Confucian" Heritage* and the Chunqiu Fanlu. Leiden: Brill, 2011.

——. *Crisis and Conflict in Han China*. London: Routledge, 1974.

——. *Divination, Mythology and Monarchy in Han China*. Cambridge: Cambridge University Press, 1994.

——. "State Funerals of the Han Empire." *Bulletin of Museum of the Far Eastern Antiquities* 71 (1999): 5–72.

——. *The Government of the Qin and Han Empires: 221 BCE–220 CE*. Indianapolis: Hackett, 2006.

——. "The Imperial Tombs of the Former Han Dynasty and their Shrines." *T'oung Pao* 78.4/5 (1992): 302–40.

——. "The Imperial Way of Death in Han China." In *State and Court Ritual in China*, ed. Joseph P. McDermott, 81–111. Cambridge: Cambridge University Press, 1999.

——. "The Tombs Built for Han Chengdi and Migrations of Population." In *Chang'an 26 BCE: An Augustan Age in China*, ed. Michael Nylan and Griet Vankeeberghen, 201–28. Seattle: University of Washington Press, 2015.

Loewe, Michael and Denis, Twichett. *The Cambridge History of China: Vol.1, "The Ch'in and Han Empires."* Cambridge: Cambridge University Press, 1986.

Louis, François. "Written Ornament—Ornamental Writing: Birdscript of the Early Han Dynasty and the Art of Enchanting." *Ars Orientalis* 33 (2003): 10–31.

Loy, Hui-chieh. "Xunzi contra Mozi." In *Dao Companion to the Philosophy of Xunzi*, ed. Eric L. Hutton, 356–58. Dordrecht: Springer, 2016.

Lu, Liancheng 盧連成 and Hu Zhisheng 胡智生. *Baoji Yu guo mudi* 寶雞強國墓地. Two volumes. Beijing: Wenwu chubanshe, 1988.

Lu, Yan 盧岩 and Shan Yueying 單月英. "Xi Han muzang chutu de dongwuwen yao-shipai" 西漢墓葬出土的動物紋腰飾牌. *Kaogu yu wenwu* 2007.4: 45–55.

Lu, Zhaoyin 盧兆蔭. "Handai guizu funü xiai de peiyu—yuwuren" 漢代貴族婦女喜愛的珮玉—玉舞人. *Shoucangjia* 收藏家1996.3: 4–7.

——. *Mancheng Han mu* 滿城漢墓. Beijing: Sanlian shudian, 2005.

——. "Shilun liang Han de yuyi" 試論兩漢的玉衣. *Kaogu* 1981.1: 51–58.

——. "Zai lun liang Han de yuyi" 再論兩漢的玉衣. *Wenwu* 1989.10: 60–67.

Lü, Shihao 呂世浩. *Cong Shiji dao Hanshu—zhuanzhe guocheng yu lishi yiyi* 從史記到漢書—轉折過程與歷史意義. Taipei: Taida chuban zhongxin, 2009.

Luan, Fengshi 欒豐實. "Shiqian guanguo de chansheng, fazhan, he guanguo zhidu de xingcheng" 史前棺槨的產生、發展和棺槨制度的形成. *Wenwu* 2006.6: 49–55.

Lullo, Sheri Lullo. "Making up Status and Authority: Practices of Beautification in War-ring States through Han Dynasty China (Fourth Century BCE–Third Century CE)." *Fashion Theory* 20.4 (2016): 415–40.

——. "Toiletry Case-sets across Life and Death in Early China (fifth c. BCE–third c. CE)." PhD diss., University of Pittsburg, 2009.

Luo, Ping 羅平. "Hebei Handan Zhao wang ling" 河北邯鄲趙王陵. *Kaogu* 1982.6: 597–605, 564.

Luoyang shi wenwu gongzuodui 洛陽市文物工作隊. "Luoyang zhenzhichang Dong Zhou mu (C1M5269) de qingli" 洛陽市針織廠東周墓 (C1M5269) 的清理. *Wenwu* 2001.12: 41–59, 64.

Ma, Duanlin 馬端臨. *Wenxian tongkao* 文獻通考. Shenduzhai 慎獨齋 edition, 1521.

Ma, Sha 馬沙. "Woguo gudai 'fumian' yanjiu" 我國古代 "覆面" 研究. *Jianghan kaogu* 1999.1: 66–74.

Ma, Yongying 馬永嬴. "Cong Jiangzuo dajiang kan Xi Han diling de bianhua" 從將作大匠看西漢帝陵的變化. *Kaogu yu wenwu* 2009.4: 72–76.

——. "'Daguan zhi yin' yu Xi Han de Taiguan" 大官之印" 與西漢的太官. *Kaogu yu wenwu* 2006.5: 77–79.

Ma, Zhenzhi 馬振智. "Shi tan Qin gong yihao damu de guozhi" 試談秦公一號大墓的槨制. *Kaogu yu wenwu* 2002.5: 56–59.

Machida, Akira 町田章. "Kahoku chihō ni okeru Kanbo no kōzō" 華北地方における漢墓の構造. *Tōhō gakuhō* 東方學報 49 (1977): 1–66.

Major, John S. et al. *The Huainanzi: A Guide to the Theory and Practice of Government in Early Han China*. New York: Columbia University Press, 2010.

Maspero, Henry. "Le Ming-t'ang et la crise religieuse Chinoise avant les Han." *Melanges chinois et bouddhiques* 9(1948–1951): 1–71.

Mayr, Ernst. *The Growth of Biological Thought*. Cambridge, MA: Harvard University Press, 1982.

Meng, Wentong 蒙文通. *Zhou Qin shaoshu minzu yanjiu* 周秦少數民族研究. Shanghai: Shanghai Longmen lianhe shuju, 1958.

Meng, Xianwu 孟憲武. "Yinxu nanqu muzang fajue zongshu—jian tan jige xiangguan wenti" 殷墟南區墓葬發掘綜述—兼談幾個相關問題. *Zhongyuan wenwu* 1986.3: 78–83.

Merleau-Ponty, Maurice. *The Visible and the Invisible*. Evanston, IL: Northwestern University Press, 1968.

Merriam-Webster's Collegiate Dictionary. Springfield, MA: Merriam-Webster at http://www.merriam-webster.com

Miao, Wenyuan 繆文遠. *Zhanguo ce xin jiaozhu* 戰國策新校注. Chengdu: Bashu shushe, 1987.

Miller, Alison. "Politics, and the Emergence of Rock-Cut Tombs in Early Han China." PhD diss., Harvard University, 2011.

Miller, Daniel. *A Theory of Shopping*. Ithaca, NY: Cornell University Press, 1998.

Mitchell, W. J. T. *Iconology: Image, Text, Ideology*. Chicago: University of Chicago Press, 1986.

Mitrović, Branko. "A Defence of Light: Ernst Gombrich, the Innocent Eye and Seeing in Perspective." *Journal of Art Historiography* 3 (2010): 3–30.

Moss, Robert. *Dao De Jing: The Book of the Way*. Berkeley: University of California Press, 2001.

Mu, Zhaona 穆朝娜. "Heibei Han mu xingzhi chu lun" 河北漢墓初論. In *Hebei sheng kaogu wenji, er* 河北省考古文集（二）, ed. Hebei sheng wenwu yanjiusuo, 386–402. Beijing: Beijing Yanshan chubanshe, 2001.

Nan, Bo 南波. "Jiangsu Lianyungang shi Haizhou Xi Han Shiqi you mu" 江蘇連雲港市海州西漢侍其繇墓. *Kaogu* 1975.3: 169–77.

Nanjing bowuyuan and Tongshan xian wenhuaguan 銅山縣文化館. "Tongshan Guishan erhao Xi Han Yadong mu" 銅山龜山二號西漢崖洞墓. *Kaogu xuebao* 1985.1:119–33.

Nanjing bowuyuan and Xuyi xian wenguang xinju 盱眙縣文廣新局. "Xuyi Dayunshan Xi Han damu muzhu keneng shi panfei daitou dage" 江蘇盱眙縣大雲山西漢江都王陵一號墓. *Kaogu* 2013.10: 3–68.

——. "Jiangsu Xuyi xian Dayunshan Xi Han Jiangdu wangling erhao mu fajue jianbao" 江蘇盱眙大雲山西漢江都王陵二號墓發掘簡報. *Wenwu* 2013.1: 42–47.

Needham, Joseph. *Science and Civilisation in China, volume 5, part 2, Spagyrical Discovery and Invention: Magisteries of Gold and Immortality*. Cambridge: Cambridge University Press, 1974.

Neimenggu wenwu gongzuodui 内蒙古文物工作隊. "Neimenggu Zizhiqu Zhunge'erqi Sujigou chutu yipi tongqi" 内蒙古自治區准格爾旗速機溝出土一批銅器. *Wenwu* 1965.2: 44–46.

Neimenggu bowuguan 内蒙古博物館 and Neimenggu wenwu gongzuodui. "Neimenggu Zhunge'erqi Yulongtai de Xiongnu mu" 内蒙古准格爾旗玉隆太的匈奴墓. *Kaogu* 1977.2: 111–14.

Nelson, Roger B. *Proofs Without Words: Exercises in Visual Thinking – Volume 1*. Mathematical Washington, DC: Association of America, 1993.

Nelson, Sarah M. "Feasting the Ancestors in Early China." In *The Archaeology and Politics of Food and Feasting in Early States and Empires*, ed. Tamara L. Bray, 65–90. New York: Kluwer Academic/Plenum Publishers, 2003.

Ni, Run'an 倪潤安. "Lun liang Han siling de yuanliu" 論兩漢四靈的源流. *Zhongyuan wenwu* 1999.1: 83–91.

Ningxia wenwu kaogu yanjiusuo 寧夏文物考古研究所 and Ningxia Guyuan bowuguan 寧夏固原博物館. "Ningxia Guyuan Yanglang qingtong wenhua mudi" 寧夏固原楊郎青銅文化墓地. *Kaogu xuebao* 1993.1: 15–56.

Nylan, Michael. "Toward an Archaeology of Writing: Text, Ritual, and the Culture of Public Display in the Classical Period (475 B.C.E–220 C.E.)." In *Text and Ritual in Early China*, ed. Martin Kern, 3–49. Seattle: University of Washington Press, 2005.

Nylan, Michael and Michael Loewe. *China's Early Empires: A Re-appraisal*. Cambridge: Cambridge University Press, 2010.

Ochi, Shigeaki 越智重明. "Shin no kokka saisei seido" 秦の国家財政制度. *Kyūshū Daigaku Tōyōshi ronshū* 15 (1986): 1–21.

———. "Zen Kan no zaisei ni tsuite" 前漢の財政について. *Kyūshū Daigaku Tōyōshi ronshū* 10 (1982): 1–21.

Ogata, Toru大形徹. "Shishin kō: Zenkan Gokan ki no shiryō o chūshin toshite" 四神考: 前漢、後漢期の資料を中心として. *Jinbengaku ronshū* 人文學論集 15 (1997): 127–43.

Okon, Etim E. "Religion and Politics in Ancient Egypt." *The American Journal of Social and Management Sciences* 3.3 (2012): 93–98.

Owen, Stephen. "One Sight: The Han shu Biography of Lady Li." In *Rhetoric and the Discourses of Power in Court Culture: China, Europe, and Japan*, ed. David R. Knechtges and Eugene Vance, 239–59. Seattle: University of Washington Press, 2005.

Panofsky, Erwin. *Studies in Iconology: Humanistic Themes in the Art of the Renaissance*. New York: Oxford University Press, 1939.

———. *Ein Beitrag zur Begriffsgeschichte der älteren Kunsttheorie*. Berlin: Wissenschaftsverlag Volker Spiess, 1993.

Pas, Julian. "Yin-Yang Polarity: A Binocular Vision of the World." *Asian Thought and Society* 8 (1983): 188–201.

Peerenboom, Randall P. *Law and Morality in Ancient China: The Silk Manuscripts of Huang-Lao*. Albany, NY: SUNY, 1993.

Pei, Puyan 裴溥言. *Xunzi yu Shijing* 荀子與詩經. *Taiwan daxue wenshi zhexue bao* 台灣大學文史哲學報 17 (1968): 151–83.

Peng, Hao 彭浩. "Du Yunmeng Shuihudi M77 Han jian zanglü" 讀雲夢睡虎地M77漢簡葬律. *Jianghan kaogu* 2009.4: 130–34.

Pi, Xirui 皮錫瑞. *Jingxue lishi* 經學歷史. Beijing: Zhonghua shuju, 1959.

Pines, Yuri. "Changing Views of tianxia in Pre-Imperial Discourse." *Oriens Extremus* 43.1/2 (2002): 101–16.

———. *Envisioning Eternal Empire: Chinese Political Thought of the Warring States*. Honolulu: University of Hawaii Press, 2009.

Pingshuo kaogudui 平朔考古隊. "Shanxi Shuoxian Qin Han mu fajue jianbao" 山西朔縣秦漢墓發掘簡報. *Wenwu* 1987.6: 1–52.

Pirazzoli-t'Serstevens, Michéle. *The Han Dynasty*. trans. Janet Seligman. New York: Rizzoli, 1982.

———. "Two Eastern Han Sites: Dahuting and Houshiguo." In *China's Early Empires: A Re-Appraisal*, ed. Michael Nylan and Michael Loewe, 83–113. Cambridge: Cambridge University Press, 2010.

Poo, Mu–chou. *Enemies of Civilization: Attitudes toward Foreigners in Ancient Mesopotamia, Egypt, and China*. Albany, NY: SUNY, 2005.

———. *In Search of Personal Welfare: A View of Ancient Chinese Religion*. Albany, NY: SUNY, 1998.

Pope, John A. "Sinology or Art History: Notes on Method in the Study of Chinese Art." *Harvard Journal of Asiatic Studies* 10.3/4 (1947): 388–417.

Portal, Jane Portal. *The First Emperor: China's Terracotta Army*. Cambridge, MA: Harvard University Press, 2007.

Porter, Deborah Lynn. *From Deluge to Discourse: Myth, History, and the Generation of Chinese Fiction*. Albany, NY: SUNY, 1996.

Powers, Martin J. *Art and Political Expressions in Early China*. New Haven, CT: Yale University Press, 1991.

——. *Pattern and Person: Ornament, Society, and Self in Classical China*. Cambridge, MA: Harvard University Asia Center, 2006.

Pregadio, Fabrizio. *The Encyclopedia of Taoism*, two volumes. London: Routledge, 2008.

Pruzinsky, Thomas and Thomas F. Cash. "Understanding Body Images: Historical and Contemporary Perspectives." In *Body Image: A Handbook of Theory, Research, and Clinical Practice*, ed. Thomas Pruzinsky and Thomas F. Cash, 3–12. New York: Guilford, 2002.

Psarras, Sophia-Karin. *Han Material Culture: An Archaeological Analysis and Vessel Typology*. Cambridge: Cambridge University Press, 2015.

Pullyblank, Edwin. "The Chinese and their Neighbors in Prehistoric and Early Historic Times." In *The Origins of Chinese Civilization*, ed. David N. Keightley, 411–66. Berkeley: University of California Press, 1983.

Pylyshyn, Zenon. *Seeing and Visualizing*. Cambridge, MA: MIT Press, 2003.

Qin Shihuang binmayong bowuguan 秦始皇兵馬俑博物館 and Shaanxi sheng kaogu yanjiusuo 陝西省省考古研究所. *Qin Shi Huang ling tongchema fajue baogao* 秦始皇陵銅車馬發掘報告. Beijing: Wenwu chubanshe, 1998.

Qin Shihuang jinshi keci zhu zhushizu 秦始皇金石刻辭注釋組. *Qin Shi Huang jinshi keci zhu* 秦始皇金石刻辭註. Shanghai: Shanghai renmin chubanshe, 1975.

Qin, Yu 秦玉. "Jiuliandun Zhanguo gumuqun: zhenjing guoneiwai de Chu wenhua faxian" 九連墩戰國古墓群：震驚國內外的楚文化發現. In *Dalian ribao* 大連日報, July 24, 2013. http://roll.sohu.com/20130724/n382399916.shtml.

Qinyong kaogudui 秦俑考古隊. "Lintong Shangjiaocun Qin mu qingli jianbao" 臨潼上焦村秦墓清理簡報. *Kaogu yu wenwu* 1980.2: 42–50.

Qiu, Xigui 裘錫圭. *Changsha Mawangdui Han mu jianbo jicheng* 長沙馬王堆漢墓簡帛集成. Seven volumes. Beijing: Zhonghua shuju, 2014.

——. "Du kaogu fajue suode wenzi ziliao biji (yi)" 讀考古發掘所得文字資料筆記 （一）. *Renwen zazhi* 人文雜誌 1981.6: 97–99.

Qiu, Yufang 裘毓芳. *Nujie zhushi* 女誡註釋. Shanghai: Shanghai yixue shuji, 1916.

Qu, Tongzu. *Han Social Structure*, ed. Jack L. Dull. Seattle & London: University of Washington Press, 1972.

Qu Yongxin 曲用心, "Lüelun Lingnan diqu Xi Han zaoqi qingtongqi de tezheng ji chengyin" 略論嶺南地區西漢早期青銅器的特徵及成因, *Dongnan wenhua* 2009.4: 64–67.

Ragon, Michel. *The Space of Death: A Study of Funerary Architecture, Decoration, and Urbanism*. Charlottesville: University of Virginia Press, 1983.

Rao, Zongyi 饒宗頤. *Laozi Xiang'er zhu jiaozheng* 老子想爾注校證. Hong Kong: Zhonghua shuju, 2015.

Raphals, Lisa Ann. *Sharing the Light: Representations of Women and Virtue in Early China*. Albany, NY: SUNY Press, 1998.

Rawson, Jessica. *Chinese Jade from the Neolithic to the Qing*. London: British Museum, 1995.

——. "Chu Influences on the Development of Han Bronze Vessels." *Arts Asiatiques* 44 (1989): 84–99.

——. "Ewige Wohnstätten: Die Gräber des Königs von Nan Yue und der kaiserlichen Prinzen in Ostchina." In *Schätze für König Zhao Mo: Das Grab von Nan Yue*, ed. Margarete Prüch, 80–95. Heidelberg: Braus, 1998.

——. "Ritual Vessel Changes in the Warring States, Qin and Han Periods." In *Regional Culture, Religion, and Arts before the Seventh Century* 中世紀以前的地域文化、宗

教與藝術, Papers from the Third International Conference on Sinology, History Section, ed. Hsing I-tien (=Xing Yitian), 1–57. Taipei: Academia Sinica, 2002.

——. "The Eternal Palaces of the Western Han: A New View of the Universe." *Artibus Asiae* 59.1/2 (1999): 5–58.

——. "The First Emperor's Tomb: The Afterlife Universe." In *The First Emperor: China's Terracotta Army*, ed. Jane Portal, 120–24. London: British Museum, 2007.

——. "The Han Empire and its Northern Neighbours: the Fascination of the Exotic." In *The Search for Immortality, Tomb Treasures of Han China*, ed. James Lin, 23–36. New Haven, CT: Yale University Press, 2012.

——. "Western Zhou Archaeology." In *Cambridge History of Ancient China: From the Origins of Civilisation to 221 B.C.*, ed. Michael Loewe and Edward Shaughnessy, 352–449. Cambridge: Cambridge University Press, 1999.

Rawson, Jessica and Emma C. Bunker. *Ancient Chinese and Ordos Bronzes*. Hong Kong: Oriental Ceramic Society of Hong Kong, 1990.

Richeson, David Scott. *Euler's Gem: The Polyhedron Formula and the Birth of Topology*. Kington, NJ: Kington University Press, 2008.

Rickett, W. Allyn. *Guanzi: Political, Economic, and Philosophical Essays from Early China. Volume 2*. Princeton, NJ: Princeton University Press, 1998.

——. *Guanzi: Political, Economic, and Philosophical Essays from Early China, Volume 1*. Revised edition. Boston: Chen and Tsui Company, 2001.

Riegel, Jeffrey. "Kou-mang and Ju-shou." *Cahiers d'Extrême-Asie* 5 (1989): 55–83.

Rolle, Renate. *The World of the Scythians*. Trans. Gayna Walls. London: B.T. Batsford, 1989.

——. *Totenkult der Skythen, Teil I. Das Steppengebiet*. Berlin: De Gruyter, 1979.

Rosemont, Henry and Roger T. Ames. *The Chinese Classic of Family Reverence: A Philosophical Translation of the Xiaojing*. Honolulu: University of Hawaii Press, 2009.

Ruan, Yuan 阮元. *Shisanjing zhushu* 十三經注疏. Beijing: Zhonghua shuju, 1980.

Sartre, Jean-Paul. *Being and Nothingness: An Essay on Phenomenological Ontology*. Translated by Hazel E. Barnes. London: Methuen, 1958.

Schilder, Paul. *The Image and Appearance of the Human Body*. New York: International University Press, 1935/1950.

Schmidt, E. F. *Persepolis III: The Royal Tombs and Other Monuments*. Chicago: University of Chicago Press, 1970.

Sekino, Tadashi 関野貞. "Rikuchō izen no bojō ni tsuyite" 六朝以前の墓塼に就いて. *Kōkogaku zasshi* 考古學雑誌 6.11 (1916): 605–24.

Sekino, Takeshi 關野雄. *Chūgoku kōkogaku kenkyū* 中國考古學研究. Tokyo: Tokyo Daigaku Shuppankai, 1963.

Seppänen, Janne. *The Power of the Gaze: An Introduction to Visual Literacy*. Trans. Aijaleena Ahonen and Kris Clarke. New York: Peter Lang, 2006.

Sellmann, James D. *Timing and Rulership in Master Lü's Spring and Autumn Annals (Lüshi chunqiu)*. Albany, NY: SUNY Press, 2002.

Shaanxi sheng kaogu yanjiusuo 陝西省考古研究所. *Qindu Xianyang kaogu baogao* 秦都咸陽考古報告. Beijing: Kexue chubanshe, 2004.

Shaanxi sheng kaogu yanjiusuo and Lintong xian wenguanhui 臨潼縣文管會. "Qin Dongling diyihao lingyuan kanchaji" 秦東陵第一號陵園勘察記. *Kaogu yu wenwu* 1987.4: 19–28.

Shaanxi sheng kaogu yanjiusuo Hanling kaogudui 陝西省考古研究所漢陵考古隊. "Han Jingdi Yangling nanqu congzangkeng fajue dierhao jianbao" 漢景帝陽陵南區從葬坑發掘第二號簡報. *Wenwu* 1994.6: 4–23.

——. "Han Jingdi Yangling nanqu congzangkeng fajue diyihao jianbao" 漢景帝陽陵南區從葬坑發掘第一號簡報. *Wenwu* 1992.4: 1–13.

——. *Zhongguo Han Yangling caiyong* 中國漢陽陵彩俑. Xi'an: Shaanxi lüyou chubanshe, 1992.

Shaanxi sheng kaogu yanjiusuo Qinling gongzuozhan. "Qin Dongling disihao lingyuan diaocha zuantan jianbao" 秦東陵第四號陵園調查鑽探簡報. *Kaogu yu wenwu* 1993.3: 48–51.

Shaanxi sheng kaogu yanjiuyuan 陝西省考古研究院. "Han Yangling diling dongce shiyi-ershiyi hao waicangkeng fajue jianbao" 漢陽陵帝陵東側11–21號外藏坑發掘簡報. *Kaogu yu wenwu* 2008.3: 3–32.

——. *Liangdaicun Rui guo mudi—2007 niandu fajue baogao* 梁帶村芮國墓地—2007年度發掘報告. Two volumes. Beijing: Wenwu chubanshe, 2010.

Shaanxi sheng kaogu yanjiusuo and Shi Huang ling Qin yongkeng kaogu fajuedui 始皇陵秦俑坑考古發掘隊. *Qin Shihuang ling bingmayongken—yihao keng fajue baogao 1974–1984* 秦始皇陵兵馬俑坑一號坑發掘報告 1974–1984. Two volumes. Beijing: Wenwu chubanshe, 1988.

Shaanx sheng kaogu yanjiusuo and Qin Shihuang bingmayong bowuguan 秦始皇兵馬俑博物館. *Qin Shihuangdi lingyuan fajue baogao 1999* 秦始皇帝陵園發掘報告 1999. Beijing: Kexue chubanshe, 2000.

Shaanxi sheng kaogu yanjiuyuan and Qin Shihuang bingmayong bowuguan. *Qin Shihuangdi lingyuan kaogu baogao 2001–2003* 秦始皇帝陵園考古報告 2001–2003. Beijing: Wenwu chubanshe, 2007.

Shaanxi sheng kaogu yanjiusuo, Weinan shi wenwu baohu kaogu yanjiusuo 渭南市文物保護考古研究所, and Hancheng shi wenwu lüyouju 韓城市文物旅遊局. "Shaanxi Hancheng Liangdaicun yizhi M26 fajue jianbao" 陝西韓城梁帶村遺址M26發掘簡報. *Wenwu* 2008.1: 4–21.

Shaanxi sheng Yongcheng kaogudui 陝西省雍城考古隊. "Fengxiang Qingong lingyuan zuantan yu shijue jianbao" 鳳翔秦公陵園鑽探與試掘簡報. *Wenwu* 1983.7: 30–37.

Shaanxi sheng Yongcheng kaogudui. "Fengxiang Qingong lingyuan dierci zuantan jianbao" 鳳翔秦公陵園第二次鑽探簡報. *Wenwu* 1987: 55–65.

Shan, Yueying. "Dong Zhou Qindai Zhongguo beifang diqu kaoguxue wenhua geju—jianlun Rong, Di, Hu yu Huaxia zhijian de hudong" 東周秦代中國北方地區考古學文化格局—兼論戎狄胡與華夏之間的互動. *Kaogu xuebao* 2015.3: 304–344.

Shan, Yuying and Lu Yan. "Xiongnu yaoshipai ji xiangguan wenti yanjiu" 匈奴腰飾牌及相關問題研究. *Gugong bowuyuan yuankan* 故宮博物院院刊2008.2: 130–58.

Shandong Heze diqu Han mu fajue xiaozu 山東菏澤地區漢墓發掘小組. "Juye Hongtushan Xi Han mu" 巨野紅土山西漢墓. *Kaogu xuebao* 1983.5: 471–500.

Shandong sheng kaogu yanjiusuo. "Zhangqiu shi Weishan Han mu peizangkeng" 章丘市危山漢墓陪葬坑. *Zhongguo kaoguxue nianjian* (2003) 中國考古學年鑑 (2003), ed. Zhongguo kaogu xuehui, 216–18. Beijing: Zhongguo shehui kexue chubanshe, 2004.

Shandong sheng wenwu kaogu yanjiusuo 山東省文物考古研究所. *Linzi Qi mu* 臨淄齊墓. Volume One. Beijing: Wenwu chubanshe, 2007.

Shandong sheng wenwu kaogu yanjiusuo and Linzi shi Linzi qu wenwu guanliju 臨淄市臨淄區文物管理局. "Shandong Linzi Shanwangcun Han dai bingmayong keng fajue jianbao" 山東臨淄山王村漢代兵馬俑坑發掘簡報. *Wenwu* 2016.6: 5–29.

Shandong sheng wenwu kaogu yanjiusuo, Linzi shi Linzi qu wenwu guanliju, Han Weidong 韓偉東, Wei Chengmin 魏成敏, and Wang Huitian 王會田. *Linzi Shanwangcun Han dai bingmayong* 臨淄山王村漢代兵馬俑. Beijing: Wenwu chubanshe, 2017.

Shanxi sheng kaogu yanjiusuo 山西省考古研究所 and Beijing daxue kaogu xi 北京大學考古系. "Tianma-Qucun yizhi—Beizhao Jin hou mudi dierci fajue" 天馬—曲村遺址—北趙晉侯墓地第二次發掘. *Wenwu* 1994.1: 4–28.

——. Tianma-Qucun yizhi—Beizhao Jin hou mudi diliuci fajue" 天馬—曲村遺址—北趙晉侯墓地第六次發掘, *Wenwu* 2001.8: 4–21, 55.

——. "Tianma-Qucun yizhi—Beizhao Jin hou mudi disanci fajue a 天馬—曲村遺址—北趙晉侯墓地第三次發掘. *Wenwu* 1994.8: 22–33, 68.

——. "Tianma-Qucun yizhi—Beizhao Jin hou mudi disici fajueo 天馬—曲村遺址—北趙晉侯墓地第四次發掘. *Wenwu* 1994.8: 4–21.

——. "Tianma-Qucun yizhi—Beizhao Jin hou mudi diwuci fajue" 天馬—曲村遺址—北趙晉侯墓地第五次發掘. *Wenwu* 1995.7: 4–39.

Shanxi sheng kaogusuo 山西省考古所 and Taiyuan shi wenwu guanli weiyuanhui太原市文物管理委員會. *Taiyuan Jin guo Zhao qin mu* 太原晉國趙卿墓. Beijing: Wenwu chubanshe, 1996.

Shanxi sheng wenwuju 山西省文物局, et al., *Jin guo qi zhen: Shanxi Jin hou muqun chutu wenwu jing pin* 晉國奇珍: 山西晉侯墓群出土文物精品. Shanghai: Shanghai renmin meishu chubanshe, 2002.

Shao, Huiqiu 邵會秋 and Xiong Zenglong 熊增瓏. "Jibei diqu Dong Zhou shiqi beifang wenhua qingtong duanjian yanjiu" 冀北地區東周時期北方文化青銅器短劍研究. *Wenwu chunqiu* 2005.4: 7–22.

Shaughnessy, Edward L. "I Chou shu." In *Early Chinese Texts: A Bibliographical Guide*, ed. William Boltz, 229–33. Berkeley, CA: Society for the Study of Early China, 1993.

——. "Once Again on Ideographs and Iconolatry." *Shijie hanzi tongbao* 世界漢字通報. 2.1 (2016): 1–31.

Shemakhanskaya, Marina Shemakhanskaya, Mikhail Treister, and Leonid Yablonsky. "The Technique of Gold Inlaid Decoration in the 5th-4th Centuries BC: Silver and Iron Finds from the Early Sarmatian Barrows of Filippovka, Southern Urals." *Archéo-Sciences* 33 (2009): 211–20.

Shen, Bingzhen 沈炳震. *Jiujing bian zi du meng* 九經辨字瀆蒙. In *Yingyin Wenyuange siku quanshu* 景印文淵閣四庫全書. 1500 volumes. Volume 194. Taipei: Xinwenfeng, 1986.

Shen, Yue 沈約. *Songshu* 宋書. Beijing: Zhonghua shuju, 1974.

Shi, Jie 施傑. "Jiaotong youming: Xi Han zhuhouwang mu zhong de jisi kongjian" 交通幽明: 西漢諸侯王墓中的祭祀空間. In *Gudai muzang meishu yanjiu (dierjuan)* 古代墓葬美術研究 (第二卷), ed. Wu Hung, Zheng Yan, and Zhu Qingsheng, 72–93. Changsha: Hunan meishu chubanshe, 2013.

——. "Incorporating All for One: The First Emperor's Tomb Mound." *Early China* 37 (2014): 359–91.

——. "Revisiting the 'Old Jade Man' at Mancheng Tomb No. 1 in Western Han China." Paper presented at the symposium Age of Empires: Chinese Art from the Qin and Han Dynasties. Metropolitan Museum of Art, New York, Apr. 2017.

——. "Rolling Between Burial and Shrine: A Tale of Two Chariot Processions at Chulan Tomb 2 in Eastern Han China (171 CE)." *Journal of American Oriental Society* 135.3 (2015): 433–52.

——. "The Mancheng Tombs: Shaping the Afterlife of the 'Kingdom within the Mountains." PhD diss., University of Chicago, 2017.

Shi, Nianhai 史念海. "Xi Zhou yu Chunqiu shiqi huazu yu fei huazu de zaju jiqi dili fenbu(shangpian)" 西周與春秋時期華族與非華族的雜居及其地理分佈（上篇）. *Zhongguo lishi dili luncong* 中國歷史地理論叢1990.1: 27–40.

——. "Xi Zhou yu Chunqiu shiqi huazu yu fei huazu de zaju jiqi dili fenbu (xiapian)" 西周與春秋時期華族與非華族的雜居及其地理分佈 (下篇). *Zhongguo lishi dili luncong* 1990.2: 9–40.

Shizishan Chuwangling kaogu fajuedui. "Xuzhou Shizishan Xi Han Chuwangling fajue jianbao" 徐州獅子山西漢楚王陵發掘簡報. *Wenwu* 1998.8: 4–33.

Shuihudi Qin mu zhujian zhengli xiaozu 睡虎地秦墓竹簡整理小組. *Shuihudi Qin mu zhujian* 睡虎地秦墓竹簡. Beijing: Wenwu chubanshe, 1990.

Sigimura, Shinji 杉村伸二. "Zen Kan keiteiki kokusei tankan no haikei" 前漢景帝期國制轉換の背景. *Tōyōshi kenkyū* 東洋史研究67.2 (2008): 161–93.

——. "Kan sho no gunkokubyō to nyūchō seido ni tsuite: Kan sho gunkokusei to ketsuen teki chūtai" 漢初の郡国廟と入朝制度について：漢初郡国制と血縁的紐帯. *Kyūshū Daigaku Tōyōshi ronshū* 37 (2009): 1–23.

Sima, Qian 司馬遷. *Shiji* 史記. Beijing: Zhonghua shuju, 1959.

Slingerland, Edward. *Effortless Action: Wu-wei As Conceptual Metaphor and Spiritual Ideal in Early China*. Oxford: Oxford University Press, 2003.

So, Jenny. (=Su Fangshu 蘇芳淑). "Guren cun gu—Yucong zai gudai muzhong zhong de zhu yiyi" 古人存古—玉琮在古代墓葬中的諸意義. In *Gudai muzang meishu yanjiu (dierji)* 古代墓葬美術研究 (第二集), ed. Wu Hung, Zheng Yan, and Zhu Qingsheng, 1–17. Changsha: Hunan meishu chubanshe, 2014.

——. "The Inlaid Bronzes of the Warring States Period." In *The Great Bronze Age of China*, ed. Wen Fong, 303–20. New York: Metropolitan Museum of Art, 1980.

Sofaer, Joanna R. *The Body as Material Culture: A Theoretical Osteoarchaeology*. Cambridge: Cambridge University Press, 2006.

Song, Rong 宋蓉. "Xuzhou diqu Xi Han muzang de fenqi he wenhua yinsu fenxi" 徐州地區西漢墓葬的分期和文化因素分析. *Huaxia kaogu* 2010. 4: 101–13.

Steele, John. *The I-li or Book of Etiquette and Ceremonial*. Two volumes. London: Probsthain, 1917.

Sterckx, Roel. "Food and Philosophy in Early China." In *Of Tripod and Palate: Food, Politics, and Religion in Traditional China*, 34–61, ed. Roel Sterckx. New York: Palgrave Macmillan, 2005.

——. *Food, Sacrifice, and Sagehood in Early China*. Cambridge: Cambridge University Press, 2011.

Su, Yu 蘇輿. *Chunqiu fanlu yizheng* 春秋繁露義證. Beijing: Zhonghua shuju, 1992.

Sun, Guanwen 孫冠文 and Zhao Chao 趙超. "You chutu yinzhang kan liangchu muzang de muzhu deng wenti" 由出土印章看兩處墓葬的墓主等問題. *Kaogu* 1981.4: 333–38.

Sun, Hua 孫華. "Banqiuxing qi yongtu lue kao" 半球形器用途略考. *Nanfang wenwu* 1995.10: 107–10.

Sun, Ji 孫機. *Han dai wuzhi wenhua ziliao tushuo* 漢代物質文化資料圖説. Beijing: Wenwu chubanshe, 1991.

——. "Han zhen yishu" 漢鎮藝術. *Wenwu* 1983.6: 69–72.

——. "Zhoudai de zu yupei" 周代的組玉佩. *Wenwu* 1998.4: 4–14.

——. *Zhongguo gu yufu luncong (zengdingben)* 中國古輿服論叢 (增訂本). Beijing: Wenwu chubanshe, 2001.

Sun, Qingwei 孫慶偉. "Jinhou mudi chutu yuqi zhaji" 晉侯墓地出土玉器札記. *Huaxia Kaogu* 1999.1: 60–71.

Sun, Weigang 孫偉剛. "Xi, Liyi, yu Lishanyuan—jian lun Qin Shihuangdi ling Liyi de gongneng yu zuoyong" 戲, 驪邑與驪山園—兼論秦始皇帝驪邑的功能與作用. *Kaogu yu wenwu* 2009.4: 61–71.

Sun, Xingyan 孫星衍 et al. *Han guan liuzhong* 漢官六种. Beijing: Zhonghua shuju, 1990.

Sun, Yiran 孫詒讓. *Mozi jiangu* 墨子閒詁. Beijing: Zhonghua shuju, 2001.

Sun, Zhixin Jason. "The Liangzhu Culture: Its Discovery and Its Jades." *Early China* 18 (1993): 1–40.

Sung, Z. D. *The Text of Yi King and its Appendixes*. Taipei: Ch'eng Wen, 1971.

Tang, Jigen 唐際根. "Yinxu jiazu mudi chutan" 殷墟家族墓地初探. In *Zhongguo Shang wenhua guoji xueshu taolunhui lunwenji* 中國商文化國際學術討論會論文集, ed. Zhongguo shehui kexueyuan kaogu yanjiusuo, 201–7. Beijing: Zhongguo dabaike quanshu chubanshe, 1998.

Tang, Jinyu 唐金裕. "Xi'an xijiao Han dai jianzhu yizhi fajue baogao" 西安西郊漢代建築遺址發掘報告. *Kaogu xuebao* 1959.2: 45–55.

Tang, Lan 唐蘭. "Mawangdui chutu Laozi yiben juanqian gu yishu de yanjiu—jianlun qi yu Han chu ru fa douzheng de guanxi" 馬王堆出土老子乙本卷前古軼書的研究—兼論其與漢初儒法鬥爭的關係. *Kaogu xuebao* 1975.1: 8–38.

Tang, Qiling 湯其領. "Yinwan Han mu jiandu zhong youguan junxian houguo lizhi de jige wenti" 尹灣漢墓簡牘中有關郡縣侯國吏治的幾個問題. *Shixue yuekan* 史學月刊 2005.11: 16–19.

Taniguchi, Yasuyo 谷口やすよ. "Kandai no 'taigō rinchō'" 漢代の太后臨朝. *Rekishi hyōron* 歷史評論159 (1980): 86–98.

Taylor, John H. *Death and the Afterlife in Ancient Egypt*. Chicago: University of Chicago Press, 2001.

——. *Journey Through the Afterlife: Ancient Egyptian Book of the Dead*. Cambridge, MA: Harvard University Press, 2010.

Teng, Mingyu 滕銘予. "Lun Guanzhong Qin mu zhong dongshimu de niandai" 論關中秦墓中洞室墓的年代. *Huaxia kaogu* 1993.2: 90–97.

——. "Zhongguo beifang diqu liang Zhou shiqi tongfu de zai tantao" 中國北方地區兩周時期銅鍑的再探討. *Bianjiang kaogu yanjiu* 邊疆考古研究 1 (2002): 34–54.

Teng, Mingyu and Wang Chunbin 王春斌. "Dong Zhou shiqi sanjin diqu de beifang wenhua" 東周時期三晉地區的北方文化. *Bianjiang kaogu yanjiu* 10 (2011): 117–22.

Thorp, Robert L. Thorp. *China in the Early Bronze Age: Shang Civilization*. Philadelphia: University of Pennsylvania Press, 2006.

——. "Mountain Tombs and Jade Burial Suits: Preparations for Eternity in the Western Han." In *Ancient Mortuary Traditions of China: Papers on Chinese Ceramic Funerary Sculptures*, ed. George Kuwayama, 26–39. Los Angeles: Los Angeles County Museum of Art, 1991.

——. "The Sui Xian Tomb: Re-Thinking the Fifth Century." *Artibus Asiae.* 43.1/2 (1981): 67–110.

Thote, Alain. "Continuities and Discontinuities: Chu Burials during the Eastern Zhou Period." In *Exploring China's Past, New Discoveries and Studies in Archaeology and Art*, ed. Roderick Whitfield and Wang Tao, 189–204. London: Saffron, 1999.

——. "Burial Practices as Seen in Rulers' Tombs of the Eastern Zhou Period: Patterns and Regional Traditions." In *Religion and Chinese Society: A Centennial Conference of the Ecole francaise d'Extreme-Orient*, 1: 65–107.

Tian, Guangjin 田廣金 and Guo Suxin 郭素新. *E'erduosi shi qingtongqi* 鄂爾多斯式青銅器. Beijing: Wenwu chubanshe, 1986.

Tian, He 田河. "Chutu Zhanguo qiance suoji mingwu fenlei huishi" 出土戰國遣冊所記名物分類彙釋. PhD diss., Jilin University, 2007.

Tian, Wei 田偉. "Shi lun liang Zhou de jishi jitan mu" 試論兩周的積石積炭墓. *Zhong-guo lishi wenwu* 2009.2: 59–67.

Tosaki, Tetsuhiko 戸崎哲彦. "Chūgoku kodai no taisō ni okeru taikō shōni tsuite" 中国古代の大喪における「大行」称について, *Shigaku zasshi* 史學雜誌 100.9 (1991): 1546–68.

Tseng, Lilian Lan-ying. *Picturing Heaven in Early China*. Cambridge, MA: Harvard University Asia Center, 2011.

——. "Princely Tombs in Han China: New Discoveries from Dayunshan and Nanchang." *Orientations* 48.2 (2017): 103–9.

Turner, Terence. "The Social Skin." In *Not Work Alone: A Cross-cultural View of Activities Superfluous to Survival*, ed. Jeremy Cherfas and Roger Lewin, 112–40. London: Temple Smith, 1980.

Umehara, Sueji 梅原末治. *Rakuyō Kin-son kobo shūei* 洛陽金村古墓聚英. Kyoto: Kobayashi Shashin Seihanjo Shuppanbu, 1937.

Wang, Aihe. *Cosmology and Political Culture in Early China*. Cambridge: Cambridge University Press, 2000.

Wang, Ganghuai 王綱懷. *Zhishui ji: Wang Ganghuai tongjing yanjiu lunji* 止水集: 王綱懷銅鏡研究論集. Shanghai: Shanghai guji chubanshe, 2010.

Wang, Guowei 王國維. "Mingtang miao qin tongkao" 明堂廟寢通考. In *Guantang ji lin* 觀堂集林, ed. Wang Guowei, 58–68. Shijiazhuang: Hebei jiaoyu, 2003.

Wang, Hui 王恢. *Han wangguo yu houguo zhi yanbian* 漢王國與侯國之演變. Taipei: Zhonghua shuju, 1984.

Wang, Hui 王輝. "Zhangjiachuan Majiayuan mudi xiangguan wenti chutan" 張家川馬家塬墓地相關問題初探. *Wenwu* 2009.10: 70–77.

Wang, Kailuan 王恺鑾. *Yin Wen zi jiaozheng* 尹文子校正. Minguo congshu edition. Shanghai: Shanghai shudian, 1989.

Wang, Kai 王恺 and Ge Mingyu 葛明宇. *Xuzhou Shizishan Chuwang ling* 徐州獅子山西漢楚王陵. Beijing: Sanlian, 2005.

Wang, Liqi 王利器. *Fengsu tongyi jiaozhu* 風俗通義校注. Beijing: Zhonghua shuju, 1981.

——. *Yantielun jiaozhu* 盐鐵論校注. Beijing: Zhonghua shuju, 1992.

Wang, Longzheng 王龍正 and Jiang Tao 姜濤. "Chutu qiwu zuiduo de Xi Zhou guojun mu" 出土器物最多的西周國君墓. In *Zhongguo shinian baida kaogu xinfaxian* 中國十年百大考古新發現, ed. Li Wenru 李文儒, 337–41. Beijing: Wenwu chubanshe, 2002.

Wang, Michelle C. *A Bronze Menagerie: Mat Weights of Early China*. Boston: Isabella Stewart Gardner Museum, 2006.

Wang, Ming 王明. *Baopuzi neipian jiaoshi* 抱朴子內篇校釋. Beijing: Zhonghua shuju, 1986.

——. *Taipingjing hejiao* 太平經合校. Beijing: Zhonghua shuju, 1979.

Wang, Mingke 王明珂. *Huaxia bianyuan, lishi jiyi yu zuqun rentong* 華夏邊緣—歷史際遇與族群認同. Taipei: Yunchen, 1997.

Wang, Niansun 王念孫. *Guangya shuzheng* 廣雅疏證. Beijing: Zhonghua shuju, 1983.

Wang Pinzhen 王聘珍. *Da Dai liji jiegu* 大戴禮記解詁. Beijing: Zhonghua shuju, 1983.

Wang, Robin Wang. *Images of Women in Chinese Thought and Culture: Writings from the Pre-Qin*. New York: Hackett, 2003.

Wang, Shuping 王叔平. "Xinzheng fajue Xugang damu" 新鄭發掘許崗大墓. In *Henan wenhua wenwu nianjian* 河南文化文物年鑑, ed. Bianweihui, 97. Zhengzhou: Henan sheng wuhuating & wenwuju, 2004.

Wang, Wei 王瑋 and Wang Jinchao 王金潮. "Dayunshan Han mu jinlü yuyi xiufu baogao" 大雲山漢墓金縷玉衣修復報告. *Jianghan kaogu* 2014.1: 113–18.

Wang, Wuyu 王武鈺 and Wang Ce 王策. "Longqingxia bieshu gongcheng zhong faxian de Chunqiu shiqi muzang" 龍慶峽別墅工程中發現的春秋時期墓葬. *Beijing wenwu yu kaogu* 北京文物與考古 1994.2: 32–45.

Wang, Xianqian 王先謙. *Shi sanjia yi jishu* 詩三家義集疏. Beijing: Zhonghua shuju, 1987.

——. *Xunzi jijie* 荀子集解. Beijing: Zhonghua shuju, 1988.

Wang, Xueli 王學理. "Qin Han xiang cheng, diwang tongzhi—lue lun Qin Han huangdi he Han zhuhouwang lingyuan de jicheng yu yanbian" 秦漢相承 帝王同制—略論秦漢皇帝和漢諸侯王陵園制度的繼承與演變. *Kaogu yu wenwu* 2000.6: 60–66, 79.

Wang, Yang 王洋. "Liangdaicun Rui Huangong fufu mu suizang qingtongqi de xingbie guancha" 梁帶村芮桓公夫婦墓隨葬青銅器的性別觀察. *Kaogyu yu wenwu* 2013.2: 69–77.

Wang, Yiliang 王貽樑. *Mutianzi zhuan huijiao jishi* 穆天子傳滙校集釋. Shanghai: Huadong shifan daxue chubanshe, 1994.

Wang, Yongbo 王永波. *Changqing Xi Han Jibei wang ling* 長清西漢濟北王陵. Beijing: Sanlian shudian, 2005.

Wang, Zhongshu. *Han Civilization*. Trans. K.C. Chang et al. New Haven, CT: Yale University Press, 1982.

Wang Zunguo 汪遵國. "Liangzhu wenhua 'yulianzang' shulüe" 良渚文化玉斂葬述略. *Wenwu* 1984.2: 23–35.

Watanabe, Shin ichirō 渡辺信一郎. *Chūgoku kodai no ōken to tenka chitsujo: Nitchū hikakushi no shiten kara* 中国古代の王権と天下秩序: 日中比較史の視点から. Tokyo: Azekura Shobō, 2003.

Watson, Burton. *Hsün Tzu: Basic Writings*. New York: Columbia University Press, 1963.

——. *Courtier and Commoner: Selections of the History of the Former Han by Pan Ku*. New York: Columbia University Press, 1974.

——. *Mozi: Basic Writings*. New York: Columbia University Press, 2003.

——. *The Analects of Confucius*. New York: Columbia University Press, 2007.

——. *The Complete Works of Zhuangzi*. New York: Columbia University Press, 2013.

Watson, James L. and Evelyn S. Rawski. *Death Ritual in Late Imperial and Modern China*. Berkeley: University of California Press, 1988.

Wells, Marnix. *The Pheasant Cap Master and the End of History: Linking Religion to Philosophy in Early China*. St. Petersburg, FL: Three Pines, 2013.

Wenwu bianji weiyuanhui 文物編輯委員會. *Wenwu kaogu gongzuo sanshinian* 文物考古工作三十年. Beijing: Wenwu chubanshe, 1979.

Winckelmann, Johann Joachim. *History of the Art of Antiquity*. Trans. Harry Francis Mallgrave. Los Angeles, CA: Getty Publications, 2006.

Windfuhr, Gernot. "The Stags of Filippovka: Mithraic Coding on the South Ural Steppes." In *The Golden Deer of Eurasia: Perspectives on the Steppe Nomads of the Ancient World*, ed. Joan Aruz et al., 46–81. New York: Metropolitan Museum of Art, 2006.

Wollheim, Richard. "Seeing-As, Seeing-In, and Pictorial Representation." In *Art and Its Objects: With Six Supplementary Essays*, ed. Wollheim, 137–51. Cambridge: Cambridge University Press, 1980.

Wood, Christopher. *The Vienna School Reader*. New York: Zone Books, 2000.

Wu, Guangping 吳廣平. *Song Yu ji* 宋玉集. Changsha: Yuelu shuyuan, 2001.

Wu, Hung. "Rethinking East Asian Tombs: A Methodological Proposal." In *Dialogues in Art History, from Mesopotamian to Modern: Readings for a New Century*, ed. Elizabeth Cropper, 139–65. Washington, DC: National Gallery of Art, 2009.

——. *The Art of the Yellow Springs: Understanding Chinese Tombs.* London: Reaktion Books, 2009.

——. "The Prince of Jade Revisited: Material Symbolism of Jade as Observed in the Mancheng Tomb." In *Chinese Jade, Colloquies on Art and Archaeology in Asia 18*, ed. Rosemary E. Scott, 147–70. London: Percival David Foundation of Chinese Art, 1997.

——. *The Wu Liang Shrine: The Ideology of Early Chinese Pictorial Art.* Stanford, CA: Stanford University Press, 1989.

Wu, Rongzeng 吳榮曾. "Xi Han wangguo guanzhi kaoshi" 西漢王國官制考實. *Beijing daxue xuebao (zhexue shehui kexue ban)* 北京大學學報（哲學社會科學版）1990.3: 110–22, 109.

Wu, Yujiang 吳毓江. *Mozi jiaozhu* 墨子校注. Beijing: Zhonghua shuju, 1993.

Wu, Shuping 吳樹平. *Dongguan Hanji jiaozhu* 東觀漢紀校注. Beijing: Zhonghua shuju, 2008.

Wu, Xiaoyun 吳曉筠. "Shang zhi Chunqiu shiqi zhongyuan diqu qingtong chemaqi xing-shi yanjiu" 商至春秋時期中原地區青銅車馬器形式研究. *Gudai wenming* 古代文明 2002.1: 180–277.

——. *Shang Zhou shiqi chema maizang yanjiu* 商周時期車馬埋葬研究. Beijing: Kexue chubanshe, 2009.

Wu, Xiaolong. *Material Culture, Power, and Identity in Ancient China.* Cambridge: Cambridge University Press, 2017.

Wuen, Yuesitu 烏恩岳斯圖 (=Wu En 烏恩). *Beifang caoyuan kaoguxue wenhua bijiao yanjiu—qingtong shidai zhi zaoqi tieqi shidai* 北方草原考古學文化研究—青銅時代至早期鐵器時代. Beijing: Kexue chubanshe, 2007.

——. "Guanyu woguo beifang de qingtong duanjian" 關於我國北方的青銅短劍. *Kaogu* 1978.5: 324–33, 360.

Wylie, Alison. *Thinking from Things: Essays in the Philosohpy of Archaeology.* Berkeley: Univeristy of California Press, 2002.

Xiang, Zonglu 向宗魯. *Shuoyuan jiaozheng* 說苑校證. Beijing: Zhonghua shuju, 1987.

Xianyang shi wenwu kaogu yanjiusuo 咸陽市文物考古研究所. *Xi Han diling zuantan diaocha baogao* 西漢帝陵鑽探調查報告. Beijing: Wenwu chubanshe, 2010.

Xie, Duanju 謝端琚. "Shilun woguo zaoqi tudongmu" 試論我國早期土洞墓. *Kaogu* 1987.12: 1097–1104.

Xing, Yitian (= Hsing I-Tien) 邢義田. *Tianxia yijia: Huangdi, guanliao yu shehui* 天下一家：皇帝、官僚與社會. Beijing: Zhonghua shuju, 2008.

Xiong, Beisheng 熊北生, Chen Wei 陳偉, and Cai Dan 蔡丹. "Hubei Yunmeng Shui-hudi 77 hao Han mu chutu jiandu gaishu" 湖北雲夢睡虎地77號漢墓出土簡牘概述. *Wenwu* 2018.3: 43–53.

Xu, Cheng 許成 and Li Jinzeng 李進增. "Dong Zhou shiqi de rongdi qingtong wenhua" 東周時期的戎狄青銅文化. *Kaogu xuebao* 1993: 1–11.

Xu, Fuguan 徐復觀. *Liang Han sixiangshi* 兩漢思想史. Three volumes. Shanghai: Hua-dong shifan chubanshe, 2001.

Xu, Gan 徐幹. *Balanced Discourses.* Translated by John Makeham. New Haven, CT: Yale University Press, 2002.

Xu, Jay. "The Cemetery of the Western Zhou Lords of Jin." *Artibus Asiae* 56.3/4 (1996): 193–231.

Xu, Yongjie 許永傑. "Changcheng yanxian Zhou Qin shiqi shuanger taoqi de chubu kaocha" 長城沿線周秦時期雙耳陶器的初步考察. *Beifang wenwu* 北方文物 1992.2: 3–11.

Xu, Yuangao 徐元誥. *Guoyu jijie* 國語集解. Beijing: Zhonghua shuju, 2000.

Xu, Yunhe 許雲和. "Han Fangzhongci yue yu Anshi fangzhongge shiqi zhang" 漢房中祠樂與安世房中歌十七章. *Zhongshan daxue xuebao* 中山大學學報 2010.2:33-44.

Xu, Zhengkao 徐正考. *Han dai tongi mingwen wenzibian* 漢代銅器銘文文字編. Changchun: Jilin daxue chubanshe, 2005.

——. *Handai tongqi mingwen zonghe yanjiu* 漢代銅器銘文綜合研究. Beijing: Zuojia chubanshe, 2007.

Xun, Yue 荀悅. *Shen jian* 申鑒. Shanghai: Shang wu yinshuguan, 1925. Hanwei congshu edition.

——. *Qian Han ji* 前漢紀, *Sibu congkan* edition.

Xuzhou bowuguan 徐州博物館. "Jiangsu Xuzhou Xiaochangshan Han mu M4 fajue jianbao" 江蘇徐州小長山漢墓M4發掘簡報. *Zhongyuan wenwu* 2010.6: 4-9.

——. "Jiangsu Xuzhou Mishan Han mu" 江蘇徐州米山漢墓. *Kaogu* 1996.4: 36-37, 44.

——. "Jiangsu Tongshan xian Xi Han erhao yadongmu cailiao de zai buchong" 江蘇銅山縣西漢二號崖洞墓材料的再補充. *Kaogu* 1997.2: 36-46.

——. "Xuzhou diqu de Handai yuyi jiqi xiangguan weni" 徐州地區的漢代玉衣及其相關問題. *Dongnan wenwu* 1996.1: 26-32.

——. "Xuzhou Shiqiao Han mu qingli baogao" 徐州石橋漢墓清理簡報. *Wenwu* 1984.11: 22-40.

——. "Xuzhou Hanshan Xi Han mu" 徐州韓山西漢墓. *Wenwu* 1997.2: 26-43.

——. "Xuzhou Shizishan bingmayong keng diyici fajue jianbao" 徐州獅子山兵馬俑坑第一次發掘簡報. *Wenwu* (1986)12: 1-12.

Yablonsky, Leonid Teodorovich. "New Excavations of the Early Nomadic Burial Ground at Filippovka (Southern Ural Region, Russia)." *American Journal of Archaeology* 114.1 (2010): 129-43.

Yamada, Katsuyoshi 山田勝芳. "Qin Han shiqi de caizheng wenti" 秦漢時期的財政問題. In *Yin Zhou Qin Han shixue de jiben wenti* 殷周秦漢史學的基本問題, ed. Satake Yasuhiko, 204-23. Beijing: Zhonghua shuju, 2008.

——. Review of Kamiya Masakazu 紙屋正和. "Zen Kan shokōō no saisei to Butei no sazei zōshū" 前漢諸侯主國の財政と武帝の財政增收. *Hōseishiki kenkyū* 法制史研究 29 (1979): 234.

Yan, Genqi 閻根齊. *Mangdangshan Xi Han Liangwang mudi* 芒碭山西漢梁王墓地. Beijing: Wenwu chubanshe, 2001.

Yang, Aiguo 楊愛國. "Handai de yuzuo shoucang" 漢代的預作壽藏. In *Handai kaogu yu Han wenhua guoji xueshu taolunhui lunwenji* 漢代考古與漢文化國際學術討論會論文集, ed. Bianhuiwei, 271-81. Ji'nan: Qilu shushe, 2006.

Yang, Baocheng 楊寶成. *Yinxu wenhua yanjiu* 殷墟文化研究. Taipei: Taiwan guji chuban youxian gongsi, 2004

Yang, Fu 楊復. *Yili tu* 儀禮圖. In *Yingyin Wenyuange siku quanshu*. Vol. 104. Taipei: Xinwenfeng, 1986.

Yang, Hong 楊泓. *Zhongguo gudai bingqi luncong* 中國古代兵器論叢. Beijing: Wenwu chubanshe, 1980.

Yang, Hongxun 楊鴻勳. "Cong yizhi kan Xi'an Chang'an Mingtang (Biyong) xing zhi" 從遺址看西漢長安明堂（辟雍）形制. In *Jianzhu kaoguxue lunwen ji* 建築考古學論文集, ed. Yang Hongxun, 169-200. Beijing: Wenwu chubanshe, 1987.

——. "Guangyu Qindai yiqian mushang jianzhu de wenti" 關於秦代以前墓上建築的問題. *Kaogu* 1982.4: 38-42.

Yang, Jianhua 楊建華. *Chunqiu Zhanguo shiqi Zhongguo beifang wenhuadai de xingcheng* 春秋戰國時期中國北方文化帶的形成. Beijing: Kexue chubanshe, 2004.

——. "Shaanxi Qingjian Lijiaya Dong Zhou mu yu 'Hexi Baidi'" 陝西清澗李家崖東周墓 與"河西白狄. *Kaogu yu wenwu* 2008.5: 34–38.

——. "Zhongguo beifang Dong Zhou shiqi liangzhong wenhua yicun bianxi—jianlun rongdi yu hu de guanxi" 中國北方東周時期兩種文化遺存辨析—兼論戎狄与胡的 關係. *Kaogu xuebao* 2009.2: 155–83.

——. "Baidi dongqian kao—cong Baidi jianli de Zhongshanguo tanqi" 白狄東遷考—從 白狄建立的中山國談起. In *E'erduosi qingtongqi guoji xueshu yantaohui lunwenji* 鄂 爾多斯青銅器國際學術研討會論文集, ed. Bianweihui, 283–94. Beijing: Kexue chubanshe, 2009.

——. "Lüe lun Qin wenhua yu beifang wenhua de guanxi" 略論秦文化與北方文化的關 係. *Kaogu yu wenwu* 2013.1: 45–51.

Yang, Kuan 楊寬. *Zhongguo gudai lingqin zhidushi yanjiu* 中國古代陵寢制度史研究. Shanghai: Shanghai guji chubanshe, 1985.

——. *Zhanguo shi* 戰國史. Shanghai: Shanghai renmin chubanshe, 1998.

——. *Xi Zhou shi* 西周史. Shanghai: Shanghai renmin chubanshe, 2008.

Yang, Shuda 楊樹達. *Han dai hunsang lisu kao* 漢代婚喪禮俗考. Shanghai: Shanghai guji chubanshe, 2000.

Yang, Xiaoneng 楊曉能. *Ling yizhong gushi: Qingtongqi wenshi, tuxing wenzi yu tuxiang mingwen de jiedu* 另一種古史：青銅器文飾、圖形文字與圖像銘文的解讀. Beijing: Sanlian shudian, 2008.

Hua, Xuecheng 華學誠. *Yang Xiong Fang yan jiao shi hui zheng* 揚雄方言校釋匯證. Beijing: Zhonghua shuju, 2005.

Yang, Zhefeng 楊哲峰. "Beifeng diqu Han mu chutu de nanfang leixing taociqi" 北方地 區漢墓出土的南方類型陶瓷器. In *Han Chang'an cheng kaogu yu Han wenhua* 漢長 安城考古與漢文化, ed. Zhongguo shehui kexueyuan kaogu yanjiusuo et al., 507–42. Beijing: Kexue chubanshe, 2008.

Yangjiawan Han mu fajue xiaozu 楊家灣漢墓發掘小組. "Xianyang Yangjiawan Han mu fajue jianbao" 咸陽楊家灣漢墓發掘簡報. *Wenwu* 1977.10: 10–16.

Yanshi Shangcheng bowuguan 偃師商城博物館. "Henan Yanshi Koudian faxian Dong Han tongqi jiaocang" 河南偃師寇店發現東漢銅器窖藏. *Kaogu* 1992.9: 803–5.

Yao, Alice. *The Ancient Highlands of Southwest China: From the Bronze Age to the Han Empire*. Oxford: Oxford University Press, 2015.

Yasunaga, Tomoaki 安永知晃. "Zen Kan zenhanki no tai shokōō seisaku: Keitei chūgonen kaikaku no igi no saikentō" 前漢前半期の対諸侯王政策: 景帝中五年改革の意義 の再檢討. *Jinbun ronkyū* 人文論究64/65 (2015): 79–95.

Yates, Robin. *Five Lost Classics: Tao, Huang-Lao, and Yin-Yang in Han China*. New York: Ballantine, 1997.

Yetts, W. Perceval. " 'Bird Script' on Ancient Chinese Swords." *The Journal of the Royal Asiatic Society of Great Britain and Ireland* 3 (1934): 547–52.

Yin, R. K. *Case Study Research: Design and Methods*. Newbury Park, CA: Sage, 1984.

Yinqueshan Han mu zhujian zhengli xiaozu 銀雀山漢墓竹簡整理小組. *Yinqueshan Han mu zhujian* 銀雀山漢墓竹簡. Two volumes. Beijing: Wenwu chubanshe, 1985.

Yokota, Kiozo 橫田恭三. "Kameyama Kanbo no saiseki kokuji ni tsuite" 龜山漢墓の 塞石刻字について. *Atomi Gakuen Joshi Daigaku kiyō* 跡見学園女子大学紀要33 (2000): 83–95.

Yu, Guanying 余冠英. *Han Wei Liuchao shixuan* 漢魏六朝詩選. Beijing: Renmin wenxue chubanshe, 1987.

Yu, Mingguang 于明光. *Huangdi sijing yu Huang-Lao sixiang* 黃帝四經與黃老思想. Harbing: Heilongjiang renmin chubanshe, 1989.

Yu, Weichao 俞偉超. "Gudai Xirong he Qiang Hu kaoguxue wenhua guishu de tantao" 古代西戎和羌胡考古學文化歸屬的探討. In *Xian-Qin Liang Han kaoguxue lunji* 先秦兩漢考古學論集, ed. Yu Weichao, 180–92. Beijing: Wenwu chubanshe, 1985.

——. "Handai zhuhouwang yu liehou muzang de xingzhi fenxi—jian lun 'Zhou zhi,' 'Han zhi' yu 'Jin zhi'de sanjieduan xing" 漢代諸侯王與列侯墓葬的性質分析—兼論 "周制"、"漢制" 和 "晉制" 的三階段性. In *Zhongguo kaoguxuehui diyici nianhui lunwenji* 中國考古學會第一次年會論文集, ed. Zhongguo kaogu xuehui, 332–37. Beijing: Wenwu chubanshe, 1979.

Yu, Ying-shih. " 'O Soul, Come Back!': A Study in the Changing Conceptions of the Soul and Afterlife in Pre-Buddhist China." *Harvard Journal of Asiatic Studies* 27 (1987): 363–95.

Yuan, Shengwen 袁勝文. "Guanguo zhidu de chansheng yu yanbian lunshu" 棺槨制度的產生與演變論述. *Nakai xuebao* 南開學報 2014.3: 94–101.

Yuan, Shengwen and Shi Wenjia 石文嘉. "Yushi fumian yanjiu" 玉石覆面研究. *Zhongyuan wenwu* 2009.3: 76–81, 108.

Zang, Zheng 臧振. "Yucong gongneng yanjiu shuping" 玉琮功能研究述評. *Wenbo* 1993.5: 61–66, 20.

Zaoqi Qin wenhua lianhe kaogudui 早期秦文化聯合考古隊 and Zhangjiachuan Huizu zizhixian bowuguan. "Gansu Zhangjiachuan Majiayuan Zhanguo mudi 2012–2014 nian fajue jianbao" 甘肅張家川馬家塬戰國墓地2012–2014年發掘簡報. *Wenwu* 2018.3: 4–25.

Zhang, Shuangdi 張雙棣. *Huainanzi jiaoshi* 淮南子校釋. Beijing: Beijing daxue chubanshe, 1997.

Zhang, Shuguo 張樹國. "Lun Anshi fangzhong ge yu Han chu zongmiao jiyue de chuangzhi" 論安世房中歌與漢初宗廟祭樂的創制. *Hangzhou shifan daxue xuebao* 杭州師範大學學報 2010.5: 70–77.

Zhang, Tian'en 張天恩. "Zai lun Qin shi duanjian" 再論秦式短劍. *Kaogu* 1995.9: 841–53.

Zhang, Wenjiang 張文江. *Qin Han jia, hu falü yanjiu—yi jia, hu falü gouzao wei shijiao* 秦漢家戶法律研究—以家戶法律構造為視角. Beijing: Renmin ribao chubanshe, 2016.

Zhang, Xunliao 張勛燎 and Bai Bing 白彬. *Zhongguo daojiao kaogu* 中國道教考古. Six volumes. Beijing: Xianzhuang shuju, 2006.

Zhang, Zhenglang 張政烺 (= Xiao Yun 肖蘊). "Guanyu Mancheng Han mu tonghu niaozhuan shiwen de taolun (sanpian)" 關於滿城漢墓銅壺鳥篆釋文的討論 (三篇). *Kaogu* 1979.4: 356–59.

——. "Mancheng Han mu chutu de cuo jinyin niaochongshu tonghu" 滿城漢墓出土的錯金銀鳥蟲書銅壺. *Kaogu* 1972.5: 49–52.

"Ai Chengshu ding shiwen" 哀成叔鼎釋文. In *Jiagu jiwen yu Shang Zhou shi yanjiu* 甲骨金文與商周史研究, ed. Zhang Zhenglang, 261–68. Beijing: Zhonghua shuju, 2012.

Zhangjiashan Han mu zhujian zhengli xiaozu 張家山漢墓竹簡整理小組. *Zhangjiashan Han mu zhujian ersiqi hao mu (shiwen xiudingben)* 張家山漢墓竹簡247號墓 (釋文修訂本). Beijing: Wenwu chubanshe, 2006.

Zhao, Deyun 趙德雲. "Tubanwen yin tonghe santi" 凸瓣紋銀銅盒三題. *Wenwu* 2007.3: 81–88.

Zhao, Dingxin. "The Han Bureaucracy: Its Origin, Nature, and Development." In *State Power in Ancient China and Rome*, ed. Walter Scheidel, 56–89. Oxford: Oxford University Press, 2015.

Zhao, Huacheng 趙化成. "Cong Shang Zhou jizhong gongmuzhi dao Qin Han duli lingyuan zhi de yanhua guiji" 從商周集中公墓制到秦漢獨立陵園制的演化軌跡. *Wenwu* 2006.7: 41–48.

——. "Qin Han diling waicang xitong (congzangkeng) de xingzhi wenti" 秦漢帝陵外藏系統(從葬坑)的性質問題. *Qin Shihuang diling bowuyuan* 秦始皇帝陵博物院 1 (2011): 119–30.

——. "Qin Shihuang lingyuan buju jiegou de zai renshi" 秦始皇陵園佈局結構的再認識. In *Yuanwangji* 遠望集, ed. Shaanxi sheng kaogu yanjiusuo, 501–8. Xi'an: Shaanxi renmin meishu chubanshe, 1998.

——. "Zhou dai guanguo duochong zhidu yanjiu" 周代棺槨多重制度研究. *Guoxue yanjiu* 國學研究 5 (1998): 27–74.

Zhao, Jianzhao 趙建朝 and Li Haixiang 李海祥. "Hebei Handan Zhaowangling erhaoling chutu de Zhanguo wenwu" 河北邯鄲趙王陵二號陵出土的趙國文物. *Wenwu* 2009.3: 89–94.

Zhao, Peng 趙鵬. "Shangcunling Guoguo mudi M2001, M2012 suo fanying de liangxing guanxi" 上村嶺虢國墓地M2001, M2012所反映的兩性關係. *Dongfang cangpin* 東方藏品 2018.7: 199–200.

Zhao, Ping'an 趙平安. "Dui Shizishan Chuwangling suochu yinzhang fengni de zairenshi" 對獅子山楚王陵所出印章封泥的再認識. *Wenwu* 1999.1: 52–55.

——. *Qin Xi Han yinzhang yanjiu* 秦西漢印章研究. Shanghai: Shanghai guji chubanshe, 2013.

Zhao, Ye 趙曄. *Wu Yue chunqiu* 吳越春秋. Nanjing: Jiangsu guji chubanshe, 1999.

Zhejiang sheng wenwu kaogu yanjiusuo 浙江省文物考古研究所 and Shaoxing xian wenwu baohu guanliju 紹興縣文物保護管理局. *Yinshan Yuewang ling* 印山越王陵. Beijing: Wenwu chubanshe, 2002.

Zheng, Liangshu 鄭良樹. *Yili gongshi kao* 儀禮宮室考. Taipei: Zhonghua shuju, 1971.

Zheng, Shaozong 鄭紹宗. *Mancheng Han mu* 滿城漢墓. Beijing: Wenwu chubanshe, 2003.

Zheng, Shaozong and Zheng Luanming 鄭灤明. "Mancheng Han mu fajue rizhi" 滿城漢墓發掘日誌. *Wenwu chunqiu* 2002.5: 55–65.

Zhong, Yiming 鐘一鳴. "Xi Han zhuhouwang zhi caiquan kaoshu" 西漢諸侯王之財權考述. *Yiyang shizhuan xuebao* 益陽師專學報 1987.3: 9–13.

Zhongguo guojia bowuguan 中國國家博物館 and Xuzhou bowuguan. *Da Han Chu wang: Xuzhou Xi Han Chu wang ling mu wenwu ji cui* 大漢楚王：徐州西漢楚王陵墓文物輯萃. Beijing: Zhongguo shehui kexue chubanshe, 2005.

Zhongguo huaxiangshi quanji bianji weiyuanhui 中國畫像石全集編輯委員會. *Zhongguo huaxiangshi quanji* 中國畫像石全集. Eight volumes. Ji'nan: Shandong meishu chubanshe, 2000.

Zhongguo kexueyuan kaogu yanjiusuo 中國科學院考古研究所. *Huixian fajue baogao* 輝縣發掘報告. Beijing: Kexue chubanshe, 1956.

——. *Luoyang Shaogou Han mu* 洛陽燒溝漢墓. Beijing: Kexue chubanshe, 1959.

——. *Shangcunling Guoguo mudi* 上村嶺虢國墓地. Beijing: Kexue chubanshe, 1959.

Zhongguo shehui kexueyuan kaogu yanjiusuo 中國社會科學院考古研究所. *Han Duling lingyuan yizhi* 漢杜陵陵園遺址. Beijing: Wenwu chubanshe, 1993.

——. "Henan Anyang shi Meiyuanzhuang dongnan de Yindai chenmakeng" 河南安陽市梅園莊東南的殷代車馬坑. *Kaogu* 1998.10: 48–65.

——. *Mancheng Han mu fajue baogao* 滿城漢墓發掘報告. Two volumes. Beijing: Wenwu chubanshe, 1980.

——. *Yinxu Fu Hao mu* 殷墟婦好墓. Beijing: Wenwu chubanshe, 1980.

——. *Zhongguo kaoguxue Liangzhou juan* 中國考古學兩周卷. Beijing: Zhongguo shehui kexueyuan chubanshe, 2004.

Zhongguo shehui kexueyuan kaogu yanjiusuo and Beijing yiqichang gongren lilunzu 北京儀器廠工人理論組. *Mancheng Han mu* 滿城漢墓. Beijing: Wenwu chubanshe, 1978.

Zhou, Nanquan 周南泉. "Zhongshan guo de yuqi" 中山國的玉器. *Gugong bowuyuan yuankan* 1979.2: 95–96.

Zhou, Baoping 周保平 and Liu Jianzhao 劉建照. "Xi Han Chu wang lingmu xingzhi yanjiu" 西漢楚王陵墓形制研究. *Zhongguo lishi wenwu* 2005.6: 66–79.

Zhou, Jun 周筠 and Chen Jing 陳靜. "Mancheng Han mu chutu tongqi mingwen yanjiu" 滿城漢墓出土銅器銘文研究. *Wenwu chunqiu* 2010.3: 51–57, 66.

Zhou, Xiaolu 周曉路. "Miao Yu muzhi dukao" 繆紆墓誌讀考. *Wenwu* 1995.4: 83–87.

Zhou, Xueying 周学鷹. "Handai jianzhu mingqi tanyuan" 漢代建筑明器探源. *Jianzhushi lunwenji* 建築史論文集 17 (2003): 12–24.

——. *Xuzhou Hanmu jianzhu—Zhongguo Handai Chu (Pengcheng) guo muzang jianzhu kao* 徐州漢墓建筑— 中國漢代楚 (彭城) 國墓葬建筑考. Beijing: Zhongguo jianzhu gongye chubanshe, 2001.

Zhou, Zhenhe 周振鶴. *Xi Han zhengqu dili* 西漢政區地理. Beijing: Renmin chubanshe, 1987.

Zhu, Jieyuan 朱捷元 and Li Yuzheng 李域錚. "Xi'an dongjiao Sandiancun Xi Han mu" 西安東郊三店村西漢墓. *Kaogu yu wenwu* 1983.2: 22–25.

Zhu, Qianzhi 朱謙之. *Laozi jiaoshi* 老子校釋. Beijing: Zhonghua shuju, 1984.

INDEX

Page numbers in *italics* represent figures or tables.

necklaces, 108–10, *109*, 118–19, 279n39
needle cases, *132*, 139
Neolithic period, 6
nested coffins, 30, *31–32*, 32–37
nine orifices, 36
noble tombs, 9
nomadic culture, 135–36, *136*, 280n47
non-ethnic-Han, 12, 22, 107, 110, 116–17, 130–31, 133, 139–40, 142, 150
nonroyal tombs, 5–6
Northern Zone culture, 110–11, *111*; burials in, 131–32; Eurasia and, 150
Nüjie, 73

objects. *See* burials; ritual objects
offerings, 275n122
ontological approaches, 16–17, 309n9
Ordos site, 110, 122–24, 137, 282n74
ornaments, 181
outer coffins, 37–43, *38–39*; imperial rituals and, 44–45; weapons in, 111
Outer Commentary to the Book of Songs (Master Han), 303n19
outfits (*fu*): 25–26, clothing and, 45; for Liu Sheng, 60

palaces, 95, 97, *98*, 99
paralleling principle, 159, 208, 211, 240. *See also* gender
Pazyrik site, 122
peace: 10, 22, 63, 105, 107, 151, 181–83, 203, 209; *jing*, 21, 22, 105, 186–92, 207
pendants, 44
petite vessels, 80
phenomenology, 309n90
philosophy: in *Annals of Lü Buwei*, 206; of Daoism, 184; of Eastern Zhou dynasty, 226; of family, 302n100; gong, 166–67; of governing states, 302n100; from *Guanzi*, 215–16; history of, 22; of immortality, 61–63; for kings, 150, 165–66; of *Laozi*, 216; of Legalism, 9–10; of *liuxing*, 46–47; of married couples, 88–93, *89*; of Mengzi, 182; of Mohism, 184; politics and, 107, 195, 206; religion and, 223–24; royalty and, 247; of sacred rulers, 220–21; of sages, 188–89, 296n112; of sexual organs, 73–74; *si*, 166–67; of tombs, 162;

in Warring States period, 9, 179–80; of Western Han dynasty, 92–93, 240–41; of *xingjie*, 45–46; of Xunzi, 150–52, 154, 178. *See also* Confucianism; Huang-Lao philosophy
pictorial art, 72
pictorialization, 230
pit graves, 27–29, 305n55; chambers for, 145–46; Liu Sheng against, 288n157; for married couples, 91–92; material abundance in, 224
plaques, 131–32
plundering, of tombs, 254n52
political ideology, 9; of governing states, 151; of kings, 155–56; of Liu Sheng, 21, 26, 186–87, 191–98, 203–7, 242–43, 246; at Mancheng site, 207–11; tombs and, 292n26
politics: art and, 255n62; in *Book of Poetry*, 215; of Confucianism, 116–17; "Cultivation of Political Power," 211; culture and, 247; family and, 272n75; of governing states, 105; of *Hanshu*, 198, 201–2; of imperialism, 129; for Liu Sheng, 84; of married couples, 104–5; of ownership, 174–75; philosophy and, 107, 195, 206; political capital, 86–88; retrograding in, 168; of ritual vessels, 129–30; of royal burials, 162–65; of royalty, 92; of *Shiji*, 198, 216; Sima Qian on, 219
poses, 70, 90
posthumous titles, 188–91, *189*, 296n96
power: "Cultivation of Political Power," 211; of Eastern Zhou dynasty, 117–18; for Huaxia civilization, 141; in married couples, 80–88, *82*, *86*
preservation: of jade suits, 67, *67*, 268n7; of tombs, 4–5
principal wives, 2–3, 6. *See also* Dou Wan
private objects, 177–78
property, 175–78
prophecies, 39
psychology, 242–43, 310n13
public funds, 169; governing states and, 295n88; in Warring States period, 178
public life: in China, 293n45; economics and, 174–76; of kings, 165–66; tombs and, 185

Qin dynasty, 75, 168, 216; kings from, 209–10, 298n19; military of, 192
Qin, first emperor of, 3, 4, 8, 10, 33, 77, 97, 130, 161, 162, 164–65, 168, 169, 183, 192, 216, 220, 233. *See also* Qin Shihuangdi
Qin, second emperor of, 48
Qin Shihuangdi, 3
quanxiu, 211
queens. *See specific queens*
Qu Yuan, 199–200

Rebellion of the Seven Kingdoms (*qiguo zhiluan*), 191–92
regional kingdoms, 7
religion: in China, 8; culture and, 9; genitalia and, 70–71; philosophy and, 223–24; in Western Han dynasty, 45–46
research: case study, 15–16; history and, 18; material culture studies in, 17
resemblance, 181–82
"Response Upon Hearing Music" (Liu Sheng), 198
retrograding, 168
Rhapsody on the Divine Lady (Song Yu), 70
rings, 32, 40–41, 109
Rites of Zhou (Liu Xin), 163, 173–74
ritual objects, 25–26; for attraction, 48–49; beautification knives, 73; bronzes for, 48–49, 49, 78, 120–21, 121, 129, 135–36, 136, 307n76; in burials, 91–92, 217; from games, 135–37, 136–38, 139; gender in, 81–82, 270n32; hairpins, 262n71; inscriptions in, 124–25, 125, 171–72, 174–75, 294n77, 305n55; jewelry, 71, 71–72; lamps, 54, 55, 100–101; for master planners, 227–29; musical instruments, 59–60; necklaces, 108–9, 109; royal tombs and, 223–30, 262n72; toiletry cases, 72–73, 269n27, 270n29; tradition of, 107, 238; weapons as, 115; for Western Han dynasty, 217–18
ritual offerings, 170–71
rituals: archaeology and, 18–19; in China, 62–63, 266n145; design and, 95; *Former Rituals of the Han*, 161, 164; in history, 22; from Mancheng site, 20; tombs and, 96–97

ritual vessels, 308n77, 308n82; inscriptions on, 177–78; for Liu Sheng, 78, 139–40; politics of, 129–30
robe: ritual, 38; for *zhaohun*, 43
Roman art, 255n62, 255n66
Rong-Di tradition, 22, 107; art from, 120–21, 121; burials in, 146; customs in, 117; Eastern Zhou dynasty and, 133; ethnicity of, 140; Huaxia civilization and, 119, 129; necklaces in, 110; in social space, 130–37, 131–38, 139–42; tombs in, 126; in Warring States period, 137, 139; weapons in, 112, 115; Western Han dynasty and, 121–22, 122; for Zhongshan kingdom, 141–42
rongyi, 262n76
royal burials: barbarism in, 108–17, 109, 111, 113–14; clothing in, 40; in Eastern Han dynasty, 32–33; history of, 10–11; inscriptions in, 176–77; as lavish, 178–85; for Liu Sheng, 28–29, 43–44, 60–63, 115, 140, 233; politics of, 162–65; as state project, 165–70
royal tombs, 1–2, 2, 43–44, 60–63; alcohol in, 57; architecture of, 93–95, 94; artifacts in, 16–20; art in, 14–15, 308n87; Bright Halls in, 54, 56; in China, 17; for Cuo, 119; for Dou Wan, 53, 64–66, 65, 74–77, 91, 204; for Duke Jing, 3; in Eastern Zhou dynasty, 61, 276n138; encasing in, 27–29, 28; food in, 57, 235, 236, 237; front chambers in, 50, 51, 52–60, 55, 57–58; for Fu Hao, 60–61; gaze in, 212–22; imperial mausoleums as, 3–4; intangible appearance in, 37–44, 38–39; for kings, 10, 15, 80–88, 82, 86, 160–62; Lamp of the Palace of Lasting Trust from, 82, 82–84; as latent pictorial narratives, 230–31, 232, 233–35, 236, 237–38; at Mancheng site, 115–16, 159–60, 178–79, 202, 239–47; for Marquis Yi, 59–60; for married couples, 77–78, 88–93, 89; master planners of, 159–60; material remains in, 26; mausoleums as, 7, 18–19; murals in, 286n141; in Neolithic period, 6; property in, 177–78; ritual objects and, 223–30,